Final

ch. 12, 13

Functional Areas of the Organization

BU121

Wilfrid Laurier University
Custom Edition

NELSON EDUCATION

NELSON EDUCATION

Printed and bound in Canada
1 2 3 4 14 13 12 11

For more information contact Nelson Education Ltd., 1120 Birchmount Road, Toronto, Ontario, M1K 5G4. Or you can visit our Internet site at http://www.nelson.com

This textbook is a Nelson custom publication. Because your instructor has chosen to produce a custom publication, you pay only for material that you will use in your course.

ISBN-13: 978-0-17-663845-0
ISBN-10: 0-17-663845-8

Consists of Selections from:

The Future of Business, 3/e
Althouse; Rose; Allan
ISBN 0-17-650140-1, © 2011

Business Communication: Process and Product, 7/e
Guffy; Loewy
ISBN 10: 0-538-46625-1, © 2011

Entrepreneurship: A Process Perspective
Baron; Shane; Reuber
ISBN 10: 0-17-610334-1, © 2008

Cover Credit:

sheelamohanachandran2010/Shutterstock

Roman Shcherbakov/Shutterstock

Kirill_M/Shutterstock

Ilin Sergey/Shutterstock

Table of Contents

Custom Chapter 3 – Organizing and Writing Business Messages 67

Custom Chapter 4 – Revising Business Messages 92

Custom Chapter 5 – Report and Research Basics 116

Custom Chapter 6 – Informal Business Reports 159

INTRODUCTION

This text on business is important whether you are working in a business today or hope to work in one in the future. Even if your major is in the arts or sciences, you will likely work in an organization that is considered to be a business. Profit or non-profit, the same principles apply.

First let's look at the nature of business.

business
An organization that strives for a profit by providing goods and services desired by its customers.

goods
Tangible items manufactured by businesses.

services
Intangible offerings of businesses that can't be touched or stored.

standard of living
A country's output of goods and services that people can buy with the money they have.

quality of life
The general level of human happiness based on such things as life expectancy, educational standards, health, sanitation, and leisure time..

risk
The potential for losing time and money or otherwise not being able to accomplish an organization's goals.

revenue
The money a company earns from providing services or selling goods to customers.

A **business** is an organization that strives for a profit by providing goods and services desired by its customers. Businesses meet the needs of consumers by providing movies, medical care, autos, and countless other goods and services. **Goods** are tangible items manufactured by businesses, such as laptop computers and BlackBerries. **Services** are intangible offerings of businesses that can't be touched or stored. Accountants, lawyers, restaurants, car washes, and airlines all provide services. Businesses also serve other organizations, such as hospitals, retailers, and governments, by providing machinery, goods for resale, computers, and thousands of other items.

Thus, businesses create the goods and services that are the basis of our standard of living. The **standard of living** of any country is measured by the output of goods and services people can buy with the money they have. This includes not o nly privately purchased goods and services but also collectively consumed goods and services, such as those provided by public utilities and governments.

Businesses play a key role in determining our quality of life by providing jobs and goods and services to society. **Quality of life** refers to the general level of human happiness based on such things as life expectancy, educational standards, health, sanitation, and leisure time. Zurich, Switzerland, is ranked as having the world's highest quality of life, followed by Vienna, Austria, and Vancouver, Canada.[1] Building a high quality of life is a combined effort of businesses, government, and not-for-profit organizations.

Creating a high quality of life is not without risks, however. **Risk** is the potential for losing time and money or otherwise not being able to accomplish an organization's goals. Without enough blood donors, for example, Canadian Blood Services faces the risk of not meeting the demand for blood by victims of disaster. Businesses like Bell Canada Enterprises face the risk of falling short of their revenue goals. **Revenue** is the money a company earns from providing services or selling goods to customers.

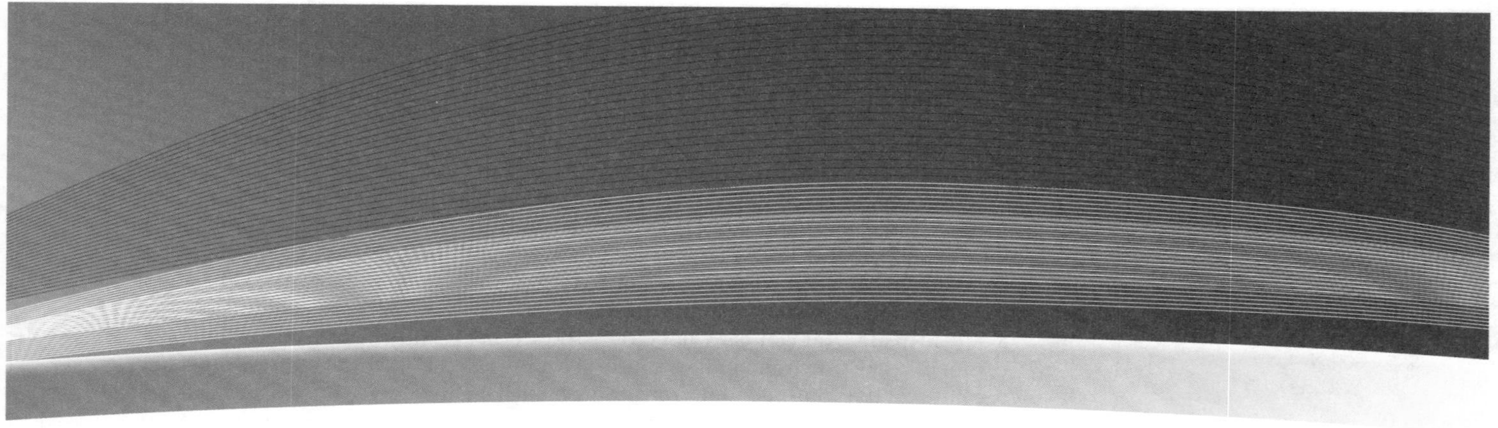

costs
Expenses incurred in creating and selling goods and services.

profit
The money left over after all expenses are paid.

not-for-profit organization
An organization that exists to achieve some goal other than the usual business goal of profit.

Costs are expenses for rent, salaries, supplies, transportation, and many other items that a company incurs from creating and selling goods and services. Some of the costs incurred by Research in Motion (featured in our opening) include expenses for research and development, building rental or purchase, advertising, and transportation. Profit is the money left over after all expenses are paid.

When a company like Research in Motion uses its resources intelligently, it can often increase sales, hold costs down, and earn a profit. Not all companies earn a profit, but that is the risk of being in business. In Canadian business today, there is generally a direct relationship between risks and profit: the greater the risks, the greater the potential profit (or loss).

Not all organizations strive to make a profit. A not-for-profit organization is an organization that exists to achieve some goal other than the usual business goal of profit. The United Way, the Canadian Cancer Society, and Greenpeace are all not-for-profit organizations.

Successful not-for-profit organizations follow sound business principles. These groups have goals they hope to accomplish, but the goals are not focused on profits. For example, a not-for-profit organization's goal might be feeding the poor, stopping destruction of the environment, increasing attendance at the ballet, or preventing drunk driving. Reaching such goals takes good planning, management, and control. Not-for-profit organizations do not compete directly with each other as, for example, Ford and Honda do, but they do compete for people's scarce volunteer time and donations.

If you want to be as successful as you can be, and make your business as successful as it can be, then it is critical that you understand how a successful business works. Most introductory textbooks and courses do a good job of introducing you to the different elements of a business, but often fail to show you how these elements fit together. This objective is achieved mostly in senior business courses. The problem is that by that point, you are so used to studying each piece separately that it's very difficult to see them working together to create the business entity as a whole. And what's important to see is that *"the whole" really is greater than the sum of its parts.* To truly understand what makes a business successful, you must accept it as a fully integrated entity and, as you study each of its parts, study them with the whole in mind.

To this end, we have used an integrative model (shown on page 5) of a successful business as the framework, or basis, of this book. Each chapter will focus on a specific part of this model, and you will be reminded of where and how each piece fits with the other aspects of the model at the beginning of each chapter.

Before we get into the model in detail, take a look at the title—*The Integrative Model of a Successful Business*. Why is this important? What does it tell you?

It Is Integrative.

All the elements of the model work together to create a unified whole. Each piece depends on the others, and they all affect one another. One of the most important lessons to learn about business is that you can't make a decision in one area of a business without considering the impact that it will have on other areas of the business.

For example, according to *Report on Business* magazine's 2008 Top 1000, EnCana Corporation, the largest natural gas producer in North America, was the number one-ranked publicly listed company in Canada on the basis of revenue. Despite the fallout from the global credit crisis and ensuing global recession when Canada's 1,000 largest publicly listed companys' earnings dropped 30% from the year before, EnCana enjoyed a 50% increase. This company has clearly shown that it knows what it takes to be successful in today's environment. Of course given the external environmental context, the top ranks of the Top 1000 were crowded by financial and resource firms, EnCana is not only successful in terms of achieving financial performance, but was also ranked #31 on Corporate Knights "Best 50 Corporate Citizens" for 2009 (**www.corporateknights.ca**), as well as being listed as one of the "Global 100 Most Sustainable Corporations in the World" for 2009 (**www.global100.org**). EnCana certainly appreciates the need to balance all of its *stakeholders*. This is an organization that provides us with an excellent example of the need to act in an integrative fashion to achieve the critical success factors. For example, if the *operations* department of EnCana was able to find a new, less-expensive process to use in its production, could it do so without any impact on other areas of the business? If the process produced a product of lesser quality, or was perceived to be of lesser quality, this would affect the image of the product in the mind of the consumer, making it difficult for the *marketing* department to sell the product. Therefore, the marketing department would be affected in terms of the sales of the product, which, in turn, means that the *finance* department would be affected, as it would affect the expected income for the year, and this might mean that the salaries negotiated in future labour contracts by the *human resources* department might be lower, and so on. All the elements of the business or areas of its *internal environment* (shown by the green circle on the model) affect one another.

By the same token, what if new *technology* was developed that would allow EnCana to produce natural gas by way of machinery exclusively, with absolutely no human input? Then layoffs would likely result and affect the *economy* of the towns where the company was located. This, in turn, would have an impact on the *social* environment of the business with respect to the relationship it has with the residents of the community, and might lead to the government's stepping in to enact a *political* solution for the community.

All the areas of the *external environment* (shown by the pink circle on the model) have an impact on each other as well as on the business as a whole. These four areas of the external environment together can be remembered as the acronym PEST—for political, economic, social, and technological. The external environment can, indeed, be a pest to business! But it can also create enormous opportunities, as you will see.

To make our model more fully integrated, changes in this external environment set off other chain reactions inside the internal environment of the business, just as society's increasing demands for business to be more responsible in the social environment have led to strategic changes within EnCana that have made it into the sustainable business that it is today. The interactions are endless. It's not necessary that you see all these connections. What is necessary is that you understand, as we go through the material section by section, that these sections of material cannot be treated as if they are separate areas of a business that can act on their own. They all work together.

It Is a *Model*

This means several things. A model represents reality—this is how a real business works! A model simplifies reality—you are learning how a successful business works, and that's very complicated. A model summarizes the essential elements in a simple form to give you a base on which to build your knowledge. A model integrates ideas into a whole, as we discussed. And finally, a model provides a framework, so that you can see how the pieces fit together and how you can build on it in later business courses.

> The Integrative Model of a Successful Business

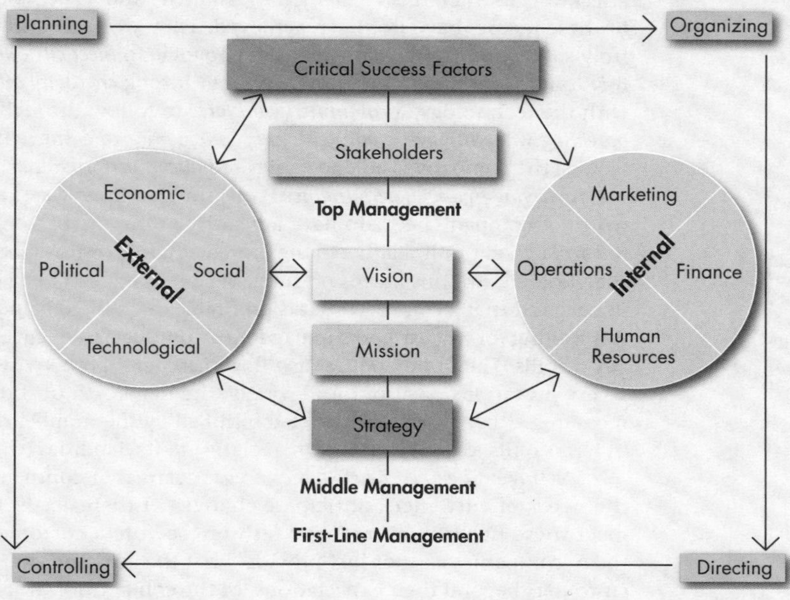

SOURCE: This material was originally published in *Business 111 Lab Manual*, 23rd ed. by Laura Allan and Jim McCutcheon, page xv. Reprinted by permission of Captus Press Inc.

It Is a Model of a *Successful* Business

We're not discussing what all businesses do. We are discussing what successful businesses do that makes them successful over time—not just one year but consistently outperforming year after year. That's how we learn about business—by studying those successful businesses that are leaders in their fields.

What does it mean to be truly successful? Is it simply making money? What does it take to make money? The *critical success factors* for any business, or the factors that indicate success, are:

- achieving financial performance
- meeting and exceeding customer needs
- providing value—quality products at a reasonable price
- encouraging creativity and innovation
- gaining employee commitment[2]

Most businesses exist to make money, but what is often left out of the discussion is how a business becomes successful in the first place. Can a business be truly successful at generating income if it ignores the other four factors? For example, can it make money by selling products that do not satisfy customers' needs, with inferior quality at an unreasonable price, using yesterday's ideas (when the competition is 10 steps ahead), while displaying a negative attitude toward the customer as demonstrated by its employees? Even one of these points would result in lower income and a less successful business. Using EnCana again as an example, according to its website (**www.encana.com**): "At the heart of EnCana's success, are the ingenuity, technical leadership and enthusiasm of (its) over 7,000 staff." Clearly EnCana appreciates the importance of the critical success factors of *gaining employee commitment* in order to *encourage* the *innovation and creativity* so important to its success.

Achieving Success

It's important to remember as well that these factors are also integrative—they all affect one another. It is virtually impossible to find a successful business in which all of these factors have not been achieved. They work together to make the company truly successful. For example, consider Toyota. To *meet customer needs,* Toyota was the first to mass-produce a hybrid vehicle, but it took *creativity and innovation* to come up with the technology, a *committed workforce* to follow through, and a commitment to *providing value through quality at a reasonable price* to achieve success. Because of these factors, the company is able to achieve *financial performance.*

Achieving financial performance is measured in three ways: profit, cash flow, and net worth. A company needs to have a healthy profit, or "bottom line," but it also needs to earn a good profit relative to the money it has invested—the equity of the owners or shareholders. But this means nothing, of course, if it can't pay its bills. It's important to understand that a company that is profitable can still go bankrupt. For instance, while it is waiting for its customers to pay for the products they have purchased, it still has to pay its bills. The timing of the cash flows can put an otherwise profitable business into a very precarious position. And finally, the net worth of the company is important, measured either by its stock price multiplied by the number of shares outstanding, or in terms of its assets (what it owns) relative to its liabilities (what it owes).

Meeting and exceeding customer needs means that companies must be sensitive to the needs of customers, anticipate changes in their needs, and, of course, work to meet these needs in a proactive fashion—before a customer complains. However, today companies cannot just provide what the customer wants. They need to satisfy customers beyond their expectations, or the competition will.

Providing value means that a business must constantly strive to improve the quality of its products and services, and do so at a reasonable cost. Customers demand quality and will stand for nothing less, but they want value for their dollar. They will pay a price that gives them value for their money—the quality that they demand at a price that makes it worthwhile or valuable to them.

Encouraging creativity and innovation involves the process of being creative (or "thinking outside the box"), as well as harnessing that creativity to generate the innovations that keep the company one step ahead of the competition. Danger exists when the company becomes comfortable with its level of success, as it might resist the change needed to stay ahead. But remember, there are only two kinds of businesses—those that constantly innovate and those that go out of business. In today's business world, one of the only constants is change. The status quo doesn't work anymore. Companies need to become "learning organizations," proactively seeking to learn and move ahead every day in everything they do.

And finally, probably the most important success factor is *gaining employee commitment.* Employees need to be empowered to act and motivated to meet the company's objectives in each of the first four factors, or those objectives won't be met. Therefore, every company needs to understand the needs of its employees. Only then can it gain their commitment, for they will be committed to meeting the goals of the company only if their own goals are met at the same time. It is, again, an integrative relationship.

Underneath the critical success factors are the *stakeholders* of the business. These are individuals and groups that have a "stake" in what the business does. They are affected by the decisions that the business makes, and therefore the business has a responsibility to consider them in those decisions.

The three most critical and obvious stakeholder groups are the owners of the business (or shareholders in the case of a corporation), the employees of the business (and their union if represented by one), and the customers. But there is a much wider world out there that must be considered—the government, special interest groups, the community surrounding the business, its suppliers, and so on. All of these groups interact with the business and keep it operating.

The business cannot operate in a vacuum, as if these groups did not exist. They must be considered in every decision the business makes. If we change this material, how will our customers react? Will they keep buying our product? If we move the business, how will it affect the community? How many employees will we lose? If we cut down these trees to build the new plant, how will the environmentalist groups respond? How will the community and the local government respond? If earnings drop in the fourth quarter as expected, will our shareholders sell their shares, making the share price fall even lower? Achieving the critical success factors clearly depends on an intimate knowledge of and relationship with the stakeholders of the business.

It is primarily *top management's* external focus that keeps the business looking at the stakeholders. It is the responsibility of the top management of the company to look outward and chart a course for the company. They examine the external environment of the business and match the threats and opportunities in the external environment with both the expectations of the stakeholders and the strengths and weaknesses of the company, to determine the direction the company should take in the future—their *vision* for the future of the company. This is further refined into a *mission* statement for the company. Next they determine the *strategy* for the company to pursue to achieve this mission—how to go about achieving the company's goals in the future.

For example, perhaps opportunities exist in the external environment to take the company global. Perhaps needs exist within foreign countries for the type of product the company sells, and little competition exists from other firms at the present time. If the company has the internal marketing, operations, human, and financial strength to achieve this objective, then top management might determine that the vision for the future of the company is to make it a strong global competitor. The strategy would then need to take into account such decisions as what countries to enter first, whether to search out foreign firms with which to form a joint venture, and whether to pursue a licensing arrangement with a foreign firm or build its own plants.

It is then *middle management's* job within each of the functional areas of the business to determine and plan out what each area needs to do to help achieve this overall corporate strategy. For example, what type of marketing campaigns will be most successful in these new foreign markets? Do we build new plants or lease/purchase and renovate existing plants? What new skills and attributes are needed to staff our operations in these new foreign markets? Where will the money come from, and how will the budgets be realigned?

First-line management manages the workers who do the actual work in each of the functional areas. It is their job to make sure the higher level plans are implemented—and, most important—by committed workers who are motivated to achieve the goals of the company.

Top managers, middle managers, and first-line managers are responsible for managing the company and its employees to ensure that all five of the critical success factors are achieved. They do this by

- *planning* what the goals are (to achieve the critical success factors) and how to achieve them,
- *organizing* the resources of the company—human, physical, and financial—to achieve the goals,
- *motivating* the workers to gain their commitment to the goals, and then
- *measuring* results and making any changes necessary to continue to steer the company in the direction of the goals, thus maintaining control over the achievement of these five critical success factors.

This is the model we will use in this text to help you integrate the different topics covered into an understanding of how a successful business works as a whole. By studying the topics presented in this textbook, you will gain a solid foundation on which to build your further understanding of successful business practices.

CHAPTER 8

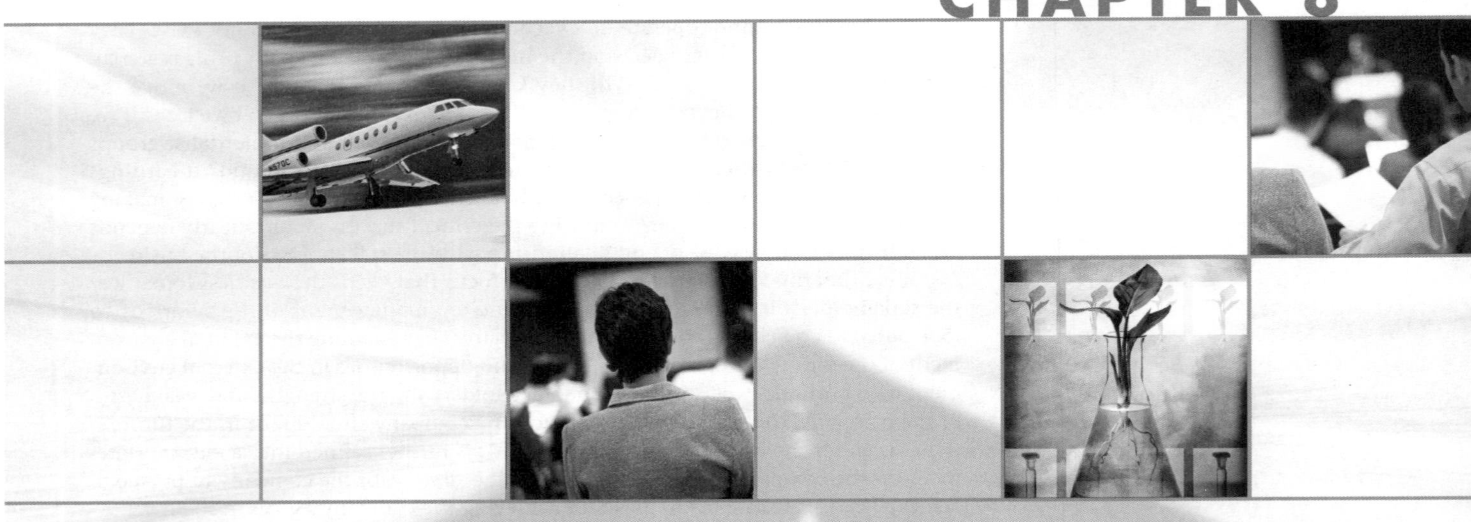

WRITING AN EFFECTIVE BUSINESS PLAN: CRAFTING A ROAD MAP TO SUCCESS

LEARNING OBJECTIVES

After reading this chapter, you should be able to:

1. Define a business plan and explain why entrepreneurs should write one.
2. Explain how the process of persuasion plays a key role in business plans and in the success of new ventures.
3. Explain why the executive summary is a very important part of any business plan.
4. Describe the major sections of a business plan and the types of information they should include.
5. Describe the seven deadly sins of business plans—errors all entrepreneurs should avoid.
6. Explain why potential investors usually ask entrepreneurs to give verbal presentations describing their idea for new products or services and their company.
7. Describe the steps entrepreneurs can take to make their verbal presentations to potential investors truly excellent.

> "There is a real magic in enthusiasm. It spells the difference between mediocrity and accomplishment." (Norman Vincent Peale, 1961)

Whether they realize it or not, most entrepreneurs accept these words as true. They are convinced that because *they* believe passionately in their ideas and their new ventures, others will, too, if given half a chance to do so. As a result, they are often dismayed when their initial efforts to obtain financial backing meet with lukewarm receptions (or worse!) from venture capitalists, business angels, and others who might readily provide the resources they need. "What's wrong with these people?" they wonder. "Can't they recognize a great thing when they see it?" The problem, of course, may not be a lack of discernment on the part of these persons. Rather, it may have much more to do with the kind of job the entrepreneur is doing in presenting her or his idea to others. Yes, the entrepreneur is enthusiastic and enthusiasm sells. But in order to induce other people—especially ones who have been taught by years of experience to view new ventures with a jaundiced eye—enthusiasm alone is rarely sufficient. In addition, entrepreneurs who want to succeed must realize that they face a very serious and very tough task, one centred around the process of persuasion—the task of inducing others to share our views and to see the world much as we do. After all, why should total strangers entrust their hard-earned money to something as risky in nature as a new venture, especially if it is going to be run by someone who has had little if any experience in starting or running a business? Would you? Unless you are like the characters shown in Figure 8.1, and have fallen in love with an idea or industry, the answer is clear: No!

If enthusiasm alone is not enough, then what can entrepreneurs do to gain the resources they need? For many entrepreneurs, a large part of the answer involves preparing a truly first-rate business plan. This document is a formal, written expression of the entrepreneur's vision for converting ideas into a profitable, going business, and in most cases, it is the entry card for serious consideration by venture capitalists, banks, and other sources of funding: Most won't even think about supporting a new venture until they have seen and carefully evaluated this document. This basic fact poses something of a dilemma for many entrepreneurs: They firmly believe in their ideas and their own ability to carry them through to success, but at the same time, they have had little practice in writing formal documents, such as business plans. In fact, unless they have a background in business (which only some entrepreneurs possess), they may not even have a clear idea about what a business plan is or what it should contain. The result? Many do not prepare such plans; in fact, statistics show that more than 60 percent of small, new companies have no business plan—or no written plans of any kind, for that matter.[1]

Figure 8.1 Overeager Investors: A Very Rare Occurrence!

Sometimes, investors rush to offer funding to start-up companies in a hot industry, as happened during the late 1990s with respect to Internet companies. In most cases, however, they are much more careful about where they put their hard-earned money!

That brings us to the main purpose of this chapter: helping you understand what a business plan is and how to write one that will assist you in attaining the support you need, financial and otherwise. In order to reach this goal, we will proceed as follows. First, we will examine the question of why you should write a business plan, even if you are in the rare and truly glorious situation of not needing financial support to get started. As we will soon note, preparing this document can be helpful in several important ways. In fact, research findings indicate that entrepreneurs who prepare excellent business plans are more likely to attain success than those who do not—for reasons that will soon become clear. For instance, one recent and very carefully conducted study found that writing business plans significantly reduced the chances of venture failure and increased the rate of new business and new product development among a random sample of Swedish entrepreneurs.[2]

After explaining why it is usually helpful to write a thorough business plan, we will turn to the task of describing this document in detail—the key sections it should contain, how these sections should be put together, and so on. Throughout this discussion, we will do more than just describe the basic requirements: We will also provide you with tips and suggestions for making your plan excellent—an instrument for transmitting your own enthusiasm and vision to others. We think this is crucial information that will serve you well as you move toward starting your own venture.

After we have described the major sections of a formal business plan, we will return to a key theme we wish to emphasize throughout this chapter: Persuasion is, indeed, the name of the game where starting a new venture is concerned. For that reason, writing an excellent business plan, though certainly a crucial activity, is only the first step in a larger process. Persuading other people to support your new venture involves several other steps as well. For instance, a plan that generates initial positive reactions on the part of venture capitalists and other investors to whom you send it (an outcome achieved by only a few percentage of all plans) will often lead to the next step: an invitation for you to make a formal presentation. This presentation often plays an important role in decisions about whether and to what extent to support your venture, so it is a task you should definitely take very seriously. How can you shine in this context? Although we agree with John Ruskin (1749) who once wrote: "He who has truth at his heart need never fear the want of persuasion on his tongue," we also know that being persuasive involves much more than personal conviction. In this section, therefore, we will provide suggestions for reaching these goals, based on both careful research and our personal experiences as entrepreneurs.

Finally, in the Appendix, we provide the example of a real, recent business plan developed by two entrepreneurs to obtain bank financing. In the Voice of Experience section, we talk with these entrepreneurs about the process of developing the business plan and the role it has played in the growth of their business.

WHY WRITE A BUSINESS PLAN? THE BENEFITS OF CLEAR-CUT GOALS

LEARNING OBJECTIVE

1 Define a business plan and explain why entrepreneurs should write one.

Make no mistake: Preparing a business plan requires a lot of hard work. In fact, it usually requires many hours of careful thought, followed by an equal or larger number of hours spent converting these thoughts into a written document. Although university professors may enjoy such activities (!), entrepreneurs often do not. Often, they are eager to get started—to launch their business and make their vision happen. Many realize that once their business has been launched, it will rarely follow the steps and time line outlined in the business plan. So why should they stop and devote so much hard work to the task of preparing a first-rate business plan, even if, as we noted earlier, they are in the rare and enviable position of *not* needing outside resources to get started? Perhaps the simplest yet most important answer we can give is this: *It is truly difficult to arrive somewhere unless you know where you want to go.* In other words, a business plan is much more than a document designed to persuade skeptical people to invest in your new venture: *It is also a detailed road map for converting your ideas and vision into a real, functioning business.* Writing a business plan requires you, as an entrepreneur, to carefully and fully address a number of complex issues relating to the process of converting your idea and its accompanying vision into reality: how your product will be produced, the price at which it will sell, how and to whom it will be marketed, how it will compare with existing or potential competitors, what financial resources are needed and how these will be used, and so on.

In other words, the term "plan" in "business plan" is really appropriate: A carefully prepared and well-reasoned business plan will indeed help you with the process of planning; it really *will* provide the road map mentioned in the title of this chapter. More specifically, a well-prepared business plan will explain what the new venture is trying to accomplish and how it will go about attaining these goals. This is the kind of information venture capitalists and others who might support a new venture often seek, and in fact, the clearer the links between the goals sought and the means for accomplishing them, the more impressive (and persuasive) the business plan will be. But remember: Entrepreneurs do not write business plans solely to persuade others to invest in their new ventures. They also write them to provide themselves with a clearer understanding of the best ways of proceeding. That, we hope you'll agree, is invaluable information that should be sought by all entrepreneurs early in the process.

Having made these points, we should now balance the scales, so to speak, by noting that a business plan is a *living document*—one that often changes—and changes often—as a new business develops. Because you can never know in advance just how your new business will develop, there is a limit to how much planning you can do. For this reason, successful entrepreneurs often avoid analysis paralysis, in which they spend countless hours in the library developing long, formal business plans with lots of data and assumptions, fancy spreadsheets, and beautiful bindings. Instead, they do just enough planning to get their new companies started, and then use the information that they gather from actually running their new ventures to refine their plans in the light of reality. In essence, the successful entrepreneur's business planning model often looks like this: (1) Develop a simple, basic business plan, (2) start the business, (3) take the information that is gained from starting and running the new business and use it to refine the plan and obtain funding as this becomes necessary.

For example, consider Alex D'Arbeloff, founder of Teradyne, a large, public, scientific instruments company. When D'Arbeloff founded his company, he wrote a short business plan only a few pages in length. He assumed that there was little benefit in developing a long, detailed business plan made up mostly of assumptions and analysis of data resting on largely unsupported assumptions. Rather, it was better to focus on the key pieces of information that he knew to be true, and get the business started. Then, once the business was up and running, he revised his business plan many times, adding new information as it was acquired. D'Arbeloff's success as an entrepreneur made him quite wealthy, and he now works as a business angel who has backed such notable companies as Lotus. As a business angel, he maintains the same philosophy that he used when he started his own company: Look for entrepreneurs who have written simple, straightforward business plans that focus on key dimensions of business opportunities that are well understood, and then treat their business plans as living documents that change and develop with the new ventures.

The advantages of this approach are obvious: Entrepreneurs can spend their time getting their business started rather than on writing a formal business plan, and thus have something tangible to sell when they finally do seek large amounts of outside funding to expand their growing businesses. (See Figure 8.2 for a summary of the model of business planning we have just described.)

So overall, is it better to start with a long, detailed business plan or a shorter and simpler one? As you can guess, the answer is "It depends." In some situations, a long and detailed plan is necessary—for instance, when large amounts of funding are required to launch the new venture. In others, a shorter and less detailed plan will suffice—as long as it provides sufficient guidance to get the business started, and it is changed on the fly to reflect new information as it becomes available. The key rule, then, is to *always* engage in careful preparation and planning, but to be flexible and to match the form of the business plan you develop to the specific needs of your new venture.

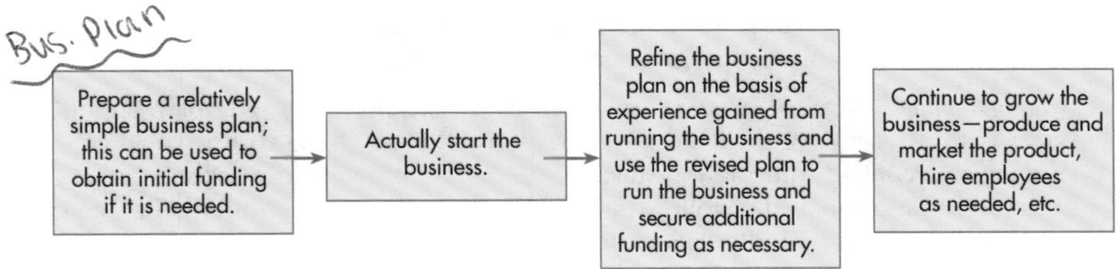

Figure 8.2 A Model of Business Planning Used by Many Successful Entrepreneurs

Many successful entrepreneurs write relatively simple business plans that are based on information they actually know rather than on lots of untested assumptions. Then they start their businesses and use the information they gain from running them to both refine their business plans and to secure additional funding as needed. The cycle continues, thus making business plans true living documents that are open to change in response to new information.

KEY POINTS

- A business plan is a formal written document that explains the entrepreneur's vision and how it will be converted into a profitable, viable business.
- Venture capitalists and other potential sources of funding generally require a formal business plan as a first step for considering investments in new ventures.
- An additional step, and one that is often very important, involves a face-to-face presentation of the plan by the entrepreneur to venture capitalists or other interested parties.
- Preparing a formal business plan is useful for most entrepreneurs because doing so encourages them to formulate specific goals and concrete plans for reaching them, and these are invaluable both for converting ideas into viable companies and for raising needed capital.
- However, many successful entrepreneurs develop a fairly simple business plan, and then refine it in the light of information they gain from actually running the new venture.

COMPONENTS OF A BUSINESS PLAN: BASIC REQUIREMENTS

Business plans are as different in their specific contents as the persons who prepare them. You will find many different business plan templates on the Internet. Overall, though, there is general agreement that they must contain a number of basic sections that, together, address key questions anyone should ask before investing in a new venture:

- *What* is the basic idea for the new product of service?
- *Why* is this new product useful or appealing—and to whom?
- *How* will the idea for the new venture be realized—what is the overall plan for producing the product, for marketing it, and for dealing with existing and future competition?
- *Who* are the entrepreneurs—do they have the required knowledge, experience, and skills to develop this idea and to run a new company?
- If the plan is designed to raise money, *how much* funding is needed, *what type of financing* is needed, *how* will it be used, and how will both the entrepreneurs and other persons realize a return on their investment?

As you can see, these are truly basic and important questions—the kind *you* would ask *yourself* before making an investment in a start-up company. A well-prepared business plan addresses all these questions and many others, too. Moreover, it does so in an *orderly*, *succinct*, and *persuasive* fashion. Pay careful attention to these terms, because they are truly crucial. As we noted earlier, the great majority of all business plans are rejected within a few minutes by experienced venture capitalists who see hundreds or even thousands of such documents each year. As a result of this experience, they employ a set of filters to determine which business plans are worthy of their time and which they can quickly discard. As an entrepreneur, you want to do everything in your power to assure that your business plan is one of the few that receive more than a cursory glance, and that requires careful attention to several basic principles:

- *The plan should be arranged and prepared in proper business form.* The plan should start with a *cover page* showing the name and address of the company and the names and contact information (telephone, e-mail, etc.) for key contact people. This information should be followed by a clear *table of contents* outlining the major sections. The table of contents should then be followed by an *executive summary*; which, in turn, should be followed by the major sections of the plan, each clearly headed and identified. Various appendices (e.g., detailed financial projections, complete résumés for the company's founders and key persons) follow, often bound separately. Overall, the entire plan should adhere to the same basic rule: It should have the appearance of a serious business document, but should *not* seek to wow readers with showy illustrations or super-creative use of type fonts and styles. Remember: The first impression you make on venture capitalists, bankers, and other people important to your company's future will be made by your business plan, so make sure that it looks like what it is: A serious document prepared by serious people!

- *The plan should be succinct.* This principle is absolutely crucial; no one—not even your own family members—will plow through hundreds of pages of dense, convoluted prose (or complex financial figures). An effective business plan, therefore, should be as short and succinct as possible. Anything more than 40 to 50 pages is almost certainly overkill, and up to a point, the shorter the better. For instance, the business plan submitted by Teradyne was six pages in length, and that for Lotus Development was ten pages. The key goal is to address the major questions listed earlier (what, why, how, who, and how much?) in a clear and intelligent manner, without needless detail or redundancy. Always keep in mind that the people you want to read your plan are busy and highly experienced: They know how to cut rapidly to the heart of what your business is all about and to tell whether you are smart enough to present it clearly.
- *The plan should be persuasive.* As we have tried to emphasize, you are facing a highly competitive situation in which you will have a small window of opportunity: Either you seize the attention of the people who read your plan early on and have additional chances to persuade them, or they conclude, within minutes, that reading further would be a waste of time. It is simply a fact of life: Experienced decision makers operate this way in many business contexts, not just with respect to evaluating business plans. For instance, research on job interviews indicates that many interviewers make their judgment about the suitability of each applicant within a minute or two.[3] Why? They simply don't have time to waste on applicants who are clearly not suitable, so they reach a decision about whether to continue the discussion very early in the process. If their decision is "this is not a suitable person," they conclude the interview very quickly. If, instead, they decide "this could be a good candidate," they keep the interview going in order to acquire more information. The same principle is at work with respect to business plans: Decisions are made very quickly by venture capitalists and other potential sources of funding and are rarely, if ever, reversed.[4] Therefore, you must begin strong, and continue strong, if you want to succeed. And the place where a business plan begins is the executive summary—the first major component of the business plan and, in some ways, the most important.

One more point: We want to emphasize that, ultimately, it is the quality of the idea behind the new venture, and the quality of the person or persons who have put it together that are crucial. If the idea is not sound and has little economic potential, experienced investors will recognize this weakness immediately, no matter how well-written or persuasive the plan appears to be. So before you decide to invest large amounts of time and effort into preparing a super-impressive business plan, you absolutely *must* get feedback on the idea behind your new venture. If the response is not encouraging, stop right there, because proceeding is almost certain to be a waste of time.

LEARNING OBJECTIVE

2 Explain how the process of persuasion plays a key role in business plans and in the success of new ventures.

The Executive Summary

LEARNING OBJECTIVE

3 Explain why the executive summary is a very important part of any business plan.

Have you ever heard the phrase "elevator pitch"? I (Robert Baron) first became familiar with it while working at a government agency (I was a program director at the National Science Foundation). I observed that many of my more experienced colleagues went to lunch at a specific time each day and that they jockeyed for position in front of the elevator. Why? Because they wanted to stand next to the division director—the person who made key decisions about how funds available to our part of the agency would be distributed—and they knew that she would be standing on the elevator when the door opened (because her office was on a higher floor). On the way down to the street, they made their elevator pitches—brief but impassioned statements about the wonderful things going on in their particular areas of science, and why funding of such work would be a great investment. The director usually made no concrete response, but in a few cases, I heard her remark, "That sounds interesting ... make an appointment so we can discuss it." That response signified great success because it meant that the one- or two-minute pitch delivered in the elevator had at least opened the door to further discussions—and the real possibility of additional funding.

The moral of such situations is clear: Often, we have just a brief opportunity to stimulate another person's interest—to get them interested enough to want to learn more. That, in essence, is the purpose of the executive summary. This part of the business plan—which should be brief and to the point (many experienced investors suggest two to three pages at most)—should provide a short, clear, and persuasive overview of what the new venture is all about. In essence, it should provide brief answers to all the questions listed earlier: What is the idea for the new product or service? Why will it be appealing—and to whom? Who are the entrepreneurs? How much funding (and in what form) are they seeking?

Can all this be accomplished within a brief format? Absolutely. But being succinct requires very careful and thoughtful writing—writing that delivers a lot of information per sentence (or even word), yet also conveys the entrepreneurs' excitement and enthusiasm. We wish we could provide you with a few simple rules for writing such a document, but in fact, we cannot: The precise contents will depend on the specific ideas you are presenting. But whatever your ideas are, the executive summary should answer key questions briefly, but in enough detail that a reader can form a clear picture of what your new venture is all about. Remember: This is an important part of the business plan, so it is worthy of special effort. It is your first and best chance (and often your only chance!) to generate interest in others, so by all means, make it your very best shot in all respects.

After the executive summary, major sections follow in an orderly arrangement. Many arrangements of these key sections are possible, but here is one that is used in many business plans and that seems quite logical. The specific order of the sections—as well as their content, however—should be dictated by the nature of your idea and what you are trying to communicate in the plan, not by any hard-and-fast preset rules.

LEARNING OBJECTIVE

4 Describe the major sections of a business plan and the types of information they should include.

- *Background and purpose.* A section describing your idea and the current state of your business.
- *Marketing.* A section describing the market for your product or service—who will want to use or buy it, and—most importantly—*why* they would want to do so. In other words, describe your target market and your value proposition. Business plans often have separate sections detailing the firm's communication strategy, pricing strategy, distribution strategy, and sales strategy.
- *Competition.* Information on the existing competition and how it will be overcome, pricing, and related issues. (Sometimes the discussion on the competition is a separate section, and sometimes it is included in the marketing section.) Readers of your plan want to know what the market gap is, how you will enter the market to fill the gap, and how you will build and sustain competitive advantage against current firms and future entrants.
- *Development, production, and location.* Where your product or service is right now in terms of development, how you will move toward actually producing or providing the product or service, and (if it is relevant to your company) where the new venture will be located. Information on operations, too, can be included in this section if it is an important factor in understanding what the business will do and why it has significant economic potential.

- *Management.* A section describing the experience, skills, and knowledge of the new venture's management team—what you have and what additional skills may be required in the months ahead. Information on current ownership should be included here.
- *Financial section.* This section provides information on the company's current financial state and offers projections for future needs, revenues, and other financial measures. It should also include information on the amount of funding being sought, when such funds are required, how they will be used, cash flow, and a breakeven analysis.
- *Risk factors.* This section discusses various risks the new venture will face and the steps the management team is taking to protect against them.
- *Harvest or exit.* Investors are interested in understanding precisely how they will gain if the company is successful, so information on this important issue (e.g., when and how the company might go public) can often be very useful.
- *Scheduling and milestones.* Information on when each phase of the new venture will be completed should be included, so that potential investors will know just when key tasks (e.g., start of production, time to first sales, projected breakeven point) will be completed. The scheduling and milestones can be a separate section, or it can be included in other sections, as appropriate.
- *Appendices.* Here is where detailed financial information and detailed résumés of the top management team should be presented.

To be complete, all business plans must cover these and closely related topics. However, depending on the specific nature of the new venture, the order can be altered, and the relative length adjusted. In other words, there are no hard-and-fast rules about how long or detailed each section should be; rather, the length and scope are matters of good business judgment.

Now that we've provided an overview of the key sections included in a sound business plan, we'll describe each of these sections in more detail.

Background, Product, and Purpose

Among the first pieces of information potential investors want to know are facts relating to the background of your product and your company and what, specifically, you hope to accomplish. As we noted in Chapters 2 and 3, ideas for new products or services do not arise in a vacuum; rather, such opportunities emerge out of changing economic, technological, and social conditions and are then recognized by specific persons who take action to develop them. A key question from potential investors, then, is "What is the nature of the idea driving your company and how did it arise?" The answer will often require discussing conditions in the industry in which your company is located, because these conditions, in part, have likely suggested the idea you are now seeking to develop.

For instance, suppose that an entrepreneur has developed a new material that gives the soles of shoes much better traction than any material now on the market. Potential investors will want to know why this feature is useful and who will want to use the new material (e.g., manufacturers of athletic shoes? manufacturers of medical devices for people who have been hurt in accidents or who have brittle bones?). In other words, this section of the business plan should explain what the product has to offer—why it is unique and valuable, and therefore has potential for generating future profits. Unless these issues can be addressed clearly and successfully, investors are likely to conclude that the risks far outweigh any potential benefits.

Investors also usually want basic information about the existing company—its legal form, its current ownership, and its current financial condition. After all, no one wants to invest in a new venture in which thorny issues of ownership exist, or where there is an excessively high overhead.

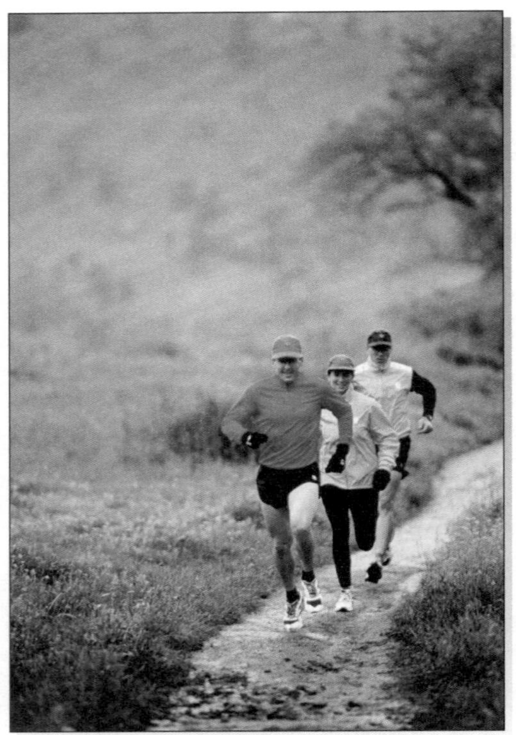

John Kelly/The Image Bank/Getty Images

Figure 8.3 Describing the New Venture's Goals or Mission

The first major section of a business plan should provide background information on the nature of the product and the start-up venture. It should also include information on the new venture's goals—a brief mission statement. For instance, a company that wants to develop a new material that gives shoes better traction might present data indicating how many athletes are injured each year in falls, and show how the company's product would help reduce the frequency of such accidents.

This section of the business plan should also address the company's goals: What does it hope to accomplish? Returning to the venture with a new material for shoes, described earlier, this section of the business plan should clarify whether the new material will be generally useful for all kinds of shoes or only for some (e.g., running shoes) and the benefits its use will confer. For instance, perhaps many thousands of persons are injured in falls each year, and perhaps many of these injuries could be prevented through use of the new material (see Figure 8.3). In that case, these potential benefits should be mentioned along with the financial benefits that will stem from the company's success. But again, the usefulness of such information depends very much on the idea behind the new venture, and it is more appropriate for some than others. Like everything else in the plan, the potential benefits should only be included if they are relevant and will contribute to both planning by the entrepreneurs and their ability to communicate the nature of the company to others.

In sum, after reading this initial section, potential investors will understand where and how the product was developed, the basic nature of the entrepreneur's company (its legal form, ownership, history), what it is that makes this product or service valuable or unique, and what the new venture will seek to accomplish—a brief statement of its mission. Together, this information provides a useful framework for understanding later sections of the business plan, so it is important that it be presented first.

Market Analysis

One reason why products fail is that no one conducted careful market analysis before they were produced; in other words, no one bothered to find out if there was a market for them—whether anyone would really want to buy or use them. The result? Disaster for the entrepreneurs who invented them and for anyone who invested in the companies that were launched to produce and sell these items.

It is not surprising, then, that sophisticated investors want to see specific and detailed information concerning marketing as part of any strong business plan. Specifically, they want information on what entrepreneurs have done to identify the market for their product (e.g., have they conducted marketing surveys? detailed market analyses?). Moreover, investors want to know how large these markets are, whether they are growing or shrinking, and how the new products or services will be promoted in these markets. This analysis often requires detailed information about *competing products*—whether they exist and, if so, how the new product will be demonstrably superior; *competing companies*—who are they, and how they are likely to respond to the entrepreneurs' new product; and *pricing*—how the new product or service will be priced relative to competing products or services, and why this pricing strategy makes sense.

For instance, consider Photowow.com, a company started by Robert Schiff in Los Angeles. Schiff's company makes large pieces of art for use in homes and businesses. This art is produced by large-format inkjet printers and can show almost anything—for instance, the buyer's children in pop montages resembling the style of a famous artist, such as Andy Warhol. This is an entirely new product, so pricing it was a challenging task and required careful consideration of existing products (e.g., art posters). Marketing, too, raised complex questions: What would be the potential market for such art? Many possibilities existed: franchises, which would want to show a picture of their founders in every outlet; corporations, which might want to have a picture of the home office in every branch. Schiff explored all these, plus others, with the help of consultants and was then able to include this information in his business plan.

In essence, this section of a new venture's business plan should be designed to convince skeptical investors that the entrepreneurs have done their homework: They have examined potential markets for their product or service carefully and have evidence indicating that consumers or other businesses (depending on the product or service) will want to buy it when it becomes available. Further, investors want to know the specifics of how the new product or service will be promoted, and at what cost. Market projections are, of course, always uncertain; no one ever knows for certain how consumers will react to new products (see Figure 8.4). But at the very least, entrepreneurs should have engaged in state-of-the-art efforts to learn why people will want to buy or use their products, and to pinpoint an effective marketing strategy. If, instead, it is simply assumed that the product or service is so wonderful that people will line up to buy it, a loud alarm will sound for sophisticated investors, and they will quickly lose interest.

Development, Production, and Location

It is not possible to market a new product or service unless it is available, so another issue that must be carefully addressed in any effective business plan is product development and production. Potential investors want information about where the new venture's products and services are in this process: Are they still under development? Are they fully developed and ready to be manufactured? If so, what are the projected costs and timetable for making the product or for delivering the service? Related issues include steps to assure quality and safety for consumers or other users (e.g., has the company applied for Underwriters Laboratory approval, or similar certification?). As I learned while running my own company, such processes can require months—and considerable fees—so investors want to know that entrepreneurs are aware of these issues and have them well in hand.

The further along a start-up company is with respect to these issues, the more attractive it will be to potential investors—not simply because the company has developed beyond the initial launch phase, but also because this progress demonstrates that the company is operating in a productive and rational manner. I (Robert Baron) recently invested in a new biotechnology company, mainly because I liked the basic idea (developing drugs for orphan diseases—ailments that afflict too few people for major drug companies to bother with) and also because I know and respect the founders. Another important consideration for me, however, was where the company stood with respect to development of effective new drugs. My conclusion was that everything was in place to allow the new venture to move ahead quickly, but only time will tell whether I was correct in this judgment. In any case, I—like other potential investors—searched for information on this issue in the company's business plan and would certainly have been less enthusiastic about investing in it if such information were not included or was too general in scope to be informative.

Figure 8.4 Market Analysis: Sometimes Uncertain, But Always Essential

Entrepreneurs should always devote careful attention to the following question: "What is the need for our product or service? Why, in other words, would anyone want to buy or use it?" Market research can often help to answer this question. The product on the left was introduced after market research indicated that consumers would want to buy it—which is exactly what happened: It was a huge success. In contrast, the product on the right was introduced mainly because the company that produced it simply assumed that a market for it existed; in fact, consumers did not want it and the product largely failed.

© Roger Ressmeyer/CORBIS

AP/ Wide World Photos/Carlos Osorio

The Management Team

Many venture capitalists note that they would rather invest in a first-rate team with a second-rate idea than a second-rate team with a first-rate idea. Although this saying is something of an exaggeration—venture capitalists and other investors actually focus on many different issues—there is actually a substantial grain of truth in such statements. What venture capitalists are saying, in essence, is that talented, experienced, and motivated people at the top of a new venture are very important for its success. For this reason, a key section of any business plan describes the people who will run the new venture.

What, specifically, do potential investors want to know? Primarily that, taken together, these people have the experience, expertise, skills, and personal characteristics needed to run the new venture successfully. We say "taken together," because as we pointed out in Chapter 5, investors want to know that the management team has complementary skills, abilities, and experience: What one person is lacking, others provide, and vice versa. Further, investors want to be reasonably certain that the members of the team have developed good working relationships: Each has clearly assigned roles and duties, and communication between them is good. Although investors may be willing to bend these requirements to a degree—for instance, they can't really require decades of experience from a very young group of entrepreneurs—they do demand at least some of them. If the management team of a new venture is lacking in experience, for instance, they may require that the entrepreneurs hire seasoned executives to assist in running the business—in other words, that they acquire needed experience from outside the new venture team itself. Similarly, if entrepreneurs are lacking in experience, investors may place greater weight on their training, their intelligence, and their interpersonal skills. Seasoned investors know from past experience that entrepreneurs who are good at getting along with others are more likely to succeed than those who are rough around the edges and annoy or irritate the people with whom they deal. After all, why should anyone give their business to a stranger who rubs them the wrong way? Surely, it would take a vastly superior product or service to tip the balance this way. In fact, research findings indicate that entrepreneurs who are high in social skills are indeed more successful in running new ventures than ones who are not.[5]

In short, potential investors place a great deal of emphasis on the qualifications of entrepreneurs, and do everything they can to assure that the companies they fund are headed by people in whom they can have confidence. The source of such confidence is, ideally, past business experience, but if this background is lacking, potential investors will seek to assure that this potential weakness is offset by other strengths brought to the table by the founding entrepreneurs: high intelligence (social and cognitive), a high level of technical skill, and yes—energy and enthusiasm!

Financial Plans and Projections

Every section of a business plan is important—of that there can be no doubt. But one section that is absolutely certain to receive close and especially careful examination is the section dealing with financial matters. This section should include several major components, each of which must be carefully prepared. As we explained in Chapter 6, these elements provide a picture of the company's current financial state, how it will use the funds it receives from investors, and how it will manage its financial resources to reach its major objectives.

The financial section should provide an assessment of what assets the venture will own, what debt it will have, and so on. As Chapter 6 explained, such information is summarized in a **proforma balance sheet**, showing projections of the company's financial condition at various times in the future; such information should be projected semiannually for the first three years. These projected balance sheets allow investors to determine whether debt-to-equity ratios, working capital, inventory turnover, and other financial indices are within acceptable limits and justify initial and future funding of the company. In addition, as Chapter 6 explained, a **proforma income statement** should be prepared to illustrate projected operating results based on profit and loss. This statement records sales, costs of goods sold, expenses, and profit or loss, and should take careful account of sales forecasts, production costs, costs of advertising, distribution, storage, and administrative expenses. In short, it should provide a reasonable projection of operating results. Finally a **cash flow statement** showing the amount and timing of expected cash inflows and outflows should be prepared, again for a period of several years. By highlighting expected sales and capital expenditures over a specific period of time, this forecast will underscore the need for and timing of further financing and needs for working capital. These forms are summarized in Table 8.1.

Another key part of the financial section—one also discussed in Chapter 6—should be a **breakeven analysis**, a table showing the level of sales (and production) needed to cover all costs. This analysis should include costs that vary with the level of production (manufacturing, labour, materials, sales) and costs that do not vary with production (interest charges, salaries, rent, and so on). The breakeven analysis is a very important reality check for entrepreneurs who often have an overly optimistic view of how quickly their new venture can become profitable, and it is often examined with considerable care by potential investors.

Overall, the financial section of the business plan should provide potential investors with a clear picture of how the new venture will use the resources it already has, resources generated by continuing operations, and resources provided by investors to move toward its financial objectives. If there is any section in which entrepreneurs should strive to hold their enthusiasm and optimism in check, it is the financial plans and projections: Many investors have learned to view entrepreneurs' financial projections with a healthy dose of skepticism. Investors have seen too many overly optimistic predictions to view the situation otherwise; in fact, many begin by discounting entrepreneurs' projections by a minimum of 50 percent!

Critical Risks: Describing What Might Go Wrong

You probably know this saying, known as Murphy's Law: "If anything can go wrong, it will." Perhaps you have also heard the corollary: "Murphy was an optimist." Entrepreneurs, filled with enthusiasm for their new ventures, are not the most likely candidates on earth to think hard and long about what can go wrong with respect to their new ventures. On the contrary, they prefer to dwell on the upside and are often genuinely dismayed when things do *not* go according to plan, which is one reason why effective business plans should contain a section specifically focused on what might potentially go wrong—critical risks that can prevent the new venture from reaching its key objectives. Thinking about these risks is good medicine for entrepreneurs, and formulating ways of responding to these potential calamities before they occur can be constructive indeed!

What are the potential risks new ventures face? Here is a partial list:

- Price cutting by competitors, who refuse to roll over and play dead for the new venture
- Unforeseen industry trends that make the new venture's product or service less desirable—or less marketable
- Sales projections that are not achieved for a variety of reasons, thus reducing cash flow
- Design, manufacturing, or shipping costs that exceed estimates. Product development or production schedules that are not met (people problems, such as low employee motivation, can play a role in each of the last three points)

INCOME STATEMENT	CASH FLOW STATEMENT
Includes sales as they are generated.	Shows sales as "cash in" only when payment is received.
Includes depreciation.	Depreciations are added back in because it is not a cash expense.
Interest on loans is included.	Both interest and principle are included.
Beginning inventory and ending inventory are included in the calculation of cost of goods sold.	Inventory purchases are recorded as bills actually paid

Table 8.1 Income Statements and Cash Flow Statements: Some Key Differences

Income statements and cash flow statements differ in several important respects.

Figure 8.5 New Ventures Face Retaliation from Existing Firms

New ventures confront many risks. One risk is litigation from existing competitors. Even if the new venture is successful in a lawsuit, legal matters can divert the firm's management from developing the market for its products. Such lawsuits can take a long time. The lawsuit by Danish company LEGO, against Montreal-based Mega Bloks, was launched in 1996 and was not completed until 2005.

- Problems stemming from top management's lack of experience (e.g., an inability to negotiate contracts with suppliers or customers on favourable terms)
- Longer than expected lead times with respect to obtaining parts or raw materials
- Difficulties in raising additional, needed financing
- Unforeseen political, economic, social, or technological trends or developments (e.g., new government legislation or the sudden start of a major recession)

These are just a few of the many potential risks that can put new ventures badly off the track. The difficulty in identifying risks is that many are truly unexpected. In particular, entrepreneurs need to think about how rivals might react to the start of their firm (see Figure 8.5). For instance, Montreal-based Mega Bloks sells interlocking plastic blocks that can be used interchangeably with LEGO blocks. Although patent protection for LEGO blocks expired in 1988, LEGO claimed that Mega Bloks infringed on its trademark because the raised studs on the toy bricks were part of its distinctive brand.[6] LEGO launched a lawsuit in 1996 that continued until 2005, when the Supreme Court of Canada ruled in Mega Blok's favour. Mega Bloks is also undefeated in the highest courts of Greece and France, and has cases pending in Spain and Italy.[7] Lawsuits such as these are time-consuming and expensive for new firms to deal with. Although Mega Bloks' management was successful in growing the firm while managing this legal issue in jurisdictions around the world, lawsuits launched by rivals can distract a new firm's management from other market priorities.

Many of the potential risks are frightening to contemplate, so why should entrepreneurs describe them in detail in their business plans? Mainly because recognizing these dangers is the first step toward coming up with strategies to deal with them if they do in fact occur. Writing an appropriate risk-related section for their business plan obliges entrepreneurs to perform this task and take these potential risks into account.

Reaping the Rewards: Harvest and Exit

All good things must come to an end, and even the most enthusiastic of entrepreneurs realizes that at some point, they may want to leave the companies they started. This decision may come about because they have reached a stage in life where they want to sit back a bit and enjoy the fruits of their labours or, alternatively, because it is they crave the excitement of starting something new, so they may choose to launch yet another new venture. Whatever the reason, every business plan should include a section that describes both *management succession*—how the founding entrepreneurs can, ultimately, be replaced—and *exit strategies for investors*—how they can ultimately reap the benefits of having funded the new venture. Initially, ownership of a new venture is not a liquid asset: Shares cannot readily be sold to other persons. Later, however, this status can change radically if the company has an initial public offering (IPO) and its shares are subsequently traded on a national exchange. The business plan should address this and other potential exit strategies for investors, and for founders, too. In fact, this section is often very important to investors who fully understand the Arab proverb: "Think of the going out before you enter."

Scheduling and Milestones

A final section in the body of the business plan should address when major activities will be performed and key milestones reached. Again, giving careful thought to the timing of when various tasks will be performed or specific goals achieved is useful both for entrepreneurs and potential investors. Identifying target dates may help entrepreneurs overcome a powerful cognitive bias known as the *planning fallacy*, which we described in Chapter 3—the tendency to assume that we can accomplish more in a given period of time than is really possible.[8] In this way, it can serve as another important reality check. From the point of view of investors, it indicates that entrepreneurs are indeed paying careful attention to the operations of their company and have developed clear plans for its future progress. What are these milestones? Included among the most important are these:

- Formal incorporation of the new venture (if this has not already occurred)
- Completion of product or service design
- Completion of prototypes
- Hiring of initial persons (sales or otherwise)
- Product display at trade shows
- Reaching agreements with distributors and suppliers
- Launch of initial production
- Receipt of initial orders
- First sales and deliveries
- Profitability

This list is just a small sample of the many milestones new ventures can include in their business plans; many others exist as well. The important point is to select milestones that make sense both from the point of view of the company's resources and the industry in which it is located.

Appendices

Because the main body of the plan should be relatively brief—as short as is adequate for presenting all essential information—several items are best included in separate appendices. Items typically included are detailed financial projections and full résumés of the founders and other members of the top management team. By including such items in appendices, entrepreneurs ensure that this important information is present for persons who wish to examine it, but at the same time keep the length of the business plan within desirable limits.

A Note on the Intangibles

In the preceding section, we described an outline of the essentials—the sections that are generally viewed as necessary for any thorough business plan. What we haven't addressed, of course, is what might be termed the *intangibles*—the extra something that leads readers of a plan to drop their slightly jaded attitude and to conclude, perhaps with some excitement, that there is indeed something here worth a closer look. We have all done a large amount of writing, so we believe that such factors as organization, clarity, choice of words, and style do indeed matter. Unfortunately, no one has yet been able to draw a bead on how these factors operate or how you can turn them to your own advantage. Given the importance of the business plan in the future of your new venture, however, we do have a concrete suggestion: Before distributing it to potential investors, have a number of people who are known to be good writers read it. If they will do it as a favour, that's great; if not, pay them for their time. Then *listen carefully to their suggestions* and revise the plan accordingly. Honestly, we can't think of anything else you can do that is likely to yield as much benefit for you and for your new venture. (What about the downside—are there specific errors you

LEARNING OBJECTIVE

5 Describe the seven deadly sins of business plans—errors all entrepreneurs should avoid.

should be careful to avoid because they can be the kiss of death to any business plan? Our answer is "Yes." And we have attempted to summarize the most important of these in the **Danger! Pitfall Ahead!** section.)

KEY POINTS

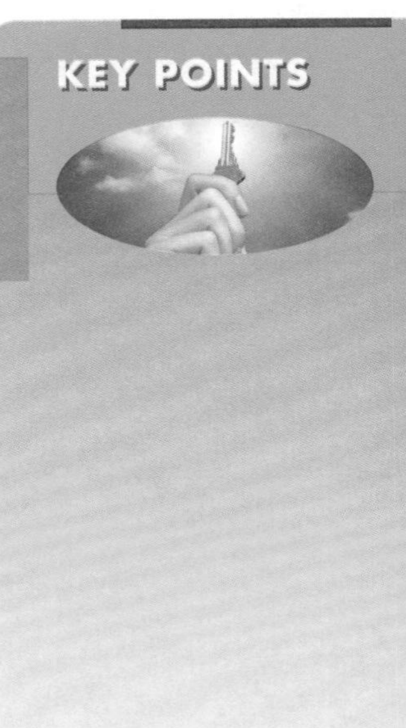

- All business plans should begin with an executive summary—a brief (two to three pages) section that provides a brief, clear, and persuasive overview of what the new venture is all about.
- Subsequent sections should include:
  Background and purpose. A section describing your idea and the current state of the business.
  Marketing. A section describing the market for the new venture's product or service, why there is a need for the product (or service) and why anyone would want to buy it, plus information on the existing competition and how it will be overcome, and pricing.
  Development, production, and location. Where the product or service is, in terms of development, how it will be produced, and (if appropriate) information on where the business will be located.
  Management. A section describing the experience, skills, and knowledge of the new venture's management team.
  Financial section. A section that provides information on the company's current financial state, and offers projections for future needs, revenues, and other financial measures, as well as a breakeven analysis.
  Risk factors. A section that discusses various risks the new venture will face, and the steps the management team is taking to protect against these threats.
  Harvest or exit. A section focused on how investors will gain if the company is successful.
  Scheduling and milestones. An overview of when each phase of the new venture will be completed, so that potential investors will know just when key tasks (e.g., start of production, time to first sales, projected breakeven point) will be completed.
  Appendices. Detailed financial information and detailed résumés of the top management team.

DANGER! PITFALL AHEAD!

The Seven Deadly Sins for New Venture Business Plans

Let us say it again: less than five minutes. That's the amount of time your plan has in the hands of many potential investors before they decide to turn thumbs up or thumbs down on it. In other words, in just a few moments, they evaluate a document that may have taken you weeks or even months to prepare. For this reason, it is absolutely imperative that you avoid errors that will doom your plan to the rejection pile no matter how good other sections of it may be. We term these the "Seven Deadly Sins of New Venture Business Plans." Here they are for you to recognize—and avoid:

Sin #1: The plan is poorly prepared and has an unprofessional look (e.g., no cover page, a cover page without contact information, glaring typos). This kind of carelessness triggers the following investor reaction: "I'm dealing with a group of amateurs."

Sin #2: The plan is far too slick (e.g., it is bound like a book, is printed on shiny paper, uses flashy graphics). This kind of glossy presentation leads investors to think: "What are they trying to hide behind all those fireworks?"

Sin #3: The executive summary is too long and rambling—it doesn't get right to the point. This excessiveness leads investors to think: "If they can't describe their own idea and company succinctly, I don't want to waste my time with them."

Sin #4: It's not clear where the product is in terms of development—does it exist or not? Can it be readily manufactured? Investors conclude: "I can't tell whether this is real or just another pipe dream; I'll pass on this one."

Sin #5: No clear answer is provided to the question: "Why would anyone ever want to buy one?" Many entrepreneurs seem to assume that their new product or service is so great that it will virtually sell itself. This type of self-assurance leads investors to think: "How naïve can you get? Even a machine that grew hair on the heads of bald men would need a marketing plan. These are truly amateurs."

Sin #6: There is no clear statement of the qualifications of the management team. This lack of information leads investors to conclude: "They probably have no relevant experience—and may not even know what relevant experience would be!"

Sin #7: Financial projections are largely an exercise in wishful thinking. This kind of optimism leads potential investors to conclude: "They have no idea about what it is like to run a company, or (even worse) they think I am incredibly naïve or stupid. Pass!" (These Seven Deadly Sins are summarized in Figure 8.6.)

The moral is clear: Keep a sharp lookout for these seven deadly errors because if you commit even one, your chance of obtaining help from sophisticated investors will drop off the bottom of the scale.

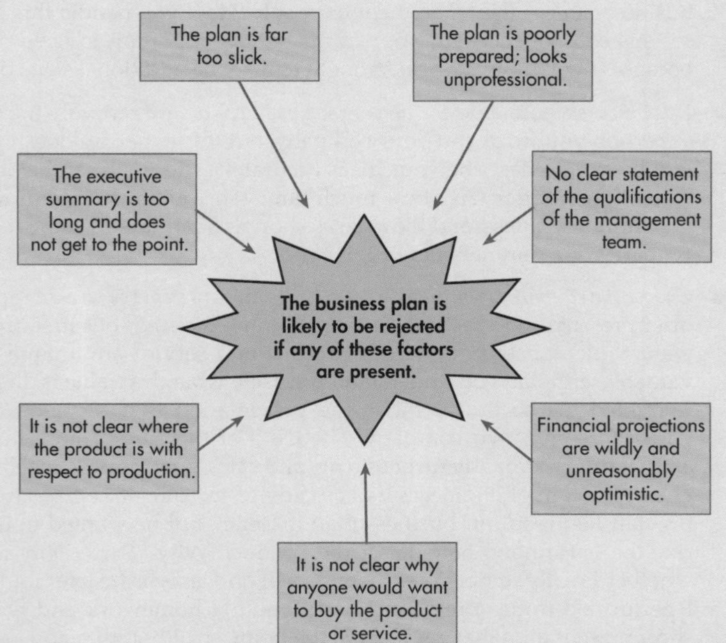

Figure 8.6 The Seven Deadly Sins for New Venture Business Plans

If one or more of these errors or problems are present in a business plan, it is likely to be rejected by potential investors, no matter how good other aspects of the plan may be.

MAKING AN EFFECTIVE BUSINESS PLAN PRESENTATION: THE BALL IS DEFINITELY IN YOUR COURT

LEARNING OBJECTIVE

6 Explain why potential investors usually ask entrepreneurs to give verbal presentations describing their idea for new products or services and their company.

LEARNING OBJECTIVE

7 Describe the steps entrepreneurs can take to make their verbal presentations to potential investors truly excellent.

Researchers who study stress agree that the way in which people think about stressful situations is a powerful determinant of how they react to them. One possible reaction is to emphasize the downside—to imagine what will happen if you simply can't cope with the stressful situation. Many people feel this way about making formal presentations: They imagine forgetting what they planned to say or harsh rejection from the audience, which causes them to experience high levels of anxiety that can, in turn, interfere with their actual performance. In contrast, another way to think about high-stress situations is to view them as a *challenge*—an opportunity to rise to the occasion and show the world what you've got. When people think about stressful situations in this way, they experience lower levels of anxiety, and their performance often matches their expectations: It *does* rise to new heights.[9]

Likewise, you should consider yourself fortunate to have the opportunity to verbally present your idea and your company to venture capitalists or other potential investors or sources of funding. The fact that you have been invited to make the presentation indicates that you have successfully passed the first major hurdle: More than 90 percent of plans do not generate an invitation to make a presentation, so you are already in a select group. Because you have done such a good job in preparing your plan, why should you doubt your ability to make a dynamite presentation? Basically, you should not; on the contrary, confidence, not doubt, should be your guiding principle. But confidence does not automatically translate into a first-rate presentation. Confidence, like writing an excellent business plan, requires a lot of preparation. Yes, some of us are better at making presentations—and at persuasion—than others, but almost all of us can improve our presentation skills if we try. Here are some concrete steps you can take (we really mean *should* take) to assure that your verbal presentation will match the high quality of your business plan—or even exceed it.

- *Remember: This really is important.* Your carefully prepared business plan has opened the door, but venture capitalists, bankers, and business angels do not give funds to business plans—they give them to people. How you handle this presentation has serious consequences for your company. It's important to keep this fact in mind because it will motivate you strongly to take the additional steps described below.
- *Prepare, prepare, and then ... prepare some more.* You are certainly the world's greatest expert on your idea and your company, but this expertise doesn't mean that you will be able to describe your ideas accurately, succinctly, and eloquently without careful preparation. Ask how much time you will have for your remarks (often it is 20 minutes or less, and it can be as short as 5 minutes in some settings) and then prepare your comments to fit this time.
- *Choose the content carefully.* What, exactly, should you try to accomplish during this brief presentation? Several areas need to be covered, but first and foremost you want to demonstrate that your product and service are unique and potentially valuable, and that you understand precisely what this value is. In this context, I'm reminded of the time I made the presentation that secured a manufacturing partner for my own company. The CEO of this large (more than $1 billion in annual sales) company turned to me and said, "OK, professor, tell us what you've got." His team of engineers had already tested our prototypes exhaustively, and his staff had read our business plan in detail, but he wanted to hear *me* summarize the nature and benefits of the product. Why? Partly, I'm sure, to find out whether I really understood them myself and also, as he later told me, to see how I performed under pressure. I had done my homework and was ready with a short presentation that got right to the point, so although many pointed questions followed later, I felt from the start that I was on the right track.

- *Remember that you are trying to persuade, not overwhelm.* One potential trap for many entrepreneurs—especially ones from a technical background—is to lapse quickly into technical language that only others in that technical field would understand. This approach can be a serious tactical error, because although the people you are addressing are highly intelligent and have a wide range of business experience, they may not have the specific training needed to understand highly technical descriptions. In general, it is far better to focus on the big picture—what the product does and why it is superior to other, competing products, rather than to slip into technical language that is easy and comfortable for the entrepreneur, but which may be largely unfamiliar to at least some potential investors.

- *Show enthusiasm—but temper it with reality checks.* Yes, you should definitely be enthusiastic; after all, this is *your* baby and *your* chance to shine, but temper your enthusiasm with hard facts and data. If you have completed marketing research, mention it briefly as you discuss marketing strategy. In any financial projections you mention, ensure that you keep at least one foot in contact with the ground; anyone can use a spreadsheet program to demonstrate sales that soon exceed the entire gross national product of the country. Your audience will certainly *not* be dazzled—or influenced—by numbers that make little or no business sense.

- *Rehearse!* There is no substitute for rehearsal where oral presentations are concerned. Some of these practice runs should be performed in front of friends and cofounders of your company so that you can get their feedback on how to improve. Others should be in front of people totally unfamiliar with your idea or company; that will help you find out whether your presentation makes sense to people learning about it for the first time. (When you give your formal presentation, some of the people in the audience will probably be in this situation, or—at most—they will have read your two-page executive summary.) Some rehearsals don't even require an audience. It is often helpful to deliver portions of your presentations to the four walls of your own room or office, just to make sure that you have committed major points to memory.

- *Don't overlook the basics.* It's amazing, but we have both personally attended many presentations that fell flat on their face because the people giving them had focused on the content, delivery, and level of their talks, but had forgotten about the basics. For instance, we have seen many talks in which the presenters spent precious time trying to figure out how to get their slides to appear on the screen, or in trying to explain charts or tables that were extremely complex or unreadable by the audience. In other cases, presenters failed to keep track of time and ran out of this precious commodity before they could make key points. *Don't overlook these basic issues.* If you do, all your hard work and careful presentation may go directly down the drain, and for very little reason.

- *Adopt a cooperative, helpful approach to questions.* One thing that is sure to happen during and after your presentation is that members of the audience will ask you pointed, searching questions. These questions should come as no surprise. First, you are asking them to give you money—perhaps large amounts of money. Second, they are an experienced group, who have seen lots of things go wrong with what seemed, at first, to be excellent start-up ventures. They are cautious and will have no qualms about asking you to hold forth on virtually any point made in your business plan—and also on issues not considered in the plan. Your answers to these questions are important and must make good sense, but so, too, is your attitude. If you bristle with obvious annoyance when asked a pointed question, or when the person who asks a question objects to your answer, this clash is a sign to potential investors that you may be lacking in the kind of emotional maturity they want to see in entrepreneurs, and you may *not* be a good bet. Your reaction to questions should be to take all questions seriously, answer them as best as possible, and maintain a helpful, cooperative attitude, no matter how intense the session becomes.

If you keep these points firmly in mind, we believe that you will have a good chance of making an excellent presentation—a much better chance than would be true if you ignore these points or minimize their importance. But suppose that despite your best efforts, and despite the fact that you did an excellent job, you still receive a "no" from a group on which you pinned high hopes. Should you be discouraged? Not at all. Very few entrepreneurs obtain support from the first potential investors they approach. In fact, highly successful entrepreneurs often note that their companies were rejected by many investors initially. In view of this fact, you should view rejections as an opportunity to learn, and you should try to obtain as much information as possible from them. Try to find out *why* your proposal was rejected, and whether there were aspects of the plan and your presentation that the potential investors found especially weak—or strong. Then, go back to the drawing boards and rework both your plan and your presentation. Along these lines, there are two key points you should keep firmly in mind: (1) There is almost always room for improvement, in virtually everything; and (2) success does *not* have to be immediate to be sweet. Good luck!

KEY POINTS

- Entrepreneurs should view invitations to give verbal presentations about their idea and their company as a challenge—a chance to shine—rather than as a high-stress situation in which they may be overwhelmed.
- Because such presentations are very important to the future of new ventures, entrepreneurs should take them very seriously and try to do an outstanding job.
- Steps that can help entrepreneurs accomplish this goal include selecting content carefully, avoiding technical jargon, showing enthusiasm tempered by reality, rehearsing carefully, paying careful attention to basic aspects of presentations (e.g., arriving early to set up audiovisual systems), and adopting a helpful cooperative attitude toward questions.
- Entrepreneurs should view rejections by potential investors as an opportunity to learn—to improve both their business plan and their verbal presentations.

THE VOICE OF EXPERIENCE

Business Planning Is More Important Than the Business Plan

Courtesy of Admiral Road

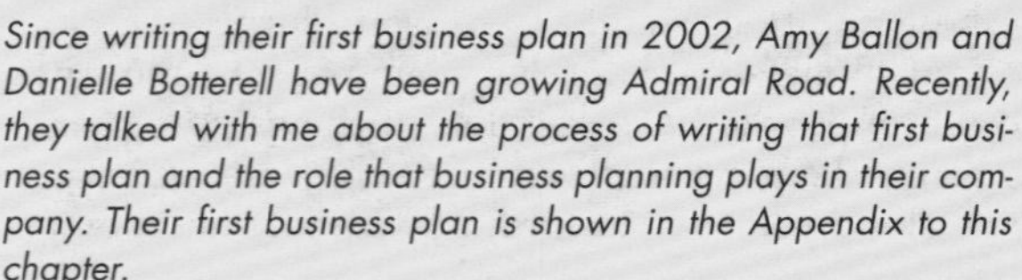

Since writing their first business plan in 2002, Amy Ballon and Danielle Botterell have been growing Admiral Road. Recently, they talked with me about the process of writing that first business plan and the role that business planning plays in their company. Their first business plan is shown in the Appendix to this chapter.

Reuber: "How did you come to found a blanket manufacturing business?"

Admiral Road: "We had a burning desire not to continue working on Bay Street and gave ourselves three months to find an alternative. We started with a list of criteria for a start-up: it had to have low capital-intensity, it had to be low-tech and we had to be able to balance the business with children." (In the four years after starting Admiral Road, Ballon and Botterell have each had two children, as you can see from the photo.) "We spent days and days making lists of possible businesses, and matching them against our skill sets, our interests, and what we thought market demands were. We have a regular Sunday night dinner group, and each week we would throw out ideas and find out what people thought of them. This feedback was valuable—for example, no one could see us being calm enough to run a spa! Within a month, we'd narrowed it down to a couple of choices. Amy had been a customer of the blanket business

continued

we ended up buying and knew people who were trying to order blankets but couldn't. So, we knew that there was demand but not supply. We met with the owner to find out what happened to the business and found out that it was a side business for her that had become increasingly difficult to run because she was located in a rural area and there was a shortage of people who could sew for the company. She agreed to sell us the assets at a very reasonable price and we had a lawyer draw up a sales agreement to transfer the rights to us. The legal agreement bought peace of mind, especially with respect to the intellectual property rights of her designs, even though the lawyer probably cost half as much as all the assets cost!

Reuber: "Can you describe the process of developing the initial business plan?"

Admiral Road: "We actually did it over a weekend. On Friday, we sat down with the Ernst & Young template for a business plan and assigned sections to each of us. We worked all weekend and met with a banker on Monday. Beforehand, though, we had collected some valuable information. We talked to loans officers at five major Canadian banks to find out what was available to us as new business owners. So, we had a good idea of what they were looking for and what bank we wanted to target. (Yes, there were differences among them.) As with any business plan, the hardest element is the demand forecasts. We were lucky because we had the sales figures from the previous owner and knew how much she'd made at different shows and through different channels. Her track record also gave us a good basis to estimate costs. We'd heard through the business community that the bank, as a matter of course, would halve our sales forecasts so we doubled what we thought were the most realistic figures."

Reuber: "How did the bank react to it?"

Admiral Road: "Our banker loved it. At one point he said to the loans officer 'give them whatever they want!' We think this reflects three things. First, we weren't asking for all that much, and it was guaranteed by our personal savings, so there was little risk for him. However, he did slash some fees and do some deals for us. Second, we got the impression that 95 percent of what he sees is 'back of the napkin.' When you have a thorough, comprehensive plan, it stands out. Third, he liked our business school credentials and work experience. It's really true that bankers pay attention to the people at least as much as the plan. We still have the same banker today. It's really important to get to know your banker and nurture the relationship. We send him media articles about Admiral Road and keep him up-to-date on our plans and progress. So, if we need additional credit at any point in time, he very much understands why and is supportive."

Reuber: "Was the plan useful for anything other than getting the line of credit from the bank?"

Admiral Road: "Yes, developing the plan forced us to think in a constructive way about what we could do when. This was especially true for the marketing plan. In setting down activities against the calendar, we were forced to answer questions about what we could afford to do at different times and what would yield the biggest payoffs."

Reuber: "What is the role of a business plan now that Admiral Road is operating successfully?"

Admiral Road: "We have switched focus from the business plan to business planning. After starting the business, we spent much of 2002 and 2003 learning about the industry—how to make blankets, how to ship, how to find and retain sewers, what our most promising customer base was, a whole host of things. We were mired in the details and too busy to step back. Then, at the start of 2004, we had what we called the G2 Summit. We sat down and talked about our priorities for the business and realized that it was important to rebrand and develop a more professional image and website. A year later, at the start of 2005, we had another summit and developed a comprehensive financial model of the business and conducted sensitivity analyses to explore various growth options. This marked a transition point for Admiral Road. Up until then, business planning meant looking at most three months ahead. For the past year, though, we have held monthly planning meetings, setting goals and projections and looking ahead five years. Business planning has become increasing and critically important to the business."

Commentary: What Amy Ballon and Danielle Botterell are saying, in essence, is that business planning matters more than the business plan itself. Through the process of planning you learn more about your business, how the various parts fit together, and how it might best evolve. When entrepreneurs approach other people, such as investors or bankers, with their business plan, it becomes obvious very quickly whether they have been deeply engaged in the planning process and, as a result, truly understand their business.

Summary and Review of Key Points

- A business plan is a formal written document that explains the entrepreneur's vision and how it will be converted into a profitable, viable business.
- Venture capitalists and other potential sources of funding generally require a formal business plan as a first step for considering investments in new ventures.
- An additional step, and one that is often very important, involves a face-to-face presentation of the plan by the entrepreneur to venture capitalists or other interested parties.
- Preparing a formal business plan is useful for most entrepreneurs because doing so encourages them to formulate specific goals and concrete plans for reaching them, and these are invaluable both for converting ideas into viable companies and for raising needed capital.
- However, many successful entrepreneurs develop a fairly simple business plan, and then refine it in the light of information they gain from actually running the new venture.
- All business plans should begin with an executive summary—a brief (two to three pages) section that provides a brief, clear, and persuasive overview of what the new venture is all about.
- Subsequent sections should include:

  Background and purpose. A section describing your idea and the current state of the business.

  Marketing. A section describing the market for the new venture's product or service, why there is a need for the product (or service) and why anyone would want to buy it, plus information on the existing competition and how it will be overcome, and pricing.

  Development, production, and location. Where the product or service is, in terms of development, how it will be produced, and (if appropriate) information on where the business will be located.

  Management. A section describing the experience, skills, and knowledge of the new venture's management team.

  Financial section. A section that provides information on the company's current financial state, and offers projections for future needs, revenues, and other financial measures, as well as a breakeven analysis.

  Risk factors. A section that discusses various risks the new venture will face, and the steps the management team is taking to protect against these threats.

  Harvest or exit. A section focused on how investors will gain if the company is successful.

  Scheduling and milestones. An overview of when each phase of the new venture will be completed, so that potential investors will know just when key tasks (e.g., start of production, time to first sales, projected breakeven point) will be completed.

  Appendices. Detailed financial information and detailed résumés of the top management team.
- Entrepreneurs should view invitations to give verbal presentations about their idea and their company as a challenge—a chance to shine—rather than as a high-stress situation in which they may be overwhelmed.
- Because such presentations are very important to the future of new ventures, entrepreneurs should take them very seriously and try to do an outstanding job.
- Steps that can help entrepreneurs accomplish this goal include selecting content carefully, avoiding technical jargon, showing enthusiasm tempered by reality, rehearsing carefully, paying careful attention to basic aspects of presentations (e.g., arriving early to set up audiovisual systems), and adopting a helpful cooperative attitude toward questions.
- Entrepreneurs should view rejections by potential investors as an opportunity to learn—to improve both their business plan and their verbal presentations.

Glossary

Breakeven Analysis: An analysis indicating the level of sales and production required to cover all costs.

Business Plan: A written expression of the entrepreneur's vision for converting ideas into a profitable, going business.

Cash Flow Statement: A written statement of actual or projected cash inflows and outflows over a specific period of time, given certain levels of sales and costs.

Persuasion: The task of inducing others to share our views and to see the world much as we do.

Proforma Balance Sheet: A form showing projections of the company's financial condition at various times in the future.

Proforma Income Statement: A form illustrating projected operating results based on profit and loss.

Discussion Questions

1. Since writing a business plan requires a lot of work, why should entrepreneurs do it? Why not just get the company started? Which approach would you prefer, and why?
2. Why is the executive summary at the start of a business plan so important? What should be its primary goal or goals?
3. Why it is important to explain where the new product or service is with respect to the production process (e.g., is an idea? a prototype? in production?)?
4. Why it is so important for a business plan to fully describe the experience and expertise of the new venture's management?
5. How much optimism should be built into financial projections? What is the potential downside of including too much optimism?
6. Why should business plans include a full disclosure and discussion of potential risk factors? Isn't this just calling attention to negatives that might prevent investors from providing financial support?
7. Some people are better than others at giving verbal presentations. Should entrepreneurs consider this factor when choosing potential cofounders?

InfoTrac Exercises

1. **The Ins and Outs of Turnons and Turnoffs.** (The Company Doctor) (developing sound business plans that will attract potential investors) (column)

   Scott Clark

   Long Island Business News, May 7, 1999 v46 i19 p35A(1)

   Record: A54896541

   Abstract: Many entrepreneurs develop, assemble, or present business plans that represent their life's dream so poorly that they fail to attract the interest of potential investors. All business plans ever written feature elements that will engage readers' interest, that may turn them on, or turn them off. Suggestions pertaining to business plan writing may help entrepreneurs to engage the immediate attention and, perhaps, the support of potential financiers.

   1. According to the article, what two purposes should a business plan achieve?
   2. What aspects of the Admiral Road business plan, presented in the appendix to this chapter, might be turnoffs to potential stakeholders?
   3. What aspects are likely to be turnons to potential stakeholders?

2. The dos and don'ts of fund raising. Barbara Jorgensen.

   Electronic Business, May 2001 v27 i5 p29

   Record: A74361522

   Abstract: More and more companies need to seek funds from venture capital companies but most don't have a clue as to the best way of going about doing so. Companies must take care to do an accurate presentation to venture capital companies, paying particular attention to important details such as their niche and importance in the market. This article also give as ten reasons why companies fail to get funding.

1. According to the text, what should you emphasize when presenting your business plan to potential stakeholders?
2. What are the most frequent problems with business plans?
3. Where should a business plan be optimistic and where should it be pessimistic?

GETTING DOWN TO BUSINESS

Writing a Great Executive Summary

A first-rate executive summary is an important ingredient in any good business plan. Excellent summaries catch the attention and interest of potential investors who generally decide, on the basis of the executive summary, whether to continue reading—or to move on to the next business plan in the pile. For this reason, learning how to write an excellent executive summary is a very useful skill for entrepreneurs. Follow these steps to improve your skill with respect to this important task.

1. **Write an executive summary for your new venture.** Be sure that it is no more than two to three pages long.
2. **Now, ask several people you know to read it and comment on it.** In particular, ask them to rate the summary on the following dimensions. (Ratings should use a 5-point scale: 1 = very poor; 2 = poor; 3 = neutral; 4 = good; 5 = excellent.)
   a. It provides a clear description of the new product or service.
   b. It explains why the new product or service will be appealing in specific markets.
   c. It identifies these markets and explains how the product will be promoted in them.
   d. It explains where the product is with respect to production.
   e. It explains who the entrepreneurs are and describes their background and experience.
   f. It explains how much funding the entrepreneurs are seeking and the purposes for which it will be used.
3. **Obtain the average score on each dimension.** The features on which you scored low (3 or below) are the areas that you should work on. Prepare an improved executive summary and have a different group of people rate it.
4. **Continue the process until the ratings on all dimensions are 4 or 5.**

Describing the New Venture's Management Team—And Putting It in a Favourable Light

Potential investors consider the quality of a new venture's management team to be a crucial factor—perhaps the most crucial—in their decision about whether to provide funding for it. Therefore, not only is it important to assemble an excellent team but it is essential to describe it fully and in terms that are as positive as possible. Unfortunately, some entrepreneurs don't seem to recognize the importance of this task. They fail to list past accomplishments or experience, and are just too modest overall. Carrying out the following steps can help you avoid these errors—and increase your chances of obtaining the funding you seek.

1. **List each member of the top management team of your new venture.**
2. **Describe their role in the new venture—what, specifically, will they do?**

3. **Next, ask each to provide information on the following items:**
    a. Where and when did they received their degrees, and in what fields.
    b. A description of all relevant experience—experience that is in any way relates to the tasks they will perform. This experience can include work experience, offices held in social and professional organizations, experience in running previous businesses (even small, informal ones), writing experience—almost anything that is relevant to their role in the new venture.
    c. Honours, awards, and prizes they have received (academic, business, athletics, etc.).
    d. Personal references—the more experienced, well-known, and prestigious, the better.
    e. Anything else in their background or experience that is relevant to their role in the new venture and places them in a favourable light (e.g., famous relatives? famous friends or associates?).
4. **Match the information that you have about the members of the top management team to the roles that you defined.** Make sure to include all the information that supports their ability to fulfill these roles, but don't include information that isn't relevant to the role. (For example, don't say that your head of marketing was the president of her high school chess club.)
5. Finally, show the finished product to other members of the top management team and brainstorm with them about whether it presents your strengths in a way that will be obvious to potential investors. If it does not, go back to the drawing board and start again!

Enhanced Learning

You may select any combination of the resources below to enhance your understanding of the chapter material.

- **Appendix 1: Case Studies** – Twelve cases provide opportunities to apply chapter concepts to realistic entrepreneurial situations. These brief cases call for careful analysis of real business problems and ask you to think about potential solutions.
- **Video Case Library** – Nine cases are tied directly to video segments from the popular PBS television series Small Business School. These cases and video segments (available on the Entrepreneurship website at http://www.entrepreneurship.nelson.com) give you unparalleled access to today's entrepreneurs, with expert advice and insights on how to start, run, and grow a business.
- **Management Interview Series Video Database** – This video interview series contains a wealth of tips on how to manage effectively. Access to the database and practical exercises are available on the book support website at http://www.entrepreneurship.nelson.com.

Notes

1 Mancuso, J.R. 1975. *How to write a winning business plan.* Englewood Cliffs, NJ: Prentice-Hall.

2 Delmar, F., & Shane, S. (2003). Does business planning facilitate the development of new ventures? *Strategic Management Journal* 24(12): 1165–1185.

3 Fletcher, C. 1979. Impression management in the selection interview. In R.A. Giacalone & P. Rosenfeld, P. (eds.). *Impression management in the selection interview* (pp. 269–272). Hillsdale, NJ: Erlbaum.

4 Zacharakis, A.L, & Shepherd, D.A. 2001. The nature of information and overconfidence on venture capialists' decision making. *Journal of Business Venturing* 16(4): 311–332.

5 Baron, R.A., & Markman, G.D. 2003. Beyond social capital: The role of entrepreneurs' social competence in their financial success. *Journal of Business Venturing* 18(1): 41–60.

6 McNish, J. 2005. Mega Bloks v. LEGO. *globeandmail.com*, November 23.

7 Marotte, B. 2005. Top court quashes LEGO big against toy rival. *Globe and Mail*, November 18: B5.

8 Buehler, R., Griffin, D., & MacDonald, H. 1997. The role of motivated reasoning in optimistic time predictions. *Personality and Social Psychology Bulletin* 23(3): 237–247.

9 Greenberg, J., & Baron, R.A. 2003. *Behavior in organizations.* 7th ed. Upper Saddle River, NJ: Prentice-Hall.

APPENDIX

ADMIRAL ROAD BUSINESS PLAN

In this section, we present a real business plan written by Amy Ballon and Danielle Botterell, two Toronto-based entrepreneurs who decided to leave Bay Street to open their own business in 2002 (see the Voice of Experience in Chapter 8 for their insights on business planning). Ballon and Botterell purchased the assets of an existing blanket manufacturer and used these assets to found Admiral Road. They used their own funds to purchase the business, and wrote the business plan to think through their development plan and to obtain a line of credit from a bank (see Figure A8.1). You can find out more about Admiral Road from the company's website at http://www.admiralroad.com.

ADMIRAL ROAD BUSINESS PLAN

1. Executive Summary

Admiral Road is a mail-order company that produces a high quality and attractive product that serves as a personalized alternative to mass-produced products for the gift or home accessory buyer.

Purchased as an established business, Admiral Road offers tested products to a receptive customer base via mail order or at craft shows. The Company has plans to sell its products via the Internet and to target corporate accounts and suitable retailers.

Admiral Road's margins are attractive and the Company expects to be net income positive in its first year of operation. The principals of the Company have solid business backgrounds and extensive personal networks through which to market the products.

2. Background

Admiral Road began when the principals, Amy Ballon and Danielle Botterell, purchased a fleece blanket and accessory business from Mazooma Inc. of Huntsville,

Courtesy of Admiral Road

Courtesy of Admiral Road

Figure A8.1 Venture Business Plans Need to Convey Clear Business Objectives

The founders of Admiral Road used their business plan to obtain funds to develop a logo and image for their business and to invest in professional photographs of their products, such as their moose blanket.

Ontario. The owner of Mazooma designed the product line and first marketed it at the Toronto One of A Kind Craft Show in December 1998, during which she generated approximately $20,000 of revenue. She continued to operate the fleece business by mail order in conjunction with her Huntsville retail store until she experienced a labour shortage, which caused her to stop producing the blankets in late 2000.

Both of the principals of Admiral Road were customers of Mazooma's blanket business. When Mazooma stopped providing the blankets, Admiral Road perceived a market niche and approached Mazooma about a purchase. The purchase was completed on March 13th, 2002 and all rights of ownership were legally transferred. During the negotiations to purchase Mazooma, the principals spent considerable time with the owner of Mazooma. During these sessions, the success and viability of each product was discussed, as was pricing, marketing and other key elements to running the business. The owner of Mazooma was extremely forthcoming and the sessions were very valuable.

As part of the purchase of Mazooma's blanket business, Admiral Road bought a mailing list with approximately 1700 customer names on it, as well as supplier lists, the exclusive rights to all of the designs, catalogue and web site artwork and the hard assets of the business (sewing machines, design table, etc.). By purchasing the Mazooma blanket business—a known and proven entity—rather than starting a business from scratch, the principals of Admiral Road believe that considerable time and funds were spared in the learning process.

3. Product

Admiral Road produces a Canadian handmade fleece product. The product line includes blankets, pillows and accessories for babies, children, adults and pets. The emphasis is on quality, bright and beautiful colours, and designs that are comforting and fun. The products are reasonably priced and yet upscale. Items in the catalogue range in price from $24 to $105 (see Exhibit 1).

Exhibit 1 Admiral Road Catalogue

4. Market Analysis

4.1 Customer Analysis

Admiral Road's products will appeal to a number of different customer groups.

4.1.1 Buyer of Baby Gifts

With the current product line, the best selling item is the Baby Name Blanket—a fleece blanket featuring brightly coloured appliquéd animals and the child's name. At $39, it makes an excellent gift from a grandparent, friend, or someone attending a baby shower. Our research shows that the price point on this product reflects the amount most people want to spend on a gift for a newborn.

While there are many options for gifts for babies, very few offer a personalized touch, which is a huge contributing factor to the popularity of the blankets.

4.1.2 Home or Cottage Owner

Admiral Road's fleece product designs are unique as well as beautiful, comfortable and durable. With motifs such as oak leaves and cottages, the big blankets and quilts are perfect accessories for casual rooms in homes or cottages. Buyers will also appreciate the ease of caring for Admiral Road products.

4.1.3 Tourists

Admiral Road's products are designed with a distinctly Canadian flair. Purchasing a throw or a pillow adorned with a moose or a polar bear will serve to remind tourists of Canada while enjoying a comfortable and well-made product. Tourists will be able to access Admiral Road's products through craft shows initially and later through retailers to whom the Company is wholesaling.

4.1.4 Retailers

Admiral Road will seek out retailers across Canada with whom the products would fit well. Participating in craft shows is an excellent way to make contacts with appropriate retailers.

4.1.5 Corporate Clients

As did its predecessor, Mazooma, Admiral Road will serve companies who wish to send unique and personal gifts to their client. The Company has already made contact with several potential corporate clients and has secured a relationship with one.

Regardless of the specific customer's attributes, Admiral Road's products will appeal to those wishing to pay a slight premium for original home accessories, each of which is handmade in Canada. Admiral Road customers will be looking for a one-of-a-kind product, rather than something mass-produced. Customers will appreciate the personalized nature of the children's and pet products, as well as the ability to have any product personalized.

4.2 Market

Admiral Road views the market potential as very broad. The Company will focus its marketing efforts on craft shows, personal contacts, and corporate clients in Southern Ontario for the remainder of 2002. Additionally, the Company will market and sell its products via the Internet. Beginning in 2003, Admiral Road will participate in craft shows outside of Ontario and will focus on wholesaling, while continuing to solicit corporate clients.

4.3 Competitors

While there are a limited number of providers of fleece blankets for infants in the local market, the Company's research shows that there are no comparable personalized products on the market. Additionally, while there is a company offering fleece blankets in Canada, its customer, marketing and design focus are very different than that of Admiral Road.

5. Marketing and Sales Channels

5.1 Marketing:

In developing the marketing plan, Admiral Road has defined its mission statement as follows: To design and produce Canadian-made textile products for babies, kids, adults and pets in a manner that emphasizes quality, fashion and fun and serves as an alternative to mass-produced products.

The marketing objectives of Admiral Road are three-fold. The first objective is to make customers in the Ontario market aware of the Admiral Road brand and product through participation in various craft shows and a launch event. Admiral Road has had replies from nine major craft shows and gained acceptance into each one. The first three craft shows were extremely successful. The second objective is to capitalize on the 1,700-person mailing list that was purchased as an asset of the former business. These existing customers will be contacted with a mailing and a follow-up telephone call. Finally, Admiral Road will promote the company name and product in the broader market using a company web site. The Company has registered the domain name "admiralroad.com."

5.2 Marketing Strategy

The marketing strategy is to create a fleece product line centred around the concepts of quality and fun. Various promotional activities will be used to support the mail order business and managed by the full-time efforts of the two principals. Marketing concepts include participation in Ontario craft shows, a launch event, a catalogue, a mailing to existing mailing list customers, promotional fliers, an email campaign, local television appearances and print media write-ups.

5.3 Sales channels:

In Year 1, distribution channels include a launch event and eight major craft shows in Ontario. Product will also be available by contacting Admiral Road directly by telephone and through the web site. The Company will also target corporate sales through the extensive personal networks of the principals. Additionally, wholesaling to retailers will be pursued via participation in craft shows and targeting selected appropriate partners. The marketing schedule has been planned for the remainder of 2002 (see Exhibit 2).

6. Management Team

Admiral Road's management team combines business expertise with creative talent. Formerly employed as management consultants, Amy Ballon and Danielle Botterell are both graduates of the MBA program at the University of Toronto. Before returning to business school Amy and Danielle held responsible positions at TSE 100 firms (see Exhibit 3).

There are many craftspeople in Ontario, many of whom make beautiful products. There are however, very few craftspeople with solid business experience and know-how. Admiral Road believes that it is uniquely positioned and qualified to grow its business exponentially.

The principals have known each other for more than 12 years and are aware of the challenges of partnership. A partnership agreement as well as a commitment to the business and a friendly relationship is in place to mitigate this challenge.

7. Funding Requirements

The Principals have each contributed $12,500 to the business for a total of $25,000 in start-up capital. To date, the Company has incurred approximately $25,000 in expenses, which includes the purchase of the Mazooma business and its assets, hard

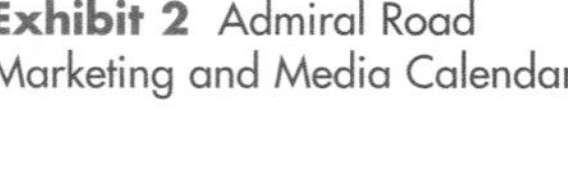

Exhibit 2 Admiral Road Marketing and Media Calendar

		May				Jun				Jul					Aug				Sep					Oct				Nov				Dec			
		6	13	20	27	3	10	17	24	1	8	15	22	29	5	12	19	26	2	9	16	23	30	7	14	21	28	4	11	18	25	2	9	16	23
1	Catalogue prod'ctn	■																																	
2	Send Launch Invites		■																																
3	Toronto Show			▒																															
4	Burlington Show					▒																													
5	Web site launch						■																												
6	Launch Party						■																												
7	Hamilton Show								▒																										
8	Goderich Show									▒																									
10	Barrie Show													▒	▒																				
9	Shaw Show																▒																		
11	Mailing to existing list																		■																
12	Ottawa Show																												▒						
13	One of a Kind Show																														▒	▒			
14	TV appearance																														■				

■ Internal event
▒ Crat Show

AMY S. BALLON

Employment

Admira Road Designs
Owner, March 2002 - Present

- Negotiated the purchase of an existing mail-order fleece blanket and pillow business
- Prepared marketing materials including packaging and a catalogue
- Developed new designs and product ideas
- Accepted to all craft shows to which the Company has applied

Mercer Management Consulting, Toronto, Ontario
Associate, 2000 – 2002

- Led a module to redesign marketing processes at a major U.S. regional bank that identified opportunities for increased efficiency
- Identified revenue growth opportunities for a major Canadian cultural institution that resulted in organizational change and an improved ability to target clients
- Prepared numerous presentations for business development purposes
- Managed and oversaw the work of analysts

TD Bank, Corporate and Investment Banking Group, Toronto, Ontario
Summer Associate, International Trade Finance, Latin America, Summer 1999

- Closed $45 million in trade finance transactions generating over $1 million in revenue
- Prepared financial and business analyses to assess the Bank's relationships in Latin America
- Developed a business case to judge the viability of opening a Representative Office in Latin America

Nesbitt Burns, Investment Banking Department, Toronto, Ontario
Coordinator, Financial Services Group, 1997 - 1998

- Advised Great-West Life in its $3.1 billion acquisition of London Life as a member of the project team
- Assisted in the research and preparation of presentations for clients in the financial services sector

Diefenbach Elkins Vandenberg (Corporate Design Consultancy), Toronto, Ontario
Account Executive, 1995 - 1996

- Compiled research data for *Bell Canada* on the strategic positioning of its retail stores
- Developed a positioning paper for *Saudi Aramco* on the branding of its retail gas stations
- Oversaw the production of promotional materials for various clients

Moment Magazine, Washington, D.C.
Marketing Assistant, 1994 - 1995

- Coordinated advertising for a national magazine with a circulation of 40,000
- Implemented a distribution program that provided communities with low-cost subscriptions and increased monthly circulation by 25%

EDUCATION

University of Toronto, *MBA, 2000*

- President of the Graduate Business Council – the elected students' representative to the faculty, administration and business community
- Winner of the Concordia International Case Competition

McGill University, *BA, Political Science, 1994*

- ***Graduated with Distinction***

The Hebrew University, Jerusalem, Israel, 1992-1993

ACHIEVEMENTS

- Trained for and successfully completed dozens of road races including six full marathons:
- – Boston 2001 (Time: 3:31), Boston 2000 (3:39), Toronto 1998 (3:38), Chicago 1997 (3:42), Washington, D.C. 1996, (3:55), Toronto 1995 (4:33)

Volunteer Activities

Proofreader, Ontario Roadrunner Magazine, 1997 - 2000

Department Coordinator, Nesbitt Burns' United Way Campaign, 1997-1998; raised over $175,000

Chairperson, Chevrolet Mother-Daughter Walk for the Heart and Stroke Foundation, 1996 - 1997

Special Skills and Interests

- Language study; French, Spanish, German, Hebrew, Arabic and Latin
- Traveled throughout the former Soviet Union, Europe, Southeast Asia and the Middle East

DANIELLE S. BOTTERELL

PROFESSIONAL EXPERIENCE

Owner
Admiral Road Designs, Toronto, Ontario Present

- Negotiated the purchase of an existing mail-order fleece blanket and pillow business
- Prepared marketing materials including packaging and a catalogue
- Developed new designs and product ideas
- Accepted to all craft shows to which the Company has applied

Associate
Mercer Management Consulting Toronto, Ontario Fall 2001-March 2002

Associate, Investment Banking
RBC Dominion Securities, Toronto, Ontario Summer 2000

- Key team member for a $350 million public-private infrastructure project
- Created complex financial models and presentations for senior client management in healthcare, retail, and auto sectors
- Designed, researched and completed a bank-wide product profile used for marketing purposes

Director, Investor Relations and Corporate Communications
TrizecHahn Corporation, Toronto, Ontario

- Managed relationships with key investors and media contacts
- Led a cross-divisional team in the implementation of an integrated company-wide web site
- Crafted speeches, news releases and other key corporate documents
- Created monthly IR/market activity report for Peter Munk and senior management
- Drafted and coordinated entire production of annual and quarterly reports
- Created and maintained IR content for corporate web site
- Negotiated key contracts and managed all supplier relationships for IR department
- Prepared department budget

Director of Investor Relations
Minorca Resources Inc., Toronto, Ontario

- Initial development of corporate communications program
- Assumed role of key contact for portfolio managers, analysts, and retail investors
- Handled all investor relations activities for two equity issues totaling $90 million
- Worked with management team and investors in restructuring of equity deal
- Handled crisis communications for shareholders and media following post-Bre-X collapse
- Developed corporate image through drafting and production of annual and quarterly reports
- Drafted, disseminated and filed press releases
- Scripted and arranged all investor meetings and presentations
- Prepared regulatory filings and contact with stock exchange market surveillance teams

EDUCATION

Masters of Business Administration
Joseph L. Rotman School of Management, Toronto, Ontario
Elected Class President 2000-2001

Canadian Securities Course

Bachelor of Arts, Honours, Political Science
McGill University, Montreal, Quebec

Dîplome, Niveau II
Université d'Aix-Marseille III, Aix en Provence, France

LANGUAGE STUDY

French (fluent), Mandarin, German

PROFESSIONAL DEVELOPMENT

Canadian Investor Relations Institute (CIRI): Board of Directors 1998-1999
Chair, Membership 1998-1999
Committee Member 1997

- Attended three annual CIRI conferences
- Attended seminars on Corporate Disclosure, Stock Exchange workings, Media Interaction
- Planned and attended seminars on IR web sites, effective investor kits, media relations and IR fundamentals
- Attended Northern Miner mining seminars, guest speaker at Northern Miner Investor Relations Conference

COMMUNITY INVOVLEMENT

Campaign Chair: TrizecHahn United Way Campaign 1998 – raised $50,000
Corporate Committee member: Kids' Help Phone - 1998-1999
Organizing Committee member: Fundraising Gala for the Toronto International Film Festival –1997

INTERESTS

Golf
Running – trained for and completed New York City marathon – November 2000
Reading – about 50 books a year

Exhibit 3 Résumés of Principals of Admiral Road

assets such as a computer, telephones and fleece inventory, as well as administrative expenses. The capital also covers all initial marketing expenses including the fees to participate in craft shows as well as a budget for a launch event.

The Company has generated approximately $8,000 of revenue to date. At this time, the Company is seeking a line of credit to finance the following:

- The placement of an advertisement in a North American publication;
- The building of an e-commerce web site;
- A logo/identity for the business;

- Professional photography of our product line for use in print and web advertising; and
- Booth space at the prestigious One of a Kind Craft Show.

8. Financial Projections

Exhibit 4 shows that Admiral Road expects to have Pro Forma 2002 revenues of nearly $100,000, with a net income of more than $43,000.

The Company currently has no debt.

9. Risks

Risks are associated with all new business ventures. In the case of Admiral Road two risks have been identified. First, the barriers to entry are quite low. Craftspeople would find it relatively easily to imitate the product by purchasing fleece and reproducing the Company's designs. However, this risk is somewhat mitigated by operational and financial expertise of the principals that is required for the successful widespread distribution of the product. The other risk is the dissolution of the partnership. To mitigate this risk the principals have drawn up a Partnership Agreement that outlines the terms of business should the partnership dissolve.

Exhibit 4 Admiral Road Projected Financials

Assumptions

1 **Depreciation:**

Computer	$ 1,200
Telephones	$ 200
Sewing Machines	$ 900
Other Equipment	$ 300
Total	$ 2,600
Industrial Machine	$ 1,400 over 20 years

All equipment is straight-line depreciated over 3 years

2 **Sales, General & Administrative Expenses/Month**

Telephone/Internet	$ 210
Car Insurance, Gas	$ 300
Craft Shows	$ 350
Mailing/Promotion	$ 200
Total	$ 1,060

3 **Tax Rate** 35%

4 **Custom Orders**

10% of orders are custom at approximately $10 revenue, $1 cost per order

5 **Growth Rate**

2003	50%
2004	25%
2005	15%

6 **Projected % of Revenue**

Cost of Goods Sold	17%
SG&A	13%

	2002									
	May	June	July	August	September	October	November	December	Total	Pro Forma 2002
Revenue	$ 1,962.00	$ 6,640.00	$ 6,640.00	$ 6,640.00	$ 3,964.00	$ 3,964.00	$ 18,718.00	$ 18,718.00	$ 67,246.00	$ 97,506.70
COGS	$ 329.99	$ 1,251.37	$ 1,251.37	$ 1,251.37	$ 547.61	$ 547.61	$ 3,241.18	$ 3,241.18	$ 11,661.69	$ 16,909.45
Gross Profit	$ 1,632.01	$ 5,388.63	$ 5,388.63	$ 5,388.63	$ 3,416.39	$ 3,416.39	$ 15,476.82	$ 15,476.82	$ 55,584.31	$ 80,597.25
SG&A	$ 1,060.00	$ 1,060.00	$ 1,060.00	$ 1,060.00	$ 1,060.00	$ 1,060.00	$ 1,060.00	$ 1,060.00	$ 8,480.00	$ 12,720.00
EBITDA	$ 1,553.95	$ 4,328.63	$ 4,328.63	$ 4,328.63	$ 2,356.39	$ 2,356.39	$ 14,416.82	$ 14,416.82	$ 48,086.25	$ 67,877.25
Depreciation	$ 78.06	$ 78.06	$ 78.06	$ 78.06	$ 78.06	$ 78.06	$ 78.06	$ 78.06	$ 624.44	$ 866.67
EBIT	$ 1,475.89	$ 4,250.58	$ 4,250.58	$ 4,250.58	$ 2,278.33	$ 2,278.33	$ 14,338.76	$ 14,338.76	$ 47,461.81	$ 67,010.58
Interest	$ -	$ -	$ -	$ -	$ -	$ -	$ -	$ -	$ -	$ -
Taxes	$ 516.56	$ 1,487.70	$ 1,487.70	$ 1,487.70	$ 797.42	$ 797.42	$ 5,018.57	$ 5,018.57	$ 16,611.63	$ 23,453.70
Net Income	$ 959.33	$ 2,762.87	$ 2,762.87	$ 2,762.87	$ 1,480.91	$ 1,480.91	$ 9,320.20	$ 9,320.20	$ 30,850.17	$ 43,556.88

	2003	2004	2005
Revenue	$ 146,260.05	$ 182,825.06	$ 210,248.82
COGS	$ 24,864.21	$ 31,080.26	$ 35,742.30
Gross Profit	$ 121,395.84	$ 151,744.80	$ 174,506.52
SG&A	$ 19,013.81	$ 23,767.26	$ 27,332.35
EBITDA	$ 102,382.04	$ 127,977.54	$ 147,174.18
Depreciation	$ 866.67	$ 866.67	$ 866.67
EBIT	$ 101,515.37	$ 127,110.88	$ 146,307.51
Interest	$ -	$ -	$ -
Taxes	$ 35,530.38	$ 44,488.81	$ 51,207.63
Net Income	$ 65,984.99	$ 82,622.07	$ 95,099.88

		Baby Blankets	Kid Blankets	Big Blankets	Cozy	Pillows	Mini	Custom	Total
May	Units	30	4	2	0	5	20	6.1	
	Revenue	$ 1,170.00	$ 196.00	$ 150.00	$ -	145	$ 240.00	$ 61.00	**$ 1,962.00**
	COGS	$ 138.91	$ 32.54	$ 28.45	$ -	$ 32.80	$ 91.20	$ 6.10	**$ 329.99**
June	Units	75	15	10	5	10	100	21.5	
	Revenue	$ 2,925.00	$ 735.00	$ 750.00	$ 525.00	290	$ 1,200.00	$ 215.00	**$ 6,640.00**
	COGS	$ 347.28	$ 122.03	$ 142.23	$ 96.74	$ 65.59	$ 456.00	$ 21.50	**$ 1,251.37**
July	Units	75	15	10	5	10	100	21.5	
	Revenue	$ 2,925.00	$ 735.00	$ 750.00	$ 525.00	290	$ 1,200.00	$ 215.00	**$ 6,640.00**
	COGS	$ 347.28	$ 122.03	$ 142.23	$ 96.74	$ 65.59	$ 456.00	$ 21.50	**$ 1,251.37**
August	Units	75	15	10	5	10	100	21.5	
	Revenue	$ 2,925.00	$ 735.00	$ 750.00	$ 525.00	290	$ 1,200.00	$ 215.00	**$ 6,640.00**
	COGS	$ 347.28	$ 122.03	$ 142.23	$ 96.74	$ 65.59	$ 456.00	$ 21.50	**$ 1,251.37**
September	Units	70	10	2	2	10	0	9.4	
	Revenue	$ 2,730.00	$ 490.00	$ 150.00	$ 210.00	290	$ -	$ 94.00	**$ 3,964.00**
	COGS	$ 324.13	$ 81.36	$ 28.45	$ 38.70	$ 65.59	$ -	$ 9.40	**$ 547.61**
October	Units	70	10	2	2	10	0	9.4	
	Revenue	$ 2,730.00	$ 490.00	$ 150.00	$ 210.00	290	$ -	$ 94.00	**$ 3,964.00**
	COGS	$ 324.13	$ 81.36	$ 28.45	$ 38.70	$ 65.59	$ -	$ 9.40	**$ 547.61**
November	Units	300	18	8	10	30	250	61.6	
	Revenue	$ 11,700.00	$ 882.00	$ 600.00	$ 1,050.00	870	$ 3,000.00	$ 616.00	**$ 18,718.00**
	COGS	$ 1,389.11	$ 146.44	$ 113.78	$ 193.48	$ 196.78	$ 1,140.00	$ 61.60	**$ 3,241.18**
December	Units	300	18	8	10	30	250	61.6	
	Revenue	$ 11,700.00	$ 882.00	$ 600.00	$ 1,050.00	870	$ 3,000.00	$ 616.00	**$ 18,718.00**
	COGS	$ 1,389.11	$ 146.44	$ 113.78	$ 193.48	$ 196.78	$ 1,140.00	$ 61.60	**$ 3,241.18**

CHAPTER 4

Planning Business Messages

Want to do well on tests and excel in your course? Go to **www.meguffey.com** for helpful interactive resources.

- **Review the Chapter 4 PowerPoint slides to prepare for the first quiz.**

OBJECTIVES

After studying this chapter, you should be able to

1. Identify four basic principles of business writing, summarize the 3-x-3 writing process, and explain how a writing process helps a writer.
2. Recognize the components of the first phase of the writing process (prewriting), including analyzing your purpose, anticipating the audience, selecting the best channel, and considering how to adapt your message to the audience.
3. Effectively apply audience benefits, the "you" view, and conversational but professional language.
4. Effectively employ positive and courteous tone, bias-free language, simple expression, and vigorous words.
5. Understand how teams approach collaborative writing projects and what collaboration tools support team writing.
6. Summarize the legal and ethical responsibilities of business communicators in the areas of investments, safety, marketing, human resources, and copyright law.

Zooming In PART 1

Suze Orman Preaches Financial Freedom in Simple Language

Personal finance guru Suze Orman has a mission. She wants to change the way people think, act, and talk about money. One of the most widely read financial authorities of our time, she has written seven best-selling financial guidance books. But she is probably best known for her television programs including specials for PBS, the syndicated *Financial Freedom Hour* on QVC network, and an advice show on CNBC. She is also a columnist for *O*, Oprah Winfrey's magazine, and for Yahoo's personal finance site.

Orman's advice is largely for people who are drowning in debt. "Sweetheart," she says to a caller, "burn those credit cards!" She delivers her gospel of financial freedom with an animated conviction and high-energy style that have become her hallmark.[1] In her books and magazine articles, she speaks with the same assurance. "Having talked to literally tens of thousands of people, I can say that what is good for America ... is not having credit card debt, not leasing a car, and not having mortgage debt. This is not good for a human being. It's just not!"[2]

Orman knows what it is like to be in debt. After graduating with a degree in sociology, she worked for seven years as a waitress at the Buttercup Bakery in Berkeley, California. With a $50,000 loan from her customers, she intended to finance her own restaurant. Because of bad advice from an investment firm, she lost her $50,000 within four months. However, "she made it all up and then some after the firm hired her as its only female broker."[3]

As a broker, she developed her financial planning skills and built a reputation for honesty and ethical advice. Her books and articles combine emotional and spiritual observations about money and how to avoid the financial problems that caused pain for her family as she was growing up. *The Money Book for the Young, Fabulous, & Broke* directs financial advice at young people early in their working lives.

She admits that her message is not new. "It's not the material that I know, but how I communicate the material I know that sets me apart."[4] Orman's advice is practical and cuts through much confusing, contradictory financial information. One of her greatest strengths is breaking complex ideas into easy-to-understand segments. Like many great communicators, she knows her audience, shapes her message accordingly, and uses simple language.

© Newscom

Critical Thinking

- Whether one is writing a book, making a speech, or composing a business letter, why is it important to anticipate the audience for the message?
- What does writing an effective financial help book have in common with writing an effective business message?
- Why is it important to follow a writing process?

http://www.suzeorman.com

Understanding the Writing Process for Business Messages

LEARNING OBJECTIVE 1

Identify four basic principles of business writing, summarize the 3-x-3 writing process, and explain how a writing process helps a writer.

The task of preparing a written business message or a presentation is easier and more efficient if you have a systematic process to follow. When financial expert Suze Orman starts a writing assignment, she focuses totally on the task at hand. She takes no phone calls, answers no e-mails, and allows no interruptions. In delivering a convincing message, she employs many of the writing techniques you are about to learn. This chapter presents a systematic writing process that you can use to approach all business communication problems, whether you are planning an e-mail message, a report, an oral presentation, or even an instant message. The 3-x-3 writing process guides you through three phases, making it easy for you to plan, organize, and complete any message. Following the 3-x-3 writing process takes the guesswork out of writing. It tells you what goes on in each phase and guides you to effective results.

Starting With the Basics

What distinguishes business writing from other kinds of writing?

The first thing you should recognize about business writing is that it differs from other writing you may have done. In preparing high school or college compositions and term papers, you probably focused on discussing your feelings or displaying your knowledge. Your instructors wanted to see your thought processes, and they wanted assurance that you had internalized the subject matter. You may have had to meet a minimum word count. Business writers, however, have different goals. For business messages and oral presentations, your writing should be:

- **Purposeful.** You will be writing to solve problems and convey information. You will have a definite purpose to fulfill in each message.
- **Persuasive.** You want your audience to believe and accept your message.
- **Economical.** You will try to present ideas clearly but concisely. Length is not rewarded.
- **Audience oriented.** You will concentrate on looking at a problem from the perspective of the audience instead of seeing it from your own.

These distinctions actually ease the writer's task. You will not be searching your imagination for creative topic ideas. You won't be stretching your ideas to make them appear longer. Writing consultants and businesspeople complain that many college graduates entering industry have at least an unconscious perception that quantity enhances quality. Wrong! Get over the notion that longer is better. Conciseness and clarity are prized in business.

The ability to prepare concise, audience-centered, persuasive, and purposeful messages does not come naturally. Very few people, especially beginners, can sit down and compose a terrific letter or report without training. However, following a systematic process, studying model messages, and practicing the craft can make nearly anyone a successful business writer or speaker.

Following the 3-x-3 Writing Process

What are the three phases of the writing process?

Whether you are preparing an e-mail message, memo, letter, or oral presentation, the process will be easier if you follow a systematic plan. The 3-x-3 writing process breaks the entire task into three phases: *prewriting, writing,* and *revising,* as shown in Figure 4.1.

To illustrate the writing process, let's say that you own a popular local McDonald's franchise. At rush times, you face a problem. Customers complain about the chaotic multiple waiting lines to approach the service counter. You once saw two customers nearly get into a fistfight over cutting into a line. What's more, customers often are so intent on looking for ways to improve their positions in line that they fail to examine the menu. Then they are

FIGURE 4.1 The 3-x-3 Writing Process

1 Prewriting	2 Writing	3 Revising
Analyze: Decide on your purpose. What do you want the receiver to do or believe? What channel or form is best? Should you deliver your message in writing, orally, electronically, or graphically?	**Research:** Gather data to provide facts. Search company files, previous correspondence, and the Internet. What do you need to know to write this message? How much does the audience already know?	**Revise:** Edit your message to be sure it is clear, conversational, concise, and readable. Revise to eliminate wordy fillers, long lead-ins, redundancies, compound prepositions, wordy noun phrases, and trite business phrases. Develop parallelism and consider using headings and numbered and bulleted lists for quick comprehension.
Anticipate: Profile the audience. What does the receiver already know? Will the receiver's response be neutral, positive, or negative? Use the direct method for positive messages; consider using the indirect method for negative or persuasive messages.	**Organize:** Group similar facts together. Organize direct messages with the big idea first, followed by an explanation and an action request in the closing. For persuasive or negative messages, use an indirect, problem-solving plan. For short messages, make quick notes. For longer messages, outline your plan and make notes.	**Proofread:** Take the time to read over every message carefully. Look for errors in spelling, grammar, punctuation, names, numbers, and format.
Adapt: What techniques can you use to adapt your message to its audience and the audience's anticipated reaction? Include audience benefits and the "you" view, as well as positive, conversational, and courteous language.	**Compose:** Prepare a first draft, usually writing quickly. Focus on short, clear sentences using the active voice. Link ideas to build paragraph coherence.	**Evaluate:** Decide whether this message will achieve your purpose. Have you thought enough about the audience to be sure this message is appropriate and appealing?

undecided when their turn arrives. You want to convince other franchise owners that a single-line (serpentine) system would work better. You could telephone the other owners. But you want to present a serious argument with good points that they will remember and be willing to act on when they gather for their next district meeting. You decide to write a letter that you hope will win their support.

What tasks are involved in the first phase of the writing process?

Prewriting. The first phase of the writing process prepares you to write. It involves *analyzing* the audience and your purpose for writing. The audience for your letter will be other franchise owners, some highly educated and others not. Your purpose in writing is to convince them that a change in policy would improve customer service. You are convinced that a single-line system, such as that used in banks, would reduce chaos and make customers happier because they would not have to worry about where they are in line.

Prewriting also involves *anticipating* how your audience will react to your message. You are sure that some of the other owners will agree with you, but others might fear that customers seeing a long single line might go elsewhere. In *adapting* your message to the audience, you try to think of the right words and the right tone that will win approval.

What tasks are involved in the second phase of the writing process?

Writing. The second phase involves researching, organizing, and then composing the message. In *researching* information for this letter, you would probably investigate other kinds of businesses that use single lines for customers. You might check out your competitors. What are Wendy's and Burger King doing? You might do some calling to see whether other franchise owners are concerned about chaotic lines. Before writing to the entire group, you might brainstorm with a few owners to see what ideas they have for solving the problem.

Once you have collected enough information, you would focus on *organizing* your letter. Should you start out by offering your solution? Or should you work up to it slowly, describing the problem, presenting your evidence, and then ending with the solution? The final step in the second phase of the writing process is actually *composing* the letter. Naturally, you will do it at your computer so that you can revise easily.

Revising. The third phase of the process involves revising, proofreading, and evaluating your letter. After writing the first draft, you will spend a lot of time *revising* the message for clarity, conciseness, tone, and readability. Could parts of it be rearranged to make your point more effectively? This is the time when you look for ways to improve the organization and tone of your message. Next, you will spend time *proofreading* carefully to ensure correct spelling, grammar, punctuation, and format. The final phase involves *evaluating* your message to decide whether it accomplishes your goal.

Scheduling the Writing Process

What percentage of your time should you spend on each phase of the writing process?

Although Figure 4.1 shows the three phases of the writing process equally, the time you spend on each varies depending on the complexity of the problem, the purpose, the audience, and your schedule. One expert gives these rough estimates for scheduling a project:

- Prewriting—25 percent (thinking and planning)
- Writing—25 percent (organizing and composing)
- Revising—50 percent (45 percent revising and 5 percent proofreading)

These are rough guides, yet you can see that good writers spend most of their time on the final phase of revising and proofreading. Much depends, of course, on your project, its importance, and your familiarity with it. What is critical to remember, though, is that revising is a major component of the writing process.

It may appear that you perform one step and progress to the next, always following the same order. Most business writing, however, is not that rigid. Although writers perform the tasks described, the steps may be rearranged, abbreviated, or repeated. Some writers revise every sentence and paragraph as they go. Many find that new ideas occur after they have begun to write, causing them to back up, alter the organization, and rethink their plan. Beginning business writers often follow the writing process closely. With experience, though, you will become like other good writers and presenters who alter, compress, and rearrange the steps as needed.

Ethics Check

Essays for Sale

Web sites with playful names such as Cramster, Course Hero, Koofers, and Spark Notes provide ready-made solutions and essays for students. Do such sites encourage cheating and undermine the mental sweat equity of day-to-day learning?

Analyzing Your Purpose and Selecting Your Channel

LEARNING OBJECTIVE 2
Recognize the components of the first phase of the writing process (prewriting), including analyzing your purpose, profiling the audience, and selecting the best channel.

We devote the remainder of this chapter to the first phase of the writing process. You will learn to analyze the purpose for writing, anticipate how your audience will react, and adapt your message to the audience. It's surprising how many people begin writing and discover only as they approach the end of a message what they are trying to accomplish. If you analyze your purpose before you begin, you can avoid backtracking and starting over.

Identifying Your Purpose

What are the primary and secondary purposes of most business messages?

As you begin to compose a message, ask yourself two important questions: (a) Why am I sending this message? and (b) What do I hope to achieve? Your responses will determine how you organize and present your information.

Your message may have primary and secondary purposes. For college work your primary purpose may be merely to complete the assignment; secondary purposes might be to make yourself look good and to earn an excellent grade. The primary purposes for sending business messages are typically to inform and to persuade. A secondary purpose is to promote goodwill. You and your organization want to look good in the eyes of your audience.

Most business messages do nothing more than *inform*. They explain procedures, announce meetings, answer questions, and transmit findings. Some business messages, however, are meant to *persuade*. These messages sell products, convince managers, motivate employees, and win over customers. Informative messages are developed differently from persuasive messages.

-purpose
-channel

Selecting the Best Channel

What factors influence your selection of the best delivery channel?

After identifying the purpose of your message, you need to select the most appropriate communication channel. Some information is most efficiently and effectively delivered orally. Other messages should be written, and still others are best delivered electronically. Whether to set up a meeting, send a message by e-mail, or write a report depends on some of the following factors:

- Importance of the message
- Amount and speed of feedback and interactivity required
- Necessity of a permanent record
- Cost of the channel
- Degree of formality desired
- Confidentiality and sensitivity of the message

An interesting theory, called the media richness theory, describes the extent to which a channel or medium recreates or represents all the information available in the original message. A richer medium, such as face-to-face conversation, permits more interactivity and feedback. A leaner medium, such as a report or proposal, presents a flat, one-dimensional message. Richer media enable the sender to provide more verbal and visual cues, as well as allow the sender to tailor the message to the audience.

Many factors help you decide which of the channels shown in Figure 4.2 on page 116 is most appropriate for delivering a workplace message.

Switching to Faster Channels

Technology and competition continue to accelerate the pace of business today. As a result, communicators are switching to ever-faster means of exchanging information. In the past business messages within organizations were delivered largely by hard-copy memos. Responses would typically take a couple of days. However, that's too slow for today's communicators. They want answers and action now! Mobile phones, instant messaging, faxes, Web sites, and especially e-mail can deliver that information much faster than can traditional channels of communication.

FIGURE 4.2 Choosing Communication Channels

Channel	Best Use
Blog	When one person needs to present digital information easily so that it is available to others.
E-mail	When you need feedback but not immediately. Lack of security makes it problematic for personal, emotional, or private messages.
Face-to-face conversation	When you need a rich, interactive medium. Useful for persuasive, bad-news, and personal messages.
Face-to-face group meeting	When group decisions and consensus are important. Inefficient for merely distributing information.
Fax	When your message must cross time zones or international boundaries, when a written record is significant, or when speed is important.
Instant message	When you are online and need a quick response. Useful for learning whether someone is available for a phone conversation.
Letter	When a written record or formality is required, especially with customers, the government, suppliers, or others outside an organization.
Memo	When you want a written record to clearly explain policies, discuss procedures, or collect information within an organization.
Phone call	When you need to deliver or gather information quickly, when nonverbal cues are unimportant, and when you cannot meet in person.
Report or proposal	When you are delivering considerable data internally or externally.
Voice mail message	When you wish to leave important or routine information that the receiver can respond to when convenient.
Video- or audioconference	When group consensus and interaction are important, but members are geographically dispersed.
Wiki	When digital information must be made available to others. Useful for collaboration because participants can easily add, remove, and edit content.

Why is e-mail so popular for business messages?

Within many organizations, hard-copy memos are still written, especially for messages that require persuasion, permanence, or formality. They are also prepared as attachments to e-mail messages. Clearly, however, the channel of choice for corporate communicators today is e-mail. It's fast, inexpensive, and easy. Businesspeople are sending fewer hard-copy interoffice memos and fewer customer letters. Customer service functions can now be served through Web sites or by e-mail.

Many businesses now help customers with live chat, shown in Figure 4.3. Customers visit the company Web site and chat with representatives by keying their questions and answers back and forth. Customer representatives must have not only good keying skills but also an ability to write conversational and correct responses. One company found that it could not easily convert its telephone customer service people to chat representatives because many lacked the language skills necessary to write clear and correct messages. They were good at talking but not at writing, again making the point that the Internet has increased the need for good writing skills.

Whether your channel choice is live chat, e-mail, a hard-copy memo, or a report, you will be showcasing your communication skills and applying the writing process. The best writers spend sufficient time in the prewriting phase.

Anticipating the Audience

A good writer anticipates the audience for a message: What is the reader or listener like? How will that person react to the message? Although you can't always know exactly who the receiver is, you can imagine some of that person's characteristics. Even writers of direct-mail sales letters have a general idea of the audience they wish to target. Picturing a typical receiver is important in guiding what you write. One copywriter at Lands' End, the catalog company, pictures his sister-in-law whenever he writes product descriptions for the catalog. By profiling your audience and shaping a message to respond to that profile, you are more likely to achieve your communication goals.

FIGURE 4.3 Live Chat Connects Service Reps and Customers

© Courtesy of clickandchat.com

Customer service reps in chat sessions require good writing skills to answer questions concisely, clearly, and conversationally. It takes special talent to be able to think and key immediate responses that are spelled correctly and are error-free.

Profiling the Audience

Why is it important to profile the audience for a business message?

Visualizing your audience is a pivotal step in the writing process. The questions in Figure 4.4 will help you profile your audience. How much time you devote to answering these questions depends on your message and its context. An analytical report that you compose for management or an oral presentation before a big group would, of course, demand considerable audience anticipation. On the other hand, an e-mail message to a coworker or a letter to a familiar supplier might require only a few moments of planning. No matter how short your message, though, spend some time thinking about the audience so that you can tailor your words to your readers or listeners. Remember that most receivers will be thinking, *What's in it for me?* or, *What am I supposed to do with this information*?

Responding to the Audience Profile

Profiling your audience helps you make decisions about shaping the message. You will discover what kind of language is appropriate, whether you are free to use specialized technical terms, whether you should explain everything, and so on. You will decide whether your tone should be formal or informal, and you will select the most desirable channel. Imagining whether the receiver is likely to be neutral, positive, or negative will help you determine how to organize your message.

Another advantage of profiling your audience is considering the possibility of a secondary audience. For example, let's say you start to write an e-mail message to your supervisor, Sheila, describing a problem you are having. Halfway through the message you realize that Sheila will probably forward this message to her boss, the vice president. Sheila will not want to summarize what you said; instead she will take the easy route and merely forward your e-mail. When you realize that the vice president will probably see this message, you decide to back up and use a more formal tone. You remove your inquiry about Sheila's family, you reduce your complaints, and you tone down your language about why things went wrong. Instead, you provide more background information, and you are more specific in identifying items the vice

Spotlight on Communicators

Warren Buffett, the second richest man in the United States and one of the most successful investors of all time, offers advice on how to improve your messages by profiling your audience and responding to that profile. When writing annual reports, he pretends that he's talking to his sisters. "I have no trouble picturing them. Though highly intelligent, they are not experts in accounting or finance. They will understand plain English but jargon may puzzle them. . . . No sisters to write to? Borrow mine. Just begin with 'Dear Doris and Bertie,'" he suggested.

© Alex Wong/Getty Images

FIGURE 4.4 Asking the Right Questions to Profile Your Audience

Primary Audience	Secondary Audience
Who is my primary reader or listener?	Who might see or hear this message in addition to the primary audience?
What are my personal and professional relationships with this person?	How do these people differ from the primary audience?
What position does this person hold in the organization?	Do I need to include more background information?
How much does this person know about the subject?	How must I reshape my message to make it understandable and acceptable to others to whom it might be forwarded?
What do I know about this person's education, beliefs, culture, and attitudes?	
Should I expect a neutral, positive, or negative response to my message?	

president might not recognize. Analyzing the task and anticipating the audience help you adapt your message so that you can create an efficient and effective message.

Adapting to the Task and Audience

LEARNING OBJECTIVE 3

Effectively apply audience benefits, the "you" view, and conversational but professional language.

After analyzing your purpose and anticipating your audience, you will begin to think about how to adapt your message to the task and the audience. Adaptation is the process of creating a message that suits your audience. One important aspect of adaptation is *tone*. Conveyed largely by the words in a message, tone affects how a receiver feels upon reading or hearing a message. Tone is how you say something. It reveals the writer's attitude toward the receiver. For example, how you would react to these statements?

You must return the form by 5 p.m.

Would you please return the form by 5 p.m.

The wording of the first message establishes an aggressive or negative tone—no one likes being told what to do. The second message is reworded in a friendlier, more positive manner. Poorly chosen words may sound demeaning, condescending, discourteous, pretentious, or demanding. Notice in the Lands' End letter in Figure 4.5 that the writer achieves a courteous and warm tone. The letter responds to a customer's concern about the changing merchandise mix available in Lands' End catalogs. The customer also wants to receive fewer catalogs. The writer explains the company's expanded merchandise line and reassures the customer that Lands' End has not abandoned its emphasis on classic styles.

What techniques help a writer achieve a positive tone?

Skilled communicators create a positive tone in their messages by using a number of adaptive techniques, some of which are unconscious. These include spotlighting audience benefits, cultivating a "you" view, sounding conversational but professional, and using positive, courteous expression. Additional adaptive techniques include using bias-free language and preferring plain language with familiar but vigorous words.

Developing Audience Benefits

Focusing on the audience sounds like a modern idea, but actually one of America's early statesmen and authors recognized this fundamental writing principle over 200 years ago. In describing effective writing, Ben Franklin observed, "To be good, it ought to have a tendency to benefit the reader."[5] These wise words have become a fundamental guideline for today's business communicators. Expanding on Franklin's counsel, a contemporary communication consultant gives this solid advice to his business clients: "Always stress the benefit to the audience of whatever it is you are trying to get them to do. If you can show them how you are going to save them frustration or help them meet their goals, you have the makings of a powerful message."[6]

What is *empathy*?

Adapting your message to the receiver's needs means putting yourself in that person's shoes. It's called *empathy*. Empathic senders think about how a receiver will decode a message. They try to give something to the receiver, solve the receiver's problems, save the receiver's

FIGURE 4.5 Customer Response Letter

LAND'S END
DIRECT MERCHANTS

February 23, 2011

Mrs. Elaine Hough
9403 Farwest Drive SW
Tacoma, WA 98498

Dear Mrs. Hough:

Your letter was a strong endorsement of our belief that we made the right choice when we devoted our company to traditional, classic styles—and that it's still the right choice.

It's true we've made changes. In the past few years, with the markets soft and tastes changing, we reexamined our merchandise, with a view to continuing to serve valued customers while introducing ourselves to new ones. We decided that our styles needed freshening and that we would offer clothes that didn't chase after trends but did have a feel for what was current.

Our commitment to the classics hasn't weakened, as I hope you'd agree, having seen recent catalogs. But we've defined "classic" more inclusively than in the past. We're using new fabrics, new colors, a more relaxed fit. There's more imagination in our product mix now, but the sweaters, rugbys, blouses, button-downs, and other basics for which you've relied on us are still here. You may not find each one in every catalog, and you may notice the new products more than those you've seen before. The classics are still here, and the selection will be growing.

I've arranged to send you just the four catalogs a year you wanted. I hope you'll keep an eye on them. I think that, more and more, you'll be able to come to us for the styles you want.

Sincerely,

Brian Finnegan

Brian Finnegan
Customer Relations

LANDS' END, INC.
1 LANDS' END LANE DODGEVILLE, WI 53595
(608) 935-9341

Explains evolving merchandise line from company's and reader's view
Emphasizes areas of agreement
Opens response to inquiry by agreeing with customer
Uses conversational language to convey warmth and sincerity
Concludes by giving customer what she wants and promoting further business

money, or just understand the feelings and position of that person. Which version of the following messages is more appealing to the audience?

Sender Focus	**Audience Focus**
The Human Resources Department requires that the enclosed questionnaire be completed immediately so that we can allocate our training resource funds to employees.	By filling out the enclosed questionnaire, you can be one of the first employees to sign up for our training resource funds.
Our warranty becomes effective only when we receive an owner's registration.	Your warranty begins working for you as soon as you return your owner's registration.
We are proud to announce our new software virus checker that we think is the best on the market!	Now you can be sure that all your computers will be protected with our real-time virus scanning.

Cultivating the "You" View

Notice that many of the previous audience-focused messages included the word *you*. In concentrating on receiver benefits, skilled communicators naturally develop the "you" view. They

Spotlight on Communicators

© AP Images/David Kohl

Voted the greatest minority entrepreneur in American history, John H. Johnson was a master at profiling potential customers and cultivating the "you" view. He always focused on what they wanted rather than on what he wanted. His emphasis on the "you" view helped him build *Ebony* and *Jet* magazines, along with *Fashion Fair Cosmetics*, into multimillion-dollar businesses. In explaining his customer approach, he said, "I want to know where they came from, what are their interests, [and] what can I talk to them about." He worked to establish rapport with people by learning their interests.

emphasize second-person pronouns (*you, your*) instead of first-person pronouns (*I/we, us, our*). Whether your goal is to inform, persuade, or promote goodwill, the catchiest words you can use are *you* and *your*. Compare the following examples.

"I/We" View	"You" View
We are requiring all employees to respond to the attached survey about health benefits.	Because your ideas count, please complete the attached survey about health benefits.
I need your account number before I can do anything.	Would you mind giving me your account number so that I can locate your records and help you solve this problem?
We have shipped your order by UPS, and we are sure it will arrive in time for your sales promotion December 1.	Your order will be delivered by UPS in time for your sales promotion December 1.

How can you use the word *you* skillfully?

Although you want to focus on the reader or listener, don't overuse or misuse the second-person pronoun *you*. Readers and listeners appreciate genuine interest; on the other hand, they resent obvious attempts at manipulation. The authors of some sales messages, for example, are guilty of overkill when they include *you* dozens of times in a direct-mail promotion. Furthermore, the word can sometimes create the wrong impression. Consider this statement: *You cannot return merchandise until you receive written approval.* The word *you* appears twice, but the reader feels singled out for criticism. In the following version the message is less personal and more positive: *Customers may return merchandise with written approval.*

Another difficulty in emphasizing the "you" view and de-emphasizing *we/I* is that it may result in overuse of the passive voice. For example, to avoid *We will give you* (active voice), you might write *You will be given* (passive voice). The active voice in writing is generally preferred because it identifies who is doing the acting. You will learn more about active and passive voice in Chapter 5.

Should you remove all incidents of *I* and *we* in your messages?

In recognizing the value of the "you" attitude, writers do not have to sterilize their writing and totally avoid any first-person pronouns or words that show their feelings. Skilled communicators are able to convey sincerity, warmth, and enthusiasm by the words they choose. Don't be afraid to use phrases such as *I'm happy* or *We're delighted,* if you truly are.

When speaking face-to-face, communicators show sincerity and warmth with nonverbal cues such as a smile and a pleasant voice tone. In letters, memos, and e-mail messages, however, only expressive words and phrases can show these feelings. These phrases suggest hidden messages that say *You are important, I hear you,* and *I'm honestly trying to please you.* Mary Kay Ash, one of the most successful cosmetics entrepreneurs of all time, gave her salespeople wise advice. She had them imagine that any person they were addressing wore a sign saying, *Make me feel important.*

Being Conversational but Professional

How can a message be conversational and also professional?

Most instant messages, e-mail messages, business letters, memos, and reports replace conversation. Thus, they are most effective when they convey an informal, conversational tone instead of a formal, pretentious tone. Workplace messages should not, however, become so casual that they sound low level and unprofessional.

Instant messaging (IM) enables coworkers to have informal, spontaneous conversations. Some companies have accepted IM as a serious workplace tool. With the increasing use of instant messaging and e-mail, however, a major problem has developed. Sloppy, unprofessional expression appears in many workplace messages. You will learn more about the dangers of e-mail in Chapter 7. At this point, though, we focus on the tone of the language.

To project a professional image, you must sound educated and mature. Overuse of expressions such as *totally awesome, you know,* and *like,* as well as reliance on needless abbreviations (*BTW* for *by the way*), make a businessperson sound like a teenager. Professional messages do not include IM abbreviations, slang, sentence fragments, and chitchat. We urge you to strive for a warm, conversational tone that avoids low-level diction. Levels of diction, as shown in Figure 4.6, range from unprofessional to formal.

FIGURE 4.6 **Levels of Diction**

Unprofessional (Low-level diction)	Conversational (Middle-level diction)	Formal (High-level diction)
badmouth	criticize	denigrate
guts	nerve	courage
pecking order	line of command	dominance hierarchy
ticked off	upset	provoked
rat on	inform	betray
rip off	steal	expropriate
Sentence example: If we just hang in there, we can snag the contract.	**Sentence example:** If we don't get discouraged, we can win the contract.	**Sentence example:** If the principals persevere, they can secure the contract.

Your goal is a warm, friendly tone that sounds professional. Although some writers are too casual, others are overly formal. To impress readers and listeners, they use big words, long sentences, legal terminology, and third-person constructions. Stay away from expressions such as *the undersigned, the writer*, and *the affected party*. You will sound friendlier with familiar pronouns such as *I, we*, and *you*. Study the following examples to see how to achieve a professional, yet conversational tone:

Unprofessional	Professional
Hey, boss, Gr8 news! Firewall now installed!! BTW, check with me b4 announcing it.	Mr. Smith, our new firewall software is now installed. Please check with me before announcing it.
Look, dude, this report is totally bogus. And the figures don't look kosher. Show me some real stats. Got sources?	Because the figures in this report seem inaccurate, please submit the source statistics.

Zooming In — PART 2

Suze Orman

America's most listened-to personal finance expert, Suze Orman, appears on TV, makes personal appearances, prepares magazine columns, and has written seven best-selling books. One might expect her to be a master multitasker, taking on many jobs at once and juggling all of them perfectly. Wrong, way wrong! When Orman starts a writing task, she focuses on that task only and allows no interruptions. "I came to this conclusion after watching the way racehorses win," she explained. "They come out of the gate with blinders on and go for the finish line." That's how she writes. "All I care about is what I do, and I do absolutely nothing else while I am doing it."[7] Trying to complete more than one task at the same time ends in the "absolute ruination" of any project, she contended. "When I'm writing, I don't answer phones. I don't care what else is going on."[8]

Her total focus enables her to target her advice to specific audiences. She seems to really care about people and is nonjudgmental toward those who have dug themselves into terrible financial trouble. Although much financial information is contradictory and confusing, she offers practical advice in simple, positive language. She explains the reasoning behind her advice and encourages others to learn to make their own financial decisions wisely.

Critical Thinking

- When writing, what are the advantages and disadvantages of multitasking?
- Suze Orman is known for using simple, familiar language to express complex ideas. Does a business writer lose credibility when using this kind of language?
- Why does it make sense for a business writer to express ideas positively instead of negatively?

Overly Formal	Conversational
All employees are herewith instructed to return the appropriately designated contracts to the undersigned.	Please return your contracts to me.
Pertaining to your order, we must verify the sizes that your organization requires prior to consignment of your order to our shipper.	We will send your order as soon as we confirm the sizes you need.

Expressing Yourself Positively

LEARNING OBJECTIVE 4
Effectively employ positive and courteous tone, bias-free language, simple expression, and vigorous words.

You can improve the clarity, tone, and effectiveness of a message if you use positive rather than negative language. Positive language generally conveys more information than negative language does. Moreover, positive messages are uplifting and pleasant to read. Positive wording tells what *is* and what *can be done* rather than what *isn't* and what *can't be done*. For example, *Your order cannot be shipped by January 10* is not nearly as informative as *Your order will be shipped January 20.* An office supply store adjacent to an ice cream parlor in Portland, Maine, posted a sign on its door that reads: *Please enjoy your ice cream before you enjoy our store.* That sounds much more positive and inviting than *No food allowed!*[9]

What are examples of loaded words that convey a negative tone?

Using positive language also involves avoiding negative words that create ill will. Some words appear to blame or accuse your audience. For example, opening a letter to a customer with *You claim that* suggests that you don't believe the customer. Other loaded words that can get you in trouble are *complaint, criticism, defective, failed, mistake,* and *neglected.* Often the writer is unconscious of the effect of these words. Notice in the following examples how you can revise the negative tone to create a more positive impression.

Negative	Positive
This plan definitely cannot succeed if we don't obtain management approval.	This plan definitely can succeed if we obtain management approval.
You failed to include your credit card number, so we can't mail your order.	We look forward to completing your order as soon as we receive your credit card number.
Your letter of May 2 claims that you returned a defective headset.	Your May 2 letter describes a headset you returned.
Employees cannot park in Lot H until April 1.	Employees may park in Lot H starting April 1.
You won't be sorry that....	You will be happy that....

Being Courteous

Why is it smart for a business communicator to remain cool and courteous even when angry?

Maintaining a courteous tone involves not just guarding against rudeness but also avoiding words that sound demanding or preachy. Expressions such as *you should, you must,* and *you have to* cause people to instinctively react with *Oh, yeah?* One remedy is to turn these demands into rhetorical questions that begin with *Will you please....* Giving reasons for a request also softens the tone.

Even when you feel justified in displaying anger, remember that losing your temper or being sarcastic will seldom accomplish your goals as a business communicator: to inform, to persuade, and to create goodwill. When you are irritated, frustrated, or infuriated, keep cool and try to defuse the situation. In dealing with customers in telephone conversations, use polite phrases such as *I would be happy to assist you with that, Thank you for being so patient,* and *It was a pleasure speaking with you.*

Less Courteous	More Courteous and Helpful
Can't you people get anything right? This is the second time I've written!	Please credit my account for $340. My latest statement shows that the error noted in my letter of May 15 has not yet been corrected.
Stewart, you must complete all performance reviews by Friday.	Stewart, will you please complete all performance reviews by Friday.

Less Courteous	More Courteous and Helpful
You should organize a car pool in this department.	Organizing a car pool will reduce your transportation costs and help preserve the environment.
Am I the only one who can read the operating manual?	Let's review the operating manual together so that you can get your documents to print correctly next time.

Choosing Bias-Free Language

In adapting a message to its audience, be sure your language is sensitive and bias-free. Few writers set out to be offensive. Sometimes, though, we all say things that we never thought might be hurtful. The real problem is that we don't think about the words that stereotype groups of people, such as *the boys in the mail room* or *the girls in the front office.* Be cautious about expressions that might be biased in terms of gender, race, ethnicity, age, and disability. Generally, you can avoid gender-biased language by leaving out the words *man* or *woman*, by using plural nouns and pronouns, or by changing to a gender-free word (*person* or *representative*). Avoid the *his or her* option whenever possible. It's wordy and conspicuous. With a little effort, you can usually find a construction that is graceful, grammatical, and unselfconscious.

What is biased language, and why should business communicators avoid it?

Specify age only if it is relevant, and avoid expressions that are demeaning or subjective (such as *spry old codger*). To avoid disability bias, do not refer to an individual's disability unless it is relevant. When necessary, use terms that do not stigmatize disabled individuals. The following examples give you a quick look at a few problem expressions and possible replacements. The real key to bias-free communication, though, lies in your awareness and commitment. Be on the lookout to be sure that your messages do not exclude, stereotype, or offend people.

Gender Biased	Improved
female doctor, woman attorney, cleaning woman	doctor, attorney, cleaner
waiter/waitress, authoress, stewardess	server, author, flight attendant
mankind, man-hour, man-made	humanity, working hours, artificial
office girls	office workers
the doctor ... he	doctors ... they
the teacher ... she	teachers ... they
executives and their wives	executives and their spouses
foreman, flagman, workman	lead worker, flagger, worker
businessman, salesman	businessperson, sales representative
Each employee had his picture taken.	Each employee had a picture taken. All employees had their pictures taken. Each employee had his or her picture taken.

Racially or Ethnically Biased	Improved
An Indian accountant was hired.	An accountant was hired.
James Lee, an African American, applied.	James Lee applied.

Age Biased	Improved
The law applied to old people.	The law applied to people over 65.
Sally Kay, 55, was transferred.	Sally Kay was transferred.
a spry old gentleman	a man
a little old lady	a woman

Disability Biased	Improved
afflicted with arthritis, suffering from ..., crippled by ...	has arthritis
confined to a wheelchair	uses a wheelchair

Using Plain Language and Familiar Words

Why should business communicators strive to use familiar language?

In adapting your message to your audience, use plain language and familiar words that you think audience members will recognize. Don't, however, avoid a big word that conveys your idea efficiently and is appropriate for the audience. Your goal is to shun pompous and pretentious language. Instead, use "GO" words. If you mean *begin*, don't say *commence* or *initiate*. If you mean *pay*, don't write *compensate*. By substituting everyday, familiar words for unfamiliar ones, as shown here, you help your audience comprehend your ideas quickly.

Unfamiliar	Familiar
commensurate	equal
interrogate	question
materialize	appear
obfuscate	confuse
remuneration	pay, salary
terminate	end

At the same time, be selective in your use of jargon. *Jargon* describes technical or specialized terms within a field. These terms enable insiders to communicate complex ideas briefly, but to outsiders they mean nothing. Human resources professionals, for example, know precisely what's meant by *cafeteria plan* (a benefits option program), but most of us would be thinking about lunch. Geologists refer to *plate tectonics,* and physicians discuss *metastatic carcinomas.* These terms mean little to most of us. Use specialized language only when the audience will understand it. In addition, don't forget to consider secondary audiences: Will those potential receivers understand any technical terms used?

- words meaning diff things

Employing Precise, Vigorous Words

How can you improve your vocabulary so that you can use precise, vigorous words?

Strong verbs and concrete nouns give receivers more information and keep them interested. Don't overlook the thesaurus (or the thesaurus program on your computer) for expanding your word choices and vocabulary. Whenever possible, use specific words as shown here.

Imprecise, Dull	More Precise
a change in profits	a 25 percent hike in profits a 10 percent plunge in profits
to say	to promise, confess, understand to allege, assert, assume, judge
to think about	to identify, diagnose, analyze to probe, examine, inspect

The accompanying checklist feature on page 126 reviews important elements in the first phase of the 3-x-3 writing process. As you review these tips, remember the three basics of prewriting: analyzing, anticipating, and adapting. Figure 4.7 on page 125 illustrates a number of poor techniques that create a negative tone in an e-mail message. Notice what a difference revision makes. Many negative ideas could have been expressed positively. After revision, the message is shorter, is more conversational, and emphasizes audience benefits.

Writing in Teams

LEARNING OBJECTIVE 5
Understand how teams approach collaborative writing projects and what collaboration tools support team writing.

As you learned in Chapter 2, many of today's workers will work with teams to deliver services, develop products, and complete projects. It is almost assumed that today's progressive organizations will employ teams in some capacity to achieve their objectives. Because much of a team's work involves writing, you can expect to be putting your writing skills to work as part of a team.

FIGURE 4.7 Improving the Tone in an E-Mail Message

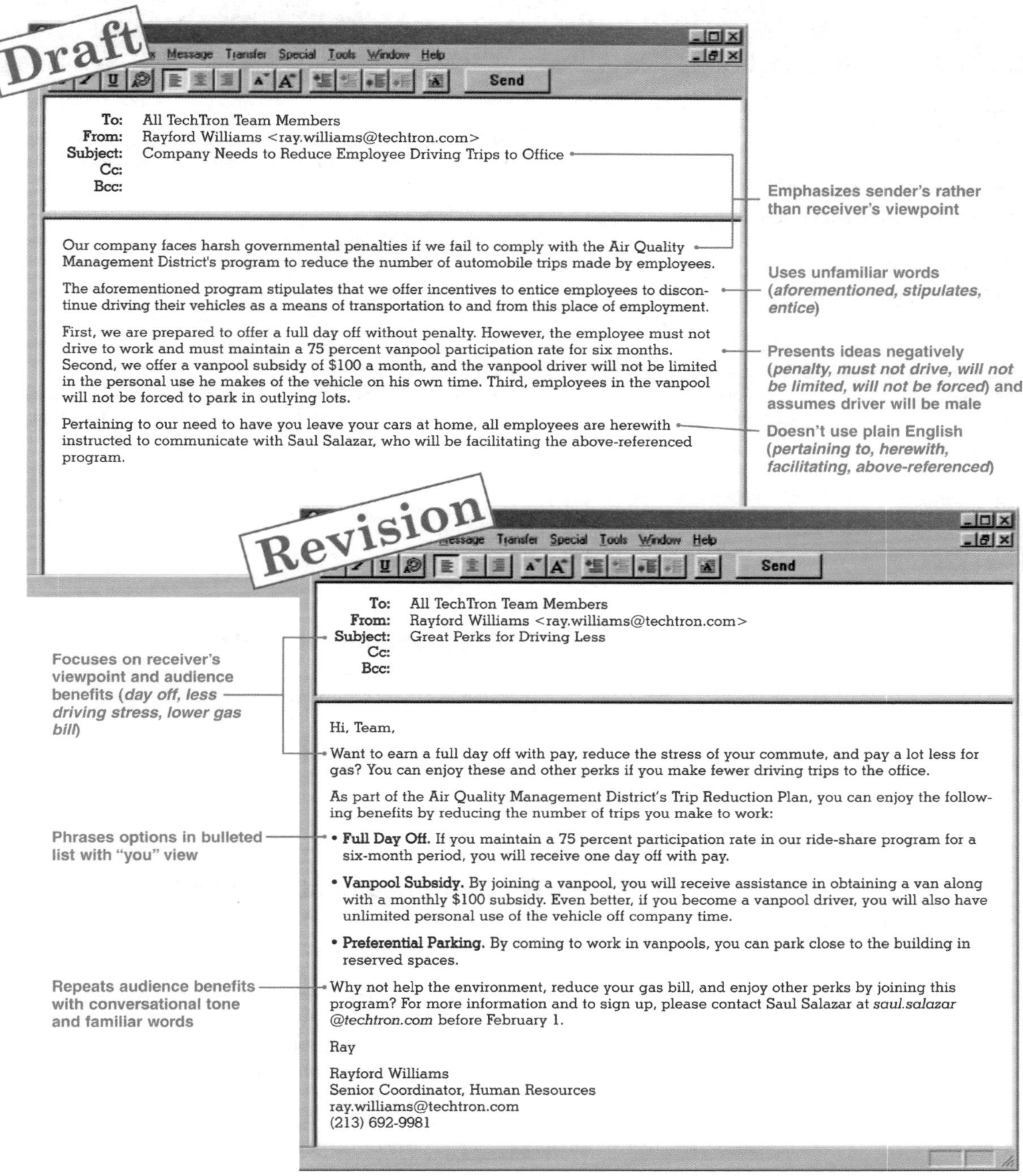

Draft

To: All TechTron Team Members
From: Rayford Williams <ray.williams@techtron.com>
Subject: Company Needs to Reduce Employee Driving Trips to Office
Cc:
Bcc:

Our company faces harsh governmental penalties if we fail to comply with the Air Quality Management District's program to reduce the number of automobile trips made by employees.

The aforementioned program stipulates that we offer incentives to entice employees to discontinue driving their vehicles as a means of transportation to and from this place of employment.

First, we are prepared to offer a full day off without penalty. However, the employee must not drive to work and must maintain a 75 percent vanpool participation rate for six months. Second, we offer a vanpool subsidy of $100 a month, and the vanpool driver will not be limited in the personal use he makes of the vehicle on his own time. Third, employees in the vanpool will not be forced to park in outlying lots.

Pertaining to our need to have you leave your cars at home, all employees are herewith instructed to communicate with Saul Salazar, who will be facilitating the above-referenced program.

Revision

To: All TechTron Team Members
From: Rayford Williams <ray.williams@techtron.com>
Subject: Great Perks for Driving Less
Cc:
Bcc:

Hi, Team,

Want to earn a full day off with pay, reduce the stress of your commute, and pay a lot less for gas? You can enjoy these and other perks if you make fewer driving trips to the office.

As part of the Air Quality Management District's Trip Reduction Plan, you can enjoy the following benefits by reducing the number of trips you make to work:

- **Full Day Off.** If you maintain a 75 percent participation rate in our ride-share program for a six-month period, you will receive one day off with pay.
- **Vanpool Subsidy.** By joining a vanpool, you will receive assistance in obtaining a van along with a monthly $100 subsidy. Even better, if you become a vanpool driver, you will also have unlimited personal use of the vehicle off company time.
- **Preferential Parking.** By coming to work in vanpools, you can park close to the building in reserved spaces.

Why not help the environment, reduce your gas bill, and enjoy other perks by joining this program? For more information and to sign up, please contact Saul Salazar at *saul.salazar @techtron.com* before February 1.

Ray

Rayford Williams
Senior Coordinator, Human Resources
ray.williams@techtron.com
(213) 692-9981

Emphasizes sender's rather than receiver's viewpoint
Uses unfamiliar words (*aforementioned, stipulates, entice*)
Presents ideas negatively (*penalty, must not drive, will not be limited, will not be forced*) and assumes driver will be male
Doesn't use plain English (*pertaining to, herewith, facilitating, above-referenced*)
Focuses on receiver's viewpoint and audience benefits (*day off, less driving stress, lower gas bill*)
Phrases options in bulleted list with "you" view
Repeats audience benefits with conversational tone and familiar words

When Are Team-Written Documents Necessary?

Collaboration on team-written documents is necessary for projects that (a) are big, (b) have short deadlines, and (c) require the expertise or consensus of many people. Businesspeople sometimes collaborate on short documents, such as memos, letters, information briefs, procedures, and policies. But more often, teams work together on big documents and presentations.

In what situations can you expect to share writing duties with a team?

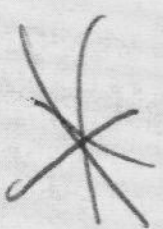

Checklist

Adapting a Message to Its Audience

- **Identify the message purpose.** Ask yourself why you are communicating and what you hope to achieve. Look for primary and secondary purposes.
- **Select the most appropriate form.** Determine whether you need a permanent record or whether the message is too sensitive to put in writing.
- **Profile the audience.** Identify your relationship with the reader and your knowledge about that individual or group. Assess how much the receiver knows about the subject.
- **Focus on audience benefits.** Phrase your statements from the readers' viewpoint, not the writer's. Concentrate on the "you" view (*Your order will arrive, You can enjoy, Your ideas count*).
- **Avoid gender and racial bias.** Use bias-free words (*businessperson* instead of *businessman; working hours* instead of *man-hours*). Omit ethnic identification unless the context demands it.
- **Avoid age and disability bias.** Include age only if relevant. Avoid potentially demeaning expressions (*spry old gentleman*), and use terms that do not stigmatize disabled people (*he is disabled* instead of *he is a cripple* or *he has a handicap*).
- **Be conversational but professional.** Strive for a warm, friendly tone that is not overly formal or familiar. Avoid slang and low-level diction.
- **Express ideas positively rather than negatively.** Instead of *Your order can't be shipped before June 1,* say *Your order can be shipped June 1.*
- **Use short, familiar words.** Use technical terms and big words only if they are appropriate for the audience (*end* not *terminate, required* not *mandatory*).
- **Search for precise, vigorous words.** Use a thesaurus if necessary to find strong verbs and concrete nouns (*announces* instead of *says, brokerage* instead of *business*).

Why Are Team-Written Documents Better?

Team-written documents and presentations are standard in most organizations because collaboration has many advantages. Most important, collaboration usually produces a better product because many heads are better than one. In addition, team members and organizations benefit from team processes. Working together helps socialize members. They learn more about the organization's values and procedures. They are able to break down functional barriers, and they improve both formal and informal chains of communication. Additionally, they buy in to a project when they are part of its development. Members of effective teams are eager to implement their recommendations.

How Are Team-Written Documents Divided?

In what phases of the writing process do team members work together and separately?

With big writing projects, teams may not actually function together for each phase of the writing process. Typically, team members gather at the beginning to brainstorm. They iron out answers to questions about the purpose, audience, content, organization, and design of their document or presentation. They develop procedures for team functioning, as you learned in Chapter 2. Then, they often assign segments of the project to individual members.

Teams work together closely in Phase 1 (prewriting) of the writing process. However, members generally work separately in Phase 2 (writing), when they conduct research, organize their findings, and compose a first draft. During Phase 3 (revising) teams may work together to synthesize their drafts and offer suggestions for revision. They might assign one person the task of preparing the final document, and another, the job of proofreading. The revision and evaluation phase might be repeated several times before the final product is ready for presentation.

What Online Collaboration Tools Support Team Writing?

One of the most frustrating tasks for teams is writing shared documents. Keeping the various versions straight and recognizing who made what comment can be difficult. Fortunately, online collaboration tools are constantly being developed and improved. They range from simple to complex, inexpensive to expensive, locally installed to remotely hosted, commercial to open source, and large to small. Online collaboration tools are especially necessary when team members are not physically in the same location. However, even when members are nearby, they may find it necessary to use online collaboration tools, such as the following:[10]

- **E-mail.** Despite its many drawbacks, e-mail remains a popular tool for online asynchronous (intermittent data transmission) collaboration. However, as projects grow more complex and involve more people who are not working nearby, e-mail becomes a clumsy, ineffective tool, especially for collaborative writing tasks.
- **Mailing lists.** With the right software, mailing lists can be archived online, providing a threaded listing of posts and full-text searching.
- **Discussion boards.** Participants can upload documents to the board instead of sending large files to everyone.
- **Instant messaging.** Because it ensures immediate availability, instant messaging is gaining acceptance. It allows members to clear up minor matters immediately, and it is helpful in initiating a quick group discussion.
- **Blogs and wikis.** A *blog* is a Web site with journal entries usually written by one person with comments added by others. A *wiki* is a Web site that allows multiple users to collaboratively create and edit pages. Wikis are good tools for building a knowledge repository that can be edited by participants. You will learn more about blogs and wikis in Chapter 7.
- **Groupware and portals.** Groupware and portals in the past involved expensive software featuring online discussion areas, document- and file-sharing areas, integrated calendaring, and collaborative authoring tools. More recently, less expensive tools including Basecamp, Box, Huddle, and Socialtext are available.

A team of investors and organic farmers in Bloomington, Indiana, began using Basecamp, an inexpensive Web-based collaboration program, to help the people in the field keep in touch with those in town. The 81-acre farm grows organic produce and sells it to Whole Foods Market, food co-ops, and farmers' markets. The farm's founders brought on four partners, but their jobs elsewhere prevented them from visiting the farm very often. One partner decided to install Basecamp on the farm house computer. For $24 a month this program offers to-do lists, a wiki, a chat room, 3 gigabytes of file storage, and a function that tracks due dates. Now the city folks can stay in the loop with the farmers and can share in decision making and farm progress.[11]

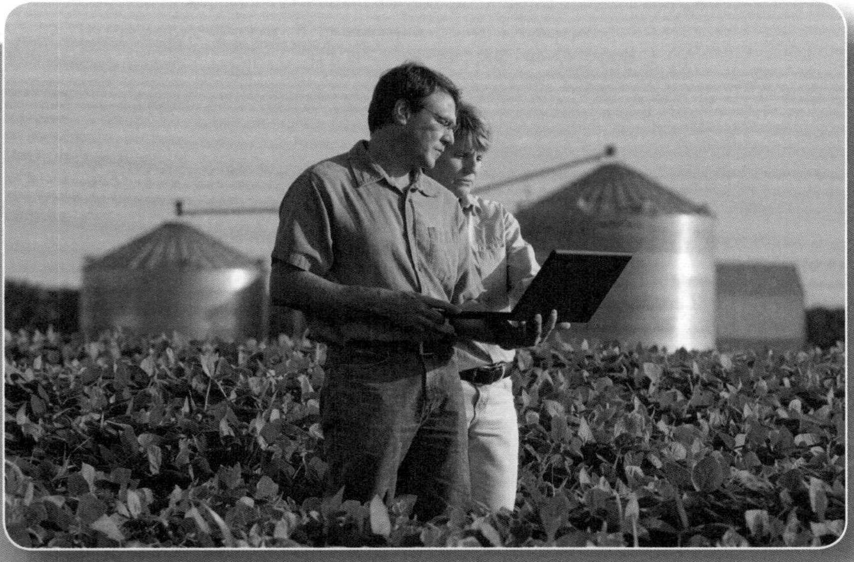

Collaboration software isn't just for multinational corporations. Stranger's Hill Organics, the oldest certified organics farm in Indiana, has joined the ranks of Adidas, Patagonia, Kellogg's and others in using Basecamp, a popular project-management tool that allows professionals to work together from different locations. The local grower, which serves markets and co-ops in Bloomington and Indianapolis, uses Basecamp to coordinate tasks, from crop maintenance and harvesting to tax planning. The results show in the farm's healthy squash, beans, cucumbers, and herbs. *How might farmers use online collaboration tools?*

PLUGGED IN

Using Technology to Edit and Revise Collaborative Documents

Collaborative writing and editing projects are challenging. Fortunately, Microsoft Word offers useful tools to help team members edit and share documents electronically. Two simple but useful editing tools are **Text Highlight Color** and **Font Color**. These tools, which are found on the **Home** tab in MS Office 2007, enable reviewers to point out errors and explain problematic passages through the use of contrast. However, some projects require more advanced editing tools such as **Track Changes** and **Comment**.

Track Changes. To suggest specific editing changes to other team members, **Track Changes** is handy. The revised wording is visible on screen, and deletions show up in callout balloons that appear in the right-hand margin (see Figure 4.2). Suggested revisions offered by various team members are identified and dated. The original writer may accept or reject these changes. In Office 2007 you will find **Track Changes** on the **Review** tab.

Comment. Probably the most useful editing tool is the **Comment** function, also shown in Figure 4.8. This tool allows users to point out problematic passages or errors, ask or answer questions, and share ideas without changing or adding text. When more than one person adds comments, the comments appear in different colors and are identified by the writer's name and a date/time stamp. To use this tool in Word 2007, click **New Comment** from the drop-down **Review** tab. Then type your comment, which can be seen in the Web or print layout view (click **View** and **Print Layout** or **Web Layout**).

Completing a Document. When a document is finished, be sure to accept or reject all changes on the **Review** tab, a step that removes the tracking information.

Career Application

Organize into groups of three. Using the latest version of Word, copy and respond to the Document for Analysis in 4.11. Set up a round-robin e-mail file exchange so that each member responds to the other group members' documents by using the **Comment** feature of Word to offer advice or suggestions for improvement. Submit a printout of the document with group comments, as well as a final edited document.

What Tools Work Well for Student Collaboration?

Student groups collaborating on assignments may find several helpful software tools. Google Docs is a free Web-based word processor, spreadsheet, presentation, and form application program that keeps documents current and lets team members update files from their own computers. A favorite feature of Google Docs is offline editing via Google Gears or the Chrome browser. In addition, Google Docs enables you to compose offline using your own word processor and upload into Docs to share and edit with teammates. Another free collaborative writing tool is Whiteboard. Check out either of these free tools by searching Google.

A number of tools accompanying Microsoft Word enable team writers to track changes and insert comments while editing one team document. The above Plugged In box discusses these tools, and Figure 4.8 illustrates how they work.

Adapting to Legal and Ethical Responsibilities

LEARNING OBJECTIVE 6

Summarize the legal and ethical responsibilities of business communicators in the areas of investments, safety, marketing, human resources, and copyright law.

One of your primary responsibilities in writing for an organization or for yourself is to avoid language that may land you in court. Another responsibility is to be ethical. Both of these concerns revolve around the use and abuse of language. You can protect yourself and avoid litigation by knowing what is legal and by adapting your language accordingly. Be especially careful when your messages address or include mentions of investments, safety, marketing, human resources, and copyright law.

Investment Information

Writers describing the sale of stocks or financial services must follow specific laws written to protect investors. Any messages—including e-mails, letters, newsletters, and pamphlets—must be free of misleading information, exaggerations, and half-truths. One company in Massachusetts inadvertently violated the law by declaring that it was "recession-proof." After going bankrupt, the company was sued by angry stockholders claiming that they had been

FIGURE 4.8 **Track Changes and Comment Features in Team Document**

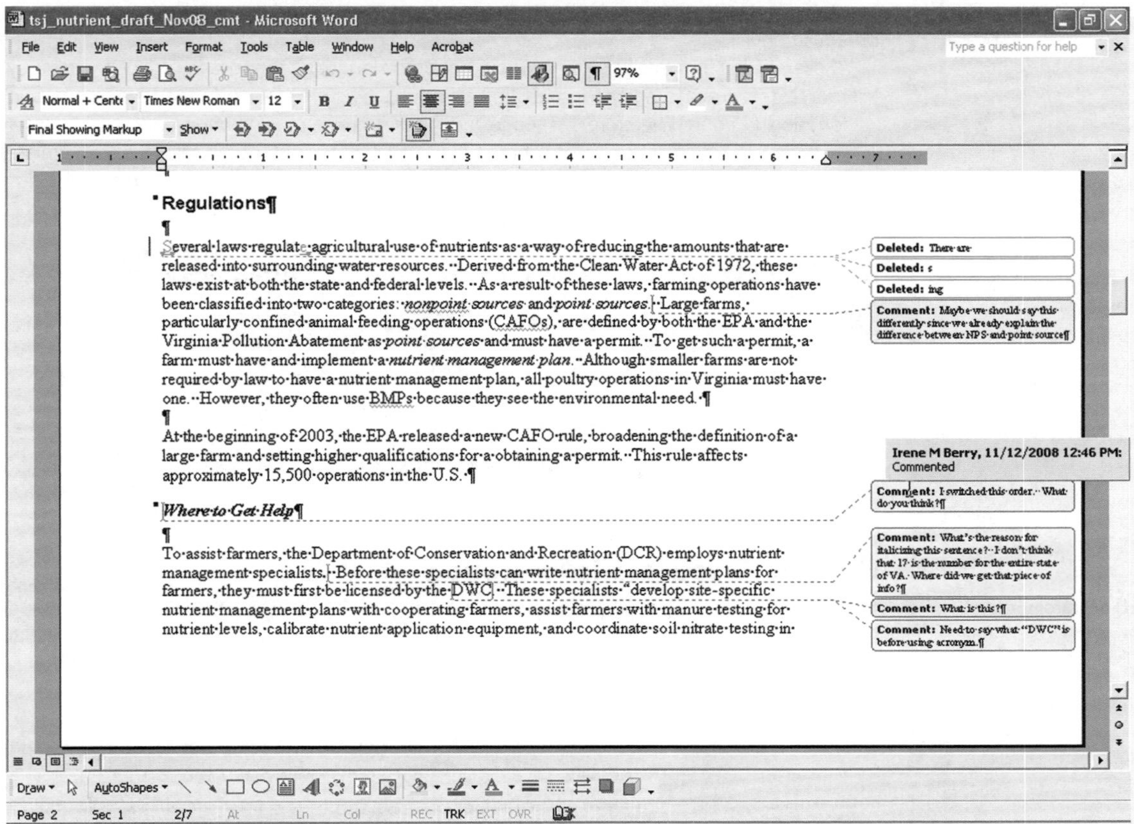

deceived. A software company caused a flurry of lawsuits by withholding information that revealed problems in a new version of one of its most popular programs. Stockholders sued, charging that managers had deliberately concealed the bad news, thus keeping stock prices artificially high. Experienced financial writers know that careless language and even poor timing may provoke litigation.

Safety Information

Why should warnings on dangerous products be written especially clearly?

Writers describing potentially dangerous products worry not only about protecting people from physical harm but also about being sued. During the past three decades, litigation arising from product liability has been one of the most active areas of tort law (*tort law* involves wrongful civil acts other than breach of contract). Manufacturers are obligated to warn consumers of any risks in their products. These warnings must do more than suggest danger; they must also clearly tell people how to use the product safely. In writing warnings, concentrate on major points. Omit anything that is not critical. In the work area describe a potential problem and tell how to solve it. For example, *Lead dust is harmful and gets on your clothes. Change your clothes before leaving work.*

Clearly written safety messages use easy-to-understand words, such as *doctor* instead of *physician*, *clean* instead of *sanitary*, and *burn* instead of *incinerate*. Technical terms are defined; for example, *Asbestos is a carcinogen (something that causes cancer)*. Effective safety messages also include highlighting techniques such as headings and bullets. In coming chapters you will learn more about these techniques for improving readability.

Marketing Information

Sales and marketing messages are illegal if they falsely advertise prices, performance capability, quality, or other product characteristics. Marketing messages must not deceive the buyer in any

What kinds of sales and marketing messages are illegal?

way. The marketers of CortiSlim and CortiStress paid huge fines and were forbidden to claim that their products caused rapid weight loss and reduced the risk of cancer, heart disease, and other ailments.[12]

Sellers of services must also be cautious about the language they use to describe what they will do. Letters, reports, and proposals that describe services to be performed are interpreted as contracts in court. Therefore, language must not promise more than intended. In Chapter 10 on page 315, you will learn more about what's legal and what's not in sales letters. Here are some dangerous words (and recommended alternatives) that have created misunderstandings leading to lawsuits.[13]

Dangerous Word	Court Interpretation	Recommended Alternative
inspect	to examine critically, to investigate and test officially, to scrutinize	to review, to study, to tour the facility
determine	to come to a decision, to decide, to resolve	to evaluate, to assess, to analyze
assure	to render safe, to make secure, to give confidence, to cause to feel certain	to facilitate, to provide further confidence, to enhance the reliability of

Human Resources Information

What kinds of statements should you avoid in evaluating employees in the workplace?

The vast number of lawsuits relating to human resources and employment makes this a treacherous area for business communicators. In evaluating employees in the workplace, avoid making unsubstantiated negative comments. It is also unwise to assess traits (*she is unreliable*) because doing so requires subjective judgment. Concentrate instead on specific incidents (*in the last month she missed four work days and was late three times*). Defamation lawsuits have become so common that some companies no longer provide letters of recommendation for former employees. To be safe, give recommendations only when the former employee authorizes the recommendation and when you can say something positive. Stick to job-related information.

Statements in employee handbooks also require careful wording, because a court might rule that such statements are "implied contracts." Consider the following handbook remark: "We at Hotstuff, Inc., show our appreciation for hard work and team spirit by rewarding everyone who performs well." This seemingly harmless statement could make it difficult to fire an employee because of the implied employment promise.[14] Companies are warned to avoid promissory phrases in writing job advertisements, application forms, and offer letters. Phrases that suggest permanent employment and guaranteed job security can be interpreted as contracts.[15]

ETHICS CHECK

Barack Rip-Off

Poster artist Shepard Fairey created a popular "Hope" poster of Barack Obama from a striking photo he saw on the Internet. Freelance photographer Mannie Garcia cried foul and demanded licensing fees, which Fairey refused. Are items on the Internet free for the taking if they have been changed a little?

In statements to existing and prospective employees, companies must recognize that oral comments may trigger lawsuits. A Minnesota television news anchor won damages when she gave up her job search because her station manager promised to extensively market her in a leading role. But he failed to follow through. A Vermont engineer won his case of negligent misrepresentation when he was not told that the defense project for which he was hired faced a potential cutback. Companies are warned to require employees to sign employment agreements indicating that all terms of employment orally agreed upon must be made in writing to be valid.[16]

In adapting messages to meet today's litigious business environment, be sensitive to the rights of others and to your own rights. The key elements in this adaptation process are awareness of laws, sensitivity to interpretations, and careful use of language.

Copyright Information

What is *fair use* in relation to copyright law?

The Copyright Act of 1976 protects authors—literary, dramatic, and artistic—of published and unpublished works. The word *copyright* refers to "the right to copy," and a key provision is *fair use*. Under fair use, individuals have limited use of copyrighted material without requiring permission. These uses are for criticism, comment, news reporting, teaching, scholarship, and research. Unfortunately, the distinctions between fair use and infringement are not clearly defined.

Four-Factor Test to Assess Fair Use. What is fair use? Actually, it is a shadowy territory with vague and often disputed boundaries—now even more so with the addition of cyberspace. Courts use four factors as a test in deciding disputes over fair use:

- **Purpose and character of the use, particularly whether for profit.** Courts are more likely to allow fair use for nonprofit educational purposes than for commercial ventures.
- **Nature of the copyrighted work.** When information is necessary for public good—such as medical news—courts are more likely to support fair use.
- **Amount and substantiality of portion used.** Copying a 200-word passage from a 200,000-word book might be allowed but not 200 words from a 1,000-word article or a substantial part of a shorter work. A total of 300 words is mistakenly thought by many to be an acceptable limit for fair use, but courts have not upheld this figure. Don't rely on it.
- **Effect of the use on the potential market.** If use of the work may interfere with the author's potential profit from the original, fair use copying would not be allowed.

How to Avoid Copyright Infringement. Whenever you borrow words, charts, graphs, photos, music, or anything created privately, be sure you know what is legal and acceptable. The following guidelines will help:

- **Assume that everything is copyrighted.** Nearly everything created privately and originally after 1989 is copyrighted and protected whether or not it has a copyright notice.
- **Realize that Internet items are NOT in the public domain.** Nothing modern is in the public domain (free to be used by anyone) unless the owner explicitly says so.
- **Observe fair-use restrictions.** Be aware of the four-factor test. Avoid appropriating large amounts of outside material.
- **Ask for permission.** You are always safe if you obtain permission. Write to the source, identify the material you wish to include, and explain where it will be used. Expect to pay for permission.
- **Don't assume that a footnote is all that is needed.** Including a footnote to a source prevents plagiarism but not copyright infringement. Anything copied beyond the boundaries of fair use requires permission. You will learn more about citation methods and ways to avoid plagiarism in Chapter 12.

For more information about *copyright law, fair use, public domain,* and *work for hire,* you can search the Web with these keywords.

Why should writers assume that everything is copyrighted?

Want to do well on tests and excel in your course? Go to **www.meguffey.com** for helpful interactive resources.

- **Review the Chapter 4 PowerPoint slides to prepare for the first quiz.**

Zooming In — YOUR TURN

Applying Your Skills With Suze Orman

As an applicant for a research assistant at the Suze Orman Financial Group, you have been asked to submit a writing sample. Your assignment is to compose a one-page memo discussing why so many college students are in debt. All applicants are to provide tips to students who want to avoid getting into college-related debt. As a writing sample, your memo will be judged on its clear expression, simple language, and precise words.

Your Task

Address your memo to Melissa M., who is a recruiter hired by Suze Orman to screen applicants. See Chapter 8 for information about preparing memos.

Summary of Learning Objectives

1 Identify four basic principles of business writing, summarize the 3-x-3 writing process, and explain how a writing process helps a writer. Business writing differs from academic writing in that it strives to solve business problems. It is also economical, persuasive, and audience oriented. Phase 1 of the 3-x-3 writing process (prewriting) involves analyzing the message, anticipating the audience, and considering ways to adapt the message to the audience. Phase 2 (writing) involves researching the topic, organizing the material, and composing the message. Phase 3 (revising) includes proofreading and evaluating the message. A writing process helps a writer by providing a systematic plan describing what to do in creating messages.

2 Recognize the components of the first phase of the writing process (prewriting) including analyzing your purpose, profiling the audience, and selecting the best channel. Communicators must decide why they are delivering a message and what they hope to achieve. Although many messages only inform, some must also persuade. After identifying the purpose of a message, communicators must choose the most appropriate channel. That choice depends on the importance of the message, the amount and speed of feedback required, the need for a permanent record, the cost of the channel, and the degree of formality desired. Communicators should also anticipate the primary and secondary audiences in order to adapt the message appropriately.

3 Effectively apply audience benefits, the "you" view, and a conversational but professional tone. Skilled communicators strive to emphasize audience benefits in business messages. This involves looking for ways to give something to the receiver, solve the receiver's problems, save the receiver's money, or just understand the feelings and position of that person. Skilled communicators look at a message from the receiver's perspective applying the "you" view without attempting to manipulate. Effective business messages convey a warm, friendly tone but avoid expressions that may make the writer sound immature or unprofessional.

4 Effectively employ positive and courteous tone, bias-free language, simple expression, and vigorous words. Skilled communicators improve the clarity, tone, and effectiveness of messages by using positive language that tells what can be done rather than what can't be done (*The project will be successful with your support* rather than *The project won't be successful without your support*). A courteous tone means guarding against rudeness and avoiding sounding preachy or demanding. Messages should also avoid language that excludes, stereotypes, or offends people, such as *lady lawyer, spry old gentlemen,* and *confined to a wheelchair*). Messages are improved by strong verbs and concrete nouns rather than imprecise, dull expressions.

5 Understand how teams approach collaborative writing projects and what collaboration tools support team writing. Team writing, which is necessary for large projects or when wide expertise is necessary, alters the writing process. Teams often work together in brainstorming and working out their procedures and assignments. Then individual members write their portions of the report or presentation during Phase 2. During Phase 3 (revising) teams may work together to combine their drafts. Teams use online collaboration tools such as e-mail, mailing lists, discussion boards, instant messaging, blogs, wikis, groupware, and portals.

6 Summarize the legal and ethical responsibilities of business communicators in the areas of investments, safety, marketing, human resources, and copyright law. In writing about investments, communicators must avoid misleading information, exaggerations, and half-truths. Safety information, including warnings, must tell consumers clearly how to use a product safely and motivate them to do so. In addition to being honest, marketing information must not promise more than intended. Communicators in human resources must use careful wording (particularly in employment recommendations and employee handbooks) to avoid lawsuits. They must also avoid oral promises that can result in lawsuits. In publication, one must be mindful of copyright laws. Writers should assume that everything is copyrighted, even items borrowed from the Internet, and know the implications and limitations of *fair use.*

Are you ready? Get more practice at **www.meguffey.com**

Chapter Review

1. Why do you think business writing differs from school essay writing? (Obj. 1)
2. List the three phases of the writing process and summarize what happens in each phase. Which phase requires the most time? (Obj. 1)
3. What six factors are important in selecting an appropriate channel to deliver a message? What makes one channel richer than another? (Obj. 2)
4. How does profiling the audience help a business communicator prepare a message? (Obj. 2)
5. What is meant by "audience benefits"? (Obj. 3)
6. When is the "you" view appropriate, and when is it inappropriate? (Obj. 3)
7. Why is it OK to use instant messaging abbreviations (such as *BTW*) and happy faces in messages to friends but not OK in business messages? (Obj. 3)
8. What is wrong with using expressions such as *you claim, complaint, criticism, defective, failed, mistake,* and *neglected?* (Obj. 4)
9. What is wrong with the following statement? *Pertaining to the above-referenced infraction, all employees are herewith warned by the undersigned not to install private software on company computers.* (Obj. 4)
10. What is bias-free language? List original examples. (Obj. 4)
11. Why should business writers strive to use short, familiar, simple words? Does this "dumb down" business messages? (Obj. 4)
12. What is *jargon*, and when is it appropriate for business writing? (Obj. 4)
13. What are the advantages and disadvantages of team-written documents? (Obj. 5)
14. Under copyright law, what does *fair use* mean? (Obj. 6)
15. What kinds of works are protected by copyright laws? (Obj. 6)

Critical Thinking

1. Why do you think employers prefer messages that are not written like high school and college essays? (Obj. 1)
2. A wise observer once said that bad writing makes smart people look dumb. Do you agree or disagree, and why? (Objs. 1–4)
3. Discuss the following statement: "The English language is a land mine—it is filled with terms that are easily misinterpreted as derogatory and others that are blatantly insulting . . . . Being fair and objective is not enough; employers must also appear to be so."[17] (Obj. 4)
4. Why do you think that writing in a natural, conversational tone is difficult for many people? (Obj. 3)
5. **Ethical Issue:** Peter Whitney, an employee at Wells Fargo, launched an Internet blog to chat about his life, his friends, and his job. After criticizing some of his coworkers in his blog, he was fired from his job handling mail and the front desk. Whitney said, "There needs to be clearer guidelines. Some people go to a bar and complain about workers. I decided to do it online. Some people say I deserve what happened, but it was really harsh. It was unfair."[18] Do you agree or disagree, and why?

Writing Improvement Exercises

4.1 Audience Benefits and the "You" View (Obj. 3)

Your Task. Revise the following sentences to emphasize the perspective of the audience and the "you" view.

a. To avoid suffering the kinds of monetary losses we have experienced in the past, our credit union prohibits the cashing of third-party checks presented by our members.
b. To help us process your order with our new database software, we need you to go to this Web site and fill out the required customer information.
c. We regret to announce that our electronics center is able to honor iPhone discounts only for a limited initial offering during the next 30 days.
d. Under a new policy, reimbursement of travel expenses will be restricted to those related to work only.
e. We are pleased to announce that you have been approved to enroll in our management trainee program.
f. To allow us to continue our policy of selling name brands at discount prices, we can give store credit but we cannot give cash refunds on returned merchandise.

4.2 Conversational but Professional (Obj. 3)

Your Task. Revise the following to make the tone conversational yet professional.

a. Under separate cover the above-referenced items (printer toner and supplies) are being sent to your Oakdale office, as per your telephone conversation of April 1.
b. Kindly inform the undersigned whether or not your representative will be making a visitation in the near future.
c. It is recommended that you conceptualize and submit your departmental budget ASAP.
d. BTW, we've had some slippage in the schedule but don't have to scrap everything and start from ground zero.
e. To facilitate ratification of this agreement, your negotiators urge that the membership respond in the affirmative.
f. She didn't have the guts to badmouth him 2 hz face.

4.3 Positive and Courteous Expression (Obj. 4)

Your Task. Revise the following sentences to reflect positive and courteous expression.

Are you ready? Get more practice at **www.meguffey.com**

a. Customers are ineligible for the 10 percent discount unless they show their membership cards.
b. Titan Insurance Company will not process any claim not accompanied by documented proof from a physician showing that the injuries were treated.
c. If you fail to follow each requirement, you will not receive your $50 rebate.
d. You have definitely not completed the job satisfactorily, and we will exercise our legal right to withhold payment until you do.
e. In the message you left at our Web site, you claim that you returned a defective headset.
f. We regret to announce that the special purchase netbook computers will be available only to the first 25 customers.

4.4 Bias-Free Language (Obj. 4)

Your Task. Revise the following sentences to reduce gender, racial, ethnic, age, and disability bias.

a. Any applicant for the position of fireman must submit a medical report signed by his physician.
b. Every employee is entitled to see his personnel file.
c. All waiters and waitresses are covered under our new benefits package.
d. A salesman would have to use all his skills to sell those condos.
e. Serving on the panel are a lady veterinarian, a female doctor, two businessmen, and an Indian CPA.
f. All conference participants and their wives are invited to the banquet.
g. How many man-hours are required to complete the project?

4.5 Plain Language and Familiar Words (Obj. 4)

Your Task. Revise the following sentences to use plain language and familiar words.

a. Please ascertain whether we must perpetuate our current contract despite perplexing profits.
b. He hypothesized that the vehicle was not operational because of a malfunctioning gasket.
c. Because we cannot monitor all cash payments, we must terminate the contract.
d. The contract stipulates that management must perpetuate the retirement plan.
e. I'll interface with Mark to access his people.
f. Unilateral nullification of the terms and conditions of the expiring agreement absent bona fide impasse is prohibited. (Legal talk!)

4.6 Precise, Vigorous Words (Obj. 4)

Your Task. From the choices in parentheses, select the most precise, vigorous words.

a. We plan to (*acknowledge, publicize, applaud*) the work of exemplary employees.
b. When replying to e-mail, (*bring in, include, put*) enough of the old message for (*someone, the person, the recipient*) to recognize the original note.
c. For a (*hard, long, complicated*) e-mail message, (*make, create, do*) the message in your word processing program.
d. If an e-mail (*thing, catch, glitch*) interferes while writing, you can easily (*get, have, retrieve*) your message.

For the following sentences provide more precise alternatives for the italicized words.

e. After (a) *going over* the proposal, I decided it was (b) *bad*.
f. In her e-mail message, she said that she would (a) *change* overtime hours in order to (b) *fix* the budget.
g. Our new manager (a) *said* that only (b) *the right kind of* applicants should apply.

4.7 Legal Language (Obj. 6)

Your Task. To avoid possible litigation, revise the italicized words in the following sentences taken from proposals.

a. We have *inspected* the environmental project and will send a complete report.
b. Our goal is to *assure* completion of the ecological program on schedule.
c. We will *determine* the amount of stress for each supporting column.

Activities

4.8 Document for Analysis: Improving the Tone of an E-Mail Message (Objs. 3–5)

Team

Your Task. Analyze the following demanding e-mail to be sent by the vice president to all employees. In teams or individually, discuss the tone and writing faults in this message. Your instructor may ask you to revise the message so that it reflects some of the writing techniques you learned in this chapter. How can you make this message more courteous, positive, and precise? Focus on conciseness, familiar words, and developing the "you" view. Consider revising this e-mail as a collaboration project using Word's **Comment** feature.

To: All Employees
From: B. A. Cartwright <bacartwright@integrity.com>
Subject: Your Excessive Use of E-Mail!
Cc:
Attached: E-Mail and Internet Policy

Once again I have the decidedly unpleasant task of reminding all employees that you may NOT utilize company computers or the Internet other than for work-related business and essential personal messages. Effective immediately a new policy will be implemented.

Our guys in IT tell me that our bandwidth is now seriously compromised by some of you boys and girls who are using company computers for gaming, blogging, shopping, chatting, and downloading streaming video. Yes, we have given you the right to use e-mail responsibly for essential personal messages. But that does not include checking your Facebook or MySpace accounts during work hours or downloading your favorite shows or sharing music.

We distributed an e-mail policy a little while ago. We have now found it necessary to amplify and extrapolate that policy to include use of the Internet. If our company does not control its e-mail and Internet use, you will continue to suffer slow downloads. You may also lose the right to use e-mail at all. In the past every employee has had the right to send a personal e-mail occasionally, but he must use that right carefully. We may have to prohibit the personal use of e-mail entirely. Don't make me do this!

You will be expected to study the attached E-Mail and Internet policy and return the signed form with your agreement to adhere to this policy. You must return this form by March 1. No exceptions!

4.9 Channel Selection: Burger King and the $1 Double Cheeseburger (Obj. 2)

To offer a budget sandwich during tough times, Burger King Holdings Inc. proposed a four-month promotion offering its double cheeseburger for $1 in the United States. But franchisees rejected the proposal because they thought it made no sense to sell the sandwich at a lower price than the cost of its ingredients. Burger King has 11,100 restaurants in more than 65 countries, and almost 90 percent of them are owned and operated by independent franchisees. Burger King management tried again by asking its U.S. franchisees to consider a six-week period for the $1 special, but operators voted against the modified plan as well. Results of the vote were delivered to franchisees in an audio recording.[19]

Your Task. Discuss the factors Burger King management may have considered before choosing a communication channel to deliver this important news. Was an audio recording (probably a recorded phone message) the best channel to deliver this news to thousands of franchisees in the United States?

4.10 Channel Selection: Various Business Scenarios (Obj. 2)

Your Task. Using Figure 4.2 on page 116, suggest the best communication channels for the following messages. Assume that all channels shown are available. Be prepared to explain your choices.

a. You need to know whether Crystal in Reprographics can produce a rush job for you in two days.
b. As part of a task force to investigate cell phone marketing, you need to establish a central location where each team member can see general information about the task as well as add comments for others to see. Task force members are located throughout the country.
c. You want to know what team members are available immediately for a quick teleconference meeting. They are all workaholics and glued to their computers.
d. As human resources manager during a company reorganization, you must tell six employees that they will lose their jobs.
e. A prospective client in Japan wants price quotes for a number of your products as soon as possible.
f. You must respond to a notice from the Internal Revenue Service insisting that you did not pay the correct amount for last quarter's employer's taxes.
g. As a member of the Information Technology Department, you must collect information about virus protection software for your office computers and make a recommendation to the hands-on company president.

4.11 Analyzing Audiences (Obj. 3)

Your Task. Using the questions in Figure 4.4 on page 118, write a brief analysis of the audience for each of the following communication tasks.

a. You are about to send an e-mail to your regional sales manager describing your visit to a new customer who is demanding special discounts.
b. You are preparing a cover letter for a job that you saw advertised in a local newspaper. You are confident that your qualifications match the job description.
c. As an administrator at the municipal water department, you must write a letter to water users explaining that the tap water may taste and smell bad; however, it poses no threats to health.
d. You are planning to write an e-mail to your boss to try to persuade her to allow you to attend a computer class that will require you to leave work early two days a week for ten weeks.
e. You are preparing an unsolicited sales letter to a targeted group of executives promoting part-time ownership in a corporate jet plane.

4.12 Copyright Confusion: Myths and Facts (Obj. 6)

Ethics

Your Task. You overheard the following statements as a group of college students discussed copyright issues.[20] Which of these statements do you think are true, and which are false?

a. If it doesn't have a copyright notice, it's not copyrighted.
b. If I don't charge for it, it's not a violation.
c. If it's posted to the Internet, it's in the public domain.
d. I can always argue that my posting was just fair use.
e. If you don't defend your copyright, you lose it.
f. If I make up my own stories, but base them on another work, my new work belongs to me.
g. They can't get me; defendants in court have powerful rights!
h. Copyright violation isn't a crime or anything, is it?
i. It doesn't hurt anybody. In fact, it's free advertising.
j. They e-mailed me a copy, so I can post it.

Video Resource

Video Library 1, Guffey's 3-x-3 Writing Process Develops Fluent Workplace Skills

This video combines narrative and role-playing to illustrate each phase of Guffey's 3-x-3 writing process. It shows three phases of the writing process including prewriting, writing, and revising. You will see how the writing process guides the development of a complete message. This video illustrates concepts in Chapters 4, 5, and 6. After viewing the film, be prepared to answer these questions:

- How can a writing process help a writer?
- Does the writing process always follow the same order?
- Why does revising take more time than any other part of the process?

Chat About It

In each chapter you will find five discussion questions related to the chapter material. Your instructor may assign these topics for you to discuss in class, in an online chat room, or on an online discussion board. Some of the discussion topics may require outside research. You may also be asked to read and respond to postings made by your classmates.

Are you ready? Get more practice at **www.meguffey.com**

Topic 1: List and analyze the steps that you followed to write a document before you started this course. Based on what you are learning in this course, which steps were effective? Which were ineffective? How will you change your approach to writing?

Topic 2: After searching an alumni database, you decide to e-mail a professional who is working in the career you hope to enter. Your goal in writing this professional is to obtain firsthand information about this person's career and to receive career advice. However, you know nothing about this person. Why might this person help you? Why might this person refuse? Should you organize your message directly or indirectly?

Topic 3: Why should you avoid words such as *really, totally, very*, and *quite* in your business writing? Provide an example of a sentence with and without such words. How did the meaning of the sentence change?

Topic 4: Think back to the last time you were involved in a team project. What did the team do that resulted in an efficient working process and a successful product? What did the team do that resulted in an inefficient working process and an unsuccessful product?

Topic 5: Find a news article online that describes a company that used careless language in its communication with its customers, stockholders, or employees. Briefly explain what the company did and what it should have done instead.

Grammar and Mechanics C.L.U.E. Review 4

Adjectives and Adverbs

Review Guides 19–20 about adjectives and adverbs in Appendix A, Grammar and Mechanics Guide, beginning on page A-9. On a separate sheet, revise the following sentences to correct errors in adjectives and adverbs. For each error that you locate, write the guide number that reflects this usage. Some sentences may have two errors. If a sentence is correct, write *C*. When you finish, check your answers on page Key-1.

1. Business writers strive to use easy to understand language and familiar words.
2. Luis said he did good in his employment interview.
3. Having prepared for months, we won the contract easy.
4. Collaboration on team written documents is necessary for big projects.
5. Jenna felt badly when her team project was completed.
6. The 3-x-3 writing plan provides step by step instructions for writing messages.
7. Our recently-revised office handbook outlined all recommended document formats.
8. The project ran smooth after Maria organized the team.
9. Locally-installed online collaboration tools are easy-to-use and work well.
10. Well written safety messages include short, familiar words.

CHAPTER 5

Organizing and Writing Business Messages

Want to do well on tests and excel in your course? Go to **www.meguffey.com** for helpful interactive resources.

- **Review the Chapter 5 PowerPoint slides to prepare for the first quiz.**

OBJECTIVES

After studying this chapter, you should be able to

1. Apply Phase 2 of the 3-x-3 writing process, which begins with formal and informal methods for researching data and generating ideas.
2. Explain how to organize data into lists and alphanumeric or decimal outlines.
3. Compare direct and indirect patterns for organizing ideas.
4. Compose the first draft of a message, avoiding sentence fragments, run-on sentences, and comma splices as well as emphasizing important ideas, avoiding misplaced modifiers, and using active and passive voice effectively.
5. Compose effective paragraphs using three classic paragraph plans as well as applying techniques for achieving paragraph coherence.

Zooming In PART 1

Once the Height of Hip, Gap Struggles to Stop Sagging Sales

From humble beginnings in San Francisco, Gap Inc. grew to become the largest clothing chain in the United States. However, after spectacular growth, it fell from favor. Critics accused it of making every bad move a retailer could. Besides major misses in fashion, the company failed to differentiate among its three major brands—Banana Republic, Gap, and Old Navy—and it opened too many stores.

The company that had pioneered the casual cool look with fitted jeans, khakis, and simple T-shirts lost its fashion compass. "The Gap doesn't seem hip any longer," said one shopper. "They're too preppy and sterile."[1] Another young shopper said, "Gap seems to be stuck in the '90s. I always think of it as the clothes my parents wear."[2] Once the king of casual but classic clothing, Gap has been stung by retailing upstarts that woo young people with trendy fashions at affordable prices. Retailers such as Zara, Mango, Hot Topic, and Hollister are snagging customers with hip styles and competitive pricing.

At its zenith in 1994, Gap launched Old Navy as a fun fashion label with good prices and street-chic attitude. Emphasizing humor and mass appeal, Old Navy gave shoppers music and bright colors while promoting a quirky image. But like Gap, Old Navy lost its cult status and its aura of campy fashion. In attempting to right the sinking ship, Old Navy overcorrected and went overboard with inexpensive fashions.

Further compounding their woes, both Gap and Old Navy have saturated the market. Gap has 2,688 U.S. stores, and Old Navy has 1,066.[3] They are almost as ubiquitous as Starbucks. In the fashion business, bigness is not necessarily a plus. With stores in nearly every shopping center, Gap has overexposed the brand. Customers are staying away because its styles no longer seem unique or special.

Under new management, Gap Inc. is working to improve its merchandise mix, reduce inventories, halt capital spending, and enhance its online and global presence. Ultimately, though, Gap and Old Navy must find a way to lure their customers back.

© AP Images/Paul Sakuma

Critical Thinking

- In what ways would research (gathering information) be important to Gap and Old Navy in getting their customers back?
- Why is it important for Gap managers, as well as other business communicators, to gather all necessary information before making management decisions?
- What techniques can business communicators at Gap Inc. and other companies use to generate ideas for new products as well as to improve business processes?

http://www.gap.com

Gathering Information Through Research

LEARNING OBJECTIVE 1

Apply Phase 2 of the 3-x-3 writing process, which begins with formal and informal methods for researching data and generating ideas.

Why is it necessary to gather information before beginning to write rather than gathering it as you write?

Business communicators at Gap and Old Navy face daily challenges that require data collection, idea generation, and concept organization. Before they can make decisions and convey those decisions in written messages or presentations, they must gather information and organize that information. These activities are part of the second phase of the 3-x-3 writing process. You will recall that the 3-x-3 writing process, as reviewed in Figure 5.1, involves three phases. This chapter focuses on the second phase of the process: researching, organizing, and writing.

No smart businessperson would begin writing a message before collecting all the needed information. We call this collection process *research*, a rather formal-sounding term. For simple documents, though, the process can be quite informal. Research is necessary before beginning to write because the information you collect helps shape the message. Discovering significant data after a message is half completed often means starting over and reorganizing. To avoid frustration and inaccurate messages, collect information that answers a primary question:

- What does the receiver need to know about this topic?

When the message involves action, search for answers to secondary questions:

- What is the receiver to do?
- How is the receiver to do it?

FIGURE 5.1 Guffey's 3-x-3 Writing Process

1 Prewriting

Analyze: Decide on the purpose of your message. What do you want the receiver to do or believe? What communication channel is best?

Anticipate: Profile the audience. What does the receiver already know? Will the receiver's response be neutral, positive, or negative?

Adapt: What writing techniques and strategies can you use to adapt your message to its audience? How can you shape the message to achieve your purpose?

2 Writing

Research: Gather background data to provide facts. Search company files, previous correspondence, and the Internet. What do you need to know to write this message?

Organize: Group similar information together. Decide whether to organize your information directly or indirectly. Outline your plan and make notes.

Compose: Prepare a first draft, usually writing quickly. Remember that you will be revising it to improve its readability and impact.

3 Revising

Revise: Edit your message to be sure it is clear, conversational, concise, and readable. Look for ways to highlight important information. Consider bullets, lists, and headings to help the reader understand related points.

Proofread: Read carefully to find and correct errors in spelling, grammar, punctuation, names, numbers, and format.

Evaluate: Will this message achieve your purpose? Have you thought enough about the audience to be sure this message is appropriate and appealing?

- When must the receiver do it?
- What will happen if the receiver doesn't do it?

Whenever your communication problem requires more information than you have in your head or at your fingertips, you must conduct research. This research may be formal or informal.

Formal Research Methods

How can you gather information formally?

Long reports and complex business problems generally require some use of formal research methods. Let's say you are part of the management team at Gap Inc. and you want to evaluate several locations for the placement of a new Old Navy store. Or, let's assume you must write a term paper for a college class. Both tasks require more data than you have in your head or at your fingertips. To conduct formal research, you could do the following:

- **Access electronically.** Much information is now available on the Internet, on CDs or DVDs, and in databases that can be accessed by computer. College and public libraries subscribe to retrieval services that permit you to access most periodic literature. You can

© Beau Lark/Fancy/Photolibrary

As consumers increasingly turn to the Internet to shop, recommend products, and rate businesses on their customer service, management teams are turning to a new kind of research to inform business decisions—online "buzz-tracking." Research firms such as Nielsen BuzzMetrics and Brandimensions traverse millions of fan sites, blogs, and chat rooms to analyze user feedback and spot consumer trends. *How can buzz-tracking research help communication professionals develop more effective written messages and presentations?*

FIGURE 5.2 Creating Cluster Diagram to Generate Ideas for an Old Navy/Gap Recruiting Brochure

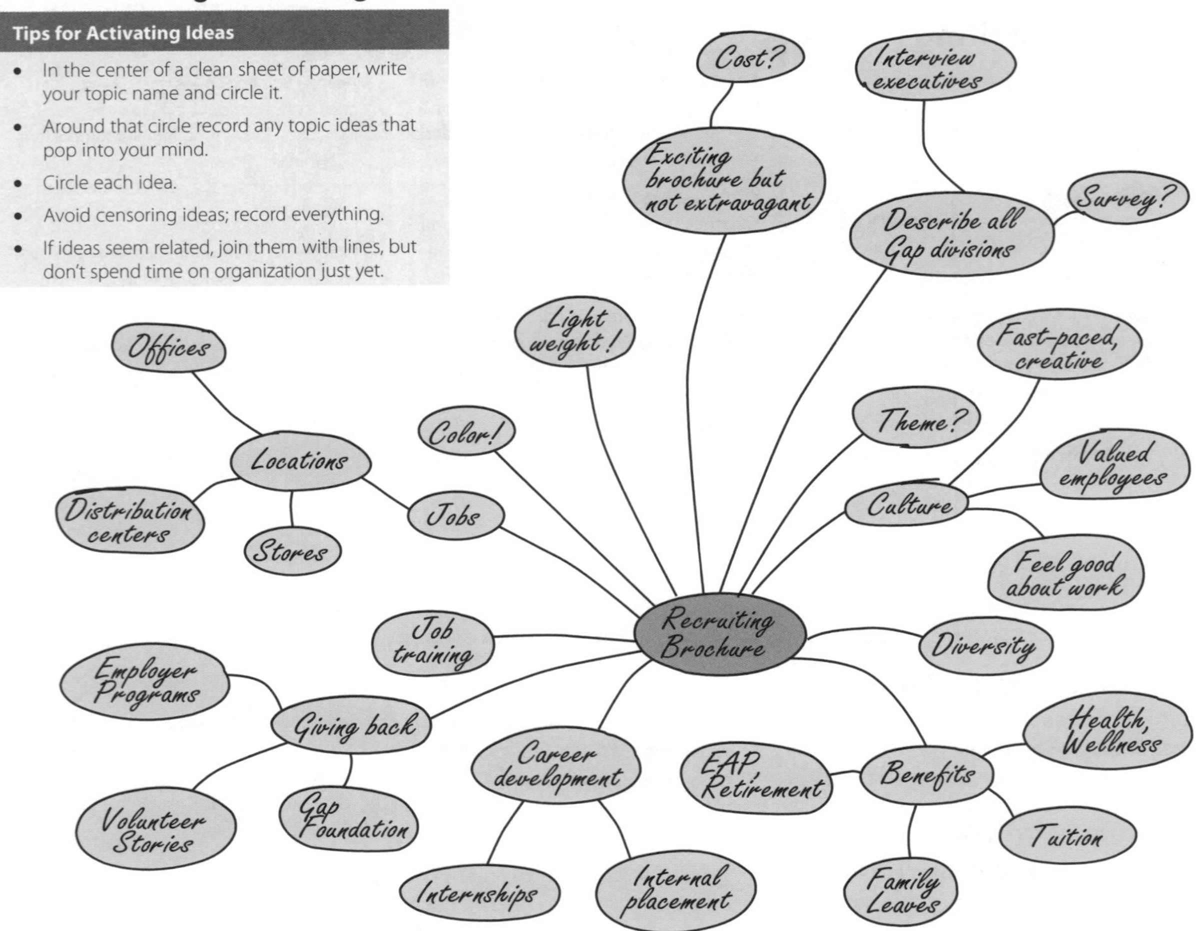

also find extraordinary amounts of information by searching the Web. You will learn more about using electronic sources in Chapter 11.

- **Search manually.** Helpful background and supplementary information is available through manual searching of resources in public and college libraries. These traditional sources include books and newspaper, magazine, and journal articles. Other sources are encyclopedias, reference books, handbooks, dictionaries, directories, and almanacs.
- **Go to the source.** For firsthand information, go directly to the source. If you were comparing the taste of Coca-Cola and Pepsi, for example, you could find out what consumers really think by conducting interviews or surveys, by putting together questionnaires, or by organizing focus groups. Formal research includes structured sampling and controls that enable investigators to make accurate judgments and valid predictions.
- **Investigate primary sources.** To develop firsthand, primary information for a project, go directly to the source. In searching for locations for Old Navy stores, you might travel to possible sites and check them out. If you need information about how many shoppers pass by a location or visit a shopping center, you might conduct a traffic count. To learn more about specific shoppers who might become Old Navy customers, you could use questionnaires, interviews, or focus groups. Formal research includes scientific sampling methods that enable investigators to make accurate judgments and valid predictions.
- **Conduct scientific experiments.** Another source of primary data is experimentation. Instead of merely asking for the target audience's opinion, scientific researchers present

FIGURE 5.3 **Organizing Ideas From a Cluster Diagram Into Subclusters**

Tips for Organizing Ideas

- Analyze the ideas generated in the original cluster diagram.
- Cross out ideas that are obviously irrelevant; simplify and clarify.
- Add new ideas that seem appropriate.
- Study the ideas for similarities.
- Group similar ideas into classifications (such as Content, Development, and Form).
- If the organization seems clear at this point, prepare an outline.
- For further visualization, make subcluster circles around each classification.

Recruiting Brochure
Development
Consult new employees
Look at other brochures
Work with our PR agency
Interview executives
Consult students
Estimate budget
Content
Job locations
Giving back
Introduction
Benefits
Diversity
Career development
Career opportunities
Gap history, culture
Form
Theme?
Color
Youthful, exciting pictures
Light in weight
Concise text

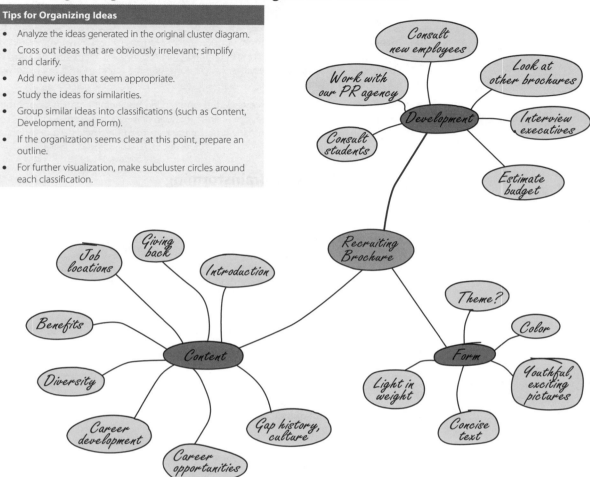

choices with controlled variables. Assume, for example, that the management team at Gap wants to know at what price and under what circumstances consumers would purchase jeans from the Gap instead of from Abercrombie & Fitch. Instead of jeans, let's say that management wants to study the time of year and type of weather conditions that motivate consumers to begin purchasing sweaters, jackets, and cold-weather gear. The results of such experimentation would provide valuable data for managerial decision making. Because formal research techniques are particularly necessary for reports, you will study resources and techniques more extensively in Unit 4.

Informal Research Methods

Most routine tasks—such as composing e-mails, memos, letters, informational reports, and oral presentations—require data that you can collect informally. For some projects, though, you rely more on your own ideas instead of—or in addition to—researching existing facts. Here are some techniques for collecting informal data and for generating ideas:

- **Look in the files.** If you are responding to an inquiry, you often can find the answer to the inquiry by investigating the company files or by consulting colleagues.

Spotlight on Communicators

Chris Heatherly and Len Mazzocco use systematic brainstorming to overhaul the Disney toy lineup every six months. A diverse group of designers, engineers, artists, animators, video game designers, marketers, and theme park employees gather 20 to 30 times a year for two- or three-day brainstorming sessions at hotels around the world. Three elements are crucial to their success: (a) icebreaker activities from 10 minutes to a half hour, (b) 45- to 60-minute brainstorming sessions in which teams list as many ideas as they can and then vote for their favorites, and (c) a product pitch including a storyboard record of the best toy ideas. When people have tried to ignore the icebreaker segment and cut to the chase, Chris says, "it just doesn't work. . . . You have to have some decompression time to be creative."

How can you gather information informally?

- **Talk with your boss.** Get information from the individual making the assignment. What does that person know about the topic? What slant should you take? What other sources would he or she suggest?
- **Interview the target audience.** Consider talking with individuals at whom the message is aimed. They can provide clarifying information that tells you what they want to know and how you should shape your remarks. Suggestions for conducting more formal interviews are presented in Chapter 11.
- **Conduct an informal survey.** Gather unscientific but helpful information through questionnaires, telephone surveys, or online surveys. In preparing a memo report predicting the success of a proposed company fitness center, for example, circulate a questionnaire asking for employee reactions.

What is brainstorming, and how should it be conducted for best results?

Generating Ideas by Brainstorming

One popular method for generating ideas is brainstorming. We should point out, however, that some critics argue that brainstorming groups "produce fewer and poorer quality ideas than the same number of individuals working alone." Even brainstorming proponents agree that, when done poorly, it can be a waste of time. But done properly, brainstorming is quite effective in unleashing ideas and creative energy.[4] One recent writer claims that groups can generate more and better ideas when "brainwriting"; that is, silently sharing written ideas in a structured group format.[5] Another group suggests using Twitter to exchange brainstorming ideas quickly.[6] Most business communicators, however, meet face to face to brainstorm, and they follow these suggestions to produce the best ideas:

- Define the problem and create an agenda that outlines the topics to be covered.
- Establish time limits, remembering that short sessions are best.
- Set a quota, such as a minimum of 100 ideas. The goal is quantity, not quality.
- Require every participant to contribute ideas, accept the ideas of others, or improve on ideas.
- Encourage wild, out-of-the-box thinking. Allow no one to criticize or evaluate ideas.
- Write ideas on flipcharts or on sheets of paper hung around the room.
- Organize and classify the ideas, retaining the best. Consider using cluster diagrams, discussed shortly.

Thousands of hospital patients die every year after receiving the wrong medicine. To prevent this tragic loss and to improve overall hospital efficiency, one large managed care facility holds brainstorming sessions bringing together doctors, nurses, patients, and vendors. Their ground rules include focusing on quantity of ideas rather than quality, withholding criticism, welcoming unusual ideas, and combining and improving ideas. The facilitator begins with a clear problem statement. Participants write ideas on Post-It notes using Sharpie pens to prevent wordiness. *Why is it necessary for successful brainstorming to begin with a clear problem statement, and what is the benefit of conciseness?*

Collecting Information and Generating Ideas on the Job

Let's assume that you work in the corporate offices of Gap Inc. and that you have been given the task of developing a college recruiting brochure for all Gap stores. You think this is a great idea because Gap Inc. has thousands of stores, and many college students don't know about the exciting career opportunities and benefits it offers. You know right away that you want the brochure to be colorful, exciting, concise, youth oriented, lightweight (because it has to be carried to college campuses), and easily updated. Beyond that, you realize that you need ideas from others on how to develop this recruiting brochure.

To collect data for this project, you decide to use both formal and informal research methods. You study recruiting brochures from other companies. You talk with college students about information they would like to see in a brochure. You conduct more formal research among recently hired employees and among Gap division presidents and executives to learn what they think a recruiting brochure should include. Working with an outside consultant, you prepare a questionnaire to use in personal interviews with employees and executives. The interviews include some open-ended questions such as, *How did you start with the company?* The questionnaire also asks specific questions about career paths, degree requirements, personality traits desired, and so forth.

Next you ask five or six fellow employees and team members to help brainstorm ideas for the brochure. In a spirited session, your team comes up the cluster diagram shown in Figure 5.2. The ideas range from the cost of the brochure to career development programs and your company's appealing location in the San Francisco Bay area.

From the jumble of ideas in the initial cluster diagram, you see that you can organize most of the information into three main categories relating to the brochure—Development, Form, and Content. You eliminate, simplify, and consolidate some ideas and add other new ideas. Then you organize the ideas into subclusters, shown in Figure 5.3. This set of subclusters could form the basis for an outline, which we will talk about shortly. Or you could make another set of subclusters, further outlining the categories.

Organizing Ideas

LEARNING OBJECTIVE 2

Explain how to organize data into lists and alphanumeric or decimal outlines.

One of the most important tasks in preparing well-organized messages is grouping similar ideas together. These groups of ideas are then sequenced in a way that helps the reader understand relationships and accept the writer's views. Unorganized messages proceed free-form, jumping from one thought to another. They look like the jumbled ideas in our Figure 5.2 cluster diagram. Such messages fail to emphasize important points. Puzzled readers can't see how the pieces fit together, and they become frustrated and irritated. Many communication experts regard poor organization as the greatest failing of business writers. Two simple techniques can help you organize data: the scratch list and the outline.

Using Lists and Outlines

What are two techniques for organizing data?

In developing simple messages, some writers make a quick scratch list of the topics they wish to cover. Writers often jot this scratch list in the margin of the letter or memo to which they are responding (the majority of business messages are written in response to other documents). These writers then compose a message at their computers directly from the scratch list.

Most writers, though, need to organize their ideas—especially if the project is complex—into a hierarchy, such as an outline. The beauty of preparing an outline is that it gives you a chance to organize your thinking before you get bogged down in word choice and sentence structure. Figure 5.4 shows two outline formats: alphanumeric and decimal. The familiar alphanumeric format uses Roman numerals, letters, and numbers to show major and minor ideas. The decimal format, which takes a little getting used to, has the advantage of showing how every item at every level relates to the whole. Both outlining formats force you to focus on the topic, identify major ideas, and support those ideas with details, illustrations, or evidence.

Probably the hardest part of outlining is grouping ideas into components or categories—ideally three to five. These categories are very important because they will become the major headings in your report. If you have more than five components, look for ways to combine smaller segments into broader topics. The following example shows how a portion of the Gap recruiting brochure subclusters (Figure 5.3) can be organized into an alphanumeric outline.[7]

FIGURE 5.4 Two Outlining Formats

Format for Alphanumeric Outline	Format for Decimal Outline
Title: Major Idea, Purpose	Title: Major Idea, Purpose
I. First major component	1.0. First major component
A. First subpoint	1.1. First subpoint
1. Detail, illustration, evidence	1.1.1. Detail, illustration, evidence
2. Detail, illustration, evidence	1.1.2. Detail, illustration, evidence
B. Second subpoint	1.2. Second subpoint
1.	1.2.1.
2.	1.2.2.
II. Second major component	2.0. Second major component
A. First subpoint	2.1. First subpoint
1.	2.1.1.
2.	2.1.2.
B. Second subpoint	2.2. Second subpoint
1.	2.2.1.
2.	2.2.2.
III. Third major component	3.0. Third major component
A.	3.1.
1.	3.1.1.
2.	3.1.2.
B.	3.2.
1.	3.2.1.
2.	3.2.2.
(This method is simple and familiar.)	*(This method relates every item to the overall outline.)*

Tips for Making Outlines

- Define the main topic (purpose of message) in the title.
- Divide the main topic into major components or classifications (preferably three to five). If necessary, combine small components into one larger category.
- Break the components into subpoints.
- Don't put a single item under a major component; if you have only one subpoint, integrate it with the main item above it or reorganize.
- Strive to make each component exclusive (no overlapping).
- Use details, illustrations, and evidence to support subpoints.

How are alphanumeric and decimal outlines different, and how are they similar?

I. Introduction
- A. Brief history of Gap Inc.
  - 1. Founding
  - 2. Milestones
- B. Corporate culture
  - 1. Emphasize upbeat attitude
  - 2. Value diversity, employees
  - 3. Value social responsibility

II. Careers
- A. Opportunities
  - 1. Internships
  - 2. Management trainee programs
  - 3. MBA programs
- B. Development
  - 1. Internal promotion
  - 2. Job training

Notice that each major category is divided into at least two subcategories. These categories are then fleshed out with examples, details, statistics, case histories, and other data. In moving

FIGURE 5.5 **Typical Major Components in Business Outlines**

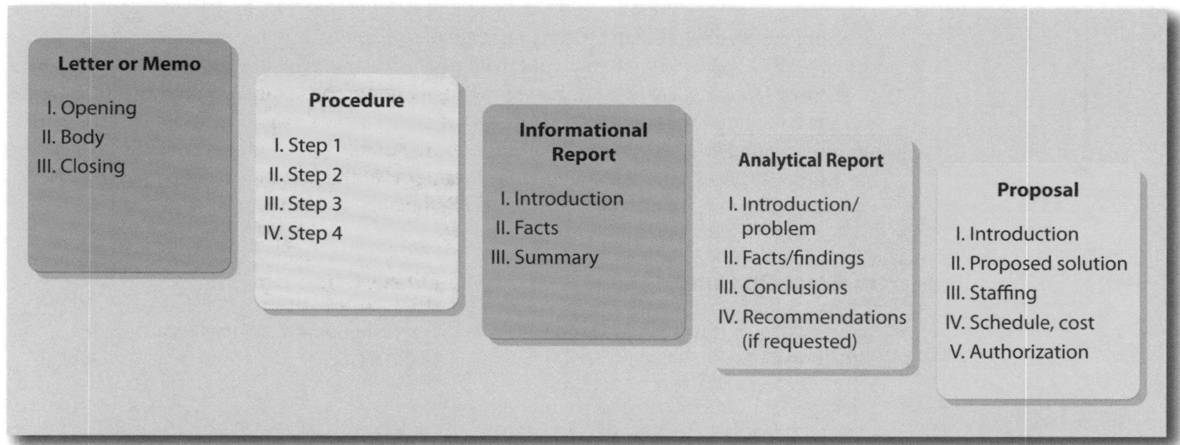

from major point to subpoint, you are progressing from large, abstract concepts to small, concrete ideas. Each subpoint could be further subdivided with more specific illustrations if you desired. You can determine the appropriate amount of detail by considering what your audience (primary and secondary) already knows about the topic and how much persuading you must do.

How you group ideas into components depends on your topic and your channel of communication. Business documents usually contain typical components arranged in traditional patterns, as shown in Figure 5.5.

Thus far, you've seen how to collect information, generate ideas, and prepare an outline. How you order the information in your outline, though, depends on the pattern or strategy you choose.

Organizing Ideas into Patterns

LEARNING OBJECTIVE 3
Compare direct and indirect patterns for organizing ideas.

Two organizational patterns provide plans of action for typical business messages: the direct pattern and the indirect pattern. The primary difference between the two patterns is where the main idea is placed. In the direct pattern, the main idea comes first, followed by details, explanation, or evidence. In the indirect pattern, the main idea follows the details, explanation, and evidence. The pattern you select is determined by how you expect the audience to react to the message, as shown in Figure 5.6.

FIGURE 5.6 **Audience Response Determines Pattern of Organization**

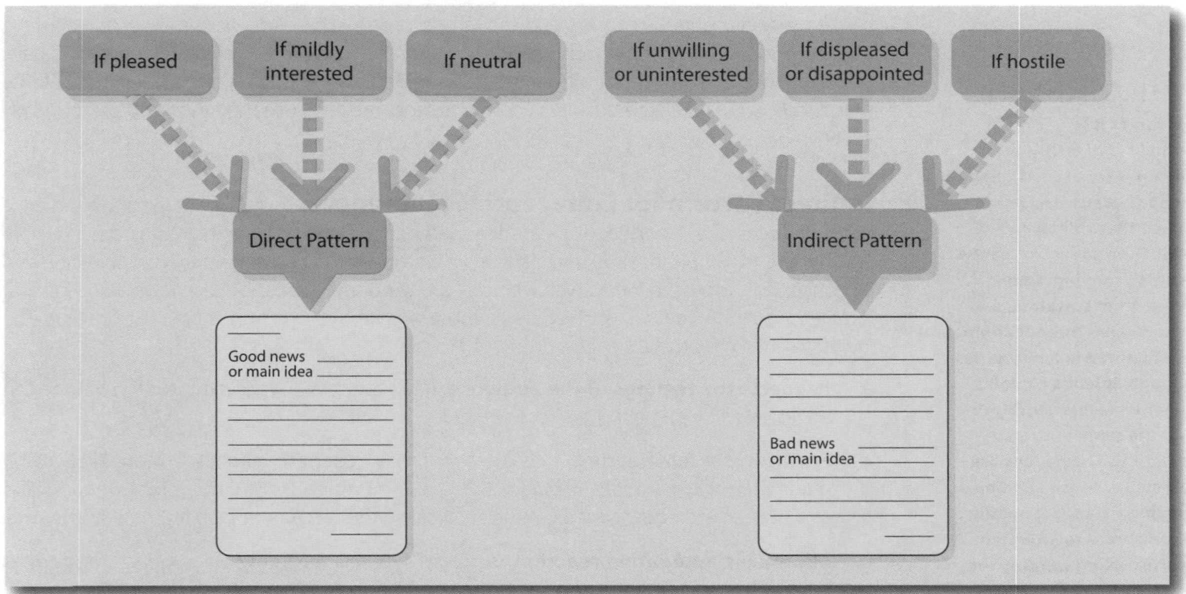

What pattern do business messages usually follow? Why?

Direct Pattern for Receptive Audiences. In preparing to write any message, you need to anticipate the audience's reaction to your ideas and frame your message accordingly. When you expect the reader to be pleased, mildly interested, or, at worst, neutral—use the direct pattern. That is, put your main point—the purpose of your message—in the first or second sentence. Dianna Booher, renowned writing consultant, pointed out that typical readers begin any message by saying, "So what am I supposed to do with this information?" In business writing you have to say, "Reader, here is my point!"[8] As quickly as possible, tell why you are writing. Compare the direct and indirect patterns in the following memo openings. Notice how long it takes to get to the main idea in the indirect opening.

Indirect Opening	Direct Opening
Our company has been concerned with attracting better-qualified prospective job candidates. For this reason, the Management Council has been gathering information about an internship program for college students. After considerable investigation, we have voted to begin a pilot program starting next fall.	The Management Council has voted to begin a college internship pilot program next fall.

What is frontloading, and how does it benefit receivers?

Explanations and details follow the direct opening. What's important is getting to the main idea quickly. This direct method, also called *frontloading*, has at least three advantages:

- **Saves the reader's time.** Many of today's businesspeople can devote only a few moments to each message. Messages that take too long to get to the point may lose their readers along the way.
- **Sets a proper frame of mind.** Learning the purpose up front helps the reader put the subsequent details and explanations in perspective. Without a clear opening, the reader may be thinking, "Why am I being told this?"
- **Reduces frustration.** Readers forced to struggle through excessive verbiage before reaching the main idea become frustrated. They resent the writer. Poorly organized messages create a negative impression of the writer.

This frontloading technique works best with audiences that are likely to be receptive to or at least not disagree with what you have to say. Typical business messages that follow the direct pattern include routine requests and responses, orders and acknowledgments, nonsensitive memos, e-mails, informational reports, and informational oral presentations. All these tasks have one element in common: none has a sensitive subject that will upset the reader. It should be noted, however, that some business communicators prefer to use the direct pattern for nearly all messages.

ETHICS CHECK

How Sweet It Is

The makers of artificial sweetener Equal sued competitor Splenda because the latter claimed that Splenda was "made from sugar." In reality, Splenda's core ingredient is made from sucralose, a nonnutritive synthetic compound manufactured in laboratories. Although Splenda contains a sugar molecule, sucralose is not the same as sucrose, the technical name for pure table sugar, despite its similar-sounding name. Is it unethical for companies to intentionally advertise using wording that would confuse consumers?

Indirect Pattern for Unreceptive Audiences. When you expect the audience to be uninterested, unwilling, displeased, or perhaps even hostile, the indirect pattern is more appropriate. In this pattern you reveal the main idea only after you have offered explanation and evidence. This approach works well with three kinds of messages: (a) bad news, (b) ideas that require persuasion, and (c) sensitive news, especially when being transmitted to superiors. The indirect pattern has these benefits:

- **Respects the feelings of the audience.** Bad news is always painful, but the trauma can be lessened by preparing the receiver for it.
- **Facilitates a fair hearing.** Messages that may upset the reader are more likely to be read when the main idea is delayed. Beginning immediately with a piece of bad news or a persuasive request, for example, may cause the receiver to stop reading or listening.
- **Minimizes a negative reaction.** A reader's overall reaction to a negative message is generally improved if the news is delivered gently.

Zooming In PART 2

Gap Inc.

Rebuilding its customer base and correcting its fashion missteps are major initiatives at Gap and its offspring, Old Navy. At the same time, the stores must be ever watchful that their garments are not made in sweatshops. Stiff competition and consumer demand for low prices have forced many U.S. apparel manufacturers to shift production offshore. Some of that production ends up in sweatshops, such as those found in Cambodia, Bangladesh, and Honduras. The worst sweatshops use child labor and demand 80-hour workweeks without overtime pay. Bosses routinely shout at workers and may send them home for talking on the job. Workers earn as little as 29 cents an hour.

Like other major apparel manufacturers, Gap Inc. strives to control working conditions with factory-monitoring and labor-standards programs. Around the world Gap Inc. has more than 90 employees whose sole focus is working to improve conditions in the factories that make its clothing. In one year these employees conducted 4,438 inspections at 2,118 garment factories around the world.[9] When a problem is found, Gap takes action. It works with contractors and factories to improve practices and conditions. If conditions don't improve, the retailer stops using errant contractors.[10] Enforcing its standards worldwide requires an ongoing effort.

When complaints from human rights activists and other watchdog groups arrive, Gap Inc. must investigate and respond to each inquiry.

© AP Images/Paul Sakuma

Critical Thinking

- When a business communicator responds to an inquiry, such as a letter about human rights violations among contractors, is "research" necessary?
- What are the differences between formal and informal research?
- What are the advantages and disadvantages of brainstorming with groups?

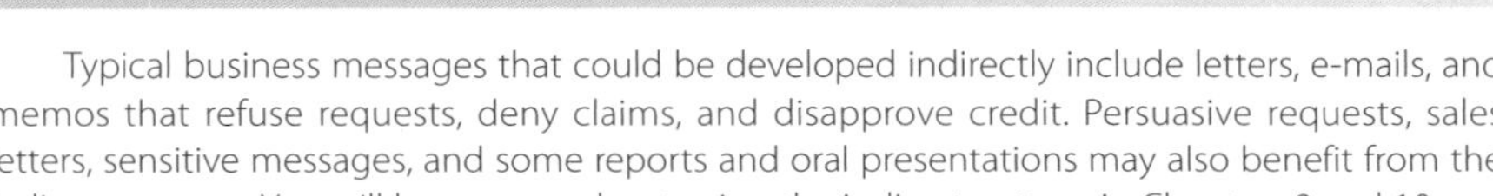

Typical business messages that could be developed indirectly include letters, e-mails, and memos that refuse requests, deny claims, and disapprove credit. Persuasive requests, sales letters, sensitive messages, and some reports and oral presentations may also benefit from the indirect strategy. You will learn more about using the indirect pattern in Chapters 9 and 10.

In summary, business messages may be organized directly, with the main idea first, or indirectly, with the main idea delayed. Although these two patterns cover many communication problems, they should be considered neither universal nor inviolate. Every business transaction is distinct. Some messages are mixed: part good news, part bad; part goodwill, part persuasion. In upcoming chapters you will practice applying the direct and indirect patterns in typical situations. Then, you will have the skills and confidence to evaluate communication problems and vary these patterns depending on the goals you wish to achieve.

Composing the First Draft

LEARNING OBJECTIVE 4

Compose the first draft of a message, avoiding sentence fragments, run-on sentences, and comma splices as well as emphasizing important ideas, avoiding misplaced modifiers, and using active and passive voice effectively.

Once you have researched your topic, organized the data, and selected a pattern of organization, you are ready to begin composing. Most writers expect to use their computers for composition, but many are unaware of all the ways a computer can help create better written messages, oral presentations, and Web pages. See the accompanying Plugged In box to learn how you can take full advantage of your computer.

Even with a computer, some writers have trouble getting started, especially if they haven't completed the preparatory work. Organizing your ideas and working from an outline are very helpful in overcoming writer's block. Composition is also easier if you have a quiet environment in which to concentrate. Businesspeople with messages to compose set aside a given time and allow no calls, visitors, or other interruptions. This is a good technique for students as well.

What is freewriting, and how is it helpful?

As you begin composing, think about what style fits you best. Some experts suggest that you write quickly (*freewriting*). Get your thoughts down now and refine them in later versions. As you take up each idea, imagine that you are talking to the reader. Don't let yourself get bogged down. If you can't think of the right word, insert a substitute or type *find perfect word later.* Freewriting works well for some writers, but others prefer to move more slowly and think through their ideas more deliberately. Whether you are a speedy or a deliberate writer, keep in mind that you are writing the first draft. You will have time later to revise and polish your sentences.

PLUGGED IN

Seven Ways Computers Can Help You Create Better Written Messages, Oral Presentations, and Web Pages

Although computers can't actually do the writing for you, they provide powerful tools that make the composition process easier and the results more professional. Here are seven ways your computer can help you improve your written documents, oral presentations, and even Web pages.

1. **Fighting writer's block.** Because word processors enable ideas to flow almost effortlessly from your brain to a screen, you can expect fewer delays resulting from writer's block. You can compose rapidly, and you can experiment with structure and phrasing, later retaining and polishing your most promising thoughts.
2. **Collecting information electronically.** As a knowledge worker in an information economy, you must find information quickly. Much of the world's information is now accessible in databases or on the Web. You will learn more about these exciting electronic resources in Unit 4.
3. **Outlining and organizing ideas.** Most word processors include some form of "outliner," a feature that enables you to divide a topic into a hierarchical order with main points and subpoints. Your computer keeps track of the levels of ideas automatically so that you can easily add, cut, or rearrange points in the outline.
4. **Improving correctness and precision.** Nearly all word processing programs today provide features that catch and correct spelling and typographical errors. Grammar checkers detect many errors in capitalization, word use (such as *it's, its*), double negatives, verb use, subject–verb agreement, sentence structure, number agreement, number style, and other writing faults. But the errors are merely highlighted—not corrected. You have to do that.
5. **Adding graphics for emphasis.** Your letters, memos, and reports may be improved by the addition of graphs and artwork to clarify and illustrate data. You can import charts, diagrams, and illustrations created in database, spreadsheet, graphics, or draw-and-paint programs. Clip art is available to symbolize or illustrate ideas.
6. **Designing and producing professional-looking documents, presentations, and Web pages.** Most software now includes a large selection of scalable fonts (for a variety of character sizes and styles), italics, boldface, symbols, and styling techniques to help you format consistently and produce professional-looking results. Presentation software enables you to incorporate illustrative slide effects, color, sound, pictures, and video clips into your talks for management or customers. Web document builders also help you design and construct Web pages.
7. **Using collaborative software for team writing.** Special programs with commenting and revision features, described in Chapter 4, allow you to make changes and to identify each team member's editing.

Career Application

Individually or in teams, identify specific software programs that perform the tasks described here. Prepare a table naming each program, its major functions, and its advantages and disadvantages for business writers in your field.

Creating Effective Sentences

In creating your first draft, you will be working at the sentence level of composition. Although you have used sentences all your life, you may be unaware of how they can be shaped and arranged to express your ideas most effectively.

Recognizing Basic Sentence Elements

To avoid writing sentence fragments and making punctuation errors, let's review some basic sentence elements. Complete sentences have subjects and verbs and make sense.

What makes a sentence complete?

SUBJECT (The manager) — VERB (sent)

The manager of Information Technology sent an e-mail to all employees.

Clauses and phrases, the key building blocks of sentences, are related groups of words. Clauses have subjects and verbs; phrases do not.

PHRASE (of Information Technology) — PHRASE (to all employees)

The manager of Information Technology sent an e-mail to all employees.

PHRASE (By reading carefully) — PHRASE (about the latest computer viruses)

By reading carefully, we learned about the latest computer viruses.

CLAUSE / CLAUSE

Because he is experienced, Adam can repair most computer problems.

CLAUSE / CLAUSE

When we have technology problems, we call a technician in our support group.

How are clauses different from phrases?

Clauses may be divided into two groups: independent and dependent. Independent clauses are grammatically complete. Dependent clauses depend for their meaning on independent clauses. In the two preceding examples the clauses beginning with *Because* and *When* are dependent. Dependent clauses are often introduced by words such as *if, when, because,* and *as.*

How are independent clauses different from dependent clauses?

INDEPENDENT CLAUSE

Adam solves our technology problems.

DEPENDENT CLAUSE / INDEPENDENT CLAUSE

When employees need help, Adam solves our technology problems.

By learning to distinguish phrases, independent clauses, and dependent clauses, you will be able to punctuate sentences correctly and avoid three basic sentence faults: the fragment, the run-on sentence, and the comma splice.

Avoiding Three Common Sentence Faults

As you craft your sentences, beware of three common traps: fragments, run-on (fused) sentences, and comma-splice sentences. If any of these faults appears in a business message, the writer immediately loses credibility.

What are sentence fragments?

Fragments. One of the most serious errors a writer can make is punctuating a fragment as if it were a complete sentence. A fragment is usually a broken-off part of a complex sentence.

Fragment	**Revision**
Because most transactions require a permanent record. Good writing skills are critical.	Because most transactions require a permanent record, good writing skills are critical.
The recruiter requested a writing sample. Even though the candidate seemed to communicate well.	The recruiter requested a writing sample even though the candidate seemed to communicate well.

Fragments often can be identified by the words that introduce them—words such as *although, as, because, even, except, for example, if, instead of, since, such as, that, which,* and *when*. These words introduce dependent clauses. Make sure such clauses always connect to independent clauses.

Run-On (Fused) Sentences. A sentence with two independent clauses must be joined by a coordinating conjunction (*and, or, nor, but*) or by a semicolon (;) or separated into two sentences. Without a conjunction or a semicolon, a run-on sentence results.

What is a run-on (fused) sentence?

Run-On Sentence	**Revision**
Most job seekers present a printed résumé some are also using Web sites as electronic portfolios	Most job seekers present a printed résumé. Some are also using Web sites as electronic portfolios.
One candidate sent an e-mail résumé another sent a traditional résumé.	One candidate sent an e-mail résumé; another sent a traditional résumé.

Comma-Splice Sentences. A comma splice results when a writer joins (splices together) two independent clauses with a comma. Independent clauses may be joined with a coordinating conjunction (*and, or, nor, but*) or a conjunctive adverb (*however, consequently, therefore,* and others). Notice that clauses joined by coordinating conjunctions require only a comma. Clauses joined by a coordinating adverb require a semicolon. On the following page are three possible revisions that rectify a comma splice.

What is a comma splice?

Comma Splice	Possible Revisions
Some employees responded by e-mail, others picked up the telephone.	Some employees responded by e-mail, and others picked up the telephone. Some employees responded by e-mail; however, others picked up the telephone. Some employees responded by e-mail; others picked up the telephone.

Sentences should average how many words?

Preferring Short Sentences

Because your goal is to communicate clearly, you should strive for sentences that average 20 words. Some sentences will be shorter; some will be longer. The American Press Institute reports that reader comprehension drops off markedly as sentences become longer.[11] Therefore, in crafting your sentences, think about the relationship between sentence length and comprehension.

Sentence Length	Comprehension Rate
8 words	100%
15 words	90%
19 words	80%
28 words	50%

Instead of stringing together clauses with *and, but,* and *however*, break some of those complex sentences into separate segments. Business readers want to grasp ideas immediately. They can do that best when thoughts are separated into short sentences. On the other hand, too many monotonous short sentences will sound "grammar schoolish" and may bore or even annoy the reader. Strive for a balance between longer sentences and shorter ones. Your computer probably can point out long sentences and give you an average sentence length.

What techniques can be used to emphasize important ideas?

Emphasizing Important Ideas

You can stress prominent ideas mechanically by underscoring, italicizing, or boldfacing. You can also emphasize important ideas with five stylistic devices.

- **Use vivid words.** Vivid words are emphatic because the reader can picture ideas clearly.

General	Vivid
One business uses personal selling techniques.	Avon uses face-to-face selling techniques.

- **Label the main idea.** If an idea is significant, tell the reader as shown here.

Unlabeled	Labeled
Explore the possibility of leasing a site, but also hire a consultant.	Explore the possibility of leasing a site; but, *most important*, hire a consultant

- **Place the important idea first or last in the sentence.** Ideas have less competition from surrounding words when they appear first or last in a sentence. Observe how the date of the meeting can be emphasized.

Unemphatic	Emphatic
All production and administrative personnel will meet on May 23, at which time we will announce a new plan of salary incentives.	On May 23 all personnel will meet to learn about salary incentives.

- **Place the important idea in a simple sentence or in an independent clause.** Don't dilute the effect of the idea by making it share the spotlight with other words and clauses.

Unemphatic	Emphatic
Although you are the first trainee that we have hired for this program, we have interviewed many candidates and expect to expand the program in the future. (Main idea lost in introductory dependent clause.)	You are the first trainee that we have hired for this program. (Simple sentence contains main idea.)

- **Make sure the important idea is the sentence subject.** You will learn more about active and passive voice shortly, but at this point just focus on making the important idea the subject.

Unemphatic	Emphatic
The environmental report was written by Courtney. (De-emphasizes *Courtney*; emphasizes the report.)	Courtney wrote the environmental report. (Emphasizes *Courtney*.)

Managing Active and Passive Voice

How are active- and passive-voice sentences different?

In sentences with active-voice verbs, the subject is the doer of the action. In passive-voice sentences, the subject is acted upon.

Passive-Voice Verb	Active-Voice Verb
The tax return *was completed* before the April 15 deadline. (The subject, *tax return*, is acted upon.)	Marcelo *completed* his tax return before the April 15 deadline. (The subject, *Marcelo*, is the doer of the action.)

In the first sentence, the passive-voice verb emphasizes the tax return. In the second sentence, the active-voice verb emphasizes Marcelo. Active-voice sentences are more direct because they reveal the performer immediately. They are easier to understand and shorter. Most

FIGURE 5.7 Using Active and Passive Voice Effectively

Use active voice for directness, vigor, and clarity.

Direct and Clear in Active Voice	Indirect and Less Clear in Passive Voice
The manager completed performance reviews for all employees.	Performance reviews were completed for all employees by the manager.
Evelyn initiated a customer service blog last year.	A customer service blog was initiated last year.
IBM will accept applications after January 1.	Applications will be accepted after January 1 by IBM.
Coca-Cola created a Sprite page in Facebook to advertise its beverage.	A Sprite page was created in Facebook by Coca-Cola to advertise its beverage.

Use passive voice to be tactful or to emphasize the action rather than the doer.

Less Tactful or Effective in Active Voice	More Tactful or Effective in Passive Voice
We cannot grant you credit.	Credit cannot be granted.
The CEO made a huge error in projecting profits.	A huge error was made in projecting profits.
I launched a successful fitness program for our company last year.	A successful fitness program was launched for our company last year.
We are studying the effects of the Sarbanes-Oxley Act on our accounting procedures.	The effects of the Sarbanes-Oxley Act on our accounting procedures are being studied.

Spotlight on Communicators

"Wordiness and murkiness come from misuse of the passive voice," says writing coach Bob Knight. The passive voice also shields people from responsibility. For example, government officials often say, *Mistakes were made.* Passive voice abounds in corporate writing, he suspects, because writers are afraid to say things clearly or they don't want to stand out. He suggests, however, using passive voice for effect, especially when the subject is overwhelmingly important, as in, *A Rembrandt was stolen by two men in janitors' uniforms.* Passive voice is also helpful when you don't know who or what the subject would be in active voice, as in, *The cargo was damaged during an intercontinental flight.*

Courtesy of Bob Knight

business writing should be in the active voice. Nevertheless, passive voice is useful in certain instances such as the following:

- **To emphasize an action or the recipient of the action.** *An investigation was launched.*
- **To de-emphasize negative news.** *Cash refunds cannot be made.*
- **To conceal the doer of an action.** *An error was made in our sales figures.*

How can you tell whether a verb is active or passive? Identify the subject of the sentence and decide whether the subject is doing the acting or is being acted upon. For example, in the sentence *An appointment was made for January 1*, the subject is *appointment*. The subject is being acted upon; therefore, the verb (*was made*) is passive. Another clue in identifying passive-voice verbs is that they generally include a *to be* helping verb, such as *is, are, was, were, be, being,* or *been*. Figure 5.7 summarizes effective uses for active and passive voice.

What happens when modifiers are not close to the words they describe or limit?

Avoiding Dangling and Misplaced Modifiers

For clarity, modifiers must be close to the words they describe or limit. A dangling modifier describes or limits a word or words that are missing from the sentence. A misplaced modifier occurs when the word or phrase it describes is not close enough to be clear. To remedy a dangling modifier, supply the missing modifier. To remedy a misplaced modifier, move the modifier closer to the word(s) it describes or limits. Introductory verbal phrases are particularly dangerous; be sure to follow them immediately with the words they logically describe or modify.

Dangling Modifier	Improved
After working nine hours, the report was finally finished. *(Did the report work nine hours? The introductory verbal phrase must be followed by a logical subject.)*	After working nine hours, we finally finished the report.
Driving through Malibu Canyon, the ocean suddenly came into view. (*Is the ocean driving through Malibu Canyon?*)	As we drove through Malibu Canyon, the ocean suddenly came into view.
Speaking before the large audience, Luke's knees began to knock. (*Are Luke's knees making a speech?*)	Speaking before the large audience, Luke felt his knees begin to knock.

Try this trick for detecting and remedying these dangling modifiers. Ask the question *Who?* or *What?* after any introductory phrase. The words immediately following should tell the reader *who* or *what* is performing the action. Try the *who?* test on the previous danglers and on the following misplaced modifiers.

Misplaced Modifier	Improved
Seeing her error too late, the envelope was immediately resealed by Luna. (*Did the envelope see the error?*)	Seeing her error too late, Luna immediately resealed the envelope.
A wart appeared on my left hand that I want removed. (*Is the left hand to be removed?*)	A wart that I want removed appeared on my left hand.
The busy recruiter interviewed only candidates who had excellent computer skills in the morning. (*Were the candidates skilled only in the morning?*)	In the morning the busy recruiter interviewed only candidates who had excellent computer skills.

Drafting Powerful Paragraphs

A paragraph is a group of sentences about one idea. To avoid muddled paragraphs, writers should be able to recognize basic paragraph elements, conventional sentence patterns, and ways to organize sentences using one of three classic paragraph plans. They must also be able to polish their paragraphs by building coherence and using transitional expressions.

Well-constructed paragraphs discuss only one topic. They reveal the primary idea in a topic sentence that usually, but not always, appears first. Paragraphs may be composed of three kinds of sentences:

LEARNING OBJECTIVE 5
Compose effective paragraphs using three classic paragraph plans as well as applying techniques for achieving paragraph coherence.

Topic Sentence Expresses the primary idea of the paragraph.

Supporting Sentences Illustrates, explains, or strengthens the primary idea.

Limiting sentence Opposes the primary idea by suggesting a negative or contrasting thought; may precede or follow the topic sentence.

How many topics should be covered in one paragraph?

These sentences may be arranged in three classic paragraph plans: direct, pivoting, and indirect.

Using the Direct Paragraph Plan to Define, Classify, Illustrate, or Describe

Paragraphs arranged in the direct plan begin with the topic sentence, followed by supporting sentences. Most business messages use this paragraph plan because it clarifies the subject immediately. This plan is useful whenever you must define (a new product or procedure), classify (parts of a whole), illustrate (an idea), or describe (a process). Start with the topic sentence; then strengthen and amplify that idea with supporting ideas, as shown here:

When should the direct paragraph plan be used?

Topic Sentence A social audit is a report on the social performance of a company.

Supporting Sentences Such an audit may be conducted by the company itself or by outsiders who evaluate the company's efforts to produce safe products, engage in socially responsible activities, and protect the environment. Many companies publish the results of their social audits in their annual reports. Ben & Jerry's Homemade, for example, devotes a major portion of its annual report to its social audit. The report discusses Ben & Jerry's efforts to support environmental restoration. Moreover, it describes workplace safety, employment equality, and peace programs.

You can alter the direct plan by adding a limiting sentence if necessary. Be sure, though, that you follow with sentences that return to the main idea and support it, as shown here:

Topic Sentence Flexible work scheduling could immediately increase productivity and enhance employee satisfaction in our entire organization.

Limiting Sentence Such scheduling, however, is impossible for all employees.

Supporting Sentences Managers would be required to maintain their regular hours. For many other employees, though, flexible scheduling permits extra time to manage family responsibilities. Feeling less stress, employees are able to focus their attention better at work; hence they become more relaxed and more productive.

Using the Pivoting Paragraph Plan to Compare and Contrast

Paragraphs using the pivoting plan start with a limiting sentence that offers a contrasting or negative idea before delivering the topic sentence. Notice in the following example how two limiting sentences about drawbacks to foreign service careers open the paragraph; only then do the topic and supporting sentences describing rewards in foreign service appear. The pivoting plan is especially useful for comparing and contrasting ideas. In using the pivoting plan, be sure you emphasize the turn in direction with an obvious *but* or *however*.

When is the pivoting paragraph plan appropriate?

Limiting Sentences	Foreign service careers are certainly not for everyone. Many representatives are stationed in remote countries where harsh climates, health hazards, security risks, and other discomforts exist.
Topic Sentence	However, careers in the foreign service offer special rewards for the special people who qualify.
Supporting Sentences	Foreign service employees enjoy the pride and satisfaction of representing the United States abroad. They enjoy frequent travel, enriching cultural and social experiences in living abroad, and action-oriented work.

Using the Indirect Paragraph Plan to Explain and Persuade

When is the indirect paragraph plan appropriate?

Paragraphs using the indirect plan start with the supporting sentences and conclude with the topic sentence. This useful plan enables you to build a rationale, a foundation of reasons, before hitting the audience with a big idea—possibly one that is bad news. It enables you to explain your reasons and then in the final sentence draw a conclusion from them. In the following example, the vice president of a large accounting firm begins by describing the trend toward casual dress and concludes with a recommendation that his firm change its dress code. The indirect plan works well for describing causes followed by an effect.

Supporting Sentences	According to a recent poll, more than half of all white-collar workers are now dressing casually at work. Many high-tech engineers and professional specialists have given up suits and ties, favoring khakis and sweaters instead. In our own business, our consultants say they stand out like "sore thumbs" because they are attired in traditional buttoned-down styles, while the businesspeople they visit are usually wearing comfortable, casual clothing.
Topic Sentence	Therefore, I recommend that we establish an optional business casual policy allowing consultants to dress casually, if they wish, as they perform their duties both in and out of the office.

You will learn more techniques for implementing direct and indirect writing strategies when you prepare letters, memos, e-mails, reports, and oral presentations in subsequent chapters.

Building Paragraph Coherence

What is coherence, and what four techniques help build it in paragraphs?

Paragraphs are coherent when ideas cohere—that is, when the ideas stick together and when one idea logically leads to the next. Well-written paragraphs take the reader through a number of steps. When the author skips from Step 1 to Step 3 and forgets Step 2, the reader is lost. You can use several techniques to keep the reader in step with your ideas.

- **Sustaining the key idea.** Repeating a key expression or using a similar one throughout a paragraph helps sustain a key idea. In the following example, notice that the repetition of *guest* and *VIP* connects ideas.

  Our philosophy holds that every customer is really a ***guest****. All new employees to our theme parks are trained to treat* ***guests*** *as* ***VIPs****. We take great pride in respecting our guests. As* ***VIPs,*** *they are never told what they can or cannot do.*

- **Dovetailing sentences.** Sentences are "dovetailed" when an idea at the end of one connects with an idea at the beginning of the next. Dovetailing sentences is especially helpful with dense, difficult topics. It is also helpful with ordinary paragraphs, such as the following.

  New hosts and hostesses learn about the theme park and its ***facilities****. These* ***facilities*** *include telephones, food services, bathrooms, and attractions, as well as the location of* ***offices****. Knowledge of* ***offices*** *and the internal workings of the company is required of all staffers.*

- **Using pronouns.** Familiar pronouns, such as *we, they, he, she,* and *it,* help build continuity, as do demonstrative pronouns, such as *this, that, these,* and *those.* These words confirm that something under discussion is still being discussed. However, be careful with such

Ethics Check

Blogging for Pay

One single mother earned nearly $500 a month by putting her writing skills to use on "opps" (opportunities) at PayPerPost .com. This site pays consumers to write favorable comments in blogs about specific products. Is it ethical for bloggers to hide their motivation and affiliation when rating products?

pronouns. They often need a noun with them to make their meaning absolutely clear. In the following example, notice how confusing *this* would be if the word *training* were omitted.

All new park employees receive a two-week orientation. They learn that every staffer has a vital role in preparing for the show. This training includes how to maintain enthusiasm.

- **Including transitional expressions.** Transitional expressions are another excellent device for showing connections and achieving paragraph coherence. These words, some of which are shown in Figure 5.8 on page 156 act as verbal road signs to readers and listeners. Transitional expressions enable the receiver to anticipate what's coming, reduce uncertainty, and speed comprehension. They signal that a train of thought is moving forward, being developed, possibly detouring, or ending. As Figure 5.8 shows, transitions can add or strengthen a thought, show time or order, clarify ideas, show cause and effect, contradict thoughts, and contrast ideas. Look back at the examples of direct, pivoting, and indirect paragraphs to see how transitional expressions and other techniques build paragraph coherence. Remember that coherence in communication rarely happens spontaneously; it requires effort and skill.

Want to do well on tests and excel in your course? Go to **www.meguffey.com** for helpful interactive resources.
▸ Review the Chapter 5 PowerPoint slides to prepare for the first quiz.

Composing Short Paragraphs for Readability

Although no rule regulates the length of paragraphs, business writers recognize that short paragraphs are more attractive and readable than longer ones. Paragraphs with eight or fewer lines look inviting. Long, solid chunks of print appear formidable. If a topic can't be covered in eight or fewer printed lines (not sentences), consider breaking it up into smaller segments.

The accompanying Checklist summarizes the key points of composing a first draft.

To be inviting and readable, paragraphs should have no more than how many printed lines?

Composing Sentences and Paragraphs

For Effective Sentences

- **Avoid common sentence faults.** To avoid un-on sentences, do not join two clauses without appropriate punctuation. To avoid comma splices, do not join two clauses with a comma. To avoid fragments, be sure to use periods only after complete sentences.
- **Control sentence length.** Use longer sentences occasionally, but rely primarily on short and medium-length sentences.
- **Emphasize important ideas.** Place main ideas at the beginning of short sentences for emphasis.
- **Apply active- and passive-voice verbs carefully.** Use active-voice verbs (*She sent the e-mail* instead of *The e-mail was sent by her*) most frequently; they immediately identify the doer. Use passive verbs to emphasize an action, to be tactful, or to conceal the performer.
- **Eliminate misplaced modifiers.** Be sure that introductory verbal phrases are followed by the words that can logically be modified. To check the placement of modifiers, ask *Who?* or *What?* after such phrases.

For Meaningful Paragraphs

- **Develop one idea.** Use topic, supporting, and limiting sentences to develop a single idea within each paragraph.
- **Use the direct plan.** Start most paragraphs with the topic sentence followed by supporting sentences. This direct plan is useful in defining, classifying, illustrating, and describing.
- **Use the pivoting plan.** To compare and contrast ideas, start with a limiting sentence; then, present the topic sentence followed by supporting sentences.
- **Use the indirect plan.** To explain reasons or causes first, start with supporting sentences. Build to the conclusion with the topic sentence at the end of the paragraph.
- **Build coherence with linking techniques.** Hold ideas together by repeating key words, dovetailing sentences (beginning one sentence with an idea from the end of the previous sentence), and using appropriate pronouns.
- **Provide road signs with transitional expressions.** Use verbal signals to help the audience know where the idea is going. Words and phrases such as *moreover, accordingly, as a result,* and *therefore* function as idea pointers.
- **Limit paragraph length.** Remember that paragraphs with eight or fewer printed lines look inviting. Consider breaking up longer paragraphs if necessary.

FIGURE 5.8 Transitional Expressions That Build Coherence

To Add or Strengthen	To Show Time or Order	To Clarify	To Show Cause and Effect	To Contradict	To Contrast
additionally	after	for example	accordingly	actually	as opposed to
accordingly	before	for instance	as a result	but	at the same time
again	earlier	I mean	consequently	however	by contrast
also	finally	in other words	for this reason	in fact	conversely
beside	first	put another way	hence	instead	on the contrary
indeed	meanwhile	that is	so	rather	on the other hand
likewise	next	this means	therefore	still	previously
moreover	now	thus	thus	yet	similarly

Zooming In — YOUR TURN

Applying Your Skills at Gap Inc.

The management team at Gap Inc. is struggling to regain its premier position in retailing. As part of a focus group, you and your team have been asked to brainstorm ideas that will help turn around its fortunes. Your team members are to visit a Gap or Old Navy store and take notes on store appearance, merchandise selection, and customer service. Team members should also look at the Gap Web site to learn about its commitment to social responsibility.

Your Task

Form teams of four or five people. Discuss your task and decide on a goal. Make assignments. Who will investigate Gap's Web site? Who will visit stores? Who will lead the brainstorming session? Hold a 10-minute brainstorming session following the suggestions in this chapter for generating ideas. What could be changed to attract more customers in your age group to Gap and Old Navy? Set a quota of at least 50 suggestions. Take notes on all suggestions. After 10 minutes, organize and classify the ideas, retaining the best. Prepare a cluster diagram. Organize the cluster diagram into an outline, and submit your cluster diagram and outline to your instructor. Your instructor may ask for individual or team submissions.

© AP Images/Paul Sakuma

Summary of Learning Objectives

1 Apply Phase 2 of the 3-x-3 writing process, which begins with formal and informal methods for researching data and generating ideas. The second phase of the writing process includes researching, organizing, and writing. Researching means collecting information using formal or informal techniques. Formal research for long reports and complex problems may involve searching electronically or manually, as well as conducting interviews, surveys, focus groups, and experiments. Informal research for routine tasks may include looking in company files, talking with your boss, interviewing the target audience, conducting informal surveys, brainstorming for ideas, and creating cluster diagrams.

2 Explain how to organize data into lists and alphanumeric or decimal outlines. One method for organizing data in simple messages is to list the main topics to be discussed. Organizing more complex messages usually requires an outline. To prepare an outline, divide the main topic into three to five major components. Break the components into subpoints consisting of details, illustrations, and evidence. For an alphanumeric outline, arrange items using Roman numerals (I, II), capital letters (A, B), and numbers (1, 2). For a decimal outline, show the ordering of ideas with decimals (1., 1.1, 1.1.1).

Are you ready? Get more practice at **www.meguffey.com**

3 Compare direct and indirect patterns for organizing ideas. The direct pattern places the main idea first. This pattern is useful when audiences will be pleased, mildly interested, or neutral. It saves the reader's time, sets the proper frame of mind, and reduces reader frustration. The indirect pattern places the main idea after explanations. This pattern is useful for audiences that will be unwilling, displeased, or hostile. It respects the feelings of the audience, encourages a fair hearing, and minimizes negative reactions.

4 Compose the first draft of a message, avoiding sentence fragments, run-on sentences, and comma splices as well as emphasizing important ideas, avoiding misplaced modifiers, and using active and passive voice effectively. Compose the first draft of a message in a quiet environment where you won't be interrupted. Compose quickly but plan to revise. Avoid fragments (breaking off parts of sentences), comma splices (joining two clauses improperly), and run-on sentences (fusing two clauses improperly). Understand the difference between clauses and phrases so that you can write complete sentences. Remember that sentences are most effective when they are short (20 or fewer words). A main idea may be emphasized by making it the sentence subject, placing it first, and removing competing ideas. Effective sentences use active-voice verbs, although passive-voice verbs may be necessary for tact or de-emphasis. Effective sentences avoid dangling and misplaced modifiers.

5 Compose effective paragraphs using three classic paragraph plans as well as applying techniques for achieving paragraph coherence. Typical paragraphs follow one of three plans. Direct paragraphs (topic sentence followed by supporting sentences) are useful to define, classify, illustrate, and describe. Pivoting paragraphs (limiting sentence followed by topic sentence and supporting sentences) are useful to compare and contrast. Indirect paragraphs (supporting sentences followed by topic sentence) build a rationale and foundation of ideas before presenting the main idea. Paragraphs are more coherent when the writer links ideas by (a) sustaining a key thought, (b) dovetailing sentences, (c) using pronouns effectively and (d) employing transitional expressions.

Chapter Review

1. Compare the first phase of the writing process with the second phase. (Obj. 1)
2. For routine writing tasks, what are some techniques for collecting informal data and generating ideas? (Obj. 1)
3. Name seven specific techniques for a productive group brainstorming session. (Obj. 1)
4. What is the difference between a list and an outline? (Obj. 2)
5. What are the major components in a letter or memo? (Obj. 2)
6. What are the major components in an analytical report? (Obj. 2)
7. Why do many readers prefer the direct method for organizing messages? (Obj. 3)
8. When is the indirect pattern appropriate, and what are the benefits of using it? (Obj. 3)
9. What is the primary difference between the direct and indirect patterns of organization? (Obj. 3)
10. List four techniques for emphasizing important ideas in sentences. (Obj. 4)
11. When should business writers use active-voice sentences? When should they use passive-voice sentences? Give an original example of each. (Obj. 4)
12. What's wrong with this sentence? *After reading it carefully, the proposal doesn't interest us.* (Obj. 4)
13. What is a topic sentence, and where is it usually found? (Obj. 5)
14. Describe three paragraph plans. Identify the uses for each. (Obj. 5)
15. What is coherence, and how is it achieved? (Obj. 5)

Critical Thinking

1. Why is cluster diagramming considered an intuitive process whereas outlining is considered an analytical process? (Obj. 2)
2. Why is audience analysis so important in the selection of the direct or indirect pattern of organization for a business message? (Obj. 3)
3. How are speakers different from writers in the way they emphasize ideas? (Obj. 4)
4. Why are short sentences and short paragraphs appropriate for business communication? (Objs. 4, 5)
5. **Ethical Issue:** Discuss the ethics of the indirect pattern of organization. Is it manipulative to delay the presentation of the main idea in a message?

Are you ready? Get more practice at **www.meguffey.com**

Writing Improvement Exercises

5.1 Sentence Elements (Obj. 4)

Your Task. Identify the following groups of words using these abbreviations: independent clause (IC), dependent clause (DC), or phrase(s) (P). For clauses, circle the subject. Be prepared to explain your choices.

a. although you want to make a good impression during your interview
b. the interviewer will size you up in about seven seconds
c. during a study conducted by neuro-scientists from New York
d. when they examined brain activity
e. MRI results showed significant activity in two brain areas
f. as a matter of fact
g. because people make 11 decisions about you in the first seven seconds
h. in the areas of education, believability, trustworthiness, and economic level

5.2 Sentence Faults (Obj. 4)

In the following, identify the sentence fault (fragment, run-on, comma splice). Then revise to remedy the fault.

a. Because 90 percent of all business transactions involve written messages. Good writing skills are critical.
b. The recruiter requested a writing sample. Even though the candidate seemed to communicate well orally.
c. Major soft-drink companies considered a new pricing strategy, they tested vending machines that raise prices in hot weather.
d. Thirsty consumers may think that variable pricing is unfair they may also refuse to use the machine.
e. About half of Pizza Hut's 7,600 outlets make deliveries, the others concentrate on walk-in customers.
f. McDonald's sold its chain of Chipotle Mexican Grill restaurants the chain's share price doubled on the next day of trading.
g. Private equity players are betting they can breathe new life into old brands. Which explains why Golden Gate Partners paid millions for defunct retailer Eddie Bauer.

5.3 Emphasis (Obj. 4)

For each of the following sentences, circle (1) or (2). Be prepared to justify your choice.

a. Which is more emphatic?
   1. Our dress code is good.
   2. Our dress code reflects common sense and good taste.
b. Which is more emphatic?
   1. A budget increase would certainly improve hiring.
   2. A budget increase of $70,000 would enable us to hire two new people.
c. Which is more emphatic?
   1. The committee was powerless to act.
   2. The committee was unable to take action.
d. Which de-emphasizes the refusal?
   1. Although our resources are committed to other projects this year, we hope to be able to contribute to your worthy cause next year.
   2. We can't contribute to your charity this year.
e. Which sentence places more emphasis on the date?
   1. The deadline is November 30 for health benefit changes.
   2. November 30 is the deadline for health benefit changes.
f. Which sentence is *less* emphatic?
   1. One division's profits decreased last quarter.
   2. Profits in beauty care products dropped 15 percent last quarter.
g. Which sentence gives more emphasis to video game sales?
   1. Sales of video game consoles and software rose 40 percent in June.
   2. During the period ending June 30, sales of video game consoles and software rose significantly.
h. Which sentence gives more emphasis to leadership?
   1. Jason has many admirable qualities, but most important is his leadership skill.
   2. Jason has many admirable qualities, including leadership skill, good judgment, and patience.
i. Which sentence format is more emphatic?
   1. We notified three departments: (a) Marketing, (b) Accounting, and (c) Distribution.
   2. We notified three departments:
      (a) Marketing
      (b) Accounting
      (c) Distribution

5.4 Active Voice (Obj. 4)

Business writing is more forceful if it uses active-voice verbs.

Passive: Antivirus software was installed by Craig on his computer.
Active: Craig installed antivirus software on his computer.

Your Task. Revise the following sentences so that verbs are in the active voice. Put the emphasis on the doer of the action.

a. Employees were given their checks at 4 p.m. every Friday by the manager.
b. New spices and cooking techniques were tried by McDonald's to improve its hamburgers.
c. Our new company logo was designed by my boss.
d. The managers with the most productive departments were commended by the CEO.
e. All team members were asked by the leader to brainstorm for 10 minutes.

5.5 Passive Voice (Obj. 4)

Your Task. Revise the following sentences so that they are in the passive voice.

a. The auditor discovered a computational error in the company's tax figures.
b. We cannot ship your order for ten monitors until June 15.
c. Stacy did not submit the accounting statement on time.
d. The Federal Trade Commission targeted deceptive diet advertisements by weight-loss marketers.
e. Thieves are stealing corporate and financial information by using data-stealing malware on the Web.

5.6 Dangling and Misplaced Modifiers (Obj. 4)

Your Task. On a separate sheet, revise the following sentences to remedy dangling and misplaced modifiers. Add subjects as needed, but retain the introductory phrases. Mark *C* if correct.

a. By advertising extensively, all the open jobs were filled quickly.
b. To apply for early admission, submit your application by November 1. (Tricky!)
c. After leaving the midtown meeting, Angela's car would not start.
d. Walking up the driveway, the Hummer parked in the garage was immediately spotted by the detectives.
e. The manager's rules were to be observed by all staff members, no matter how silly they seemed.
f. To complete the project on time, a new deadline was established by the team.

g. Acting as manager, several new employees were hired by Mr. Lopez.
h. Michelle Mitchell presented a talk about workplace drug problems in our boardroom.

5.7 Paragraph Organization (Obj. 5)

In a memo to the college president, the athletic director is arguing for a new stadium scoreboard. One paragraph will describe the old scoreboard and why it needs to be replaced. Study the following list of ideas for that paragraph.

1. The old scoreboard is a tired warhorse that was originally constructed in the 1960s.
2. It's now hard to find replacement parts for it when something breaks.
3. The old scoreboard is not energy efficient.
4. Coca-Cola has offered to buy a new sports scoreboard in return for exclusive rights to sell soda on campus.
5. The old scoreboard should be replaced for many reasons.
6. It shows only scores for football games.
7. When we have soccer games or track meets, we are without a functioning scoreboard.
   a. Which sentence should be the topic sentence? ______
   b. Which sentence(s) should be developed in a different paragraph? ______
   c. Which supporting sentences should follow the topic sentence? ______
   d. Now write a well-organized paragraph using the preceding information. Strive to incorporate coherence techniques described in this chapter.

5.8 Paragraph Organization and Revision (Obj. 5)

Your Task. The following paragraphs are poorly organized and poorly expressed. Decide what the main idea is in each paragraph. Then revise each paragraph so that it has a topic sentence and is organized directly. Improve the sentence flow, structure, coherence, and correctness by using the techniques described in this chapter and the previous chapter.

a. We feel that the "extreme" strategy has not been developed fully in the fast-food market. Pizza Hut is considering launching a new product called The Extreme. We plan to price this new pizza at $19.99. It will be the largest pizza on the market. It will have double the cheese. It will also have double the toppings. The plan is to target the X and Y Generations. The same target audience that would respond to an extreme product also reacts to low prices. The X and Y Generations are the fastest-growing segments in the fast-food market. These population segments have responded well to other marketing plans using the extreme strategy.
b. You should always have your sound and video files ready for your PowerPoint presentation. When you move the presentation to a network folder or send it to someone else, the presentation has no sound. A common problem in PowerPoint involves lost sound and video files. Create a new folder for your presentation, and copy the sound and video files to that folder before you put them in your presentation. Then you will always have your sound files ready for use with your presentation.
c. Current employees may be interested in applying for new positions within the company. The Human Resources Department has a number of jobs available immediately. The positions are at a high level. Current employees may apply immediately for open positions in production, for some in marketing, and jobs in administrative support are also available. Interested people should come to the Human Resources Department. We have a list showing the open positions, what the qualifications are, and job descriptions are shown. Many of the jobs are now open, but application must be made immediately. That's why we are sending this now. To be hired, an interview must be scheduled within the next two weeks.

Activities

Note: All Documents for Analysis may be downloaded from **www.meguffey.com** so that you do not have to rekey the entire message.

5.9 Document for Analysis: Weak E-Mail Message (Objs. 3–5)

Team

Your Task. The following e-mail suffers from numerous writing faults such as dangling modifiers, overuse of passive voice, and fragments. Notice that small superscript numbers identify each sentence. Individually or in a group, analyze this message. For each sentence or group of words, identify the following faults: dangling modifier (DM), passive voice (PV), and fragment (FR). Your group should agree on its analysis. Your instructor may ask you to revise the message to remedy its faults.

To: Jeremy.Gibbons12@aol.com
From: Andrea Kelly <akelly@bodyfitness.com>
Subject: Improving Your Experience at Body Fitness Center
Cc:
Bcc:

Dear Mr. Gibbons,

[1]Body Fitness Center here in Scottsdale was probably chosen by you because it is one of the top-rated gyms in the Southwest. [2]Our principal goal has always been making your workouts enjoyable. [3]To continue to provide you with the best equipment and programs, your feedback is needed.

[4]An outstanding program with quality equipment and excellent training programs has been provided by Body Fitness. [5]However, more individual attention could be given by us to our customers if our peak usage time could be extended. [6]You have probably noticed that attendance at the gym increases from 4 p.m. to 8 p.m. [7]We wish it were possible to accommodate all our customers on their favorite equipment during those hours. [8]Although we can't stretch an hour. [9]We would like to make better use of the time between 8 p.m. and 11 p.m. [10]With more members coming later, we would have less crush from 4 p.m. to 8 p.m.

[11]To encourage you to stay later, security cameras for our parking area are being considered by my partner and me. [12]Cameras for some inside facilities may also be added. [13]This matter has been given a lot of thought. [14]Although Body Fitness has never previously had an incident that endangered a member.

[15]Please fill in the attached interactive questionnaire. [16]Which will give us instant feedback about scheduling your workouts. [17]By completing this questionnaire, your workouts and training sessions can be better planned so that you can enjoy exactly the equipment and trainers you prefer.

Cordially,

Are you ready? Get more practice at **www.meguffey.com**

5.10 Collaborative Brainstorming (Obj. 1)

Team

Brainstorming can be a productive method for generating problem-solving ideas. You can improve your brainstorming skills through practice.

Your Task. In teams of four or five, analyze a problem on your campus such as the following: unavailable classes, unrealistic degree requirements, a lack of student intern programs, poor parking facilities, an inadequate registration process, a lack of diversity among students on campus, and so forth. Use brainstorming techniques to generate ideas that clarify the problem and explore its solutions. Each team member should prepare a cluster diagram to record the ideas generated. Either individually or as a team, organize the ideas into an outline with three to five main points and numerous subpoints. Assume that your ideas will become part of a letter to be sent to an appropriate campus official or to your campus newspaper discussing the problem and your solution. Remember, however, your role as a student. Be polite, positive, and constructive—not negative, hostile, or aggressive.

5.11 Individual Brainstorming (Objs. 1, 2)

Brainstorming techniques can work for individuals as well as groups. Assume that your boss or department chair wants you to submit a short report analyzing a problem.

Your Task. Analyze a problem that exists where you work or go to school, such as long lines at the copy or fax machines, overuse of express mail services, understaffing during peak customer service hours, poor scheduling of employees, inappropriate cell phone use, an inferior or inflexible benefits package, outdated equipment, or one of the campus problems listed in **Activity 5.10.** Select a problem about which you have some knowledge. Prepare a cluster diagram to develop ideas. Then, organize the ideas into an outline with three to five main points and numerous subpoints. Be polite, positive, and constructive. E-mail the outline to your boss (your instructor). Include an introduction (such as, *Here is the outline you requested in regard to . . .*). Include a closing that offers to share your cluster diagram if your boss would like to see it.

5.12 Brainstorming Tips for Productive Sessions (Obj. 1)

Web

Casandra M., your supervisor at Gap Inc., has been asked to lead a brainstorming group in an effort to generate new ideas for the company's product line. Although Casandra knows a great deal about the company and its products, she doesn't know much about brainstorming. She asks you to research the topic quickly and give her a concise guide on how to brainstorm. One other thing—Casandra doesn't want to read a lot of articles. She wants you to outline tips for productive brainstorming.

Your Task. Conduct an Internet or database keyword search for brainstorming tips. Locate a number of articles with helpful tips. Prepare an outline that tells how to (a) prepare for a brainstorming session, (b) conduct the session, and (c) follow up after the meeting. Submit your outline in a memo or an e-mail to your supervisor (your instructor).

5.13 Collecting Primary Information: Research Interviewing (Obj. 1)

Team

In your follow-up meeting with Casandra M. from **Activity 5.12**, she asks you to complete one more task in preparation for the brainstorming session. She needs further insight in defining the problem and creating an agenda for the outline of topics to be covered in the brainstorming session. She asks you to conduct informal interviews of Gap and Old Navy shoppers.

Your Task. Form five-member class groups. Two members of each group, if possible, should be familiar with Gap and Old Navy. Decide who will role-play the interviewer and the two interviewees (those most familiar with Gap and Old Navy), and who will act as recorder and group spokesperson. If your group has fewer than five members, some will have to fill more than one role. The interviewer asks both interviewees the same three questions outlined below. The recorder takes notes, and the group spokesperson summarizes the group's research results during the class discussion. Use the following interview questions:

a. During your last two visits to Gap or Old Navy, were there any products you expected the two stores to carry but couldn't find?
b. Can you think of any seasonal products you would like Gap or Old Navy to carry? Specifically, identify products for winter, spring, summer, and fall.
c. If you were in charge of Gap or Old Navy's product lines, what three changes would you make to the existing product lines? What three totally new product lines would you want to create?

As a team or individually, prepare an outline that summarizes the information gathered from the in-class interviews.

5.14 Brainstorming: Are Ethics Programs Helpful? (Obj. 1)

Ethics Team Web

In the wake of the banking collapse and previous corporate scandals, more companies are hiring ethics officers—sometimes called "ethics cops." Companies are also investing in expensive interactive Web-based ethics training. You have been named to a team to discuss ethics compliance in your company, a large firm with thousands of employees. It has no current program. Other companies have ethics codes, conflicts-of-interest policies, ethics officers, training programs, and hotlines. Some authorities, however, say that ethics failures are usually not the result of ignorance of laws or regulations.[12] A variety of pressures may cause ethics lapses.

Your Task. Your boss, the Human Resources vice president, wants to learn more about employee feelings in regard to ethics programs. In teams, brainstorm to find reactions to these questions. What kinds of ethical dilemmas do typical entry-level and midlevel managerial employees face? Do you think ethics codes help employees be more ethical? What conditions might force employees to steal, lie, or break the rules? Can ethics be taught? What kind of workplace ethics program would you personally find helpful? Before your brainstorming session, you might want to investigate the topic of ethics programs on the Web. Record your ideas during the session. Then organize the best ones into an outline to be presented to Rita Romano, Human Resources Vice President.

5.15 Researching, Brainstorming, and Organizing: Student Loans (Objs. 1–3)

Team Web

Sarah was all smiles when she graduated and got that degree in her hand. Soon, however, she began to worry about her student loans. Student debt has risen 58 percent in the last decade, according to the College Board, a New York–based college testing and information firm. One study showed that about one third of all recent graduates are unprepared to make their first student loan payment.[13] Another report stated that the average borrower leaves college owing more than $22,000.[14]

Your Task. In teams collect information about student debt. Who has it? How much debt does an average student carry? How do most students repay their loans? What strategies are proposed for helping students avoid, reduce, and repay educational loans? As a group, discuss your findings. Brainstorm for additional strategies. Then organize your findings into an outline with a title, an introduction, and recommendations for helping current students avoid, reduce, and repay their student loans. Submit your outline to your instructor.

Video Resource

Video Library 1, Guffey's 3-x-3 Writing Process Develops Fluent Workplace Skills

If you didn't see *Guffey's 3-x-3 Writing Process Develops Fluent Workplace Skills* when you studied a previous chapter, your instructor may show it with this chapter. It shows all three phases of the writing process so that you can see how it guides the development of a complete message. This video illustrates concepts in Chapters 4, 5, and 6.

Chat About It

In each chapter you will find five discussion questions related to the chapter material. Your instructor may assign these topics for you to discuss in class, in an online chat room, or on an online discussion board. Some of the discussion topics may require outside research. You may also be asked to read and respond to postings made by your classmates.

Topic 1: This chapter describes various techniques for generating ideas. Explore other methods by using Google to search for *generating writing ideas*. Select a method that appeals to you and explain why it would be effective.

Topic 2: In which phase of the 3-x-3 writing process do you suppose most beginners at business writing spend their time? In which phase have you been spending most of your time?

Topic 3: Some writers have trouble writing the opening sentence of a message. Occasionally, a quotation makes for an appropriate opening. Assume that you need to motivate an employee to achieve more at work. Find a famous quotation online about motivation that might be an appropriate opening for such a message. In addition, write a sentence that would effectively transition from this opening.

Topic 4: In your opinion, how many business managers know what a comma splice is? If some managers don't know what a comma splice is, then is it critical that you avoid comma splices in your writing?

Topic 5: Learn how to display the average sentence length in a document using Microsoft Office Word 2007. Not everyone using Word 2007 knows how to do that. Explain the process briefly.

Grammar and Mechanics C.L.U.E. Review 5

Commas

Review Guides 21–26 about commas in Appendix A, Grammar and Mechanics Guide, beginning on page A-10. On a separate sheet, revise the following sentences to correct errors in comma usage. For each error that you locate, write the guide number and abbreviation that reflects this usage. The more you recognize the reasons, the better you will learn these punctuation guidelines. If a sentence is correct, write *C*. When you finish, check your answers on page Key-1.

Guide 21, CmSer (Comma series)	Guide 24, CmDate (Comma, dates, addresses, geographical names, etc.)
Guide 22, CmIntr (Comma introductory)	Guide 25, CmIn (Comma, internal sentence interrupters)
Guide 23, CmConj (Comma conjunction)	

Example: Before beginning a message always collect the necessary information.
Revision: Before beginning a message, always collect the necessary information. [Guide 22, Cm Intr]

1. The 3-x-3 writing process includes prewriting, writing and revising.
2. Before asking others for information see what you can find yourself.
3. Formal research methods include accessing electronically, searching manually and investigating primary sources.
4. If a project is complex consider organizing it by outlining the major points.
5. Careful writers define the main topic and they divide it into three to five components.
6. We decided that Jill Hawkins who is the best writer on the team should prepare the final draft.
7. The company's executives expected new office construction to be finished by September 1, 2012 in Boulder Colorado.
8. Grammar checkers by the way often highlight passive voice as a grammar fault.
9. When you must be tactful and avoid naming the doer of an action the passive voice can be helpful.
10. The direct paragraph plan is useful when you want to define a process or when you must describe something such as a product.

Are you ready? Get more practice at **www.meguffey.com**

CHAPTER 6

Revising Business Messages

OBJECTIVES

After studying this chapter, you should be able to

1. Complete business messages by revising for conciseness, which includes eliminating flabby expressions, long lead-ins, *there is/are* and *it is/was* fillers, redundancies, and empty words.
2. Improve clarity in business messages by keeping the ideas simple, dumping trite business phrases, dropping clichés and slang, unburying verbs, and controlling exuberance.
3. Enhance readability by understanding document design including the use of white space, margins, typefaces, fonts, numbered and bulleted lists, and headings.
4. Recognize proofreading problem areas and apply effective techniques to proofread both routine and complex documents.
5. Evaluate a message to judge its success.

Want to do well on tests and excel in your course? Go to **www.meguffey.com** for helpful interactive resources.

- **Review the Chapter 6 PowerPoint slides to prepare for the first quiz.**

© iStockphoto.com/Josh Hodge

Zooming In PART 1

Taco Bell Tweaks Menu to Rebuild Customer Base

After an outbreak of *E. coli* linked to its restaurants in five states followed by a highly publicized video of rats cavorting in one of its New York restaurants, Taco Bell struggled to regain its reputation. Eventually the restaurant chain overcame the bad publicity, and customers returned to its tacos, burritos, and tostadas. Taco Bell realized, however, that it had to keep rebuilding its customer base by improving its image and its menu.

Yum Brands—owner of Taco Bell, Pizza Hut, and KFC—is the world's largest restaurant company, with more than 36,000 restaurants around the world.[1] Although Taco Bell is the most successful of Yum's fast-food chains, it must compete for customers with McDonald's, Burger King, and Wendy's as well as with trendy upstarts Baja Fresh, Chipotle, and Qdoba. Despite the competition, Taco Bell holds a commanding lead in the Mexican fast-food market.

In overcoming its bad image, Taco Bell plans to remodel or rebuild 375 locations. Major emphasis, however, goes to revamping its menu. One portion of the plan focuses on new breakfast products such as a sausage and bacon Grilled Stuft burrito; a Southwest sausage burrito; an egg, bacon, and cheese burrito; and cinnamon Toastadas.

Looking beyond breakfast fare, Emil Brolick, president of brand building at Yum, suggested that Taco Bell had higher aspirations. "[W]e believe we have a unique opportunity because while all the sandwich players are trying to one-up each other in the same game, we're going to play a different game."[2] His interest lies in unique flavors and better products. However, Taco Bell is also concerned with healthful food. Stinging from criticism that fast food contributes to the worldwide obesity epidemic, Taco Bell is looking for more nutritious menu choices.[3]

In the increasingly crowded fast-food market, customers are slowly but surely shifting away from the traditional burger and chicken fast foods. One food industry executive said, "Burgers are your dad's food, and Mexican is the choice of the new generation."[4] Poised to capitalize on this movement, Taco Bell remains keenly

© AP Images/Phil Coale

aware that (a) it sells a quasi-Mexican food, and (b) its customers are changing. Although its products cannot veer too far from what appeals to the masses, Taco Bell must also compete with new flavors, low-fat items, and fresh ingredients. A recently hired culinary product manager is charged with the task of coming up with menu suggestions and communicating them to management. You will learn more about this case on page 171.

Critical Thinking

- When new ideas must be generated and sold to management, what role does communication skill play in the process?
- Do you think the Taco Bell culinary product manager will be making an oral or a written presentation of new menu ideas?
- Why is a writing process helpful in developing a presentation of new ideas?

http://www.tacobell.com

Applying Phase 3 of the Writing Process

LEARNING OBJECTIVE 1

Complete business messages by revising for conciseness, which includes eliminating flabby expressions, long lead-ins, *there is/are* and *it is/was* fillers, redundancies, and empty words.

The final phase of the 3-x-3 writing process focuses on revising, proofreading, and evaluating. Revising means improving the content and sentence structure of your message. Proofreading involves correcting its grammar, spelling, punctuation, format, and mechanics. Evaluating is the process of analyzing whether your message achieves its purpose. One would not expect people in the restaurant business to require these kinds of skills. However, the new culinary product manager at Taco Bell—and many other similar businesspeople—realize that bright ideas are worth little unless they can be communicated effectively to fellow workers and to management. In the communication process, the techniques of revision can often mean the difference between the acceptance or rejection of ideas.

Although the composition process differs depending on the person and the situation, this final phase should occupy a significant share of the total time you spend on a message. As you learned earlier, some experts recommend devoting about half the total composition time to revising and proofreading.[5]

Why is the revision stage of the writing process so important?

Rarely is the first or even second version of a message satisfactory. Only amateurs expect writing perfection on the first try. The revision stage is your chance to make sure your message says what you mean. Many professional writers compose the first draft quickly without worrying about language, precision, or correctness. Then they revise and polish extensively. Other writers, however, prefer to revise as they go—particularly for shorter business documents.

Whether you revise immediately or after a break, you will want to examine your message critically. You should be especially concerned with ways to improve its conciseness, clarity, and readability.

Revising for Conciseness

In business, time is indeed money. Translated into writing, this means that concise messages save reading time and, thus, money. In addition, messages that are written directly and efficiently are easier to read and comprehend. In the revision process, look for shorter ways to say what you mean. Examine every sentence that you write. Could the thought be conveyed in fewer words? Your writing will be more concise if you eliminate flabby expressions, drop unnecessary introductory words, get rid of redundancies, and purge empty words.

Eliminating Flabby Expressions

Why is conciseness so important in business messages?

As you revise, focus on eliminating flabby expressions. This takes conscious effort. As one expert copyeditor observed, "Trim sentences, like trim bodies, usually require far more effort than flabby ones."[6] Turning out slim sentences and lean messages means that you will strive to "trim the fat." For example, notice the flabbiness in this sentence: *Due to the fact that sales are booming, profits are good*. It could be said more concisely: *Because sales are booming, profits are good.* Many flabby expressions can be shortened to one concise word as shown here and illustrated in Figure 6.1. Also notice in this figure that you may use different methods for revising printed documents and digital documents.

Flabby	**Concise**
as a general rule	generally
at a later date	later
at this point in time	now, presently
despite the fact that	although
due to the fact that, inasmuch as, in view of the fact that	because
feel free to	please
for the period of	for
in addition to the above	also
in all probability	probably
in the event that	if
in the near future	soon
in very few cases	seldom
until such time as	until

Limiting Long Lead-Ins

Why should you avoid long lead-ins in your messages?

Another way to create concise sentences is to delete unnecessary introductory words. Consider this sentence: *I am sending you this e-mail to announce that we have hired a new manager*. A more concise and more direct sentence deletes the long lead-in: *We have hired a*

FIGURE 6.1 Revising Manually and Digitally

Revising Digital Documents Using Strikethrough and Color
When revising digital documents, you can use simple word processing tools such as strikethrough and color. In this example, strikethroughs in red identify passages to be deleted. The strikethrough function is located on the **Font** tab. We used blue to show inserted words, but you may choose any color you prefer. If you need to add comments, use the MS Word **Comment** feature, shown in Chapter 4, Figure 4.8, on page 129.

~~This is a short note to let you know that, as~~ As you requested, I ~~made an investigation of~~ investigated several of our competitors' Web sites. Attached ~~hereto~~ is a summary of my findings. ~~of my investigation.~~ I was ~~really~~ most interested in ~~making a comparison of the employment of strategies for~~ comparing marketing strategies as well as ~~the use of~~ navigational graphics ~~used~~ to guide visitors through the sites. ~~In view of the fact that~~ Because we will be revising our own Web site ~~in the near future~~ soon, I was ~~extremely~~ intrigued by the organization, ~~kind of~~ marketing tactics, and navigation at ~~each and~~ every site I visited.

Revising Printed Documents Using Proofreading Symbols
When revising printed documents, use standard symbols to manually show your revisions.

~~This is a short note to let you know that,~~ as you requested, I ~~made an~~ investigat~~ion of~~ [ed] several of our competitors' Web sites. Attached ~~hereto~~ is a summary of my findings ~~of my investigation.~~ I was ~~really~~ most interested in ~~making a comparison of the employment of~~ [comparing] [marketing] strategies ~~for marketing~~ as well as ~~the use of~~ navigational graphics ~~used~~ to guide visitors through the sites. ~~In view of the fact that~~ [Because] we will be revising our own Web site [soon] ~~in the near future,~~ I was ~~extremely~~ intrigued by the organization, ~~kind of~~ marketing tactics, and navigation at ~~each and~~ every site I visited.

Popular Proofreading Symbols

Delete	ℊ
Capitalize	≡
Insert	∧
Insert comma	∧,
Insert period	⊙
Start paragraph	¶

new manager. The meat of the sentence often follows the words *that* or *because,* as shown in the following:

Wordy	**Concise**
We are sending this announcement to let everyone know that new parking permits will be available January 1.	New parking permits will be available January 1.
This is to inform you that you may find lower airfares at our Web site.	You may find lower airfares at our Web site.
I am writing this letter because Professor John Donnellan suggested that your organization was hiring trainees.	Professor John Donnellan suggested that your organization was hiring trainees.

Dropping Unnecessary *there is/are* and *it is/was* Fillers

In many sentences the expressions *there is/are* and *it is/was* function as unnecessary fillers. In addition to taking up space, these fillers delay getting to the point of the sentence. Eliminate them by recasting the sentence. Many—but not all—sentences can be revised so that fillers are unnecessary.

Wordy	**Concise**
There are only two administrative assistants to serve five managers.	Only two administrative assistants serve five managers.
There was an unused computer in the back office.	An unused computer was in the back office.
It was our auditor who discovered the theft.	Our auditor discovered the theft.

What are redundancies?

Rejecting Redundancies

Expressions that repeat meaning or include unnecessary words are redundant. Saying *unexpected surprise* is like saying *surprise surprise* because *unexpected* carries the same meaning as *surprise*. Excessive adjectives, adverbs, and phrases often create redundancies and wordiness. Redundancies do not add emphasis, as some people think. Instead, they identify a writer as inexperienced. As you revise, look for redundant expressions such as the following:

Redundant	**Concise**
absolutely essential	essential
adequate enough	adequate
basic fundamentals	fundamentals *or* basics
big in size	big
combined together	combined
exactly identical	identical
each and every	each *or* every
necessary prerequisite	prerequisite
new beginning	beginning
refer back	refer
repeat again	repeat
true facts	facts

Purging Empty Words

Familiar phrases roll off the tongue easily, but many contain expendable parts. Be alert to these empty words and phrases: *case, degree, the fact that, factor, instance, nature,* and *quality*. Notice how much better the following sentences sound when we remove all the empty words:

> ~~*In the case of*~~ USA Today, ~~*the newspaper*~~ *improved its readability.*
>
> *Because of* ~~*the degree of*~~ *active participation by our sales reps, profits soared.*
>
> *We are aware* ~~*of the fact*~~ *that many managers need assistance.*
>
> *Except for* ~~*the instance of*~~ *Toyota, Japanese imports sagged.*
>
> *She chose a career in a field that was analytical* ~~*in nature*~~. [OR: *She chose a career in an analytical field.*]
>
> *Student writing in that class is excellent* ~~*in quality*~~.

Also avoid saying the obvious. In the following examples, notice how many unnecessary words we can omit through revision:

> ~~*When it arrived*~~, *I cashed your check immediately.* (Announcing the check's arrival is unnecessary. That fact is assumed in its cashing.)
>
> ~~*We need printer cartridges; therefore*~~, *please send me two dozen laser cartridges.* (The first clause is obvious.)

Finally, look carefully at clauses beginning with *that, which,* and *who*. They can often be shortened without loss of clarity. Search for phrases such as *it appears that*. These phrases often can be reduced to a single adjective or adverb, such as *apparently*.

> *Changing the name of a* ^ *[successful] company* ~~*that is successful*~~ *is always risky.*
>
> *All employees* ~~*who are among those*~~ *completing the course will be reimbursed.*
>
> *Our* ^ *[final] proposal,* ~~*which was*~~ *slightly altered* ~~*in its final form*~~, *won approval.*
>
> *We plan to schedule* ^ *[weekly] meetings* ~~*on a weekly basis*~~.

Revising for Clarity

LEARNING OBJECTIVE 2
Improve clarity in business messages by keeping the ideas simple, dumping trite business phrases, dropping clichés and slang, unburying verbs, and controlling exuberance.

A major revision task involves assessing the clarity of your message. A clear message is one that is immediately understood. Employees, customers, and investors increasingly want to be addressed in a clear and genuine way. Fuzzy and bombastic writing alienates these stakeholders.[7] Business writers appreciate clear messages that are immediately understandable. Techniques that improve clarity include applying the KISS formula (Keep It Short and Simple), dumping trite business phrases, and avoiding clichés and slang.

Keep It Short and Simple

What is the KISS formula, and how does it apply to business messages?

To achieve clarity, resist the urge to show off or be fancy. Remember that your goal is not to impress a reader. Instead, the goal of business writing is to *express*, not *impress*. One way to achieve clear writing is to apply the familiar KISS formula. Use active-voice sentences that avoid indirect, pompous language.

Wordy and Unclear	Improved
Employees have not been made sufficiently aware of the potentially adverse consequences regarding the use of these perilous chemicals.	Warn your employees about these dangerous chemicals.

Communicating in clear, simple language is an uphill battle for some firms. That's why plain-language advocate Christopher Balmford founded Cleardocs.com, a document management company that helps law firms, accounting firms, and other highly technical businesses communicate clearly and effectively with clients. Cleardocs' online technology turns complex documents into market-focused plain language, transforming elaborate or technical letters and reports into easily understandable written communications. *What types of businesses have difficulty producing simple, conversational messages, and why?*

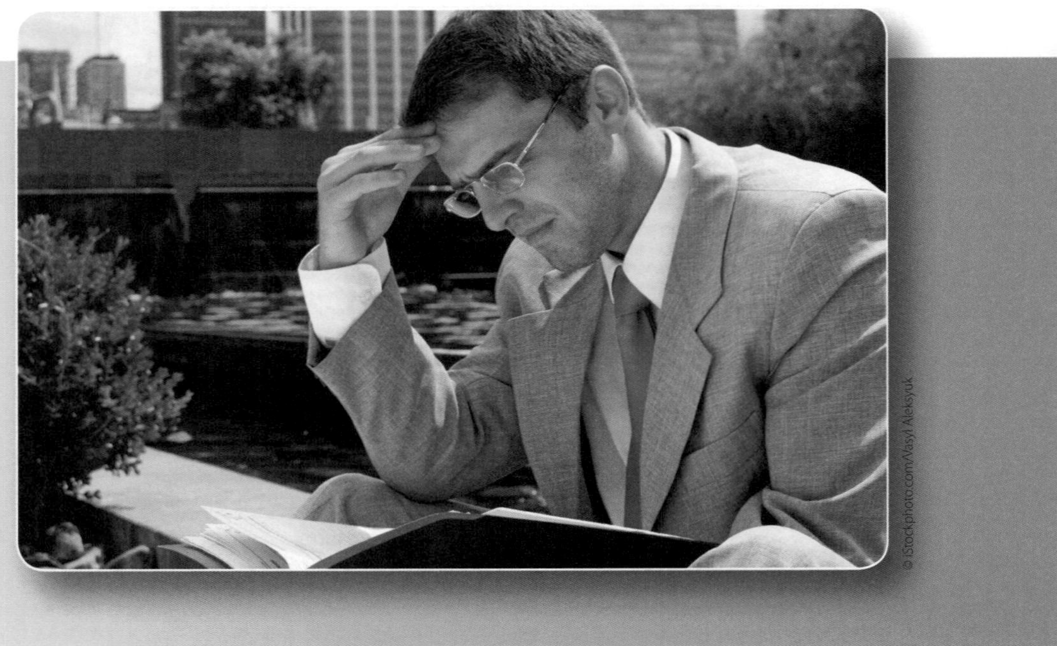
© iStockphoto.com/Vasyl Aleksyuk

Wordy and Unclear	Improved
In regard to the matter of obtaining optimal results, it is essential that employees be given the implements that are necessary for jobs to be completed satisfactorily.	To get the best results, give employees the tools they need to do the job.

Dumping Trite Business Phrases

To sound "businesslike," many writers repeat the same stale expressions that other writers have used over the years. Your writing will sound fresher and more vigorous if you eliminate these trite phrases or find more original ways to convey the idea.

Trite Phrase	Improved
as per your request	as you request
pursuant to your request	at your request
enclosed please find	enclosed is
every effort will be made	we'll try
in accordance with your wishes	as you wish
in receipt of	have received
please do not hesitate to	please
thank you in advance	thank you
under separate cover	separately
with reference to	about

Dropping Clichés and Slang

Clichés are expressions that have become exhausted by overuse. Many cannot be explained, especially to those who are new to our culture. Clichés lack not only freshness but also clarity. Instead of repeating clichés such as the following, try to find another way to say what you mean.

below the belt	last but not least
better than new	make a bundle
beyond a shadow of a doubt	pass with flying colors
easier said than done	quick as a flash
exception to the rule	shoot from the hip
fill the bill	stand your ground
first and foremost	think outside the box
good to go	true to form

Spotlight on Communicators

© AP Images/Jack Plunket

Former Secretary of State Colin Powell believes that effective leaders apply the KISS formula in keeping things simple. They articulate vivid, overarching goals and values. Their visions and priorities are lean and compelling, not cluttered and laden with buzzwords. One of Secretary Powell's favorite quotations illustrates his conviction: "Great leaders are almost always great simplifiers, who can cut through argument, debate and doubt, to offer a solution everybody can understand."

What is slang, and when is it appropriate in business messages?

Slang is composed of informal words with arbitrary and extravagantly changed meanings. Slang words quickly go out of fashion because they are no longer appealing when everyone begins to understand them. Consider the following statement of a government official who had been asked why his department was dropping a proposal to lease offshore oil lands: "The Administration has an awful lot of other things in the pipeline, and this has more wiggle room so they just moved it down the totem pole." He added, however, that the proposal might be offered again since "there is no pulling back because of hot-potato factors."

The meaning here, if the speaker really intended to impart any, is considerably obscured by the use of slang. If you want to sound professional, avoid expressions such as *snarky, lousy, blowing the budget, bombed,* and *getting burned.*

Unburying Verbs

What is a buried verb?

Buried verbs are those that are needlessly converted to wordy noun expressions. This happens when verbs such as *acquire, establish,* and *develop* are made into nouns such as *acquisition, establishment,* and *development.* Such nouns often end in *-tion, -ment,* and *-ance.* Using these nouns increases sentence length, drains verb strength, slows the reader, and muddies the thought. Notice how you can make your writing cleaner and more forceful by avoiding wordy verb/noun conversions:

Buried Verbs	Unburied Verbs
conduct a discussion of	discuss
create a reduction in	reduce
engage in the preparation of	prepare
give consideration to	consider
make an assumption of	assume
make a discovery of	discover
perform an analysis of	analyze
reach a conclusion that	conclude
take action on	act

Controlling Exuberance

Occasionally we show our exuberance with words such as *very, definitely, quite, completely, extremely, really, actually,* and *totally*. These intensifiers can emphasize and strengthen your meaning. Overuse, however, sounds unbusinesslike. Control your enthusiasm and guard against excessive use.

Excessive Exuberance	Businesslike
We *totally* agree that we *actually* did not *really* give his proposal a *very* fair trial.	We agree that we did not give his proposal a fair trial.
The manufacturer was *extremely* upset to learn that its printers were *definitely* being counterfeited.	The manufacturer was upset to learn that its printers were being counterfeited.

Designing Documents for Readability

LEARNING OBJECTIVE 3

Enhance readability by understanding document design including the use of white space, margins, typefaces, fonts, numbered and bulleted lists, and headings.

Well-designed documents improve your messages in two important ways. First, they enhance readability and comprehension. Second, they make readers think you are a well-organized and intelligent person. In the revision process, you have a chance to adjust formatting and make other changes so that readers grasp your main points quickly. Significant design techniques to improve readability include the appropriate use of white space, margins, typefaces, numbered and bulleted lists, and headings for visual impact.

Employing White Space

Empty space on a page is called *white space*. A page crammed full of text or graphics appears busy, cluttered, and unreadable. To increase white space, use headings, bulleted or numbered lists, and effective margins. As discussed earlier, short sentences (20 or fewer words) and short paragraphs (eight or fewer printed lines) improve readability and comprehension. As you revise, think about shortening long sentences. Consider breaking up long paragraphs into shorter chunks. Be sure, however, that each part of the divided paragraph has a topic sentence.

Understanding Margins and Text Alignment

What is a ragged-right margin?

Margins determine the white space on the left, right, top, and bottom of a block of type. They define the reading area and provide important visual relief. Business letters and memos usually have side margins of 1 to 1 ½ inches.

Your word processing program probably offers four forms of margin alignment: (a) lines align only at the left, (b) lines align only at the right, (c) lines align at both left and right (*justified*), and (d) lines are centered. Nearly all text in Western cultures is aligned at the left and reads from left to right. The right margin may be *justified* or *ragged right*. The text in books, magazines, and other long works is often justified on the left and right for a formal appearance.

However, justified text may require more attention to word spacing and hyphenation to avoid awkward empty spaces or "rivers" of spaces running through a document. When right margins are "ragged"—that is, without alignment or justification—they provide more white space and improve readability. Therefore, you are best served by using left-justified text and ragged-right margins without justification. Centered text is appropriate for headings but not for complete messages.

Choosing Appropriate Typefaces

What is the difference between serif and sans serif fonts?

Business writers today may choose from a number of typefaces on their word processors. A typeface defines the shape of text characters. As shown in Figure 6.2, a wide range of typefaces is available for various purposes. Some are decorative and useful for special purposes. For most business messages, however, you should choose from *serif* or *sans serif* categories.

Serif typefaces have small features at the ends of strokes. The most common serif typeface is Times New Roman. Other popular serif typefaces are Century, Georgia, and Palatino. Serif typefaces suggest tradition, maturity, and formality. They are frequently used for body text in

FIGURE 6.2 Typefaces With Different Personalities for Different Purposes

All-Purpose Sans Serif	Traditional Serif	Happy, Creative Script/Funny	Assertive, Bold Modern Display	Plain Monospaced
Arial	Century	Brush Script	Britannic Bold	Courier
Calibri	Garamond	Comic Sans	Broadway	Letter Gothic
Helvetica	Georgia	Gigi	Elephant	Monaco
Tahoma	Goudy	Jokerman	Impact	Prestige Elite
Univers	Palatino	Lucinda	Bauhaus 93	
Verdana	Times New Roman	Kristen	SHOWCARD	

business messages and longer documents. Because books, newspapers, and magazines favor serif typefaces, readers are familiar with them.

Sans serif typefaces include Arial, Calibri, Helvetica, Tahoma, Univers, and Verdana. These clean characters are widely used for headings, signs, and material that does not require continuous reading. Web designers often prefer sans serif typefaces for simple, pure pages. For longer documents, however, sans serif typefaces may seem colder and less accessible than familiar serif typefaces.

For less formal messages or special decorative effects, you might choose one of the happy fonts such as Comic Sans or a bold typeface such as Impact. You can simulate handwriting with a script typeface. Despite the wonderful possibilities available on your word processor, don't get carried away with fancy typefaces. All-purpose sans serif and traditional serif typefaces are most appropriate for your business messages. Generally, use no more than two typefaces within one document.

Capitalizing on Type Fonts and Sizes

Font refers to a specific style (such as *italic*) within a typeface family (such as Times New Roman). Most typeface families offer various fonts such as CAPITALIZATION, SMALL CAPS, **boldface**, *italic*, and underline, as well as fancier fonts such as outline and shadow.

How can font styles and typeface families be used to emphasize your words?

Font styles are a mechanical means of adding emphasis to your words. ALL CAPS, SMALL CAPS, and **bold** are useful for headings, subheadings, and single words or short phrases in the text. ALL CAPS, HOWEVER, SHOULD NEVER BE USED FOR LONG STRETCHES OF TEXT BECAUSE ALL THE LETTERS ARE THE SAME HEIGHT, MAKING IT DIFFICULT FOR READERS TO DIFFERENTIATE WORDS. In addition, excessive use of all caps feels like shouting and irritates readers. **Boldface,** *italics*, and underlining are effective for calling attention to important points and terms. Be cautious, however, when using fancy or an excessive number of font styles. Don't use them if they will confuse, annoy, or delay readers.

During the revision process, think about type size. Readers are generally most comfortable with 10- to 12-point type for body text. Smaller type enables you to fit more words into a space. Tiny type, however, makes text look dense and unappealing. Slightly larger type makes material more readable. Overly large type (14 points or more), however, looks amateurish and out of place for body text in business messages. Larger type, however, is appropriate for headings.

Numbering and Bulleting Lists for Quick Comprehension

What is "skim value," and how can it be enhanced in business messages?

One of the best ways to ensure rapid comprehension of ideas is through the use of numbered or bulleted lists. Lists provide high "skim value." This means that readers can browse quickly and grasp main ideas. By breaking up complex information into smaller chunks, lists improve readability, understanding, and retention. They also force the writer to organize ideas and write efficiently.

In the revision process, look for ideas that could be converted to lists and follow these techniques to make your lists look professional:

- **Numbered lists:** Use for items that represent a sequence or reflect a numbering system.
- **Bulleted lists:** Use to highlight items that don't necessarily show a chronology.

Spotlight on Communicators

© AP Images/Jennifer Szymaszek

Arthur Levitt, former chair of the U.S. Securities and Exchange Commission, is said to have been the most activist chair in the SEC's history. As a champion of "plain English," he was instrumental in requiring that disclosure documents written for investors be readable. To improve their readability, he advocated using the active voice, familiar words, and graphic techniques. He recommended emphasizing important ideas with boldface, graphics, headings, lists, and color. All of these techniques can vastly improve the readability of any business document.

- **Capitalization:** Capitalize the initial word of each line.
- **Punctuation:** Add end punctuation only if the listed items are complete sentences.
- **Parallelism:** Make all the lines consistent; for example, start each with a verb.

In the following examples, notice that the list on the left presents a sequence of steps with numbers. The bulleted list does not show a sequence of ideas; therefore, bullets are appropriate. Also notice the parallelism in each example. In the numbered list, each item begins with a verb. In the bulleted list, each item follows an adjective/noun sequence. Business readers appreciate lists because they focus attention. Be careful, however, not to use so many that your messages look like grocery lists.

What helps you decide whether to use a bulleted or a numbered list?

Numbered List

Our recruiters follow these steps when hiring applicants:

1. Examine the application.
2. Interview the applicant.
3. Check the applicant's references.

Bulleted List

To attract upscale customers, we feature the following:

- Quality fashions
- Personalized service
- A generous return policy

Should headings be used in business messages other than reports?

Adding Headings for Visual Impact

Headings are an effective tool for highlighting information and improving readability. They encourage the writer to group similar material together. Headings help the reader separate major ideas from details. They enable a busy reader to skim familiar or less important information. They also provide a quick preview or review. Headings appear most often in reports, which you will study in greater detail in Chapters 9 and 10. However, main headings, subheadings, and

Zooming In PART 2

Taco Bell

The newly hired culinary product manager at Taco Bell has her job cut out for her. Management expects her to anticipate trends in Mexican foods and improve restaurant menus. Part of the challenge is recognizing trends that consumers haven't even picked up yet and then working these trends into restaurant products. In her words, "We want to kick it up a notch, but we still have to deliver to mainstream consumers." She needs to read the market and then create innovative menu ideas. The new chef is eager to incorporate some of the rich, complex flavors of authentic Mexican cuisine. But she must do it in ways that are acceptable to fast-food customers. Although she has excellent culinary references, the new chef has not been trained in communication. She has plenty of ideas to put into a memo or a presentation. Her job now depends on how well she can communicate these ideas to management.

© AP Images/Phil Coale

Critical Thinking

- Based on what you learned in this chapter, what specific advice can you give about keeping a message clear? Should a business message be conversational?
- Why is conciseness important, and what techniques can be used to achieve it?
- Would you advise the culinary chef to be direct with her ideas? What advice can you give for improving the directness and readability of a business message?

category headings can also improve readability in e-mails, memos, and letters. In the following example, they are used with bullets to summarize categories:

Category Headings

Our company focuses on the following areas in the employment process:

- **Attracting applicants.** We advertise for qualified applicants, and we also encourage current employees to recommend good people.
- **Interviewing applicants.** Our specialized interviews include simulated customer encounters as well as scrutiny by supervisors.
- **Checking references.** We investigate every applicant thoroughly. We contact former employers and all listed references.

In Figure 6.3 on page 174, the writer was able to convert a dense, unappealing e-mail message into an easier-to-read version by applying document design. Notice that the all-caps font in the first paragraph makes its meaning difficult to decipher. Justified margins and lack of white space further reduce readability. In the revised version, the writer changed the all-caps font to upper- and lowercase and also used ragged-right margins to enhance visual appeal. One of the best document design techniques in this message is the use of headings and bullets to help the reader see chunks of information in similar groups. All of these improvements are made in the revision process. You can make any message more readable by applying the document design techniques presented here.

ETHICS CHECK

Costly Writing

Bad writing can be expensive: A Philadelphia lawyer was charged with malpractice to the tune of $6.6 million for drafting a poor commercial lease. The judge in Los Angeles said the draft was "inartfully written and done so in a confusing fashion, which lends itself to ambiguities and disagreements." Can you think of other situations in which writing can be deliberately or accidentally misleading and cost money?

Proofreading

Once you have the message in its final form, it's time to proofread. Don't proofread earlier because you may waste time checking items that eventually are changed or omitted. Important messages—such as those you send to management or to customers or turn in to instructors for grades—deserve careful revision and proofreading. When you finish a first draft, plan for a cooling-off period. Put the document aside and return to it after a break, preferably after 24 hours or longer. Proofreading is especially difficult because most of us read what we thought we wrote. That's why it's important to look for specific problem areas.

LEARNING OBJECTIVE 4

Recognize proofreading problem areas and apply effective techniques to proofread both routine and complex documents.

What to Watch for in Proofreading

Careful proofreaders check for problems in the following areas.

- **Spelling.** Now is the time to consult the dictionary. Is *recommend* spelled with one or two *c*'s? Do you mean *affect* or *effect*? Use your computer spell checker, but don't rely on it totally.
- **Grammar.** Locate sentence subjects; do their verbs agree with them? Do pronouns agree with their antecedents? Review the grammar and mechanics principles in Appendix A if necessary. Use your computer's grammar checker, but be suspicious, as explained in the Plugged In box on page 175.
- **Punctuation.** Make sure that introductory clauses are followed by commas. In compound sentences put commas before coordinating conjunctions *(and, or, but, nor)*. Double-check your use of semicolons and colons.
- **Names and numbers.** Compare all names and numbers with their sources because inaccuracies are not always visible. Especially verify the spelling of the names of individuals receiving the message. Most of us immediately dislike someone who misspells our name.
- **Format.** Be sure that your document looks balanced on the page. Compare its parts and format with those of standard documents shown in Appendix B. If you indent paragraphs, be certain that all are indented.

Spotlight on Communicators

Pulitzer Prize–winning *Washington Post* columnist William Raspberry frequently promotes the value of language skills in relation to career success: "Misused words, haphazard sentences, failed subject–verb agreement can distract people from our ideas and get them concentrating on our inadequacies. Good English, carefully spoken and written, can open more doors than a college degree. Bad English can slam doors we don't even know about."

Courtesy of The Washington Post Writers Group - www.washpost.com

FIGURE 6.3 **Using Document Design to Improve E-Mail Readability**

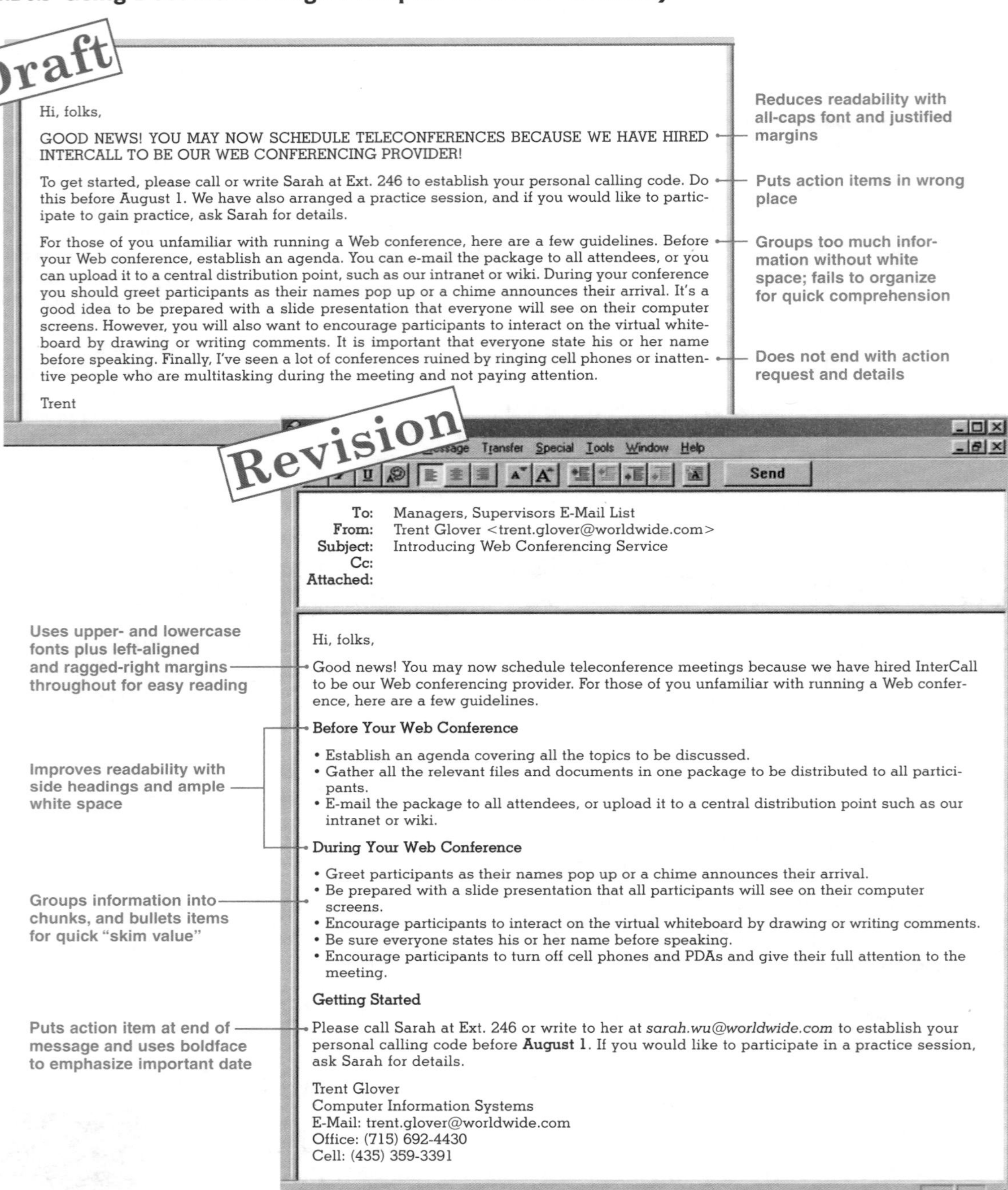

How does proofreading routine documents differ from proofreading complex documents?

How to Proofread Routine Documents

Most routine documents require a light proofreading. If you read on screen, use the down arrow to reveal one line at a time. This focuses your attention at the bottom of the screen. A safer proofreading method, however, is reading from a printed copy. Regardless of which method you use, look for typos and misspellings. Search for easily confused words, such as *to* for *too* and *then* for *than*. Read for missing words and inconsistencies. For handwritten or printed messages, use standard proofreading marks, shown in Figure 6.4, to indicate changes. For digital documents and collaborative projects, use the simple word processing tools shown in Figure 6.1 or use the **Comment** and **Track Changes** functions described in Figure 4.8 on page 129.

How to Proofread Complex Documents

Long, complex, or important documents demand more careful proofreading. Apply the previous suggestions but also add the following techniques:

- Print a copy, preferably double-spaced, and set it aside for at least a day. You will be more alert after a breather.
- Allow adequate time to proofread carefully. A common excuse for sloppy proofreading is lack of time.
- Be prepared to find errors. One student confessed, "I can find other people's errors, but I can't seem to locate my own." Psychologically, we don't expect to find errors, and we don't want to find them. You can overcome this obstacle by anticipating errors and congratulating, not criticizing, yourself each time you find one.
- Read the message at least twice—once for word meanings and once for grammar and mechanics. For very long documents (book chapters and long articles or reports), read a third time to verify consistency in formatting.
- Reduce your reading speed. Concentrate on individual words rather than ideas.
- For documents that must be perfect, enlist a proofreading buddy. Have someone read the message aloud. Spell names and difficult words, note capitalization, and read punctuation.
- Use standard proofreading marks shown in Figure 6.4 to indicate changes.

PLUGGED IN

Using Spell Checkers and Grammar/Style Checkers Wisely

Spell-checking and grammar-checking software are two useful tools that can save you from many embarrassing errors. They can also greatly enhance your revision techniques—if you know how to use them wisely.

Spell Checking

Although some writers dismiss spell checkers as an annoyance, most of us are only too happy to have our typos, repeated words, and misspelled words detected. If you are using Microsoft Word 2007, you need to set relevant options. (Click the **MS Office** button, choose **Word Options,** select **Proofing,** and check **Flag repeated words, Check spelling as you type,** and **Use contextual spelling**). When you see a wavy line under a word, you know that the highlighted word may be faulty. Right-click for a list of suggested replacements and other actions. Word 2007 can even detect the misuse of words in context. For example, it usually knows whether *they're, their,* and *there* are being used correctly and may automatically correct errors.

The latest spell checkers are indeed wonderful, but they are far from perfect. When you mistype a word, the spell checker may not be sure what you meant and the suggested replacements may be way off target. What's more, a spell checker cannot know when you type *form* that you meant *from*. Lesson: Don't rely totally on spell checkers to find all typos and spelling errors.

Grammar and Style Checking

Like spell checkers, today's grammar and style checkers are amazingly sophisticated. Microsoft Word marks faults in capitalization, possessives, plurals, punctuation, subject–verb agreement, and gender-specific words as well as misused words, double negatives, fragments, wordiness, and many other problems.

How does a grammar checker work? Say you typed the sentence, *The office and its equipment is for sale*. You would see a wavy line appear under *is*. If you right-click on it, a box identifies the subject–verb agreement error and suggests the verb *are* as a correction. When you click **Change**, the error is corrected. Be sure to set your grammar and style options (**MS Office** button → **Word Options** → **Proofing** → **When correcting spelling and grammar in Word** → **Settings**). However, before you decide that a grammar checker will solve all your writing problems, think again. Even Word's highly developed software misses plenty of errors, and it also mismarks some correct expressions.

Career Application

Study the spelling and grammar/style settings on your computer. Decide which settings are most useful to you. As you prepare written messages for this class, analyze the suggestions made by your spell checker and grammar checker. For one or two documents, list the spelling, grammar, and style corrections suggested by Word. How many were valid?

FIGURE 6.4 Proofreading Marks

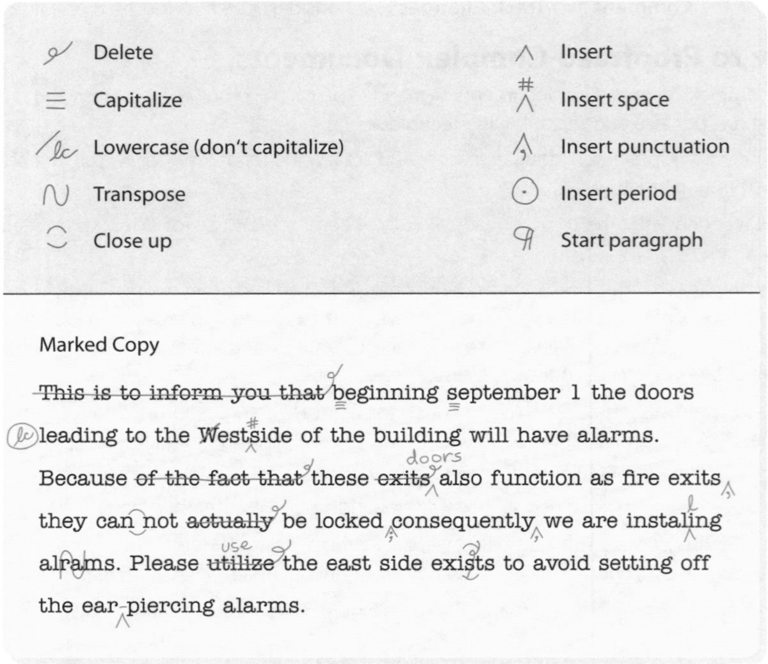

℘	Delete	∧	Insert
≡	Capitalize	# ∧	Insert space
/lc	Lowercase (don't capitalize)	∧	Insert punctuation
∿	Transpose	⊙	Insert period
⌒	Close up	¶	Start paragraph

Marked Copy

~~This is to inform you that~~ beginning september 1 the doors leading to the Westside of the building will have alarms. Because ~~of the fact that~~ these ~~exits~~ doors also function as fire exits they can not ~~actually~~ be locked consequently we are instaling alrams. Please ~~utilize~~ use the east side exists to avoid setting off the ear piercing alarms.

Many of us struggle with proofreading our own writing because we are seeing the same information over and over. We tend to see what we expect to see as our eyes race over the words without looking at each one carefully. We tend to know what is coming next and glide over it. To change the appearance of what you are reading, you might print it on a different colored paper or change the font. If you are proofing on screen, enlarge the page view or change the background color of the screen.

ETHICS CHECK

Overly Helpful

Students may visit writing centers where they receive useful advice and help. However, some well-meaning tutors take over, revising documents until they don't resemble the original student work. Instructors worry that the resulting documents amount to cheating. Yet in the workplace today, writers must collaborate, and drafts go through multiple revisions. Individual authorship is often not relevant. How much revision is acceptable in a college setting? How much is acceptable in the workplace?

How to Proofread and Revise PDF Files

As documents are increasingly sent as PDF (portable document format) files, business writers are learning to proof without a pen. "Soft proofing" involves using Adobe Acrobat markup tools. The advantages of soft proofing include enabling collaborators in distant locales to proof each other's work electronically and saving days of time in sending hard-copy proofs back and forth. Corrections and edits can be transferred electronically among authors, editors, proofreaders, and typesetters—and then on to the printer without pen ever touching paper. The disadvantages of soft proofing include tired eyes, especially if you are working on long documents, and the fear of losing your work because of a computer crash.

Adobe Acrobat Pro and Standard provide a rich array of tools that can make markup and work flow fairly intuitive. You can insert, replace, highlight, delete, or underline material as well as add notes, all with an insertion point that looks like that used in traditional proofreading, as shown in Figure 6.5. Adobe Acrobat enables you to add comment easily, but the markup tools require practice to use effectively. You can even make your own proofreading marks using the **Create Custom Stamp** feature.

Evaluating

LEARNING OBJECTIVE 5

Evaluate a message to judge its success.

As part of applying finishing touches, take a moment to evaluate your writing. Remember that everything you write, whether for yourself for someone else, takes the place of a personal appearance. If you were meeting in person, you would be certain to dress appropriately and professionally. The same standard applies to your writing. Evaluate what

FIGURE 6.5 Proofreading and Marking PDF Files

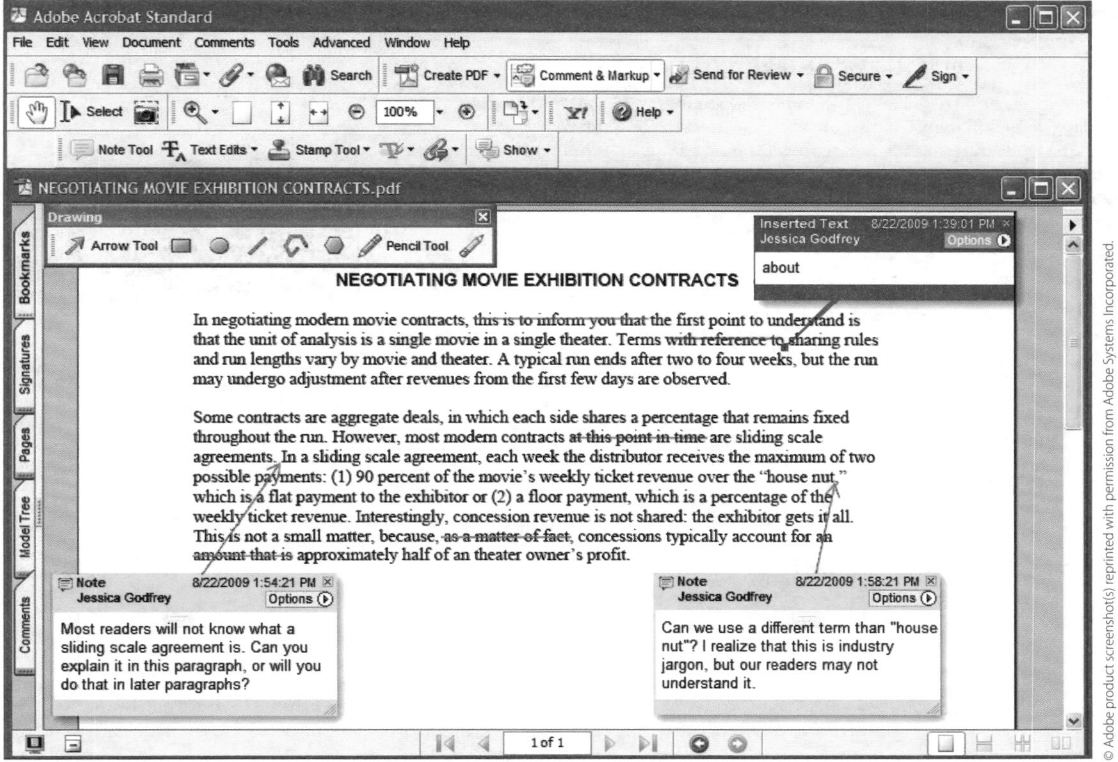

You may proofread and edit PDF files by using Adobe Acrobat software that allows you to insert, replace, highlight, delete, and underline material as well as add notes.

Checklist

Proofreading, Revising, and Evaluating

- **Eliminate flabby expressions.** Strive to reduce wordy phrases to single words (*as a general rule* becomes *generally*; *at this point in time* becomes *now*).
- **Avoid opening fillers and long lead-ins.** Revise sentences so that they don't start with fillers (*there is, there are, it is, it was*) and long lead-ins (*this is to inform you that*).
- **Shun redundancies.** Eliminate words that repeat meanings, such as *refer back*. Watch for repetitious adjectives, adverbs, and phrases.
- **Tighten your writing.** Check phrases that include *case, degree, the fact that, factor*, and other words and phrases that unnecessarily increase wordiness. Avoid saying the obvious.
- **Keep the message simple.** Express ideas directly. Don't show off or use fancy language.
- **Avoid trite business phrases.** Keep your writing fresh, direct, and contemporary by skipping such expressions as *enclosed please find* and *pursuant to your request*.
- **Don't use clichés or slang.** Avoid expressions that are overused and unclear (*below the belt, shoot from the hip*). Don't use slang, which is not only unprofessional but also often unclear to a wide audience.
- **Unbury verbs.** Keep your writing vigorous by not converting verbs to nouns ((*analyze* not *make an analysis of*).
- **Control exuberance.** Avoid overusing intensifiers such as *really, very, definitely, quite, completely, extremely, actually,* and *totally.*
- **Improve readability through document design.** Use bullets, lists, headings, capital letters, underlining, boldface, italics, and blank space to spotlight ideas and organization.
- **Proofread for correctness.** Check spelling, grammar, and punctuation. Compare names and numbers with their sources. Double-check the format to be sure you have been consistent.
- **Evaluate your final product.** Will your message achieve its purpose? Could it be improved? How will you know whether it is successful?

Zooming In — YOUR TURN

Applying Your Skills at Taco Bell

Upgrading the menu at Taco Bell is an exciting challenge for the new culinary product manager. In response to management's request, she comes up with terrific ideas for capitalizing on eating trends and converting them to mainstream tastes. She has been asked to submit a memo summarizing her longer report, which will be presented at a management meeting next week.

Although the new culinary product manager has exceptional talent in cuisine, she realizes that her writing skills are not as well developed as her cooking skills. She comes to the corporate communication department and shows your boss the first draft of her memo. Your boss is a nice guy; and, as a favor, he revises the first two paragraphs, as shown in Figure 6.6.

Your Task

Your boss, the head of corporate communication, has many important tasks to oversee. He hands the product manager's memo to you, his assistant, and tells you to finish cleaning it up. He adds, "Her ideas are right on target, but the main points are totally lost in wordy sentences and solid paragraphs. Revise this and concentrate on conciseness, clarity, and readability. Don't you think some bulleted lists would help this memo a lot?" Revise the remaining four paragraphs of the memo using the techniques you learned in this chapter. Prepare a copy of the complete memo to submit to your boss (your instructor).

© AP Images/Phil Coale

you have written to be certain that it attracts the reader's attention. Is it polished and clear enough to convince the reader that you are worth listening to? How successful will this message be? Does it say what you want it to? Will it achieve your purpose? How will you know whether it succeeds?

How is feedback helpful in evaluating the effectiveness of a message?

As you learned in Chapter 1, the best way to judge the success of your communication is through feedback. For this reason you should encourage the receiver to respond to your message. This feedback will tell you how to modify future efforts to improve your communication technique.

Your instructor will also be evaluating some of your writing. Although any criticism is painful, try not to be defensive. Look on these comments as valuable advice tailored to your specific writing weaknesses—and strengths. Many businesses today spend thousands of dollars bringing in communication consultants to improve employee writing skills. You are getting the same training in this course. Take advantage of this chance—one of the few you may have—to improve your skills. The best way to improve your skills, of course, is through instruction, practice, and evaluation.

In this class you have all three elements: instruction in the writing process, practice materials, and someone to guide and evaluate your efforts. Those three elements are the reasons this book and this course may be the most valuable in your entire curriculum. Because it's almost impossible to improve your communication skills alone, take advantage of this opportunity.

The task of revising, proofreading, and evaluating, summarized in the checklist on the preceding page, is hard work. It demands objectivity and a willingness to cut, cut, cut. Though painful, the process is also gratifying. It's a great feeling when you realize your finished message is clear, concise, and effective.

Want to do well on tests and excel in your course?
Go to **www.meguffey.com** for helpful interactive resources.

- **Review the Chapter 6 PowerPoint slides to prepare for the first quiz.**

FIGURE 6.6 Partially Revised First Draft

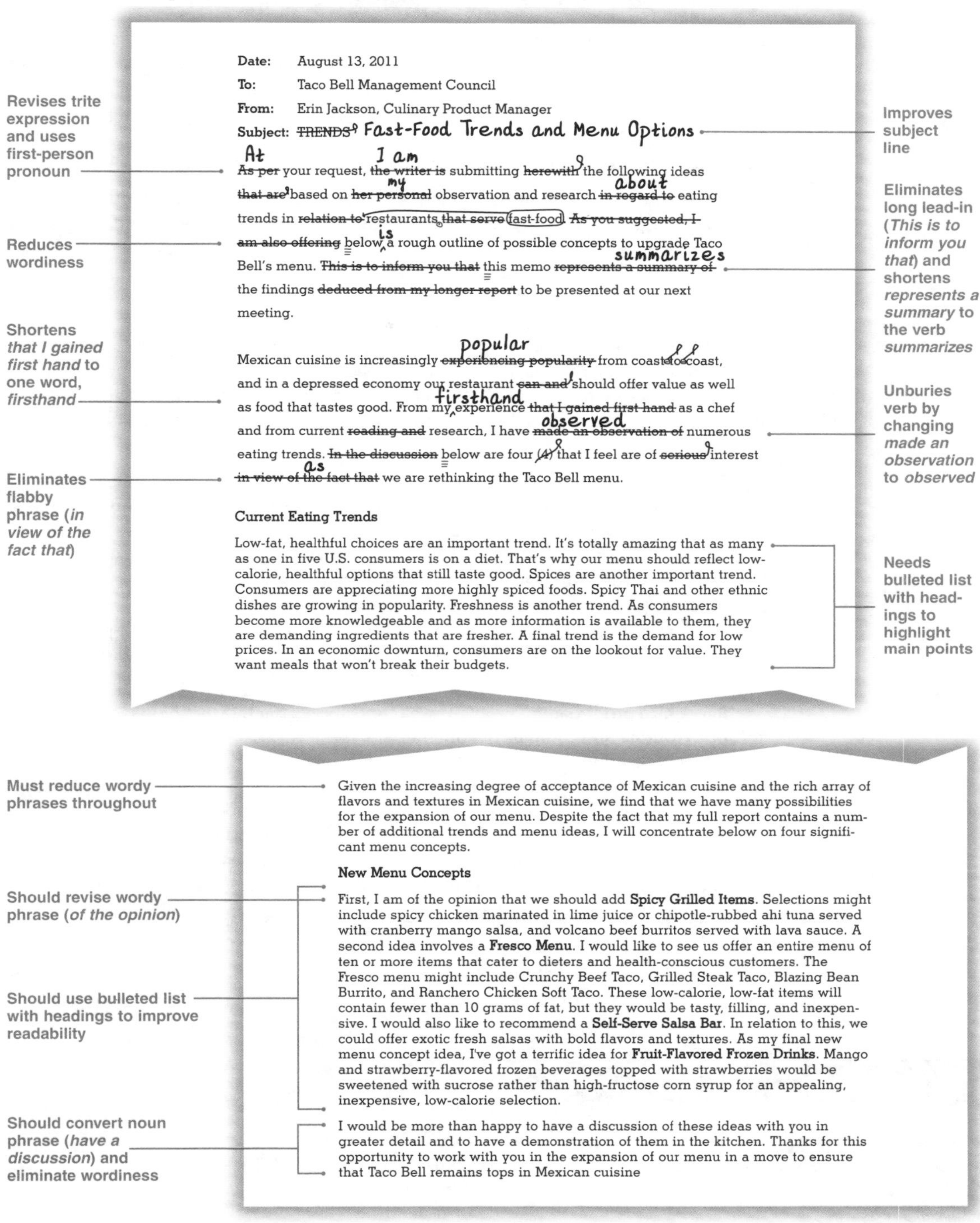

Date: August 13, 2011
To: Taco Bell Management Council
From: Erin Jackson, Culinary Product Manager
Subject: ~~TRENDS~~ Fast-Food Trends and Menu Options

~~As per~~ At your request, ~~the writer is~~ I am submitting ~~herewith~~ the following ideas ~~that are~~ based on ~~her personal~~ my observation and research ~~in regard to~~ about eating trends in ~~relation to~~ restaurants ~~that serve~~ fast-food. ~~As you suggested, I am also offering~~ below is a rough outline of possible concepts to upgrade Taco Bell's menu. ~~This is to inform you that~~ this memo ~~represents a summary of~~ summarizes the findings ~~deduced from my longer report~~ to be presented at our next meeting.

Mexican cuisine is increasingly ~~experiencing popularity~~ popular from coast ~~to~~ coast, and in a depressed economy our restaurant ~~can and~~ should offer value as well as food that tastes good. From my firsthand experience ~~that I gained first hand~~ as a chef and from current ~~reading and~~ research, I have ~~made an observation of~~ observed numerous eating trends. ~~In the discussion~~ below are four ~~(4)~~ that I feel are of ~~serious~~ interest ~~in view of the fact that~~ as we are rethinking the Taco Bell menu.

Current Eating Trends

Low-fat, healthful choices are an important trend. It's totally amazing that as many as one in five U.S. consumers is on a diet. That's why our menu should reflect low-calorie, healthful options that still taste good. Spices are another important trend. Consumers are appreciating more highly spiced foods. Spicy Thai and other ethnic dishes are growing in popularity. Freshness is another trend. As consumers become more knowledgeable and as more information is available to them, they are demanding ingredients that are fresher. A final trend is the demand for low prices. In an economic downturn, consumers are on the lookout for value. They want meals that won't break their budgets.

Given the increasing degree of acceptance of Mexican cuisine and the rich array of flavors and textures in Mexican cuisine, we find that we have many possibilities for the expansion of our menu. Despite the fact that my full report contains a number of additional trends and menu ideas, I will concentrate below on four significant menu concepts.

New Menu Concepts

First, I am of the opinion that we should add **Spicy Grilled Items**. Selections might include spicy chicken marinated in lime juice or chipotle-rubbed ahi tuna served with cranberry mango salsa, and volcano beef burritos served with lava sauce. A second idea involves a **Fresco Menu**. I would like to see us offer an entire menu of ten or more items that cater to dieters and health-conscious customers. The Fresco menu might include Crunchy Beef Taco, Grilled Steak Taco, Blazing Bean Burrito, and Ranchero Chicken Soft Taco. These low-calorie, low-fat items will contain fewer than 10 grams of fat, but they would be tasty, filling, and inexpensive. I would also like to recommend a **Self-Serve Salsa Bar**. In relation to this, we could offer exotic fresh salsas with bold flavors and textures. As my final new menu concept idea, I've got a terrific idea for **Fruit-Flavored Frozen Drinks**. Mango and strawberry-flavored frozen beverages topped with strawberries would be sweetened with sucrose rather than high-fructose corn syrup for an appealing, inexpensive, low-calorie selection.

I would be more than happy to have a discussion of these ideas with you in greater detail and to have a demonstration of them in the kitchen. Thanks for this opportunity to work with you in the expansion of our menu in a move to ensure that Taco Bell remains tops in Mexican cuisine

Revises trite expression and uses first-person pronoun
Reduces wordiness
Shortens *that I gained first hand* to one word, *firsthand*
Eliminates flabby phrase (*in view of the fact that*)
Improves subject line
Eliminates long lead-in (*This is to inform you that*) and shortens *represents a summary* to the verb *summarizes*
Unburies verb by changing *made an observation* to *observed*
Needs bulleted list with headings to highlight main points
Must reduce wordy phrases throughout
Should revise wordy phrase (*of the opinion*)
Should use bulleted list with headings to improve readability
Should convert noun phrase (*have a discussion*) and eliminate wordiness

Summary of Learning Objectives

1 Complete business messages by revising for conciseness, which includes eliminating flabby expressions, long lead-ins, *there is/are* and *it is/was* fillers, redundancies, and empty words. Concise messages make their points using the least number of words. Revising for conciseness involves eliminating flabby expressions (*as a general rule, at a later date, at this point in time*). Concise writing also excludes opening fillers (*there is, there are*), redundancies (*basic essentials*), and empty words (*in the case of, the fact that*).

2 Improve clarity in business messages by keeping the ideas simple, dumping trite business phrases, dropping clichés and slang, unburying verbs, and controlling exuberance. To be sure your messages are clear, apply the KISS formula: Keep It Short and Simple. Avoid foggy, indirect, and pompous language. Do not include trite business phrases (*as per your request, enclosed please fine, pursuant to your request*), clichés (*better than new, beyond a shadow of a doubt, easier said than done*), and slang (*snarky, lousy, bombed*). Also avoid transforming verbs into nouns (*to conduct an investigation* rather than *to investigate, to perform an analysis* rather than *to analyze*). Noun conversion lengthens sentences, saps the force of the verb, and muddies the message. Finally, do not overuse intensifiers that show exuberance (*totally, actually, very, definitely*). These words can emphasize and strengthen meaning, but overusing them makes your messages sound unbusinesslike.

3 Enhance readability by understanding document design including the use of white space, margins, typefaces, fonts, numbered and bulleted lists, and headings. Well-designed messages enhance readability and comprehension. The most readable messages have ample white space, appropriate side margins, and ragged-right (not justified) margins. Serif typefaces (fonts with small features at the ends of strokes, such as Times New Roman, Century, and Palatino) are most used for body text. Sans serif typefaces (clean fonts without small features, such as Arial, Helvetica, and Tahoma) are often used for headings and signs. Numbered and bulleted lists provide high "skim value" in messages. Headings add visual impact and aid readability in business messages as well as in reports.

4 Recognize proofreading problem areas and apply effective techniques to proofread both routine and complex documents. Proofreaders must be especially alert to spelling, grammar, punctuation, names, numbers, and document format. Routine documents may be proofread immediately after completion. They may be read line by line on the computer screen or, better yet, from a printed draft copy. More complex documents, however, should be proofread after a breather. To do a good job, you must read from a printed copy, allow adequate time, reduce your reading speed, and read the document at least three times—for word meanings, for grammar and mechanics, and for formatting.

5 Evaluate a message to judge its success. Encourage feedback from the receiver so that you can determine whether your communication achieved its goal. Try to welcome any advice from your instructor on how to improve your writing skills. Both techniques help you evaluate the success of a message.

Chapter Review

1. How is proofreading different from revising? (Objs. 1, 4)
2. Why should business writers strive for conciseness? (Obj. 1)
3. What's wrong with expressions such as *due to the fact that* and *in view of the fact that*? (Obj. 1)
4. What is a redundancy? Give an example. Why should writers avoid redundancies? (Obj. 1)
5. Why should a writer avoid the opening *I am sending this e-mail because we have just hired a new manager, and I would like to introduce her*? (Obj. 1)
6. Why should writers avoid opening a sentence with *There is* or *There are*? (Obj. 1)
7. What is a buried verb? Give an original example. Why should they be avoided? (Obj. 2)
8. Why would a good writer avoid this sentence? *When it arrived, I read your message and am now replying.* (Obj. 2)
9. What are five document design techniques that business writers can use to enhance readability? (Obj. 3)

Are you ready? Get more practice at **www.meguffey.com**

10. How can writers increase white space to improve readability? (Obj. 3)
11. What is the difference between serif and sans serif typefaces? What is the preferred use for each? (Obj. 3)
12. What are five specific items to check in proofreading? Be ready to discuss methods you find useful in spotting these errors. (Obj. 4)
13. In proofreading, why is it difficult to find your own errors? How can you overcome this barrier? (Obj. 4)
14. List four or more effective techniques for proofreading complex documents. (Obj. 4)
15. How can you overcome defensiveness when your writing is criticized constructively? (Obj. 5)

Critical Thinking

1. Is the revision and proofreading process different for short and long documents? Can you skip revising if your message is brief? (Objs. 1, 4)
2. Would you agree or disagree with the following statement by writing expert William Zinsser? "Plain talk will not be easily achieved in corporate America. Too much vanity is on the line." (Objs. 1–5)
3. Because business writing should have high "skim value," why not write everything in bulleted lists? (Obj. 3)
4. Conciseness is valued in business. However, can messages be too short? (Obj. 1)
5. **Ethical Issue:** What advice would you give in this ethical dilemma? Becky is serving as interim editor of the company newsletter. She receives an article written by the company president describing, in abstract and pompous language, the company's goals for the coming year. Becky thinks the article will need considerable revising to make it readable. Attached to the president's article are complimentary comments by two of the company vice presidents. What action should Becky take?

Writing Improvement Exercises

6.1 Flabby Expressions (Obj. 1)

Your Task. Revise the following sentences to eliminate flabby expressions.

a. Despite the fact that we lost the contract, we must at this time move forward.
b. Inasmuch as prices are falling, we will invest in the very near future.
c. We cannot fill the order until such time as payment is received for previous shipments.
d. As a general rule, we would not accept the return; however, we will in all probability make an exception in this case.

6.2 Long Lead-Ins (Obj. 1)

Your Task. Revise the following to eliminate long lead-ins.

a. This message is to let you know that I received your e-mail and its attachments.
b. This memo is to notify everyone that we will observe Monday as a holiday.
c. I am writing this letter to inform you that your homeowner's coverage expires soon.
d. This is to warn everyone that the loss of laptops endangers company security.

6.3 *There is/are* and *It is/was* Fillers (Obj. 1)

Your Task. Revise the following to avoid unnecessary *there is/are* and *it is/was* fillers.

a. There are many businesses that are implementing strict e-mail policies.
b. It is the CEO who must approve the plan.
c. There are several Web pages you must update.
d. The manager says that there are many employees who did not return the health surveys.

6.4 Redundancies (Obj. 1)

Your Task. Revise the following to avoid redundancies.

a. Because the proposals are exactly identical, we need not check each and every item.
b. All requests for iPods and BlackBerrys were combined together in our proposal.
c. The office walls were painted beige in color.
d. Our supervisor requested that team members return back to the office.

6.5 Empty Words (Obj. 1)

Your Task. Revise the following to eliminate empty words and saying the obvious.

a. He scheduled the meeting for 11 a.m. in the morning.
b. Because of the surprising degree of response, the company expanded its free gift program.
c. I have before me your proposal sent by FedEx, and I will distribute it immediately.
d. Are you aware of the fact that our budget has a deficit in the amount of approximately $100,000?

6.6 Trite Business Phrases (Obj. 2)

Your Task. Revise the following sentences to eliminate trite business phrases.

a. As per your request, we will no longer send you e-mail offers.
b. Thank you in advance for considering our plea for community support.
c. Pursuant to your request, we are sending the original copies under separate cover.
d. Enclosed please find a check in the amount of $700.

6.7 Clichés, Slang, and Wordiness (Obj. 2)

Your Task. Revise the following sentences to avoid confusing slang, clichés, and wordiness.

a. Although our last presentation bombed, we think that beyond the shadow of a doubt our new presentation will fly.
b. Our team must be willing to think outside the box in coming up with marketing ideas that pop.
c. True to form, our competitor has made a snarky claim that we think is way below the belt.

Are you ready? Get more practice at **www.meguffey.com**

d. If you will refer back to the budget, you will see that there are provisions that prevent blowing the budget.

6.8 Buried Verbs (Obj. 2)

Your Task. Revise the following to unbury the verbs.

a. Ms. Nelson gave an appraisal of the home's value.
b. Web-based customer service causes a reduction in overall costs.
c. Management made a recommendation affirming abandonment of the pilot project.
d. The board of directors will give consideration to the contract at its next meeting.

6.9 Lists, Bullets, and Headings (Obj. 3)

a. Use the information in the following dense paragraph to compose a concise, easy-to-read bulleted vertical list with an introductory statement.

   Here at SecurityPlus we specialize in preemployment background reports, which we describe in the following. Among our preemployment background reports are ones that include professional reference interviews, criminal reports, driving records, employment verification, and credit information.

b. Create an introduction and a list from the following wordy paragraph.

   A high-powered MBA program costs hundreds of dollars an hour. Our program covers the same information. That information includes how to start a business. You will also learn information about writing a business plan and understanding taxes. In addition, our MBA program covers how to go about writing a marketing feasibility study. Another topic that students cover in our program is employment benefits plans and licensing requirements.

c. From the following wordy paragraph, create a concise bulleted list with category headings.

   This is to inform you that our on-site GuruGeek computer technicians can provide you with fast, affordable solutions to residential and also to small business clients. Our most popular offerings include antivirus security. This service involves having our GuruGeek protect your computer against viruses, worms, and spyware as well as help you avoid e-mail attacks, identity theft, and malicious hacker programs. Our wireless networking service enables you to share Internet access through a single wireless router so that many computer users use one network at the same time. They are all using the same network. Another popular service is data backup and recovery. Our technicians focus on helping small businesses and home users protect their data without making an investment of a lot of time and energy.

Activities

Note: All Documents for Analysis may be downloaded from **www.meguffey.com** so that you do not have to rekey the entire message.

6.10 Document for Analysis: Ineffective Customer Letter (Objs. 1–5)

Your Task. Study the following message. In teams or in class discussion, list at least five specific weaknesses. If your instructor directs, revise to remedy flabby expressions, long lead-ins, *there is/are* fillers, trite business expressions, clichés, slang, buried verbs, lack of parallelism, and general wordiness. Look for ways to improve readability with bulleted or numbered points.

Current date

Mr. Michael Chatham
329 Sycamore Street
Pikeville, KY 41605

Dear Mr. Chatham:

This is to inform you that we are changing your World Bank Credit Card Agreement. These changes will be effective for all billing periods that will be beginning on or after the date of February 3.

First, we want to tell you about the change in how the calculation of your APR is done. We are increasing your variable APR (annual percentage rate) for purchases. Your APR will be exactly identical to the U.S. prime rate plus 10.99 percent with a minimum APR of 16.99 percent.

Second, we must make an explanation of how the default APR will change. All of your APRs on all balances may automatically increase to the default APR in the event that you default under any card agreement you have with us because for either of the two following reasons: You do not make the minimum payment when due. You make a payment to us that is not honored.

The default APR takes effect as of the first day of the billing period in which you default. However, every effort will be made to lower the APR for new purchases or cash advances if you are able to meet the terms of all card agreements that you have with us for six billing periods.

To Opt Out
To opt out of these changes, call or write us by the date of March 31. It is absolutely essential for you to include your name, address, and account number in the letter that you write. Should you decide to opt out of these changes, you may use your account under the current terms until the ultimate end of your current membership year or the expiration date on your card. We will close your account at that point in time. You must then repay the balance under the current terms.

Please do not hesitate to take advantage of your World Card revolving line of credit and all the benefits and services we offer you.

Sincerely,

6.11 Document for Analysis: Poorly Written E-Mail Message (Objs. 1–5)

Your Task. Study the following message. In teams or in class discussion, list at least five specific weaknesses. If your instructor directs, revise to remedy flabby expressions, long lead-ins, *there is/are* fillers, trite business expressions, clichés, slang, buried verbs, lack of parallelism, and general wordiness. Look for ways to improve readability with bulleted or numbered points.

To: Marcy Love <marcy.love@sokia.com>
From: Shelton Matthews <shelton.matthews@sokia.com>
Subject: Improving Presentation Techniques
Cc:

Marcy,

I am writing this message because, pursuant to your request, I attended a seminar about the use of PowerPoint in business presentations. You suggested that there might be tips that I would learn that we could share with other staff members, many of whom make presentations that almost always include PowerPoint. The speaker, Gary Dixon, made some very good points on the subject of PowerPoint. There were several points of an important nature that are useful in avoiding what he called a "PowerPoint slumber party." Our staff members should give consideration to the following:

Create first the message, not the slide. Only after preparing the entire script should you think about how to make an illustration of it.

You should prepare slides with short lines. Your slides should have only four to six words per line. Short lines act as an encouragement to people to listen to you and not read the slide.

Don't put each and every thing on the slide. If you put too much on the slide, your audience will be reading Item C while you are still talking about Item A. As a last and final point, she suggested that presenters think in terms of headlines. What is the main point? What does it mean to the audience?

Please let me know whether you want me to elaborate and expand on these presentation techniques subsequent to the next staff meeting.

Shelton

6.12 Document for Analysis: Poorly Written Response Letter (Objs. 1–5)

Your Task. Study the following message. In teams or in class discussion, list at least five specific weaknesses. If your instructor directs, revise to remedy flabby expressions, long lead-ins, *there is/are* fillers, trite business expressions, clichés, slang, buried verbs, lack of parallelism, and general wordiness. Look for ways to improve readability with bulleted or numbered points.

Current date

Mr. DeJuan Wilson
Fairfield Associates, Inc.
4290 Park Avenue
Fairfield, CT 06435

Dear Mr. Wilson:

We have received your request for information. As per your request, the undersigned is transmitting to you the attached documents with regard to the improvement of security in your business. To ensure the improvement of your after-hours security, you should initially make a decision with regard to exactly what you contemplate must have protection. You are, in all probability, apprehensive not only about your electronic equipment and paraphernalia but also about your company records, information, and data.

Due to the fact that we feel you will want to obtain protection for both your equipment and data, we will make suggestions for taking a number of judicious steps to inhibit crime. First and foremost, we make a recommendation that you install defensive lighting. A consultant for lighting, currently on our staff, can design both outside and inside lighting, which brings me to my second point. Exhibit security signs, because of the fact that nonprofessional thieves are often as not deterred by posted signs on windows and doors.

As my last and final recommendation, you should install space alarms, which are sensors that look down over the areas that are to receive protection, and activate bells or additional lights, thus scaring off intruders.

After reading the materials that are attached, please call me to initiate a verbal discussion regarding protection of your business.

Sincerely,

6.13 Document for Analysis: Poorly Written Customer Letter (Objs. 1–5)

Your Task. Study the following message. In teams or in class discussion, list at least five specific weaknesses. If your instructor directs, revise to remedy flabby expressions, long lead-ins, *there is/are* fillers, trite business expressions, clichés, slang, buried verbs, lack of parallelism, and general wordiness. Look for ways to improve readability with bulleted or numbered points.

Current date

Ms. Monique Faria
Grey Wolf BioSolutions
4210 Geddes Road
Ann Arbor, MI 48105

Dear Ms. Faria:

This message is an opportunity to thank you for your interest in employee leasing through Enterprise Staffing Services. Small businesses like yours can, at this point in time, enjoy powerful personnel tools previously available only to firms that were larger.

The employee leasing concept allows you to outsource personnel duties so that you can focus on the basic fundamentals of running your business. There are many administrative burdens that you can reduce such as monthly payroll, quarterly taxes, and records related to personnel matters. There is also expert guidance available in the areas of human resources, compliance, and matters of a safety nature. In view of the fact that we have extensive experience, your employer liability can be reduced by a significant degree. You can be assured that the undersigned, as well as our entire staff, will assemble together a plan that will save you time and money as well as protect you from employee hassles and employer liability.

Whether or not you offer no benefits or a full benefits package, Enterprise Staffing Services can make an analysis of your needs and help you return back to the basics of running your business and improvement in profits. Please allow me to call you to arrange a time to meet and talk about your specific needs.

Cordially,

6.14 Learning About Writing Techniques in Your Field (Objs. 1–5)

How much writing is required by people working in your career area? The best way to learn about on-the-job writing is to talk with someone who has a job similar to the one you hope to have one day.

Your Task. Interview someone working in your field of study. Your instructor may ask you to present your findings orally or in a written report. Ask questions such as these: *What kind of writing do you do? What kind of planning do you do before writing? Where do you get information? Do you brainstorm? Make lists? Do you compose with pen and paper, a computer, or a dictating machine? How many e-mail messages do you typically write in a day? How long does it take you to compose a routine one- or two-page memo or letter? Do you revise? How often? Do you have a preferred method for proofreading? When you have questions about grammar and mechanics, what or whom do you consult? Does anyone read your drafts and make suggestions? Can you describe your entire composition process? Do you ever work with others to produce a document? How does this process work? What makes writing easier or harder for you? Have your writing methods and skills changed since you left school?*

6.15 Searching for Deadwood (Objs. 1, 2)

Team | Web

Many writers and speakers are unaware of "deadwood" phrases they use. Some of these are flabby expressions, redundancies, or trite business phrases.

Your Task. Using your favorite Web browser, locate two or three sites devoted to deadwood phrases. Your instructor may ask you to (a) submit a list of ten deadwood phrases (and their preferred substitutes) not mentioned in this textbook, or (b) work in teams to prepare a comprehensive "Dictionary of Deadwood Phrases," including as many as you can find. Be sure to include a preferred substitute.

6.16 Conciseness Is Hard Work (Objs. 1, 2)

Just as most people are unmotivated to read wordy documents, most are unmotivated to listen to wordy speakers. Effective communicators work to eliminate "rambling" in both their written and spoken words.

Abraham Lincoln expressed the relationship between conciseness and hard work with his reply to the question, "How long does it take you to prepare a speech?" "Two weeks for a 20-minute speech," he replied. "One week for a 40-minute speech; and I can give a rambling, two-hour talk right now." Rambling takes little thought and effort; conciseness takes a great deal of both.

Your Task. For a 24-hour period, think about conciseness violations in spoken words. Consider violations in five areas you studied in this chapter: (a) fillers, (b) long lead-ins, (c) redundancies, (d) buried verbs, and (e) empty words. Identify the source of the violation using descriptors such as *friend, family member, coworker, boss, instructor, actor in TV sitcom, interviewer or interviewee on a radio or TV talk show*, and so forth. Include the communication medium for each example (telephone, conversation, radio, television, etc.). Be prepared to share the results of this activity during a class discussion.

6.17 Communicating With a Nonnative English Speaker

Intercultural | Web

In the three chapters devoted to the writing process, most of the advice focuses on communicating clearly and concisely. As the world becomes more globally connected, businesspeople may be increasingly communicating with nonnative speakers and writers. Assume that you have been asked to present a talk to businesspeople in your area. What additional advice would you give to speakers and writers in communicating with nonnative English speakers?

© Juice Images/Photolibrary

Your Task. Search the Web for advice in communicating with nonnative English speakers. Prepare a list of ten significant suggestions.

6.18 How Plain Is the English in Your Apartment Lease? (Objs. 1–3)

E-mail | Ethics | Team

Have you read your apartment lease carefully? Did you understand it? Many students—and their friends and family members—are intimidated, frustrated, or just plain lost when they try to comprehend an apartment lease.

Your Task. Locate an apartment lease—yours, a friend's, or a family member's. In teams, analyze its format and readability. What size is the paper? How large are the margins? Is the type large or small? How much white space appears on the page? Are paragraphs and sentences long or short? Does the lease contain legalese or obscure language? What makes it difficult to understand? In an e-mail message to your instructor, summarize your team's reaction to the lease. Your instructor may ask you to revise sections or the entire lease to make it more readable. In class, discuss how ethical it is for an apartment owner to expect a renter to read and comprehend a lease while sitting in the rental office.

Video Resource

Video Library 2, Writing Skills: The Little Guys

The Little Guys Home Electronics specializes in selling and installing home theater equipment. In just 12 years, it has grown from a start-up company to an established business with annual sales of more than $10 million. The owners—Dave and Evie Wexler and Paul Gerrity—describe their goals, motivations, and experiences in making their business successful. As you watch this video, look for (a) good business practices that helped the owners launch a successful business, (b) characteristics of successful entrepreneurs, and (c) reasons some small businesses remain successful whereas others fail.

Your Task. After watching the video, assume that you have been asked to summarize reasons for the success of The Little Guys. Building on what you have learned in this writing process chapter, compose a bulleted list with ten or more items. Use this opening sentence: *The Little Guys Home Electronics business succeeded because the owners did the following.*

Chat About It

In each chapter you will find five discussion questions related to the chapter material. Your instructor may assign these topics for you to discuss in class, in an online chat room, or on an online discussion board. Some of the discussion topics may require outside research. You may also be asked to read and respond to postings made by your classmates.

Topic 1: When you tackle a serious writing project, do you prefer freewriting, in which you rapidly record your thoughts, or do you prefer to polish and revise as you go? What are the advantages and disadvantages of each method for you? Do you use the same method for both short and long messages?

Topic 2: Think about your own speaking and writing. Do you recognize some favorite redundancies that you use in spoken or written messages? When did you realize that you could be more concise and precise by eliminating these expressions?

Topic 3: The default font in Microsoft Word used to be Times New Roman, a serif typeface. With Word 2007, the new default font is Calibri, a sans serif typeface. Why do you think Microsoft made the switch? In your opinion, is Calibri more readable than Times New Roman in printed documents, documents displayed on a computer screen, both, or neither?

Topic 4: What proofreading tasks can you safely ask a proofreading buddy to perform? What if that person is not a skilled writer?

Topic 5: Are you a good proofreader? Is it easier to find other people's errors than your own? Why? What are you good at finding? What do you frequently miss?

Grammar and Mechanics C.L.U.E. Review 6

Semicolons, Colons

Review Guides 27–30 about semicolons and colons in Appendix A, Grammar and Mechanics Guide, beginning on page A-12. On a separate sheet, revise the following sentences to correct errors in semicolon and colon usage. Do not start new sentences. For each error that you locate, write the guide number that reflects this usage. The more you recognize the reasons, the better you will learn these punctuation guidelines. If a sentence is correct, write *C*. When you finish, check your answers on page Key-1.

Example: Companies find it difficult to name new products consequently they often hire specialists.
Revision: Companies find it difficult to name new products; consequently, they often hire specialists. [Guide 27]

1. Successful product names may appear to have been named by magic, however the naming process is methodical and deliberate.
2. Choosing the right name and tagline is critical consequently companies are eager to hire specialists.
3. Naming is a costly endeavor, fees may range up to $70,000 for a global name.
4. Expanding markets are in Paris France Beijing China and Dubai City United Arab Emirates.
5. As she was about to name a fashion product, Rachel Hermes said "If I am launching a new fashion label, the task becomes very difficult. I have to find a name that communicates the creative style that the brand is to embody."
6. For a new unisex perfume, Hermes considered the following names Declaration, Serenity, and Earth.
7. Naming is not a problem for small companies however it is a big problem for global brands.
8. Hermes started with a thorough competitive analysis it included quantifying the tone and strength of competing names.
9. Attending the naming sessions were James Harper, marketing director, Reva Cruz, product manager, and Cheryl Chang, vice president.
10. Distribution of goods has become global therefore names have to be registered in many countries.

Are you ready? Get more practice at **www.meguffey.com**

CHAPTER 11

Report and Research Basics

OBJECTIVES

After studying this chapter, you should be able to

1. Describe basic features of business reports, including functions, strategies (indirect or direct), writing style, and formats.
2. Apply the 3-x-3 writing process to business reports to create well-organized documents that show a firm grasp of audience and purpose.
3. Find, evaluate, and use print and electronic secondary sources.
4. Understand how to generate and use primary data while avoiding researcher bias.
5. Comprehend fast-changing communication technology: the Web, electronic databases, and other resources for business writers and researchers.
6. Recognize the purposes and techniques of documentation in business reports, and avoid plagiarism.
7. Create meaningful and interesting graphics; display numeric information in the appropriate graphic form; and skillfully generate, use, and convert data to visual aids.

Want to do well on tests and excel in your course? Go to **www.meguffey.com** for helpful interactive resources.

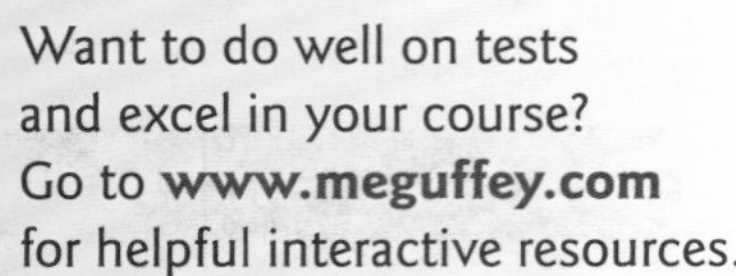

▸ **Review the Chapter 11 PowerPoint slides to prepare for the first quiz.**

Zooming In PART 1

"Pawsengers" Enjoy Creature Comforts With Pet Airways

Zoe, a Jack Russell terrier, may have inspired a nifty business idea and helped Dan Wiesel and Alysa Binder launch a successful enterprise, Pet Airways. The unique start-up is the first pet-only carrier, transporting cats and dogs (more animals are to follow) between regional airports in nine major U.S. cities. The company's three Beech 1900 aircraft, reliable 19-passenger turboprop planes, were modified to accommodate up to 50 four-legged travelers. One-way fares start as low as $150 and average about $250. Most customers of Pet Airways are pet owners going on vacation or relocating; others include rescue and adoption missions and organizers of animal shows. Typically, business owners preface the big step of starting a company with research. In most cases they must then raise capital. To accomplish this difficult task, they need to persuade potential investors and banks that their proposed venture, usually presented in a business plan, is worthy of support and economically viable. Like many pet owners, Dan and Alysa were unhappy with commercial airlines' treating their precious dog like baggage or, recently reclassified, as cargo on commercial flights. If Fido or Fluffy doesn't fit into a pet crate stowed under a passenger seat in the main cabin, the critter is banned to the cargo section, a potentially terrifying, uncomfortable, even deadly place for a pet. Each year animals freeze to death, are lost, or die from a lack of cabin pressure en route. Only since 2005 are airlines required to report injuries, losses, and deaths of companion animals.[1] At the same time, commercial and private transport of live animals is a multimillion-dollar business for the major airlines.

This is how the husband-and-wife team describes the origins of their pet enterprise: "Of course, there's one thing Zoe is certainly not, and that's cargo. As we're fond of telling our neighbor Janet, her boxer Samson isn't Samsonite, and she agreed. In fact, we met lots of neighbors, friends, and even complete strangers who felt exactly the same way." The couple relied on their consulting and business experience and wondered: "Instead of trying to convince the human airlines to treat pets better, why not start up an airline just for pets?" The response, so far, has been overwhelming. The secret? Dan and Alysa write on the company Web site: "You see, on Pet Airways, your pets aren't packages; they're 'pawsengers.' And every step of the journey, we'll take care of them as if they were our own. Because that's exactly the way we'd want Zoe to be treated."

Although quizzing friends and neighbors does not qualify as a representative sample in empirical research, it could lead in the right direction and accurately reflect what a greater sample of the

© Benassi/Splash News/Newscom

population may want or believe. Observation has many limitations; nevertheless, it can be applied effectively in primary research, as this chapter shows.

Hatching a brilliant business idea is only the start. To make generalizations and predictions and to secure funds, entrepreneurs need solid data. You will learn more about business plans and other formal reports and proposals in Chapter 13. We will revisit Pet Airways on page 347.

Critical Thinking

- Why might a U.S. airline dedicated strictly to traveling pets be an easy sell to the public? Why might it not be?[2]
- Today's entrepreneurs have many technological resources at their disposal to do research and spread the news when launching a new business. What channels may Dan Wiesel and Alysa Binder have used to explore their business idea and to find potential customers?
- To hear Dan Wiesel and Alysa Binder tell it on their Web site, before launching Pet Airways, they apparently relied a great deal on anecdotal evidence, a very limited empirical research method. Do you think an entrepreneur's hunch is enough on which to start a business?

http://petairways.com/

Understanding Report Essentials

LEARNING OBJECTIVE 1
Describe basic features of business reports, including functions, strategies (indirect or direct), writing style, and formats.

Reports are indispensable in business. The larger an organization, the more vital the exchange and flow of information becomes. Employees report their activities vertically to supervisors. At the same time, the various divisions of a business communicate horizontally with each other through reports. Occasionally, reports are generated for outside organizations or government agencies. In North America, a low-context culture, our values and attitudes seem to prompt us to write reports. We analyze problems, gather and study the facts, and then assess the alternatives. We pride ourselves on being practical and logical as we apply scientific procedures. When we wish to persuade financiers that our business merits a capital investment, as Dan Wiesel and Alysa Binder have, we generally write a business plan or a report outlining our case.

Management decisions in many organizations are based on information submitted in the form of reports. Routine reports keep managers informed about completed tasks, projects, and work in progress. Reports help us understand and study systematically the challenges we encounter in business before we can outline the steps toward solving them. Historian and author David McCullough said it best: "Trying to plan for the future without a sense of the past is like trying to plant cut flowers."[2] Business solutions are unthinkable without a thorough examination of the problems that prompted them.

This chapter examines the functions, strategies, writing style, and formats of typical business reports. It also introduces the report-writing process and discusses methods of collecting, documenting, and illustrating data.

What are the purposes of effective business reports?

Business reports range from informal bulleted lists and half-page trip reports to formal 200-page financial forecasts. Reports may be presented orally in front of a group or electronically on a computer screen. In many organizations, reports still take the form of paper documents such as traditional memos and letters. Other reports present primarily numerical data, such as tax reports and profit-and-loss statements. Increasingly, reports are delivered and presented digitally—for instance, as e-mail messages, PDF (portable document format) files, or electronic "slide decks." These files can then be e-mailed, distributed on the company intranet, or posted on the Internet. Hyperlinks tie together content within the document, between associated files, and with Web sources. Such linking adds depth and flexibility to traditional linear texts.

Some reports provide information only; others analyze and make recommendations. Although reports vary greatly in length, content, form, and formality level, they all have one or more of the following purposes: *to convey information, answer questions, and solve problems.*

Report Functions and Types

In terms of what they do, most reports fit into two broad categories: informational reports and analytical reports.

What is the difference between informational and analytical reports?

Informational Reports. Reports that present data without analysis or recommendations are primarily informational. For such reports, writers collect and organize facts, but they do not analyze the facts for readers. A trip report describing an employee's visit to a trade show, for example, presents information. Weekly bulleted status reports distributed by e-mail to a team record the activities of each group member and are shared with supervisors. Other reports that present information without analysis involve routine operations, compliance with regulations, and company policies and procedures.

Analytical Reports. Reports that provide data or findings, analyses, and conclusions are analytical. If requested, writers also supply recommendations. Analytical reports may intend to persuade readers to act or change their beliefs. For example, if you were writing a yardstick report that compares several potential manufacturing locations for a new automobile plant, you might conclude by recommending one site after discussing several criteria. Alternatively, let's say you work for a company that is considering a specific building for a women-only gym, and you are asked to study the location's suitability. You may have to write a feasibility report, an analysis of alternatives and a recommendation, that attempts to persuade readers to accept that site.

To distinguish among findings, conclusions, and recommendations, consider the example of an audit report. The auditor compiles facts and figures—the findings of the report—to meet the purpose or objective of the audit. Drawing inferences from the findings, the auditor arrives at conclusions. With the audit objectives in mind, the auditor may then propose corrective steps or actions, the recommendations.

Organizational Strategies

Like other business messages, reports may be organized directly or indirectly. The reader's expectations and the content of a report determine its development strategy, as illustrated in Figure 11.1. In long reports, such as corporate annual reports, some parts may be developed directly whereas other parts are arranged indirectly.

Where do the conclusions and recommendations appear in an analytical report written using the direct strategy, and why?

Direct Strategy. When the purpose for writing is presented close to the beginning of a report, the organizational strategy is direct. Informational reports, such as the letter report

FIGURE 11.1 Audience Analysis and Report Organization

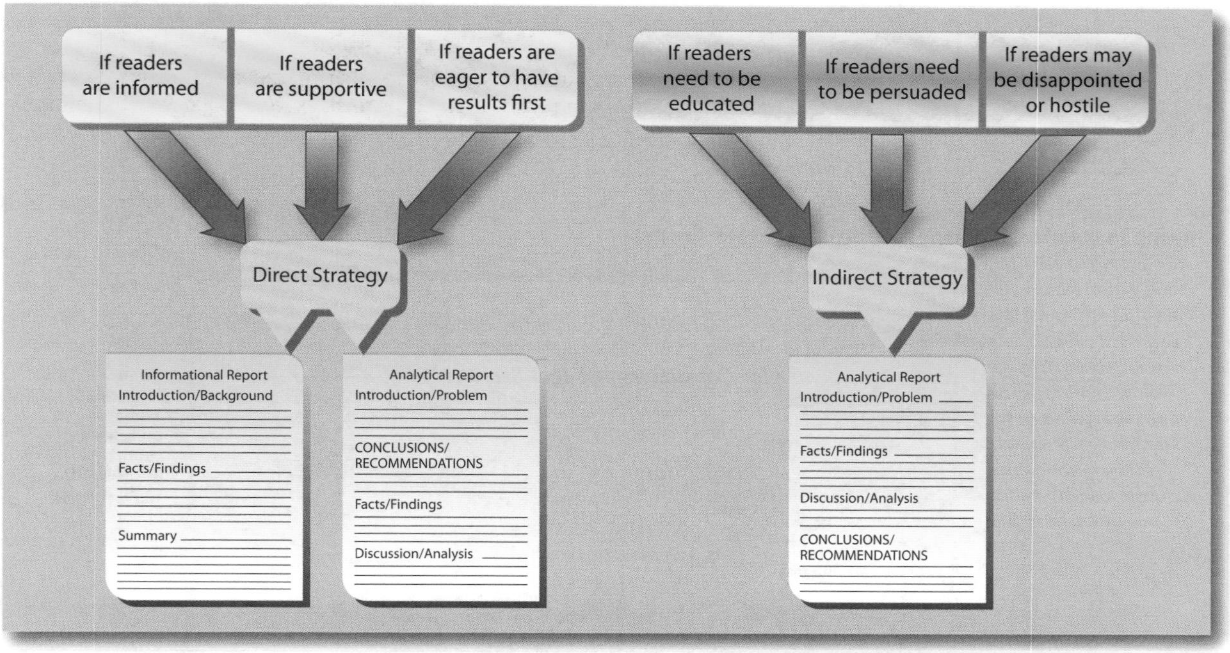

shown in Figure 11.2, are usually arranged directly. They open with an introduction, which is followed by the facts and a summary. In Figure 11.2 the writer explains a legal services plan using a letter report. The report begins with an introduction. The facts, divided into three subtopics and identified by descriptive headings, follow. The report ends with a summary and a complimentary close.

Analytical reports may also be organized directly, especially when readers are supportive of or familiar with the topic. Many busy executives prefer this strategy because it gives them the results of the report immediately. They don't have to spend time wading through the facts, findings, discussion, and analyses to get to the two items they are most interested in—the conclusions and recommendations. Figure 11.3 illustrates such an arrangement. This analytical memo report describes environmental hazards of a property that a realtor has just listed. The realtor is familiar with the investigation and eager to find out the recommendations. Therefore, the memo is organized directly. You should be aware, though, that unless readers are familiar with the topic, they may find the direct strategy confusing. Many readers prefer the indirect strategy because it seems logical and mirrors the way they solve problems.

When is the indirect strategy the best choice for analytical reports?

Indirect Strategy. The organizational strategy is indirect when the conclusions and recommendations, if requested, appear at the end of the report. Such reports usually begin with an introduction or description of the problem, followed by facts and interpretations from the writer. They end with conclusions and recommendations. This pattern is helpful when readers are unfamiliar with the problem. This pattern is also useful when readers must be persuaded or when they may be disappointed in or hostile toward the report's findings. The writer is more likely to retain the reader's interest by first explaining, justifying, and analyzing the facts and then making recommendations. This strategy also seems most rational to readers because it follows the normal thought process: problem, alternatives (facts), solution.

Writing Style

When should you use a formal report-writing style, and when should you use an informal style?

Like other business messages, reports can range from informal to formal, depending on their purpose, audience, and setting. Research reports from consultants to their clients tend to be rather formal. Such reports must project objectivity, authority, and impartiality. However, depending on the industry, a report to your boss describing a trip to a conference would probably be informal.

An office worker once called a grammar hotline service with this problem: "We've just sent a report to our headquarters, and it was returned with this comment, 'Put it in the third person.' What do they mean?" The hotline experts explained that management apparently wanted a more formal writing style, using third-person constructions *(the company* or *the researcher* instead of *we* and *I*). Figure 11.4, which compares the characteristics of formal and informal

FIGURE 11.2 Informational Report—Letter Format

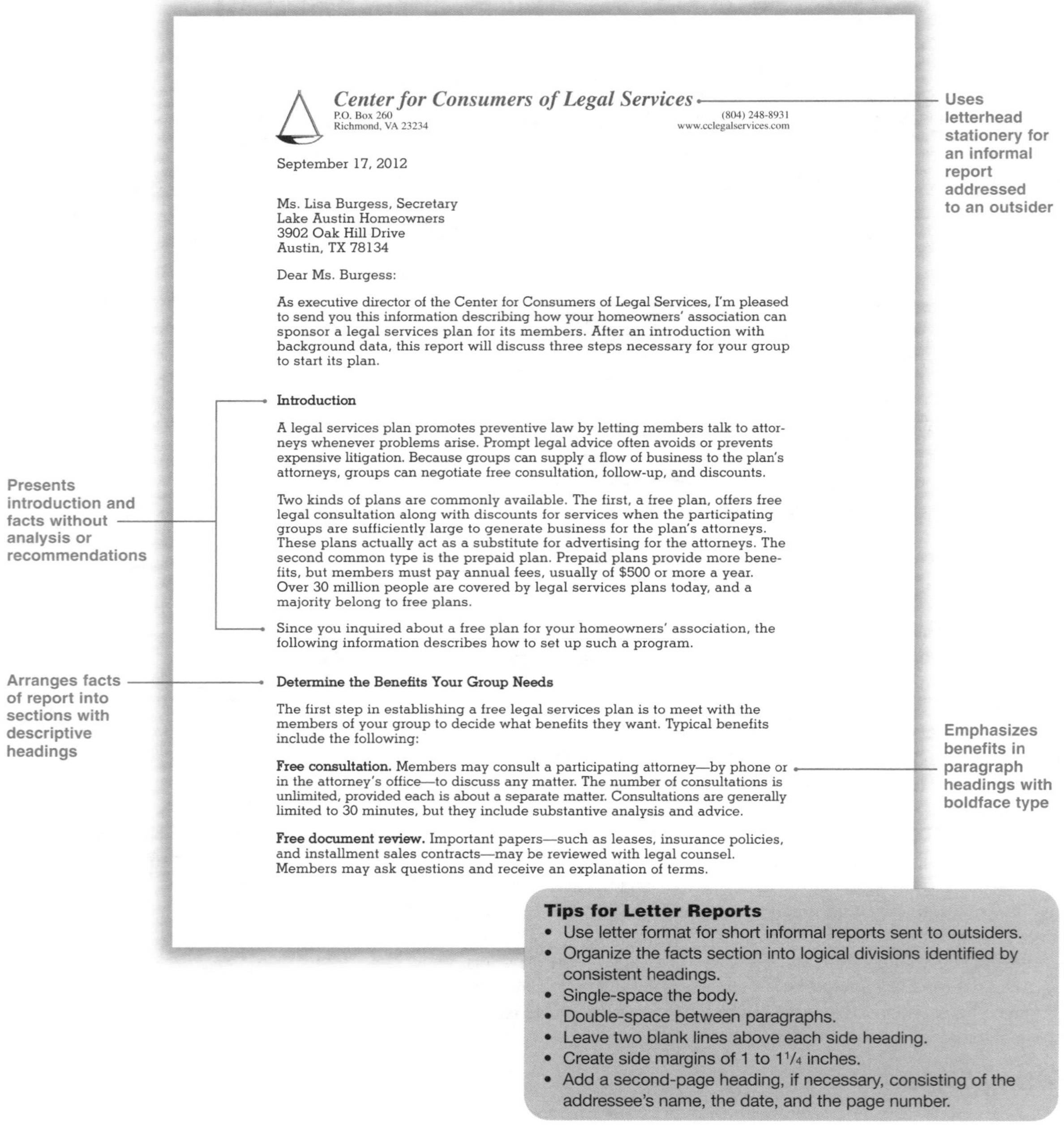
Center for Consumers of Legal Services
P.O. Box 260
Richmond, VA 23234
(804) 248-8931
www.cclegalservices.com

September 17, 2012

Ms. Lisa Burgess, Secretary
Lake Austin Homeowners
3902 Oak Hill Drive
Austin, TX 78134

Dear Ms. Burgess:

As executive director of the Center for Consumers of Legal Services, I'm pleased to send you this information describing how your homeowners' association can sponsor a legal services plan for its members. After an introduction with background data, this report will discuss three steps necessary for your group to start its plan.

Introduction

A legal services plan promotes preventive law by letting members talk to attorneys whenever problems arise. Prompt legal advice often avoids or prevents expensive litigation. Because groups can supply a flow of business to the plan's attorneys, groups can negotiate free consultation, follow-up, and discounts.

Two kinds of plans are commonly available. The first, a free plan, offers free legal consultation along with discounts for services when the participating groups are sufficiently large to generate business for the plan's attorneys. These plans actually act as a substitute for advertising for the attorneys. The second common type is the prepaid plan. Prepaid plans provide more benefits, but members must pay annual fees, usually of $500 or more a year. Over 30 million people are covered by legal services plans today, and a majority belong to free plans.

Since you inquired about a free plan for your homeowners' association, the following information describes how to set up such a program.

Determine the Benefits Your Group Needs

The first step in establishing a free legal services plan is to meet with the members of your group to decide what benefits they want. Typical benefits include the following:

Free consultation. Members may consult a participating attorney—by phone or in the attorney's office—to discuss any matter. The number of consultations is unlimited, provided each is about a separate matter. Consultations are generally limited to 30 minutes, but they include substantive analysis and advice.

Free document review. Important papers—such as leases, insurance policies, and installment sales contracts—may be reviewed with legal counsel. Members may ask questions and receive an explanation of terms.

Uses letterhead stationery for an informal report addressed to an outsider
Presents introduction and facts without analysis or recommendations
Arranges facts of report into sections with descriptive headings
Emphasizes benefits in paragraph headings with boldface type

Tips for Letter Reports

- Use letter format for short informal reports sent to outsiders.
- Organize the facts section into logical divisions identified by consistent headings.
- Single-space the body.
- Double-space between paragraphs.
- Leave two blank lines above each side heading.
- Create side margins of 1 to $1^1/_4$ inches.
- Add a second-page heading, if necessary, consisting of the addressee's name, the date, and the page number.

FIGURE 11.2 **(Continued)**

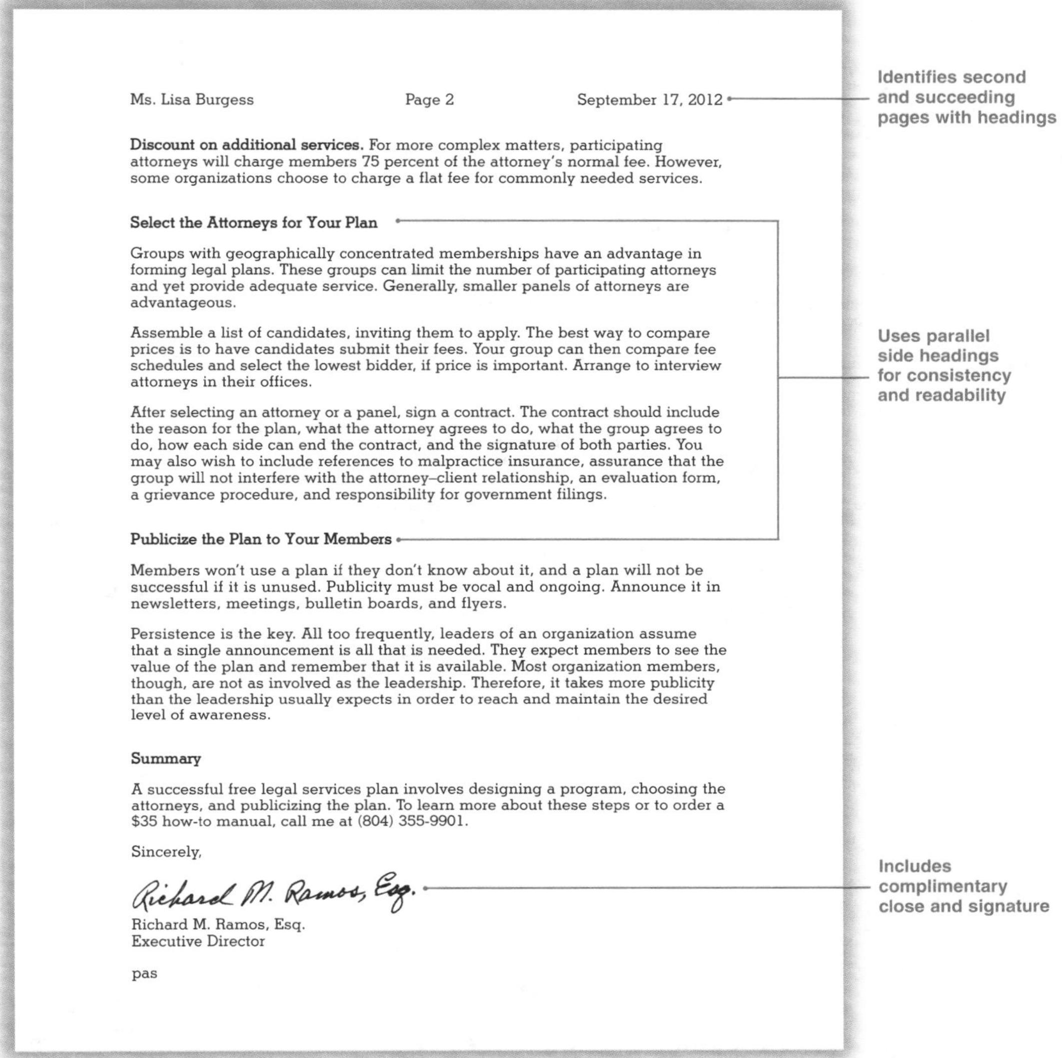

Ms. Lisa Burgess Page 2 September 17, 2012

Discount on additional services. For more complex matters, participating attorneys will charge members 75 percent of the attorney's normal fee. However, some organizations choose to charge a flat fee for commonly needed services.

Select the Attorneys for Your Plan

Groups with geographically concentrated memberships have an advantage in forming legal plans. These groups can limit the number of participating attorneys and yet provide adequate service. Generally, smaller panels of attorneys are advantageous.

Assemble a list of candidates, inviting them to apply. The best way to compare prices is to have candidates submit their fees. Your group can then compare fee schedules and select the lowest bidder, if price is important. Arrange to interview attorneys in their offices.

After selecting an attorney or a panel, sign a contract. The contract should include the reason for the plan, what the attorney agrees to do, what the group agrees to do, how each side can end the contract, and the signature of both parties. You may also wish to include references to malpractice insurance, assurance that the group will not interfere with the attorney–client relationship, an evaluation form, a grievance procedure, and responsibility for government filings.

Publicize the Plan to Your Members

Members won't use a plan if they don't know about it, and a plan will not be successful if it is unused. Publicity must be vocal and ongoing. Announce it in newsletters, meetings, bulletin boards, and flyers.

Persistence is the key. All too frequently, leaders of an organization assume that a single announcement is all that is needed. They expect members to see the value of the plan and remember that it is available. Most organization members, though, are not as involved as the leadership. Therefore, it takes more publicity than the leadership usually expects in order to reach and maintain the desired level of awareness.

Summary

A successful free legal services plan involves designing a program, choosing the attorneys, and publicizing the plan. To learn more about these steps or to order a $35 how-to manual, call me at (804) 355-9901.

Sincerely,

Richard M. Ramos, Esq.

Richard M. Ramos, Esq.
Executive Director

pas

Identifies second and succeeding pages with headings
Uses parallel side headings for consistency and readability
Includes complimentary close and signature

report-writing styles, can help you decide which style is appropriate for your reports. Note that, increasingly, formal reports are written with contractions and in the active voice. Today, report writers try to avoid awkward third-person references to themselves as *the researchers* or *the authors* because it sounds stilted and outdated.

Report Formats

The format of a report depends on its length, topic, audience, and purpose. After considering these elements, you will probably choose from among the following formats.

What criteria determine a report's format?

Letter Format. Use letter format for short informal reports (usually eight or fewer pages) addressed outside an organization. Prepared on office stationery, a letter report contains a date, inside address, salutation, and complimentary close, as shown in Figure 11.2. Although they may carry information similar to that found in correspondence, letter reports usually are longer and show more careful organization than most letters. They also include headings.

FIGURE 11.3 Analytical Report—Memo Format

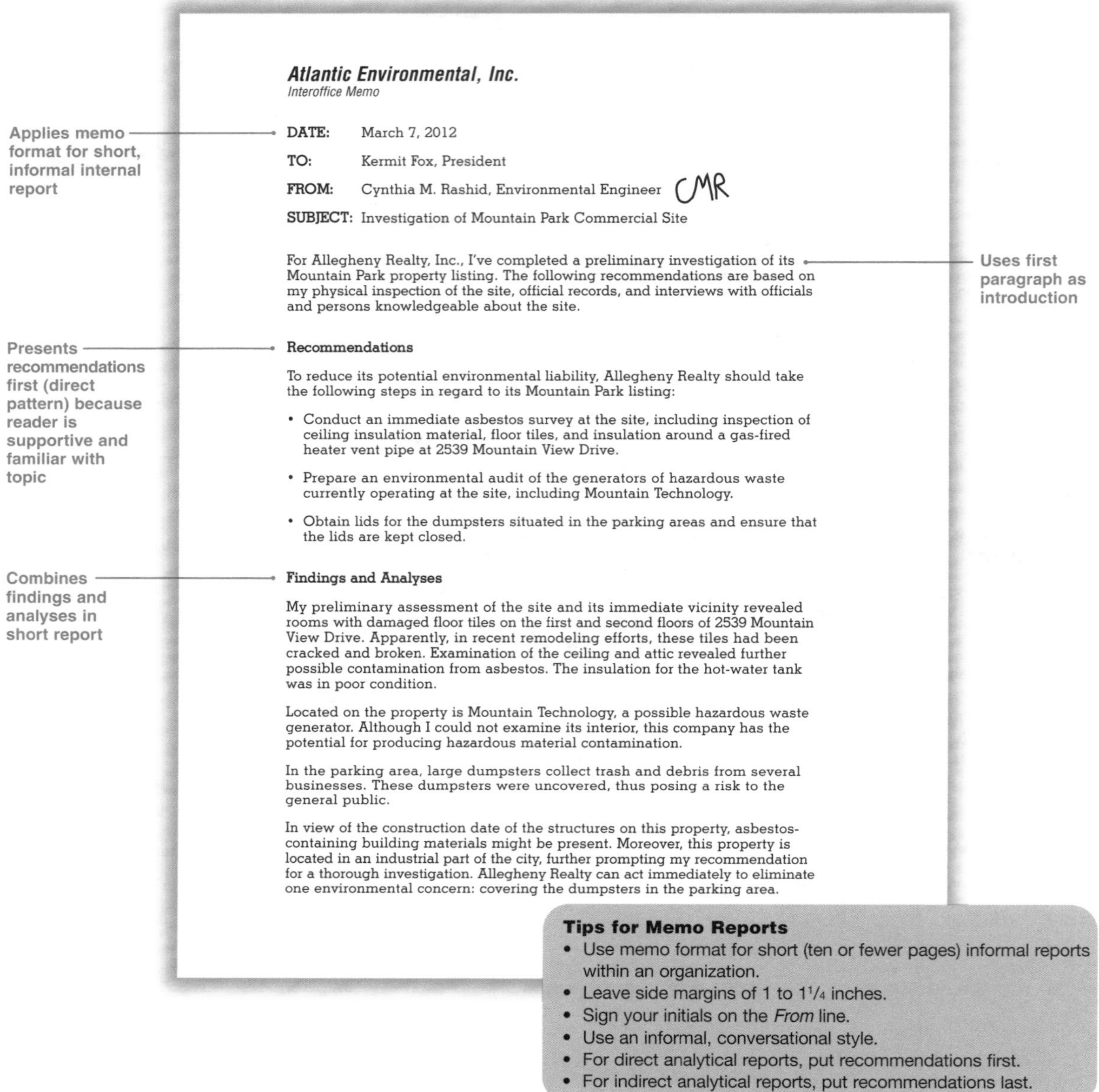

Atlantic Environmental, Inc.
Interoffice Memo

DATE: March 7, 2012

TO: Kermit Fox, President

FROM: Cynthia M. Rashid, Environmental Engineer CMR

SUBJECT: Investigation of Mountain Park Commercial Site

For Allegheny Realty, Inc., I've completed a preliminary investigation of its Mountain Park property listing. The following recommendations are based on my physical inspection of the site, official records, and interviews with officials and persons knowledgeable about the site.

Recommendations

To reduce its potential environmental liability, Allegheny Realty should take the following steps in regard to its Mountain Park listing:

- Conduct an immediate asbestos survey at the site, including inspection of ceiling insulation material, floor tiles, and insulation around a gas-fired heater vent pipe at 2539 Mountain View Drive.
- Prepare an environmental audit of the generators of hazardous waste currently operating at the site, including Mountain Technology.
- Obtain lids for the dumpsters situated in the parking areas and ensure that the lids are kept closed.

Findings and Analyses

My preliminary assessment of the site and its immediate vicinity revealed rooms with damaged floor tiles on the first and second floors of 2539 Mountain View Drive. Apparently, in recent remodeling efforts, these tiles had been cracked and broken. Examination of the ceiling and attic revealed further possible contamination from asbestos. The insulation for the hot-water tank was in poor condition.

Located on the property is Mountain Technology, a possible hazardous waste generator. Although I could not examine its interior, this company has the potential for producing hazardous material contamination.

In the parking area, large dumpsters collect trash and debris from several businesses. These dumpsters were uncovered, thus posing a risk to the general public.

In view of the construction date of the structures on this property, asbestos-containing building materials might be present. Moreover, this property is located in an industrial part of the city, further prompting my recommendation for a thorough investigation. Allegheny Realty can act immediately to eliminate one environmental concern: covering the dumpsters in the parking area.

Applies memo format for short, informal internal report
Uses first paragraph as introduction
Presents recommendations first (direct pattern) because reader is supportive and familiar with topic
Combines findings and analyses in short report
Tips for Memo Reports
• Use memo format for short (ten or fewer pages) informal reports within an organization.
• Leave side margins of 1 to 1¼ inches.
• Sign your initials on the *From* line.
• Use an informal, conversational style.
• For direct analytical reports, put recommendations first.
• For indirect analytical reports, put recommendations last.

Memo and E-Mail Formats. For short informal reports that stay within organizations, the memo format is appropriate. Memo reports begin with essential background information, using standard headings: *Date, To, From,* and *Subject*, as shown in Figure 11.3. Like letter reports, memo reports differ from regular memos in length, use of headings, and deliberate organization. Today, memo reports are rarely distributed in hard copy; rather, they are attached to e-mails or, if short, contained in the body of e-mails.

FIGURE 11.4 Report-Writing Styles

	Formal Writing Style	Informal Writing Style
Use	Theses Research studies Controversial or complex reports (especially to outsiders)	Short, routine reports Reports for familiar audiences Noncontroversial reports Most reports for company insiders
Effect	Impression of objectivity, accuracy, professionalism, fairness Distance created between writer and reader	Feeling of warmth, personal involvement, closeness
Characteristics	Traditionally, no first-person pronouns; use of third person *(the researcher, the writer)*; increasingly, however, first-person pronouns and contractions are beginning to gain acceptance. Absence of contractions *(can't, don't)* Use of passive-voice verbs *(the study was conducted)* Complex sentences; long words Absence of humor and figures of speech Reduced use of colorful adjectives and adverbs Elimination of "editorializing" (author's opinions, perceptions)	Use of first-person pronouns *(I, we, me, my, us, our)* Use of contractions Emphasis on active-voice verbs *(I conducted the study)* Shorter sentences; familiar words Occasional use of humor, metaphors Occasional use of colorful speech Acceptance of author's opinions and ideas

Manuscript Format. For longer, more formal reports, use the manuscript format. These reports are usually printed on plain paper instead of letterhead stationery or memo forms. They begin with a title followed by systematically displayed headings and subheadings. You will see examples of proposals and formal reports using the manuscript format in Chapter 13.

Preprinted Forms. Preprinted forms are often used for repetitive data, such as monthly sales reports, performance appraisals, merchandise inventories, and personnel and financial reports. Standardized headings on these forms save time for the writer. Preprinted forms also make similar information easy to locate and ensure that all necessary information is provided.

Digital Format. Digital media allow writers to produce and distribute reports in electronic form, not in hard copy. With Adobe Acrobat any report can be converted into a PDF document that retains its format and generally cannot be changed. In addition, today's communicators can use programs such as Microsoft's PowerPoint or Apple's Keynote to create electronic presentations in the form of slides. Because the purpose of such presentations is to concisely display the contents of reports, they are often not intended for verbal delivery. Rather, these text-heavy slides are often posted online or e-mailed. When printed out, the stacks of hard-copy slides resemble decks of playing cards, which is why they are called slide decks. Digital delivery has also changed Microsoft Word documents. This popular program lets users hyperlink multimedia content within the document or with associated text or media files. Thus, such digital documents create a nonlinear reading experience similar to that of browsing Web pages.

Applying the 3-x-3 Writing Process to Reports

LEARNING OBJECTIVE 2
Apply the 3-x-3 writing process to business reports to create well-organized documents that show a firm grasp of audience and purpose.

Because business reports are systematic attempts to compile often complex information, answer questions, and solve problems, the best reports are developed methodically. In earlier chapters the 3-x-3 writing process was helpful in guiding short projects such as e-mails, memos, and letters. That same process is even more necessary when preparing longer projects such as reports and proposals. After all, an extensive project poses a greater organizational challenge than a short one and, therefore, requires a rigorous structure to help readers grasp the message. Let's channel the writing process into seven specific steps:

What are the seven steps of the report-writing process?

Step 1: Analyze the problem and purpose.

Step 2: Anticipate the audience and issues.

Step 3: Prepare a work plan.

Step 4: Conduct research.

Step 5: Organize, analyze, interpret, and illustrate the data.

Step 6: Compose the first draft.

Step 7: Revise, proofread, and evaluate.

How much time you spend on each step depends on your report task. A short informational report on a familiar topic might require a brief work plan, little research, and no data analysis. A complex analytical report, on the other hand, might demand a comprehensive work plan, extensive research, and careful data analysis. In this section we consider the first three steps in the process—analyzing the problem and purpose, anticipating the audience and issues, and preparing a work plan.

To illustrate the planning stages of a report, we will watch Diane Camas develop a report she's preparing for her boss, Mike Rivers, at Mycon Pharmaceutical Laboratories. Mike asked Diane to investigate the problem of transportation for sales representatives. Currently, some Mycon reps visit customers (mostly doctors and hospitals) using company-leased cars. A few reps drive their own cars, receiving reimbursements for use. In three months Mycon's leasing agreement for 14 cars expires, and Mike is considering a major change. Diane's task is to investigate the choices and report her findings to Mike.

Analyzing the Problem and Purpose

What is a problem statement, and why should you prepare one as you begin work on a report?

The first step in writing a report is understanding the problem or assignment clearly. For complex reports, prepare a written problem statement to clarify the task. In analyzing her report task, Diane had many questions: Is the problem that Mycon is spending too much money on leased cars? Does Mycon wish to invest in owning a fleet of cars? Is Mike unhappy with the paperwork involved in reimbursing sales reps when they use their own cars? Does he suspect that reps are submitting inflated mileage figures? Before starting research for the report, Diane talked with Mike to define the problem. She learned several dimensions of the situation and wrote the following statement to clarify the problem—both for herself and for Mike.

Problem statement: *The leases on all company cars will be expiring in three months. Mycon must decide whether to renew them or develop a new policy regarding transportation for sales reps. Expenses and paperwork for employee-owned cars seem excessive.*

Diane further defined the problem by writing a specific question that she would try to answer in her report:

Problem question: *What plan should Mycon follow in providing transportation for its sales reps?*

Now Diane was ready to concentrate on the purpose of the report. Again, she had questions: Exactly what did Mike expect? Did he want a comparison of costs for buying and leasing cars? Should she conduct research to pinpoint exact reimbursement costs when employees drive their own cars? Did he want her to do all the legwork, present her findings in a report, and let him make a decision? Or did he want her to evaluate the choices and recommend a course of action? After talking with Mike, Diane was ready to write a simple purpose statement for this assignment.

What function does a simple purpose statement serve?

Simple statement of purpose: *To recommend a plan that provides sales reps with cars to be used in their calls.*

Preparing a written purpose statement is a good idea because it defines the focus of a report and provides a standard that keeps the project on target. In writing useful purpose statements, choose action verbs telling what you intend to do: *analyze, choose, investigate, compare, justify, evaluate, explain, establish, determine,* and so on. Notice that Diane's statement begins with the action verb *recommend.*

Some reports require only a simple statement of purpose: *to investigate expanded teller hours, to select a manager from among four candidates, to describe the position of accounts supervisor.* Many assignments, though, demand additional focus to guide the project. An expanded statement of purpose considers three additional factors: scope, limitations, and significance.

What is the value of setting boundaries to determine the scope of a report?

Scope and Limitations. What issues or elements will be investigated? The scope statement prepares the audience by clearly defining which problem or problems will be analyzed and solved. To determine the scope, Diane brainstormed with Mike and others to pin down her task. She learned that Mycon currently had enough capital to consider purchasing a fleet of cars outright. Mike also told her that employee satisfaction was almost as important as cost-effectiveness. Moreover, he disclosed his suspicion that employee-owned cars were costing Mycon more than leased cars. Diane had many issues to sort out in setting the boundaries of her report.

What conditions affect the generalizability and utility of a report's findings? As part of the scope statement, the limitations further narrow the subject by focusing on constraints or exclusions. For this report Diane realized that her conclusions and recommendations might apply only to reps in her Kansas City sales district. Her findings would probably not be reliable for reps in Seattle, Phoenix, or Atlanta. Another limitation for Diane was time. She had to complete the report in four weeks, thus restricting the thoroughness of her research.

Significance. Why is the topic worth investigating at this time? Some topics, after initial examination, turn out to be less important than originally thought. Others involve problems that cannot be solved, making a study useless. For Diane and Mike the problem had significance because Mycon's leasing agreement would expire shortly and decisions had to be made about a new policy for transportation of sales reps.

Diane decided to expand her statement of purpose to define the scope, describe the limitations of the report, and explain the significance of the problem.

What are the components of an expanded purpose statement?

> ***Expanded statement of purpose:*** *The purpose of this report is to recommend a plan that provides sales reps with cars to be used in their calls. The report will compare costs for three plans: outright ownership, leasing, and compensation for employee-owned cars. It will also measure employee reactions to each plan. The report is significant because Mycon's current leasing agreement expires April 1 and an improved plan could reduce costs and paperwork. The study is limited to costs for sales reps in the Kansas City district.*

After expanding her statement of purpose, Diane checked it with Mike Rivers to be sure she was on target.

Sports fans aren't the only ones who follow March Madness. Each year, interactive marketing firm Unicast issues its NCAA Basketball Tournament Fever Report to identify where hoops watchers get their daily fix of scores, highlights, bracket updates, and pool information. The agency's 2010 report found that 44% of March Madness fans tracked the tournament online, and 10% followed along using mobile devices. Not surprisingly, favorite online destinations included ESPN.com and Yahoo Sports—familiar brands that own the loyalty of sports enthusiasts online. *Who are the primary and secondary readers of this report?*

Anticipating the Audience and Issues

After defining the purpose of a report, a writer must think carefully about who will read it. Concentrating solely on a primary reader is a major mistake. Although one individual may have solicited the report, others within the organization may eventually read it, including upper management and people in other departments. A report to an outside client may first be read by someone who is familiar with the problem and then be distributed to others less familiar with the topic. Moreover, candid statements to one audience may be offensive to another audience. Diane could make a major blunder, for instance, if she mentioned Mike's suspicion that sales reps were padding their mileage statements. If the report were made public—as it probably would be to explain a new policy—the sales reps could feel insulted that their integrity was questioned.

How can you take into account both primary and secondary readers?

As Diane considered her primary and secondary readers, she asked herself these questions:

- *What do my readers need to know about this topic?*
- *What do they already know?*
- *What is their educational level?*
- *How will they react to this information?*
- *Which sources will they trust?*
- *How can I make this information readable, believable, and memorable?*

Answers to these questions help writers determine how much background material to include, how much detail to add, whether to include jargon, what method of organization and presentation to follow, and what tone to use.

Why should major report problems be broken down into subproblems, and what is this process called?

In the planning stages, a report writer must also break the major investigative problem into subproblems. This process, sometimes called factoring, identifies issues to be investigated or possible solutions to the main problem. In this case Mycon must figure out the best way to transport sales reps. Each possible solution or issue that Diane considers becomes a factor or subproblem to be investigated. Diane came up with three tentative solutions to provide transportation to sales reps: (a) purchase cars outright, (b) lease cars, or (c) compensate employees for using their own cars. These three factors form the outline of Diane's study.

Diane continued to factor these main points into the following subproblems for investigation:

What plan should Mycon use to transport its sales reps?

I. Should Mycon purchase cars outright?
   A. How much capital would be required?
   B. How much would it cost to insure, operate, and maintain company-owned cars?
   C. Do employees prefer using company-owned cars?

II. Should Mycon lease cars?
   A. What is the best lease price available?
   B. How much would it cost to insure, operate, and maintain leased cars?
   C. Do employees prefer using leased cars?

III. Should Mycon compensate employees for using their own cars?
   A. How much has it cost in the past to compensate employees who used their own cars?
   B. How much paperwork is involved in reporting expenses?
   C. Do employees prefer being compensated for using their own cars?

Each subproblem would probably be further factored into additional subproblems. These issues may be phrased as questions, as Diane's are, or as statements. In factoring a complex problem, prepare an outline showing the initial problem and its breakdown into subproblems. Make sure your divisions are consistent (don't mix issues), exclusive (don't overlap categories), and complete (don't skip significant issues).

Preparing a Work Plan

After analyzing the problem, anticipating the audience, and factoring the problem, you are ready to prepare a work plan. A good work plan includes the following:

What role does a work plan play in the completion of a report?

- Statement of the problem (based on key background/contextual information)
- Statement of the purpose including scope with limitations and significance
- Research strategy including a description of potential sources and methods of collecting data
- Tentative outline that factors the problem into manageable chunks
- Work schedule

Preparing a plan encourages you to evaluate your resources, set priorities, outline a course of action, and establish a schedule. Having a plan keeps you on track and provides management a means of measuring your progress.

A work plan gives a complete picture of a project. Because the usefulness and quality of any report rest primarily on its data, you will want to develop a clear research strategy, which includes allocating plenty of time to locate sources of information. For firsthand information you might interview people, prepare a survey, or even conduct a scientific experiment. For secondary information you will probably search electronic materials on the Internet and printed materials such as books and magazines. Your work plan describes how you expect to generate or collect data. Because data collection is a major part of report writing, the next section of this chapter treats the topic more fully.

Figure 11.5 shows a complete work plan for a proposal pitched by BzzAgent's advertising executive Dave Balter to his client Lee Jeans. A work plan is useful because it outlines the issues to be investigated. Notice that considerable thought and discussion and even some preliminary research are necessary to be able to develop a useful work plan.

Zooming In PART 2

"Bone Voyage" on Pet Airways

As cute as ferrying animals in style across the United States may sound, it is not easy to turn an appealing idea into a profitable business. Nor is it easy to secure financing for a fledgling pet airline, least of all during severe economic turbulences. To obtain funding, most would-be entrepreneurs must write a business plan, as you will see in Chapter 13. You can assume that Dan and Alysa worked hard to chart the potential market, their competition, and the road to success.

The odds of start-up success vary greatly, depending on the source. Some claim that first-time entrepreneurs and those who have previously failed in a business venture face a 20 percent chance of succeeding. The U.S. Census Bureau pegs the success rate much higher, suggesting that 65 percent of new businesses still operate four years after launching. Dan and Alysa took the plunge after researching opportunities and potential threats. They had to figure out what makes their business special, what, in advertising terms, its unique selling point is. Other relocation specialists offer to move animals, not only domestically but also globally. Pet Airways, however, is the first pet-only carrier offering pet-friendly "Travel For Your Best Friend" (company motto), not in cargo but in a climate-controlled main cabin.

Pet Airways hopes to differentiate itself from the competition by providing a comfortable and safe travel experience for its four-legged "pawsengers." Cat and dog owners drop off their darlings at the airline's Pet Lounge located at the airport. The animals get potty breaks less than two hours before the flight and also along the way. They board the plane escorted by "pet attendants," and their pet carriers are securely stowed. When airborne, the animals are monitored every 15 minutes and given a last potty break after disembarking at their destination. They are then ready for pickup at the Pet Lounge.

Critical Thinking

- When writing their funding proposal or business plan, do you think Dan and Alysa chose an informational or analytical approach? Why?
- Do you think Dan's and Alysa's proposal was developed directly or indirectly? Why? Should it have been written formally or informally?
- What are some of the questions Dan and Alysa should have asked themselves about their audience before pitching their business idea or writing their proposal?

FIGURE 11.5 **Work Plan for a Formal Report**

Statement of Problem

Many women between the ages of 18 and 34 have trouble finding jeans that fit. Lee Jeans hopes to remedy that situation with its One True Fit line. We want to demonstrate to Lee that we can create a word-of-mouth campaign that will help it reach its target audience.

Statement of Purpose

Defines purpose, scope, limits, and significance of report

The purpose of this report is to secure an advertising contract from Lee Jeans. We will examine published accounts about the jeans industry and Lee Jeans in particular. In addition, we will examine published results of Lee's current marketing strategy. We will conduct focus groups of women in our company to generate campaign strategies for our pilot study of 100 BzzAgents. The report will persuade Lee Jeans that word-of-mouth advertising is an effective strategy to reach women in this demographic group and that Bzz Agent is the right company to hire. The report is significant because an advertising contract with Lee Jeans would help our company grow significantly in size and stature.

Research Strategy (Sources and Methods of Data Collection)

Describes primary and secondary data

We will gather information about Lee Jeans and the product line by examining published marketing data and conducting focus group surveys of our employees. In addition, we will gather data about the added value of word-of-mouth advertising by examining published accounts and interpreting data from previous marketing campaigns, particularly those with similar age groups. Finally, we will conduct a pilot study of 100 BzzAgents in the target demographic.

Tentative Outline

Factors problem into manageable chunks

I. How effectively has Lee Jeans marketed to the target population (women, ages 22–35)?
   A. Historically, who has typically bought Lee Jeans products? How often? Where?
   B. How effective are the current marketing strategies for the One True Fit line?
II. Is this product a good fit for our marketing strategy and our company?
   A. What do our staff members and our sample survey of BzzAgents say about this product?
   B. How well does our pool of BzzAgents correspond to the target demography in terms of age and geographic distribution?
III. Why should Lee Jeans engage BzzAgent to advertise its One True Fit line?
   A. What are the benefits of word of mouth in general and for this demographic in particular?
   B. What previous campaigns have we engaged in that demonstrate our company's credibility?
   C. What are our marketing strategies, and how well did they work in the pilot study?

Work Schedule

Estimates time needed to complete report tasks

Investigate Lee Jeans and the One True Fit line's current marketing strategy	July 15–25
Test product using focus groups	July 15–22
Create campaign materials for BzzAgents	July 18–31
Run a pilot test with a selected pool of 100 BzzAgents	August 1–21
Evaluate and interpret findings	August 22–25
Compose draft of report	August 26–28
Revise draft	August 28–30
Submit final report	September 1

Tips for Preparing a Work Plan

- Start early; allow plenty of time for brainstorming and preliminary research.
- Describe the problem motivating the report.
- Write a purpose statement that includes the report's scope, significance, and limitations.
- Describe the strategy including data collection sources and methods.
- Divide the major problem into subproblems stated as questions to be answered.
- Develop a realistic work schedule citing dates for completion of major tasks.
- Review the work plan with whoever authorized the report.

Although this tentative outline guides the investigation, it does not determine the content or order of the final report. You may, for example, study five possible solutions to a problem. If two prove to be useless, your report may discuss only the three winners. Moreover, you will organize the report to accomplish your goal and satisfy the audience. Remember that a busy executive who is familiar with a topic may prefer to read the conclusions and recommendations before a discussion of the findings. If someone authorizes the report, be sure to review the work plan with that person (your manager, client, or professor, for example) before proceeding with the project.

Gathering Information From Secondary Sources

LEARNING OBJECTIVE 3
Find, evaluate, and use print and electronic secondary sources.

One of the most important steps in the process of writing a report is that of gathering information (research). As the philosopher Goethe once said: "The greater part of all mischief in the world arises from the fact that men do not sufficiently understand their own aims. They have undertaken to build a tower, and spend no more labor on the foundation than would be necessary to erect a hut." Think of your report as a tower. Because a report is only as good as its foundation—the questions you ask and the data you gather to answer those questions—the remainder of this chapter describes the fundamental work of finding, documenting, and illustrating data.

Why are data important in report writing?

As you analyze a report's purpose and audience and prepare your research strategy, you will identify and assess the data you need to support your argument or explain your topic. As you do, you will answer questions about your objectives and audience: Will the audience need a lot of background or contextual information? Will your readers value or trust statistics, case studies, or expert opinions? Will they want to see data from interviews or surveys? Will summaries of focus groups be useful? Should you rely on organizational data? Figure 11.6 lists five forms of data and provides questions to guide you in making your research accurate and productive.

What are the main differences between primary data and secondary data?

Data fall into two broad categories: primary and secondary. Primary data result from firsthand experience and observation. Secondary data come from reading what others have experienced or observed and written down. Coca-Cola and Pepsi-Cola, for example, produce primary data when they stage taste tests and record the reactions of consumers. These same sets

FIGURE 11.6 Gathering and Selecting Report Data

Form of Data	Questions to Ask
Background or historical	How much do my readers know about the problem?
	Has this topic/issue been investigated before?
	Are those sources current, relevant, and/or credible?
	Will I need to add to the available data?
Statistical	What or who is the source?
	How recent are the data?
	How were the figures derived?
	Will this data be useful in this form?
Expert opinion	Who are the experts?
	What are their biases?
	Are their opinions in print?
	Are they available for interviewing?
	Do we have in-house experts?
Individual or group opinion	Whose opinion(s) would the readers value?
	Have surveys or interviews been conducted on this topic?
	If not, do questionnaires or surveys exist that I can modify and/or use?
	Would focus groups provide useful information?
Organizational	What are the proper channels for obtaining in-house data?
	Are permissions required?
	How can I learn about public and private companies?

of data become secondary after they have been published and, let's say, a newspaper reporter uses them in an article about soft drinks. Secondary data are easier and cheaper to gather than primary data, which might involve interviewing large groups or sending out questionnaires.

We discuss secondary data first because that is where nearly every research project should begin. Often, something has already been written about your topic. Reviewing secondary sources can save time and effort and prevent you from reinventing the wheel. Most secondary material is available either in print or electronically.

Print Resources

Are print sources and libraries irrelevant today?

Although we are seeing a steady movement away from print data and toward electronic data, print sources are still the most visible part of most libraries. Much information is available only in print.

By the way, if you are an infrequent library user, begin your research by talking with a reference librarian about your project. Librarians won't do your research for you, but they will steer you in the right direction. Moreover, they are very accommodating. Several years ago a *Wall Street Journal* poll revealed that librarians are perceived as among the friendliest, most approachable people in the working world. Many librarians help you understand their computer, cataloging, and retrieval systems by providing advice, brochures, handouts, and workshops.

Books. Although quickly outdated, books provide excellent historical, in-depth data. Books can be located through print or online listings.

- **Card catalogs.** A few small public or high school libraries still maintain card catalogs with all books indexed on 3-by-5 cards alphabetized by author, title, and subject.
- **Online catalogs.** Most libraries today have computerized their card catalogs. Some systems are fully automated, thus allowing users to learn not only whether a book is located in the library but also whether it is currently available. Moreover, online catalogs can help you trace and retrieve items from other area libraries if your college doesn't own them.

Periodicals. Magazines, pamphlets, and journals are called *periodicals* because of their recurrent, or periodic, publication. Journals are compilations of scholarly articles. Articles in journals and other periodicals are extremely useful because they are concise, limited in scope, and current and can supplement information in books.

What is the main difference between books and periodicals, and when would you want to use each?

- **Print indexes.** Most university libraries now offer online access to *The Readers' Guide to Periodical Literature*. You may still find print copies of this valuable index of general-interest magazine article titles in small libraries. It includes such magazines as *Time, Newsweek, The New Yorker*, and *U.S. News & World Report*. However, business writers today rely almost totally on electronic indexes and databases.
- **Electronic indexes.** Online indexes are stored in digital databases. Most libraries now provide such databases to help you locate references, abstracts, and full-text articles from magazines, journals, and newspapers, such as *The New York Times*. When using Web-based online indexes, follow the on-screen instructions or ask for assistance from a librarian. Beginning with a subject search such as *manufacturers' recalls* is helpful because it generally turns up more relevant citations than keyword searches—especially when searching for names of people (*Akio Toyoda*) or companies (*Toyota*). Once you locate usable references, print a copy of your findings, save them to a portable flash memory device, or send them to your e-mail address.

Electronic Databases

As a writer of business reports today, you will probably begin your secondary research with electronic resources. Online databases have become the staple of secondary research. Most writers turn to them first because they are fast and easy to use. You can conduct detailed searches without ever leaving your office, home, or dorm room.

Where do most researchers begin to look?

A database is a collection of information stored electronically so that it is accessible by computer and digitally searchable. Databases provide bibliographic information (titles of documents and brief abstracts) and full-text documents. Most researchers prefer full-text

FIGURE 11.7 **ABI/INFORM (ProQuest) Search Result**

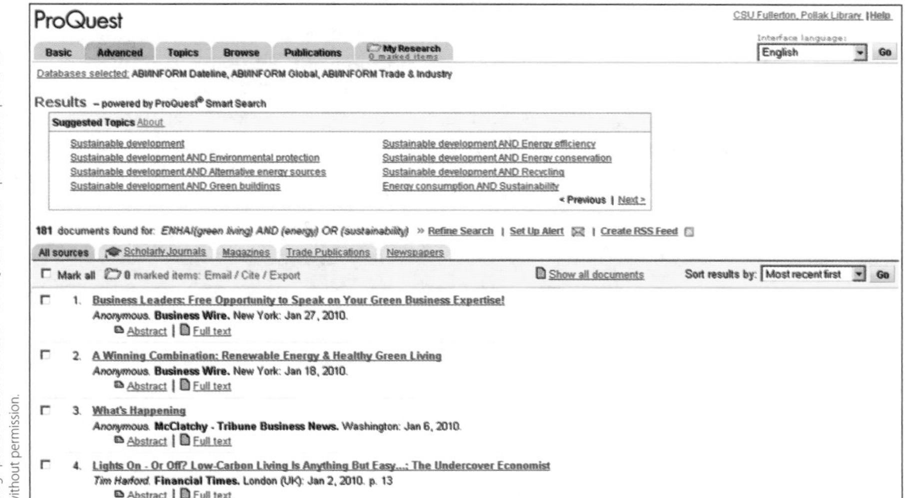

ABI/INFORM indexes over 4,000 journals and features 3,000 full-text documents about business topics. Users can access newspapers, magazines, reports, dissertations, book reviews, scholarly journals, and trade publications. Figure 11.7 shows that the search terms *green living* and energy or *sustainability* brought up 181 full-text search results.

documents because they are convenient. Various databases contain a rich array of magazine, newspaper, and journal articles, as well as newsletters, business reports, company profiles, government data, reviews, and directories. The four databases most useful to business writers for general searches are ABI/INFORM (ProQuest), Factiva (Dow Jones), LexisNexis Academic, and Academic Search Elite (EBSCO). Your college library and many businesses probably subscribe to these expensive resources and perhaps to other, more specialized commercial databases. Figure 11.7 shows the ABI/INFORM search menu.

What kind of information can be found in commercial databases?

Developing a search strategy and narrowing your search can save time. Think about the time frame for your search, the language of publication, and the types of materials you will need. Most databases enable you to focus a search easily. For example, if you were researching the banking crisis that occurred recently and wanted to look at articles published in a specific year, most search tools would enable you to limit your search to that period. All databases and search engines allow you to refine your search and increase the precision of your hits. In addition, for research in international business, don't limit yourself to English-language articles only; some Web sites, most notably AltaVista's Babel Fish, offer rough but free translations. What's more, many organizations overseas present their Web content in multiple languages.

Electronic resources may take time to master. Therefore, before wasting time and retrieving lots of useless material, talk to a university librarian. College and public libraries as well as some employers offer free access to several commercial databases, sparing you the high cost of individual subscriptions.

Gathering Information From Primary Sources

LEARNING OBJECTIVE 4
Understand how to generate and use primary data while avoiding researcher bias.

Up to this point, we have been talking about secondary data. You should begin nearly every business report assignment by evaluating the available secondary data. However, you will probably need primary data to give a complete picture. Business reports that solve specific current problems typically rely on primary, firsthand data. If, for example, management wants to discover the cause of increased employee turnover in its Seattle office, it must investigate conditions in Seattle by collecting recent information. Providing answers to business problems often means generating primary data through surveys, interviews, observation, or experimentation.

What are primary data, and when would you want to use them?

Surveys

What are the advantages and disadvantages of surveys and mailed questionnaires?

Surveys collect data from groups of people. Before developing new products, for example, companies often survey consumers to learn their needs. The advantages of surveys are that they gather data economically and efficiently. Snail-mailed or e-mailed surveys reach big groups nearby or at great distances. Moreover, people responding to mailed or e-mailed surveys have time to consider their answers, thus improving the accuracy of the data.

Mailed or e-mailed surveys, of course, have disadvantages. Most of us rank them with junk mail or spam, so response rates may be no higher than 5 percent. Furthermore, those who do respond may not represent an accurate sample of the overall population, thus invalidating generalizations from the group. Let's say, for example, that an insurance company sends out a questionnaire asking about provisions in a new policy. If only older people respond, the questionnaire data cannot be used to generalize what people in other age groups might think. If a survey is only e-mailed, it may miss audiences that do not use the Internet.

A final problem with surveys has to do with truthfulness. Some respondents exaggerate their incomes or distort other facts, thus causing the results to be unreliable. Nevertheless, surveys may be the best way to generate data for business and student reports. In preparing print or electronic surveys, consider these pointers:

- **Select the survey population carefully.** Many surveys question a small group of people (a sample) and project the findings to a larger population. Let's say that a survey of your class reveals that the majority prefer *phở*, the Vietnamese beef and rice noodle soup. Can you then say with confidence that all students on your campus (or in the nation) prefer pho? To be able to generalize from a survey, you need to make the sample as large as possible. In addition, you need to determine whether the sample represents the larger population. For important surveys you will want to consult books on or experts in sampling techniques. As for pho, in a recent Sodexo survey, the soup ranked among the top three comfort foods favored by American college students.[3]

What are the characteristics of effective surveys?

- **Explain why the survey is necessary.** In a cover letter or an opening paragraph, describe the need for the survey. Suggest how someone or something other than you will benefit. If appropriate, offer to send recipients a copy of the findings.
- **Consider incentives.** If the survey is long, persuasive techniques may be necessary. Response rates can be increased by offering money (such as a $1 bill), coupons, gift certificates, free books, or other gifts.
- **Limit the number of questions.** Resist the temptation to ask for too much. Request only information you will use. Don't, for example, include demographic questions (income, gender, age, and so forth) unless the information is necessary to evaluate responses.
- **Use questions that produce quantifiable answers.** Check-off, multiple-choice, yes–no, and scale (or rank-order) questions, illustrated in Figure 11.8, provide quantifiable data that are easily tabulated. Responses to open-ended questions (*What should the bookstore do about plastic bags?*) reveal interesting, but difficult-to-quantify perceptions.[4] To obtain workable data, give interviewees a list of possible responses, as shown in items 5 through 8 of Figure 11.8. For scale and multiple-choice questions, try to present all the possible answer choices. To be safe, add an *Other* or *Don't know* category in case the choices seem insufficient to the respondent. Many surveys use scale questions because they capture degrees of feelings. Typical scale headings are *Agree strongly, Agree somewhat, Neutral, Disagree somewhat,* and *Disagree strongly.*

Why is it important to craft survey questions carefully?

- **Avoid leading or ambiguous questions.** The wording of a question can dramatically affect responses to it.[5] When respondents were asked, "Are we spending too much, too little, or about the right amount on *assistance to the poor?*" [emphasis added], 13 percent responded *Too much.* When the same respondents were asked, "Are we spending too much, too little, or about the right amount on *welfare?*"[emphasis added], 44 percent responded *Too much.* Because words have different meanings for different people, you must strive to use objective language and pilot test your questions with typical respondents. Stay away from questions that suggest an answer (*Don't you agree that the salaries of CEOs are obscenely high?*). Instead, ask neutral questions (*Do CEOs earn too much, too little, or about the right amount?*). Also, avoid queries that really ask two or more things (*Should the salaries of CEOs be reduced or regulated by government legislation?*). Instead, break them into separate questions (*Should the salaries of CEOs be reduced by government legislation? Should the salaries of CEOs be regulated by government legislation?*).

FIGURE 11.8 **Preparing a Survey**

1 Prewriting

Analyze: The purpose is to help the bookstore decide if it should replace plastic bags with cloth bags for customer purchases.

Anticipate: The audience will be busy students who will be initially uninterested.

Adapt: Because students will be unwilling to participate, the survey must be short and simple. Its purpose must be significant and clear.

2 Writing

Research: Ask students how they would react to cloth bags. Use their answers to form question response choices.

Organize: Open by explaining the survey's purpose and importance. In the body ask clear questions that produce quantifiable answers. Conclude with appreciation and instructions.

Compose: Write the first draft of the questionnaire.

3 Revising

Revise: Try out the questionnaire with a small representative group. Revise unclear questions.

Proofread: Read for correctness. Be sure that answer choices do not overlap and that they are complete. Provide an *Other* category if appropriate (as in No. 9).

Evaluate: Is the survey clear, attractive, and easy to complete?

North Shore College Bookstore
STUDENT SURVEY

The North Shore College Bookstore wants to do its part in protecting the environment. Each year we give away 45,000 plastic bags for students to carry off their purchases. We are considering changing from plastic to cloth bags or some other alternative, but we need your views.

Explains need for survey (use cover letter for longer surveys

Please place checks below to indicate your responses.

1. How many units are you presently carrying?
   ___ 15 or more units
   ___ 9 to 14 units
   ___ 8 or fewer units

   ___ Male
   ___ Female

Uses groupings that do not overlap (not 9 to 15 and 15 or more)

2. How many times have you visited the bookstore this semester?
   ___ 0 times ___ 1 time ___ 2 times ___ 3 times ___ 4 or more times
3. Indicate your concern for the environment.
   ___ Very concerned ___ Concerned ___ Unconcerned
4. To protect the environment, would you be willing to change to another type of bag when buying books?
   ___ Yes
   ___ No

Indicate your feeling about the following alternatives.

For major purchases the bookstore should	Agree	Undecided	Disagree
5. Continue to provide plastic bags.	_____	_____	_____
6. Provide no bags; encourage students to bring their own bags.	_____	_____	_____
7. Provide no bags; offer cloth bags at reduced price (about $3).	_____	_____	_____
8. Give a cloth bag with each major purchase, the cost to be included in registration fees.	_____	_____	_____

9. Consider another alternative, such as
   ____

Uses scale questions to channel responses into quantifiable alternatives, as opposed to open-ended questions

Allows respondent to add an answer in case choices provided seem insufficient

Please return the completed survey form to your instructor or to the survey box at the North Shore College Bookstore exit. Your opinion counts.

Tells how to return survey form

Thanks for your help!

- **Make it easy for respondents to return the survey.** Researchers often provide prepaid self-addressed envelopes or business-reply envelopes. Low-cost Web survey software such as SurveyMonkey and Zoomerang help users develop simple, template-driven questions and allow survey takers conveniently to follow a link to take the survey.
- **Conduct a pilot study.** Try the questionnaire with a small group so that you can remedy any problems. For example, the survey shown in Figure 11.8 revealed that female students generally favored cloth bags and were willing to pay for them. Male students opposed purchasing cloth bags. By adding a gender category, researchers could verify this finding. The pilot study also revealed the need to ensure an appropriate representation of male and female students in the survey.

When are interviews with experts appropriate?

Interviews

Some of the best report information, particularly on topics about which little has been written, comes from individuals. These individuals are usually experts or veterans in their fields. Consider both in-house and outside experts for business reports. Tapping these sources will call for in-person, telephone, or online interviews. To elicit the most useful data, try these techniques:

- **Locate an expert.** Ask managers and individuals who are considered to be most knowledgeable in their areas. Check membership lists of professional organizations, and consult articles about the topic or related topics. Most people enjoy being experts or at least recommending them. You could also post an inquiry to an Internet newsgroup. An easy way to search newsgroups in a topic area is through the **Browse all groups** category indexed by the popular search tool Google.
- **Prepare for the interview.** Learn about the individual you are interviewing, and make sure you can pronounce the interviewee's name. Research the background and terminology of the topic. Let's say you are interviewing a corporate communication expert about producing an in-house newsletter. You ought to be familiar with terms such as *font* and software such as QuarkXPress and Adobe InDesign. In addition, be prepared by making a list of questions that pinpoint your focus on the topic. Ask the interviewee if you may record the talk. Practice using the recording device so that you are familiar with it by the time of the interview.
- **Maintain a professional attitude**. Call before the interview to confirm the arrangements, and then arrive on time. Be prepared to take notes if your recorder fails (and remember to ask permission beforehand if you want to record). Use your body language to convey respect.
- **Make your questions objective and friendly.** Adopt a courteous and respectful attitude. Don't get into a debating match with the interviewee, and don't interrupt. Remember that you are there to listen, not to talk! Use open-ended rather than yes-or-no questions to draw experts out.
- **Watch the time.** Tell interviewees in advance how much time you expect to need for the interview. Don't overstay your appointment. If your subject rambles, gently try to draw him or her back to the topic; otherwise, you may run out of time before asking all your questions.
- **End graciously.** Conclude the interview with a general question, such as *Is there anything you would like to add?* Express your appreciation, and ask permission to telephone later if you need to verify points.

When do firsthand observation and investigation provide useful report data?

Observation and Experimentation

Some kinds of primary data can be obtained only through firsthand observation and investigation. If you determine that the questions you have require observational data, then you need to plan the observations carefully. Most important is deciding what or whom you are observing and how often those observations are necessary to provide reliable

Spotlight on Communicators

© AP Images/Toby Talbot

Premier management consultant and best-selling author Tom Peters recognizes the value of ongoing primary and secondary research. He recommends collecting data not only about the performance of your own company but also about that of the competition. To stay abreast of rivals and their techniques, businesses must (a) collect data, (b) update them regularly, and (c) share them widely within the firm.

data. For example, if you want to learn more about an organization's telephone customer service, you probably need to conduct an observation (along with interviews and perhaps even surveys). You will want to answer questions such as *How long does a typical caller wait before a customer service rep answers the call?* and *Is the service consistent?* Recording observations for 60-minute periods at various times throughout a week will give you a better picture than just observing for an hour on a Friday before a holiday.

When you observe, plan ahead. Arrive early enough to introduce yourself and set up whatever equipment you think is necessary. Make sure you have received permissions beforehand, particularly if you are recording. In addition, take notes, not only of the events or actions but also of the settings. Changes in environment often have an effect on actions. Famous for his out-of-the box thinking, Howard Schultz, the CEO of Starbucks, is known to hate research, advertising, and customer surveys. Instead of relying on sophisticated marketing research, Schultz visits 25 Starbucks locations a week to learn about his customers.[6]

Experimentation produces data suggesting causes and effects. Informal experimentation might be as simple as a pretest and posttest in a college course. Did students expand their knowledge as a result of the course? More formal experimentation is undertaken by scientists and professional researchers, who control variables to test their effects. Assume, for example, that Hershey's wants to test the hypothesis (which is a tentative assumption) that chocolate lifts people out of the doldrums. An experiment testing the hypothesis would separate depressed people into two groups: those who ate chocolate (the experimental group) and those who did not (the control group). What effect did chocolate have? Such experiments are not done haphazardly, however. Valid experiments require sophisticated research designs and careful attention to matching the experimental and control groups.

Ethics Check

Cribbing From References?
Doing last-minute research for a class or work project, you are in a hurry; therefore, you decide to copy some sources from the list of references that you found in an article on your topic to boost your number of works cited. Is it unethical to list sources you have not actually read?

The World Wide Web

LEARNING OBJECTIVE 5

Comprehend fast-changing communication technology: the Web, electronic databases, and other resources for business writers and researchers.

If you are like most adults today, you probably use the Web for entertainment and work every day. You stay in touch with your friends by instant messaging and e-mail, not to mention text and picture messages you exchange between increasingly more capable smartphones. Chances are you have a personal page on a social networking site such as Facebook or MySpace, and perhaps you play one of the countless free online games. You have probably looked up directions on Google Maps and may have bid on or sold items on eBay. You are likely to download ringtones for your cell phone, and perhaps you obtain your favorite music from iTunes, not some illegal file-sharing site. Your generation is much more likely to follow the news online than in the daily paper or even on TV. In short, you rely on the Internet daily for information and entertainment. You are part of a vast virtual community that, in turn, consists of many smaller communities all over the world. The Web and the Internet as a whole are referred to as a global village for a reason.

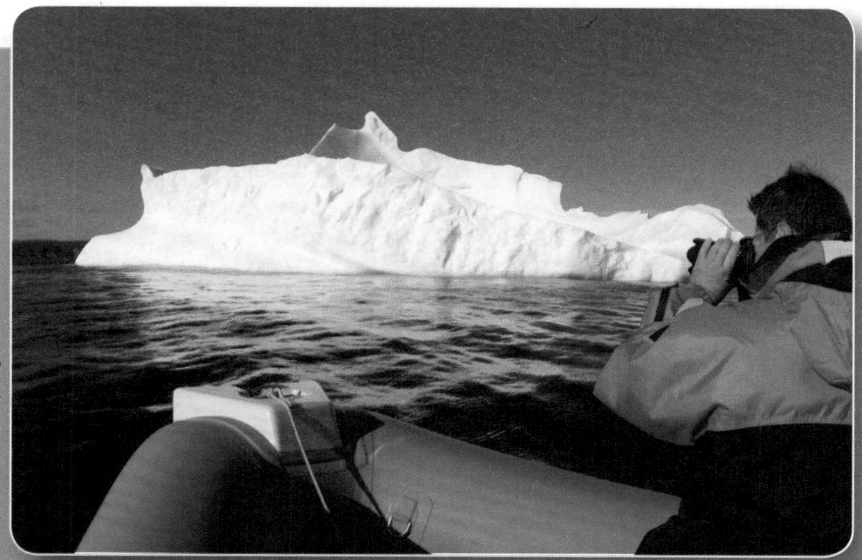

It's back to basics for scientists at the Intergovernmental Panel on Climate Change (IPCC) after the group's world-renowned Assessment Report had its most sensational claims rescinded due to invalid data. Among the claims lacking scientific backing were the assertion that the Himalayan glaciers would melt away by 2035 and that nearly half of the Amazon rainforest would disappear. The IPCC said it hoped to restore public confidence by submitting to an independent scientific review board and by adopting quality standards for future reports. *How do researchers produce valid primary data?*

Spotlight on Communicators

© Courtesy of Eric Dezenhall

One of America's top crisis management gurus explains the unbridled power of the Web: "The CEOs of the largest 50 companies in the world are practically hiding under their desks in terror about Internet rumors." Eric Dezenhall, author of *Damage Control*, adds that "[m]illions of dollars of labor are being spent discussing whether or not you should respond to the Web."

Ethics Check

Legitimate Gripe or Character Assassination?

Few would deny that customers should have an outlet for reasonable complaints against companies that slighted them. However, today, increasingly anonymous cyber threats against companies often erupt suddenly and turn nasty, leaving firms unsure about how to deal with them, whether to respond, and if so, how. In this light, can we trust the information on the Web?

How has the Web changed how we access information, and what types of information are available?

Why is it important to learn to navigate the depths of the Web?

Understanding the Dynamic Complexity of the Web. The Web is an amazing resource. It started as a fast, but exclusive network linking scientists, academics, military people, and other "tech heads." In the beginning information traveled purely in text form. Today the Web is interactive, mobile, and user-friendly with multimedia content ranging from digital sound files to vivid images and video files. Most important for report writers, the Web is considered an ever-expanding democratic medium where anyone can be a publisher and consume most of its boundless content free of charge. Armed with camera phones, average citizens post their videos on the hugely popular site YouTube and act as virtual reporters. Interest groups of all stripes gather in Usenet communities or newsgroups (digital bulletin boards and discussion forums). They exchange news, opinions, and other information.

- **Virtual communities.** The so-called Web 2.0 has fostered interactive environments that have resulted in the emergence of virtual communities that encourage teamwork among strangers all over the United States and the world. One such democratic, free-access tool is wiki. This group communication software enables users to create and change Web pages. The best known perhaps is Wikipedia, a free online reference that can be edited even by a layperson. Behind company firewalls many wikis help technical experts and other specialists collaborate.
- **Information mobility.** Digital content on the Web has also become more mobile in recent years. Thanks to browser-enabled smartphones and wireless personal digital assistants (PDAs), businesspeople can surf Web pages and retrieve text messages, instant messages, and e-mails on the go with devices that fit into their pockets. Similarly, users can listen to podcasts (digital recordings of radio or TV programs) and other media files on demand. Podcasts are distributed for downloading to a computer, a smartphone such as the iPhone or BlackBerry, or an MP3 audio player such as the iPod.

As we have seen in Chapter 7, the fastest-growing sector of the Internet is social networking sites. Social networking is a boon, but it also presents risks. On the one hand, online social media and a growing variety of prominent blogs, sometimes labeled the blogosphere, have empowered citizens to get their voices heard and to voice discontent. Online social media such as Twitter and blogs allow users to comment on any imaginable topic or event and post their views instantly. Companies have recognized the potential of the new media to reach vast audiences. Corporate blogs and social networks are growing as companies begin to understand their marketing potential.

However, the dark side of the power in the hands of "netizens" is that rumors and savage, no-holds-barred attacks can go "viral," which means they travel around the globe overnight, ruining reputations and tarnishing carefully honed brands. Therefore, more and more businesses engage in damage control after online threats surface. In short, the Web is an invaluable resource, but report writers must approach it with caution and sound judgment.

With nearly 80 percent of Americans online[7] and literally trillions of pages of information available on the World Wide Web, odds are that if you have a question, an answer exists online. To a business researcher, the Web offers a wide range of organizational and commercial information. You can expect to find such items as product and service facts, public relations material, mission statements, staff directories, press releases, current company news, government information, selected article reprints, collaborative scientific project reports, and employment information.

Although a wealth of information is available, finding exactly what you need can be frustrating and time-consuming. The constantly changing contents of the Web and its lack of organization make it more problematic for research than searching commercial databases, such as LexisNexis. Moreover, Web content is uneven, and often the quality is questionable. The problem of gathering information is complicated by the fact that the total number of Web sites recently surpassed 200 million, growing at the rate of about 4 million new domain addresses each month.[8]

To succeed in your search for information and answers, you need to understand the search tools available to you. You also need to understand how to evaluate the information you find.

Identifying Search Tools. Finding what you are looking for on the Web is hopeless without powerful, specialized search tools, such as Google, Bing, Yahoo Search, AOL, and Ask.com. These search tools can be divided into two types: subject (or Web) directories and search engines. In addition, some search engines specialize in "metasearching." This means they combine several powerful search engines into one (e.g., Dogpile). See Figure 11.9 for an overview of useful Web search tools. Large search sites such as Yahoo and Google Directory are actually search engines and subject directories combined. Subject directories fall into two categories—commercial (e.g., Yahoo, About.com, and others) and academic (e.g., InfoMine).

What can Google, Bing, and Yahoo do for a researcher?

FIGURE 11.9 **Web Search Tools for Business Writers**

Business Databases (Subscription based, commercial)	**Features**
ABI/INFORM Complete (ProQuest)	Best database for reliable, scholarly sources; recommended first stop for business students
LexisNexis Academic	Database of over 5,000 newspapers, magazines, etc.; very current; forces users to limit their search to fewer than 1,000 hits
Factiva	Stores over 5,000 periodicals; very current; best with a narrow search subject or to add results to other searches (unlimited results)
JSTOR	Scholarly articles; best for historical, not current, information
Search Engines (open-access business information)	
Business.com http://www.business.com	Search engine and subject directory/portal in one; features all business-related subjects
CEO Express http://www.ceoexpress.com	Human-selected directories of subjects relevant to business executives and researchers
Google Scholar http://scholar.google.com	Scholarly articles in various disciplines, including business, administration, finance, and economics
Search Engines (general)	
Google http://www.google.com	Relevance ranking; most popular search site or portal (65 percent of Web searches); advanced search options and subject directories
Yahoo http://www.yahoo.com	Search engine and directory; popular free e-mail site; relevance ranking; ranks second after Google with 16 percent of Web searches
Bing http://www.bing.com/	Microsoft's latest search engine indexing 200 million Web sites; MSN/Bing is in third place with nearly 11 percent of Web searches
All the Web http://www.alltheweb.com	Advanced search option; searches for audio and video files
Ask http://www.ask.com	Plain English (natural language) questions
Metasearch Engines (results from several search sites)	
Vivísimo/Clusty http://vivisimo.com http://clusty.com	Metasearch function clusters results into categories; offers advanced search options and help
InfoSpace http://search.infospace.com http://www.dogpile.com	Metasearch technology; searches Google, Yahoo, Bing, Ask, and more; owns other metasearch engines (e.g., Dogpile, WebCrawler, MetaCrawler)
Search http://www.search.com	Searches Google, Ask, LookSmart, and dozens of other leading search engines
Subject Directories or Portals	
About http://www.about.com	Directory that organizes content from over 2 million sites with commentary from 750 "guides" (chosen experts on 70,000+ topics)
Ipl2 http://www.ipl.org/	Award-winning public service organization and learning/teaching environment maintained by librarians of several universities

FIGURE 11.10 **Business.com**

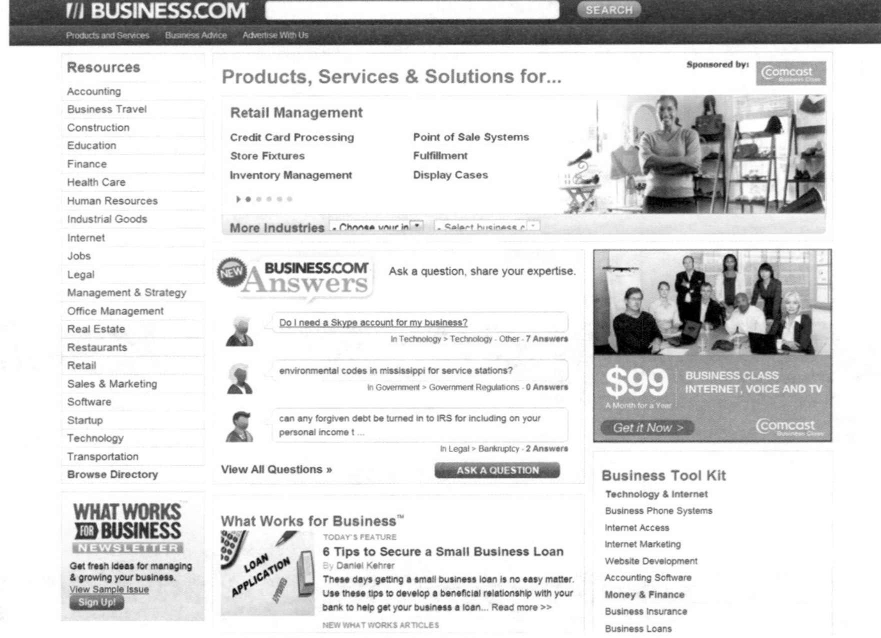

Courtesy of Business.com

Business.com is a resource that indexes any imaginable business-related topic and is very useful to business communicators and researchers.

Can any single search engine or directory index all Web pages?

Organized into subject categories, these human-compiled directories contain a collection of links to Internet resources submitted by site creators or evaluators.

Search engines differ in the way they trawl the vast amount of data on the Web. Google uses automated software "spiders" that crawl through the Web at regular intervals to collect and index the information from each location visited. Clusty by Vivísimo not only examines several search engines, but also groups results into topics called clusters. Some search tools (e.g., Ask.com) use natural-language-processing technology to enable you to ask questions to gather information. Both search engines and subject directories will help you find specific information. Figure 11.10 shows Business.com, a search engine and subject directory in one.

Search engines such as Google used to boast about the numbers of items they had indexed, but they stopped after hitting the 1 trillion milestone of unique links, recognizing that the number of individual Web pages is potentially infinite.[9] No single search engine or directory can come close to indexing all pages on the Internet. However, if you try a multiple-search site such as Dogpile, you can save much time because its metasearch technology compares the results of at least seven major search engines, eliminates duplicates, and then ranks the best hits for you.[10] To search for data effectively, consider using the search tools listed in Figure 11.9.

How can you make Web research less time-consuming and frustrating?

Applying Internet Search Strategies and Techniques. To conduct a thorough search for the information you need, build a (re)search strategy by understanding the tools available.

- **Use two or three search tools.** Begin by conducting a topic search. Use a subject directory such as Yahoo, About.com, or Open Directory Project (dmoz.org). Once you have narrowed your topic, switch to a search engine or metasearch engine.
- **Know your search tool.** When connecting to a search site for the first time, always read the description of its service, including its FAQs (frequently asked questions), Help, and How to Search sections. Often there are special features (e.g., the News, Images, Video, Books, and other categories on Google) that can speed up the search process.
- **Understand case sensitivity.** Generally use lowercase for your searches, unless you are looking for a term that is usually written in upper- and lowercase, such as a person's name.
- **Use nouns as search words and up to eight words in a query.** The right keywords—and more of them—can narrow the search effectively.

- **Combine keywords into phrases.** Phrases, marked by the use of quotation marks (e.g., "business ethics"), will limit results to specific matches.
- **Omit articles and prepositions.** Known as stop words, articles and prepositions do not add value to a search. Instead of *request for proposal*, use *proposal request*.
- **Use wild cards.** Most search engines support wildcards, such as asterisks. For example, the search term *cent** will retrieve *cents*, while *cent*** will retrieve both *center* and *centre*.
- **Learn basic Boolean search strategies.** You can save yourself a lot of time and frustration by narrowing your search with the following Boolean operators:

AND	Identifies only documents containing all of the specified words: **employee AND productivity AND morale**
OR	Identifies documents containing at least one of the specified words: **employee OR productivity OR morale**
NOT	Excludes documents containing the specified word: **employee productivity NOT morale**
NEAR	Finds documents containing target words or phrases within a specified distance, for instance, within ten words: **employee NEAR productivity**.

- **Bookmark the best.** To keep track of your favorite Internet sites, save them as bookmarks or favorites.
- **Keep trying.** If a search produces no results, check your spelling. If you are using Boolean operators, check the syntax of your queries. Try synonyms and variations on words. Try to be less specific in your search term. If your search produces too many hits, try to be more specific. Use the Advanced feature of your search engine to narrow your search. Think of words that uniquely identify what you are looking for. Use as many relevant keywords as possible.

How do search engines vary in their ability to retrieve data, and why should you learn about their advanced features?

- **Repeat your search a week later.** For the best results, return to your search a couple of days or a week later. The same keywords will probably produce additional results. That's because millions of new pages are being added to the Web every day. The ranking of hits can also change depending on how often a link is accessed by Internet users.

Remember, subject directories and search engines vary in their contents, features, selectivity, accuracy, and retrieval technologies. Only through clever cyber searching can you uncover the jewels hidden in the Internet.

Evaluating Web Sources. Most of us using the Web have a tendency to assume that any information turned up by a search engine has somehow been evaluated as part of a valid selection process. Wrong! The truth is that the Internet is rampant with unreliable sites that reside side by side with reputable ones. Anyone with a computer and an Internet connection can publish anything on the Web. Unlike library-based research, information at many sites has not undergone the editing or scrutiny of scholarly publication procedures. The information we read in journals and most reputable magazines is reviewed, authenticated, and evaluated. That's why we have learned to trust these sources as valid and authoritative.

Which four criteria should you consider when judging the value of a Web site?

Information on the Web is much less reliable than data from traditional sources. Wikis, blogs, and discussion forum entries are a case in point. Although they turn up in many Internet searches, they are mostly useless because they are short-lived. They change constantly and may disappear fast, so that your source can't be verified. Many don't provide any references or reveal sources that are either obscure or suspect. Academic researchers prefer lasting, scholarly sources. Many professors will not allow you to cite from Wikipedia, for example, because this collaborative tool and online reference can be edited by almost any contributor and is considered to be unreliable. Moreover, citing from an encyclopedia shows poor research skills. Some Web sites exist to propagandize; others want to sell you something. To use the Web meaningfully, you must scrutinize what you find and check who authored and published it. Here are specific criteria to consider as you examine a site:

- **Currency.** What is the date of the Web page? When was it last updated? Is some of the information obviously out-of-date? If the information is time sensitive and the site has not been updated recently, the site is probably not reliable.
- **Authority.** Who publishes or sponsors this Web page? What makes the presenter an authority? Is information about the author or creator available? Is a contact address available for the presenter? Learn to be skeptical about data and assertions from individuals and organizations whose credentials are not verifiable.
- **Content.** Is the purpose of the page to entertain, inform, convince, or sell? How would you classify this page (e.g., news, personal, advocacy, reference)? Who is the intended audience, based on content, tone, and style? Can you judge the overall value of the content compared with the other resources on this topic? Web presenters with a slanted point of view cannot be counted on for objective data. Be particularly cautious with blogs. They often abound with grandstanding and ranting but lack factual information. Read them side by side with reputable news sources.
- **Accuracy.** Do the facts that are presented seem reliable to you? Do you find errors in spelling, grammar, or usage? Do you see any evidence of bias? Are footnotes provided? If you find numerous errors and if facts are not referenced, you should be alert that the data may be questionable.

PLUGGED IN

Staying on Top of Research Data

In collecting electronic search results, you can easily lose track of Web sites and articles you quoted. To document Web data that may change, as well as to manage all your electronic sources, you need a specific plan for saving the information. At the very least, you will want to create a *working bibliography* or list of *references* in which you record the URL of each electronic source and its access date. Here are techniques that can help you build your list of references and stay in control of your electronic data:

- **Saving sources to disk or portable flash memory device** has advantages, including being able to open the document in a browser even if you don't have access to the Internet. More important, saving sources to disk or memory stick ensures that you will have access to information that may or may not be available later. Using either the **File** and **Save As** or the **File** and **Save Page As** menu command in your browser, you will be able to store the information permanently. Saving images and other kinds of media can be accomplished with your mouse by either right-clicking or command clicking on the item, followed by a command such as **Save Picture As** or **Save Image As** from a pop-up window.
- **Copying and pasting** information you find on the Web into word processing documents is an easy way to save and store it. Remember to copy and paste the URL into the file as well, and record the URL in your working bibliography. If you invest in Adobe's PDF Converter, you can save a Web page or an MS Word document in the portable document format simply by choosing the **Print** command and selecting Adobe PDF in the **Printer** window of the **Print** menu. The URL, access date, and time stamp will be automatically saved on the document. You can keep your PDF documents as electronic files or print out paper copies later.
- **Printing** pages is a handy way to gather and store information. Doing so enables you to have copies of important data that you can annotate or highlight. Make sure the URL prints with the document (usually on the bottom of the page). If not, write it on the page.
- **Bookmarking favorites** is an option within browsers to enable you to record and store the URLs for important sources. The key to using this option is creating folders with names that are relevant and using names for bookmarks that make sense and are not redundant. Pay attention or the browser will provide the information for you, relying on the name the Web page creator gave it. If no name is provided, the browser will default to the URL.
- **E-mailing** documents, URLs, or messages to yourself is another useful strategy. Many databases and online magazines permit you to e-mail information and sometimes the entire article to your account. If you combine the copy-and-paste function with e-mail, you can send yourself nearly any information you find on the Web.

Career Application

Use Google or another search engine that supports Boolean searches to investigate a topic such as carbon footprint or sustainability. Explore the same topic using (a) keywords and (b) Boolean operators. Which method produces more relevant hits? Save two relevant sources from each search using two or more of the strategies presented here. Remember to include the URL for each article. In a memo to your instructor, list the bibliographic information from all four sources and explain briefly which method was more productive.

Documenting Information

In writing business and other reports, you will often build on the ideas and words of others. In Western culture, whenever you "borrow" the ideas of others, you must give credit to your information sources. This is called *documentation*.

LEARNING OBJECTIVE 6

Recognize the purposes and techniques of documentation in business reports, and avoid plagiarism.

Recognizing the Purposes of Documentation

As a careful writer, you should take pains to document report data properly for the following reasons:

Why is it necessary to document data you use to write reports?

- **To strengthen your argument.** Including good data from reputable sources will convince readers of your credibility and the logic of your reasoning.
- **To protect yourself against charges of plagiarism.** Acknowledging your sources keeps you honest. Plagiarism, which is unethical and in some cases illegal, is the act of using others' ideas without proper documentation.
- **To instruct the reader.** Citing references enables readers to pursue a topic further and make use of the information themselves.

Distinguishing Between Academic Documentation and Business Practices

In the academic world, documentation is critical. Especially in the humanities and sciences, students are taught to cite sources by using quotation marks, parenthetical citations, footnotes, and bibliographies. College term papers require full documentation to demonstrate that a student has become familiar with respected sources and can cite them properly in developing an argument. Giving credit to the author is extremely important. Students who plagiarize risk a failing grade in a class and even expulsion from school.

Do business writers follow the same strict documentation standards as academic writers do?

In the business world, however, documentation and authorship are sometimes viewed differently. Business communicators on the job may find that much of what is written does not follow the standards they learned in school. In many instances, individual authorship is unimportant. For example, employees may write for the signature of their bosses. The writer receives no credit. Similarly, teams turn out documents for which none of the team members receive individual credit. Internal business reports, which often include chunks of information from previous reports, also fail to acknowledge sources or give credit. Even information from outside sources may lack proper documentation. However, if facts are questioned, business writers must be able to produce their source materials.

Although both internal and external business reports are not as heavily documented as school assignments or term papers, business communication students are well advised to learn proper documentation methods. In the workplace, stealing the ideas of others and passing them off as one's own can be corrosive to the business because it leads to resentment and worse. One writer suggests that the wronged employee may quit and speak about the unethical behavior, destroying the integrity of the business.[11]

Plagiarism of words or ideas is a serious charge and can lead to loss of a job. Famous historians, several high-level journalists, and even college professors[12] suffered serious consequences for copying from unnamed sources. Your instructor may use a commercial plagiarism detection service such as Turnitin.com, which can cross-reference much of the information on the Web, looking for documents with similar phrasing. The result, an "originality report," provides the instructor with a clear idea of whether you have been accurate and honest. You can avoid charges of plagiarism as well as add clarity to your work by knowing what to document and by developing good research habits.

Spotlight on Communicators

In academic circles, plagiarism remains a serious offense. But many see the Internet as a free-for-all. A Pew Research study found that nearly half of all bloggers have admitted to having appropriated text, images, and other media without attributing them to their original sources. "People are incredibly sloppy," says CRMMastery.com blog author Jim Berkowitz, who insists that he clearly identifies content that he borrows from others. "It's like the Wild West out there," Berkowitz claims.

© iStockphoto.com/Brasil2

When do you have to give credit?

Learning What to Document

When you write reports, especially in college, you are continually dealing with other people's ideas. You are expected to conduct research, synthesize ideas, and build on the work of others. But you are also expected to give proper credit for borrowed material. To avoid plagiarism, you must give credit whenever you use the following:[13]

- Another person's ideas, opinions, examples, or theory
- Any facts, statistics, graphs, and drawings that are not common knowledge
- Quotations of another person's actual spoken or written words
- Paraphrases of another person's spoken or written words

Information that is common knowledge requires no documentation. For example, the statement *The Wall Street Journal is a popular business newspaper* would require no citation. Statements that are not common knowledge, however, must be documented. For example, *Eight of the nation's top-ten fastest-growing large cities (100,000 or more population) since Census 2000 lie in the Western states of Arizona, Nevada, and California* would require a citation because most people do not know this fact. Cite sources for proprietary information such as statistics organized and reported by a newspaper or magazine. You probably know to use citations to document direct quotations, but you must also cite ideas that you summarize in your own words.

Developing Good Research Habits

Report writers who are gathering information have two methods available for recording the information they find. The time-honored manual method of notetaking works well because information is recorded on separate cards, which can then be arranged in the order needed to develop a thesis or argument. Today, however, writers rely heavily on electronic researching. Traditional notetaking methods may seem antiquated and laborious in comparison. Let's explore both methods.

What are the advantages of handwritten note cards?

Manual Notetaking. To make sure you know whose ideas you are using, train yourself to take excellent notes. If possible, know what you intend to find before you begin your research so that you won't waste time on unnecessary notes. Here are some pointers on taking good notes:

- Record all major ideas from various sources on separate note cards.
- Include all publication information (author, date, title, and so forth) along with precise quotations.
- Consider using one card color for direct quotes and a different color for your paraphrases and summaries.
- Put the original source material aside when you are summarizing or paraphrasing.

How can you stay safe from charges of plagiarism when taking notes electronically?

Electronic Notetaking. Instead of recording facts on note cards, savvy researchers today take advantage of electronic tools, as noted in the earlier Plugged In box. Beware, however, of the risk of cutting and pasting your way into plagiarism. Here are some pointers on taking good electronic notes:

- Begin your research by setting up a folder on your hard drive. On the go, you can use a storage device such as a USB flash drive (memory stick) or a rewritable disk (CD-RW) to carry your data.
- Create subfolders for major sections, such as introduction, body, and closing.
- When you find facts on the Web or in electronic databases, highlight the material you want to record, copy it, and paste it into a document in an appropriate folder.
- Be sure to include all publication data.
- As discussed in the section on managing research data, consider archiving on a memory stick or external USB drive those Web pages or articles used in your research in case the data must be verified.

Practicing the Fine Art of Paraphrasing

In writing reports and using the ideas of others, you will probably rely heavily on *paraphrasing*, which means restating an original passage in your own words and in your own style. To do a good job of paraphrasing, follow these steps:

What is paraphrasing, and how can you do it correctly?

1. Read the original material intently to comprehend its full meaning.
2. Write your own version without looking at the original.
3. Avoid repeating the grammatical structure of the original and merely replacing words with synonyms.
4. Reread the original to be sure you covered the main points but did not borrow specific language.

To better understand the difference between plagiarizing and paraphrasing, study the following passages. Notice that the writer of the plagiarized version uses the same grammatical construction as the source and often merely replaces words with synonyms. Even the acceptable version, however, requires a reference to the source author.

Source
While the BlackBerry has become standard armor for executives, a few maverick leaders are taking action to reduce e-mail use. . . . The concern, say academics and management thinkers, is misinterpreted messages, as well as the degree to which e-mail has become a substitute for the nuanced conversations that are critical in the workplace.[14]

What exactly is wrong with the plagiarized version, and what makes the acceptable paraphrase correct and ethical?

Plagiarized version
Although smartphones are standard among business executives, some pioneering bosses are acting to lower e-mail usage. Business professors and management experts are concerned that messages are misinterpreted and e-mail substitutes for nuances in conversations that are crucial on the job (Brady, 2006).

Acceptable paraphrase
E-mail on the go may be the rage in business. However, some executives are rethinking its use, as communication experts warn that e-mail triggers misunderstandings. These specialists believe that e-mail should not replace the more subtle face-to-face interactions needed on the job (Brady, 2006).

Knowing When and How to Quote

On occasion, you will want to use the exact words of a source. But beware of overusing quotations. Documents that contain pages of spliced-together quotations suggest that writers have few ideas of their own. Wise writers and speakers use direct quotations for three purposes only:

What are appropriate uses of direct quotations?

- To provide objective background data and establish the severity of a problem as seen by experts
- To repeat identical phrasing because of its precision, clarity, or aptness
- To duplicate exact wording before criticizing

When you must use a long quotation, try to summarize and introduce it in your own words. Readers want to know the gist of a quotation before they tackle it. For example, to introduce a quotation discussing the shrinking staffs of large companies, you could precede it with your words: *In predicting employment trends, Charles Waller believes the corporation of the future will depend on a small core of full-time employees.* To introduce quotations or paraphrases, use wording such as the following:

According to Waller, ...

Waller argues that . . . .

In his recent study, Waller reported . . . .

Use quotation marks to enclose exact quotations, as shown in the following: *"The current image," says Charles Waller, "of a big glass-and-steel corporate headquarters on landscaped grounds directing a worldwide army of tens of thousands of employees may soon be a thing of the past" (2006, p. 51).*

Using Citation Formats

You can direct readers to your sources with parenthetical notes inserted into the text and with bibliographies. The most common citation formats are those presented by the Modern Language Association (MLA) and the American Psychological Association (APA). Learn more about how to use these formats in Appendix C.

Creating Effective Visual Aids

LEARNING OBJECTIVE 7
Create meaningful and interesting graphics; display numeric information in the appropriate graphic form; and skillfully generate, use, and convert data to visual aids.

What purpose should graphics serve to be effective?

After collecting and interpreting information, you need to consider how best to present it. If your report contains complex data and numbers, you may want to consider graphics such as tables and charts. These graphics clarify data, create visual interest, and make numerical data meaningful. By simplifying complex ideas and emphasizing key data, well-constructed graphics make key information easier to remember. However, the same data can be shown in many forms; for example, in a chart, table, or graph. That's why you need to know how to match the appropriate graphic with your objective and how to incorporate it into your report.

Matching Graphics and Objectives

In developing the best graphics, you must decide what data you want to highlight and which graphics are most appropriate to your objectives. Tables? Bar charts? Pie charts? Line charts? Surface charts? Flowcharts? Organization charts? Pictures? Figure 11.11 summarizes appropriate uses for each type of graphic. The following sections discuss each type in more detail.

Tables. Probably the most frequently used graphic in reports is the table. Because a table presents quantitative or verbal information in systematic columns and rows, it can clarify large quantities of data in small spaces. The disadvantage is that tables do not readily display

FIGURE 11.11 **Matching Graphics to Objectives**

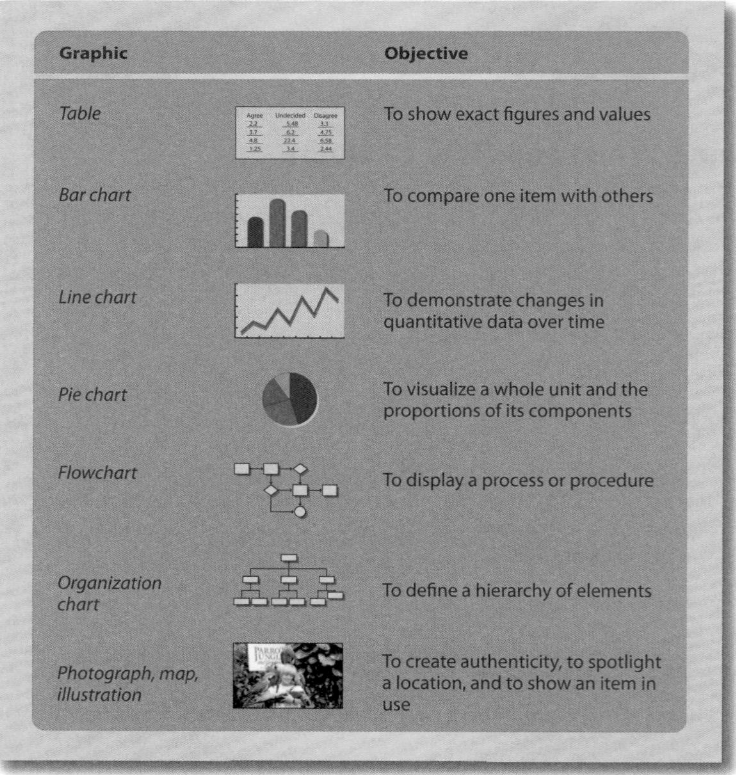

Graphic	Objective
Table	To show exact figures and values
Bar chart	To compare one item with others
Line chart	To demonstrate changes in quantitative data over time
Pie chart	To visualize a whole unit and the proportions of its components
Flowchart	To display a process or procedure
Organization chart	To define a hierarchy of elements
Photograph, map, illustration	To create authenticity, to spotlight a location, and to show an item in use

FIGURE 11.12 Table Summarizing Precise Data

Figure 1 MPM ENTERTAINMENT COMPANY Income by Division (in millions of dollars)				
	Theme Parks	**Motion Pictures**	**DVDs & Videos**	**Total**
2008	$15.8	$39.3	$11.2	$66.3
2009	18.1	17.5	15.3	50.9
2010	23.8	21.1	22.7	67.6
2011	32.2	22.0	24.3	78.5
2012 (projected)	35.1	21.0	26.1	82.2

Source: *Industry Profiles* (New York: DataPro, 2011) 225.

trends. You may have made rough tables to help you organize the raw data collected from questionnaires or interviews. In preparing tables for your readers or listeners, however, you need to pay more attention to clarity and emphasis. Here are tips for making good tables, one of which is provided in Figure 11.12:

What are the relative advantages of tables as opposed to charts and graphs, and when would tables be used?

- Place titles and labels at the top of the table.
- Arrange items in a logical order (alphabetical, chronological, geographical, highest to lowest), depending on what you need to emphasize.
- Provide clear headings for the rows and columns.
- Identify the units in which figures are given (percentages, dollars, units per worker hour) in the table title, in the column or row heading, with the first item in a column, or in a note at the bottom.
- Use *N/A* (*not available*) for missing data.
- Make long tables easier to read by shading alternate lines or by leaving a blank line after groups of five.
- Place tables as close as possible to the place where they are mentioned in the text.

How do we determine which graphic is appropriate?

Figure 11.11 shows the purposes of various graphics. Tables, as illustrated in Figure 11.12, are especially suitable for illustrating exact figures in systematic rows and columns. The table in our figure is particularly useful because it presents data about the MPM Entertainment Company over several years, making it easy to compare several divisions. Figures 11.13 through 11.16 highlight some of the data shown in the MPM Entertainment Company table, illustrating vertical, horizontal, grouped, and segmented 100 percent bar charts, each of which creates a unique effect.

Bar Charts. Although they lack the precision of tables, bar charts enable you to make emphatic visual comparisons by using horizontal or vertical bars of varying lengths. Bar charts are useful for comparing related items, illustrating changes in data over time, and showing segments as a part of the whole. Note how the varied bar charts present information in differing ways.

Many techniques for constructing tables also hold true for bar charts. Here are a few additional tips:

- Keep the length and width of each bar and segment proportional.
- Include a total figure in the middle of the bar or at its end if the figure helps the reader and does not clutter the chart.
- Start dollar or percentage amounts at zero.
- Place the first bar at some distance (usually half the amount of space between bars) from the *y* axis.
- Avoid showing too much information, thus avoiding clutter and confusion.
- Place each bar chart as close as possible to the place where it is mentioned in the text.

FIGURE 11.13 Vertical Bar Chart

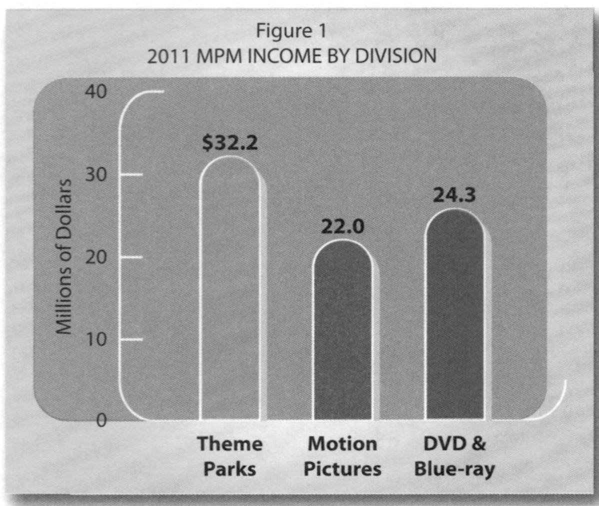

Source: *Industry Profiles*(New York: DataPro, 2011), 225.

FIGURE 11.14 Horizontal Bar Chart

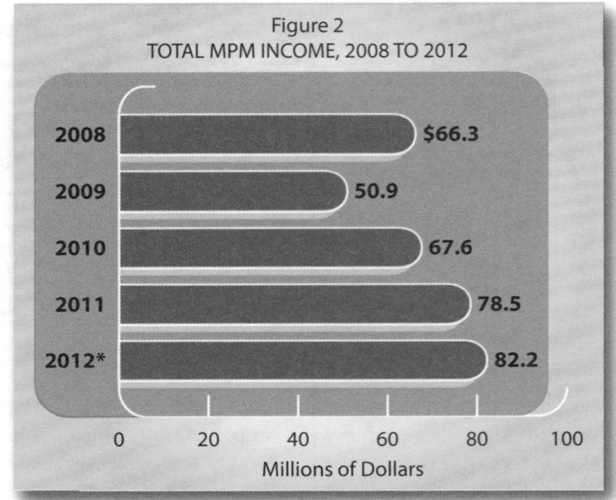

*Projected
Source: *Industry Profiles*(New York: DataPro, 2011), 225.

FIGURE 11.15 Grouped Bar Chart

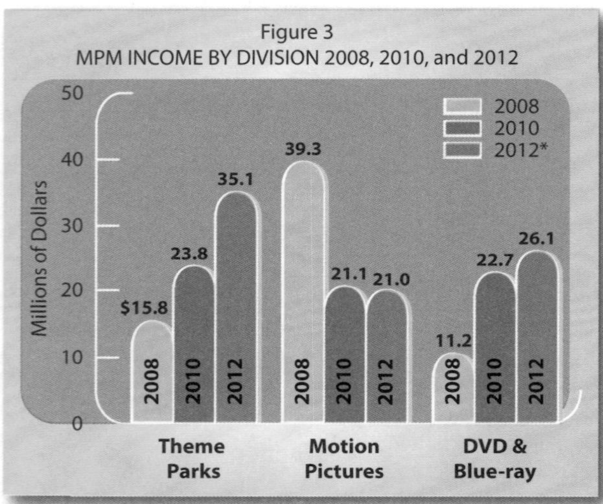

*Projected
Source: *Industry Profiles*

FIGURE 11.16 Segmented 100 Percent Bar Chart

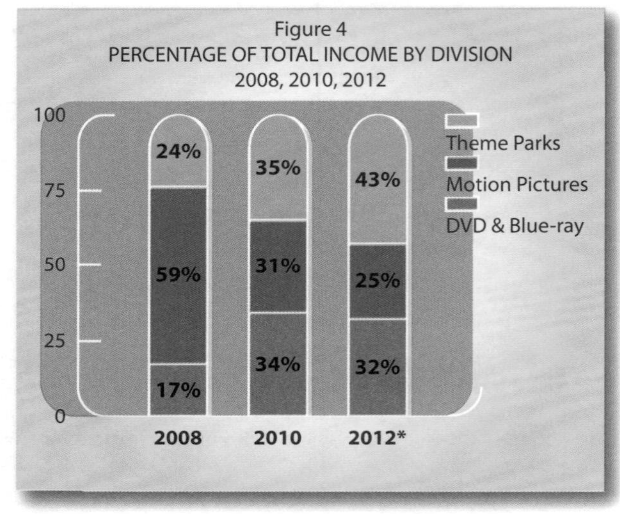

*Projected
Source: *Industry Profiles*

What is the purpose of line charts?

Line Charts. The major advantage of line charts is that they show changes over time, thus indicating trends. The vertical axis is typically the dependent variable; and the horizontal axis, the independent one. Simple line charts (Figure 11.17) show just one variable. Multiple line charts compare items, such as two or more data sets, using the same variable (Figure 11.18). Segmented line charts (Figure 11.19), also called surface charts, illustrate how the components of a whole change over time. To prepare a line chart, remember these tips:

- Begin with a grid divided into squares.
- Arrange the time component (usually years) horizontally across the bottom; arrange values for the other variable vertically.
- Draw small dots at the intersections to indicate each value at a given year.
- Connect the dots and add color if desired.

FIGURE 11.17 Simple Line Chart

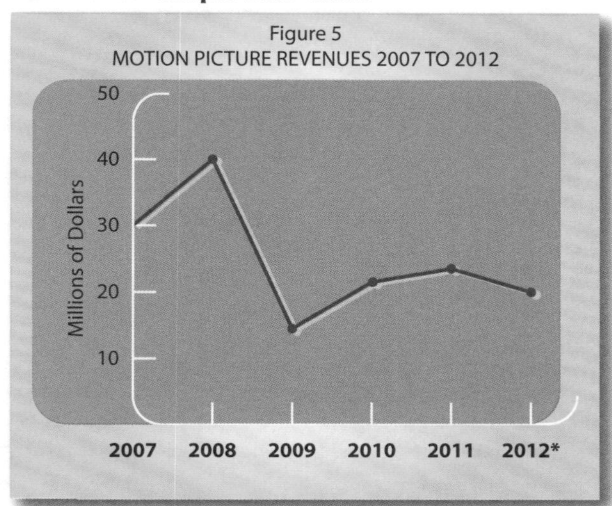

*Projected
Source: *Industry Profiles*

FIGURE 11.18 Multiple Line Chart

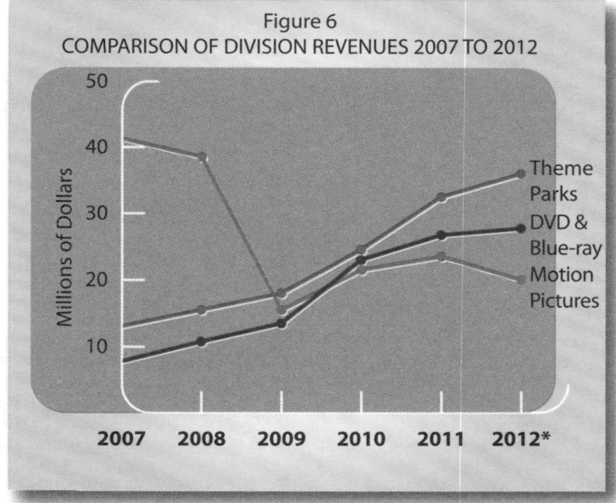

*Projected
Source: *Industry Profiles*

FIGURE 11.19 Segmented Line (Area) Chart

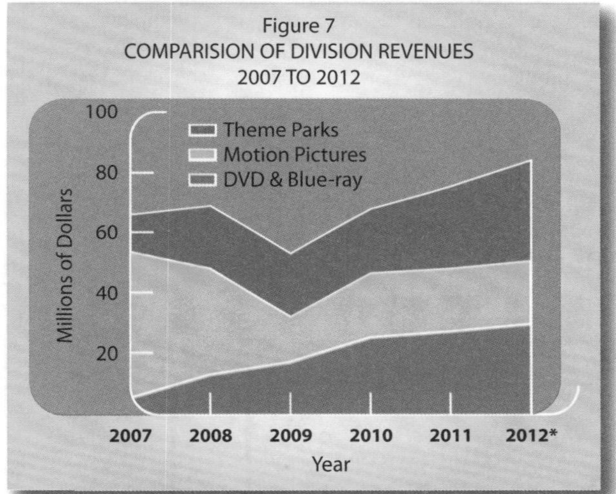

*Projected
Source: *Industry Profiles*

FIGURE 11.20 Pie Chart

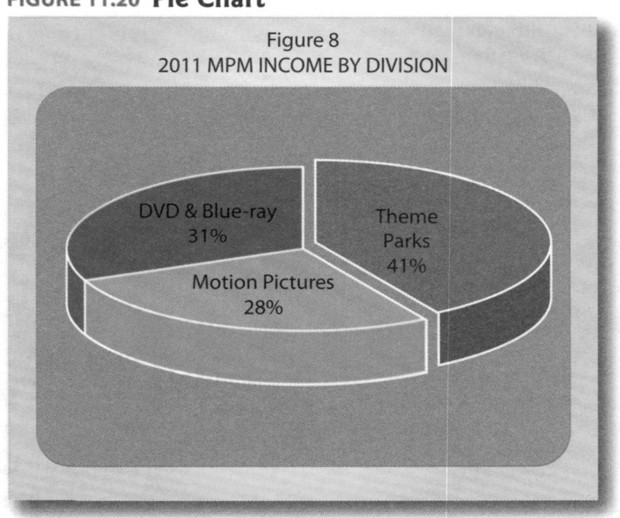

Source: *Industry Profiles*

- To prepare a segmented (surface) chart, plot the first value (say, DVD and Blu-ray disc income) across the bottom; add the next item (say, motion picture income) to the first figures for every increment; for the third item (say, theme park income), add its value to the total for the first two items. The top line indicates the total of the three values.

When are pie charts most suitable and useful?

Pie Charts. Pie charts, or circle graphs, enable readers to see a whole and the proportion of its components, or wedges. Although less flexible than bar or line charts, pie charts are useful for showing percentages, as Figure 11.20 illustrates. They are very effective for lay, or nonexpert, audiences. Notice that a wedge can be "exploded," or popped out, for special emphasis, as seen in Figure 11.20. MS Excel and other spreadsheet programs provide a selection of three-dimensional pie charts. For the most effective pie charts, follow these suggestions:

- Make the biggest wedge appear first. Computer spreadsheet programs correctly assign the biggest wedge first (beginning at the 12 o'clock position) and arrange the others in order of decreasing size as long as you list the data representing each wedge on the spreadsheet in descending order.
- Include, if possible, the actual percentage or absolute value for each wedge.
- Use four to six segments for best results; if necessary, group small portions into a wedge called *Other.*
- Draw radii from the center.
- Distinguish wedges with color, shading, or cross-hatching.
- Keep all the labels horizontal.

Flowcharts. Procedures are simplified and clarified by diagramming them in a flowchart, as shown in Figure 11.21. Whether you need to describe the procedure for handling a customer's purchase, highlight steps in solving a problem, or display a problem with a process, flowcharts help the reader visualize the process. Traditional flowcharts use the following symbols:

- Ovals to designate the beginning and end of a process
- Diamonds to designate decision points
- Rectangles to represent major activities or steps

What purpose do flowcharts and organization charts serve, and when are they most appropriate?

Organization Charts. Many large organizations are so complex that they need charts to show the chain of command, from the boss down to the line managers and employees. Organization charts provide such information as who reports to whom, how many subordinates work for each manager (the span of control), and what channels of official communication

FIGURE 11.21 **Flowchart**

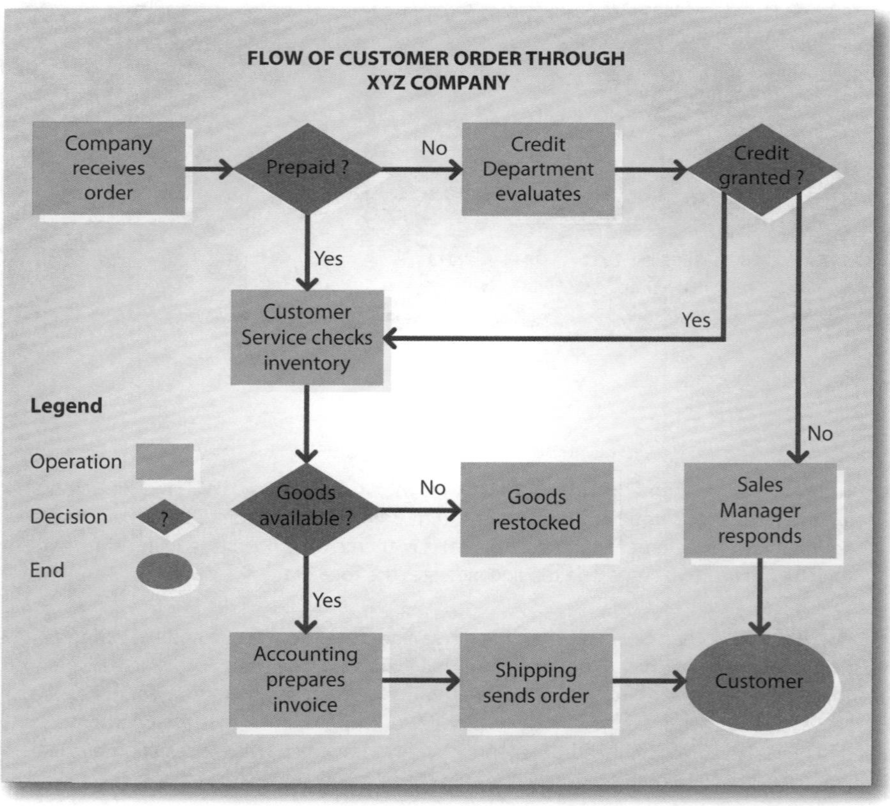

exist. These charts may illustrate a company's structure—for example, by function, customer, or product. They may also be organized by the work being performed in each job or by the hierarchy of decision making.

Photographs, Maps, and Illustrations. Some business reports include photographs, maps, and illustrations to serve specific purposes. Photos, for example, add authenticity and provide a visual record. An environmental engineer may use photos to document hazardous waste sites. Maps enable report writers to depict activities or concentrations geographically, such as dots indicating sales reps in states across the country. Illustrations and diagrams are useful in indicating how an object looks or operates. A drawing showing the parts of a printer with labels describing their functions, for example, is more instructive than a photograph or verbal description. With today's computer technology, photographs, maps, and illustrations can be scanned directly into business reports, or accessed through hyperlinks within electronically delivered documents.

When are photographs, maps, and illustrations suitable enhancements for reports?

Incorporating Graphics in Reports

Used appropriately, graphics make reports more interesting and easier to understand. In putting graphics into your reports, follow these suggestions for best effects:

How can you ensure that you use graphics accurately and ethically?

- **Evaluate the audience.** Consider the reader, the content, your schedule, and your budget. Graphics take time and can be costly to print in color, so think carefully before deciding

ETHICAL INSIGHT

Making Ethical Charts and Graphics

Business communicators must present graphical data in the same ethical, honest manner required for all other messages. Remember that the information shown in your charts and graphics will be used to inform others or help them make decisions. If this information is not represented accurately, the reader will be incorrectly informed; any decisions based on the data are likely to be faulty. And mistakes in interpreting such information may have serious and long-lasting consequences.

Chart data can be distorted in many ways. Figure 1 shows advertising expenses displayed on an appropriate scale. Figure 2 shows the same information, but the horizontal scale, from 2007 to 2012, has been lengthened. Notice that the data have not changed, but the increases and decreases are smoothed out, so changes in expenses appear to be slight. In Figure 3 the vertical scale is taller and the horizontal scale is shortened, resulting in what appear to be sharp increases and decreases in expenses.

To avoid misrepresenting data, keep the following pointers in mind when designing your graphics:

- Use an appropriate type of chart or graphic for the message you wish to convey.
- Design the chart so that it focuses on the appropriate information.
- Include all relevant or important data; don't arbitrarily leave out necessary information.
- Don't hide critical information by including too much data in one graphic.
- Use appropriate scales with equal intervals for the data you present.

Career Application

Locate one or two graphics in a newspaper, magazine article, or annual report. Analyze the strengths and weaknesses of each graphic. Is the information presented accurately? Select a bar or line chart. Sketch the same chart but change the vertical or horizontal scales on the graphic. How does the message of the chart change?

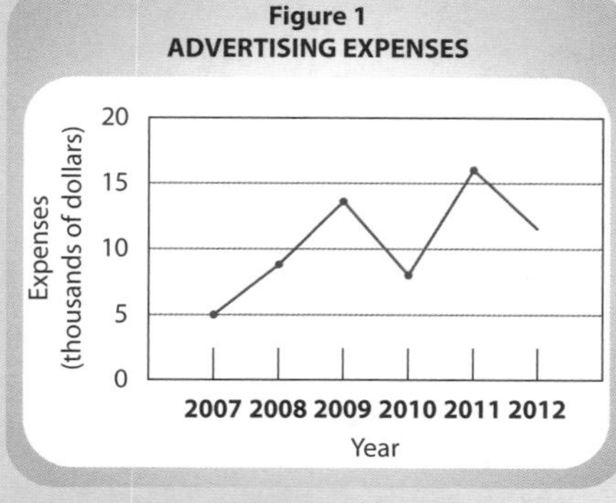

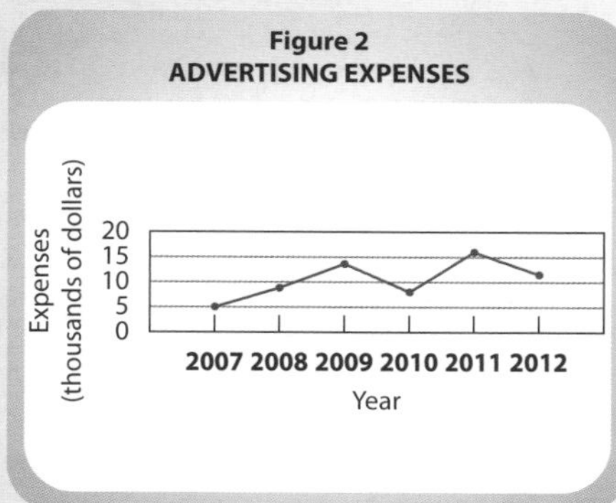

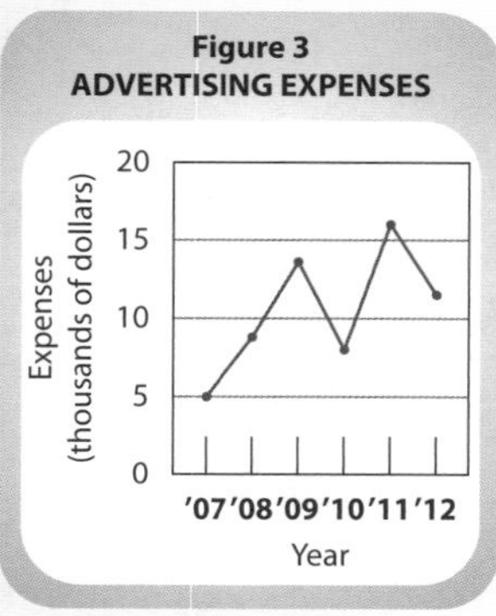

Zooming In — YOUR TURN

Applying Your Skills at Pet Airways

Although Pet Airways is a start-up and the carrier's long-term survival will depend on the viability of its business model, its current prospects seem bright. With average one-way ticket prices at $250, the pet airline is booked two months in advance. Serving nine cities today, the company is planning to expand in the next two years to new routes carrying its furry pawsengers between as many as 25 U.S. cities. In the future Pet Airways is also planning to accommodate creatures other than cats and dogs—for example, birds and reptiles.

To do good and create media buzz, Pet Airways works with pet rescue organizations to save animals from euthanasia. The airline occasionally flies discarded animals to new homes. Recently, the carrier took 35 saved pets from Kern County, California, and 29 tiny pooches from Los Angeles to Colorado, where they were greeted by their new owners. This Los Angeles Chihuahua rescue drew the attention of the George Lopez show, whose host is a dog lover.

Your Task

As writing and research consultants, you and several of your colleagues have been asked by Dan and Alysa to help with a persuasive proposal that outlines the strategies and predicts the success of the pending expansion to new cities and, potentially, to other types of pets. You have been assigned the task of researching the prospects of Pet Airways and gathering general market information about pet relocation. Using both electronic databases and the Web, put together a short report that lists articles that will be useful for the report writers. Add a short summary of your findings as an introduction. Submit your results in a memo or e-mail message to your instructor.

© Benassi/Splash News/Newscom

Want to do well on tests and excel in your course? Go to **www.meguffey.com** for helpful interactive resources.

▸ **Review the Chapter 11 PowerPoint slides to prepare for the first quiz.**

how many graphics to use. Six charts in an internal report to an executive may seem like overkill; however, in a long technical report to outsiders, six may be too few.

- **Use restraint.** Don't overuse color or decorations. Although color can effectively distinguish bars or segments in charts, too much color can be distracting and confusing. Remember, too, that colors themselves sometimes convey meaning: reds suggest deficits or negative values; blues suggest calmness and authority; and yellow may suggest warning.
- **Be accurate and ethical.** Double-check all graphics for accuracy of figures and calculations. Be certain that your visuals aren't misleading—either accidentally or intentionally. Manipulation of a chart scale can make trends look steeper and more dramatic than they really are. Moreover, be sure to cite sources when you use someone else's facts. The accompanying Ethical Insights box discusses in more detail how to make ethical charts and graphs.

Why should graphics be accompanied by introductory statements or captions?

- **Introduce a graph meaningfully.** Refer to every graphic in the text, and place the graphic close to the point where it is mentioned. Most important, though, help the reader understand the significance of the graphic. You can do this by telling your audience what to look for or by summarizing the main point of the graphic. Don't assume the reader will automatically draw the same conclusions you reached from a set of data. Instead of saying, *The findings are shown in Figure 3,* tell the reader what to look for: *Two thirds of the responding employees, as shown in Figure 3, favor a flextime schedule.* The best introductions for graphics interpret them for readers.
- **Choose an appropriate caption or title style.** Like reports, graphics may use "talking" titles or generic, descriptive titles. Talking titles are more persuasive; they tell the reader what to think. Descriptive titles describe the facts more objectively.

Talking Title	Descriptive Title
Rising Workplace Drug Testing Unfair and Inaccurate	Workplace Drug Testing Up 277 Percent
Rising Random Drug Testing Unfair and Often Inaccurate	Workplace Drug Testing up 277 Percent Since 1987

Summary of Learning Objectives

1 **Describe basic features of business reports, including functions, strategies (indirect or direct), writing style, and formats.** Business reports generally function either as informational reports (without analysis or recommendations) or as analytical reports (with analysis, conclusions, and possibly recommendations). Reports organized directly present the purpose and conclusions immediately. This strategy is appropriate when the audience is supportive and familiar with the topic. Reports organized indirectly provide the conclusions and recommendations last. This strategy is helpful when the audience is unfamiliar with the problem or may be disappointed or hostile. Reports written in a formal style use third-person constructions (*the researcher* instead of *I*), avoid contractions (*do not* instead of *don't*), and may include passive-voice verbs (*the findings were analyzed*). Reports written informally use first-person constructions, contractions, shorter sentences, familiar words, and active-voice verbs. Reports may be formatted as letters, memos, e-mails, manuscripts, prepared forms, or electronic slides.

2 **Apply the 3-x-3 writing process to business reports to create well-organized documents that show a firm grasp of audience and purpose.** Report writers begin by analyzing a problem and writing a problem statement, which may include the scope, significance, and limitations of the project. Writers then analyze the audience and define major issues. They prepare a work plan, including a tentative outline and work schedule. They collect, organize, interpret, and illustrate their data. Then they compose the first draft. Finally, they revise (often many times), proofread, and evaluate.

3 **Find, evaluate, and use print and electronic secondary sources.** Secondary data may be located by searching for books, periodicals, and newspapers through print or electronic indexes. Writers can look for information using electronic databases such as ABI/INFORM and LexisNexis. They may also find information on the Internet, but searching for it requires a knowledge of search tools and techniques. Popular search tools include Google, Yahoo, and Bing. Once found, however, information obtained on the Internet should be scrutinized for currency, authority, content, and accuracy.

4 **Understand how to generate and use primary data while avoiding researcher bias.** Researchers generate firsthand, primary data through surveys (in-person, print, and online), interviews, observation, and experimentation. Surveys are most economical and efficient for gathering information from large groups of people. Interviews are useful when working with experts in a field. Firsthand observation can produce rich data, but they must be objective. Experimentation produces data suggesting causes and effects. Valid experiments require sophisticated research designs and careful attention to matching the experimental and control groups.

5 **Comprehend fast-changing communication technology: the Web, electronic databases, and other resources for business writers and researchers.** The World Wide Web is used every day by individuals and organizations for business and pleasure. A vast resource, the Web offers a wealth of varied and often uneven secondary data. It is a complex network of information from private citizens, businesses, and other institutions that form a global virtual community. At the same time, these users also announce and advertise their local presence. Business communicators must be aware that information online changes rapidly and is not considered as lasting as scholarly sources. Making the most of Web sites means being a critical consumer of the information retrieved and understanding the function of Web search tools. Honest researchers keep track of the retrieved data and incorporate them ethically into their documents.

6 **Recognize the purposes and techniques of documentation in business reports, and avoid plagiarism.** Documentation means giving credit to information sources. Careful writers document data to strengthen an argument, protect against charges of plagiarism, and instruct readers. Although documentation is less strict in business reports than in academic reports, business writers should learn proper techniques to be able to verify their sources and

Are you ready? Get more practice at **www.meguffey.com**

to avoid charges of plagiarism. Report writers should document others' ideas, facts that are not common knowledge, quotations, and paraphrases. Good notetaking, either manual or electronic, enables writers to give accurate credit to sources. Paraphrasing involves putting another's ideas into one's own words. Quotations may be used to provide objective background data, to repeat memorable phrasing, and to duplicate exact wording before criticizing.

7 Create meaningful and interesting graphics; display numeric information in the appropriate graphic form; and skillfully generate, use, and convert data to visual aids. Good graphics improve reports by clarifying, simplifying, and emphasizing data. Tables organize precise data into rows and columns. Bar and line charts enable data to be compared visually. Line charts are especially helpful in showing changes over time. Pie charts show a whole and the proportion of its components. Organization charts, pictures, maps, and illustrations serve specific purposes. In choosing or crafting graphics, effective communicators evaluate their audience, purpose, topic, and budget to determine the number and kind of graphics. They write "talking" titles (telling readers what to think about the graphic) or descriptive titles (summarizing the topic objectively). Finally, they work carefully to avoid distorting visual aids.

Chapter Review

1. What are the main purposes of business reports? (Obj. 1)
2. Describe the writing style of typical business reports. (Obj. 1)
3. Name five common report formats. (Obj. 1)
4. List the seven steps in the report-writing process. (Obj. 2)
5. What is a statement of purpose, and what function does it serve? (Obj. 2)
6. Compare primary data and secondary data. Give an original example of each. (Objs. 3, 4)
7. Name at least two of the top four business databases and identify their chief strengths. (Objs. 3, 5)
8. List four major sources of primary information. (Obj. 4)
9. How can you ensure that your survey will be effective and appeal to as many respondents as possible? (Obj. 4)
10. Why are your professors likely to discourage your use of Wikipedia, blogs, and many other sources found on the Web as sources in your reports? (Obj. 5)
11. Can any single search engine index all Web pages? How can you optimize your search of Web sources? (Obj. 5)
12. Describe what documentation is and why it is necessary in reports. (Obj. 6)
13. In what way is documentation of sources different in colleges and universities than in business? (Obj. 6)
14. Briefly compare the advantages and disadvantages of illustrating data with charts (bar and line) versus tables. (Obj. 7)
15. Name five techniques you can use to ensure that visual aids do not distort graphic information. (Obj. 7)

Critical Thinking

1. Howard Schultz, Starbucks president and CEO, has been described as a "classic entrepreneur: optimistic, relentless, mercurial, and eager to prove people wrong." Before Starbucks' latest stumbles, Schultz successfully followed his gut instinct, not established management practices. Unlike other executives, until recently he was not interested in cost control, advertising, and customer research. "I despise research," he said. "I think it's a crutch. But people smarter than me pushed me in this direction, and I've gone along." Starbucks continues to be the most followed company on Facebook. It made $300 million in profit last year.[15] What do you think Howard Schultz meant when he called consumer research a "crutch"? Can you explain why the corporate maverick hates it so much? (Obj. 4)
2. Why must report writers anticipate their audiences and issues? (Obj. 2)
3. Is information obtained on the Web as reliable as information obtained from journals, newspapers, and magazines? (Obj. 5)
4. Some people say that business reports never contain footnotes. If you were writing your first report for a business and you did considerable research, what would you do about documenting your sources? (Obj. 6)
5. **Ethical Issue:** You are conducting one-hour-long interviews with high-level banking executives using a questionnaire featuring open-ended questions (qualitative survey) for a market research firm. You receive $75 per completed interview when you deliver legible notes. You tape the talks for accuracy, but then you transcribe the conversations, and you are not required to hand in the tapes. Busy executives are reluctant to sit down with you; you struggle to find the ten top bankers you were contracted to interview. The other interviewer hired for this study tells you that she invented at least two interviews and suggests you do the same. Should you follow her example? Should you not follow her example but stay silent, or should you tell the supervisor that your colleague has been falsifying survey results? (Obj. 4)

Activities

11.1 Report Functions, Strategies, and Formats (Obj. 1)

Your Task. For the following reports, (1) name the report's primary function (informational or analytical), (2) recommend a direct or indirect strategy of development, and (3) select a report format (memo or e-mail, letter, or manuscript).

a. A proposal from a group of citizens to their county government asking for funds to silence the train whistles and create a "quiet zone" around private residences near above-ground railroad tracks.
b. A yardstick report in the leisure industry put together by consultants who compare the potential of a future theme park at three different sites.
c. A report submitted by a sales rep to her manager describing her attendance at a marathon pre-race exhibition, including the reactions of runners to a new low-carbohydrate energy drink.
d. A feasibility report from an administrative assistant to his boss exploring the savings from buying aftermarket ink-jet cartridges as opposed to the original refills recommended by the manufacturer.
e. A progress report from a location manager to a Hollywood production company describing safety, fire, and environmental precautions taken for the shooting of a stunt involving blowing up a power boat in the Downtown Long Beach marina.
f. A report from a national shipping company telling state authorities how it has improved its safety program so that its trucks now comply with state regulations. The report describes but doesn't interpret the program.
g. A report prepared by an outside consultant examining whether a sports franchise should refurbish its stadium or look to relocate to another city.

11.2 Collaborative Project: Report Portfolio (Obj. 1)

Team

Your Task. In teams of three or four, collect several corporate annual reports. For each report identify and discuss the following characteristics:

a. Function (informational or analytical)
b. Strategy (primarily direct or indirect)
c. Writing style (formal or informal)
d. Format (memo or e-mail, letter, manuscript, preprinted form, digital)
e. Effectiveness (clarity, accuracy, expression)

In an informational memo report to your instructor, describe your findings.

11.3 Data Forms and Questions (Obj. 3)

Your Task. In conducting research for the following reports, name at least one form of data you will need and questions you should ask to determine whether that set of data is appropriate (see Figure 11.6).

a. A report about the suitability of a university campus–adjacent location for a low-cost health food store and snack bar.
b. A report on business attire in banking that you must submit to your company's executives, who want to issue a formal professional dress code on the job.
c. A report by the Center for Science in the Public Interest investigating the nutritional value of products advertised during afternoon and Saturday kids' television shows[16]
d. A report by the Agricultural Research Service of the U.S. Department of Agriculture on the nutritional value of oats.
e. A report examining the effectiveness of ethics codes in American businesses.

11.4 Problem, Purpose, and Scope Statements (Obj. 2)

Your Task. The following situations require reports. For each situation write (1) a concise problem question, (2) a simple statement of purpose, and (3) a scope statement with limitations if appropriate.

a. The use of handheld cell phones while driving has been banned in many U.S. states and in a number of countries around the world. The penalties vary in severity and enforcement. Most jurisdictions allow hands-free units, although recent studies have cast suspicion on the effectiveness of hands-free kits in preventing accidents. It seems that drivers are distracted when making emotional phone calls regardless of the device used. A Minnesota state government task force is exploring the connection between cell phone use and accident rates.
b. Car buyers regularly complain in postpurchase surveys about the persuasive tactics of the so-called closers (salespeople trained to finalize the deal). Your car dealership wishes to improve customer satisfaction in the stressful price negotiation process.
c. Last winter a severe ice storm damaged well over 50 percent of the pecan trees lining the main street in the small town of Ardmore. The local university's experts believe that well over 70 percent of the damaged trees will die in the next two years and that this variety is not the best one for providing shade (one of the major goals behind planting them ten years ago).
d. New York enacted strict regulations banning trans fats in restaurant fare. Food processors nationwide are wondering if they need to make changes before being forced to switch to nonhydrogenated fats by law. Food and Drug Administration regulations have already changed the definitions of common terms such as *fresh, fat free, low in cholesterol,* and *light*. The Thin Crust Bakery worries that it may have to change its production process and rewrite all its package labels. Thin Crust doesn't know whether to hire a laboratory or a consultant for this project.
e. Customers placing telephone orders for outdoor gear with REI typically order only one or two items. The company wonders whether it can train telephone service reps to motivate customers to increase the number of items ordered per call.

11.5 Problem and Purpose Statements (Obj. 2)

Your Task. Identify a problem in your current job or a previous job, such as inadequate use of technology, inefficient procedures, spotty customer service, poor product quality, low morale, or a personnel problem. Assume your boss agrees with your criticism and asks you to prepare a report. Write (a) a two- or three-sentence statement describing the problem, (b) a problem question, and (c) a simple statement of purpose for your report.

11.6 Plagiarism, Paraphrasing, and Citing Sources (Obj. 6)

One of the biggest problems of student writers is paraphrasing secondary sources correctly to avoid plagiarism.

Your Task. For each of the following, read the original passage. Analyze the paraphrased version. List the weaknesses in relation to what you have learned about plagiarism and the use of references. Then write an improved version.

a. **Original Passage**
Developing casual online game titles can be much less risky than trying to create a game that runs on a console such as an Xbox.

Casual games typically cost less than $200,000 to produce, and production cycles are only six months to a year. There's no shelf space, packaging, or CD production to pay for. Best of all, there's more room for innovation.[17]

Paraphrased Passage
The development of casual online games offers less risk than creating games running on Xbox and other consoles. Usually, casual games are cheaper, costing under $200,000 to create and six to twelve months to produce. Developers save on shelf space, packaging, and CD production too. Moreover, they have more freedom to innovate.

b. **Original Passage**
The collapse in the cost of computing has made cellular communication economically viable. Worldwide, one in two new phone subscriptions is cellular. The digital revolution in telephony is most advanced in poorer countries because they have been able to skip the outdated technological step of relying on landlines.

Paraphrased Passage
The drop in computing costs now makes cellular communication affordable around the world. In fact, one out of every two new phones is cellular. The digital revolution in cellular telephones is developing faster in poorer countries because they could skip the outdated technological process of using landlines (Henderson 44).

c. **Original Passage**
Search site Yahoo kept world news prominent on its front page because users feel secure knowing that it is easily accessible, even if they don't often click it. Conspicuous placement also went to entertainment, which draws heavy traffic from people seeking a diversion at work. By contrast, seemingly work-related content such as finance gets ample use in the evening when people pay bills and manage personal portfolios.[18]

Paraphrased Passage
Search giant Yahoo kept news prominent on its portal since its customers feel good knowing it is there, even though they don't read it much. Such noticeable placement was also used for entertainment news that attracts heavy traffic from users searching for a distraction at work. As opposed to that, what may seem work related, such as finance, is much visited at night when people pay their bills and manage their portfolios.

d. **Original Passage**
The bid to offer more fashionable apparel was a bid for Target's business. With designer names and fashion flair, Target has made customers comfortable buying dental floss and flirty dresses under one giant, uber-hip roof. . . . Wal-Mart found out that though its edgier Metro7 line for women sold well in several hundred stores, the line's skinny jeans and other higher-style fashions bombed when the company expanded it to 3,000 stores.[19]

Paraphrased Passage
By offering more fashionable clothes, Wal-Mart was bidding for Target's business. With fashion flair and designer names, Target had attracted customers who would buy dental floss and sexy dresses under one roof. Wal-Mart learned that its hip Metro7 line for women sold well in hundreds of stores, but the skinny jeans and higher-style clothes misfired when the retailer took them to 3,000 of its stores.

11.7 Factoring and Outlining a Problem (Obj. 2)

Virgin America has asked your company, Connections International, to prepare a proposal for a training school for tour operators. Virgin America wants to know whether Burbank would be a good spot for its school. Burbank interests Virgin America, but only if nearby entertainment facilities can be used for tour training. The airline also needs an advisory committee consisting, if possible, of representatives of the travel community and perhaps executives of other major airlines. The real problem is how to motivate these people to cooperate with Virgin America.

You have heard that NBC Studios in Burbank offers training seminars, guest speakers, and other resources for tour operators. You wonder whether Magic Mountain in Valencia would also be willing to cooperate with the proposed school. Moreover, you remember that Griffith Park is nearby and might make a good tour training spot. Before Virgin America will settle on Burbank as its choice, it wants to know if access to air travel is adequate. Virgin America's management team is also concerned about available school building space. Moreover, the carrier wants to know whether city officials in Burbank would be receptive to this tour training school proposal.

Your Task. To guide your thinking and research, factor this problem into an outline with several areas to investigate. Further divide the problem into subproblems, phrasing each entry as a question. For example, *Should the Virgin America tour training program be located in Burbank?* (See the work plan model in Figure 11.5.)

11.8 Developing a Work Plan (Obj. 2)

Any long report project requires a structured work plan.

Your Task. Select a report topic from those listed at the ends of Chapters 12 and 13 and at **www.meguffey.com**. For that report prepare a work plan that includes the following:

a. Statement of the problem
b. Expanded statement of purpose (including scope, limitations, and significance)
c. Research strategy to answer the questions
d. Tentative outline of key questions to answer
e. Work schedule (with projected completion dates)

11.9 Using Secondary Sources (Obj. 3)

Web

Secondary sources can provide quite different information depending on your mode of inquiry.

Your Task. Pick a business-related subject you want to know more about, and run it through a search engine such as Google. Compare your results with Dogpile, a metasearch site. Write a short memo or e-mail message to your instructor explaining the differences in the search results. In your message describe what you have learned about the advantages and disadvantages of each search tool.

11.10 Creating an Online Survey With SurveyMonkey or Zoomerang (Obj. 4)

Team Web

Your University Business Club (UBC) is abuzz about a Sodexo study that surveyed American college students about their favorite comfort foods. Food service provider Sodexo tracks flavor trends, holds taste test focus groups with students, and consults with top-notch chefs to identify students' favorite college foods. The current top three items are apricot-glazed turkey, meatloaf with frizzle-dried onions, and pho, a wholesome Vietnamese beef and rice noodle soup. You read the Sodexo press release and decide to use this quotation in your report:

> "Comfort food is trendy for students because familiar favorites can alleviate stress linked to studying and being away from

home," said Tom Post, Sodexo president of campus services. "The biggest change we're seeing is that students are expanding the category of feel-good foods to include comfort world cuisine, such as a Mexican stew or a Vietnamese noodle soup and they are more open to vegetarian dishes with a flair."[20]

UBC wants to advocate for a new small student-run restaurant in the campus food court. Your club colleagues have chosen you to create an online survey to poll fellow students, staff, and faculty about their preferences. You hope to generate data that will support the feasibility of the eatery.

The two main providers of online survey software, SurveyMonkey and Zoomerang, make creating questionnaires fast, fun, and easy. Depending on their research needs and the survey features they desire, businesses subscribe to the two survey creation services for fees ranging from $17 to $20 (SurveyMonkey) or $20 to $150 (Zoomerang) per month. As long as you sign up for the free no-frills basic plans, you can create brief online questionnaires and e-mail the links to your targeted respondents. The programs analyze and display the results for you—at no charge.

Your Task. In pairs or teams of three, design a questionnaire to survey students on your campus about comfort food options in the campus cafeteria. Visit **http://www.surveymonkey.com** or **http://www.zoomerang.com**, and sign up for the basic plan. You may also want to view the Sodexo Web site at **http://www.sodexousa.com**. After creating the online survey, e-mail the survey link to as many members of the campus community as possible. Interpret the results. As a team, write a memo to the campus food services advocating for the top-scoring national or regional comfort food type.

Your instructor may ask you to complete this activity as a report or proposal assignment after you study Chapter 12. If so, write a feasibility report or proposal for the campus food services and support your advocacy with the survey results.

11.11 Researching Secondary Sources: Debunking Myths About Young People (Obj. 3)

E-mail | Web

Are you tired of hearing that you are spending too much time online? The perception that teens and college students are the biggest consumers of Internet content is intractable—a largely unexamined assumption based on little more than anecdotal evidence. To learn more about teens' true media usage, you could turn to Nielsen Company research.

Your boss, Akiko Kimura, doesn't believe in stereotyping. She encourages her market researchers to be wary of all data. She asked you to explore so-called niche marketing opportunities in targeting teens, a notoriously fickle consumer group. Primarily, Ms. Kimura wants to know how teenagers spend their free time, and, more specifically, how they use media. Understanding teen behavior is invaluable for the success of any promotional or ad campaign.

A casual glance at the latest Nielsen numbers reveals surprising key findings: Teens watch more TV than ever and spend much less time browsing the Internet than adults 25 to 34 years of age do (11 hours versus the average of 29 hours, 15 minutes for adults). They also spend 35 percent less time watching online videos than adults do. In their preferences for TV shows, top Web sites, and across media, they mirror the tastes of their parents. They also read newspapers, listen to the radio, and like advertising more than most. In short, "teens are actually pretty normal in their usage and more attentive than most give them credit for," said Nic Covey, director of insights for The Nielsen Company.[21]

Your Task. Ms. Kimura requested a brief informational e-mail report summarizing the main Nielsen findings. Paraphrase correctly and don't just copy from the online report. Ms. Kimura may ask you later to analyze more comprehensive data in an analytical report and create a media use profile of U.S. teens. You have already identified additional teenager-related Nielsen studies titled "Special Report: What Do Teens Want?," "Breaking Teen Myths," and "Teens Don't Tweet; Twitter's Growth Not Fueled by Youth."

11.12 Finding Secondary Data: The Future of Tech (Objs. 3, 5, and 6)

Team | Web | E-mail

Are you a member of the "thumb generation"? Can you work the keyboard of your cell phone or personal digital assistant faster than most people can speak? The term *thumb generation* was coined in South Korea and Japan and is applied to people under 25 who furiously finger their handheld devices to text, e-mail, and complete other electronic functions at lightning speeds.

More technological innovations are coming that are likely to transform our lives. WiMAX is a new wireless supertechnology that will cover entire cities at cable speeds. Near-field communication (NFC) takes the Bluetooth technology a step further to connect cell phones and other devices. NFC is touted for its boundless commercial applications enabling Americans soon to complete many sales transactions by cell phone, as is already customary in Korea, Japan, and Finland. These and other trends were described in a *BusinessWeek* article titled "The Future of Tech,"[22] which your boss pulled out of his files to show you. However, you know that you can find more current discussions of future trends on MIT's Technology Review Web site at **http://www.technologyreview.com**.

Your Task. You are one of several marketing interns at MarketNet Global, a worldwide e-commerce specialist. Your busy boss, Jack Holden, wants to be up to speed on cutting-edge tech and communication trends, especially those that could be successfully used in selling and marketing. Individually or as a team, research one or several high-tech concepts. On the MIT Technology Review Web site, focus on the tabs **Business, Computing, Web,** and **Communications**. Chances are you will not find scholarly articles on these subjects because peer-reviewed publications take years to complete. Instead, you must rely on the Web and on electronic databases to find up-to-date information. If you use search engines, you will retrieve many forum and discussion board contributions as well. Examine them critically for authority and validity. In teams or individually, write an e-mail or informational memo to Jack Holden, complete with a short list of references in MLA or APA documentation style. Explain what each new trend is. Your instructor may ask you to complete this activity as a report assignment after you study Chapter 12. You could use your research to write a short informational memo report describing to Jack Holden what your sources suggest the new trends may mean for the future of business, specifically e-commerce and online marketing.

11.13 Researching and Evaluating Data: How Wired Is the World? (Objs. 3, 5)

Team | Web | E-mail

Out of more than 1.7 billion global Internet users, North America is in third place behind Asia and Europe as the continent with the most people online, according to Internet World Stats.[23] Data analyzing which nations have the most connected populations suggest that Scandinavians rank high; the tiny country of Iceland is often cited as the top Internet presence per resident. On the opposite side of the spectrum, Internet access is very low in Africa, where less than 1 percent of the population is online. This is why chip maker AMD and scientists at MIT have independently announced plans to build and distribute low-cost computers to poor children in developing countries.

As an entry-level employee at AMD, you are part of a young team entrusted with the task of researching global Internet use and market saturation with computers. In other words, you are to examine access to computers and the Internet in a given population or geographic region. Find Internet World Stats or comScore's World Metrix data and examine how they were collected. Are they credible? Do other reputable sources reference this survey? Retrieve other statistical information from the Internet or electronic databases that discuss online access and Internet use in relation to population size. How does a focus on absolute numbers as opposed to percentages of the population skew the outcome? What conclusions can you draw from such information?

Your Task. As a team, write an e-mail or a memo to the head of the task force at AMD, Patricia Charbonneau, about the challenges of interpreting such numeric data. In addition, Ms. Charbonneau is looking for volunteers to research attempts by competitors and independent organizations (e.g., the United Nations, other corporations, and universities) to provide basic computing devices to developing countries. Write an informational e-mail or memo to Ms. Charbonneau listing your findings without comments or recommendations. Your instructor may ask you to complete this activity as an analytical report after you study Chapters 12 and 13.

11.14 Researching Data: Target Aims at Charitable Giving (Objs. 3, 6, and 7)

Team Web

Lauren Bacall and Robert Redford have both promoted it. And Oprah Winfrey thinks it is so chic that she pronounces its name in mock French (*Tar-jay*). Unlike its big-box competitors, Target is an American discount retailer that appeals to many female shoppers with trendy and edgy but affordable fashions. However, Target is also proud of its positive corporate image. The company has been praised for giving back to the community with higher-than-usual charitable contributions. At 5 percent of pretax earnings, Target's annual donations are more than double the national average among big corporations (in absolute dollars recently as high as $101 million a year). The company gives 5 percent of pretax profits consistently, in fat and in lean times.

This tradition was established six decades ago by Target's founder, George Dayton. Such generosity is more than a public relations move because Target polls its core group of shoppers, 35- to 45-year-old mothers, about their favorite causes. Then it distributes funds to those community charities. The company even managed to regain the goodwill of the Salvation Army after driving out its bell ringers citing no-solicitation rules.[24]

Your Task. Select one of the following tasks.

a. As a summer intern at Wal-Mart, you are asked to prepare an informational memo to your boss, Salvador Ramirez, about Target's charitable practices. Wal-Mart is seeking greater community involvement to boost its public image. What types of projects does the Target Corporation fund? What other policies set this company apart from its competitors when it comes to giving back to the community? Write an individual informational e-mail or memo or one collaborative e-mail or memo as a team of summer interns. Alternatively, Salvador Ramirez could ask you to write an e-mail or memo describing how Target handled the Salvation Army controversy and what its actions say about the company's management and its philosophy.
b. As a team of summer interns for Wal-Mart, research charitable giving of Target and other major corporations. Prepare an informational memo comparing and contrasting corporate practices. Target ranks fourth behind Wal-Mart, Home Depot, and Lowe's in size. How much of their pretax earnings are these and other big chain stores spending on philanthropy? What types of causes do they embrace, and why? Do their policies seem consistent and purposeful over the long term? How do they justify charitable giving to their shareholders?

In each case, compile a bibliography of sources you used. Whenever appropriate, display numbers visually by creating charts, graphs, and tables.

You may want to start by viewing company mission statements and annual reports for discussions of corporate social responsibility, charitable giving, and worthy causes companies support. Then, go to independent sources for a more detached, objective perspective.

11.15 Gathering Data: Fortune 100 Best Companies to Work For (Objs. 3, 4)

Web

Even in these tough economic times, some companies continue to spend lavishly on unusual employee perks such as massages and sauna visits, hold on to generous compensation and benefits, and don't lay off workers as a matter of principle. At the same time, they remain profitable. Chances are that you haven't heard of the newest top three among *Fortune*'s 100 Best Companies to Work For—tech giant SAS, investment advisor Edward Jones, and New York–based Wegmans Food Markets. The perennial favorite, Google, slipped to fourth place. Fourteenth-ranked outdoor powerhouse REI attracts active types who may bring their dogs to work, go on a midday bike ride, and test the products they sell. Sound nice? Just as companies have their distinctive corporate cultures, they also differ in why they are perceived as ideal employers.

Your Task. Visit the *Fortune* magazine Web site at **http://www.fortune.com/bestcompanies** for the most current 100 Best Companies to Work For. Examine the information about the top 20 or 25 highest-ranked companies. Watch the short video clips profiling each business. After studying the information, identify factors that attract and please workers. Take note of features shared across the board, but don't overlook quirky, unusual benefits. Summarize these trends in an informational memo report. Alternatively, prepare an analytical report investigating employee satisfaction gleaned from the secondary data obtained on the *Fortune* site.

11.16 Selecting Graphics (Obj. 7)

Your Task. Identify the best graphics form to illustrate the following data.

a. Properties listed for sale in a beach community
b. Month-to-month unemployment figures by the Bureau of Labor Statistics
c. Government unemployment data by industry and sector in percent
d. Figures showing the distribution of the H1N1 virus in humans by state
e. Figures showing the process of delivering electricity to a metropolitan area
f. Areas in the United States most likely to have earthquakes
g. Figures showing what proportion of every state tax dollar is spent on education, social services, transportation, debt, and other expenses

h. Academic, administrative, and operation divisions of a college, from the president to department chairs and division managers
i. Figures comparing the sales of smartphones, netbooks, and laptop computers over the past five years

11.17 Evaluating Graphics (Obj. 7)

Your Task. Select four graphics from newspapers or magazines, in hard copy or online. Look in *The Wall Street Journal, USA Today, BusinessWeek, U.S. News & World Report, Fortune,* or other business news publications. In an e-mail or memo to your instructor, critique each graphic based on what you have learned in this chapter. What is correctly shown? What is incorrectly shown? How could the graphic be improved?

11.18 Creating a Bar Chart (Obj. 7)

Your Task. Prepare a bar chart comparing the tax rates in eight industrial countries: Canada, 33 percent; France, 45 percent; Germany, 41 percent; Japan, 28 percent; Netherlands, 38 percent; Sweden, 49 percent; United Kingdom, 38 percent; United States, 28 percent. These figures represent a percentage of the gross domestic product for each country. The sources of the figures are the rankings of "fiscal freedom" established by the Heritage Foundation. Arrange the entries logically. Write two titles: a talking title and a descriptive title. What should you emphasize in the chart and title?

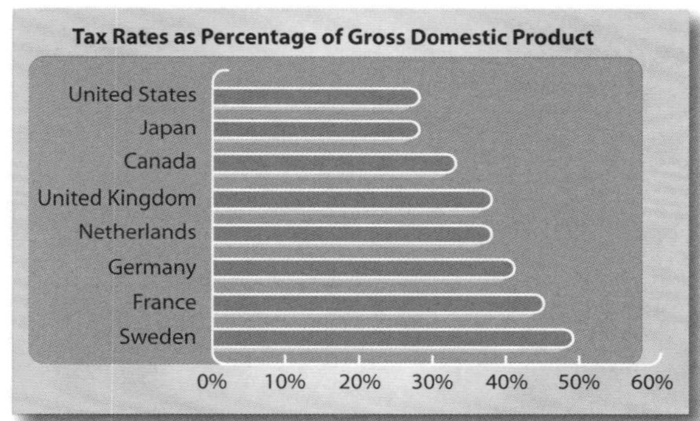

11.19 Creating a Line Chart (Obj. 7)

Your Task. Prepare a line chart showing the sales of Sidekick Athletic Shoes, Inc., for these years: 2011, $6.7 million; 2010, $5.4 million; 2009, $3.2 million; 2008, $2.1 million; 2007, $2.6 million; 2006, $3.6 million. In the chart title, highlight the trend you see in the data.

11.20 Studying Graphics in Annual Reports(Obj. 7)

Your Task. In an e-mail or memo to your instructor, evaluate the use and effectiveness of graphics in three to five corporation annual reports. Critique their readability, clarity, and effectiveness in visualizing data. How were they introduced in the text? What suggestions would you make to improve them?

11.21 Avoiding Huge Credit Card Debt for College Students (Objs. 3, 5, and 6)

Web

College students represent a new push for credit card companies. An amazing 84 percent of students carried at least one credit card in the most recent study of undergraduate card use, and half of college students had four or more cards.[25] Credit cards are a contributing factor when students graduate with an average of $20,000 debt. Because they can't buy cars, rent homes, or purchase insurance, graduates with big credit debt see a bleak future for themselves.

A local newspaper plans to run a self-help story about college credit cards. The editor asks you, a young part-time reporter, to prepare a memo with information that could be turned into an article. The article would focus on parents of students who are about to leave for college. What can parents do to help students avoid sinking deeply into credit card debt?

Your Task. Using ABI/INFORM, Factiva, or LexisNexis and the Web, locate basic information about student credit card options. In an e-mail or memo discuss shared credit cards and other options. Your goal is to be informative, not to reach conclusions or make recommendations. Use one or more of the techniques discussed in this chapter to track your sources. Address your memo to Janice Arrington, editor.

11.22 Netflix & Co.: Movies After DVD and Blu-Ray (Objs. 3, 5, and 6)

Web E-mail

The competition for consumer film rental dollars is fierce. A 400-employee company, Netflix offers online flat rates for DVD and Blu-ray disc rentals by mail. Users can also stream certain movie titles on the Web and view them on their computers. Netflix has joined the race against Blockbuster, Amazon, Apple, and the cable companies all jostling to become the leading provider of online films. Netflix is waging a battle on two fronts, against Blockbuster for online DVD rentals and with Apple for leadership in digital streaming services. Experts predict that DVDs and Blu-ray discs will go the way of such dinosaurs as VHS tapes and, eventually, music CDs. Apple's release of the iPad only intensifies the rivalry among the competing streaming services. Netflix CEO Reed Hastings has no plans to stream films to the Apple device.

Your Task. Using ABI/INFORM, Factiva, or LexisNexis and the Web, find information about the movie rental market today. Research the latest trends in the use of DVD/Blu-ray discs and Web streaming. In a memo or e-mail report, discuss the future of this important entertainment sector. Based on your research, expert opinion, and other resources, reach conclusions about the current state and future prospects of the movie rental business. If possible, make recommendations detailing how the business model could be modified to help Netflix survive the cutthroat competition. Use one or more of the techniques discussed in this chapter to track your sources. Address your memo or e-mail to Netflix CEO Reed Hastings.

Chat About It

In each chapter you will find five discussion questions related to the chapter material. Your instructor may assign these topics for you to discuss in class, in an online chat room, or on an online discussion board. Some of the discussion topics may require outside research. You may also be asked to read and respond to postings made by your classmates.

Topic 1: What is your biggest concern about writing a long report? How might you overcome this concern?
Topic 2: Why do you suppose reports created using Microsoft PowerPoint are becoming popular?

Are you ready? Get more practice at **www.meguffey.com**

Topic 3: What questions would you create to factor the problem for a report about improving the course registration process at your college or university?
Topic 4: Why is it important for a non-expert on a topic to use professional journals as report sources?
Topic 5: Is plagiarism worth the risk of being caught? Why or why not?

Grammar/Mechanics C.L.U.E. Review 11

Total Review

The first ten chapters reviewed specific guides from Appendix A: Grammar and Mechanics Guide. The exercises in this and the remaining chapters are total reviews, covering all of the grammar and mechanics guides plus confusing words and frequently misspelled words.

Each of the following sentences has **three** errors in grammar, punctuation, capitalization, usage, or spelling. On a separate sheet, write a correct version. Avoid adding new phrases, starting new sentences, or rewriting in your own words. When finished, compare your responses with the key beginning on page Key-1.

Example: To succede as a knowledge worker in todays digital workplace you need highly developed communication skills.
Revision: To **succeed** as a knowledge worker in **today's** digital **workplace**, you need highly developed communication skills.

1. The recruiter cited studys showing that mangers leave, when they lose autonomy.
2. As they work more than forty hours a week without overtime pay, most proffesionals today are wondering whether there jobs can survive the recession.
3. One organization paid three thousand dollars each for twelve employees to attend a one week workshop in communication training.
4. My company spend five hundred dollars on ink cartridges every month, but the cost doesn't worry my partner and I because our printed materials look sharp and professional.
5. If you find a open document on a colleague's computer screen its inappropriate to peek.
6. Todays workers should brush up their marketable skills otherwise they may not find another job after being laid off.
7. On June 1st our company President revealed a four million dollar drop in profits, which was bad news for everyone.
8. Most of us prefer to be let down gently, when we are being refused something, that is why the reasons before refusal pattern is effective.
9. Between you and I, if we where to share a ride each morning we would save a lot of money.
10. Despite the recent economic downturn our President and CEO gave an optimistic assessment of the companys outlook.

CHAPTER 12

Informal Business Reports

Want to do well on tests and excel in your course?
Go to **www.meguffey.com** for helpful interactive resources.
- **Review the Chapter 12 PowerPoint slides to prepare for the first quiz.**

OBJECTIVES

After studying this chapter, you should be able to

1. Tabulate information, use statistical techniques, and create decision matrices to sort and interpret business report data skillfully and accurately.
2. Draw meaningful conclusions and make practical report recommendations after sound and valid analysis.
3. Organize report data logically and provide cues to aid comprehension.
4. Write short informational reports that describe routine tasks.
5. Compose short analytical reports that solve business problems.

Zooming In PART 1

Starbucks Perks Up: Recapturing the Soul of the Coffeehouse

As Starbucks customers face shrinking disposable incomes, the purveyor of premium exotic drinks such as Iced Caramel Macchiato and Espresso Frappuccino has introduced lower-cost alternatives. Simple drip coffee, Pike Place Roast, and most notably, Via Ready Brew, Starbucks' line of instant coffee, signal attempts by chairman and CEO Howard Schultz to lead his company back to recovery in recessionary times. A costly indulgence, the $4 latte is now competing with Starbucks' own coffee drinks priced $3 on average; the chain has also introduced $3.95 breakfast meals. Howard Schultz returned to the helm of his company after an eight-year absence determined to restore Starbucks to its former glory by taking it back to its roots.

Despite setbacks, Starbucks continues to reign as the world's largest coffee shop chain, with some 16,000 retail locations in North America, Latin America, Europe, the Middle East, and the Pacific Rim—50 countries in all. Before the recession hit, the company served more than 50 million customers weekly and generated $10 billion in annual sales. Adding to its accolades, Starbucks has until recently ranked among the top ten in the *Fortune* magazine list of America's Most Admired Companies. Moreover, the retailer was repeatedly named among *Fortune's* 100 Best Companies to Work For, even after being forced to close 800 U.S. stores and cutting 30,000 employees worldwide. (As a result, Starbucks slid from position 24 to 93.) However, last year alone more than 150,000 applicants vied for jobs with the company.

Before the economy turned sour, Starbucks bucked traditional retail wisdom. As it grew explosively, the company regularly broke the retail rule about locating stores so closely that they cannibalize each other's sales. In metropolitan areas such as London and New York City, you may find as many as 170 Starbucks outlets within a five-mile radius. This "being everywhere" approach created several distinct advantages. Its numerous locations meant that Starbucks intercepted consumers on their way to work, home, or anywhere in between. Moreover, ubiquity builds brand awareness.

However, explosive growth may have led to complacency: "We got swept up," says Schultz. "We stopped asking: How can we do better? We had a sense of entitlement."[1] Fearing for his company's "soul," Schultz revamped Starbucks, at one point closing 7,100 stores for three hours to retrain employees on the Starbucks experience. He also abandoned flavor-locked packaging and introduced improved espresso machines. You will learn more about this case on page 401.

© AP Images/Seth Perlman

Critical Thinking

- What kind of information should Starbucks gather to help it decide how closely to locate its stores?
- How could Howard Schultz test his impression that the intimate communal coffee-drinking experience is fading at Starbucks?
- How can collected information be transmitted to Starbucks' decision makers?

http://www.starbucks.com

Interpreting Data

LEARNING OBJECTIVE 1

Tabulate information, use statistical techniques, and create decision matrices to sort and interpret business report data skillfully and accurately.

How can you extract meaningful information from data?

To respond nimbly to changing economic times, Starbucks and other businesses need information to stay abreast of what is happening inside and outside of their firms. Much of the information that allows decision makers to run their organizations efficiently comes to them in the form of reports. This chapter focuses on interpreting and organizing data, drawing conclusions, providing reader cues, and writing informal business reports.

Collecting information is effortless today, given the easy access to electronic databases, the Web, and other sources of digitized information. However, making sense of the massive amounts of data you may collect is much harder. You may feel overwhelmed as you look at a jumble of digital files, printouts, note cards, copies of articles, interview notes, questionnaire results, and statistics. It is a little like being a contractor who allowed suppliers to dump all the building materials for a new house in a monstrous pile. Like the contractor, you must sort the jumble of raw material into meaningful, usable groups. Unprocessed data become meaningful information through skillful and accurate sorting, analysis, combination, and recombination. You will be examining each item to see what it means by itself and what it means when connected with other data. You are looking for meanings, relationships, and answers to the research questions posed in your work plan.

Tabulating and Analyzing Responses

If you have collected considerable numerical and other information, you must tabulate and analyze it. Fortunately, several tabulating and statistical techniques can help you create order from the chaos. These techniques are used to simplify, summarize, and classify large amounts of data into meaningful terms. From the condensed data, you are more likely to be able to draw valid conclusions and make reasoned recommendations. The most helpful summarizing techniques include tables, statistical concepts (mean, median, and mode), correlations, grids, and decision matrices.

Tables. Numerical data from questionnaires or interviews are usually summarized and simplified in tables. Using systematic columns and rows, tables make quantitative information easier to comprehend. After assembling your data, you will want to prepare preliminary tables to enable you to see what the information means. Here is a table summarizing the response to one question from a campus survey about student parking:

Question: Should student fees be increased to build parking lots?

	Number	Percent	
Strongly agree	76	11.5	To simplify the table, combine these items.
Agree	255	38.5	
No opinion	22	3.3	
Disagree	107	16.1	To simplify the table, combine these items.
Strongly disagree	203	30.6	
Total	**663**	**100.0**	

Notice that this preliminary table includes a total number of responses and a percentage for each response. (To calculate a percentage, divide the figure for each response by the total number of responses times 100.) To simplify the data and provide a broad overview, you can join categories. For example, combining *Strongly agree* (11.5 percent) and *Agree* (38.5 percent) reveals that 50 percent of the respondents supported the proposal to finance new parking lots with increased student fees.

Sometimes data become more meaningful when cross-tabulated. This process allows analysis of two or more variables together. By breaking down our student survey data into male and female responses, shown in the following table, we make an interesting discovery.

Question: Should student fees be increased to build parking lots?

	Total		Male		Female	
	Number	**Percent**	**Number**	**Percent**	**Number**	**Percent**
Strongly agree	76	11.5	8	2.2	68	22.0
Agree	255	38.5	54	15.3	201	65.0
No opinion	22	3.3	12	3.4	10	3.2
Disagree	107	16.1	89	25.1	18	5.8
Strongly disagree	203	30.6	191	54.0	12	4.0
Total	**663**	**100.0**	**354**	**100.0**	**309**	**100.0**

Although 50 percent of all student respondents supported the proposal, among females the approval rating was much stronger. Notice that 87 percent of female respondents (combining 22 percent *Strongly agree* and 65 percent *Agree*) endorsed the proposal to increase fees for new parking lots. However, among male students, only 17 percent agreed with the proposal. You naturally wonder why such a disparity exists. Are female students unhappier than male

Ethics Check

Starbucks CEO Howard Schultz explains his company's Shared Planet initiative: "We feel now is the time to invest—truly and authentically—in ways to help create a better future for the world we share." Starbucks also teamed up with (Product) RED, the global anti-AIDS project spearheaded by U2's Bono. The coffee chain wishes to pursue its vision of community involvement, commitment to the environment, and ethical sourcing of coffee. Do you view favorably companies that are "green" and wish to appear ethical? Do such considerations influence your buying decisions?

What are some techniques to bring order to raw numerical data?

students with the current parking situation? If so, why? Is safety a reason? Are male students more concerned with increased fees than female students are?

By cross-tabulating the findings, you sometimes uncover data that may help answer your problem question or that may prompt you to explore other possibilities. Do not, however, undertake cross-tabulation unless it serves more than merely satisfying your curiosity. Tables also help you compare multiple data collected from questionnaires and surveys. Figure 12.1 shows, in raw form, responses to several survey items. To convert these data into a more usable form, you need to calculate percentages for each item. Then you can arrange the responses in some rational sequence, such as largest percentage to smallest.

Once the data are displayed in a table, you can more easily draw conclusions. As Figure 12.1 shows, South Bay College students apparently are not interested in public transportation or shuttle buses from satellite lots. They want to park on campus, with restricted visitor parking; and only half are willing to pay for new parking lots.

FIGURE 12.1 Converting Survey Data into Finished Tables

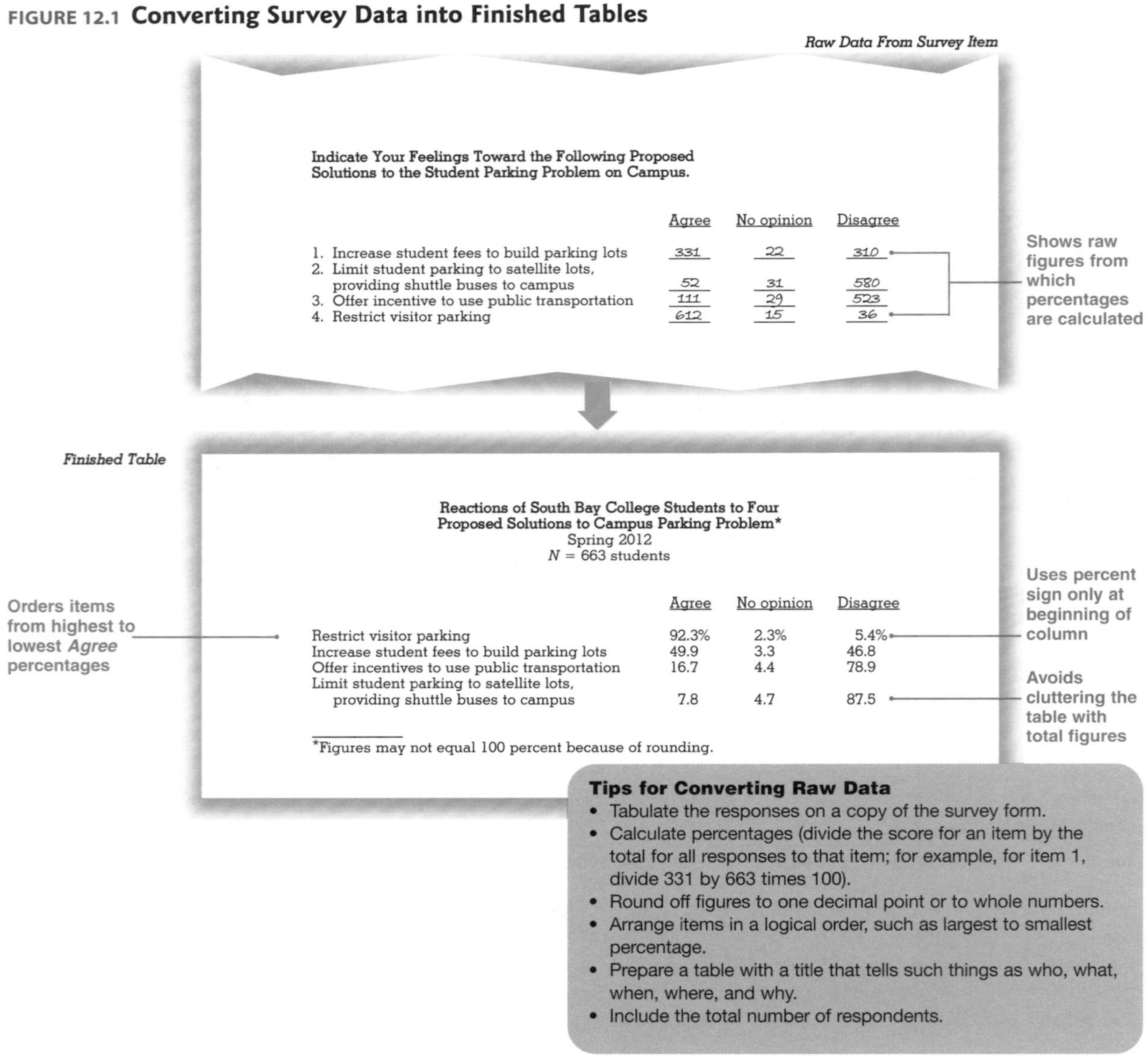

Raw Data From Survey Item

Indicate Your Feelings Toward the Following Proposed Solutions to the Student Parking Problem on Campus.

	Agree	No opinion	Disagree
1. Increase student fees to build parking lots	331	22	310
2. Limit student parking to satellite lots, providing shuttle buses to campus	52	31	580
3. Offer incentive to use public transportation	111	29	523
4. Restrict visitor parking	612	15	36

Finished Table

Reactions of South Bay College Students to Four Proposed Solutions to Campus Parking Problem*
Spring 2012
N = 663 students

	Agree	No opinion	Disagree
Restrict visitor parking	92.3%	2.3%	5.4%
Increase student fees to build parking lots	49.9	3.3	46.8
Offer incentives to use public transportation	16.7	4.4	78.9
Limit student parking to satellite lots, providing shuttle buses to campus	7.8	4.7	87.5

*Figures may not equal 100 percent because of rounding.

Shows raw figures from which percentages are calculated
Orders items from highest to lowest *Agree* percentages
Uses percent sign only at beginning of column
Avoids cluttering the table with total figures

Tips for Converting Raw Data

- Tabulate the responses on a copy of the survey form.
- Calculate percentages (divide the score for an item by the total for all responses to that item; for example, for item 1, divide 331 by 663 times 100).
- Round off figures to one decimal point or to whole numbers.
- Arrange items in a logical order, such as largest to smallest percentage.
- Prepare a table with a title that tells such things as who, what, when, where, and why.
- Include the total number of respondents.

The Three Ms: Mean, Median, Mode. Tables help you organize data, and the three Ms help you describe it. These statistical terms—mean, median, and mode—are all occasionally used loosely to mean "average." To be safe, though, you should learn to apply these statistical terms precisely.

What are three statistical concepts that help you describe data and make them meaningful?

When people say *average*, they usually intend to indicate the *mean*, or arithmetic average. Let's say that you are studying the estimated starting salaries of graduates from various disciplines, ranging from education to medicine:

Education	$41,000	*Mode (figure occurring most frequently)*
Sociology	41,000	
Humanities	41,000	
Biology	45,000	
Health sciences	50,000	*Median (middle point in continuum)*
Business	56,000	*Mean (arithmetic average)*
Engineering	60,000	
Law	65,000	
Medicine	105,000	

To find the mean, you simply add up all the salaries and divide by the total number of items ($504,000 ÷ 9 = $56,000). Therefore, the mean salary is $56,000. Means are very useful to indicate central tendencies of figures, but they have one major flaw: extremes at either end cause distortion. Notice that the $105,000 figure makes the mean salary of $56,000 deceptively high. It does not represent a valid average for the group. Because means can be misleading, you should use them only when extreme figures do not distort the result.

What are the differences among the mean, the median, and the mode?

The *median* represents the midpoint in a group of figures arranged from lowest to highest (or vice versa). In our list of salaries, the median is $50,000 (health sciences). In other words, half the salaries are above this point and half are below it. The median is useful when extreme figures may warp the mean. Although salaries for medicine distort the mean, the median, at $50,000, is still a representative figure.

The *mode* is simply the value that occurs most frequently. In our list $41,000 (for education, sociology, and the humanities) represents the mode because it occurs three times. The mode has the advantage of being easily determined—just a quick glance at a list of arranged values reveals it. Although researchers use mode infrequently, knowing the mode is useful in some situations. Assume that 7-Eleven sampled its customers to determine what Big Gulp fountain drink size they preferred: 20-ounce, 32-ounce, or Super Big Gulp 44-ounce. Finding the mode—the most frequently named figure—makes more sense than calculating the median, which might yield a size that 7-Eleven does not even offer. (To remember the meaning of *mode*, think about fashion: the most frequent response, the mode, is the most fashionable.)

Mean, median, and mode figures are especially helpful when the range of values is also known. Range represents the span between the highest and lowest values. To calculate the range, you simply subtract the lowest figure from the highest. In starting salaries for graduates, the range is $64,000 (105,000 – 41,000). Knowing the range enables readers to put mean and median figures into perspective. This knowledge also prompts researchers to wonder why such a range exists, thus stimulating hunches and further investigation to solve problems.

Correlations. In tabulating and analyzing data, you may see relationships among two or more variables that help explain the findings. If your data for graduates' starting salaries also included years of education, you would doubtless notice that graduates with more years of education received higher salaries. For example, beginning teachers, with four years of schooling, earn less than beginning physicians, who have completed nine or more years of education. Therefore, a correlation may exist between years of education and starting salary.

What are correlations among variables?

Intuition suggests correlations that may or may not prove to be accurate. Is there a relationship between studying and good grades? Between new office computers and increased productivity? Between the rise and fall of hemlines and the rise and fall of the stock market (as some newspaper writers have suggested)? If a correlation seems to exist, can we say that one event caused the other? Does studying cause good grades? Does more schooling guarantee increased salary? Although one event may not be said to cause another, the business researcher who sees a correlation begins to ask why and how the two variables are related. In this way, apparent correlations stimulate investigation and present possible solutions to be explored.

In reporting correlations, you should avoid suggesting that a cause-and-effect relationship exists when none can be proved. Only sophisticated research methods can statistically prove correlations. Instead, present a correlation as a possible relationship (*The data suggest that beginning salaries are related to years of education*). Cautious statements followed by explanations gain you credibility and allow readers to make their own decisions.

How can grids help you analyze raw verbal data?

Grids. Another technique for analyzing raw data—especially verbal data—is the grid. Let's say you have been asked by the CEO to collect opinions from all vice presidents about the CEO's four-point plan to build cash reserves. The grid shown in Figure 12.2 enables you to summarize the vice presidents' reactions to each point. Notice how this complex verbal information is transformed into concise, manageable data; readers can see immediately which points are supported and which are opposed. Imagine how long you could have struggled to comprehend the meaning of this verbal information without a grid.

Arranging data in a grid also works for projects such as feasibility studies and yardstick reports that compare many variables. Assume you must recommend a new printer to your manager. To see how four models compare, you could lay out a grid with the names of printer models across the top. Down the left side, you would list such significant variables as price, warranty, service, capacity, compatibility, and specifications. As you fill in the variables for each model, you can see quickly which model has the lowest price, longest warranty, and so forth. *Consumer Reports* often uses grids to show information.

In addition, grids help classify employment data. For example, suppose your boss asks you to recommend one individual from among many job candidates. You could arrange a grid with names across the top and distinguishing characteristics—experience, skills, education, and other employment interests—down the left side. Summarizing each candidate's points offers a helpful tool for drawing conclusions and writing a report.

Decision Matrices. A decision matrix is a special grid that helps managers make the best choice among complex options. Designed to eliminate bias and poor judgment, decision matrices are helpful in many fields. Assume you need to choose the most appropriate laptop computer for your sales representatives. You are most interested in weight, battery life, price, and hard drive size. You want to compare these features in four laptop models. Figure 12.3 shows a simple decision matrix to help you make the choice. In this case, the most important criteria were weight, battery, price, and hard drive. In Table 1, you evaluate each of these features on a scale of 1 to 5. Because the Dell Inspiron has a spacious hard drive, you give it a score of 5. However, its battery life is less desirable, and you give it a score of 2.

FIGURE 12.2 Grid to Analyze Complex Verbal Data About Building Cash Reserves

	Point 1	Point 2	Point 3	Point 4	Overall Reaction
Vice President 1	Disapproves. "Too little, too late."	Strong support. "Best of all points."	Mixed opinion. "Must wait and see market."	Indifferent.	Optimistic, but "hates to delay expansion for six months."
Vice President 2	Disapproves. "Creates credit trap."	Approves.	Strong disapproval.	Approves. "Must improve receivable collections."	Mixed support. "Good self–defense plan."
Vice President 3	Strong disapproval.	Approves. "Key to entire plan."	Indifferent.	Approves, but with "caveats."	"Will work only with sale of unproductive fixed assets."
Vice President 4	Disapproves. "Too risky now."	Strong support. "Start immediately."	Approves, "but may damage image."	Approves. "Benefits far outweigh costs."	Supports plan. Suggests focus on Pacific Rim markets.

FIGURE 12.3 **Decision Matrix Used to Choose a Laptop for Sales Reps**

Unweighted Decision Matrix—Table 1

Features	Weight	Battery Life	Price	Hard Drive	Total
Laptop Options					
Dell Inspiron i1464-4382OBK: 2.13 GHz, Intel Core i3 330M, 4.8 lbs, 3:20 hrs, $699, 500 GB	3	2	5	5	
Apple MacBook Pro: 2.26 GHz, Intel Core 2 Duo P7550, 4.5 lbs, 4:44 hrs, $1,200, 160 GB	4	3	1	1	
Acer Aspire Timeline AS4810TZ-4120: 1.3 GHz, Intel Dual-Core SU4100, 5.1 lbs, 9:10 hrs, $830, 320 GB	2	5	2	3	
HP Pavilion dv4-2153cl: 2.13 GHz, Intel Core i3 330M, 5.2 lbs, 3:13 hrs, $780, 320 GB	2	2	3	3	

Weighted Decision Matrix—Table 2

Features	Weight	Battery LIfe	Price	Hard Drive	Total
Laptop Options **Weights:**	**5**	**10**	**5**	**7**	
Dell Inspiron i1464-4382OBK: 2.13 GHz, Intel Core i3 330M, 4.8 lbs, 3:20 hrs, $699, 500 GB	15	20	25	35	95
Apple MacBook Pro: 2.26 GHz, Intel Core 2 Duo P7550, 4.5 lbs, 4:44 hrs, $1,200, 160 GB	20	30	5	7	62
Acer Aspire Timeline AS4810TZ-4120: 1.3 GHz, Intel Dual-Core SU4100, 5.1 lbs, 9:10 hrs, $830, 320 GB	10	50	10	21	91
HP Pavilion dv4-2153cl: 2.13 GHz, Intel Core i3 330M, 5.2 lbs, 3:13 hrs, $780, 320 GB	10	20	15	21	66

Tips for Creating a Decision Matrix

- **Select the most important criteria.** For a laptop computer, the criteria were weight, battery life, price, and size of hard drive.
- **Create a matrix.** List each laptop model (Dell, Apple, and others) down the left side. Place the features across the top of the columns.
- **Evaluate the criteria.** Use a scale of 1 (lowest) to 5 (highest). Rate each feature for each option, as shown in Table 1.
- **Assign relative weights.** Decide how important each feature is and give it a weight.
- **Multiply the scores.** For each feature in Table 1, multiply by the weights in Table 2 and write the score in the box.
- **Total the scores.** The total reveals the best choice.

After you have evaluated all of the laptop models in Table 1, you assign relative weights to each feature. You decide to assign a factor of 5 to weight as well as to unit price because these two aspects are of average importance. However, your field sales reps want laptops with batteries that last. Therefore, battery life is twice as important; you assign it a factor of 10. You assign a factor of 7 to the size of the hard drive because this option is slightly more important than price, but somewhat less important than battery life. Then you multiply the scores in Table 1 with the weights and total them, as shown in Table 2. According to the weighted matrix and the rating system used, the Dell Inspiron should be purchased for the sales reps because it received the highest score of 95 points, closely followed by the Acer Aspire with 91 points.

Drawing Conclusions and Making Recommendations

LEARNING OBJECTIVE 2

Draw meaningful conclusions and make practical report recommendations after sound and valid analysis.

The most widely read portions of a report are the sections devoted to conclusions and recommendations. Knowledgeable readers go straight to the conclusions to see what the report writer thinks the data mean. Because conclusions summarize and explain the findings, they represent the heart of a report.

Your value in an organization rises considerably if you can draw conclusions that analyze information logically and show how the data answer questions and solve problems. To tap into a potential $1 billion market for cellular phones in developing countries, Finnish mobile phone manufacturer Nokia researched the needs of its customers. It created handsets that can withstand the tough living conditions and harsh weather in India and Africa. To reach customers, the company sent vans into rural India. Kai Oistamo, executive vice president and general manager for mobile phones, said: "You have to understand where people live, what the shopping patterns are. You have to work with local means to reach people—even bicycles or rickshaws."[2] Doing research and drawing logical conclusions from data are crucial to business success.

Analyzing Data to Arrive at Conclusions

What kind of information is included in conclusions?

Any set of data can produce a variety of meaningful conclusions. Always bear in mind, though, that the audience for a report wants to know how these data relate to the problem being studied. What do the findings mean in terms of solving the original report problem?

For example, the Marriott Corporation recognized a serious problem among its employees. Conflicting home and work requirements seemed to be causing excessive employee turnover and decreased productivity. To learn the extent of the problem and to consider solutions, Marriott surveyed its staff. It learned, among other things, that nearly 35 percent of its employees had children under age twelve, and 15 percent had children under age five. Other findings, shown in Figure 12.4, indicated that one third of its staff with young children took time off because of child care difficulties. Moreover, many current employees left previous jobs because of work and family conflicts. The survey also showed that managers did not consider child care or family problems to be appropriate topics for discussion at work.

A sample of possible conclusions that could be drawn from these findings is shown in Figure 12.4. Notice that each conclusion relates to the initial report problem. Although only a few possible findings and conclusions are shown here, you can see that the conclusions try to explain the causes for the home/work conflict among employees. Many report writers would expand the conclusion section by explaining each item and citing supporting evidence. Even for simplified conclusions, such as those shown in Figure 12.4, you will want to itemize each item separately and use parallel construction (balanced sentence structure).

How can you ensure that your conclusions are effective?

Although your goal is to remain objective, drawing conclusions naturally involves a degree of subjectivity. Your goals, background, and frame of reference all color the inferences you make. When the Big Three automakers posted staggering losses just before the federal rescue plan kicked in, a public debate raged over whether to give loan guarantees to the companies or let them go bankrupt. The facts could not be disputed. But what conclusions could be drawn? The CEOs of GM, Ford, and Chrysler went to Washington to ask for loans because they wanted to buy time until they retooled their operations and before they ran out of cash. The workers and the government concluded that the potential for up to 3 million job losses was reason enough to bail out the Detroit companies. The taxpayers, still reeling from a $700 billion bank bailout, viewed even the relatively small rescue package with suspicion. Moreover, consumers kept fleeing big gas guzzlers in favor of smaller, more efficient imports. All writers interpret findings from their own perspectives, but they should not manipulate them to achieve a preconceived purpose.

You can make your report conclusions more objective by using consistent evaluation criteria. Let's say you are comparing computers for an office equipment purchase. If you evaluate each by the same criteria (such as price, specifications, service, and warranty), your conclusions are more likely to be bias-free.

You also need to avoid the temptation to sensationalize or exaggerate your findings or conclusions. Be careful of words such as *many, most,* and *all.* Instead of *many of the respondents felt...,* you might more accurately write *some of the respondents felt....* Examine your motives before drawing conclusions. Do not let preconceptions or wishful thinking color your reasoning.

Preparing Report Recommendations

Conclusions explain what the problem is, whereas recommendations tell how to solve it. Typically, readers prefer specific, practical recommendations. They want to know exactly how to implement the suggestions. The specificity of your recommendations depends on your authorization. What are you commissioned to do, and what does the reader expect? In the

What is the difference between conclusions and recommendations?

FIGURE 12.4 Report Conclusions and Recommendations

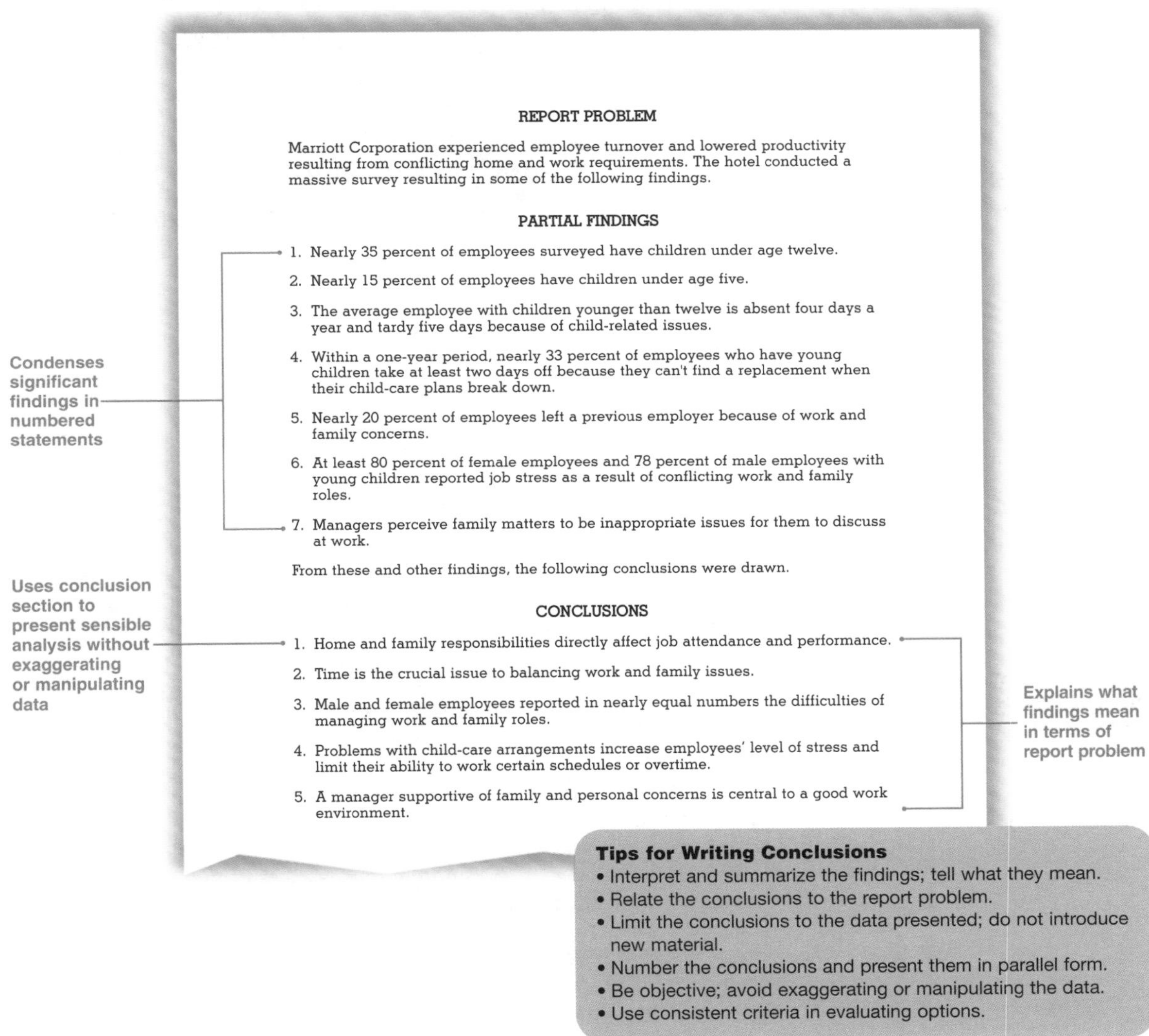

REPORT PROBLEM

Marriott Corporation experienced employee turnover and lowered productivity resulting from conflicting home and work requirements. The hotel conducted a massive survey resulting in some of the following findings.

PARTIAL FINDINGS

1. Nearly 35 percent of employees surveyed have children under age twelve.
2. Nearly 15 percent of employees have children under age five.
3. The average employee with children younger than twelve is absent four days a year and tardy five days because of child-related issues.
4. Within a one-year period, nearly 33 percent of employees who have young children take at least two days off because they can't find a replacement when their child-care plans break down.
5. Nearly 20 percent of employees left a previous employer because of work and family concerns.
6. At least 80 percent of female employees and 78 percent of male employees with young children reported job stress as a result of conflicting work and family roles.
7. Managers perceive family matters to be inappropriate issues for them to discuss at work.

From these and other findings, the following conclusions were drawn.

CONCLUSIONS

1. Home and family responsibilities directly affect job attendance and performance.
2. Time is the crucial issue to balancing work and family issues.
3. Male and female employees reported in nearly equal numbers the difficulties of managing work and family roles.
4. Problems with child-care arrangements increase employees' level of stress and limit their ability to work certain schedules or overtime.
5. A manager supportive of family and personal concerns is central to a good work environment.

Condenses significant findings in numbered statements
Uses conclusion section to present sensible analysis without exaggerating or manipulating data
Explains what findings mean in terms of report problem
Tips for Writing Conclusions
• Interpret and summarize the findings; tell what they mean.
• Relate the conclusions to the report problem.
• Limit the conclusions to the data presented; do not introduce new material.
• Number the conclusions and present them in parallel form.
• Be objective; avoid exaggerating or manipulating the data.
• Use consistent criteria in evaluating options.

FIGURE 12.4 **(Continued)**

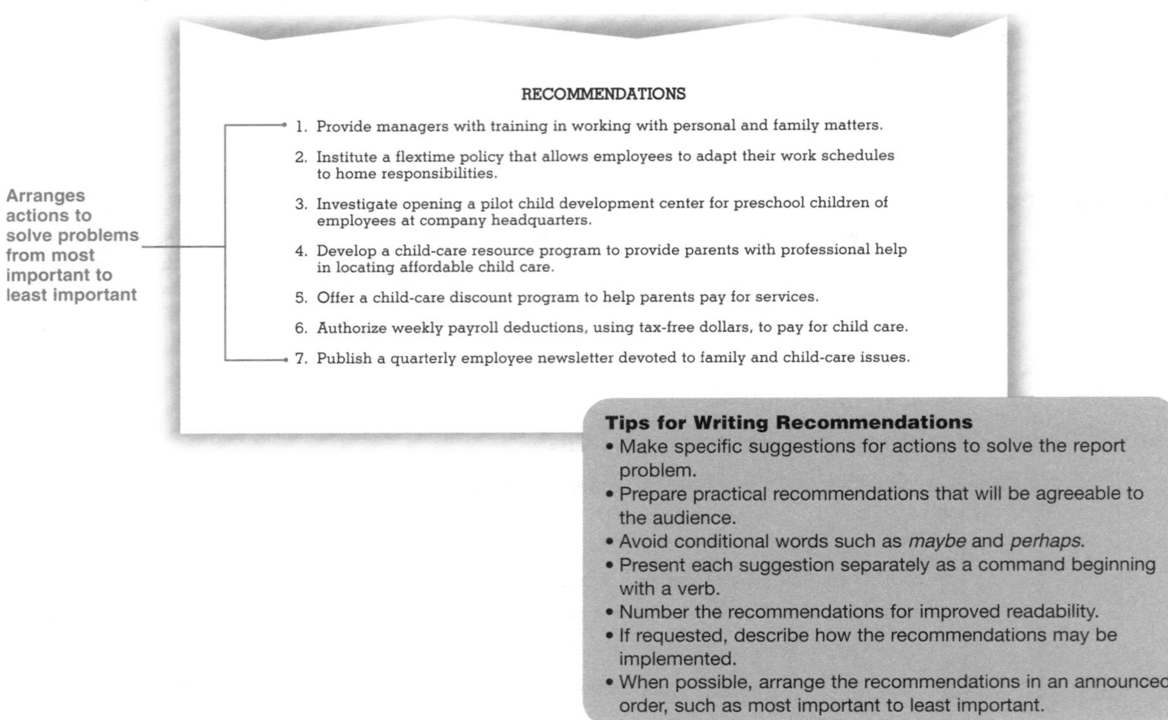
RECOMMENDATIONS

1. Provide managers with training in working with personal and family matters.
2. Institute a flextime policy that allows employees to adapt their work schedules to home responsibilities.
3. Investigate opening a pilot child development center for preschool children of employees at company headquarters.
4. Develop a child-care resource program to provide parents with professional help in locating affordable child care.
5. Offer a child-care discount program to help parents pay for services.
6. Authorize weekly payroll deductions, using tax-free dollars, to pay for child care.
7. Publish a quarterly employee newsletter devoted to family and child-care issues.

Arranges actions to solve problems from most important to least important

Tips for Writing Recommendations

- Make specific suggestions for actions to solve the report problem.
- Prepare practical recommendations that will be agreeable to the audience.
- Avoid conditional words such as *maybe* and *perhaps*.
- Present each suggestion separately as a command beginning with a verb.
- Number the recommendations for improved readability.
- If requested, describe how the recommendations may be implemented.
- When possible, arrange the recommendations in an announced order, such as most important to least important.

planning stages of your report project, you anticipate what the reader wants in the report. Your intuition and your knowledge of the audience indicate how far your recommendations should be developed.

In the recommendations section of the Marriott employee survey, shown in Figure 12.4, many of the recommendations are summarized. In the actual report, each recommendation could have been backed up with specifics and ideas for implementing them. For example, the child care resource recommendation would be explained: it provides parents with names of agencies and professionals who specialize in locating child care across the country.

How can you ensure that your recommendations are received well by your audience?

A good report provides practical recommendations that are agreeable to the audience. In the Marriott survey, for example, report researchers knew that the company wanted to help employees cope with conflicts between family and work obligations. As a result, the report's conclusions and recommendations focused on ways to resolve the conflict. If Marriott's goal had been merely to save money by reducing employee absenteeism, the recommendations would have been quite different.

If possible, make each recommendation a command. Note in Figure 12.4 that each recommendation begins with a verb. This structure sounds forceful and confident and helps the reader comprehend the information quickly. Avoid words such as *maybe* and *perhaps*; they suggest conditional statements that reduce the strength of recommendations.

Experienced writers may combine recommendations and conclusions. In short reports writers may omit conclusions and move straight to recommendations. An important point about recommendations is that they include practical suggestions for solving the report problem. Furthermore, they are always the result of prior logical analysis.

Moving From Findings to Recommendations

Recommendations evolve from the interpretation of the findings and conclusions. Consider the following examples from the Marriott survey:

Finding
Managers perceive family matters to be inappropriate issues to discuss at work.

Conclusion
Managers are neither willing nor trained to discuss family matters that may cause employees to miss work.

Recommendation
Provide managers with training in recognizing and working with personal and family matters that affect work.

Finding
Within a one-year period, nearly 33 percent of employees who have young children take at least two days off because they can't find a replacement when their child care plans break down.

Conclusion
Problems with child care arrangements increase employees' level of stress and limit their ability to work certain schedules or overtime.

Recommendation
Develop a child care resource program to provide parents with professional help in locating affordable child care.

Organizing Data

LEARNING OBJECTIVE 3
Organize report data logically and provide cues to aid comprehension.

After collecting sets of data, interpreting them, drawing conclusions, and thinking about the recommendations, you are ready to organize the parts of the report into a logical framework. Poorly organized reports lead to frustration. Readers will not understand, remember, or be persuaded. Wise writers know that reports rarely "just organize themselves." Instead, organization must be imposed on the data, and cues must be provided so the reader can follow the logic of the writer.

When would you choose the direct strategy to organize data, and when would the indirect strategy be more appropriate?

Informational reports, as you learned in Chapter 11, generally present data without interpretation. As shown in Figure 12.5, informational reports typically consist of three parts: (a) introduction/background, (b) facts/findings, and (c) summary/concluding remarks. Analytical reports, which generally analyze data and draw conclusions, typically contain four parts: (a) introduction/problem, (b) facts/findings, (c) discussion/analysis, and (d) conclusions/recommendations. However, the parts in analytical reports do not always follow this sequence. For readers who know about the project, are supportive, or are eager to learn the results quickly, the direct strategy is appropriate. Conclusions and recommendations, if requested,

FIGURE 12.5 Organizational Patterns for Informational and Analytical Reports

	Analytical Reports	
Informational Reports	**Direct Pattern**	**Indirect Pattern**
I. Introduction/background	I. Introduction/problem	I. Introduction/problem
II. Facts/findings	II. Conclusions/recommendations	II. Facts/findings
III. Summary/conclusion	III. Facts/findings	III. Discussion/analysis
	IV. Discussion/analysis	IV. Conclusions/recommendations

appear up front. For readers who must be educated or persuaded, the indirect strategy works better. Conclusions/recommendations appear last, after the findings have been presented and analyzed.

Although every report is unique, the overall organizational patterns described here typically hold true. The real challenge, though, lies in (a) organizing the facts/findings and discussion/analysis sections and (b) providing reader cues.

Ordering Information Logically

What are some organizational patterns that help readers comprehend data?

Whether you are writing informational or analytical reports, the data you have collected must be structured coherently. Five common organizational methods are by time, component, importance, criteria, or convention. Regardless of the method you choose, be sure that it helps the reader understand the data. Reader comprehension, not writer convenience, should govern organization. For additional examples of organizational principles, please go to page 460 in Chapter 14.

Time. Ordering data by time means establishing a chronology of events. Agendas, minutes of meetings, progress reports, and procedures are usually organized by time. For example, a report describing an eight-week training program would most likely be organized by weeks. A plan for step-by-step improvement of customer service would be organized by steps. A monthly trip report submitted by a sales rep might describe customers visited Week 1, Week 2, and so on. Beware of overusing chronologies (time) as an organizing method for reports, however. Although this method is easy and often mirrors the way data are collected, chronologies—like the sales rep's trip report—tend to be boring, repetitious, and lacking in emphasis. Readers cannot always pick out what is important.

Component. Especially for informational reports, data may be organized by components such as location, geography, division, product, or part. For instance, a report detailing company expansion might divide the plan into West Coast, East Coast, and Midwest expansion. The report could also be organized by divisions: personal products, consumer electronics, and household goods. A report comparing profits among makers of athletic shoes might group the data by company: Nike, Reebok, Adidas, and so forth. Organization by components works best when the classifications already exist.

What are the advantages of organizing data by level of importance?

Importance. Organization by importance involves beginning with the most important item and proceeding to the least important—or vice versa. For example, a report discussing the reasons for declining product sales would present the most important reason first followed by less important ones. The Marriott report describing work/family conflicts might begin by discussing child care, if the writer considered it the most important issue. Using importance to structure findings involves a value judgment. The writer must decide what is most important, always keeping in mind the readers' priorities and expectations. Busy readers appreciate seeing important points first; they may skim or skip other points. On the other hand, building to a climax by moving from least important to most important enables the writer to focus attention at the end. Thus, the reader is more likely to remember the most important item. Of course, the writer also risks losing the reader's attention along the way.

Criteria. Establishing criteria by which to judge helps writers to treat topics consistently. Let's say your report compares health plans A, B, and C. For each plan you examine the same standards: Criterion 1, cost per employee; Criterion 2, amount of deductible; and Criterion 3, patient benefits. The resulting data could then be organized either by plans or by criteria:

How can you make sure that you evaluate choices or plans fairly?

By Plan	**By Criteria**
Plan A	Criterion 1
Criterion 1	Plan A
Criterion 2	Plan B
Criterion 3	Plan C

By Plan	By Criteria
Plan B	Criterion 2
Criterion 1	Plan A
Criterion 2	Plan B
Criterion 3	Plan C
Plan C	Criterion 3
Criterion 1	Plan A
Criterion 2	Plan B
Criterion 3	Plan C

Although you might favor organizing the data by plans (because that is the way you collected the data), the better way is by criteria. When you discuss patient benefits, for example, you would examine all three plans' benefits together. Organizing a report around criteria helps readers make comparisons, instead of forcing them to search through the report for similar data.

What are the advantages of organizing by convention?

Convention. Many operational and recurring reports are structured according to convention. That is, they follow a prescribed plan that everyone understands. For example, an automotive parts manufacturer might ask all sales reps to prepare a weekly report with these headings: *Competitive observations* (competitors' price changes, discounts, new products, product problems, distributor changes, product promotions), *Product problems* (quality, performance, needs), and *Customer service problems* (delivery, mailings, correspondence). Management gets exactly the information it needs in an easy-to-read form.

Like operating reports, proposals are often organized conventionally. They might use such groupings as background, problem, proposed solution, staffing, schedule, costs, and authorization. As you might expect, reports following these conventional, prescribed structures greatly simplify the task of organization. Proposals and long reports are presented in Chapter 13.

Providing Reader Cues

When you finish organizing a report, you probably see a neat outline in your mind: major points, supported by subpoints and details. Readers, however, do not know the material as well as you do; they cannot see your outline. To guide them through the data, you need to provide the equivalent of a map and road signs. For both formal and informal reports, devices such as introductions, transitions, and headings prevent readers from getting lost.

What purpose does a good opener serve?

Introduction. One of the best ways to point a reader in the right direction is to provide a report introduction that does three things:

- Tells the purpose of the report
- Describes the significance of the topic
- Previews the main points and the order in which they will be developed

The following paragraph includes all three elements in introducing a report on computer security:

This report examines the security of our current computer operations and presents suggestions for improving security. Lax computer security could mean loss of information, loss of business, and damage to our equipment and systems. Because many former employees released during recent downsizing efforts know our systems, major changes must be made. To improve security, I will present three recommendations: (a) begin using smart cards that limit access to our computer system, (b) alter sign-on and log-off procedures, (c) move central computer operations to a more secure area.

This opener tells the purpose (examining computer security), describes its significance (loss of information and business, damage to equipment and systems), and outlines how the report is organized (three recommendations). Good openers in effect set up a contract with the reader. The writer promises to cover certain topics in a specified order. Readers expect the writer to fulfill the contract. They want the topics to be developed as promised—using the same wording and presented in the order mentioned. For example, if in your introduction you state that you will discuss the use of *smart cards*, do not change the heading for that section to *access cards*. Remember that the introduction provides a map to a report; switching the names on the map will ensure that readers get lost. To maintain consistency, delay writing the introduction until after you have completed the report. Long, complex reports may require introductions, brief internal summaries, and previews for each section.

What are the benefits of transitional expressions?

Transitions. Expressions such as *on the contrary, at the same time*, and *however* show relationships and help reveal the logical flow of ideas in a report. These transitional expressions enable writers to tell readers where ideas are headed and how they relate. Notice how abrupt the following two sentences sound without a transition: *The Microsoft Zune player offers several technological advances that exceed the capabilities of Apple's iPod devices. The Zune [however] is locked into a clunky online music store that isn't likely to win many fans.*

The following transitional expressions (see Chapter 5, Figure 5.8 for a complete list) enable you to show readers how you are developing your ideas.

To present additional thoughts: *additionally, again, also, moreover, furthermore*

To suggest cause and effect: *accordingly, as a result, consequently, therefore*

To contrast ideas: *at the same time, but, however, on the contrary, though, yet*

To show time and order: *after, before, first, finally, now, previously, then, to conclude*

To clarify points: *for example, for instance, in other words, that is, thus*

In using these expressions, recognize that they do not have to sit at the head of a sentence. Listen to the rhythm of the sentence, and place the expression where a natural pause occurs. If you are unsure about the placement of a transitional expression, position it at the beginning of the sentence. Used appropriately, transitional expressions serve readers as guides; misused or overused, they can be as distracting and frustrating as too many road signs on a highway.

What makes for good headings, and why are they important?

Headings. Good headings are another structural cue that assists readers in comprehending the organization of a report. They highlight major ideas, allowing busy readers to see the big picture at a glance. Moreover, headings provide resting points for the mind and for the eye, breaking up large chunks of text into manageable and inviting segments.

Report writers may use functional or talking headings. Functional headings (for example, *Background, Findings, Personnel*, and *Production Costs*) describe functions or general topics. They show the outline of a report but provide little insight for readers. Functional headings are useful for routine reports. They are also appropriate for sensitive topics that might provoke emotional reactions. By keeping the headings general, experienced writers hope to minimize reader opposition or response to controversial subjects. Talking headings (for example, *Lack of Space and Cost Compound Campus Parking Problem* or *Survey Shows Support for Parking Fees*) provide more information and spark interest. Unless carefully written, however, talking headings can fail to reveal the organization of a report. With some planning, though, headings can be both functional and talking, such as *Parking Recommendations: Shuttle and New Structures*.

The best strategy to help you create helpful talking headings is to write a few paragraphs first and then generate talking headings that sum up the major point of each paragraph. To create the most effective headings, follow a few basic guidelines:

- **Use appropriate heading levels.** The position and format of a heading indicate its level of importance and relationship to other points. Figure 12.6 illustrates and discusses a commonly used heading format for business reports. For an overview of alphanumeric and decimal outlines, please see page 144.

- **Capitalize and emphasize carefully.** Most writers use all capital letters (without underlines) for main titles, such as the report, chapter, and unit titles. For first- and second-level headings, they capitalize only the first letter of main words such as nouns, verbs, adjectives, adverbs, names, and so on. Articles (*a, an, the*), conjunctions (*and, but, or, nor*), and prepositions with three or fewer letters (*in, to, by, for*) are not capitalized unless they appear at the beginning or ending of the heading. For additional emphasis, most writers use a bold font, as shown in Figure 12.6.

- **Try to balance headings within levels.** Although it may not be always possible, attempt to create headings that are grammatically similar at a given level. For example, *Developing Product Teams* and *Presenting Plan to Management* are balanced, but *Development of Product Teams* and *Presenting Plan to Management* are not.

- **For short reports use first-level or first- and second-level headings.** Many business reports contain only one or two levels of headings. For such reports use first-level headings (centered, bolded) and, if needed, second-level headings (flush left, bolded). See Figure 12.6.

- **Include at least one heading per report page, but don't end the page with a heading.** Headings increase the readability and attractiveness of report pages. Use at least one per page to break up blocks of text. Move a heading that is separated from the text that follows from the bottom of the page to the top of the following page.

FIGURE 12.6 **Levels of Headings in Reports**

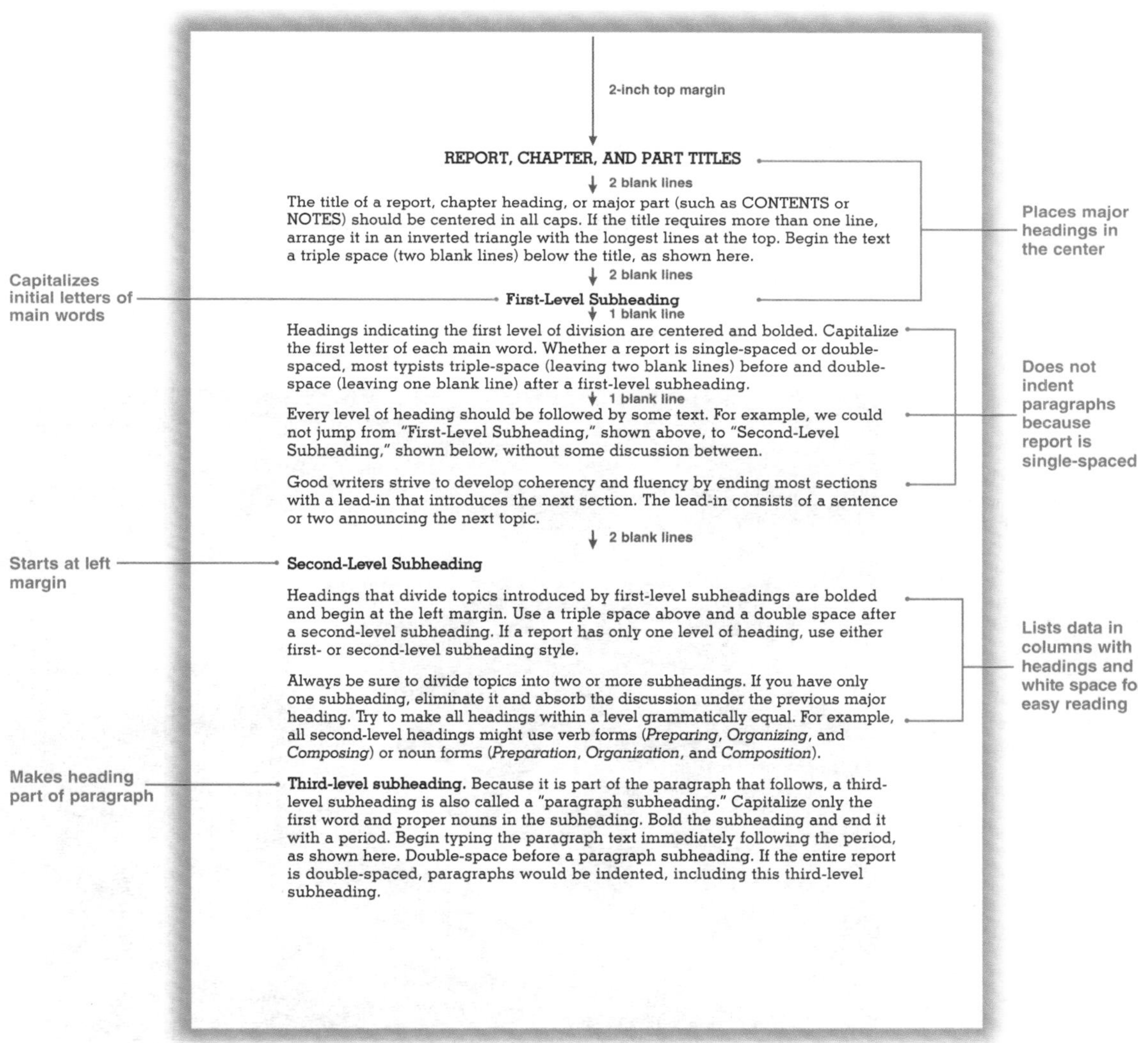
2-inch top margin

REPORT, CHAPTER, AND PART TITLES

2 blank lines

The title of a report, chapter heading, or major part (such as CONTENTS or NOTES) should be centered in all caps. If the title requires more than one line, arrange it in an inverted triangle with the longest lines at the top. Begin the text a triple space (two blank lines) below the title, as shown here.

2 blank lines

First-Level Subheading

1 blank line

Headings indicating the first level of division are centered and bolded. Capitalize the first letter of each main word. Whether a report is single-spaced or double-spaced, most typists triple-space (leaving two blank lines) before and double-space (leaving one blank line) after a first-level subheading.

1 blank line

Every level of heading should be followed by some text. For example, we could not jump from "First-Level Subheading," shown above, to "Second-Level Subheading," shown below, without some discussion between.

Good writers strive to develop coherency and fluency by ending most sections with a lead-in that introduces the next section. The lead-in consists of a sentence or two announcing the next topic.

2 blank lines

Second-Level Subheading

Headings that divide topics introduced by first-level subheadings are bolded and begin at the left margin. Use a triple space above and a double space after a second-level subheading. If a report has only one level of heading, use either first- or second-level subheading style.

Always be sure to divide topics into two or more subheadings. If you have only one subheading, eliminate it and absorb the discussion under the previous major heading. Try to make all headings within a level grammatically equal. For example, all second-level headings might use verb forms (*Preparing*, *Organizing*, and *Composing*) or noun forms (*Preparation*, *Organization*, and *Composition*).

Third-level subheading. Because it is part of the paragraph that follows, a third-level subheading is also called a "paragraph subheading." Capitalize only the first word and proper nouns in the subheading. Bold the subheading and end it with a period. Begin typing the paragraph text immediately following the period, as shown here. Double-space before a paragraph subheading. If the entire report is double-spaced, paragraphs would be indented, including this third-level subheading.

- **Apply punctuation correctly.** Omit end punctuation in first- and second-level headings. End punctuation is required in third-level headings because they are capitalized and punctuated like sentences. Proper nouns (names) are capitalized in third-level headings as they would be in a sentence.

- **Keep headings short but clear.** One-word headings are emphatic but not always clear. For example, the heading *Budget* does not adequately describe figures for a summer project involving student interns for an oil company in Texas. Try to keep your headings brief (no more than eight words), but make sure they are understandable. Experiment with headings that concisely tell who, what, when, where, and why.

Writing Short Informational Reports

LEARNING OBJECTIVE 4
Prepare short informational reports that describe routine tasks.

What is the purpose of informational reports?

Now that we have covered the basics of gathering, interpreting, and organizing data, we are ready to put it all together into short informational or analytical reports. Informational reports often describe periodic, recurring activities (such as monthly sales or weekly customer calls) as well as situational, nonrecurring events (such as trips, conferences, and progress on special projects). Short informational reports may also include summaries of longer publications. What all these reports have in common is delivering information to readers who do not have to be persuaded. Informational report readers usually are neutral or receptive.

You can expect to write many informational reports as an entry-level or middle-management employee. Because these reports generally deliver nonsensitive data and, therefore, will not upset the reader, they are organized directly. Often they need little background material or introductory comments because readers are familiar with the topics. Although they are generally conversational and informal, informational reports should not be so casual that the reader struggles to find the important points. Main points must be immediately visible. Headings, lists, bulleted items, and other graphic design elements, as well as clear organization, enable readers to grasp major ideas immediately. The lessons that you have learned about conciseness, clarity, courtesy, and effective writing in general throughout earlier chapters apply to report writing as well. After all, competent reports can boost your visibility in the company and promote your advancement. The accompanying Career Coach box provides additional pointers on design features and techniques that can improve your reports.

Film production crews have tight deadlines, and unforeseen studio mishaps can throw a multi-million dollar blockbuster off schedule. Producers at England's Leavesden Film Studios struggled to keep *Harry Potter and the Deathly Hallows* on track following the injury of Harry's stunt double and a pyrotechnics fire at Hogwart's Castle. Despite setbacks, executives announced that the studio would deliver the boy wizard's big screen adventure on time. *How do informational reports help managers keep projects on schedule?*

Summaries

A summary compresses the main points from a book, report, article, Web site, meeting, or convention. A summary saves time because it can reduce a report or article 85 to 95 percent. Employees are sometimes asked to write summaries that condense technical reports, periodical articles, or books so that their staffs or superiors may grasp the main ideas quickly. Students may be asked to write summaries of articles, chapters, or books to sharpen their writing skills and to confirm their knowledge of reading assignments. In writing a summary, you will follow these general guidelines:

- Present the goal or purpose of the document being summarized. Why was it written?
- Highlight the research methods (if appropriate), findings, conclusions, and recommendations.
- Omit illustrations, examples, and references.
- Organize for readability by including headings and bulleted or enumerated lists.
- Include your reactions or an overall evaluation of the document if asked to do so.

An *executive summary* summarizes a long report, proposal, or business plan. It concentrates on what management needs to know from a longer report. How to prepare an executive summary is covered in Chapter 13 on page 430.

Spotlight on Communicators

"We believe that the traditional methods of communicating government financial information—through reams of audited financial statements that have little relevance to the taxpayer—must be supplemented by government financial reporting that expresses complex financial details in an understandable form," said Relmond Van Daniker, executive director of the Association of Government Accountants (AGA). The association he heads recommends that government financial information be clear and understandable, updated regularly, delivered to all, easy to locate, and honest in breadth yet technically accurate in detail. A recent AGA survey revealed that the public overwhelmingly believes government has the obligation to report and explain how it generates and spends its money, but is failing to meet expectations.

Periodic (Activity) Reports

Most businesses—especially larger ones—require periodic reports (sometimes called *activity reports)* to keep management informed of operations. These recurring reports are written at regular intervals—weekly, monthly, yearly—so that management can monitor business strategies and, if necessary, remedy any problems. Some periodic reports simply contain figures, such as sales volume, number and kind of customer service calls, shipments delivered, accounts payable, and personnel data. More challenging periodic reports require descriptions and discussions of activities. In preparing a narrative description of their activities, employees writing periodic reports usually do the following:

What do summaries cover and what are their advantages?

Why are periodic reports written?

- Summarize regular activities and events performed during the reporting period
- Describe irregular events deserving the attention of management
- Highlight special needs and problems

Managers naturally want to know that routine activities are progressing normally. Employees today enjoy a great deal of independence and shoulder much responsibility due to flattened hierarchies on the job. They often work flexible hours in far-flung locations. Keeping track of their activities and the tasks they were assigned is crucial in such an environment. Increasingly, routine reports are sent by e-mail and take the form of efficient bulleted lists without commentary.

Figure 12.7 shows a weekly activity report prepared by Siddharth Singh, a senior Web producer at the information technology firm Sygnal Macro in Silicon Valley. Sid is responsible for his firm's Web presence in Asian countries or territories, mainly Japan, China, Hong Kong, and Vietnam. In his weekly reports to his supervisor, Tomas Esposito, Sid neatly divides his projects into *completed*, *in progress*, and *ongoing*. Tomas, the manager, then combines the activity reports from all his subordinates into a separate periodic report detailing the department's activities to his superiors.

Sid justifies the use of jargon, missing salutation and complimentary close, and ultrashort bulleted items as follows: "We e-mail our reports internally, so some IT jargon can be expected. The readers will understand it. Tomas and upper management all want reporting to be brief and to the point. Bullets fit us just fine." Periodic reports ensure that information within the company flows steadily and that supervisors know the status of current and pending projects. This efficient information flow is all the more important because Sid works at home two days a week to spend time with his young children. Several of his coworkers also telecommute.

Trip, Convention, and Conference Reports

What is the purpose of trip and conference reports, and what information do they convey?

Employees sent on business trips or to conventions and conferences typically must submit reports when they return. Organizations want to know that their money was well spent in funding the travel. These reports inform management about new procedures, equipment, and laws as well as supply information affecting products, operations, and service.

The hardest parts of writing these reports are selecting the most relevant material and organizing it coherently. Generally, it is best not to use chronological sequencing (*in the morning we did X, at lunch we heard Y, and in the afternoon we did Z*). Instead, you should focus on three to five topics in which your reader will be interested. These items become the body of the report.

CAREER COACH

The Top Ten Tips for Designing Better Documents

Desktop publishing packages, high-level word processing programs, and advanced printers now make it possible for you to turn out professional-looking documents and promotional materials. Resist the temptation, however, to overdo it by incorporating too many features in one document. Here are the top ten design tips for applying good sense and solid design principles in "publishing" your documents.

1. Analyze your audience. Sales brochures and promotional letters can be flashy—with color print, oversized type, and fancy borders—to attract attention. However, such effects are out of place for most traditional business documents. Also, will your readers be reading painstakingly or merely browsing? Lists and headings help those readers who are in a hurry.

2. Avoid amateurish effects. Strive for simple, clean, and forceful effects. Many beginning writers, eager to display every graphic device a program offers, produce busy, cluttered documents. Too many typefaces, ruled lines, oversized headlines, and images will overwhelm readers.

3. Choose an appropriate type size. For most business memos, letters, and reports, the body text should be 11 to 12 points tall (a point is 1/72 of an inch). Larger type looks amateurish, and smaller type is hard to read and faxes poorly.

4. Use a consistent type font. Although your software may provide a variety of fonts, stay with a single family of type within one document—at least until you become more expert. The most popular fonts are Times New Roman and Arial. In Word 2007, Cambria and Calibri are the two default fonts and, as a result, may become more popular. For emphasis and contrast, you can vary the font size and weight with **bold**, *italic*, ***bold italic***, and other selections.

5. Do not justify right margins. Textbooks, novels, newspapers, magazines, and other long works are usually set with justified (even) right margins. However, for shorter works ragged-right margins are recommended because such margins add white space and help readers locate the beginnings of new lines. Slower readers find ragged-right copy more legible.

6. Separate paragraphs and sentences appropriately. In single-spaced business documents, the first line of a paragraph is preceded by a blank line, and the line begins flush left. In double-spaced documents, the first line is indented five spaces from the left margin, and no space. To separate sentences, typists have traditionally left two spaces after the period. This spacing is still acceptable, and proponents argue that this practice enhances readability, but most writers now follow printers' standards and leave only one space. Whichever standard you adopt, maintain it consistently.

7. Design readable headings. Presenting headings in all caps is generally discouraged because solid blocks of capital letters interfere with the recognition of word patterns. To further improve readability, select a sans serif typeface (one without cross strokes or embellishment), such as Arial or Calibri.

8. Strive for an attractive page layout. In designing title pages or graphics, provide a balance between print and white space. Also consider placing the focal point (something that draws the reader's eye) at the optical center of a page—about three lines above the actual center. Moreover, remember that the average reader scans a page from left to right and top to bottom in a *Z* pattern. Plan your graphics accordingly.

9. Use graphics and clip art with restraint. You can import, copy, or scan charts, original drawings, photographs, and clip art into documents. Use such images, however, only when they are well drawn, relevant, purposeful, and appropriately sized.

10. Develop expertise. Learn to use the desktop publishing features of your current word processing software, or investigate one of the special programs, such as QuarkXPress, Adobe's InDesign, and Corel's Ventura. Although the learning curve for many of these programs is steep, such effort is well spent if you will be producing newsletters, brochures, announcements, visual aids, and promotional literature.

Career Application

Buy or borrow a book or two on designing documents, and select ten tips that you could share with the class. In teams of three or four, analyze the design and layout of three or four annual reports. Evaluate the appropriateness of typeface and type size, white space, headings, and graphics.

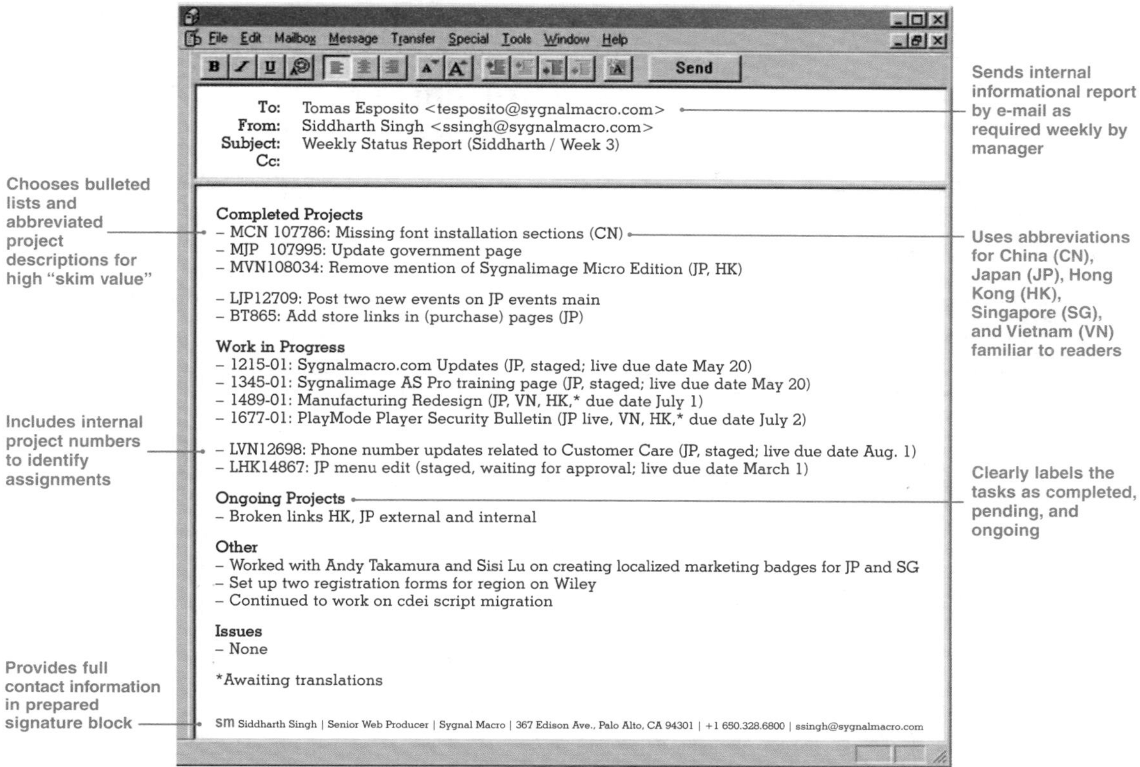

To: Tomas Esposito <tesposito@sygnalmacro.com>
From: Siddharth Singh <ssingh@sygnalmacro.com>
Subject: Weekly Status Report (Siddharth / Week 3)
Cc:

Completed Projects
- MCN 107786: Missing font installation sections (CN)
- MJP 107995: Update government page
- MVN108034: Remove mention of Sygnalimage Micro Edition (JP, HK)

- LJP12709: Post two new events on JP events main
- BT865: Add store links in (purchase) pages (JP)

Work in Progress
- 1215-01: Sygnalmacro.com Updates (JP, staged; live due date May 20)
- 1345-01: Sygnalimage AS Pro training page (JP, staged; live due date May 20)
- 1489-01: Manufacturing Redesign (JP, VN, HK,* due date July 1)
- 1677-01: PlayMode Player Security Bulletin (JP live, VN, HK,* due date July 2)

- LVN12698: Phone number updates related to Customer Care (JP, staged; live due date Aug. 1)
- LHK14867: JP menu edit (staged, waiting for approval; live due date March 1)

Ongoing Projects
- Broken links HK, JP external and internal

Other
- Worked with Andy Takamura and Sisi Lu on creating localized marketing badges for JP and SG
- Set up two registration forms for region on Wiley
- Continued to work on cdei script migration

Issues
- None

*Awaiting translations

SM Siddharth Singh | Senior Web Producer | Sygnal Macro | 367 Edison Ave., Palo Alto, CA 94301 | +1 650.328.6800 | ssingh@sygnalmacro.com

Sends internal informational report by e-mail as required weekly by manager
Chooses bulleted lists and abbreviated project descriptions for high "skim value"
Uses abbreviations for China (CN), Japan (JP), Hong Kong (HK), Singapore (SG), and Vietnam (VN) familiar to readers
Includes internal project numbers to identify assignments
Clearly labels the tasks as completed, pending, and ongoing
Provides full contact information in prepared signature block

FIGURE 12.7 **Periodic (Activity) Report—E-Mail Format**

Then simply add an introduction and closing, and your report is organized. Here is a general outline for trip, conference, and convention reports:

- Begin by identifying the event (exact date, name, and location) and previewing the topics to be discussed.
- Summarize in the body three to five main points that might benefit the reader.
- Itemize your expenses, if requested, on a separate sheet.
- Close by expressing appreciation, suggesting action to be taken, or synthesizing the value of the trip or event.

Jack Horn was recently named employment coordinator in the Human Resources Department of an electronics appliance manufacturer headquartered in central Ohio. Recognizing his lack of experience in interviewing job applicants, he asked permission to attend a one-day conference on the topic. His boss, Elizabeth Greene, encouraged Jack to attend, saying, "We all need to brush up on our interviewing techniques. Come back and tell us what you learned." When he returned, Jack wrote the conference report shown in Figure 12.8. Here is how he described its preparation: "I know my boss values brevity, so I worked hard to make my report no more than a page and a quarter. The conference saturated me with great ideas, far too many to cover in one brief report. So, I decided to discuss three topics that would be most useful to our staff. Although I had to be brief, I nonetheless wanted to provide as many details—especially about common interviewing mistakes—as possible. By the third draft, I had compressed my ideas into a manageable size without sacrificing any of the meaning."

FIGURE 12.8 Conference Report—Memo Format

//TriCom
Total HR Services
Interoffice Memo

DATE: April 22, 2011

TO: Elizabeth Greene

FROM: Jack Horn *JH*

SUBJECT: Conference on Employment Interviews

I enjoyed attending the "Interviewing People" training conference sponsored by the National Business Foundation. This one-day meeting, held in Columbus on April 19, provided excellent advice that will help us strengthen our interviewing techniques. Although the conference covered many topics, this report concentrates on three areas: structuring the interview, avoiding common mistakes, and responding to new legislation.

Identifies topic and previews how the report is organized

Structuring the Interview

Job interviews usually have three parts. The opening establishes a friendly rapport with introductions, a few polite questions, and an explanation of the purpose for the interview. The body of the interview consists of questions controlled by the interviewer. The interviewer has three goals: (a) educating the applicant about the job, (b) eliciting information about the applicant's suitability for the job, and (c) promoting goodwill about the organization. In closing, the interviewer should encourage the applicant to ask questions, summarize main points, and indicate what actions will follow.

Sets off major topics with centered headings

Avoiding Common Mistakes

Probably the most interesting and practical part of the conference centered on common mistakes made by interviewers, some of which I summarize here:

1. Not taking notes at each interview. Recording important facts enables you to remember the first candidate as easily as you remember the last—and all those in between.
2. Not testing the candidate's communication skills. To be able to evaluate a candidate's ability to express ideas, ask the individual to explain some technical jargon from his or her current position.
3. Having departing employees conduct the interviews for their replacements. Departing employees may be unreliable as interviewers because they tend to hire candidates not quite as strong as they are.
4. Failing to check references. As many as 45 percent of all résumés may contain falsified data. The best way to check references is to network: ask the person whose name has been given to suggest the name of another person.

Covers facts that will most interest and help reader

Elizabeth Greene Page 2 April 22, 2011

Responding to New Legislation

Current federal provisions of the Americans With Disabilities Act prohibit interviewers from asking candidates—or even their references—about candidates' disabilities. A question we frequently asked ("Do you have any physical limitations which would prevent you from performing the job for which you are applying?") would now break the law. Interviewers must also avoid asking about medical history; prescription drug use; prior workers' compensation claims; work absenteeism due to illness; and past treatment for alcoholism, drug use, or mental illness.

Concludes with offer to share information

Sharing This Information

This conference provided me with valuable training that I would like to share with other department members at a future staff meeting. Let me know when it can be scheduled.

Progress and Interim Reports

Continuing projects often require progress or interim reports to describe their status. These reports may be external (advising customers regarding the headway of their projects) or internal (informing management of the status of activities). Progress reports typically follow this pattern of development:

What type of information do progress and interim reports describe, and which audiences do they address?

- Specify in the opening the purpose and nature of the project.
- Provide background information if the audience requires filling in.
- Describe the work completed.
- Explain the work currently in progress, including personnel, activities, methods, and locations.
- Describe current problems and anticipate future problems and possible remedies.
- Discuss future activities and provide the expected completion date.

As a location manager for Eagle Video Productions, Gina Genova frequently writes progress reports, such as the one shown in Figure 12.9. Producers want to know what she is doing, and a phone call does not provide a permanent record. Here is how she described the reasoning behind her progress report: "I usually include background information in my reports because a director does not always know or remember exactly what specifications I was given for a location search. Then I try to hit the high points of what I have completed and what I plan to do next, without getting bogged down in tiny details. Although it would be easier to skip them, I have learned to be up front with any problems that I anticipate. I do not tell how to solve the problems, but I feel duty-bound to at least mention them."

Investigative Reports

Investigative reports deliver data for a specific situation—without offering interpretation or recommendations. These nonrecurring reports are generally arranged using the direct strategy with three segments: introduction, body, and summary. The body—which includes the facts, findings, or discussion—may be organized by time, component, importance, criteria, or convention. What is important is dividing the topic into logical segments—say, three to five areas that are roughly equal and do not overlap.

What are the main characteristics of investigative reports?

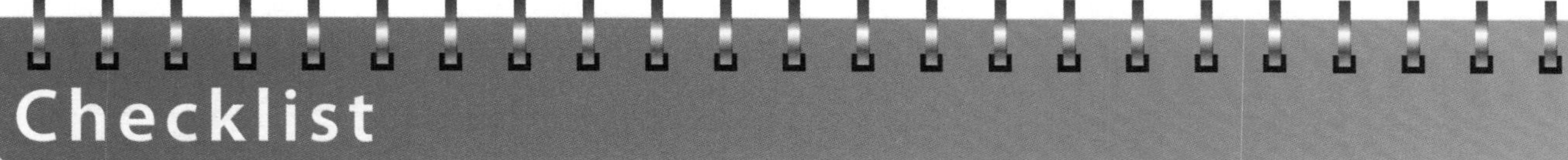

Writing Informational Reports

Introduction

- **Begin directly.** Identify the report and its purpose.
- **Provide a preview.** If the report is over a page long, give the reader a brief overview of its organization.
- **Supply background data selectively.** When readers are unfamiliar with the topic, briefly fill in the necessary details.
- **Divide the topic.** Strive to group the facts or findings into three to five roughly equal segments that do not overlap.

Body

- **Arrange the subtopics logically.** Consider organizing by time, component, importance, criteria, or convention.
- **Use clear headings.** Supply functional or talking headings (at least one per page) that describe each important section.
- **Determine degree of formality.** Use an informal, conversational writing style unless the audience expects a more formal tone.
- **Enhance readability with graphic highlighting.** Make liberal use of bullets, numbered and lettered lists, headings, underlined items, and white space.

Summary/Concluding Remarks

- **When necessary, summarize the report.** Briefly review the main points and discuss what action will follow.
- **Offer a concluding thought.** If relevant, express appreciation or describe your willingness to provide further information.

FIGURE 12.9 **Progress Report**

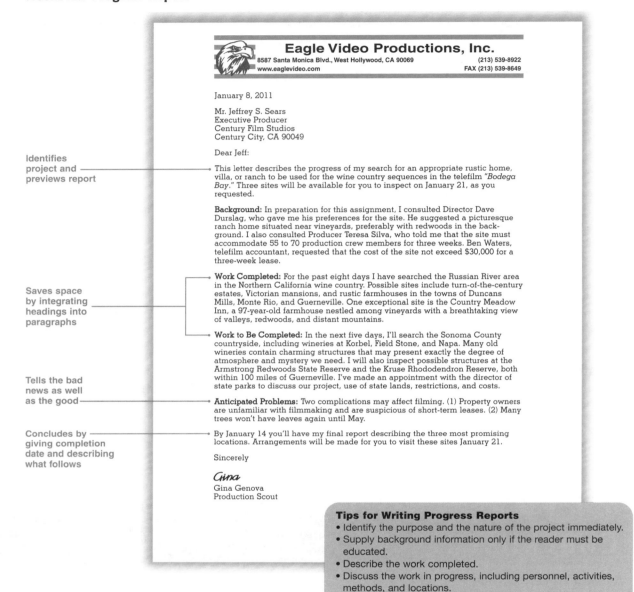

Eagle Video Productions, Inc.
8587 Santa Monica Blvd., West Hollywood, CA 90069 (213) 539-8922
www.eaglevideo.com FAX (213) 539-8649

January 8, 2011

Mr. Jeffrey S. Sears
Executive Producer
Century Film Studios
Century City, CA 90049

Dear Jeff:

Identifies project and previews report

This letter describes the progress of my search for an appropriate rustic home, villa, or ranch to be used for the wine country sequences in the telefilm "*Bodega Bay*." Three sites will be available for you to inspect on January 21, as you requested.

Background: In preparation for this assignment, I consulted Director Dave Durslag, who gave me his preferences for the site. He suggested a picturesque ranch home situated near vineyards, preferably with redwoods in the background. I also consulted Producer Teresa Silva, who told me that the site must accommodate 55 to 70 production crew members for three weeks. Ben Waters, telefilm accountant, requested that the cost of the site not exceed $30,000 for a three-week lease.

Saves space by integrating headings into paragraphs

Work Completed: For the past eight days I have searched the Russian River area in the Northern California wine country. Possible sites include turn-of-the-century estates, Victorian mansions, and rustic farmhouses in the towns of Duncans Mills, Monte Rio, and Guerneville. One exceptional site is the Country Meadow Inn, a 97-year-old farmhouse nestled among vineyards with a breathtaking view of valleys, redwoods, and distant mountains.

Work to Be Completed: In the next five days, I'll search the Sonoma County countryside, including wineries at Korbel, Field Stone, and Napa. Many old wineries contain charming structures that may present exactly the degree of atmosphere and mystery we need. I will also inspect possible structures at the Armstrong Redwoods State Reserve and the Kruse Rhododendron Reserve, both within 100 miles of Guerneville. I've made an appointment with the director of state parks to discuss our project, use of state lands, restrictions, and costs.

Tells the bad news as well as the good

Anticipated Problems: Two complications may affect filming. (1) Property owners are unfamiliar with filmmaking and are suspicious of short-term leases. (2) Many trees won't have leaves again until May.

Concludes by giving completion date and describing what follows

By January 14 you'll have my final report describing the three most promising locations. Arrangements will be made for you to visit these sites January 21.

Sincerely

Gina

Gina Genova
Production Scout

Tips for Writing Progress Reports

- Identify the purpose and the nature of the project immediately.
- Supply background information only if the reader must be educated.
- Describe the work completed.
- Discuss the work in progress, including personnel, activities, methods, and locations.
- Identify problems and possible remedies.
- Consider future activities.
- Close by telling the expected date of completion.

Zooming In PART 2

Starbucks Perks Up: Recapturing the Soul of the Coffeehouse

Under the leadership of chairman, president, and CEO Howard Schultz, Starbucks shelved plans to expand the number of stores and to pursue other avenues of growth beyond its coffeehouse business. The recession required a new approach, "to transform Starbucks and return the company to sustainable, profitable growth while at the same time [remaining] true to our core values and guiding principles" in the words of Howard Schultz.[3]

An entrepreneur who thinks outside the box, Schultz grudgingly introduced new efficiencies to reinvigorate Starbucks. Instead of relying on his instincts and free-flowing growth, he has agreed to do advertising and follows store sales data to understand customer preferences for drinking coffee in the morning (out of necessity) as opposed to in the afternoon (when it becomes a treat). Schultz also started to pay attention to controlling costs and simplifying operations. He reluctantly standardized how baristas prepare coffee, from "anything goes" to a consistent six-step process.

Pursuing the right business strategy is difficult, and Starbucks has experienced flops. The chain scaled back its music business by handing over Hear Music, its short-lived label, to Concord Music Group. Starbucks also abandoned plans to allow customers to customize CDs in its stores and got burned by promoting at least one film that became a box office dud. The poor economy forced the company to rethink its strategy. CEO Schultz said: "We are committed to examining all aspects of our business that are not directly related to our core."[4]

As for competition, Starbucks still remains the front-runner. Specialty retailers such as Caribou Coffee—the second-largest nonfranchised coffee chain in the United States—The Coffee Bean & Tea Leaf, and Peet's Coffee & Tea are all much smaller than the market leader. However, Starbucks knows that competitors never sleep. In a lagging economy, its biggest rivals are the low-end, low-cost coffee powerhouses Dunkin' Donuts and McDonald's. Ironically, Starbucks has led the coffee revolution of the last 20 years and forced its competitors to improve their coffee quality and selection. The question now is whether the in-store experience at Starbucks is so unique that customers will pay higher prices for it. Both McDonald's and Dunkin' Donuts have taken direct potshots at Starbucks' premium prices and attitude in their advertising, eager to draw away Starbucks' customers. You will learn more about this case on page 412.

© AP Images/Seth Perlman

Critical Thinking

- How important to Starbucks are the collection, organization, and distribution of up-to-date information regarding food and beverage trends, competition, and product development?
- In what ways could Starbucks use the Internet to monitor its main competitors, Caribou Coffee, McDonald's McCafé, and Dunkin' Donuts?
- What kind of reports might employees assigned the task of monitoring Starbucks' competition write to management?

The subject matter of the report usually suggests the best way to divide or organize it. Beth Givens, an information specialist for a Minneapolis health care consulting firm, was given the task of researching and writing an investigative report for St. John's Hospital. Her assignment: study the award-winning patient service program at Good Samaritan Hospital and report how it improved its patient satisfaction rating from 6.2 to 7.8 in just one year. Beth collected data and then organized her findings into four parts: management training, employee training, patient services, and follow-up program. Although we do not show Beth's complete report here, you can see a similar informational report in Chapter 11, Figure 11.2.

Whether you are writing a periodic, trip, conference, progress, or investigative report, you will want to review the suggestions found in the accompanying checklist.

Preparing Short Analytical Reports

LEARNING OBJECTIVE 5
Compose short analytical reports that solve business problems.

Analytical reports differ significantly from informational reports. Although both seek to collect and present data clearly, analytical reports also analyze the data and typically try to persuade the reader to accept the conclusions and act on the recommendations. Informational reports emphasize facts; analytical reports emphasize reasoning and conclusions.

What purpose do analytical reports serve, and how do they present information?

For some readers you may organize analytical reports directly with the conclusions and recommendations near the beginning. Directness is appropriate when the reader has confidence in the writer, based on either experience or credentials. Frontloading the recommendations also works when the topic is routine or familiar and the reader is supportive.

Directness can backfire, though. If you announce the recommendations too quickly, the reader may immediately object to a single idea. You may have had no suspicion that this idea would trigger a negative reaction. Once the reader is opposed, changing an unfavorable mind-set may be difficult or impossible. A reader may also think you have oversimplified or overlooked something significant if you lay out all the recommendations before explaining how you arrived at them. When you must lead the reader through the process of discovering the solution or recommendation, use the indirect strategy: present conclusions and recommendations last.

Most analytical reports answer questions about specific problems and aid in decision making. How can we use a Web site most effectively? Should we close the El Paso plant? Should we buy or lease company cars? How can we improve customer service? Three typical analytical reports answer business questions: justification/recommendation reports, feasibility reports, and yardstick reports. Because these reports all solve problems, the categories are not mutually exclusive. What distinguishes them are their goals and organization.

Ethics Check

Is This $100 Bill Yours?

Purchasing managers at Frito-Lay, Safeway, and B&G Foods have pleaded guilty to taking bribes that led to tainted foods purchased at inflated prices. Company officials relied on false reports and documentation supplied by their managers. How did food suppliers know whom to bribe? New Jersey businessman and food broker Randall Rahal said he could guess who would be susceptible to bribery by dropping a $100 bill on the floor, then picking it up and saying, "You must have dropped this. Is it yours?" Is this a good test?

Justification/Recommendation Reports

Both managers and employees must occasionally write reports that justify or recommend something, such as buying equipment, changing a procedure, hiring an employee, consolidating departments, or investing funds. These reports may also be called *internal proposals* because their persuasive nature is similar to that of external proposals (presented in Chapter 13). Large organizations sometimes prescribe how these reports should be organized; they use forms with conventional headings. When you are free to select an organizational plan yourself, however, let your audience and topic determine your choice of the direct or indirect strategy.

When would you follow the direct strategy in a justification/recommendation report, and when would you choose the indirect strategy?

Direct Strategy. For nonsensitive topics and recommendations that will be agreeable to readers, you can organize directly according to the following sequence:

- Identify the problem or need briefly.
- Announce the recommendation, solution, or action concisely and with action verbs.

© AP Images/Tony Ding

The Big Ten Conference may soon grow to twelve or more teams, if officials adopt a recent recommendation report by investment firm William Blair & Company. In examining whether league expansion would be profitable, the report concluded that adding teams like Rutgers, Syracuse, or Notre Dame would boost the $22 million in annual revenue that universities receive from league play. Notably, the recommended expansion would include a Big Ten title game to generate $15 million in the postseason. *What are the key elements of a persuasive justification report?*

- Explain more fully the benefits of the recommendation or steps necessary to solve the problem.
- Include a discussion of pros, cons, and costs.
- Conclude with a summary specifying the recommendation and necessary action.

Here is how Cory Black applied the process in justifying a purchase. Cory is operations manager in charge of a fleet of trucks for a large parcel delivery company in Atlanta. When he heard about a new Goodyear smart tire with an electronic chip, Cory thought his company should give the new tire a try. Because new tires would represent an irregular purchase and because they would require a pilot test, he wrote the justification/recommendation report shown in Figure 12.10 to his boss. Cory described his report in this way: "As more and more parcel delivery companies crop up, we have to find ways to cut costs so that we can remain competitive. Although more expensive initially, smart tires may solve many of our problems and save us money in the long run. I knew Jim Jordan, operations vice president, would be interested in them, especially in view of a recent Toyo truck tire recall and the huge Firestone tire fiasco that is still a vivid memory.[5] Because Jim would be most interested in what the smart tires could do for us, I concentrated on benefits. In my first draft, the benefits were lost in a couple of long paragraphs. Only after I read what I had written did I see that I was really talking about four separate benefits. Then I looked for words to summarize each one as a heading. So that Jim would know exactly what he should do, I concluded with specifics. All he had to do was say 'Go.'"

Indirect Strategy. When a reader may oppose a recommendation or when circumstances suggest caution, do not rush to reveal your recommendation. Consider using the following sequence for an indirect approach to your recommendations:

- Refer to the problem in general terms, not to your recommendation, in the subject line.
- Describe the problem or need your recommendation addresses. Use specific examples, supporting statistics, and authoritative quotes to lend credibility to the seriousness of the problem.
- Discuss alternative solutions, beginning with the least likely to succeed.
- Present the most promising alternative (your recommendation) last.
- Show how the advantages of your recommendation outweigh its disadvantages.
- Summarize your recommendation. If appropriate, specify the action it requires.
- Ask for authorization to proceed if necessary.

Why is it important to footnote or otherwise document sources in justification/recommendation reports?

Lara Brown, an executive assistant at a large petroleum and mining company in Grand Prairie, Texas, received a challenging research assignment. Her boss, the director of Human Resources, asked her to investigate ways to persuade employees to quit smoking. Here is how she described her task: "We banned smoking many years ago inside our buildings, but we never tried very hard to get smokers to actually kick their habits. My job was to gather information about the problem and learn how other companies have helped workers stop smoking. The report would go to my boss, but I knew he would pass it along to the management council for approval. If the report were just for my boss, I would put my recommendation right up front, because I'm sure he would support it. But the management council is another story. They need persuasion because of the costs involved—and because some of them are smokers. Therefore, I put the alternative I favored last. To gain credibility, I footnoted my sources. I had enough material for a ten-page report, but I kept it to two pages in keeping with our company report policy."

Lara single-spaced her report, shown in Figure 12.11, because her company prefers this style. Some companies prefer the readability of double spacing. Be sure to check with your organization for its preference before printing your reports.

Feasibility Reports

What is the purpose of feasibility reports?

Feasibility reports examine the practicality and advisability of following a course of action. They answer this question: Will this plan or proposal work? Feasibility reports typically are internal reports written to advise on matters such as consolidating departments, offering a wellness

FIGURE 12.10 **Justification/Recommendation Report—Memo Format**

1 Prewriting

Analyze: The purpose of this report is to persuade the manager to authorize the purchase and pilot testing of smart tires.

Anticipate: The audience is a manager who is familiar with operations but not with this product. He will probably be receptive to the recommendation.

Adapt: Present the report data in a direct, straightforward manner.

2 Writing

Research: Collect data on how smart tires could benefit operations.

Organize: Discuss the problem briefly. Introduce and justify the recommendation by noting its cost-effectiveness and paperwork benefits. Explain the benefits of smart tires. Describe the action to be taken.

Compose: Write and print first draft.

3 Revising

Revise: Revise to break up long paragraphs about benefits. Isolate each benefit in an enumerated list with headings.

Proofread: Double-check all figures. Be sure all headings are parallel.

Evaluate: Does this report make its request concisely but emphatically? Will the reader see immediately what action is required?

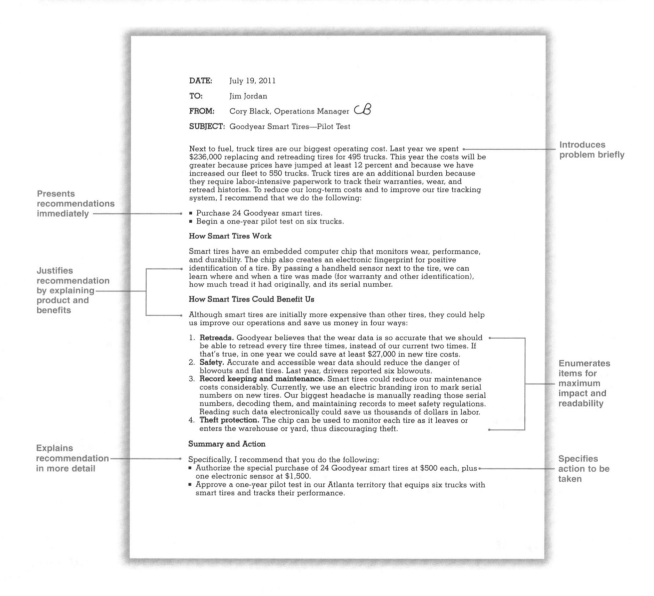

DATE: July 19, 2011

TO: Jim Jordan

FROM: Cory Black, Operations Manager *CB*

SUBJECT: Goodyear Smart Tires—Pilot Test

Next to fuel, truck tires are our biggest operating cost. Last year we spent $236,000 replacing and retreading tires for 495 trucks. This year the costs will be greater because prices have jumped at least 12 percent and because we have increased our fleet to 550 trucks. Truck tires are an additional burden because they require labor-intensive paperwork to track their warranties, wear, and retread histories. To reduce our long-term costs and to improve our tire tracking system, I recommend that we do the following: *(Introduces problem briefly)*

- Purchase 24 Goodyear smart tires.
- Begin a one-year pilot test on six trucks.

(Presents recommendations immediately)

How Smart Tires Work

Smart tires have an embedded computer chip that monitors wear, performance, and durability. The chip also creates an electronic fingerprint for positive identification of a tire. By passing a handheld sensor next to the tire, we can learn where and when a tire was made (for warranty and other identification), how much tread it had originally, and its serial number.

How Smart Tires Could Benefit Us

Although smart tires are initially more expensive than other tires, they could help us improve our operations and save us money in four ways:

(Justifies recommendation by explaining product and benefits)

1. **Retreads.** Goodyear believes that the wear data is so accurate that we should be able to retread every tire three times, instead of our current two times. If that's true, in one year we could save at least $27,000 in new tire costs.
2. **Safety.** Accurate and accessible wear data should reduce the danger of blowouts and flat tires. Last year, drivers reported six blowouts.
3. **Record keeping and maintenance.** Smart tires could reduce our maintenance costs considerably. Currently, we use an electric branding iron to mark serial numbers on new tires. Our biggest headache is manually reading those serial numbers, decoding them, and maintaining records to meet safety regulations. Reading such data electronically could save us thousands of dollars in labor.
4. **Theft protection.** The chip can be used to monitor each tire as it leaves or enters the warehouse or yard, thus discouraging theft.

(Enumerates items for maximum impact and readability)

Summary and Action

Specifically, I recommend that you do the following: *(Explains recommendation in more detail)*

- Authorize the special purchase of 24 Goodyear smart tires at $500 each, plus one electronic sensor at $1,500. *(Specifies action to be taken)*
- Approve a one-year pilot test in our Atlanta territory that equips six trucks with smart tires and tracks their performance.

FIGURE 12.11 **Justification/Recommendation Report, MLA Style**

DATE: October 11, 2011

TO: Gordon McClure, Director, Human Resources

FROM: Lara Brown, Executive Assistant *LB*

SUBJECT: Smoking Cessation Programs for Employees

At your request, I have examined measures that encourage employees to quit smoking. As company records show, approximately 23 percent of our employees still smoke, despite the antismoking and clean-air policies we adopted in 2009. To collect data for this report, I studied professional and government publications; I also inquired at companies and clinics about stop-smoking programs.

Introduces purpose of report, tells method of data collection, and previews organization

Avoids revealing recommendation immediately

This report presents data describing the significance of the problem, three alternative solutions, and a recommendation based on my investigation.

Uses headings that combine function and description

Significance of Problem: Health Care and Productivity Losses

Employees who smoke are costly to any organization. The following statistics show the effects of smoking for workers and for organizations:

- Absenteeism is 40 to 50 percent greater among smoking employees.
- Accidents are two to three times greater among smokers.
- Bronchitis, lung and heart disease, cancer, and early death are more frequent among smokers (Arhelger 4).

Documents data sources for credibility, uses MLA style citing author and page number in the text

Although our clean-air policy prohibits smoking in the building, shop, and office, we have done little to encourage employees to stop smoking. Many workers still go outside to smoke at lunch and breaks. Other companies have been far more proactive in their attempts to stop employee smoking. Many companies have found that persuading employees to stop smoking was a decisive factor in reducing their health insurance premiums. Below is a discussion of three common stop-smoking measures tried by other companies, along with a projected cost factor for each (Rindfleisch 4).

Discuss least effective alternative first

Alternative 1: Literature and Events

The least expensive and easiest stop-smoking measure involves the distribution of literature, such as "The Ten-Step Plan" from Smokefree Enterprises and government pamphlets citing smoking dangers. Some companies have also sponsored events such as the Great American Smoke-Out, a one-day occasion intended to develop group spirit in spurring smokers to quit. "Studies show, however," says one expert, "that literature and company-sponsored events have little permanent effect in helping smokers quit" (Mendel 108).

Cost: Negligible

program to employees, or hiring an outside firm to handle a company's accounting or computing operations. These reports may also be written by consultants called in to investigate a problem. The focus in these reports is on the decision: rejecting or proceeding with the proposed option. Because your role is not to persuade the reader to accept the decision, you will want to present the decision immediately. In writing feasibility reports, consider these suggestions:

- Announce your decision immediately.
- Provide a description of the background and problem necessitating the proposal.
- Discuss the benefits of the proposal.
- Describe the problems that may result.
- Calculate the costs associated with the proposal, if appropriate.
- Show the time frame necessary for implementing the proposal.

FIGURE 12.11 (Continued)

Gordon McClure October 11, 2011 Page 2

Alternative 2: Stop-Smoking Programs Outside the Workplace

Local clinics provide treatment programs in classes at their centers. Here in Houston we have the Smokers' Treatment Center, ACC Motivation Center, and New-Choice Program for Stopping Smoking. These behavior-modification stop-smoking programs are acknowledged to be more effective than literature distribution or incentive programs. However, studies of companies using off-workplace programs show that many employees fail to attend regularly and do not complete the programs.

Cost: $1,200 per employee, three-month individual program (New-Choice Program)
$900 per employee, three-month group session

Highlights costs for easy comparison

Alternative 3: Stop-Smoking Programs at the Workplace

Many clinics offer workplace programs with counselors meeting employees in company conference rooms. These programs have the advantage of keeping a firm's employees together so that they develop a group spirit and exert pressure on each other to succeed. The most successful programs are on company premises and also on company time. Employees participating in such programs had a 72 percent greater success record than employees attending the same stop-smoking program at an outside clinic (Honda 35). A disadvantage of this arrangement, of course, is lost work time—amounting to about two hours a week for three months.

Arranges alternatives so that most effective is last

Cost: $900 per employee, three-month program for two hours per week release time for three months

Conclusions and Recommendation

Summarizes findings and ends with specific recommendation

Smokers require discipline, counseling, and professional assistance in kicking the nicotine habit, as explained at the University of Michigan Health System Web site (Guide to Quitting Smoking). Workplace stop-smoking programs on company time are more effective than literature, incentives, and off-workplace programs. If our goal is to reduce health care costs and lead our employees to healthful lives, we should invest in a workplace stop-smoking program with release time for smokers. Although the program temporarily reduces productivity, we can expect to recapture that loss in lower health care premiums and healthier employees.

Therefore, I recommend that we begin a stop-smoking treatment program on company premises with two hours per week of release time for participants for three months.

Reveals recommendation only after discussing all alternatives

Lists all references in MLA Style

3

Works Cited

Magazine — Arhelger, Zack. "The End of Smoking." *The World of Business* 5 Nov. 2010: 3-8. Print.

Web site article — "Guide to Quitting Smoking." *The American Cancer Society*.org. Web. 27 Oct. 2010.

Journal article, database — Honda, Emeline Maude. "Managing Anti-Smoking Campaigns: The Case for Company Programs." *Management Quarterly* 32 (2009): 29–47. ABI-Inform. Web. 25 Oct. 2010.

Book — Mendel, I. A. *The Puff Stops Here*. Chicago: Science Publications, 2009.

Newspaper article — Rindfleisch, Terry. "Smoke-Free Workplaces Can Help Smokers Quit, Expert Says." *Evening Chronicle* 4 Dec. 2010: 4+. Print.

Ashley Denton-Tait, human resources manager for a large public accounting firm in San Antonio, Texas, wrote the feasibility report shown in Figure 12.12. Because she discovered that the company was losing time and money as a result of personal e-mail and Internet use by employees, she talked with the vice president, Eileen Heffernan, about the problem. Eileen didn't want Ashley to take time away from her job to investigate what other companies were doing to prevent this type of problem. Instead, she suggested that they hire a consultant to investigate what other companies were doing to prevent or limit personal e-mail and Internet use. The vice president then wanted to know whether the consultant's plan was feasible. Although Ashley's report is only one page long, it provides all the necessary information: background, benefits, employee acceptance, costs, and time frame.

What are the components of a typical feasibility report?

Yardstick Reports

Yardstick reports examine problems with two or more solutions. To determine the best solution, the writer establishes criteria by which to compare the alternatives. The criteria then act as a yardstick against which all the alternatives are measured. The yardstick approach is effective

What is a yardstick report, and what purpose does it serve?

FIGURE 12.12 Feasibility Report—Memo Format

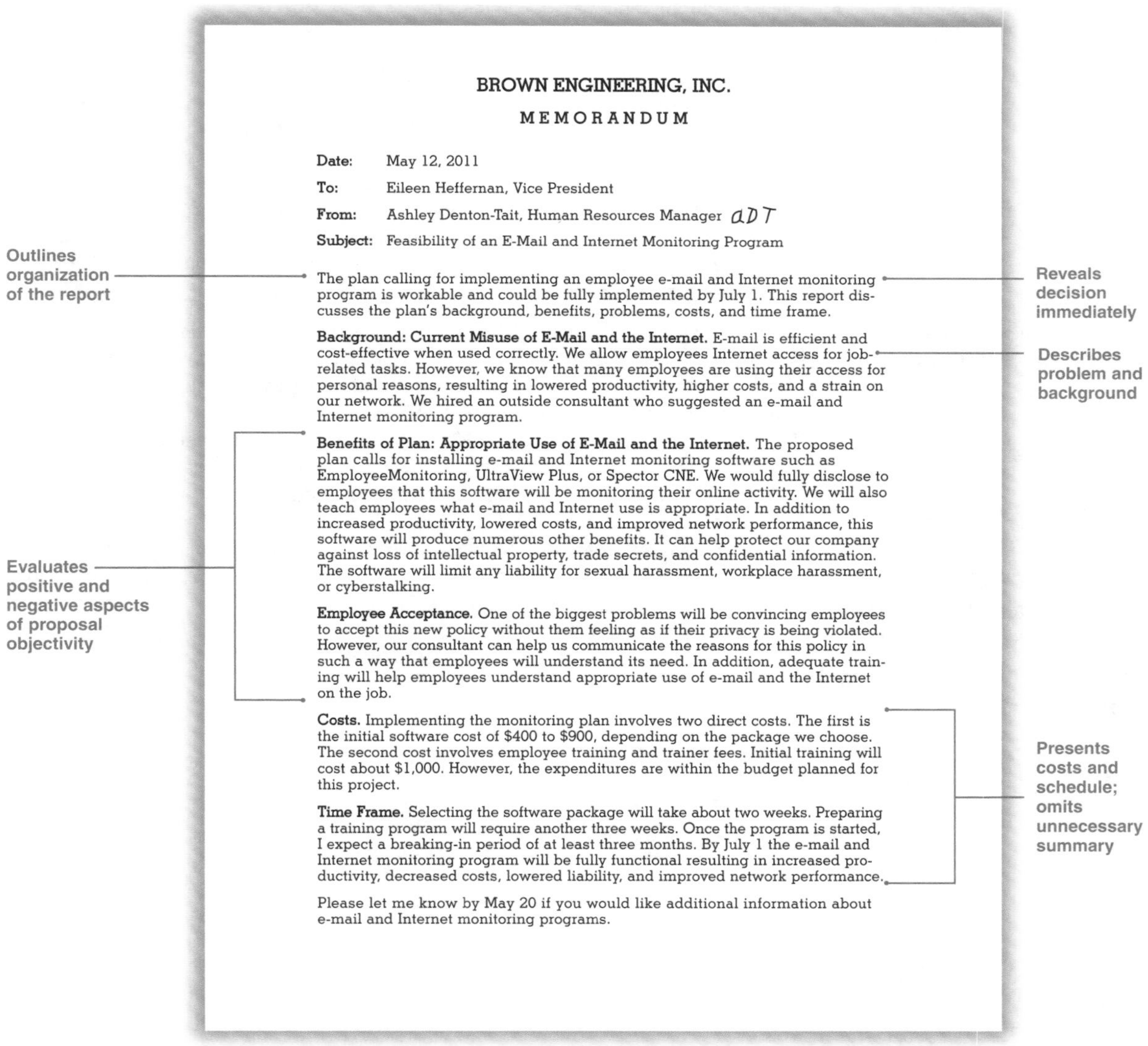

BROWN ENGINEERING, INC.

MEMORANDUM

Date: May 12, 2011

To: Eileen Heffernan, Vice President

From: Ashley Denton-Tait, Human Resources Manager ADT

Subject: Feasibility of an E-Mail and Internet Monitoring Program

The plan calling for implementing an employee e-mail and Internet monitoring program is workable and could be fully implemented by July 1. This report discusses the plan's background, benefits, problems, costs, and time frame.

Background: Current Misuse of E-Mail and the Internet. E-mail is efficient and cost-effective when used correctly. We allow employees Internet access for job-related tasks. However, we know that many employees are using their access for personal reasons, resulting in lowered productivity, higher costs, and a strain on our network. We hired an outside consultant who suggested an e-mail and Internet monitoring program.

Benefits of Plan: Appropriate Use of E-Mail and the Internet. The proposed plan calls for installing e-mail and Internet monitoring software such as EmployeeMonitoring, UltraView Plus, or Spector CNE. We would fully disclose to employees that this software will be monitoring their online activity. We will also teach employees what e-mail and Internet use is appropriate. In addition to increased productivity, lowered costs, and improved network performance, this software will produce numerous other benefits. It can help protect our company against loss of intellectual property, trade secrets, and confidential information. The software will limit any liability for sexual harassment, workplace harassment, or cyberstalking.

Employee Acceptance. One of the biggest problems will be convincing employees to accept this new policy without them feeling as if their privacy is being violated. However, our consultant can help us communicate the reasons for this policy in such a way that employees will understand its need. In addition, adequate training will help employees understand appropriate use of e-mail and the Internet on the job.

Costs. Implementing the monitoring plan involves two direct costs. The first is the initial software cost of $400 to $900, depending on the package we choose. The second cost involves employee training and trainer fees. Initial training will cost about $1,000. However, the expenditures are within the budget planned for this project.

Time Frame. Selecting the software package will take about two weeks. Preparing a training program will require another three weeks. Once the program is started, I expect a breaking-in period of at least three months. By July 1 the e-mail and Internet monitoring program will be fully functional resulting in increased productivity, decreased costs, lowered liability, and improved network performance.

Please let me know by May 20 if you would like additional information about e-mail and Internet monitoring programs.

Outlines organization of the report
Reveals decision immediately
Describes problem and background
Evaluates positive and negative aspects of proposal objectivity
Presents costs and schedule; omits unnecessary summary

for companies that must establish specifications for equipment purchases and then compare each manufacturer's product with the established specs. The yardstick approach is also effective when exact specifications cannot be established.

For example, before Nissan Motor Company decided to move its U.S. headquarters from Los Angeles to Franklin, Tennessee, the No. 8 global carmaker evaluated several sites, including Dallas, Texas, and multiple locations in the Nashville, Tennessee, region. For each site, Nissan compared tax incentives, real estate and utility costs, workforce education levels, proximity to its existing plant in Smyrna (Tennessee), and other criteria that would allow the company to save money.[6]

The real advantage to yardstick reports is that alternatives can be measured consistently using the same criteria. Writers using a yardstick approach typically do the following:

- Begin by describing the problem or need.
- Explain possible solutions and alternatives.
- Establish criteria for comparing the alternatives; tell how the criteria were selected or developed.
- Discuss and evaluate each alternative in terms of the criteria.
- Draw conclusions and make recommendations.

Jenny Gomez, benefits administrator for computer manufacturer CompuTech, was called on to write a report comparing outplacement agencies. These agencies counsel discharged employees and help them find new positions; fees are paid by the former employer. Jenny knew that times were bad for CompuTech and that extensive downsizing would take place in the next two years. Her task was to compare outplacement agencies and recommend one to CompuTech.

After collecting information, Jenny found that her biggest problem was organizing the data and developing a system for making comparisons. All the outplacement agencies she investigated seemed to offer the same basic package of services. Here is how she described her report, shown in Figure 12.13:

How can grids help you when you are writing a yardstick report?

"With the information I gathered about three outplacement agencies, I made a big grid listing the names of the agencies across the top. Down the side I listed general categories—such as services, costs, and reputation. Then I filled in the information for each agency. This grid, which began to look like a table, helped me organize all the bits and pieces of information. After studying the grid, I saw that all the information could be grouped into four categories: counseling services, administrative and research assistance, reputation, and costs. I made these the criteria I would use to compare agencies. Next, I divided my grid into two parts, which became Table 1 and Table 2. In writing the report, I could have made each agency a separate heading, followed by a discussion of how it measured up to the criteria. Immediately, though, I saw how repetitious that would become. So I used the criteria as headings and discussed how each agency met each criterion—or failed to meet it. Making a recommendation was easy once I had made the tables and could see how the agencies compared."

Want to do well on tests and excel in your course? Go to **www.meguffey.com** for helpful interactive resources.

▸ **Review the Chapter 12 PowerPoint slides to prepare for the first quiz.**

FIGURE 12.13 **Yardstick Report**

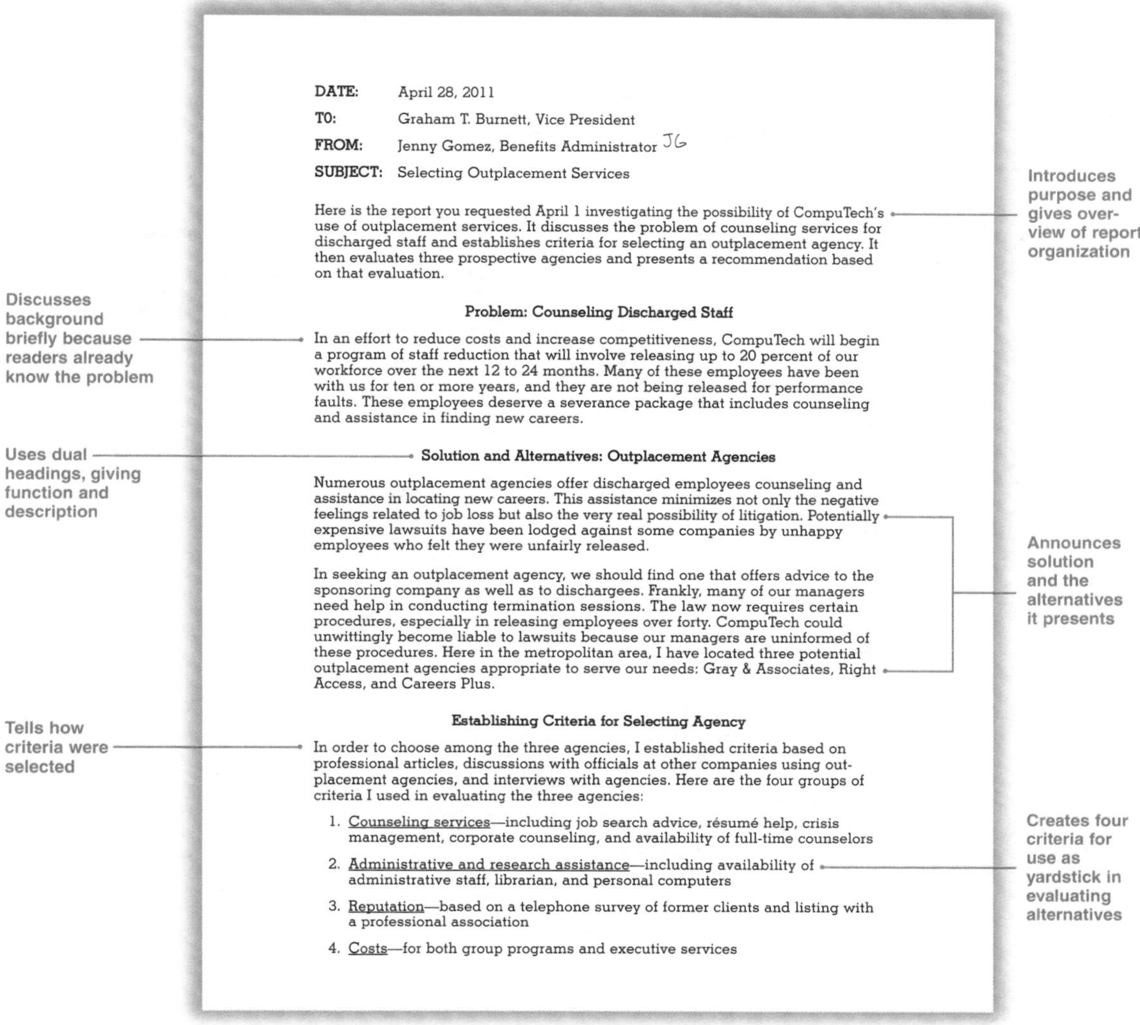

DATE: April 28, 2011

TO: Graham T. Burnett, Vice President

FROM: Jenny Gomez, Benefits Administrator JG

SUBJECT: Selecting Outplacement Services

Here is the report you requested April 1 investigating the possibility of CompuTech's use of outplacement services. It discusses the problem of counseling services for discharged staff and establishes criteria for selecting an outplacement agency. It then evaluates three prospective agencies and presents a recommendation based on that evaluation.

Problem: Counseling Discharged Staff

In an effort to reduce costs and increase competitiveness, CompuTech will begin a program of staff reduction that will involve releasing up to 20 percent of our workforce over the next 12 to 24 months. Many of these employees have been with us for ten or more years, and they are not being released for performance faults. These employees deserve a severance package that includes counseling and assistance in finding new careers.

Solution and Alternatives: Outplacement Agencies

Numerous outplacement agencies offer discharged employees counseling and assistance in locating new careers. This assistance minimizes not only the negative feelings related to job loss but also the very real possibility of litigation. Potentially expensive lawsuits have been lodged against some companies by unhappy employees who felt they were unfairly released.

In seeking an outplacement agency, we should find one that offers advice to the sponsoring company as well as to dischargees. Frankly, many of our managers need help in conducting termination sessions. The law now requires certain procedures, especially in releasing employees over forty. CompuTech could unwittingly become liable to lawsuits because our managers are uninformed of these procedures. Here in the metropolitan area, I have located three potential outplacement agencies appropriate to serve our needs: Gray & Associates, Right Access, and Careers Plus.

Establishing Criteria for Selecting Agency

In order to choose among the three agencies, I established criteria based on professional articles, discussions with officials at other companies using outplacement agencies, and interviews with agencies. Here are the four groups of criteria I used in evaluating the three agencies:

1. Counseling services—including job search advice, résumé help, crisis management, corporate counseling, and availability of full-time counselors
2. Administrative and research assistance—including availability of administrative staff, librarian, and personal computers
3. Reputation—based on a telephone survey of former clients and listing with a professional association
4. Costs—for both group programs and executive services

Introduces purpose and gives overview of report organization
Discusses background briefly because readers already know the problem
Uses dual headings, giving function and description
Announces solution and the alternatives it presents
Tells how criteria were selected
Creates four criteria for use as yardstick in evaluating alternatives

FIGURE 12.13 (Continued)

Vice President Burnett | Page 2 | April 28, 2011

Discussion: Evaluating Agencies by Criteria

Each agency was evaluated using the four criteria just described. Data comparing the first three criteria are summarized in Table 1.

Table 1

A COMPARISON OF SERVICES AND REPUTATIONS FOR THREE LOCAL OUTPLACEMENT AGENCIES

	Gray & Associates	Right Access	Careers Plus
Counseling services			
Résumé advice	Yes	Yes	Yes
Crisis management	Yes	No	Yes
Corporate counseling	Yes	No	No
Full-time counselors	Yes	No	Yes
Administrative, research assistance			
Administrative staff	Yes	Yes	Yes
Librarian, research library	Yes	No	Yes
Personal computers	Yes	No	Yes
Listed by National Association of Career Consultants	Yes	No	Yes
Reputation (telephone survey of former clients)	Excellent	Good	Excellent

Counseling Services

All three agencies offered similar basic counseling services with job-search and résumé advice. They differed, however, in three significant areas.

Right Access does not offer crisis management, a service that puts the discharged employee in contact with a counselor the same day the employee is released. Experts in the field consider this service especially important to help the dischargee begin "bonding" with the counselor immediately. Immediate counseling also helps the dischargee through the most traumatic moments of one of life's great disappointments and helps him or her learn how to break the news to family members. Crisis management can be instrumental in reducing lawsuits because dischargees immediately begin to focus on career planning instead of concentrating on their pain and need for revenge. Moreover, Right Access does not employ full-time counselors; it hires part-timers according to demand. Industry authorities advise against using agencies whose staff members are inexperienced and employed on an "as-needed" basis.

In addition, neither Right Access nor Careers Plus offers regular corporate counseling, which I feel is critical in training our managers to conduct terminal interviews. Careers Plus, however, suggested that it could schedule special workshops if desired.

Administrative and Research Assistance

Both Gray & Associates and Careers Plus offer complete administrative services and personal computers. Dischargees have access to staff and equipment to assist them in their job searches. These agencies also provide research libraries, librarians, and databases of company information to help in securing interviews.

Places table close to spot where it is first mentioned

Summarizes complex data in table for easy reading and reference

Highlights the similarities and differences among the alternatives

Does not repeat obvious data from table

FIGURE 12.13 **(Continued)**

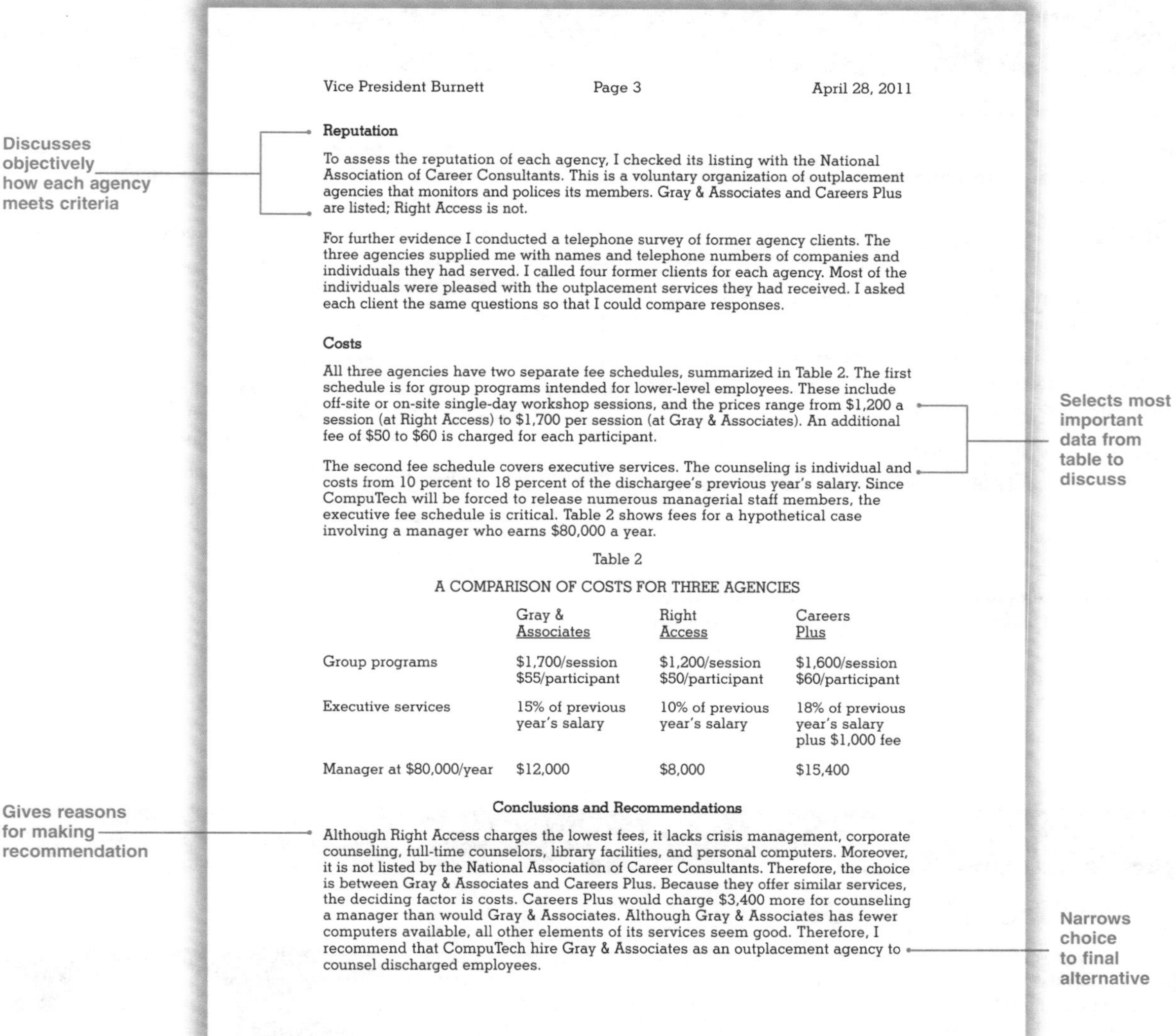

Vice President Burnett — Page 3 — April 28, 2011

Reputation

To assess the reputation of each agency, I checked its listing with the National Association of Career Consultants. This is a voluntary organization of outplacement agencies that monitors and polices its members. Gray & Associates and Careers Plus are listed; Right Access is not.

For further evidence I conducted a telephone survey of former agency clients. The three agencies supplied me with names and telephone numbers of companies and individuals they had served. I called four former clients for each agency. Most of the individuals were pleased with the outplacement services they had received. I asked each client the same questions so that I could compare responses.

Costs

All three agencies have two separate fee schedules, summarized in Table 2. The first schedule is for group programs intended for lower-level employees. These include off-site or on-site single-day workshop sessions, and the prices range from $1,200 a session (at Right Access) to $1,700 per session (at Gray & Associates). An additional fee of $50 to $60 is charged for each participant.

The second fee schedule covers executive services. The counseling is individual and costs from 10 percent to 18 percent of the dischargee's previous year's salary. Since CompuTech will be forced to release numerous managerial staff members, the executive fee schedule is critical. Table 2 shows fees for a hypothetical case involving a manager who earns $80,000 a year.

Table 2

A COMPARISON OF COSTS FOR THREE AGENCIES

	Gray & Associates	Right Access	Careers Plus
Group programs	$1,700/session $55/participant	$1,200/session $50/participant	$1,600/session $60/participant
Executive services	15% of previous year's salary	10% of previous year's salary	18% of previous year's salary plus $1,000 fee
Manager at $80,000/year	$12,000	$8,000	$15,400

Conclusions and Recommendations

Although Right Access charges the lowest fees, it lacks crisis management, corporate counseling, full-time counselors, library facilities, and personal computers. Moreover, it is not listed by the National Association of Career Consultants. Therefore, the choice is between Gray & Associates and Careers Plus. Because they offer similar services, the deciding factor is costs. Careers Plus would charge $3,400 more for counseling a manager than would Gray & Associates. Although Gray & Associates has fewer computers available, all other elements of its services seem good. Therefore, I recommend that CompuTech hire Gray & Associates as an outplacement agency to counsel discharged employees.

Discusses objectively how each agency meets criteria
Selects most important data from table to discuss
Gives reasons for making recommendation
Narrows choice to final alternative

Checklist

Writing Analytical Reports

Introduction

- **Identify the purpose of the report.** Explain why the report is being written.
- **Describe the significance of the topic.** Explain why the report is important.
- **Preview the organization of the report.** Especially for long reports, explain how the report will be organized.
- **Summarize the conclusions and recommendations for receptive audiences.** Use the direct strategy only if you have the confidence of the reader.

Findings

- **Discuss pros and cons.** In recommendation/justification reports, evaluate the advantages and disadvantages of each alternative. For unreceptive audiences consider placing the recommended alternative last.
- **Establish criteria to evaluate alternatives.** In yardstick reports, create criteria to use in measuring each alternative consistently.
- **Support the findings with evidence.** Supply facts, statistics, expert opinion, survey data, and other proof from which you can draw logical conclusions.
- **Organize the findings for logic and readability.** Arrange the findings around the alternatives or the reasons leading to the conclusion. Use headings, enumerations, lists, tables, and graphics to focus emphasis.

Conclusions/Recommendations

- **Draw reasonable conclusions from the findings.** Develop conclusions that answer the research question. Justify the conclusions with highlights from the findings.
- **Make recommendations, if asked.** For multiple recommendations prepare a list. Use action verbs. Explain fully the benefits of the recommendation or steps necessary to solve the problem or answer the question.

Zooming In — YOUR TURN

Applying Your Skills at Starbucks

In an attempt to infuse his company with fresh ideas and reinvigorate the Starbucks experience, CEO Howard Schultz went back to basics—to the coffee chain's heady beginnings. He turned to current Starbucks employees and asked them to reinvent a new, improved coffeehouse. The result was the opening of several concept stores in Seattle under different names, not under the famous Starbucks banner, one of the most recognized brands in the world.

Schultz had asked a handpicked group of employees: If you were going to open a store to compete with Starbucks, how would you do it? The team received a moderate budget and was free to improvise. The concept of 15th Ave. Coffee & Tea was born. This new Seattle coffeehouse features reused, recycled, and locally sourced design elements and furnishings. It was inspired by Starbucks and even sells Starbucks brand products, but the materials are raw and repurposed to create the vibe of a neighborhood store. Gone are the automated espresso machines that Schultz has always scorned. The food is baked locally. The same philosophy was brought to bear on Seattle's Roy Street Coffee & Tea, another highly customized take on the original Starbucks concept. Schultz is proud of the Starbucks partners' creativity: "It reminds me of the early days, when we were fighting for survival, for respect. To me this hearkens back to when we were at our best."[7]

Both new creations are in line with Schultz's latest "green" initiative. The Starbucks CEO is pursuing the ambitious goal to have all new company-owned stores worldwide LEED-certified beginning in late 2010. LEED, short for Leadership in Energy and Environmental Design, was established by the U.S. Green Building Council and applied originally to energy-efficient office buildings. Starbucks seems bent on leading the field in environmental stewardship.

© AP Images/Seth Perlman

Your Task

As assistant to Howard Schultz, you are asked to form two research teams. One is to study the feasibility of creating additional environmentally sound, locally sourced concept stores. The Starbucks CEO is considering this back-to-basics approach for cities other than Seattle. The other team must decide whether to recommend phasing out Starbucks Entertainment, the label under which the coffee chain is offering music, books, and films to its customers.

http://www.starbucks.com

Summary of Learning Objectives

1 **Tabulate information, use statistical techniques, and create decision matrices to sort and interpret business report data skillfully and accurately.** Report data are more meaningful when sorted into tables or when analyzed by mean (the arithmetic average), median (the midpoint in a group of figures), and mode (the most frequent response). Range represents a span between the highest and lowest figures. Grids help organize complex data into rows and columns. Decision matrices employ a special grid with weights to help decision makers choose objectively among complex options. Accuracy in applying statistical techniques is crucial to gain and maintain credibility with the reader.

2 **Draw meaningful conclusions and make practical report recommendations after sound and valid analysis.** Conclusions tell what the survey data mean—especially in relation to the original report problem. They interpret key findings and may attempt to explain what caused the report problem. They are usually enumerated. In reports that call for recommendations, writers make specific suggestions for actions that can solve the report problem. Recommendations should be feasible, practical, and potentially agreeable to the audience. They should all relate to the initial problem. Recommendations may be combined with conclusions.

3 **Organize report data logically and provide cues to aid comprehension.** Reports may be organized in many ways, including by (a) time (establishing a chronology or history of events), (b) component (discussing a problem by geography, division, or product), (c) importance (arranging data from most important to least important, or vice versa), (d) criteria (comparing items by standards), or (e) convention (using an already established grouping). To help guide the reader through the text, introductions, transitions, and headings serve as cues.

4 **Write short informational reports that describe routine tasks.** Periodic, trip, convention, progress, and investigative reports are examples of typical informational reports. Such reports include an introduction that may preview the report purpose and supply background data if necessary. The body of the report is generally divided into three to five segments that may be organized by time, component, importance, criteria, or convention. The body should include clear headings and may use an informal, conversational style unless the audience expects a more formal tone. The summary or conclusion reviews the main points and discusses the action that will follow. The conclusion may offer a final thought, express appreciation, or signal a willingness to provide further information. Like all professional business documents, a clear, concise, well-written report cements the writer's credibility with the audience. Because they are so important, reports require writers to apply all the writing techniques addressed in Chapters 4, 5, and 6.

5 **Compose short analytical reports that solve business problems.** Typical analytical reports include justification/recommendation reports, feasibility reports, and yardstick reports. Justification/recommendation reports organized directly identify a problem, immediately announce a recommendation or solution, explain and discuss its merits, and summarize the action to be taken. Justification/recommendation reports organized indirectly describe a problem, discuss alternative solutions, prove the superiority of one solution, and ask for authorization to proceed with that solution. Feasibility reports study the advisability of following a course of action. They generally announce the author's proposal immediately. Then they describe the background of, advantages and disadvantages of, costs of, and time frame for implementing the proposal. Yardstick reports compare two or more solutions to a problem by measuring each against a set of established criteria. They usually describe a problem, explain possible solutions, establish criteria for comparing alternatives, evaluate each alternative in terms of the criteria, draw conclusions, and make recommendations. The advantage to yardstick reports is consistency in comparing alternatives. Most reports serve as a basis for decision making in business.

Are you ready? Get more practice at **www.meguffey.com**

Chapter Review

1. What is cross-tabulation, and when is it useful? (Obj. 1)
2. Calculate the mean, median, and mode for these figures: 5, 15, 15, 15, 30. (Obj. 1)
3. What are correlations? (Obj. 1)
4. Why is a decision matrix a valuable managerial tool? (Obj. 1)
5. Why is the ability to do research and draw conclusions likely to increase your value to your employer? (Obj. 2)
6. How can you make your report conclusions as objective and bias-free as possible? (Obj. 2)
7. Name five methods for organizing report data. Be prepared to discuss each. (Obj. 3)
8. What three devices can report writers use to prevent readers from getting lost in the text? (Obj. 3)
9. Name at least four guidelines for creating effective headings, and be prepared to explain them (Obj. 3)
10. How do business writers organize most informational reports, and what can writers assume about the audience? (Obj. 4)
11. Describe periodic reports and what they generally contain. (Obj. 4)
12. What should progress reports include? (Obj. 4)
13. When is the indirect strategy appropriate for justification/recommendation reports? (Obj. 5)
14. What is a feasibility report? Are such reports generally intended for internal or external audiences? (Obj. 5)
15. What is a yardstick report? (Obj. 5)

Critical Thinking

1. When tabulating and analyzing data, you may discover relationships among two or more variables that help explain the findings. Can you trust these correlations and assume that their relationship is one of cause and effect? (Obj. 1)
2. Researchers can draw various conclusions from a set of data. How do you know how to shape conclusions and recommendations? (Obj. 2)
3. How can you increase your chances that your report recommendations will be implemented? (Obj. 2)
4. Should all reports be organized so that they follow the sequence of investigation—that is, a description of the initial problem, an analysis of the issues, data collection, data analysis, and conclusions? Why or why not? (Obj. 3)
5. What are the major differences between informational and analytical reports? (Objs. 4, 5)
6. **Ethical Issue:** You have learned that drawing conclusions involves subjectivity, although your goal is to remain objective. Even the most even-handed researchers bring their goals, background, and frame of reference to bear on the inferences they make. Consider the contentious issue of climate change. Most mainstream scientists now believe climate change to be real and induced by human activity. However, some scientists cast doubt on the extent to which global warming is human-made and constitutes an imminent threat. How can something objectively measurable be so contentious? (Obj. 2)

Activities

12.1 Tabulation and Interpretation of Survey Results (Obj. 1)

Your business communication class at South Bay College was asked by the college bookstore manager, Harry Locke, to conduct a survey. Concerned about the environment, Locke wants to learn students' reactions to eliminating plastic bags, of which 45,000 are given away annually by the bookstore. Students answered questions about a number of proposals, resulting in the following raw data:

For major purchases the bookstore should:

	Agree	Undecided	Disagree
1. Continue to provide plastic bags	132	17	411
2. Provide no bags; encourage students to bring their own bags	414	25	121
3. Provide no bags; offer cloth bags at a reduced price (about $3)	357	19	184
4. Give a cloth bag with each major purchase, the cost to be included in registration fees	63	15	482

Your Task. In groups of four or five, do the following:

a. Convert the data into a table (see Figure 12.1) with a descriptive title. Arrange the items in a logical sequence.
b. How could these survey data be cross-tabulated? Would cross-tabulation serve any purpose?
c. Given the conditions of this survey, name at least three conclusions that could be drawn from the data.
d. Prepare three to five recommendations to be submitted to Mr. Locke. How could they be implemented?
e. Role-play a meeting in which the recommendations and implementation plan are presented to Mr. Locke. One student plays the role of Mr. Locke; the remaining students play the role of the presenters.

12.2 Evaluating Conclusions (Obj. 2)

E-mail

Your Task. Read an in-depth article (800 or more words) in *BusinessWeek, Fortune, Forbes*, or *The Wall Street Journal*. What conclusions does the author draw? Are the conclusions valid, based on the evidence presented? In an e-mail message to your instructor, summarize the main points in the article and analyze the conclusions. What conclusions would you have drawn from the data?

Are you ready? Get more practice at **www.meguffey.com**

12.3 Distinguishing Between Conclusions and Recommendations (Obj. 2)

A study of red light traffic violations produced the following findings: Red light traffic violations were responsible for more than 25,000 crashes in one state. Crashes from running red lights decreased by 10 percent in areas using camera programs to cite offenders. Two out of seven local governments studied showed a profit from the programs; the others lost money.[8]

Your Task. Based on the preceding facts, indicate whether the following statements are conclusions or recommendations:

a. Red light violations are dangerous offenses.
b. Red light cameras are an effective traffic safety tool.
c. Local governments should be allowed to implement red light camera programs.
d. Although red light camera programs are expensive, they prevent crashes and are, therefore, worthwhile.
e. The city of Centerville should not implement a red light program because of the program's cost.
f. Red light programs are not necessarily profitable for local governments.

12.4 Using Decision Matrices (Objs. 1, 2)

You want to buy a low-cost laptop for your college work and consider price the most important feature.

Your Task. Study Figure 12.3 on page 385 and change the weights in Table 2 to reflect your emphasis on low price, to which you will assign a factor of 10 because it is twice as important to you as unit weight, which receives a factor of 5. The hard drive is likewise secondary to you, so you give it a 5 also. Last, you change battery life to a factor of 7 from 10 because it is less important than price, but more important than unit weight and hard drive size. Calculate the new scores. Which low-budget computer wins this time?

12.5 Buying a Car: Create a Decision Matrix (Objs. 1, 2)

David, an outrigger canoe racer, needs to buy a new car. He wants a vehicle that will carry his disassembled boat and outrigger. At the same time he will need to travel long distances on business. His passion is soft-top sports cars, but he is also concerned about gas mileage. These four criteria are impossible to find in one vehicle.

David has the following choices:

- Station wagon
- SUV with or without a sun roof
- Four-door sedan, a high-miles-per-gallon "family car"
- Sports car, convertible

He wants to consider the following criteria:

- Price
- Ability to carry cargo such as a canoe
- Fuel efficiency
- Comfort over long distances
- Good looks and fun
- Quality build/manufacturer's reputation

Your Task. Follow the steps outlined in Figure 12.3 to determine an assessment scale and to assign a score to each feature. Then, consider which weights are probably most important to David, given his needs. Calculate the totals to find the vehicle that's most suitable for David.

Table 1: Unweighted Matrix (scale from 1 to 5, from worst to best)

Features:	Price	Cargo	Fuel	Comfort	Look	Quality	Total
Weights:							
Station wagon	3	4	3	4	1	2	
4-door sedan	4	2	5	3	1	4	
SUV	1	5	1	4	3	2	
Sports car	1	1	1	1	5	4	

Table 2: Weighted Matrix (factors range from 1 to 5)

Features:	Price	Cargo	Fuel	Comfort	Look	Quality	Total
Weights:	**4**	**5**	**3**	**2**	**4**	**3**	
Station wagon	12	20	9	8	4	6	59
4-door sedan	16	10	15	6	4	12	63
SUV	4	25	3	8	12	6	58
Sports car	4	5	3	2	20	12	46

12.6 Organizing Data (Obj. 3)

Team

Your Task. In groups of three to five, discuss how the findings in the following reports could be best organized. Consider these methods: time, component, importance, criteria, and convention.

a. A weekly bulleted activity report sent by e-mail to the supervisor.
b. An agenda previewing a week-long management retreat and training program.
c. A report comparing the benefits of buying or leasing a fleet of hybrid vehicles. The report presents data on depreciation, upfront cost, maintenance, emissions, fuel consumption, and other factors.
d. A report describing the history of the development of dwarf and spur apple trees, starting with the first genetic dwarfs discovered about 100 years ago and progressing to today's grafted varieties on dwarfing rootstocks.
e. A report comparing the sales volume among the largest fast-food outlets in the United States.
f. A recommendation report to be submitted to management presenting four building plans to improve access to your building, in compliance with federal regulations. The plans range considerably in feasibility and cost.
g. An informational report describing a company's expansion plans in South America, Europe, Australia, and Southeast Asia.
h. An employee performance appraisal submitted annually.

12.7 Evaluating Headings and Titles (Obj. 3)

Your Task. Identify the following report headings and titles as *functional, talking,* or *combination.* Discuss the usefulness and effectiveness of each.

a. Disadvantages
b. Why Fast Food Has Slowed Down
c. Discussion
d. Balancing Worker Productivity and Social Media Use
e. Case History: Glatfelter's Direct-Mail Campaign Heralds Sustainability
f. Recommendations: Solving Our Applicant-Tracking Problem
g. Comparing Costs of Hiring Exempt and Nonexempt Employees
h. Equipment

12.8 Writing a Survey: Studying Employee Use of Instant Messaging (Obj. 1)

Web

Instant messaging (IM) is a popular way to exchange messages in real time. It offers the convenience of telephone conversations and e-mail. Best of all, it allows employees to contact anyone in the world while retaining a written copy of the conversation—without a whopping telephone bill! But instant messaging is risky for companies. They may lose trade secrets or confidential information over insecure lines. They also may be liable if inappropriate material is exchanged. Moreover, IM opens the door to viruses that can infect a company's entire computer system.

Your boss just read an article stating that 40 percent of companies now use IM for business and up to 90 percent of employees use instant messaging WITHOUT their manager's knowledge or authorization. She asks you to prepare a survey of your 48-member staff to learn how many are using IM. She wants to know what type of IM software they have downloaded, how many hours a day they spend on IM, what the advantages of IM are, and so forth. The goal is not to identify those using or abusing IM. Instead, the goal is to learn when, how, and why employees use instant messaging so that appropriate policies can be designed.

Your Task. Use the Web or an electronic database to learn more about instant messaging. Then prepare a short employee survey (see Figure 11.8). Include an appropriate introduction that explains the survey and encourages a response. Should you ask for names on the survey? How can you encourage employees to return the forms? Your instructor may wish to expand this survey into a report by having you produce fictitious survey results, analyze the findings, draw conclusions, and make recommendations.

12.9 Executive Summary: Condensing the Facts for Your Boss (Obj. 4)

Web

Like many executives, your boss is too rushed to read long journal articles. But she is eager to keep up with developments in her field. Assume she has asked you to help her stay abreast of research in her field. She asks you to submit to her one summary every month on an article of interest.

Your Task. In your field of study, select a professional journal, such as the *Journal of Management*. Using an electronic database search or a Web search, look for articles in your target journal. Select an article that is at least five pages long and is interesting to you. Write an executive summary in memo format. Include an introduction that might begin with *As you requested, I am submitting this executive summary of. . . .* Identify the author, article name, journal, and date of publication. Explain what the author intended to do in the study or article. Summarize three or four of the most important findings of the study or article. Use descriptive rather than functional headings. Summarize any recommendations you make. Your boss would also like a concluding statement indicating your reaction to the article. Address your memo to Susan Wright.

12.10 Periodic Report: Filling in the Boss (Obj. 4)

E-mail

You work hard at your job, but you rarely see your boss. He or she has asked to be informed of your activities and accomplishments and any problems you are encountering.

Your Task. For a job that you currently hold or a previous one, describe your regular activities, discuss irregular events that management should be aware of, and highlight any special needs or problems you are having. If you don't have a job, communicate to your instructor your weekly or monthly activities as they are tied to your classes, homework, and writing assignments. Establish components or criteria such as those in the bulleted e-mail in Figure 12.7. Use the memo format or write an e-mail report in bullet form as shown in Figure 12.7. Address the memo or the e-mail report to your boss or, alternatively, to your instructor.

12.11 Progress Report: Checking In (Obj. 4)

E-mail

Students writing a long report either for another course or for the long report assignment described in Chapter 13 will want to keep their instructors informed of their progress.

Your Task. Write a progress report informing your instructor of your work. Briefly describe the project (its purpose, scope, limitations, and methodology), work completed, work yet to be completed, problems encountered, future activities, and expected completion date. Address the e-mail report to your instructor. If your instructor allows, try your hand at the bulleted e-mail report introduced in Figure 12.7.

12.12 Investigative Report: Ensuring Fair Employment Practices Abroad (Obj. 4)

Intercultural Web

Nike's image took a big hit in the late 1990s when the company became associated with sweatshop conditions in Asian factories that supplied its shoes and apparel. Other sports and garment companies also became targets of criticism and campus boycotts in the United States for their ties to sweatshop labor. Since then, American companies have tried to investigate and end the abuses.

However, oversight is difficult, and Chinese factories dodge the labor auditors sponsored by American retail chains and manufacturers. To complicate matters, China is the largest supplier of American imports, to the tune of $280 billion annually. U.S. consumers have come to expect inexpensive goods—athletic shoes, clothing, and electronic gadgets. The pressure to keep prices down may be prompting the Chinese suppliers to cut corners and ignore the fair labor regulations of American companies. According to *BusinessWeek*, U.S. corporations are struggling with imposing "Western labor standards on a nation that lacks real labor unions and a meaningful rule of law."[9]

Your Task. Investigate the efforts of the Fair Labor Association, a coalition of 20 retailers and apparel manufacturers, such as Nike, Adidas, Nordstrom, and Eddie Bauer. The problem is not confined to the garment industry; violations also occur in offshore suppliers producing household appliances, computers, and electronics. Explore the types of abuses and the obstacles to reform. Then recommend actions that could make offshore factories play by the rules. Start by visiting the Fair Labor Association's Web site: **http://www.fairlabor.org.**

12.13 Investigative Report: Exploring a Possible Place to Work (Obj. 4)

Web

You are thinking about taking a job with a Fortune 500 company, and you want to learn as much as possible about the company.

Your Task. Select a Fortune 500 company, and collect information about it on the Web. Visit **http://www.hoovers.com** for basic facts. Then take a look at the company's Web site; check its background, news releases, and annual report. Learn about its major product, service, or emphasis. Find its Fortune 500 ranking, its current stock price (if listed), and its high and low range for the year. Look up its profit-to-earnings ratio. Track its latest marketing plan, promotion, or product. Identify its home office, major officers, and number of employees. In a memo report to your instructor, summarize your research findings.

Explain why this company would be a good or bad employment choice.

12.14 Investigative Report: Marketing Abroad (Obj. 4)

Intercultural | Web

You have been asked to prepare a training program for U.S. companies doing business outside the country.

Your Task. Select a country to investigate. Check to see whether your school or library subscribes to CultureGrams, an online resource with rich data about the daily lives and cultures of the world's peoples. Collect data from CultureGrams files, the CountryWatch Web site, or from the country's embassy in Washington. Interview on-campus international students. Use the Web to discover data about the country. See Activity 13.7 and Figure 13.5 in Chapter 13 for additional ideas on gathering information on intercultural communication. Collect information about formats for written communication, observance of holidays, customary greetings, business ethics, and other topics of interest to businesspeople. Remember that your report should promote business, not tourism. Prepare a memo report addressed to Kelly Johnson, editor for the training program materials.

12.15 Investigative Report: Expanding Operations Abroad (Obj. 4)

Intercultural | Team | Web

You have been asked to brief your boss, Dori Lundy, about the status of women in business, customs, and general business etiquette in a country that may not be friendly to Western businesswomen. Ms. Lundy is planning an international trip to expand her high-tech company.

Your Task. Select a country to investigate that has a culture markedly different from our own—for example, Saudi Arabia, Egypt, Iran, Japan, or South Korea, but don't forget Italy, Spain, Germany, or the Scandinavian countries. Collect data from CultureGrams, to which many libraries subscribe; search CountryWatch and other Web sites. Interview international students on campus. See Activity 13.7 and Figure 13.5 in Chapter 13 for additional ideas on gathering information on intercultural communication. Collect information about customary greetings, business ethics, dress codes, and other topics of interest to a traveling businesswoman. The purpose of your report is to promote business, not tourism, and to help your boss avoid embarrassment or worse. Prepare a memo report addressed to Dori Lundy, president of Paradigm CompuTech.

12.16 Progress Report: Heading Toward That Degree (Obj. 4)

You have made an agreement with your parents (or spouse, relative, or significant friend) that you would submit a progress report at this time.

Your Task. Prepare a progress report in letter format. Describe your headway toward your educational goal (such as employment, degree, or certificate). List your specific achievements, and outline what you have left to complete.

12.17 Conference or Trip Report: In Your Dreams (Obj. 4)

You have been sent to a meeting, conference, or seminar in an exotic spot at company expense.

Your Task. From a business periodical, select an article describing a conference or meeting connected with your major area of study. The article must be at least 500 words long. Assume you attended the meeting. Prepare a memo report to your supervisor.

12.18 Justification/Recommendation Report: Searching for the Best Philanthropic Project (Obj. 5)

Web

Great news! MegaTech, the start-up company where you work, has become enormously successful. Now the owner wants to support some kind of philanthropic program. He does not have time to check out the possibilities, so he asks you, his assistant, to conduct research and report to him and the board of directors.

Your Task. He wants you to investigate the philanthropic projects at 20 high-profile companies of your choice. Visit their Web sites and study programs such as volunteerism, cause-related marketing, matching funds, charitable donations, and so forth. In a recommendation report, discuss five of the best programs and recommend one that can serve as a philanthropic project model for your company.

12.19 Justification/Recommendation Report: Solving a Campus Problem (Obj. 5)

Team

Your Task. In groups of three to five, investigate a problem on your campus, such as inadequate parking, slow registration, limited dining options, poor class schedules, inefficient bookstore, weak job placement program, unrealistic degree requirements, or lack of internship programs. Within your group develop a solution to the problem. If possible, consult the officials involved to ask for their input in arriving at a feasible solution. Do not attack existing programs; strive for constructive discussion and harmonious improvements. After reviewing the persuasive techniques discussed in Chapter 10, write a group or individual justification/recommendation report. Address your report to the vice president of student affairs or the college president. Copy your instructor.

12.20 Justification/Recommendation Report: Developing an Organizational Media Use Policy (Obj. 5)

Team | Web

As a manager in a midsized engineering firm, you are aware that members of your department frequently use e-mail, social networking sites, instant messaging, and texting for private messages, shopping, and games. In addition to the strain on computer facilities, you worry about declining productivity as well as security problems. When you walked by one worker's computer and saw what looked like pornography on the screen, you knew you had to do something. Although workplace privacy is a hot-button issue for unions and employee rights groups, employers have legitimate reasons for wanting to know what is happening on their computers or during the time they are paying their employees to work. A high percentage of lawsuits involve the use and abuse of e-mail and increasingly more often other media as well. You think that the executive council should establish some kind of e-mail policy. The council is generally receptive to sound suggestions, especially if they are inexpensive. At present no explicit media use policy exists, and you fear that the executive council is not fully aware of the dangers. You decide to talk with other managers about the problem and write a justification/recommendation report.

Your Task. In teams discuss the need for a comprehensive media use policy. Using the Web and electronic databases, find information about other firms' adoption of such policies. Look for examples of companies struggling with lawsuits over abuse of technology on the job. In your report, should you describe suitable policies? Should you recommend computer monitoring and surveillance software? Should the policy cover instant messaging, social networking sites, blogging, and smartphone use? Each member of the team should present and support his or her ideas regarding what should be included in the report. Individually or as a team, write a convincing justification/recommendation report to the executive council based on the conclusions you draw from your research and discussion. Decide whether you should be direct or indirect.

12.21 Feasibility Report: International Organization (Obj. 5)

Intercultural

To fulfill a senior project in your department, you have been asked to submit a letter report to the dean evaluating the feasibility of starting an organization of international students on campus.

© Image Source/Photolibrary

Your Task. Find out how many international students are on your campus, what nations they represent, how one goes about starting an organization, and whether a faculty sponsor is needed. Assume that you conducted an informal survey of international students. Of the 39 who filled out the survey, 31 said they would be interested in joining.

12.22 Feasibility Report: Improving Employee Fitness (Obj. 5)

Your company is considering ways to promote employee fitness and morale.

Your Task. Select a fitness program that seems reasonable for your company. Consider a softball league, bowling teams, a basketball league, lunchtime walks, lunchtime fitness speakers and demos, company-sponsored health club memberships, a workout room, a fitness center, a fitness director, and so on. Assume that your boss has tentatively agreed to the programs you select and has asked you to write a memo report investigating its feasibility.

12.23 Yardstick Report: Evaluating Equipment (Obj. 5)

You recently complained to your boss that you were unhappy with a piece of equipment that you use (printer, computer, copier, fax, or the like). After some thought, the boss decided that your complaint was valid and told you to go shopping.

Your Task. Compare at least three manufacturers' models and recommend one. Because the company will be purchasing ten or more units and because several managers must approve the purchase, write a careful report documenting your findings. Establish at least five criteria for comparing the models. Submit a memo report to your boss.

12.24 Yardstick Report: Measuring the Alternatives (Obj. 5)

Your Task. Identify a problem or procedure that must be changed at your work or in an organization you know. Consider challenges such as poor scheduling of employees, outdated equipment, slow order processing, failure to encourage employees to participate fully, restrictive rules, inadequate training, or disappointed customers. Consider several solutions or courses of action (retaining the present status could be one alternative). Develop criteria that you could use to evaluate each alternative. Write a report measuring each alternative by the yardstick you have created. Recommend a course of action to your boss or to the organization head.

Self-Contained Report Activities

No Additional Research Required

12.25 Justification/Recommendation Report: Faster Service at Seguiti Family Pizza's Service* (Obj. 5)

You work for Paul Seguiti, the owner of Seguiti Family Pizza, a small, casual pizza shop he founded 30 years ago. Its signature items are eight-inch-diameter individual pizzas. The no-frills eatery also serves fries, onion rings, and assorted beverages.

The pizza shop is located in the warehouse district of Chicago, where it originally served truckers who delivered their meat, fruits, and vegetables in the middle of the night and then whisked off to the next city. Just for the truckers, Seguiti designed a pizza that was large enough to be satisfying, yet small enough for a driver to fold in half and eat with one hand while driving with the other hand. Later the pizza shop caught on with the nightclub crowd and with students who studied late. The shop opens at 11 p.m. and closes at 6 a.m.

The concept was a hit. However, success brings competition. Three imitators opened their pizza shops within a five-mile radius of Seguiti Family Pizza. You know that the family has been using the same system of delivering orders to customers that it has for years, and you know service could be faster.

The current system at Seguiti's works as follows. A counter clerk records the customer's order and table number on a ticket. The customer pays, and the counter person gives the order to the pizza makers. The pizza makers remove the dough from the refrigerator, shape it, add the sauce and other ingredients, put the pie in the oven, and remove it from the oven when baked. The counter clerk takes the order to the customer's table. Seguiti Family Pizza has three counter clerks, two pizza makers, and one cash register that is shared by the counter clerks. It takes two minutes to prep a pizza before it can go in the oven. The pizza shop uses an old-fashioned Bartho Model A pizza deck oven, which cooks a pizza in eight minutes.

You think the entire system is inefficient, and when you discuss the problem with Mr. Seguiti, he says, "Although the old ways are comfortable for me, I see that change is needed."

You suggest observing the three competitors' methods of serving customers to understand why their service is faster. Currently, the average time it takes a customer to receive an order at Seguiti Family Pizza is 18 minutes. The following are notes from your observations of the competitors.

* Instructors: See the Instructor's Manual for additional report-writing resources.

Crunchy Crust Pizza

- Similar menu
- Orders are taken using an electronic system that includes the customer's number
- Customers pay immediately
- Customers pick up their orders after their numbers have been called
- One counter employee at one register; two pizza makers
- Preprepared dough; prep time: one minute
- One state-of-the art TurboCrust Model 100 convection oven—six minutes to cook a pizza
- Average time a customer waits to receive an order: 11 minutes

Tomasia's

- Similar menu
- Order takers call out the menu item as the order is taken
- Customers pay immediately
- Customers wait at the counter to pick up their orders
- Four counter employees at four registers; two pizza makers
- Preprepared dough; prep time: one minute
- One state-of-the art TurboCrust Model 100 convection oven—six minutes to cook a pizza
- Average time a customer waits to receive an order: nine minutes

Velluti's Pizza

- Similar menu
- Tickets are used to record the customers' orders
- Customers pay immediately
- Counter staff take the order to customers' tables
- Three counter staff, two pizza makers, and one cash register
- Pizza prep the same as Seguiti Family Pizza: two minutes
- One Baker's Friend Model AC3 pizza deck oven—seven minutes to cook a pizza
- Average time a customer waits to receive an order: 17 minutes

Your Task. Now it is up to you to analyze the data you have collected. In a short memo report to Paul Seguiti, present your findings, discuss your conclusions, and make recommendations. You may want to present the data using visual aids, but you also realize you must emphasize the important findings by presenting them in an easy-to-read list.

12.26 Justification/Recommendation Report: Analyzing Service at Sporting World (Obj. 5)

Sporting World is one of the largest sporting goods retail chains in the United States, operating 102 stores across the Midwest. Paula Taylor opened the first Sporting World Store in Beckland, Missouri, in 1953 and sold military surplus supplies. Over the years, Sporting World evolved into one of the premier sporting goods chains, offering golf equipment and apparel; footwear; camping, hunting, and fishing gear; and general outdoor apparel. It has established a reputation for outstanding customer service, a great selection, and discount prices.

As an in-house consultant who reports to the vice president of operations, you have been assigned the task of analyzing checkout and customer service lanes to ensure efficient service. Employees have already been cross-trained to work in multiple departments, and all employees already know how to operate the cash registers. Remote cash registers are located in several departments to reduce customer flow at the registers nearest the exit. To improve communication among employees, Sporting World recently started to equip employees in some of its stores with headsets.

Despite these efforts, things can go wrong, and this usually happens during holidays such as Christmas, Memorial Day, Fourth of July, and Labor Day. With the Labor Day weekend only one month away, you want to help avoid the occasional gridlock encountered last Labor Day at one of the chain's busiest stores.

Sporting World's goal is to achieve at least a 35 percent *Excellent* response rating from customers. Often, ratings of *Good* are acceptable to businesses, but not to Sporting World and certainly not to its founder, Paula Taylor, who accepts nothing less than *Excellent* ratings.

Customer Survey Data

To gather information from customers, you decide to tabulate responses to questions from surveys the store received last month. You are particularly interested in the time customers spent in the checkout lines. Here are the results of 442 customer surveys:

	Responses/Score (5 = Excellent, 4 = Very good, 3 = Good, 2 = Fair, 1 = Poor)				
Customer Survey Questions	**5**	**4**	**3**	**2**	**1**
1. Based on your shopping experience, how would you rate this Sporting World store?	155	141	87	40	19
2. Based on your shopping experience, how would you rate the likelihood that you will return to this Sporting World store?	233	134	61	11	3
3. How would you rate the likelihood that you would recommend this Sporting World store to a friend?	163	122	105	32	20
4. How would you rate the efficiency of checkout at the register?	70	111	199	44	18
5. How would you rate the efficiency of service at the customer service counter?	26	52	177	133	54
6. How would you rate the service staff's handling of problems?	36	133	75	177	21

Staff Survey

To gather additional information, you conduct a survey of 33 staff members, including cashiers, customer service representatives, and salespeople. Here are the results of your survey:

Which of the following has caused a delay at a register?

Soft tag (security tag) removal	64
Approval or override	86
Register malfunction	3
Price check	7
Purchase of hunting and fishing licenses	23
Employee error	6

Figures do not total 100 percent because of multiple answers.

Your Observations

Finally, you selected nine registers at random (five near the front entrance, two in customer service, and one each in the fishing and footwear departments) and observed them for five minutes, as you took notes. You chose Saturday for these observations because of the typically higher volume of business. Following is a summary of your observations:

- During all five of your visits to registers near the front entrance, you noticed that most of the delays were caused when a manager was needed for a check approval or override. You also observed five instances in which an employee needed to go to another cash register to remove security tags because the employee's security tag remover wasn't working. Finally, you noticed six customers in the line for fishing rods and fishing reels and overheard that they really wanted to buy fishing licenses.
- In both of your visits to the service counter, only one employee was operating one of two available registers. For this reason, three customers were left waiting in line for service. During one visit, you observed that when a product needed to be opened to make sure all parts were included before it could be exchanged, the employee had to walk to the technical department to locate a technician, causing further delay.
- During your visits to the fishing and footwear departments, the two highest-volume departments in the store, you saw that floor personnel were overwhelmed with customers asking questions about the goods. In other words, no one seemed to be available to handle transactions at the open registers. You then walked to the camping department (the department with the lowest sales in the store), where you saw three customers and four employees in the area.

Your Task. After carefully comparing customer and employee perceptions, present your findings in a memo report to Red Armbruster, vice president of operations, Sporting World. In your report, include as much information from the tables as possible, but present it in an easy-to-understand way. What conclusions can you draw from your findings? What recommendations will you make to Mr. Armbruster to ensure a successful Labor Day weekend?

12.27 Yardstick Report: Comparing Textbook Options (Obj. 5)

Assume you are the finance committee chairperson for Lambda Gamma Phi, a business association at your college or university. After some members bought textbooks at the campus bookstore recently, they complained about how expensive the textbooks were and how their costs were steadily rising. Some members said that because of the expense, they didn't buy some of their textbooks last semester, which hurt their grades. Lower grades could lead to the loss of scholarships and reduced job opportunities.

The executive committee of Lambda Gamma Phi asks you to identify alternatives to buying full-priced hard-copy books at the campus bookstore. What factors are most important? The committee is most interested in the best price (including shipping charges) and availability. Even a good price is useless if the book is not readily available. Another big concern is readability.

One option for students, of course, is to continue buying books at the campus bookstore. Some instructors and students, however, are buying books for the Fleetfoot Reader. This is a proprietary hardware/software device for reading e-books, but books play only on this device. Some publishers and bookstores are now renting books, which is a distinct possibility. Students can also buy books online, or they can download e-books as PDF files. All of these options seem like reasonable alternatives to buying full-priced hard-copy books at the campus bookstore.

For the study, you choose a representative sample of four textbooks: *Calculus Classics*, *The Basics of College Writing*, *Art History: The Impressionists and Beyond*, and *Physics Is Fun*. You check the prices and availability of the books at the campus bookstore, on Web sites that specialize in renting textbooks, on Web sites that sell hard-copy books, and on Web sites that sell e-books. You check the price of the Fleetfoot Reader as well as the prices and availability of books that play on this device. You evaluate readability by seeing how easy a textbook is to read (only a concern with e-books and the Fleetfoot Reader). Delivery times for books purchased online are immaterial because most online vendors deliver books in two business days.

Price is easily the most important criterion, so you assign it a weight of 5. You assign availability a weight of 3 and readability a weight of 1.

Average Price

At the campus bookstore, the average price of each book is \$170 and the average buyback price is \$40, making the average net price \$130. The better the condition of the book is when you return it, the more the campus bookstore pays. The lowest price on the Fleetfoot Reader is \$259 at handheldgadgets.com, and the average price of books is \$10, making the average price of a book \$259 / 4 + \$10 = \$74.75. The average price to rent the four books for one semester is \$38 per book. The average price is \$65 per book to buy the four books online. None of the online booksellers has a buyback option. The average price of the four books as e-books is \$80 per book. The following chart shows those data.

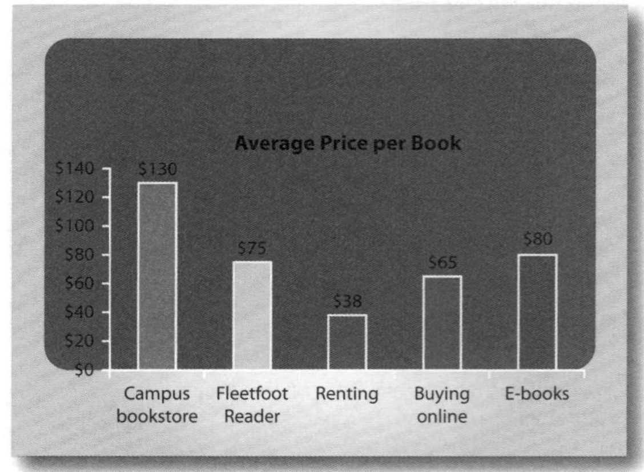

Availability

The campus bookstore has all four of the books in stock. Only one of the four books is available for the Fleetfoot Reader. A much wider selection of books for the Fleetfoot Reader is available for the mass market than for the college market. Bookrentingsite.com says it has over 2.1 million textbooks for rent and offers prepaid return shipping. Three of the four books are available on this site, which consistently offered the lowest prices on book rentals. Two online booksellers excelled in availability—reallycheap.com and savvybuyer.com. Each had three of the four books. Smartclass.com had two of the four books as e-books. No other e-bookseller came close to its selection.

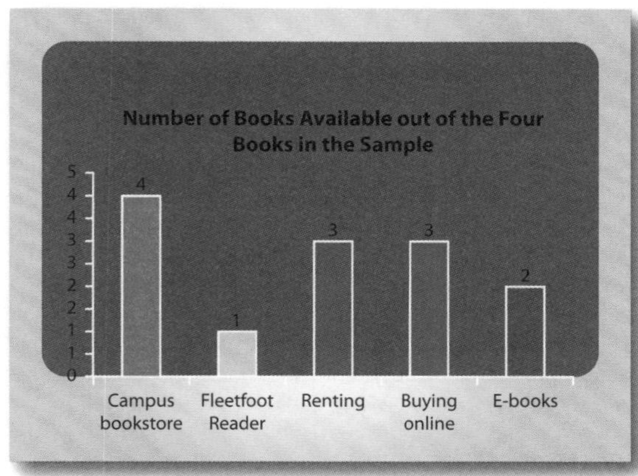

Readability

You judge all hard-copy books most readable. Formatting issues and small print on small screens, especially on iPods, make e-books the least readable. Although books on the Fleetfoot Reader are easier to read than e-books, the device is hard to use.

Your Task. Write a memo report of five or fewer pages and address it to the organization's members. Include conclusions and recommendations, a bar chart showing the availability of books, and a decision matrix.

12.28 Feasibility Report: Can Rainbow Precision Instruments Afford a Children's Center? (Obj. 5)

Rainbow Precision Instruments (RPI) is a $60 million manufacturer of specialty gauges for the aerospace industry, mainly flight deck or cockpit instruments, located in a small town in the Pacific Northwest. To accommodate its workforce of approximately 55 percent female employees, the company has been operating a state-of-the art Children's Center. More than a child care center, the facility is an award-winning and well-equipped learning center that covers two shifts, from 7:00 a.m. until 10:30 p.m.

Such innovation and extensive coverage are not cheap. A recent overhaul of the facility cost $150,000, and the annual budget to instruct and care for 145 children reached $300,000. The Children's Center provides a state-certified curriculum taught by professional preschool faculty. The children also receive their meals at the facility. At its inception, the costly investment seemed fully justified. However, the number of employee children started slowly dropping until fewer than 10 percent of enrollees were children of RPI workers. The company responded by opening the Center to surrounding communities, where quality day care is scarce.

YEAR	2003	2008	2010
Percent of employee children at the Center	55 percent	25 percent	10 percent

Instead of raising the tuition to market levels to recoup some of its investment, RPI continues to subsidize the Center annually with approximately $200,000, not differentiating between Rainbow employees and parents from the local area. The annual tuition is $696 per child.

To make matters worse, RPI has suffered financial setbacks and is currently losing about $2.5 million annually. Finding alternatives for looking after the few remaining company children would seem less expensive than keeping the Center open. RPI has unsuccessfully pursued other options, such as selling the Children's Center or finding an independent operator to run it.

Your Task. From the available evidence, decide whether it is advisable for the company to close the Children's Center or keep it open. If you choose to keep it open, you will need to argue for some substantial changes in company operations. In your memo report, announce the decision, describe the problem, and discuss both the advantages and disadvantages of your proposal. Last, focus on costs and the time frame needed to implement your decision.

12.29 Feasibility Report: Should We Continue to Outsource Personal Computer Manufacturing Jobs to India? (Obj. 5)

You are a senior analyst for the prestigious Cyberdynamic Systems Corporation (CSC), a multinational computer company. Its core products are servers and workstations, but it also manufactures personal computers (PCs). During the past three years, as the economy has slumped, overall CSC profits have slipped by 44 percent. When the economy slumps, companies outsource more activities and jobs to cut costs.

Two years ago, CSC started outsourcing PC manufacturing to India, an initiative the company calls Project India. The problem is that laying off employees and outsourcing their jobs to foreign countries is unpopular with the public. It also slightly lowers the morale of the remaining employees. In a recent Gallup survey, 74 percent of the American public had a negative opinion of outsourcing, 19 percent had a positive opinion, and 7 percent were neutral.

Your boss asks you to recommend whether CSC should continue to outsource PC manufacturing to India. As part of the study, your boss also wants you to evaluate alternatives to outsourcing and potential savings in operating costs that the company is trying or considering. You decide to interview employees to learn their views about Project India, research the pros and cons of outsourcing, and analyze the effectiveness of the alternatives to outsourcing the company is trying or considering.

Benefits of Outsourcing PC Manufacturing

From your research, you discover four main benefits to outsourcing PC manufacturing. First, outsourcing noncore operations such as PC manufacturing enables CSC to focus on its core products—servers and workstations. Second, outsourcing lowers labor costs. CSC pays an Indian employee $22 per hour to make a PC, while it pays a U.S. employee $98 per hour to make the same PC.

Third, product quality reports suggest that Indian-made PCs have a 0.14 percent defect rate, the same as domestically made PCs. Fourth, profits and market share increase because of outsourcing. Last year, CSC profits after outsourcing PC manufacturing were $1.65 billion, while profits were only $900 million before outsourcing (roughly half). Market share after outsourcing of PC manufacturing increased from 34 percent to 45 percent.

Equal Job Program
You learn that, as an alternative to layoffs, CSC created Equal Job, a program designed to deflect criticism from its outsourcing actions. Equal Job offers affected employees the option of keeping their jobs by relocating to the country to which their jobs will be outsourced. Employees who choose relocation remain employed by CSC but work for lower, local wages. Although some outsiders think the approach is creative, 88 percent of employees surveyed about the program are against it and in fact were shocked and angry at the program's announcement. Only 8 percent of the employees who were offered the relocation accepted it.

Operation Web Office
As another alternative to layoffs, you discover that CSC launched an experimental program called Operation Web Office. Still under development, the program involves creating a virtual online workplace in which each employee sits at his or her own computer at home and is connected to other employees by the Internet through an application on each employee's computer. The projected savings from Operation Web Office are about $23 million per year in reduced costs for office space. Eighty-three percent of the test group of 218 employees like the program. However, development efforts have been plagued by server crashes, software malfunctions, and computer viruses. Worse, the company has to date been unable to uncover the sources of these problems.

Onshoring
You also investigate the possibility of "onshoring"—relocating workers to areas in the United States with lower costs of living and paying them less. Based on your interviews, only 17 percent of the employees surveyed said they would consider relocation accepted it. In addition, 56 percent of the American public had a negative opinion of onshoring.
Your Task. Write a memo report of three or fewer pages addressed to your boss. Include conclusions, recommendations, and a pie chart illustrating public opinion of outsourcing. Should Cyberdynamic Systems Corporation continue to outsource its PC manufacturing?

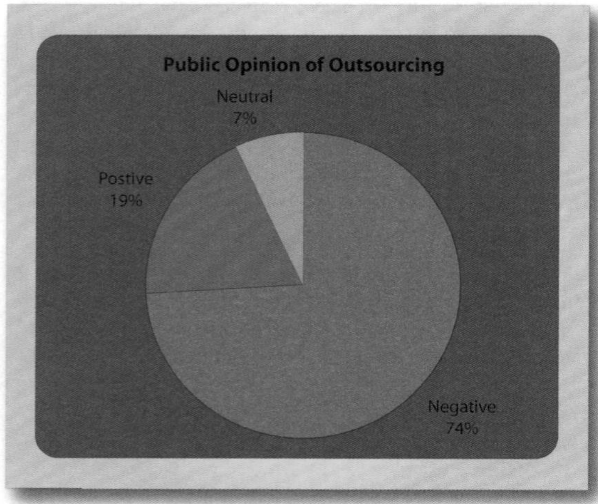

12.30 Yardstick Report: Parking Problem at Caputi's Italian Restaurant (Obj. 5)

You have always enjoyed the great food at Caputi's Italian Restaurant, owned by your Uncle Guido. Caputi's is a formal, upscale dining Italian food restaurant in downtown Tempe, Arizona, near the campus of a major university where you are a student. Because of its steadily increasing business, Caputi's has outgrown its small parking lot, which has only 20 parking spaces.

Frustrated over their inability to park in the restaurant's lot, some potential customers give up and go elsewhere to eat. Some of the regulars have also disappeared. Caputi's cannot add parking spaces because adjacent land is unavailable. However, according to Guido, "The problem is not a lack of parking spaces; it's a lack of willingness on the part of customers to walk from where they parked to the restaurant." To pay its debts, the restaurant needs to continue to grow. Uncle Guido says, "Relocation is out of the question—this spot is too good!"

Guido wants you to evaluate options to ease the parking problem, using criteria that he and you develop. The options are to (a) use a valet service, attendants who park and later retrieve cars for patrons, (b) run a free shuttle service between the restaurant and a nearby parking garage, and (c) advertise the availability of nearby parking garages and bus routes on the restaurant's Web site and in the restaurant. The criteria are (a) the cost to the restaurant to implement the solution, (b) the cost to the customer to use the solution, (c) the ease of implementation for the restaurant, and (d) convenience to the customer.

Besides talking to Guido, you interview a valet parking company about its services and fees, and you interview the managers of the nearby parking garages about availability and prices. You survey 40 of the restaurant's customers about their willingness to use a valet service and the price they would be willing to pay for the service.

Decision Matrix
You explain what a decision matrix is to Guido, and together you decide on the weights of the criteria. The net profit (or loss) to the restaurant to implement the solution receives a weight of 10. The cost to the customer to use the solution receives a weight of 6. The ease of implementation for the restaurant receives a weight of 4. The convenience to the customer receives a weight of 8.

Cost to the Restaurant to Implement a Solution
The least expensive valet service in town sent you a quotation that pegs a patron's charge at $7 per car, an amount that includes a $2 flat fee for parking at a nearby parking garage. The valet parking company has offered its service free of charge to the restaurant.

The major costs of operating a shuttle service are about $1,500 to buy a van and $200 per week to pay an employee to drive the van between the garage and the restaurant during dinner hours. Costs to advertise available parking options on the restaurant's Web site and at the restaurant are about $200.

Cost to the Customer
The per-vehicle charge of $7 plus a customer tips for valet service of about $3 makes the valet service the costliest option. The shuttle service is free to customers. Similarly, learning about the availability of nearby parking garages and bus routes on the restaurant's Web site and at the restaurant is free to customers.

Ease of Implementation
Advertising parking options is the most convenient option for the restaurant because it takes the least amount of time and effort. Offering a valet service is the second most convenient option for the restaurant. Although the valet service does most of the work, this option requires more weekly administrative work for the restaurant than advertising requires. Caputi's may also need to provide food and beverages for valets. Operating a shuttle service is the least convenient option for the

restaurant because it requires the restaurant to buy a van; pay a driver; and provide fuel, maintenance, and insurance.

Convenience to the Customer

A valet service is the most convenient option for customers because this option results in the fastest entry into the restaurant. Your survey shows that 90 percent of the customers are willing to use the service. A shuttle service is the second most convenient option for customers. It is not as convenient as driving to the restaurant entrance and leaving a car with a valet. Advertising offers information to customers but not any significant convenience, making it the least convenient option.

Your Task. Uncle Guido is relying on you to analyze the data and help him make a decision. Write a memo report of three or fewer pages to him. Prepare a decision matrix with the weights provided. For each criterion in the decision matrix, give the option that ranks highest a ranking of 3, the option that ranks second highest a ranking of 2, and the option that ranks lowest a ranking of 1. Multiply each weight by the ranking, repeat for the other criteria, and then sum up the results to compute a total. From your decision matrix, draw conclusions and then make recommendations. Overall, which option is best? Should you still recommend advertising the parking options?

Chat About It

In each chapter you will find five discussion questions related to the chapter material. Your instructor may assign these topics for you to discuss in class, in an online chat room, or on an online discussion board. Some of the discussion topics may require outside research. You may also be asked to read and respond to postings made by your classmates.

Topic 1: If you were asked to study the relationship between traffic speeds and traffic accidents, what statistic might be most useful: the mean, median, or mode? Why?

Topic 2: What criteria would you use to determine whether required courses for a given academic major are necessary?

Topic 3: Provide a simple example that illustrates the differences between findings, conclusions, and recommendations.

Topic 4: What do you think might be a good rule of thumb regarding the number of graphics (charts, tables, and so on) to put in a report and the size of the graphics? Why?

Topic 5: If your boss asked you to write a report that is formatted differently or with ideas sequenced differently than how you're learning in this course, what would you do? Would you ask your boss if you could instead write the report the way you learned to write reports? Would you identify the differences to your boss?

Grammar/Mechanics C.L.U.E. Review 12

Total Review

The first ten chapters reviewed specific guides from Appendix A, Grammar and Mechanics Guide. The exercises in this and the remaining chapters are total reviews, covering all of the grammar and mechanics guides plus confusing words and frequently misspelled words.

Each of the following sentences has a total of **three** errors in grammar, punctuation, capitalization, usage, or spelling. On a separate sheet, write a correct version. Avoid adding new phrases, starting new sentences, or rewriting in your own words. When finished, compare your responses with the key beginning on page Key-1.

Example: After our supervisor and her returned from their meeting at 2:00 p.m. we were able to sort the customers names more quickly.

Revision: After our supervisor and **she** returned from their meeting at **2 p.m.**, we were able to sort the **customers'** names more quickly.

1. Toyota, the best-selling japanese carmaker, had enjoyed a strong favorable perception of high quality therefore it long remained unharmed by a string of much-publicized recalls.
2. The auditors report, which my boss and me read very closely, featured the following three main flaws, factual inaccuracies, omissions, and incomprehensible language.
3. 8 of the 20 workers in my department were fired, as a result, we had to work much harder to acheive our objectives.
4. As a matter of principal, we offer some form of financial support to more than sixty percent of our current MBA candidates. Which proves our commitment to executive education.
5. To post easily to your blog on the Web you could use Mozilla's web browser firefox and an add-on called ScribeFire.
6. Peters presentation to a nonprofit group on advanced Internet marketing netted him only two hundred dollars, a fifth of his usual honorarium but he believes in pro bono work.
7. The old company manual covers the basics of: searching, selecting interpreting and organizing data.
8. Our latest press release which was written in our Corporate Communication Department announces the opening of 3 Canadian offices.
9. Letter reports usualy has side margins of one and one quarter inches.
10. The CEO and Manager, who had went to a meeting in the West, delivered a report to Jeff and I when they returned.

Are you ready? Get more practice at **www.meguffey.com**

CHAPTER 13

Proposals, Business Plans, and Formal Business Reports

OBJECTIVES

After studying this chapter, you should be able to

1. Discuss the general uses and basic components of informal proposals, and grasp their audience and purpose.
2. Discuss formal proposals and their specific components.
3. Identify the components of typical business plans, and ethically create buy-in for your business ideas.
4. Describe the components of the front matter in formal business reports, and show how they further the purpose of your report.
5. Describe the body and back matter of formal business reports and how they serve the purpose of your report.
6. Specify tips that aid writers of formal business reports.

Want to do well on tests and excel in your course? Go to **www.meguffey.com** for helpful interactive resources.
Review the Chapter 13 PowerPoint slides to prepare for the first quiz.

Zooming In

PART 1

Writing Winning Proposals at Raytheon

It was a sunny November morning in Southern California. The director of operations at Raytheon Company's Santa Barbara business unit stood in front of an audience of about 20 engineers and managers—the individuals selected by management to write a proposal for the Aerosol Polarimetry Sensor on the National Polar-Orbiting Operational Environmental Satellite System. He began by telling them, "The request for proposal (RFP) has finally arrived. I know that many of you have been thinking about how to win this contract for more than a year. Now it's time to turn that thinking into words—time to write the proposal!"[1]

He then introduced the proposal volume managers. They would be directing most of the team's writing efforts. Finally, he identified the proposal team's newest member, Dr. Mark Grinyer, a Raytheon proposal specialist who had been asked to write the vitally important executive summary volume. He closed with a final comment: "Remember, everyone, we're on the clock now. We've got less than 60 days to build a winning proposal for almost $100 million in new business."

As Dr. Grinyer listened, he thought, "It'll be a busy holiday season." Such schedules, however, are typical for aerospace industry proposals. Several companies were competing for this contract, and only one proposal would win.

A leading aerospace company, Raytheon is a Fortune 500 giant with about 75,000 employees worldwide. Most are technicians, engineers, scientists, and managers involved in high-technology military and government programs. Raytheon's Remote Sensing business unit in Santa Barbara specializes in high-quality electro-optical sensor systems for weather satellites and other space-based vehicles. The company's sensors on weather satellites provide images seen on TV every day and enable quality weather predictions around the world.

Like most aerospace companies, Raytheon's success depends on its ability to produce winning proposals selling complex systems that involve many disciplines. High-tech companies use a structured proposal development process. This process enables teams of employees who are neither professional writers nor proposal experts to work together, often under pressing time constraints. Their goal is to develop winning proposals against tough competition.

©PAT GREENHOUSE/Boston Globe /Landov

Critical Thinking

- Why are proposals vitally important to a company like Raytheon?
- How are proposals written at Raytheon similar to and different from proposals or long reports written by students?
- How can team members maintain consistency and meet deadlines when writing important, time-constrained, multivolume documents such as this proposal?

http://www.raytheon.com

Preparing Informal Proposals

LEARNING OBJECTIVE 1
Discuss the general uses and basic components of informal proposals, and grasp their audience and purpose.

Proposals are written offers to solve problems, provide services, or sell equipment. Some proposals are internal, often taking the form of justification and recommendation reports. You learned about these persuasive reports in Chapter 12. Most proposals, however, are external, such as those written at Raytheon. They are a critical means of selling equipment and services that generate income for the giant aerospace company.

Why do government agencies and many companies use requests for proposals (RFPs)?

Proposals may be divided into two categories: solicited and unsolicited. When government organizations or firms know exactly what they want, they prepare a request for proposal (RFP), specifying their requirements. Government agencies as well as private businesses use RFPs to solicit competitive bids from vendors. Most proposals are solicited, such as that presented by the city of Las Vegas, Nevada. Its 30-page RFP was seeking bids for a parking initiative from public and private funding sources.[2] Enterprising companies looking for work or a special challenge might submit unsolicited proposals—for example, the world-renowned architect who designed the Louvre Museum pyramid in Paris, among other landmarks. I. M. Pei was so intrigued by the mission of the Buck Institute for Age Research that he submitted an unsolicited proposal to design the biomedical research facility in Novato, California.[3]

While many companies tout the benefits of wind and solar energy, the Free Flow Power Corporation (FFP) has a different idea for renewable energy: water power. The Massachusetts-based firm recently drafted a proposal to submerge dozens of hydroelectric turbines along the Mississippi River. If the Federal Energy Regulatory Commission approves the proposal, the turbines could transform natural river currents into electricity for thousands of homes, delivering hundreds of times more energy than wind or solar installations. *What persuasive "hooks" might FFP include in the introduction of its proposals?*

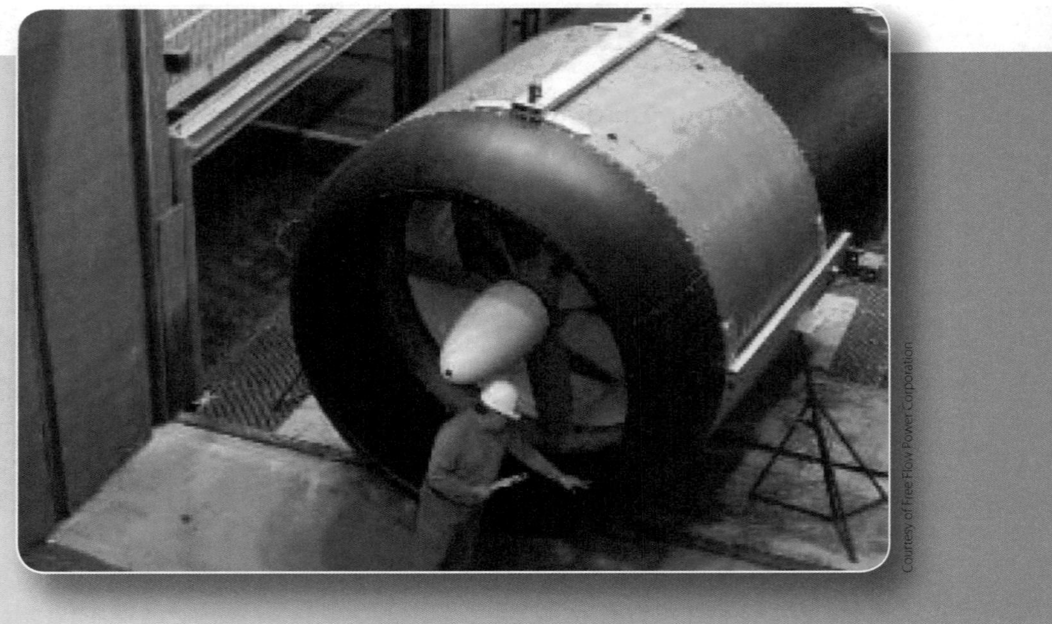

Courtesy of Free Flow Power Corporation

Components of Informal Proposals

Informal proposals may be presented in short (two- to four-page) letters. Sometimes called *letter proposals*, they may contain six principal components: introduction, background, proposal, staffing, budget, and authorization request. As you can see in Figure 13.1, both informal and formal proposals contain these six basic parts. Figure 13.2, an informal letter proposal to a Boston dentist to improve patient satisfaction, illustrates the six parts of letter proposals.

FIGURE 13.1 Components of Formal and Informal Proposals

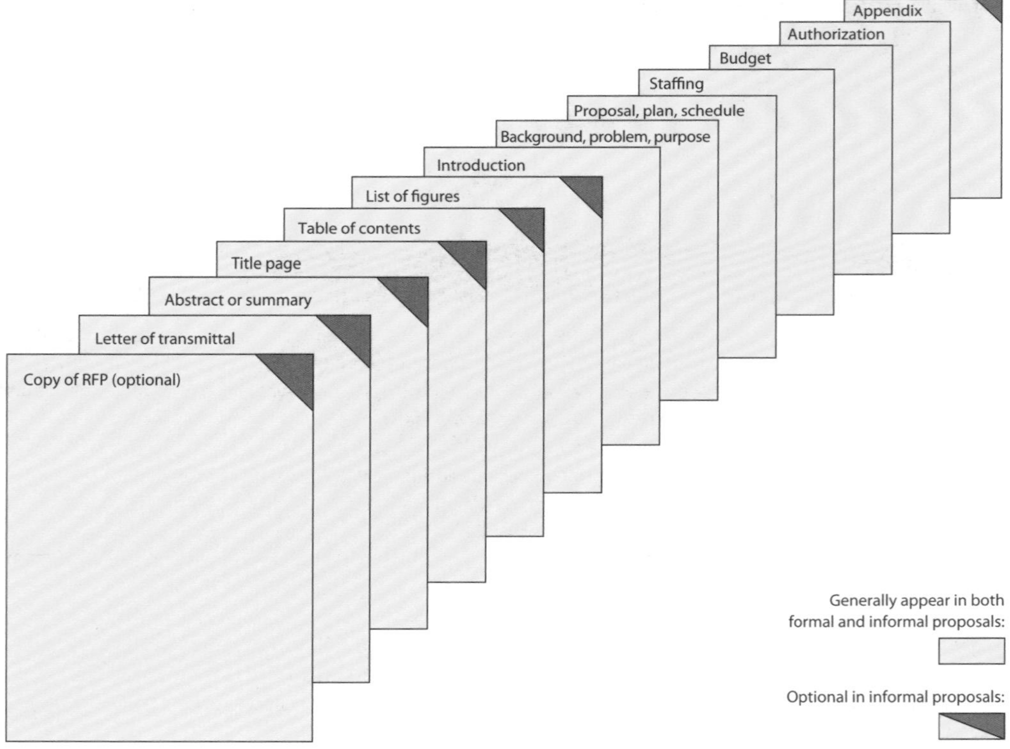

FIGURE 13.2 **Informal Proposal**

Prewriting

Analyze: The purpose is to persuade the reader to accept this proposal.

Anticipate: The reader must be convinced that this survey project is worth its hefty price.

Adapt: Because the reader will be resistant at first, use a persuasive approach that emphasizes benefits.

Writing

Research: Collect data about the reader's practice and other surveys of patient satisfaction.

Organize: Identify four specific purposes (benefits) of this proposal. Specify the survey plan. Promote the staff, itemize the budget, and ask for approval.

Compose: Prepare for revision by composing at a word processor.

Revising

Revise: Revise to emphasize benefits. Improve readability with functional headings and lists. Remove jargon and wordiness.

Proofread: Check spelling of client's name. Verify dates and calculation of budget figures. Recheck all punctuation.

Evaluate: Is this proposal convincing enough to sell the client?

---

approach market research
research | PR | consulting

205 Carlton Place | Watertown, MA 02478
phone 617.900.2005 | fax 617.900.2020
e-mail: info@approach.com

June 2, 2012

Diane Corbett, DDS
1600 Beacon Street, Suite 105
Boston, MA 02215

Dear Dr. Corbett:

Grabs attention with "hook" that focuses on key benefit

Uses opening paragraph in place of introduction

Understanding the views of your patients is the key to meeting their needs. Approach Market Research is pleased to propose a plan to help you become even more successful by learning what patients expect of your practice, so that you can improve your services.

Background and Goals

Identifies four purposes of survey

We know that you have been incorporating a total quality management system in your practice. Although you have every reason to believe your patients are pleased with your services, you may want to give them an opportunity to discuss what they like and possibly don't like about your office. Specifically, your purposes are to survey your patients to (a) determine the level of their satisfaction with you and your staff, (b) elicit their suggestions for improvement, (c) learn more about how they discovered you, and (d) compare your "preferred" and "standard" patients.

Announces heart of proposal

Proposed Plan

Describes procedure for solving problem or achieving goals

On the basis of our experience in conducting many local and national customer satisfaction surveys, Approach proposes the following plan:

Divides total plan into logical segments for easy reading

Survey. We will develop a short but thorough questionnaire probing the data you desire. Although the survey instrument will include both open-ended and closed questions, it will concentrate on the latter. Closed questions enable respondents to answer easily; they also facilitate systematic data analysis. The questionnaire will gauge patients' views of courtesy, professionalism, accuracy of billing, friendliness, and waiting time. After you approve it, the questionnaire will be sent to a carefully selected sample of 300 patients whom you have separated into groupings of "preferred" and "standard."

Analysis. Survey data will be analyzed by demographic segments, such as patient type, age, and gender. Using state-of-the art statistical tools, our team of seasoned experts will study (a) satisfaction levels, (b) the reasons for satisfaction or dissatisfaction, and (c) the responses of your "preferred" compared to "standard" patients. Moreover, our team will give you specific suggestions for making patient visits more pleasant.

Report. You will receive a final report with the key findings clearly spelled out, Dr. Corbett. Our expert staff will draw conclusions based on the results. The report will include tables summarizing all responses, divided into preferred and standard clients.

FIGURE 13.2 **(Continued)**

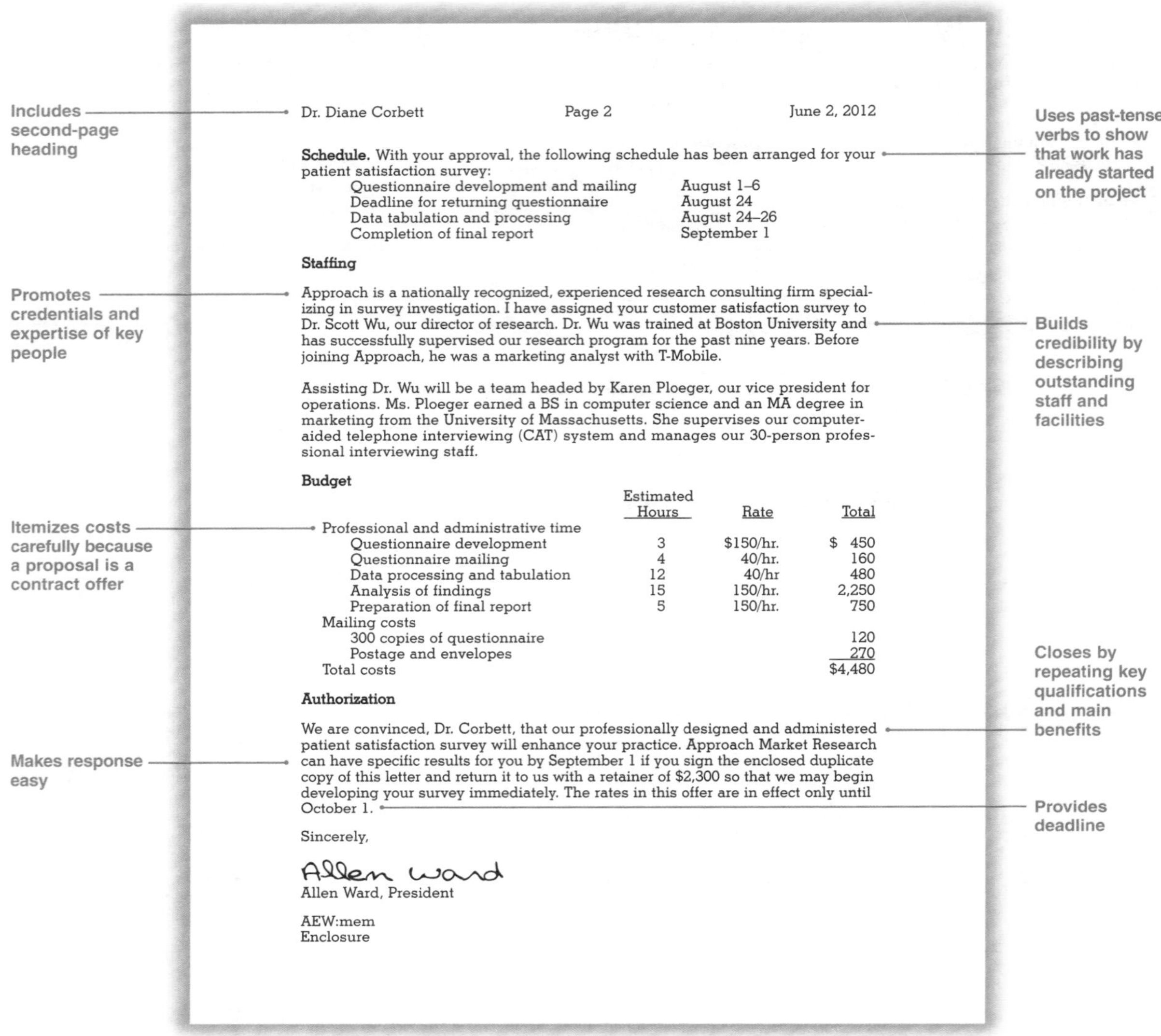

Dr. Diane Corbett Page 2 June 2, 2012

Schedule. With your approval, the following schedule has been arranged for your patient satisfaction survey:

Questionnaire development and mailing	August 1–6
Deadline for returning questionnaire	August 24
Data tabulation and processing	August 24–26
Completion of final report	September 1

Staffing

Approach is a nationally recognized, experienced research consulting firm specializing in survey investigation. I have assigned your customer satisfaction survey to Dr. Scott Wu, our director of research. Dr. Wu was trained at Boston University and has successfully supervised our research program for the past nine years. Before joining Approach, he was a marketing analyst with T-Mobile.

Assisting Dr. Wu will be a team headed by Karen Ploeger, our vice president for operations. Ms. Ploeger earned a BS in computer science and an MA degree in marketing from the University of Massachusetts. She supervises our computer-aided telephone interviewing (CAT) system and manages our 30-person professional interviewing staff.

Budget

	Estimated Hours	Rate	Total
Professional and administrative time			
Questionnaire development	3	$150/hr.	$ 450
Questionnaire mailing	4	40/hr.	160
Data processing and tabulation	12	40/hr	480
Analysis of findings	15	150/hr.	2,250
Preparation of final report	5	150/hr.	750
Mailing costs			
300 copies of questionnaire			120
Postage and envelopes			270
Total costs			$4,480

Authorization

We are convinced, Dr. Corbett, that our professionally designed and administered patient satisfaction survey will enhance your practice. Approach Market Research can have specific results for you by September 1 if you sign the enclosed duplicate copy of this letter and return it to us with a retainer of $2,300 so that we may begin developing your survey immediately. The rates in this offer are in effect only until October 1.

Sincerely,

Allen Ward

Allen Ward, President

AEW:mem
Enclosure

Includes second-page heading
Promotes credentials and expertise of key people
Itemizes costs carefully because a proposal is a contract offer
Makes response easy
Uses past-tense verbs to show that work has already started on the project
Builds credibility by describing outstanding staff and facilities
Closes by repeating key qualifications and main benefits
Provides deadline

What are the six main components of informal proposals?

Introduction. Most proposals begin by briefly explaining the reasons for the proposal and highlighting the writer's qualifications. To make your introduction more persuasive, you need to provide a "hook," such as the following:

- Hint at extraordinary results with details to be revealed shortly.
- Promise low costs or speedy results.
- Mention a remarkable resource (well-known authority, new computer program, well-trained staff) available exclusively to you.
- Identify a serious problem (worry item) and promise a solution, to be explained later.
- Specify a key issue or benefit that you feel is the heart of the proposal.

Although writers may know what goes into the proposal introduction, many face writer's block before they can get started. Proposal expert Tom Sant recommends a method he calls *cognitive webbing* to overcome the paralyzing effects of writer's block and arrive at a proposal writing plan. Dr. Sant advises that proposal writers (a) identify the outcome the client seeks, (b) brainstorm by writing down every idea and detail that will help the client achieve that objective, and (c) prioritize by again focusing on the client's most pressing needs.[4] You may have brainstormed using a very similar technique, mind mapping, by creating cluster diagrams to generate ideas for your papers.

In the proposal introduction shown in Figure 13.2, Allen Ward focused on what the customer was looking for. He analyzed the request of the Boston dentist, Dr. Diane Corbett, and decided that she was most interested in specific recommendations for improving service to her patients. However, Ward did not hit on this hook until he had written a first draft and had come back to it later. Indeed, it is often a good idea to put off writing the proposal introduction until after you have completed other parts. In longer proposals the introduction also describes the scope and limitations of the project, as well as outlining the organization of the material to come.

Background, Problem, and Purpose. The background section identifies the problem and discusses the goals or purposes of the project. In an unsolicited proposal, your goal is to convince the reader that a problem exists. Therefore, you must present the problem in detail, discussing such factors as monetary losses, failure to comply with government regulations, or loss of customers. In a solicited proposal, your aim is to persuade the reader that you understand the problem completely. Therefore, if you are responding to an RFP, this means repeating its language. For example, if the RFP asks for the *design of a maintenance program for wireless communication equipment*, you would use the same language in explaining the purpose of your proposal. This section might include segments titled *Basic Requirements, Most Critical Tasks*, or *Most Important Secondary Problems*.

Where do you discuss the problem and goals of the project?

Proposal, Plan, and Schedule. In the proposal section itself, you should discuss your plan for solving the problem. In some proposals this is tricky because you want to disclose enough of your plan to secure the contract without giving away so much information that your services aren't needed. Without specifics, though, your proposal has little chance, so you must decide how much to reveal. Tell what you propose to do and how it will benefit the reader. Remember, too, that a proposal is a sales presentation. Sell your methods, product, and "deliverables" (items that will be left with the client). In this section some writers specify how the project will be managed and how its progress will be audited. Most writers also include a schedule of activities or timetable showing when events will take place.

What role does the actual proposal section play, and how much detail must it provide?

Staffing. The staffing section of a proposal describes the credentials and expertise of the project leaders. It may also identify the size and qualifications of the support staff, along with other resources such as computer facilities and special programs for analyzing statistics. The staffing section is a good place to endorse and promote your staff and to demonstrate to the client that your company can do the job. Some firms, like Raytheon, follow industry standards and include staff qualifications in an appendix. Raytheon features the résumés of the major project participants, such as the program manager, the technical director, and team leaders. If key contributors must be replaced in the course of the project, Raytheon commits to providing only individuals with equivalent qualifications. The first rule is to give clients exactly what they asked for regarding staff qualifications, the number of project participants, and proposal details.

What is the purpose of the staffing section?

Budget. A central item in most proposals is the budget, a list of proposed project costs. You need to prepare this section carefully because it represents a contract; you cannot raise the price later—even if your costs increase. You can—and should—protect yourself from rising costs with a deadline for acceptance. In the budget section, some writers itemize hours and costs; others present a total sum only. A proposal to install a complex computer system might, for example, contain a detailed line-by-line budget. Similarly, Allen Ward felt that he needed to justify the budget for his firm's patient satisfaction survey, so he itemized the costs, as shown in Figure 13.2. However, the budget included for a proposal to conduct a one-day seminar to improve employee communication skills might be a lump sum only. Your analysis of the project will help you decide what kind of budget to prepare.

Why must you carefully research the proposal budget?

Authorization Request. Informal proposals often close with a request for approval or authorization. In addition, the closing should remind the reader of key benefits and motivate action. It might also include a deadline beyond which the offer is invalid. At Raytheon authorization information can be as simple as naming in the letter of transmittal the company official who would approve the contract resulting from the proposal. However, in most cases, a *model contract* is sent along that responds to the requirements specified by the RFP. This model contract almost always results in negotiations before the final project contract is awarded.

Preparing Formal Proposals

LEARNING OBJECTIVE 2
Discuss formal proposals and their specific components.

Proposals became a staple in the aerospace industry in the 1950s to streamline the bidding for government defense projects. Because proposals are vital to their success, high-tech companies and defense contractors maintain specialists, like Dr. Mark Grinyer at Raytheon, who do nothing but write proposals. Such proposals typically tell how a problem can be solved, what procedure will be followed, who will do it, how long it will take, and how much it will cost. When receiving bids, companies today want to be able to "compare apples with apples." They also want the protection offered by proposals, which are legal contracts. As you can imagine, writing a formal proposal to bid on a multimillion-dollar contract requires careful preparation, expertise, and countless staff hours.

Special Components of Formal Proposals

Formal proposals differ from informal proposals not in style but in size and format. Formal proposals respond to big projects and may range from 5 to 200 or more pages. To facilitate comprehension and reference, they are organized into many parts, as shown in Figure 13.1. In addition to the six basic components described for informal proposals, formal proposals may contain some or all of the following front matter and back matter components.

Which additional components might formal proposals contain that are usually missing in informal proposals?

Copy of the RFP. A copy of the request for proposal may be included in the front matter of a formal proposal. Large organizations may have more than one RFP circulating, and identification is necessary.

Letter of Transmittal. A letter of transmittal, usually bound inside formal proposals, addresses the person who is designated to receive the proposal or who will make the final decision. The letter describes how you learned about the problem or confirms that the proposal responds to the enclosed RFP. This persuasive letter briefly presents the major features and benefits of your proposal. Here, you should assure the reader that you are authorized to make the bid and mention the time limit for which the bid stands. You may also offer to provide additional information and ask for action, if appropriate.

What are the main differences between an abstract and an executive summary in proposals?

Abstract or Executive Summary. An abstract is a brief summary (typically one page) of a proposal's highlights intended for specialists or technical readers. An executive summary also reviews the proposal's highlights, but it is written for managers and should be less technically oriented. An executive summary tends to be longer than an abstract, up to 10 percent of the original text. In reports and proposals, the executive summary typically represents a nutshell version of the entire document and addresses all its sections or chapters. Formal proposals may contain either an abstract or an executive summary or both. For more information about writing executive summaries and abstracts, use a search engine such as Google.

Title Page. The title page includes the following items, generally in this order: title of proposal, name of client organization, RFP number or other announcement, date of submission, authors' names, and/or the name of their organization.

Table of Contents. Because most proposals do not contain an index, the table of contents becomes quite important. A table of contents should include all headings and their beginning page numbers. Items that appear before the contents (copy of RFP, letter of transmittal, abstract, and title page) typically are not listed in the contents. However, any appendixes should be listed.

Spotlight on Communicators

© Michael Asner

Author, coach, and proposal-writing expert Michael Asner considers a successful bid as nothing short of a work of art: "Given the complexity of meeting the demands stipulated in government documents—being able to satisfy them and compose a successful bid takes a tremendous amount of knowledge and discipline and it's really an art form." Asner is offering the first online library and how-to guide to composing proposals for government contracts on the Internet.

Checklist

Writing Proposals

Introduction

- **Indicate the purpose.** Specify why you are making the proposal.
- **Develop a persuasive "hook."** Suggest excellent results, low costs, or exclusive resources. Identify a serious problem or name a key issue or benefit.

Background, Problem, Purpose

- **Provide necessary background.** Discuss the significance of the proposal and the goals or purposes that matter to the client.
- **Introduce the problem.** For unsolicited proposals convince the reader that a problem exists. For solicited proposals show that you fully understand the customer's problem and its ramifications.

Proposal, Plan, Schedule

- **Explain the proposal.** Present your plan for solving the problem or meeting the need.
- **Discuss plan management and evaluation.** If appropriate, tell how the plan will be implemented and evaluated.
- **Outline a timetable.** Furnish a schedule showing what will be done and when.

Staffing

- **Promote the qualifications of your staff.** Explain the specific credentials and expertise of the key personnel for the project.
- **Mention special resources and equipment.** Show how your support staff and resources are superior to those of the competition.

Budget

- **Show project costs.** For most projects itemize costs. Remember, however, that proposals are contracts.
- **Include a deadline.** Here or in the conclusion, present a date beyond which the bid figures are no longer valid.

Authorization

- **Ask for approval.** Make it easy for the reader to authorize the project (for example, *Sign and return the duplicate copy*).

List of Illustrations. Proposals with many tables and figures often contain a list of illustrations. This list includes each figure or table title and its page number. If you have just a few figures or tables, however, you may omit this list.

Appendix. Ancillary material of interest to only some readers goes in appendixes. Appendix A might include résumés of the principal investigators or testimonial letters. Appendix B

Zooming In PART 2

Writing Winning Proposals at Raytheon

Raytheon's proposal process involves adapting the writing process to a team-writing environment. Dr. Mark Grinyer, who was assigned the task of writing the important executive summary, described how he used this process to complete his portion of Raytheon's Aerosol Polarimetry Sensor proposal.

First, he studied the customer's RFP looking for what the client really cared about. Then he talked to proposal team members and read descriptions of the company's offering. He turned this information into persuasive themes, outlines, and visuals, which he organized into ten storyboards (graphic organizers), one for each section of the summary. Proposal team members and a "Pink Team" of company executives reviewed these storyboards and made suggestions for improvement. "They focused on content quality, organization, and accuracy," Dr. Grinyer said.

Using the storyboards, Dr. Grinyer quickly wrote the first draft working section by section. He and his teammates revised the draft until all contributors were satisfied that it effectively addressed the interests of its audience of decision makers. A formal "Red Team" of company executives confirmed this assessment. The proposal was then ready for final corrections, formatting, proofreading, printing, and submission to the customer. "Overall," Dr. Grinyer explained, "the guidance provided by my teammates and reviewers kept me on target throughout the proposal effort."

©PAT GREENHOUSE/Boston Globe /Landov

Critical Thinking

- What aspects of Raytheon's proposal writing process can you apply to your own work?
- How do you think the various reviewers and their reviews help ensure the success of a proposal effort?
- Why do you think Raytheon puts so much effort into proposal executive summaries?

might include examples or a listing of previous projects. Other appendixes could include audit procedures, technical graphics, or professional papers cited in the body of the proposal.

Proposals in the past were always paper-based and delivered by mail or special messenger. Today, however, companies increasingly prefer *online proposals*. Receiving companies may transmit the electronic proposal to all levels of management without ever printing a page; this appeals to many environmentally conscious organizations.

Well-written proposals win contracts and business for companies and individuals. Many companies depend entirely on proposals to generate their income, so proposal writing is extremely important. The accompanying checklist summarizes key elements to remember in writing proposals.

Creating Effective Business Plans

LEARNING OBJECTIVE 3
Identify the components of typical business plans, and ethically create buy-in for your business ideas.

Another form of proposal is a business plan. Let's say you want to start your own business. Unless you can count on the Bank of Mom and Dad, you will need financial backing such as a bank loan, seed money from an individual angel investor, or funds supplied by venture capitalists. A business plan is critical for securing financial support of any kind. Such a plan also ensures that you have done your homework and know what you are doing in launching your business. It provides you with a detailed road map to chart a course to success.

According to the Small Business Administration, most entrepreneurs spend about 400 hours writing a good business plan. The average consultant can do it in about 40 hours.[5] Nevertheless, many budding entrepreneurs prefer to save the cash and do it themselves. Increasingly sophisticated software such as Business Plan Pro, PlanWrite, and PlanMagic is available for those who have done their research, assembled the relevant data, and just want formatting help. Free shareware can also be found on the Internet.[6]

Components of Typical Business Plans

If you are serious about starting a business, the importance of a comprehensive, thoughtful business plan cannot be overemphasized, says the Small Business Administration. Your business plan is more likely to secure the funds you need if it is carefully written and includes the following elements:

Letter of Transmittal and/or Executive Summary With Mission Statement. Explain your reason for writing. Provide your name, address, and telephone number, along with contact information for all principals. Include a concise mission statement for your business. Describe your business explaining the reasons it will succeed. Because potential investors will be looking for this mission statement, consider highlighting it with a paragraph heading (*Mission Statement*) or use bolding or italics. Some consultants say that you should be able to write your mission statement on the back of a business card. Others think that one or two short paragraphs might be more realistic. To give it special treatment, you could make the mission statement a section of its own following the table of contents. Your executive summary is a business plan in miniature and should not exceed two pages. It should conclude by introducing the parts of the following plan and asking for financial backing.

Table of Contents. List the page numbers and topics included in your plan. Free sample business plans featuring typical components and headings are available on the Internet from the U.S. Small Business Administration or private outfits such as Bplans.com.

Company Description. Identify the form of your business (proprietorship, partnership, or corporation) and its type (merchandising, manufacturing, or service). For existing companies, describe the company's founding, growth, sales, and profit.

Product or Service Description. In jargon-free language, explain what you are providing, how it will benefit customers, and why

Spotlight on Communicators

Courtesy of Tim Berry

President of Palo Alto Software and *Entrepreneur* magazine columnist Tim Berry advises would-be business owners not to delay writing their business plans: "Don't wait to write your plan until you think you'll have enough time. 'I can't plan. I'm too busy getting things done,' business people say." Berry suggests dropping the excuses: "The busier you are, the more you need to plan. If you are always putting out fires, you should build firebreaks or a sprinkler system. You can lose the whole forest for paying too much attention to the individual burning trees."

it is better than existing products or services. For start-ups, explain why the business will be profitable. Investors aren't always looking for a unique product or service. Instead, they are searching for a concept whose growth potential distinguishes it from others competing for funds.

Market Analysis. Discuss market characteristics, trends, projected growth, customer behavior, complementary products and services, and barriers to entry. Identify your customers and how you will attract, hold, and increase your market share. Discuss the strengths and weaknesses of your direct and indirect competitors.

Operations and Management. Explain specifically how you will run your business, including location, equipment, personnel, and management. Highlight experienced and well-trained members of the management team and your advisors. Many investors consider this the most important factor in assessing business potential. Can your management team implement this business plan?

Financial Analysis. Outline a realistic start-up budget that includes fees for legal and professional services, occupancy, licenses and permits, equipment, insurance, supplies, advertising and promotions, salaries and wages, accounting, income, and utilities. Also present an operating budget that projects costs for personnel, insurance, rent, depreciation, loan payments, salaries, taxes, repairs, and so on. Explain how much money you have, how much you will need to start up, and how much you will need to stay in business.

Appendixes. Provide necessary extras such as managers' résumés, promotional materials, and product photos. Most appendixes contain tables that exhibit the sales forecast, a personnel plan, anticipated cash flow, profit and loss, and a balance sheet.

Seeing Sample Business Plans on the Web

Writing a business plan is easier if you can see examples and learn from experts' suggestions. On the Web you will find many sites devoted to business plans. Some sites want to sell you something; others offer free advice. One of the best sites **(http://www.bplans.com)** does try to sell business plans and software. However, in addition to useful advice and blogs from experts, the site also provides over 100 free samples of business plans ranging from aircraft rental to wedding consultant businesses. These simple but helpful plans, provided by Palo Alto Software, Inc., illustrate diverse business start-ups.

At the Small Business Administration (SBA) Web site **(http://www.sba.gov/smallbusinessplanner/)**, you will find more business plan advice. In addition to suggestions for writing and using a business plan, the SBA site provides helpful business start-up information about financing, marketing, employees, taxes, and legal matters. The SBA site also provides local resources and tools for the budding entrepreneur.

ETHICS CHECK

Honesty Is Key

A business plan's purpose is to help manage a company and raise capital; hence, it is a persuasive document that must be accurate and honest. Whether the goal is to persuade a lender or investors or whether it is the blueprint for running operations, the business plan must be realistic. What are the risks of "fudging" numbers or sugarcoating potential challenges?

Writing Formal Business Reports

Formal business reports are similar to formal proposals in length, organization, and serious tone. Instead of making an offer, however, formal reports represent the end product of thorough investigation and analysis. They present ordered information to decision makers in business, industry, government, and education. In many ways formal business reports are extended versions of the analytical business reports presented in Chapter 12. Figure 13.3 shows the components of typical formal reports, their normal sequence, and parts that might be omitted in informal reports.

LEARNING OBJECTIVE 4

Describe the components of the front matter in formal business reports, and show how they further the purpose of your report.

Front Matter Components of Formal Business Reports

A number of front matter and back matter items lengthen formal reports but enhance their professional tone and serve their multiple audiences. Formal reports may be read by many levels of managers, along with technical specialists and financial consultants. Therefore, breaking a long, formal report into small segments makes its information more accessible and easier to understand

What is the purpose of formal business reports?

FIGURE 13.3 Components of Formal and Informal Reports

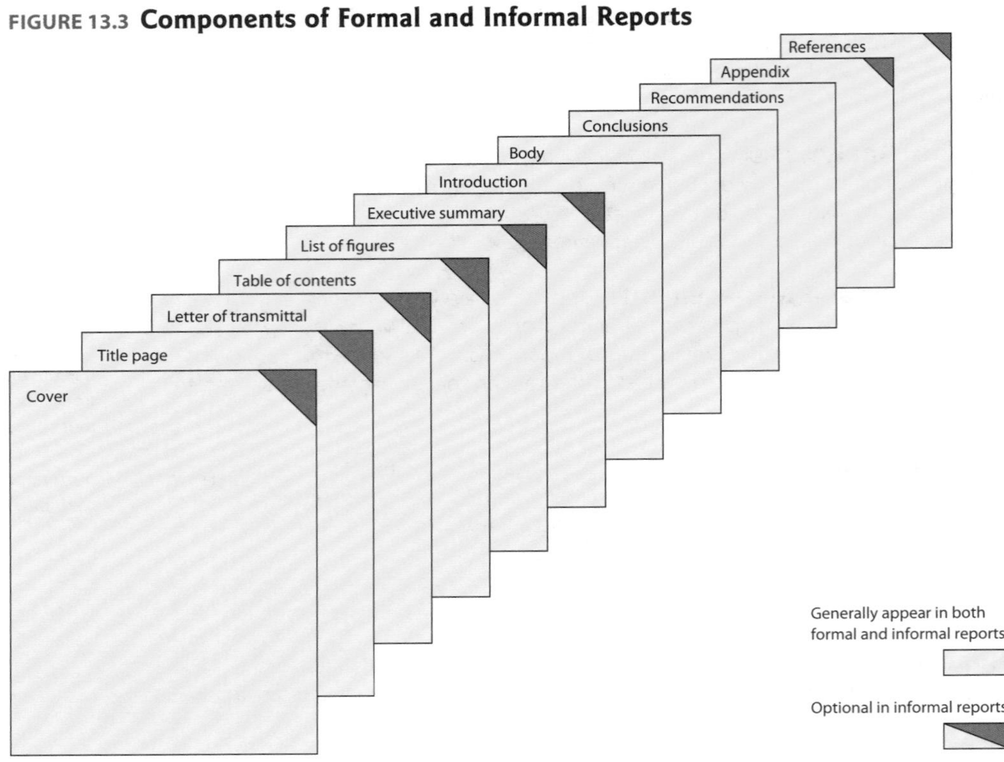

for all readers. The segments in the front of the report, called front matter or preliminaries, are discussed in this section. They are also illustrated in the model report shown later in the chapter (Figure 13.4). This analytical report studies the economic impact of an industrial park on Flagstaff, Arizona, and makes recommendations for increasing the city's future revenues.

Why are formal reports divided into many segments?

Cover. Formal reports are usually enclosed in vinyl or heavy paper binders to protect the pages and to give a professional, finished appearance. Some companies have binders imprinted with their name and logo. The title of the report may appear through a cut-out window or may be applied with an adhesive label. Good stationery and office supply stores usually stock an assortment of report binders and labels.

Title Page. A report title page, as illustrated in the Figure 13.4 model report, begins with the name of the report typed in uppercase letters (no underscore and no quotation marks). Next comes *Prepared for* (or *Submitted to*) and the name, title, and organization of the individual receiving the report. Lower on the page is *Prepared by* (or *Submitted by*) and the author's name plus any necessary identification. The last item on the title page is the date of submission. All items after the title are typed in a combination of upper- and lowercase letters.

What is the purpose of a letter or memo of transmittal?

Letter or Memo of Transmittal. Generally written on organization stationery, a letter or memorandum of transmittal introduces a formal report. You will recall that letters are sent to outsiders and memos to insiders. A transmittal letter or memo uses the direct strategy and is usually less formal than the report itself (for example, the letter or memo may use contractions and the first-person pronouns *I* and *we*). The transmittal letter or memo typically (a) announces the topic of the report and tells how it was authorized; (b) briefly describes the project; (c) highlights the report's findings, conclusions, and recommendations, if the reader is expected to be supportive; and (d) closes with appreciation for the assignment, instruction for the reader's follow-up actions, acknowledgement of help from others, or offers of assistance in answering questions. If a report is going to various readers, a special transmittal letter or memo should be prepared for each, anticipating how each reader will use the report.

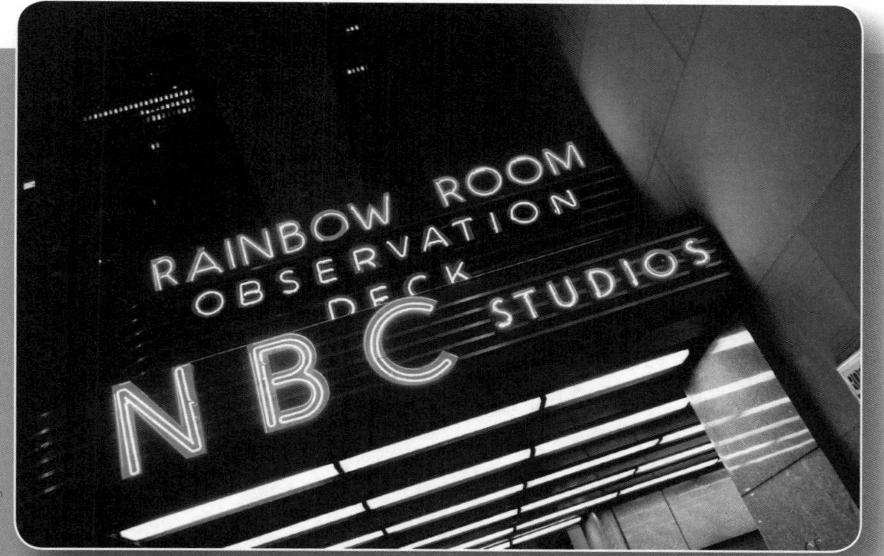

© AP Images/Mark Lennihan

When Comcast and NBC announced plans to combine their businesses in a $28.2 billion joint venture, the move launched a lengthy merger process governed by the FCC and other regulators. Opponents claimed that merging NBC with the top U.S. cable provider would increase prices and drive out independent media. Proponents argued that integrating cable with NBC would give consumers unprecedented access to popular programming on mobile phones and computers. *In what section of a formal report do businesses generally deliver a full written justification of their proposed actions?*

Table of Contents. The table of contents shows the headings in the report and their page numbers. It gives an overview of the report topics and helps readers locate them. You should wait to prepare the table of contents until after you have completed the report. For short reports you should include all headings. For longer reports you might want to list only first- and second-level headings. Leaders (spaced or unspaced dots) help guide the eye from the heading to the page number. Items may be indented in outline form or typed flush with the left margin.

List of Illustrations. For reports with several figures or tables, you may wish to include a list to help readers locate them. This list may appear on the same page as the table of contents, space permitting. For each figure or table, include a title and page number. Some writers distinguish between tables and all other illustrations, which they call figures. If you make the distinction, you should prepare separate lists of tables and figures. Because the model report in Figure 13.4 has few illustrations, the writer labeled them all "figures," a method that simplifies numbering.

What purpose does an executive summary serve in a long formal report?

Executive Summary. The purpose of an executive summary is to present an overview of a longer report to people who may not have time to read the entire document. Generally, an executive summary is prepared by the author of the report. However, occasionally you may be asked to write an executive summary of a published report or article written by someone else. In either case you will probably do the following:

- **Summarize key points.** Your goal is to summarize the important points including the purpose of the report; the problem addressed; and the findings, conclusions, and recommendations. You might also summarize the research methods, if they can be stated concisely.
- **Look for strategic words and sentences.** Read the completed report carefully. Pay special attention to the first and last sentences of paragraphs, which often contain summary statements. Look for words that enumerate (*first, next, finally*) and words that express causation (*therefore, as a result*). Also look for words that signal essentials (*basically, central, leading, principal, major*) and words that contrast ideas (*however, consequently*).
- **Prepare an outline with headings.** At a minimum, include headings for the purpose, findings, and conclusions/recommendations. What kernels of information would your reader want to know about these topics?
- **Fill in your outline.** Some writers use their computers to cut and paste important parts of the text. Then they condense with careful editing. Others find it more efficient to create new sentences as they prepare the executive summary.

- **Begin with the purpose.** The easiest way to begin an executive summary is with the words *The purpose of this report is to ....* Experienced writers may be more creative.
- **Follow the report sequence.** Present all your information in the order in which it is found in the report.
- **Eliminate nonessential details.** Include only main points. Do not include anything not in the original report. Use minimal technical language.
- **Control the length.** An executive summary is usually no longer than 10 percent of the original document. Thus, a 100-page report might require a 10-page summary. A 10-page report might need only a 1-page summary—or no summary at all. The executive summary for a long report may also include graphics to adequately highlight main points.

To see a representative executive summary, look at Figure 13.4 on page 442. Although it is only one page long, this executive summary includes headings to help the reader see the main divisions immediately. Let your organization's practices guide you in determining the length and form of an executive summary.

What is the role of the introduction to a formal report?

Introduction. Formal reports begin with an introduction that sets the scene and announces the subject. Because they contain many parts serving different purposes, formal reports are somewhat redundant. The same information may be included in the letter of transmittal, summary, and introduction. To avoid sounding repetitious, try to present the data slightly differently. However, do not skip the introduction because you have included some of its information elsewhere. You cannot be sure that your reader saw the information earlier. A good report introduction typically covers the following elements, although not necessarily in this order:

- **Background.** Describe events leading up to the problem or need.
- **Problem or purpose.** Explain the report topic and specify the problem or need that motivated the report.
- **Significance.** Tell why the topic is important. You may wish to quote experts or cite newspapers, journals, books, Web resources, and other secondary sources to establish the importance of the topic.
- **Scope.** Clarify the boundaries of the report, defining what will be included or excluded.
- **Organization.** Orient readers by giving them a road map that previews the structure of the report.

Beyond these minimal introductory elements, consider adding any of the following information that is relevant to your readers:

- **Authorization.** Identify who commissioned the report. If no letter of transmittal is included, also tell why, when, by whom, and to whom the report was written.
- **Literature review.** Summarize what other authors and researchers have published on this topic, especially for academic and scientific reports.
- **Sources and methods.** Describe your secondary sources (periodicals, books, databases). Also explain how you collected primary data, including survey size, sample design, and statistical programs used.
- **Definitions of key terms.** Define words that may be unfamiliar to the audience. Also define terms with special meanings, such as *small business* when it specifically means businesses with fewer than 30 employees.

LEARNING OBJECTIVE 5

Describe the body and back matter of formal business reports and how they serve the purpose of your report.

Body and Back Matter Components of Formal Business Reports

The body of a formal business report is the "meat" of the document. In this longest and most substantive section of the text, the author or team discusses the problem and findings, before reaching conclusions and making recommendations. Extensive and bulky materials that don't fit in the text belong in the appendix. Although some very long reports may have additional components, the back matter usually concludes with a list of sources. The body and back matter of formal business reports are discussed in this section. Figure 13.3 shows the parts of typical reports, the order in which they appear, and elements usually found only in formal reports.

Because formal business reports can be long and complex, they usually include more sections than routine informal business reports do. These components are standard and conventional; that is, the audience expects to see them in a professional report. Documents that conform to such expectations are easier to read and deliver their message more effectively. You will find most of the components addressed here in the model report in Figure 13.4, the analytical report studying the economic impact of an industrial park on Flagstaff, Arizona.

Body. The principal section in a formal report is the body. It discusses, analyzes, interprets, and evaluates the research findings or solution to the initial problem. This is where you show the evidence that justifies your conclusions. Organize the body into main categories following your original outline or using one of the organizational methods described in Chapter 12 (i.e., time, component, importance, criteria, or convention).

Although we refer to this section as the body, it does not carry that heading. Instead, it contains clear headings that explain each major section. Headings may be functional or talking. Functional heads (such as *Results of the Survey, Analysis of Findings,* or *Discussion*) help readers identify the purpose of the section but do not reveal what is in it. Such headings are useful for routine reports or for sensitive topics that may upset readers. Talking heads (for example, *Findings Reveal Revenue and Employment Benefits*) are more informative and interesting, but they do not help readers see the organization of the report. The model report in Figure 13.4 uses combination headings; as the name suggests, they combine functional heads for organizational sections (*Introduction, Conclusions and Recommendations*) with talking heads that reveal the content. The headings divide the body into smaller parts.

Conclusions. This important section tells what the findings mean, particularly in terms of solving the original problem. Some writers prefer to intermix their conclusions with the analysis of the findings—instead of presenting the conclusions separately. Other writers place the conclusions before the body so that busy readers can examine the significant information immediately. Still others combine the conclusions and recommendations. Most writers, though, present the conclusions after the body because readers expect this structure. In long reports this section may include a summary of the findings. To improve comprehension, you may present the conclusions in a numbered or bulleted list. See Chapter 12 for more suggestions on drawing conclusions.

What is the purpose of the recommendations section of a formal report?

Recommendations. When asked, you should submit recommendations that make precise suggestions for actions to solve the report problem. Recommendations are most helpful when they are practical, reasonable, feasible, and ethical. Naturally, they should evolve from the findings and conclusions. Do not introduce new information in the conclusions or recommendations sections. As with conclusions, the position of recommendations is somewhat flexible. They may be combined with conclusions, or they may be presented before the body, especially when the audience is eager and supportive. Generally, though, in formal reports they come last.

Recommendations require an appropriate introductory sentence, such as *The findings and conclusions in this study support the following recommendations*. When making many recommendations, number them and phrase each as a command, such as *Begin an employee fitness program with a workout room available five days a week.* If appropriate, add information describing how to implement each recommendation. Some reports include a timetable describing the who, what, when, where, why, and how for putting each recommendation into operation. Chapter 12 provides more information about writing recommendations.

Appendix. Incidental or supporting materials belong in appendixes at the end of a formal report. These materials are relevant to some readers but not to all. They may also be too bulky to include in the text. Appendixes may include survey forms, copies of other reports, tables of data, large graphics, and related correspondence. If additional appendixes are necessary, they are named *Appendix A, Appendix B*, and so forth.

What does the works-cited or references section of a formal report contain?

Works Cited or References. If you use the MLA (Modern Language Association) referencing format, list all sources of information alphabetically in a section titled *Works Cited*. If you use the APA (American Psychological Association) format, your list is called *References*. Your listed sources must correspond to in-text citations in the report whenever you are borrowing words or ideas from published and unpublished resources.

Regardless of the documentation format, you must include the author, title, publication, date of publication, page number, and other significant data for all ideas or quotations used in your report. For electronic references include the preceding information plus a description of the Internet address or URL leading to the citation. Also include the retrieval date on which you located the electronic reference. To see electronic and other citations, examine the list of references at the end of Figure 13.4. Appendix C of this textbook contains additional documentation information.

LEARNING OBJECTIVE 6
Specify tips that aid writers of formal business reports.

Final Writing Tips

Formal business reports are not undertaken lightly. They involve considerable effort in all three phases of writing, beginning with analysis of the problem and anticipation of the audience (as discussed in Chapter 4). Researching the data, organizing it into a logical presentation, and composing the first draft (Chapter 5) make up the second phase of writing. Revising, proofreading, and evaluating (Chapter 6) are completed in the third phase. Although everyone approaches the writing process somewhat differently, the following tips offer advice in problem areas faced by most writers of formal reports:

- **Allow sufficient time.** The main reason given by writers who are disappointed with their reports is "I just ran out of time." Develop a realistic timetable and stick to it.
- **Finish data collection.** Do not begin writing until you have collected all the data and drawn the primary conclusions. Starting too early often means backtracking. For reports based on survey data, complete the tables and figures first.

How do smart report writers approach time management, research, and their writing task?

- **Work from a good outline.** A big project such as a formal report needs the order and direction provided by a clear outline, even if the outline has to be revised as the project unfolds.
- **Provide a proper writing environment.** You will need a quiet spot where you can spread out your materials and work without interruption. Formal reports demand blocks of concentration time.
- **Use the features of your computer wisely.** Your word processor enables you to keyboard quickly; revise easily; and check spelling, grammar, and synonyms readily. A word of warning, though: save your document often and keep backup copies on disks or memory sticks. Print out important materials so that you have a hard copy. Take these precautions to guard against the grief caused by lost files, power outages, and computer malfunctions.

ETHICS CHECK
Cheater on the Team
If one of your teammates cowriting a formal report with you has been found to have plagiarized a portion of your writing project, typically the instructor will punish the entire group, assuming ownership by the entire team. After all, researchers are expected to deliver a product that they have jointly prepared. Is this fair?

- **Write rapidly; revise later.** Some experts advise writers to record their ideas quickly and save revision until after the first draft is completed. They say that quick writing avoids wasted effort spent in polishing sentences or even sections that may be cut later. Moreover, rapid writing encourages fluency and creativity. However, a quick-and-dirty first draft does not work for everyone. Many business writers prefer a more deliberate writing style, so consider this advice selectively and experiment with the method that works best for you.
- **Save difficult sections.** If some sections are harder to write than others, save them until you have developed confidence and a rhythm working on easier topics.

When should you use the past tense, and when should you use the present tense in formal reports?

- **Be consistent in verb tense.** Use past-tense verbs to describe completed actions (for example, *the respondents said* or *the survey showed*). Use present-tense verbs, however, to explain current actions (*the purpose of the report is, this report examines, the table shows*). When citing references, use past-tense verbs (*Jones reported that*). Do not switch back and forth between present- and past-tense verbs in describing related data.

[The list of Final Writing Tips continues on page 448.]

FIGURE 13.4 **Model Format Report with APA Citation Style**

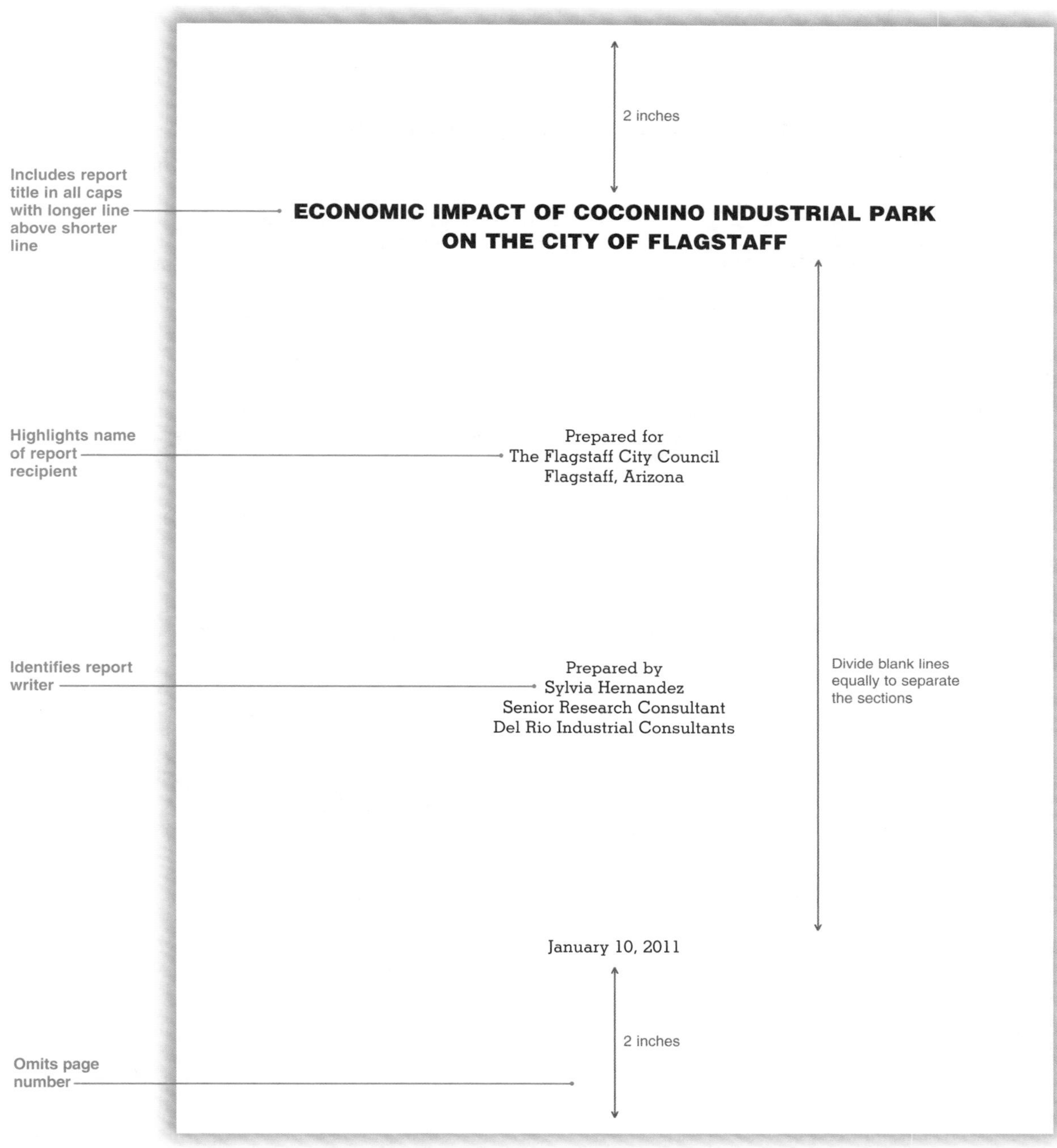

The title page is usually arranged in four evenly balanced areas. If the report is to be bound on the left, move the left margin and center point ¼ inch to the right (i.e., set the left margin to 1.25 inches). Notice that no page number appears on the title page, although it counts as page i. In designing the title page, be careful to avoid anything unprofessional—such as too many type fonts, italics, oversized print, and inappropriate graphics. Keep the title page simple and professional.

This model report uses APA documentation style. However, it does not use double-spacing, the recommended format for research papers using APA style. Instead, this model uses single-spacing, which saves space and is more appropriate for business reports.

FIGURE 13.4 (Continued) Letter of Transmittal

Announces report and identifies authorization

Gives broad overview of report purposes

Describes primary and secondary research

Offers to discuss report; expresses appreciation

Uses Roman numerals for prefatory pages

DEL RIO INDUSTRIAL CONSULTANTS

110 West Route 66
Flagstaff, Arizona 86001

www.delrio.com
(928) 774-1101

January 12, 2011

City Council
City of Flagstaff
211 West Aspen Avenue
Flagstaff, AZ 86001

Dear Council Members:

The attached report, requested by the Flagstaff City Council in a letter to Goldman-Lyon & Associates dated October 20, describes the economic impact of Coconino Industrial Park on the city of Flagstaff. We believe you will find the results of this study useful in evaluating future development of industrial parks within the city limits.

This study was designed to examine economic impact in three areas:

- Current and projected tax and other revenues accruing to the city from Coconino Industrial Park
- Current and projected employment generated by the park
- Indirect effects on local employment, income, and economic growth

Primary research consisted of interviews with 15 Coconino Industrial Park (CIP) tenants and managers, in addition to a 2010 survey of over 5,000 CIP employees. Secondary research sources included the Annual Budget of the City of Flagstaff, county and state tax records, government publications, periodicals, books, and online resources. Results of this research, discussed more fully in this report, indicate that Coconino Industrial Park exerts a significant beneficial influence on the Flagstaff metropolitan economy.

We would be pleased to discuss this report and its conclusions with you at your request. My firm and I thank you for your confidence in selecting our company to prepare this comprehensive report.

Sincerely,

Sylvia Hernandez

Sylvia Hernandez
Senior Research Consultant

SMH:mef
Attachment

ii

A letter or memo of transmittal announces the report topic and explains who authorized it. It briefly describes the project and previews the conclusions, if the reader is supportive. Such messages generally close by expressing appreciation for the assignment, suggesting follow-up actions, acknowledging the help of others, or offering to answer questions. The margins for the transmittal should be the same as for the report, about 1 to 1¼ inches on all sides. The letter should be left-justified. A page number is optional.

FIGURE 13.4 **(Continued) Table of Contents and List of Figures**

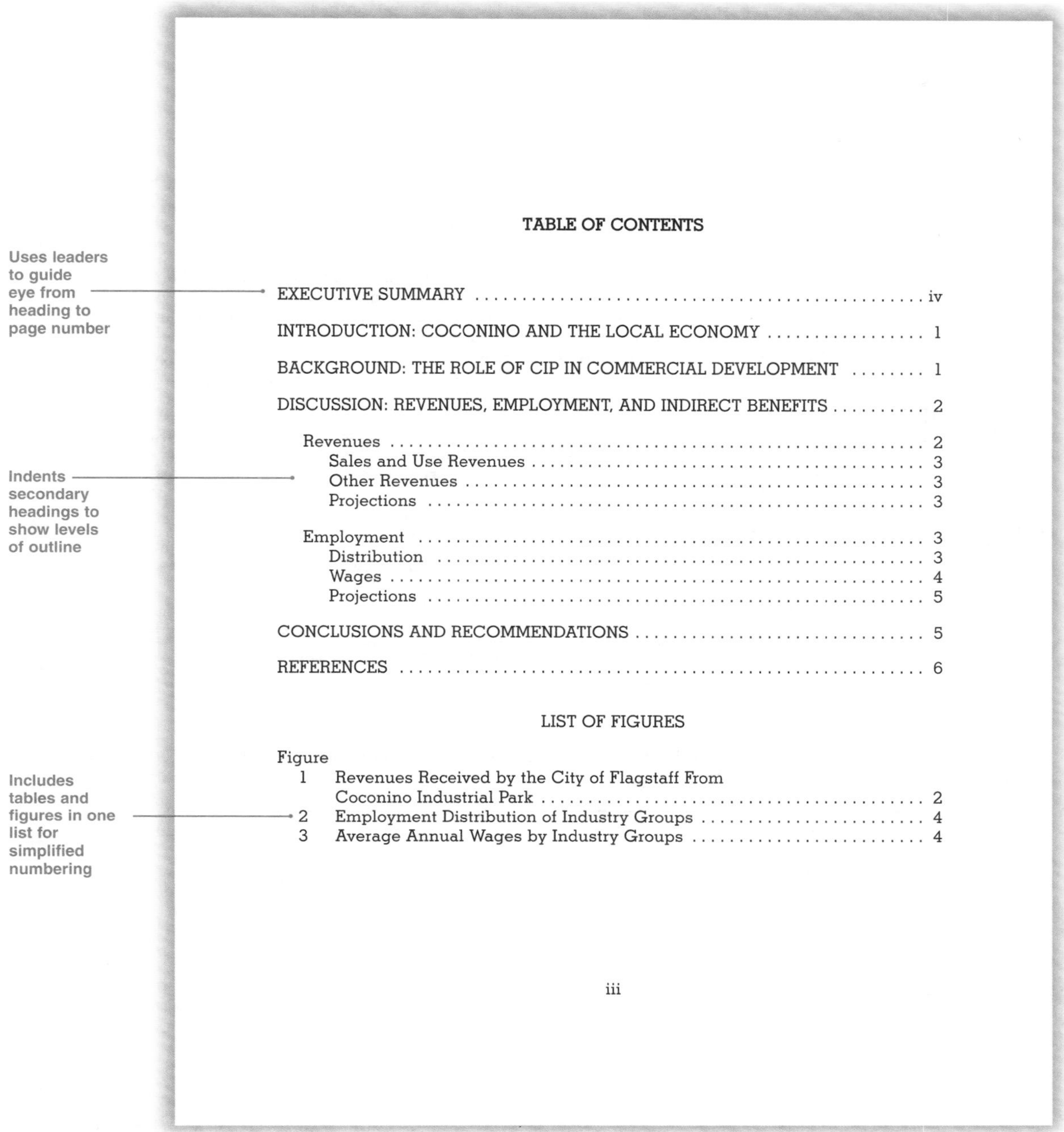

TABLE OF CONTENTS

LIST OF FIGURES

iii

Uses leaders to guide eye from heading to page number
Indents secondary headings to show levels of outline
Includes tables and figures in one list for simplified numbering

Because the table of contents and the list of figures for this report are small, they are combined on one page. Notice that the titles of major report parts are in all caps, while other headings are a combination of upper- and lowercase letters. This duplicates the style within the report. Advanced word processing capabilities enable you to generate a contents page automatically, including leaders and accurate page numbering—no matter how many times you revise. Notice that the page numbers are right-justified. Multiple-digit page numbers must line up properly (say, the number 9 under the 0 of 10).

FIGURE 13.4 (Continued) Executive Summary

Opens directly with major research findings

Identifies data sources

Summarizes organization of report

Condenses recommendations

EXECUTIVE SUMMARY

The city of Flagstaff can benefit from the development of industrial parks like the Coconino Industrial Park. Both direct and indirect economic benefits result, as shown by this in-depth study conducted by Del Rio Industrial Consultants. The study was authorized by the Flagstaff City Council when Goldman-Lyon & Associates sought the City Council's approval for the proposed construction of a G-L industrial park. The City Council requested evidence demonstrating that an existing development could actually benefit the city.

Our conclusion that the city of Flagstaff benefits from industrial parks is based on data supplied by a survey of 5,000 Coconino Industrial Park employees, personal interviews with managers and tenants of CIP, city and state documents, and professional literature.

Analysis of the data revealed benefits in three areas:

- **Revenues.** The city of Flagstaff earned nearly $2 million in tax and other revenues from the Coconino Industrial Park in 2009. By 2015 this income is expected to reach $3.4 million (in constant 2009 dollars).
- **Employment.** In 2009, CIP businesses employed a total of 7,035 workers, who earned an average wage of $56,579. By 2015, CIP businesses are expected to employ directly nearly 15,000 employees who will earn salaries totaling over $998 million.
- **Indirect benefits.** Because of the multiplier effect, by 2015 Coconino Industrial Park will directly and indirectly generate a total of 38,362 jobs in the Flagstaff metropolitan area.

On the basis of these findings, it is recommended that development of additional industrial parks be encouraged to stimulate local economic growth. The city would increase its tax revenues significantly, create much-needed jobs, and thus help stimulate the local economy in and around Flagstaff.

iv

For readers who want a quick overview of the report, the executive summary presents its most important elements. Executive summaries focus on the information the reader requires for making a decision related to the issues discussed in the report. The summary may include some or all of the following elements: purpose, scope, research methods, findings, conclusions, and recommendations. Its length depends on the report it summarizes. A 100-page report might require a 10-page summary. Shorter reports may contain one-page summaries, as shown here. Unlike letters of transmittal (which may contain personal pronouns and references to the writer), the executive summary of a long report is formal and impersonal. It uses the same margins as the body of the report. See the discussion of executive summaries in this chapter.

FIGURE 13.4 **(Continued) Page 1**

Uses a bulleted list for clarity and ease of reading

Lists three problem questions

Describes authorization for report and background of study

Includes APA citation with page number to help readers find reference

INTRODUCTION: COCONINO AND THE LOCAL ECONOMY

This study was designed to analyze the direct and indirect economic impact of Coconino Industrial Park on the city of Flagstaff. Specifically, the study seeks answers to these questions:

- What current tax and other revenues result directly from this park? What tax and other revenues may be expected in the future?
- How many and what kinds of jobs are directly attributable to the park? What is the employment picture for the future?
- What indirect effects has Coconino Industrial Park had on local employment, incomes, and economic growth?

BACKGROUND: THE ROLE OF CIP IN COMMERCIAL DEVELOPMENT

The development firm of Goldman-Lyon & Associates commissioned this study of Coconino Industrial Park at the request of the Flagstaff City Council. Before authorizing the development of a proposed Goldman-Lyon industrial park, the city council requested a study examining the economic effects of an existing park. Members of the city council wanted to determine to what extent industrial parks benefit the local community, and they chose Coconino Industrial Park as an example.

For those who are unfamiliar with it, Coconino Industrial Park is a 400-acre industrial park located in the city of Flagstaff about 4 miles from the center of the city. Most of the land lies within a specially designated area known as Redevelopment Project No. 2, which is under the jurisdiction of the Flagstaff Redevelopment Agency. Planning for the park began in 1994; construction started in 1996.

The original goal for Coconino Industrial Park was development for light industrial users. Land in this area was zoned for uses such as warehousing, research and development, and distribution. Like other communities, Flagstaff was eager to attract light industrial users because such businesses tend to employ a highly educated workforce, are relatively quiet, and do not pollute the environment (Cohen, 2010, p. C1). The city of Flagstaff recognized the need for light industrial users and widened an adjacent highway to accommodate trucks and facilitate travel by workers and customers coming from Flagstaff.

1

Titles for major parts of a report are centered in all caps. In this model document we show several combination headings. As the name suggests, combination heads are a mix of functional headings, such as *INTRODUCTION, BACKGROUND, DISCUSSION,* and *CONCLUSIONS,* and talking heads that reveal the content. Most business reports would use talking heads or a combination, such as *FINDINGS REVEAL REVENUE* and *EMPLOYMENT BENEFITS*. First-level headings (such as Revenues on page 2) are printed with bold upper- and lowercase letters. Second-level headings (such as Distribution on page 3) begin at the side, are bolded, and are written in upper- and lowercase letters. See Figure 12.6 for an illustration of heading formats. This business report is shown with single-spacing, although some research reports might be double-spaced. Always check with your organization to learn its preferred style.

FIGURE 13.4 **(Continued) Page 2**

The park now contains 14 building complexes with over 1.25 million square feet of completed building space. The majority of the buildings are used for office, research and development, marketing and distribution, or manufacturing uses. Approximately 50 acres of the original area are yet to be developed.

Provides specifics for data sources

Data for this report came from a 2009 survey of over 5,000 Coconino Industrial Park employees; interviews with 15 CIP tenants and managers; the annual budget of the city of Flagstaff; county and state tax records; and current books, articles, journals, and online resources. Projections for future revenues resulted from analysis of past trends and "Estimates of Revenues for Debt Service Coverage, Redevelopment Project Area 2" (Miller, 2009, p. 79).

Usess combination heads

DISCUSSION: REVENUES, EMPLOYMENT, AND INDIRECT BENEFITS

Previews organization of report

The results of this research indicate that major direct and indirect benefits have accrued to the city of Flagstaff and surrounding metropolitan areas as a result of the development of Coconino Industrial Park. The research findings presented here fall into three categories: (a) revenues, (b) employment, and (c) indirect benefits.

Revenues

Coconino Industrial Park contributes a variety of tax and other revenues to the city of Flagstaff, as summarized in Figure 1. Current revenues are shown, along with projections to the year 2015. At a time when the economy is unstable, revenues from an industrial park such as Coconino can become a reliable income stream for the city of Flagstaff.

Places figure close to textual reference

Figure 1

REVENUES RECEIVED BY THE CITY OF FLAGSTAFF
FROM COCONINO INDUSTRIAL PARK

Current Revenues and Projections to 2015

	2010	2015
Sales and use taxes	$ 904,140	$1,335,390
Revenues from licenses	426,265	516,396
Franchise taxes	175,518	229,424
State gas tax receipts	83,768	112,134
Licenses and permits	78,331	112,831
Other revenues	94,039	141,987
Total	$1,762,061	$2,448,162

Source: Arizona State Board of Equalization Bulletin. Phoenix: State Printing Office, 2010, p. 28.

2

Notice that this formal report is single-spaced. Many businesses prefer this space-saving format. However, some organizations prefer double-spacing, especially for preliminary drafts. If you single-space, do not indent paragraphs. If you double-space, do indent the paragraphs. Page numbers may be centered 1 inch from the bottom of the page or placed 1 inch from the upper right corner at the margin. Your word processor can insert page numbers automatically. Strive to leave a minimum of 1 inch for top, bottom, and side margins. References follow the parenthetical citation style (or in-text citation style) of the American Psychological Association (APA). Notice that the author's name, the year of publication, and page number appear in parentheses. The complete bibliographic entry for any in-text citation appears at the end of report in the references section.

FIGURE 13.4 (Continued) Page 3

Continues interpreting figures in table

Includes ample description of electronic reference

Sets stage for next topic to be discussed

Sales and Use Revenues

As shown in Figure 1, the city's largest source of revenues from CIP is the sales and use tax. Revenues from this source totaled $904,140 in 2010, according to figures provided by the Arizona State Board of Equalization (2010, p. 28). Sales and use taxes accounted for more than half of the park's total contribution to the city of $1,762,061.

Other Revenues

Other major sources of city revenues from CIP in 2010 include alcohol licenses, motor vehicle in lieu fees, trailer coach licenses ($426,265), franchise taxes ($175,518), and state gas tax receipts ($83,768). Although not shown in Figure 1, other revenues may be expected from the development of recently acquired property. The U.S. Economic Development Administration has approved a grant worth $975,000 to assist in expanding the current park eastward on an undeveloped parcel purchased last year. Revenues from leasing this property may be sizable.

Projections

Total city revenues from CIP will nearly double by 2015, producing an income of $2.45 million. This estimate is based on an annual growth rate of 0.65 percent, as projected by the Bureau of Labor Statistics and reported at the Web site of Infoplease.com ("Economic Outlook Through 2010").

Employment

One of the most important factors to consider in the overall effect of an industrial park is employment. In Coconino Industrial Park the distribution, number, and wages of people employed will change considerably in the next six years.

Distribution

A total of 7,035 employees currently work in various industry groups at Coconino Industrial Park. The distribution of employees is shown in Figure 2. The largest number of workers (58 percent) is employed in manufacturing and assembly operations. The next largest category, computer and electronics, employs 24 percent of the workers. Some overlap probably exists because electronics assembly could be included in either group. Employees also work in publishing (9 percent), warehousing and storage (5 percent), and other industries (4 percent).

Although the distribution of employees at Coconino Industrial Park shows a wide range of employment categories, it must be noted that other industrial parks would likely generate an entirely different range of job categories.

3

Only the most important research findings are interpreted and discussed for readers. The depth of discussion depends on the intended length of the report, the goal of the writer, and the expectations of the reader. Because the writer wants this report to be formal in tone, she avoids *I* and *we* in all discussions.

As you type a report, avoid widows and orphans (ending a page with the first line of a paragraph or carrying a single line of a paragraph to a new page). Strive to start and end pages with at least two lines of a paragraph, even if a slightly larger bottom margin results.

FIGURE 13.4 **(Continued) Page 4**

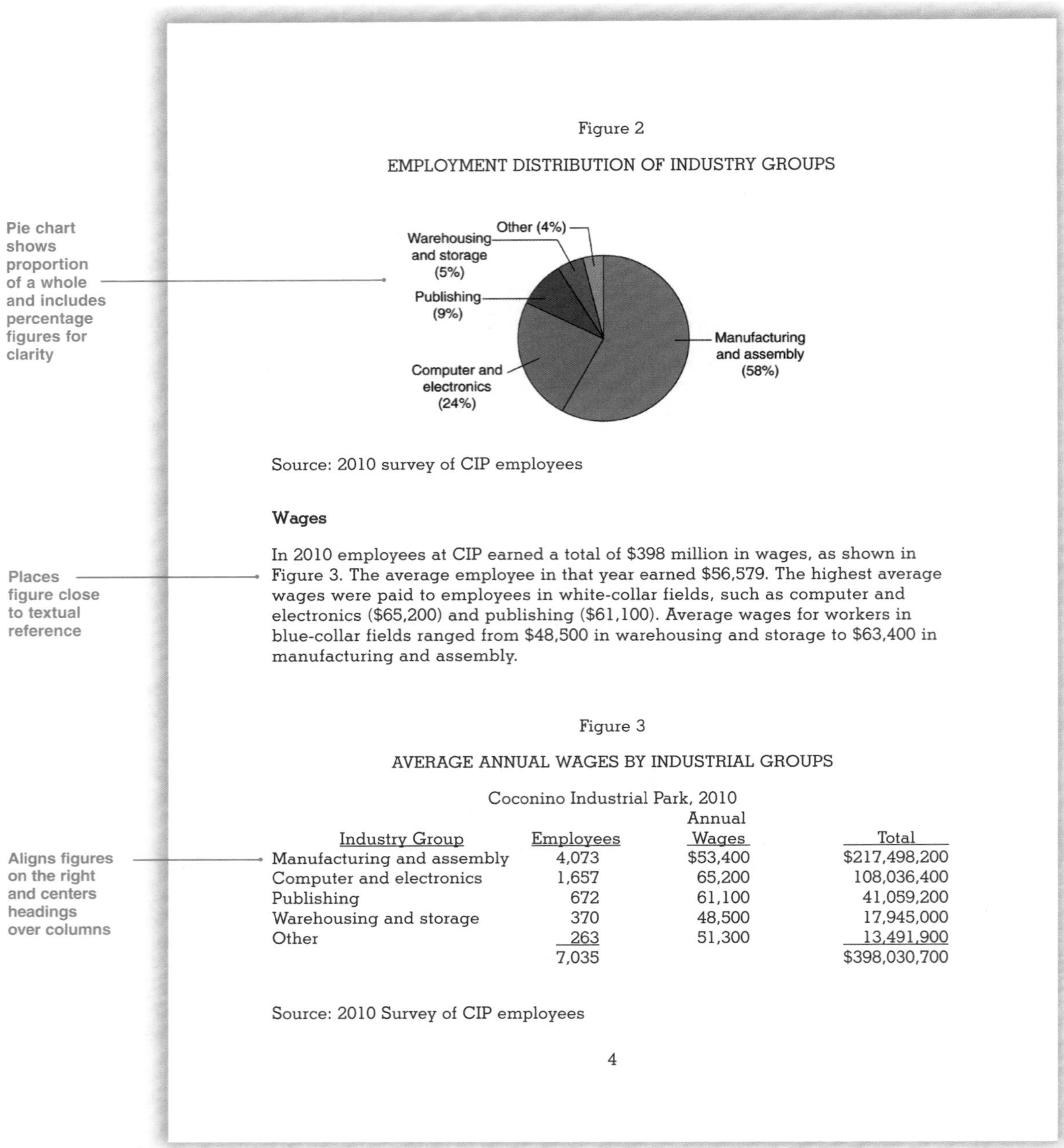

Pie chart shows proportion of a whole and includes percentage figures for clarity
Figure 2
EMPLOYMENT DISTRIBUTION OF INDUSTRY GROUPS
Other (4%)
Warehousing and storage (5%)
Publishing (9%)
Computer and electronics (24%)
Manufacturing and assembly (58%)
Source: 2010 survey of CIP employees
Places figure close to textual reference
Aligns figures on the right and centers headings over columns

Wages

In 2010 employees at CIP earned a total of $398 million in wages, as shown in Figure 3. The average employee in that year earned $56,579. The highest average wages were paid to employees in white-collar fields, such as computer and electronics ($65,200) and publishing ($61,100). Average wages for workers in blue-collar fields ranged from $48,500 in warehousing and storage to $63,400 in manufacturing and assembly.

Figure 3

AVERAGE ANNUAL WAGES BY INDUSTRIAL GROUPS

Coconino Industrial Park, 2010

Industry Group	Employees	Annual Wages	Total
Manufacturing and assembly	4,073	$53,400	$217,498,200
Computer and electronics	1,657	65,200	108,036,400
Publishing	672	61,100	41,059,200
Warehousing and storage	370	48,500	17,945,000
Other	263	51,300	13,491,900
	7,035		$398,030,700

Source: 2010 Survey of CIP employees

4

If you use figures or tables, be sure to introduce them in the text (for example, *as shown in Figure 3*). Although it is not always possible, try to place them close to the spot where they are first mentioned. To save space, you can print the title of a figure at its side. Because this report contains few tables and figures, the writer named them all "Figures" and numbered them consecutively. Graphics that serve for reference only and aren't discussed in the text belong in the appendix.

FIGURE 13.4 **(Continued) Page 5**

Clarifies information and tells what it means in relation to original research questions

Projections

By 2015 Coconino Industrial Park is expected to more than double its number of employees, bringing the total to over 15,000 workers. The total payroll in 2015 will also more than double, producing over $998 million (using constant 2010 dollars) in salaries to CIP employees. These projections are based on an 9 percent growth rate (Miller, 2009, p. 78), along with anticipated increased employment as the park reaches its capacity.

Future development in the park will influence employment and payrolls. One CIP project manager stated in an interview that much of the remaining 50 acres is planned for medium-rise office buildings, garden offices, and other structures for commercial, professional, and personal services (I. M. Novak, personal communication, November 30, 2010). Average wages for employees are expected to increase because of an anticipated shift to higher-paying white-collar jobs. Industrial parks often follow a similar pattern of evolution (Badri, 2010, p. 41). Like many industrial parks, CIP evolved from a warehousing center into a manufacturing complex.

Combines conclusions and recommendations

CONCLUSIONS AND RECOMMENDATIONS

Analysis of tax revenues, employment data, personal interviews, and professional literature leads to the following conclusions and recommendations about the economic impact of Coconino Industrial Park on the city of Flagstaff:

1. Sales tax and other revenues produced nearly $1.8 million in income to the city of Flagstaff in 2010. By 2015 sales tax and other revenues are expected to produce $2.5 million in city income.

Uses a numbered list for clarity and ease of reading

2. CIP currently employs 7,035 employees, the majority of whom are working in manufacturing and assembly. The average employee in 2010 earned $56,579.

3. By 2015 CIP is expected to employ more than 15,000 workers producing a total payroll of over $998 million.

4. Employment trends indicate that by 2015 more CIP employees will be engaged in higher-paying white-collar positions.

On the basis of these findings, we recommend that the City Council of Flagstaff authorize the development of additional industrial parks to stimulate local economic growth. The direct and indirect benefits of Coconino Industrial Park strongly suggest that future commercial development would have a positive impact on the Flagstaff community and the surrounding region as population growth and resulting greater purchasing power would trigger higher demand.

As the Coconino example shows, gains in tax revenue, job creation, and other direct and indirect benefits would follow the creation of additional industrial parks in and around Flagstaff.

5

After discussing and interpreting the research findings, the writer articulates what she considers the most important conclusions and recommendations. Longer, more complex reports may have separate sections for conclusions and resulting recommendations. In this report they are combined. Notice that it is unnecessary to start a new page for the conclusions.

FIGURE 13.4 **(Continued) Page 6 References**

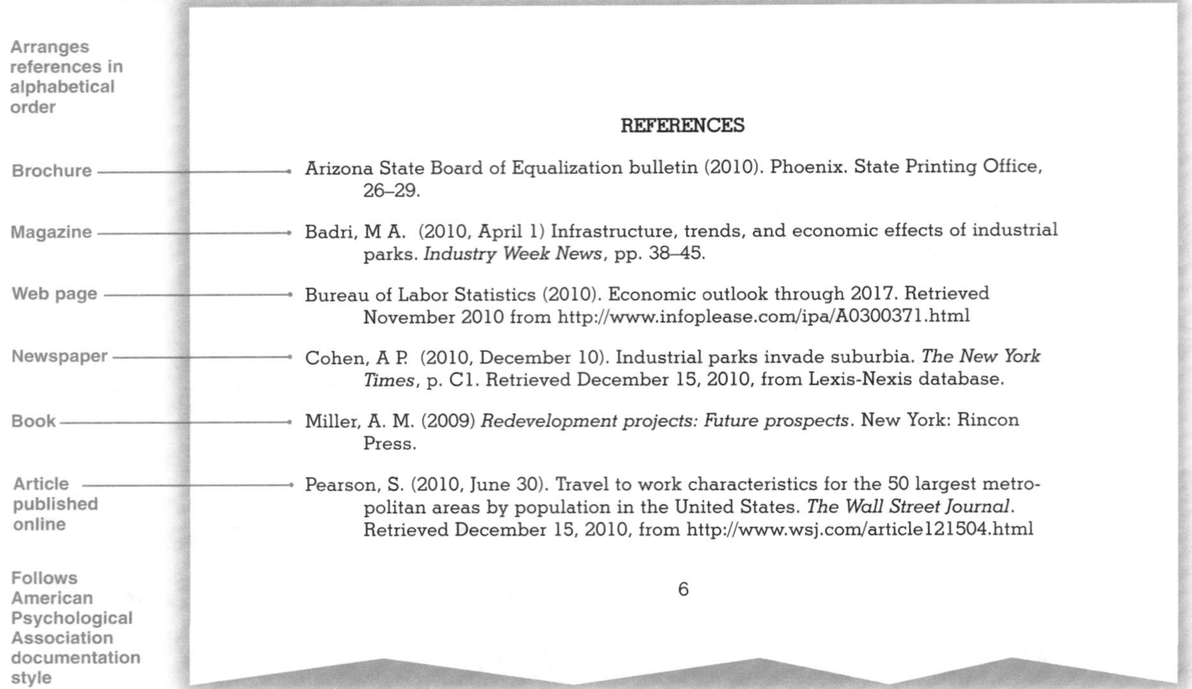

REFERENCES

Arizona State Board of Equalization bulletin (2010). Phoenix. State Printing Office, 26–29.

Badri, M A. (2010, April 1) Infrastructure, trends, and economic effects of industrial parks. *Industry Week News*, pp. 38–45.

Bureau of Labor Statistics (2010). Economic outlook through 2017. Retrieved November 2010 from http://www.infoplease.com/ipa/A0300371.html

Cohen, A P. (2010, December 10). Industrial parks invade suburbia. *The New York Times*, p. C1. Retrieved December 15, 2010, from Lexis-Nexis database.

Miller, A. M. (2009) *Redevelopment projects: Future prospects*. New York: Rincon Press.

Pearson, S. (2010, June 30). Travel to work characteristics for the 50 largest metropolitan areas by population in the United States. *The Wall Street Journal*. Retrieved December 15, 2010, from http://www.wsj.com/article121504.html

6

On this page the writer lists all references cited in the text as well as others that she examined during her research. The writer lists these citations following the APA referencing style. Notice that all entries are arranged alphabetically. Book and periodical titles are italicized, but they could be underlined. When referring to online items, she shows the full name of the citation and then identifies the URL as well as the date on which she accessed the electronic reference. This references page is shown with single-spacing, which is preferable for business reports. However, APA style recommends double-spacing for research reports, including the references page. APA style also shows "References" in upper- and lowercase letters. However, the writer preferred to use all caps to be consistent with other headings in this business report.

[Final Writing Tips continued from page 438.]

- **Generally avoid *I* and *we*.** To make formal reports seem as objective and credible as possible, most writers omit first-person pronouns. This formal style sometimes results in the overuse of passive-voice verbs (for example, *periodicals were consulted* and *the study was conducted*). Look for alternative constructions (*periodicals indicated* and *the study revealed*). It is also possible that your organization may allow first-person pronouns, so check before starting your report.
- **Let the first draft sit.** After completing the first version, put it aside for a day or two. Return to it with the expectation of revising and improving it. Do not be afraid to make major changes.
- **Revise for clarity, coherence, and conciseness.** Read a printed copy out loud. Do the sentences make sense? Do the ideas flow together naturally? Can wordiness and flabbiness be cut out? Make sure that your writing is so clear that a busy manager does not have to reread any part. See Chapter 6 for specific revision suggestions.
- **Proofread the final copy three times.** First, read a printed copy slowly for word meanings and content. Then read the copy again for spelling, punctuation, grammar, and other mechanical errors. Finally, scan the entire report to check its formatting and consistency (page numbering, indenting, spacing, headings, and so forth).

Putting It All Together

Formal reports in business generally aim to study problems and recommend solutions. Sylvia Hernandez, senior research assistant with Del Rio Industrial Consultants, was asked to study the economic impact of a local industrial park on the city of Flagstaff, Arizona, resulting in the formal report shown in Figure 13.4.

Checklist

Preparing Formal Business Reports

Report Process

- **Analyze the report and purpose.** Develop a problem question (*How is e-mail affecting productivity and security at MegaTech?*) and a purpose statement (*The purpose of this report is to investigate the use of e-mail at MegaTech and recommend policies and procedures that enhance company productivity and security*).
- **Anticipate the audience and issues.** Consider primary and secondary audiences. What do they already know? What do they need to know? Divide the major problem into subproblems for investigation.
- **Prepare a work plan.** Include problem and purpose statements, as well as a description of the sources and methods of collecting data. Prepare a tentative project outline and work schedule with anticipated dates of completion for all segments of the project.
- **Collect data.** Begin by searching secondary sources (electronic databases, books, magazines, journals, newspapers) for information on your topic. Then, if necessary, gather primary data by surveying, interviewing, observing, and experimenting.
- **Document data sources.** Establish a system for keeping track of your sources. When saving files from business databases or the Internet, be sure to record the complete publication information. Some researchers like to prepare note cards or separate sheets of paper citing all references (author, date, source, page, and quotation). Select a documentation format and use it consistently.
- **Interpret and organize the data.** Arrange the collected information in tables, grids, or outlines to help you visualize relationships and interpret meanings. Organize the data into an outline (Chapter 5).
- **Prepare graphics.** Make tables, charts, graphs, and illustrations—but only if they serve a function. Use graphics to help clarify, condense, simplify, or emphasize your data.
- **Compose the first draft.** At a computer write the first draft from your outline. Use appropriate headings as well as transitional expressions (such as *however, on the contrary,* and *in addition*) to guide the reader through the report.
- **Revise and proofread.** Revise to eliminate wordiness, ambiguity, and redundancy. Look for ways to improve readability, such as bulleted or numbered lists. Proofread three times for (a) word and content meaning, (b) grammar and mechanical errors, and (c) formatting.
- **Evaluate the product.** Examine the final report. Will it achieve its purpose? Encourage feedback so that you can learn how to improve future reports.

Report Components

- **Title page.** Balance the following lines on the title page: (a) name of the report (in all caps); (b) name, title, and organization of the individual receiving the report; (c) author's name, title, and organization; and (d) date submitted.
- **Letter of transmittal.** Announce the report topic and explain who authorized it. Briefly describe the project and preview the conclusions, if the reader is supportive. Close by expressing appreciation for the assignment, suggesting follow-up actions, acknowledging the help of others, or offering to answer questions.
- **Table of contents.** Show the beginning page number where each report heading appears in the report. Connect the page numbers and headings with leaders (spaced dots) using your word processing software. In MS Word 2007, for example, select the **Home** tab, open the **Paragraph** menu and click **Tabs** at the bottom left of the window.
- **List of illustrations.** Include a list of tables, illustrations, or figures showing the title of the item and its page number. If space permits, put these lists on the same page with the table of contents.
- **Executive summary.** Summarize the report purpose, findings, conclusions, and recommendations. Gauge the length of the summary by the length of the report and by your organization's practices.
- **Introduction.** Explain the problem motivating the report; describe its background and significance. Clarify the scope and limitations of the report. Optional items include a review of the relevant literature and a description of data sources, methods, and key terms. Close by previewing the report's organization.
- **Body.** Discuss, analyze, and interpret the research findings or the proposed solution to the problem. Arrange the findings in logical segments following your outline. Use clear, descriptive headings.
- **Conclusions and recommendations.** Explain what the findings mean in relation to the original problem. If asked, make enumerated recommendations that suggest actions for solving the problem.
- **Appendix.** Include items of interest to some, but not all, readers, such as questionnaires, transcripts of interviews, data sheets, and other information that is not essential to explain your findings, but that supports your analysis. Add large graphics—pictures, maps, figures, tables, charts, and graphs—that are not discussed directly in the text.
- **Works cited or references.** If footnotes are not provided in the text, list all references in a section called *Works Cited* or *References*.

Zooming In — YOUR TURN

Applying Your Skills at Raytheon

Proposals and reports are written, often in teams, to accomplish serious business purposes. Both require research, and sometimes resources are unavailable. Assume that you are an intern at Raytheon working with Dr. Grinyer. He has asked you to help him develop materials to improve Raytheon reports and proposals. He suggests two possible tasks:

1. A short (three to five pages) business report recommending a structured writing process to be used for team-written company documents
2. A memo evaluating several (two to four) proposal consulting companies that might be able to help Raytheon teams write good proposals when the company's proposal specialists are unavailable

Your Task

Select one of the suggested tasks. For Option 1, in a two- or three-person team, plan the required report and have each team member prepare an outline of his or her assigned section. As a team, review and improve the outlines with written comments and annotations. For Option 2, individually research, plan, and write the required one- to two-page memo for your instructor.

©PAT GREENHOUSE/Boston Globe /Landov

Want to do well on tests and excel in your course? Go to **www.meguffey.com** for helpful interactive resources.

- **Review the Chapter 13 PowerPoint slides to prepare for the first quiz.**

The city council hired the consultants to evaluate Coconino Industrial Park and to assess whether future commercial development would stimulate further economic growth. Sylvia Hernandez subdivided the economic impact into three aspects: Revenue, Employment, and Indirect Benefits. The report was compiled from survey data as well as from secondary sources that Sylvia researched.

Sylvia's report illustrates many of the points discussed in this chapter. Although it is a good example of the typical report format and style, it should not be viewed as the only way to present a report. Wide variation exists in reports.

The accompanying checklist feature on the previous page summarizes the report process and report components in one handy list.

Summary of Learning Objectives

1 Discuss the general uses and basic components of informal proposals, and grasp their audience and purpose. Although they may vary, most proposals have certain standard parts in common. Informal proposals contain the following: a persuasive introduction that explains the purpose of the proposal and qualifies the writer; background material identifying the problem and project goals; a proposal, plan, or schedule outlining the project; a section describing staff qualifications; a budget showing expected costs; and a request for approval or authorization.

2 Discuss formal proposals and their specific components. Beyond the six components generally contained in informal proposals, formal proposals may include these additional parts: a copy of the RFP (request for proposal), a letter of transmittal, an executive summary, a title page, a table of contents, a list of illustrations, and an appendix.

3 Identify the components of typical business plans, and ethically create buy-in for your business ideas. Business plans help entrepreneurs secure start-up funding and also provide a road map to follow as a business develops. Typical business plans include the following: letter of transmittal or an executive summary, table of contents, company description, product or service description, market analysis, description of operations and management, financial analysis, and appendixes. For start-up businesses seeking financial backing, the product or service description as well as the operations and management analyses are particularly important. They must promote growth potential and promise a management team capable of implementing the business plan.

Are you ready? Get more practice at **www.meguffey.com**

4 Describe the components of the front matter in formal business reports, and show how they further the purpose of your report. Formal business reports may include these beginning components: a vinyl or heavy paper cover, a title page, a letter of transmittal, a table of contents, a list of illustrations, and an executive summary. The introduction to a formal report sets the scene by discussing some or all of the following topics: background material, problem or purpose, significance of the topic, scope and organization of the report, authorization, review of relevant literature, sources and methods, and definitions of key terms.

5 Describe the body and back matter of formal business reports and how they serve the purpose of your report. The body of a report discusses, analyzes, interprets, and evaluates the research findings or solution to a problem. The conclusion states what the findings mean and how they relate to the report's purpose. The recommendations tell how to solve the report problem. The last portions of a formal report are the appendix and references or works cited.

6 Specify tips that aid writers of formal business reports. Before writing, develop a realistic timetable and collect all necessary data. During the writing process, work from a good outline, work in a quiet place, and use a computer. Also, try to write rapidly, revising later. While writing, use verb tenses consistently, and avoid *I* and *we*. A few days after completing the first draft, revise to improve clarity, coherence, and conciseness. Proofread the final copy three times.

Chapter Review

1. What purpose do proposals serve? (Objs. 1, 2)
2. Who uses requests for proposals (RFPs), and why? (Objs. 1, 2)
3. What are the six principal components of an informal letter proposal? (Obj. 1)
4. Why is the budget section in a proposal particularly important? (Obj. 2)
5. Why does an entrepreneur need to write a business plan? (Obj. 3)
6. Name eight components of typical business plans. (Obj. 3)
7. What should a business plan mission statement include, and how long should it be? (Obj. 3)
8. Why are formal reports written in business? Give an original example of a business-related formal report. (Obj. 4)
9. What is a letter or memorandum of transmittal? (Obj. 4)
10. How long should a typical executive summary be? (Obj. 4)
11. Name the steps necessary to write an executive summary in a formal business report. (Obj. 4)
12. What should be included in the introduction to a formal business report? (Obj. 4)
13. What should the writer strive to do in the body of a formal business report? (Obj. 5)
14. Why must writers list their sources and identify them in the text? (Obj. 5)
15. In your view, what are six of the most important tips for the writer of a formal report? Explain each of your choices. (Obj. 6)

Critical Thinking

1. Which category of proposal, solicited or unsolicited, is more likely to succeed, and why? (Obj. 1)
2. Compare and contrast proposals and business plans. (Objs. 1–3)
3. What is the purpose of a business plan, and what should it communicate to investors? (Obj. 3)
4. How do formal business reports differ from informal business reports? (Objs. 4–6)
5. **Ethical Issue:** How can a team of writers ensure that each member shoulders an equal or fair amount of the work on an extensive writing project, such as a formal proposal or business report?

Activities

13.1. Proposals: Solving a Workplace Problem in an Unsolicited Informal Proposal (Obj. 1)

The ability to spot problems before they turn into serious risks is prized by most managers. Draw on your internship and work experience. Can you identify a problem that could be solved with a small to moderate financial investment? Look for issues such as missing lunch or break rooms for staff; badly needed health initiatives such as gyms or sports club memberships; switching to low-gas-mileage, high-emission company vehicles; or lack of recycling efforts.

Your Task. Discuss with your instructor the workplace problem that you have identified. Make sure you choose a relatively weighty problem that can nevertheless be lessened or eliminated with a minor expenditure. Be sure to include a cost–benefit analysis. Address your unsolicited letter or memo proposal to your current or former boss and copy your instructor.

13.2 Proposals: Think Like an Entrepreneur (Obj. 1)

Web

Perhaps you have fantasized about one day owning your own company, or maybe you have already started a business. Proposals are offers to a very specific audience whose business you are soliciting. Think of a product or service that you like or know much about. On the Web or in electronic databases, research the market so that you understand going rates, prices, and costs. Search the Small Business Administration's Web site **(http://www.sba.gov)** for valuable tips on how to launch and manage a business.

Your Task. Choose a product or service you would like to offer to a particular audience, such as a window cleaning business, an online photography business, a new vehicle on the U.S. market, or a new European hair care line. Discuss products and services as well as target audiences with your instructor. Write a letter proposal promoting your chosen product or service.

13.3 Proposals: Comparing Real Proposals (Objs. 1, 2)

Web

Many new companies with services or products to offer would like to land corporate or government contracts. However, they are intimidated by the proposal (RFP process). You have been asked for help by your friend Mikayla, who has started her own designer uniform company. Her goal is to offer her colorful yet functional uniforms to hospitals and clinics. Before writing a proposal, however, she wants to see examples and learn more about the process.

Your Task. Use the Web to find at least two examples of business proposals. Do not waste time on sites that want to sell templates or books. Find actual examples. Then prepare a memo to Mikayla in which you do the following:

a. Identify two sites with sample business proposals.
b. Outline the parts of each proposal.
c. Compare the strengths and weaknesses of each proposal.
d. Draw conclusions. What can Mikayla learn from these examples?

13.4 Proposals: Medicus Associates Solicits Your Proposal (Obj. 1)

Team

In university towns, sports medicine is increasingly popular. A new medical clinic, Medicus Associates, is opening its doors in your community. A friend recommended your small business to the administrator of the clinic, and you received a letter asking you to provide information about your service. The new medical clinic specializes in sports medicine, physical therapy, and cardiac rehabilitation services. It is interested in retaining your company, rather than hiring its own employees to perform the service your company offers.

Your Task. Working in teams, first decide what service you will offer. It could be landscaping, uniform supply, laundry of uniforms, general cleaning, computerized no-paper filing systems, online medical supplies, patient transportation, supplemental hospice care, temporary office support, or food service. As a team, develop a letter proposal outlining your plan, staffing, and budget. Use persuasion to show why contracting your services is better than hiring in-house employees. In the proposal letter, request a meeting with the administrative board. In addition to a written proposal, you may be expected to make an oral presentation that includes visual aids and/or handouts. Send your proposal to Dr. Pat Leigh, Director, Medicus Associates. Supply a local address.

13.5 Proposal and Grant Writing: Learning From the Nonprofits (Objs. 1, 2)

Web

You would like to learn more about writing business proposals and especially about writing grants. Grants are written to solicit funding from institutions, foundations, or the government. You might one day even decide to become a professional grant/proposal writer. However, first you need experience.

Your Task. Volunteer your proposal or grant writing services at a local nonprofit organization, such as a United Way **(http://national.unitedway.org)** member agency, an educational institution, or your local religious community. To learn more about writing proposals and grants, use a search engine to look up *proposal*. Try categories such as *business proposal writing* and *grant proposal writing*. In the browser window, enclose the search terms in quotation marks. Your instructor may ask you to submit a preliminary memo report outlining ten or more pointers you learn about writing proposals and grants for nonprofit organizations.

13.6 Business Plans: Can Your Team Write a Winning Business Plan? (Obj. 3)

Team Web

Business plans at many schools are more than classroom writing exercises. They have won regional, national, and worldwide prizes. Although some contests are part of MBA programs, other contests are available for undergraduates. One business plan project at the University of California, Santa Barbara, resulted in the development of a portable oxygen concentrator. Three students wrote a proposal that not only won one of the school's business plan writing contests but also attracted venture capital backing of over $500,000. The trio was challenged to come up with a hypothetical business plan. One of the team members suggested making a portable oxygen device to improve the mobility and quality of life for her grandmother. The students didn't actually make the device—they just outlined the concept. Contest judges recognized the commercial potential and helped bring the device into production.[7]

As part of a business plan project, you and your team are challenged to come up with an idea for a new business or service. For example, you might want to offer a lunch service with fresh sandwiches or salads delivered to office workers' desks. You might propose building a better Web site for an organization. You might want to start a document preparation business that offers production, editing, and printing services. You might have a terrific idea for an existing business to expand with a new product or service.

Your Task. Working in teams, explore entrepreneurial ventures based on your experience and expertise. Conduct team meetings to decide on a product or service, develop a work plan, assign responsibilities, and create a schedule. Your goal is to write a business plan proposal that will convince potential investors (sometimes your own management) that you have an excellent business idea and that you can pull it off. Check out sample business plans on the Web. The two "deliverables" from your project will be your written business plan and an oral presentation. Your written report should include a cover, transmittal document (letter or memo), title page, table of contents, executive summary, proposal (including introduction, body, and conclusion), appendix items, glossary (optional), and sources. In the body of the proposal, be sure to explain your mission and vision, the market, your marketing strategy, operations, and financials. Address your business plan proposal to your instructor.

*A complete instructional module for this activity is available at **www.meguffey.com**.

Are you ready? Get more practice at **www.meguffey.com**

13.7 Business Plans: Studying Samples and Selecting the Best (Obj. 3)

Web

As a member of a group of venture capitalists with money to invest in start-up companies, you must make a choice. Assume your group has received three business plan proposals.

Your Task. Visit either Bplans.com at **http://www.bplans.com** or the Small Business Administration site at **http://www.sba.gov/smallbusiness planner**. Search for sample business plans. Browse the list and select three business plans to study. Analyze all parts of each plan. Then, select one that you will recommend for funding. Prepare a memo to your investor group explaining why you think this start-up business will succeed. Also comment on the organization, format, and writing style of the business plan. What are its strengths and weaknesses? Address your memo to your instructor.

13.8 Formal Business Reports: Intercultural Communication (Objs. 4–6)

Web Intercultural Team

U.S. businesses are expanding into foreign markets with manufacturing plants, sales offices, and branches abroad. Most Americans, however, have little knowledge of or experience with people from other cultures. To prepare for participation in the global marketplace, you are to collect information for a report focused on an Asian, Latin American, or European country where English is not regularly spoken. Before selecting the country, though, consult your campus international student program for volunteers who are willing to be interviewed. Your instructor may make advance arrangements with international student volunteers.

Your Task. In teams of three to five, collect information about your target country from electronic databases, the Web, and other sources. Then invite an international student representing your target country to be interviewed by your group. As you conduct primary and secondary research, investigate the topics listed in Figure 13.5. Confirm what you learn in your secondary research by talking with your interviewee. When you complete your research, write a report for the CEO of your company (make up a name and company). Assume that your company plans to expand its operations abroad. Your report should advise the company's executives of the social customs, family life, attitudes, religions, education, and values in the target country. Remember that your company's interests are business oriented; do not dwell on tourist information. Write your report individually or in teams.

13.9 Proposal, Business Plan, and Business Report Topics (Objs. 1–6)

Web

A list of nearly 100 report topics is available at **www.meguffey.com**. The topics are divided into the following categories: accounting, finance, personnel/human resources, marketing, information systems, management, and general business/education/campus issues. You can collect information for many of these reports by using electronic databases and the Web. Your instructor may assign them as individual or team projects. All involve critical thinking in organizing information, drawing conclusions, and making recommendations. The topics include assignments appropriate for proposals, business plans, and formal business reports. Also, a number of self-contained report activities that require no additional research are provided at the end of Chapter 12.

13.10 Executive Summary: Reviewing Articles (Objs. 4, 5)

Web E-mail

Many managers and executives are too rushed to read long journal articles, but they are eager to stay current in their fields. Assume your boss has asked you to help him stay abreast of research in his field. He asks you to submit to him one executive summary every month on an article of interest.

Your Task. In your field of study, select a professional journal, such as the *Journal of Management*. Using ProQuest, Factiva, EBSCO, or some other database, look for articles in your target journal. Select an article that is at least five pages long and is interesting to you. Write an executive summary in a memo format. Include an introduction that might begin with *As you requested, I am submitting this executive summary of ...*. Identify the author, article title, journal, and date of publication. Explain what the author intended to do in the study or article. Summarize three or four of the most important findings of the study or article. Use descriptive, or "talking," headings rather than functional headings. Summarize any recommendations made. Your boss would also like a concluding statement indicating your reaction to the article. Address your memo to Marcus E. Fratelli. Alternatively, your instructor may ask you to e-mail your executive summary in the body of a properly formatted message or as an MS Word attachment in correct memo format.

13.11 Executive Summary: Locating Expert Information About Business Plans (Obj. 3)

Web Team E-mail

To supplement your knowledge of business plans and draw on various sources, search electronic databases to find recent articles about business plans and business models. This activity can be completed in teams, with each member contributing valuable tips and insights about business plans from an article or two.

Your Task. Using ProQuest, Factiva, EBSCO, or some other business database, search for the keywords *business plan,* and if you want more sources, for *business model*. You may also try searching *BusinessWeek Online* and similar business publications on the Internet. Select an article that is at least 1,200 words long and discusses business plans fully. Write an executive summary in memo format, or write an e-mail, if requested by your instructor. Identify the author, article title, periodical, and date of publication. Summarize the most important findings of the article. Use "talking" rather than functional headings if helpful.

13.12 Unsolicited Proposal: Requesting Funding for Your Campus Business Club (Obj. 1)

Let's say you are a member of a campus business club, such as the Society for the Advancement of Management (SAM), the American Marketing Association (AMA), the American Management Association (AMA), the Accounting Society (AS), the Finance Association (FA), or the Association of Information Technology Professionals (AITP). You have managed your finances well, and therefore, you are able to fund your monthly activities. However, membership dues are insufficient to cover any extras. Identify a need such as for a hardware or software purchase,

FIGURE 13.5 Intercultural Interview Topics and Questions

Social Customs
- How do people react to strangers? Are they friendly? Hostile? Reserved?
- How do people greet each other?
- What are the appropriate manners when you enter a room? Bow? Nod? Shake hands with everyone?
- How are names used for introductions? Is it appropriate to inquire about one's occupation or family?
- What are the attitudes toward touching?
- How does one express appreciation for an invitation to another's home? Bring a gift? Send flowers? Write a thank-you note? Are any gifts taboo?
- Are there any customs related to how or where one sits?
- Are any facial expressions or gestures considered rude?
- How close do people stand when talking?
- What is the attitude toward punctuality in social situations? In business situations?
- What are acceptable eye contact patterns?
- What gestures indicate agreement? Disagreement?

Family Life
- What is the basic unit of social organization? Basic family? Extended family?
- Do women work outside of the home? In what occupations?

Housing, Clothing, and Food
- Are there differences in the kinds of housing used by different social groups? Differences in location? Differences in furnishings?
- What occasions require special clothing?
- Are some types of clothing considered taboo?
- What is appropriate business attire for men? For women?
- How many times a day do people eat?
- What types of places, food, and drink are appropriate for business entertainment? Where is the seat of honor at a table?

Class Structure
- Into what classes is society organized?
- Do racial, religious, or economic factors determine social status?
- Are there any minority groups? What is their social standing?

Political Patterns
- Are there any immediate threats to the political survival of the country?
- How is political power manifested?
- What channels are used for expressing political opinions?
- What information media are important?
- Is it appropriate to talk politics in social situations?

Religion and Folk Beliefs
- To which religious groups do people belong? Is one predominant?
- Do religious beliefs influence daily activities?
- Which places are considered sacred? Which objects? Which events?
- How do religious holidays affect business activities?

Economic Institutions
- What are the country's principal products?
- Are workers organized in unions?
- How are businesses owned? By family units? By large public corporations? By the government?
- What is the standard work schedule?
- Is it appropriate to do business by telephone? By computer?
- How has technology affected business procedures?
- Is participatory management used?
- Are there any customs related to exchanging business cards?
- How is status shown in an organization? Private office? Secretary? Furniture?
- Are businesspeople expected to socialize before conducting business?

Value Systems
- Is competitiveness or cooperation more prized?
- Is thrift or enjoyment of the moment more valued?
- Is politeness more important than factual honesty?
- What are the attitudes toward education?
- Do women own or manage businesses? If so, how are they treated?
- What are your people's perceptions of Americans? Do Americans offend you? What has been hardest for you to adjust to in America? How could Americans make this adjustment easier for you?

a special one-time event that would benefit a great number of students, or officer training.

Your Task. Request one-time funding to cover what you need by writing an unsolicited letter or memo proposal to your assistant dean, who oversees student business clubs. Identify your need or problem, show the benefit of your request, support your claims with evidence, and provide a budget (if necessary).

13.13 Unsolicited Proposal: Thwarting Dorm Room Thievery (Objs. 1, 2)

Team | Web

As an enterprising college student, you recognized a problem as soon as you arrived on campus. Dorm rooms filled with pricey digital doodads were very attractive to thieves. Some students move in with more than $3,000 in gear, including laptop computers, flat-screen TVs, digital cameras, MP3 players, video game consoles, PDAs, and DVD players. You solved the problem by buying an extra-large steel footlocker to lock away your valuables. However, shipping the footlocker was expensive (nearly $100), and you had to wait for it to arrive from a catalog company. Your bright idea is to propose to the Associated Student Organization (ASO) that it allow you to offer these steel footlockers to students at a reduced price and with campus delivery. Your footlocker, which you found by searching the Web, is extremely durable and works great as a coffee table, nightstand, or card table. It comes with a smooth interior liner and two compartments.

Your Task. Working individually or with a team, imagine that you have made arrangements with a manufacturer to act as an intermediary selling footlockers on your campus at a reduced price. Consult the Web for manufacturers and make up your own figures. How can you get the ASO's permission to proceed? Give that organization a cut? Use your imagination in deciding how this plan might work on a college campus. Then prepare an unsolicited proposal to your ASO. Outline the problem and your goals of protecting students' valuables and providing convenience. Check the Web for statistics regarding on-campus burglaries. Such figures should help you develop one or more persuasive "hooks." Then explain your proposal, project possible sales, discuss a timetable, and describe your staffing. Submit your proposal to Billie White, president, Associated Student Organization.

Chat About It

In each chapter you will find five discussion questions related to the chapter material. Your instructor may assign these topics for you to discuss in class, in an online chat room, or on an online discussion board. Some of the discussion topics may require outside research. You may also be asked to read and respond to postings made by your classmates.

Topic 1: Why is being precise about the deliverables of a project so important?

Topic 2: Some consulting firms use experienced managers, but they also employ inexperienced, lower-paid staff to lower costs. How would you write the staffing section of a proposal with experienced managers but inexperienced staff?

Topic 3: If you managed a team of proposal-writing professionals, how would you organize the work to prepare a 200-page formal proposal? How many professionals do you think you would need? What tasks would each professional be assigned?

Topic 4: Discuss the pros and cons of the following two methods for completing the outline of the executive summary of a formal report: (a) cutting and pasting existing report sentences, or (b) creating new sentences.

Topic 5: Is it ethical for a student team to "borrow" and then substantially revise a report from a team that wrote about the same topic during the previous semester? What does your school say about such a practice?

Grammar/Mechanics C.L.U.E. Review 13

Total Review

Each of the following sentences has a total of **three** errors in grammar, punctuation, capitalization, usage, or spelling. On a separate sheet, write a correct version. Avoid adding new phrases, starting new sentences, or rewriting in your own words. When finished, compare your responses with the key beginning on page Key-3.

Example: The following 3 statistical terms frequently describe data, Mean, median, and mode.
Revision: The following three statistical terms frequently describe data: mean, median, and mode.

1. Lack of job security and high unemployment is here to stay. Even if we do our work really good.
2. Managers in 3 departments' complained that there departments were over budget for supplies.
3. After sending many e-mails to Frank and I, the client felt badly about barraging us with messages to solicit a response from our two teams'.
4. The new vice president and her decided to move up the launch to May 3rd, as a result, the software was buggy.
5. Managers of big corporations' sometimes do not know how to motivate, consequently, the executives miss an opportunity to develop their worker's.
6. The Director of marketing wanted to speak to you and I about the poor moral in our division.
7. Laura and him decided to except assistance with their proposal, therefore, they completed the project by the deadline.
8. We invited seventy-five employees to hear 2 experts disberse information about wellness.
9. Memo's usually contain four necessary parts, subject line, opening, body and action closing.
10. Darrin Jizmejian who was recently evaluated, wondered whether his formal report would be presented at the March 13th meeting?

CHAPTER 14

Business Presentations

OBJECTIVES

After studying this chapter, you should be able to

1. Discuss two important first steps in preparing effective business presentations.
2. Explain the major elements in organizing a presentation, including the introduction, body, and conclusion.
3. Identify techniques for gaining audience rapport, including (a) using effective imagery, (b) providing verbal signposts, and (c) sending appropriate nonverbal messages.
4. Discuss designing visual aids, handouts, and multimedia presentations and using presentation technology competently.
5. Specify delivery techniques for use before, during, and after a presentation, and apply reflective thinking skills.
6. Organize team-based written and oral presentations, and understand how to communicate in teams.
7. Explain effective techniques for adapting oral presentations to intercultural audiences, and demonstrate intercultural and diversity understanding.
8. List techniques for improving telephone and voice mail skills to project a positive image.

Want to do well on tests and excel in your course?
Go to **www.meguffey.com** for helpful interactive resources.

- **Review the Chapter 14 PowerPoint slides to prepare for the first quiz.**

Zooming In

PART 1

Apple's Steve Jobs and His Keynotes

Come January, when CEO Steve Jobs launches yet another hot new Apple product during one of his famously simple, yet striking keynote presentations, the world listens. Weeks and months of feverish preparation and secrecy precede the "Stevenote" at the annual Macworld conference. Understandably, the tech world is abuzz on the Web. The pundits weigh in with their speculations about the latest unveiling, kept tightly under wraps until Jobs announces it. Sometimes not even the name of the newest gizmo is known, as was the case with the Apple iPad, a sleek tablet device promising to revolutionize computing. Until the last moment, the technorati were guessing at its specifications and names, ranging from iSlate, iBook, and iTablet to Canvas. A few hundred industry insiders, analysts, and members of the media gathered expectantly at the Yerba Buena Center in San Francisco.

During the launch of the iPad—a large iPhone or iPod Touch look-alike—some invited guests were covering the event live in their blogs and tweets. Bobbie Johnson, technology correspondent for the UK newspaper *The Guardian*, was one of them. His readers and Twitter followers all over the world were able to witness not only the actual keynote presentation, but rumors and speculation even before the event unfolded. Steve Jobs' impressive images, passionate delivery, and nearly messianic zeal are legendary. Johnson remarked later in his first hands-on review of the iPad: "Jobs trumpeted it as exactly that, a magical device that will change the way we use computers in our everyday lives. And while playing with the iPad was not exactly a religious experience, it's not hard to see that the gadget, or at least the ideas it contains, will be with us for a long time to come."[1]

The long buildup and the secrecy are calculated communication strategies. They work to stoke excitement and fascination, as one blogger put it: "The iPhone ... blew people away not only because of what it was capable of, but also because many of its features came as a complete surprise to even the most well-informed of Apple bloggers."[2] This expert also suggests that Jobs is hedging

© Tony Avelar/Bloomberg via Getty Images

against the risk of hyping up products that are still under development. Instead of revealing unfinished devices too soon, Apple manages the public's expectations and prevents consumer disappointment. A master showman, Jobs calls himself "a big-bang guy,"[3] meaning that he likes flashy and fast launches. You will learn about the Apple executive's storied presentation techniques in Part 2 of this feature on page 467.

Critical Thinking

- What kinds of oral presentations might you have to make in your chosen career field?
- Why are most people fearful of making presentations?
- How do you think people become effective speakers?

http://www.apple.com/contact/

Preparing Effective Oral Presentations

LEARNING OBJECTIVE 1

Discuss two important first steps in preparing effective business presentations.

Like his archnemesis Bill Gates of Microsoft, Steve Jobs is a college dropout, but he is one who has elevated communication with the public to an art form. Few of us will ever talk to an audience of millions, whether face-to-face or mediated by technology, about a spectacular new product. At some point, however, all businesspeople have to inform others or sell an idea. Such information and persuasion are often conveyed in person and involve audiences of various sizes. If you are like most people, you have some apprehension when speaking in public. That's normal. Good speakers are made, not born. The good news is that you can conquer the fear of public speaking and hone your skills with instruction and practice.

Many future businesspeople fail to take advantage of opportunities in college to develop speaking skills. However, such skills often play an important role in a successful career. In fact, the No. 1 predictor of success and upward mobility, according to an AT&T and Stanford University study, is how much you enjoy public speaking and how effective you are at it.[4] Speaking skills are useful at every career stage. You might, for example, have to make a sales pitch before customers or speak to a professional gathering. You might need to describe your company's expansion plans to your banker, or you might need to persuade management to support your proposed marketing strategy. This chapter prepares you to use speaking skills in making oral presentations, whether alone or as part of a team.

For any presentation, you can reduce your fears and lay the foundation for a professional performance by focusing on five areas: preparation, organization, audience rapport, visual aids, and delivery.

Spotlight on Communicators

© Kim White/Bloomberg via Getty Images

How long should a PowerPoint presentation be? Business leader and venture capitalist Guy Kawasaki says that ten-slide presentations are plenty. And e-mail messages should be no more than five sentences. Why? No one wants to read *War and Peace* e-mails or sit through hour-long presentations of 50 plus slides. What you learn in schools, he asserts, is just the opposite of what happens in the real world. In school you're always worried about minimum word count and slide numbers, he says. In business, that's not the case.

Knowing Your Purpose

The most important part of your preparation is deciding what you want to accomplish. Do you want to sell a health care program to a prospective client? Do you want to persuade management to increase the marketing budget? Do you want to inform customer service reps of three important ways to prevent miscommunication? Whether your goal is to persuade or to inform, you must have a clear idea of where you are going. At the end of your presentation, what do you want your listeners to remember or do?

Mark Miller, a loan officer at First Fidelity Trust, faced such questions as he planned a talk for a class in small business management. Mark's former business professor had asked him to return to campus and give the class advice about borrowing money from banks in order to start new businesses. Because Mark knew so much about this topic, he found it difficult to extract a specific purpose statement for his presentation. After much thought he narrowed his purpose to this: *To inform potential entrepreneurs about three important factors that loan officers consider before granting start-up loans to launch small businesses.* His entire presentation focused on ensuring that the class members understood and remembered three principal ideas.

Before you can prepare your business presentation, which two important pieces of information do you need?

Knowing Your Audience

What are the elements of audience analysis, and how will they affect your message?

A second key element in preparation is analyzing your audience, anticipating its reactions, and making appropriate adaptations. Audiences may fall into four categories, as summarized in Figure 14.1. By anticipating your audience, you have a better idea of how to organize your presentation. A friendly audience, for example, will respond to humor and personal experiences. A neutral audience requires an even, controlled delivery style. The talk would probably be filled with facts, statistics, and expert opinions. An uninterested audience that is forced to attend requires a brief presentation. Such an audience might respond best to humor, cartoons, colorful visuals, and startling statistics. A hostile audience demands a calm, controlled delivery style with objective data and expert opinion.

Other elements, such as age, gender, education, experience, and the size of the audience will affect your style and message content. Analyze the following questions to help you determine your organizational pattern, delivery style, and supporting material.

- *How will this topic appeal to this audience?*
- *How can I relate this information to my listeners' needs?*
- *How can I earn respect so that they accept my message?*
- *What would be most effective in making my point? Facts? Statistics? Personal experiences? Expert opinion? Humor? Cartoons? Graphic illustrations? Demonstrations? Case histories? Analogies?*
- *What measures must I take to ensure that this audience remembers my main points?*

If you have agreed to speak to an audience with which you are unfamiliar, ask for the names of a half dozen people who will be in the audience. Contact them and learn about their backgrounds and expectations for the presentation. This information can help you answer questions about what they want to hear and how deeply you should explore the subject. You will want to thank these people when you start your speech. Doing this kind of homework will impress the audience.

Organizing the Content for a Powerful Impact

LEARNING OBJECTIVE 2
Explain the major elements in organizing a presentation, including the introduction, body, and conclusion.

Once you have determined your purpose and analyzed the audience, you are ready to collect information and organize it logically. Good organization and intentional repetition are the two most powerful keys to audience comprehension and retention. In fact, many speech experts recommend the following admittedly repetitious, but effective, plan:

- **Step 1:** Tell them what you are going to say.
- **Step 2:** Say it.
- **Step 3:** Tell them what you have just said.

FIGURE 14.1 **Succeeding With Four Audience Types**

Audience Members	Organizational Pattern	Delivery Style	Supporting Material
Friendly			
They like you and your topic.	Use any pattern. Try something new. Involve the audience.	Be warm, pleasant, and open. Use lots of eye contact and smiles.	Include humor, personal examples, and experiences.
Neutral			
They are calm, rational; their minds are made up, but they think they are objective.	Present both sides of the issue. Use pro/con or problem/solution patterns. Save time for audience questions.	Be controlled. Do nothing showy. Use confident, small gestures.	Use facts, statistics, expert opinion, and comparison and contrast. Avoid humor, personal stories, and flashy visuals.
Uninterested			
They have short attention spans; they may be there against their will.	Be brief—no more than three points. Avoid topical and pro/con patterns that seem lengthy to the audience.	Be dynamic and entertaining. Move around. Use large gestures.	Use humor, cartoons, colorful visuals, powerful quotations, and startling statistics.
	Avoid darkening the room, standing motionless, passing out handouts, using boring visuals, or expecting the audience to participate.		
Hostile			
They want to take charge or to ridicule the speaker; they may be defensive, emotional.	Organize using a noncontroversial pattern, such as a topical, chronological, or geographical strategy.	Be calm and controlled. Speak evenly and slowly.	Include objective data and expert opinion. Avoid anecdotes and humor.
	Avoid a question-and-answer period, if possible; otherwise, use a moderator or accept only written questions.		

In other words, repeat your main points in the introduction, body, and conclusion of your presentation. Although it seems redundant, this strategy works surprisingly well. Let's examine how to construct the three parts of an effective presentation.

Capturing Attention in the Introduction

What are some openers that grab the audience's attention?

How many times have you heard a speaker begin with, *It's a pleasure to be here.* Or, *I'm honored to be asked to speak.* Boring openings such as these get speakers off to a dull start. Avoid such banalities by striving to accomplish three goals in the introduction to your presentation:

- Capture listeners' attention and get them involved.
- Identify yourself and establish your credibility.
- Preview your main points.

If you are able to appeal to listeners and involve them in your presentation right from the start, you are more likely to hold their attention until the finish. Consider some of the same techniques that you used to open sales letters: a question, a startling fact, a joke, a story, or a quotation. Some speakers achieve involvement by opening with a question or command that requires audience members to raise their hands or stand up. Additional techniques to gain and keep audience attention are presented in the accompanying Career Coach box.

To establish your credibility, you need to describe your position, knowledge, or experience—whatever qualifies you to speak. Try also to connect with your audience. Listeners respond particularly well to speakers who reveal something of themselves and identify with them. A consultant addressing office workers might reminisce about how she started as an administrative assistant; a CEO might tell a funny story in which the joke is on himself.

After capturing attention and establishing yourself, you will want to preview the main points of your topic, perhaps with a visual aid. You may wish to put off actually writing your introduction, however, until after you have organized the rest of the presentation and crystallized your principal ideas.

CAREER COACH

The 10/20/30 Rule of PowerPoint

Would you like to pitch a business idea to one of Silicon Valley's most successful venture capitalists? If yes, you had better whip your PowerPoint skills into shape. Former Apple man Guy Kawasaki is tired of lousy pitches from would-be entrepreneurs and their endless slides laden with fuzzy jargon. An early advocate of customer evangelism in high tech, Kawasaki decided to evangelize the 10/20/30 Rule of PowerPoint: 10 slides, 20 minutes, and 30-point typeface. In his blog, Kawasaki writes that this rule applies to any presentation aiming to reach agreement:

> **Ten slides.** Ten is the optimal number of slides in a PowerPoint presentation because a normal human being cannot comprehend more than ten concepts in a meeting—and venture capitalists are very normal. (The only difference between you and a venture capitalist is that he is getting paid to gamble with someone else's money.) If you must use more than ten slides to explain your business, you probably don't have a business. The ten topics that a venture capitalist cares about are:
>
> 1. Problem
> 2. Your solution
> 3. Business model
> 4. Underlying magic/technology
> 5. Marketing and sales
> 6. Competition
> 7. Team
> 8. Projections and milestones
> 9. Status and timeline
> 10. Summary and call to action
>
> **Twenty minutes.** You should give your ten slides in twenty minutes.... [P]eople will arrive late and have to leave early. In a perfect world, you give your pitch in twenty minutes, and you have forty minutes left for discussion.
>
> **Thirty-point font.** The reason people use a small font is twofold: first, they don't know their material well enough; second, they think that more text is more convincing. Total bozosity. Force yourself to use no font smaller than thirty points. I guarantee it will make your presentations better because it requires you to find the most salient points and to know how to explain them well. If "thirty points" is too dogmatic, then I offer you an algorithm: find out the age of the oldest person in your audience and divide it by two. That's your optimal font size.

Career Application

Revise an existing PowerPoint presentation, preferably a persuasive one, based on Guy Kawasaki's 10/20/30 rule. Use one of your own presentations or peruse a few slideshows from several thousand selections on SlideShare.net. Go to the Business category. To download a presentation, you may need to register with the Web site. Which topics lend themselves the most to the 10/20/30 principle? When might this rule be difficult to follow?

To visit Guy Kawasaki's blog, go to **http://www.blog.guykawasaki.com** or follow him on Twitter: **http://twitter.com/Guykawasaki**

Take a look at Mark Miller's introduction, shown in Figure 14.2, to see how he integrated all the elements necessary for a good opening.

Organizing the Body

How does the saying "less is more" apply to oral presentations?

The biggest problem with most oral presentations is a failure to focus on a few principal ideas. This is why the body of your short presentation (20 or fewer minutes) should include a limited number of main points, say, two to four. Develop each main point with adequate, but not excessive, explanation and details. Too many details can obscure the main message, so keep your presentation simple and logical. Remember, listeners have no pages to leaf back through should they become confused.

How can you organize main ideas in a presentation?

When Mark Miller began planning his presentation, he realized immediately that he could talk for hours on his topic. He also knew that listeners are not good at separating major and minor points. Therefore, instead of submerging his listeners in a sea of information, he sorted out a few main ideas. In the banking industry, loan officers generally ask the following three questions of each applicant for a small business loan: (a) Are you ready to "hit the ground running" in starting your business? (b) Have you done your homework? and (c) Have you made realistic projections of potential sales, cash flow, and equity investment? These questions would become his main points, but Mark wanted to streamline them further so that his audience would be sure to remember them. He encapsulated the questions in three words: *experience, preparation,* and *projection*. As you can see in Figure 14.2, Mark prepared a sentence outline showing these three main ideas. Each is supported by examples and explanations.

FIGURE 14.2 Oral Presentation Outline

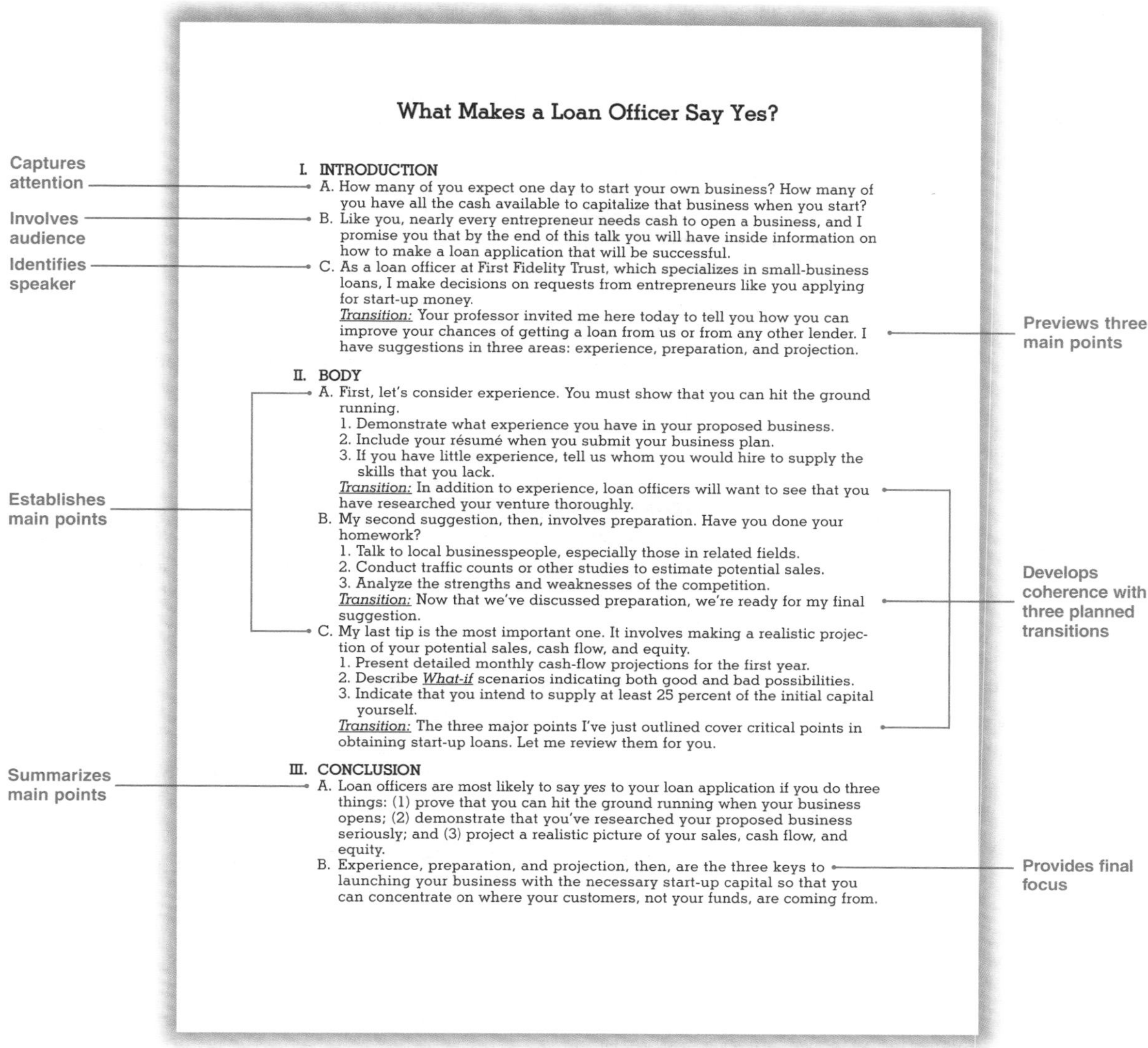

What Makes a Loan Officer Say Yes?

I. INTRODUCTION

A. How many of you expect one day to start your own business? How many of you have all the cash available to capitalize that business when you start?

B. Like you, nearly every entrepreneur needs cash to open a business, and I promise you that by the end of this talk you will have inside information on how to make a loan application that will be successful.

C. As a loan officer at First Fidelity Trust, which specializes in small-business loans, I make decisions on requests from entrepreneurs like you applying for start-up money.

<u>Transition:</u> Your professor invited me here today to tell you how you can improve your chances of getting a loan from us or from any other lender. I have suggestions in three areas: experience, preparation, and projection.

II. BODY

A. First, let's consider experience. You must show that you can hit the ground running.

1. Demonstrate what experience you have in your proposed business.
2. Include your résumé when you submit your business plan.
3. If you have little experience, tell us whom you would hire to supply the skills that you lack.

<u>Transition:</u> In addition to experience, loan officers will want to see that you have researched your venture thoroughly.

B. My second suggestion, then, involves preparation. Have you done your homework?

1. Talk to local businesspeople, especially those in related fields.
2. Conduct traffic counts or other studies to estimate potential sales.
3. Analyze the strengths and weaknesses of the competition.

<u>Transition:</u> Now that we've discussed preparation, we're ready for my final suggestion.

C. My last tip is the most important one. It involves making a realistic projection of your potential sales, cash flow, and equity.

1. Present detailed monthly cash-flow projections for the first year.
2. Describe <u>*What-if*</u> scenarios indicating both good and bad possibilities.
3. Indicate that you intend to supply at least 25 percent of the initial capital yourself.

<u>Transition:</u> The three major points I've just outlined cover critical points in obtaining start-up loans. Let me review them for you.

III. CONCLUSION

A. Loan officers are most likely to say *yes* to your loan application if you do three things: (1) prove that you can hit the ground running when your business opens; (2) demonstrate that you've researched your proposed business seriously; and (3) project a realistic picture of your sales, cash flow, and equity.

B. Experience, preparation, and projection, then, are the three keys to launching your business with the necessary start-up capital so that you can concentrate on where your customers, not your funds, are coming from.

How to organize and sequence main ideas may not be immediately obvious when you begin working on a presentation. The following methods, which review and amplify those discussed in Chapter 12, provide many possible strategies and examples to help you organize a presentation:

- **Chronology.** Example: A presentation describing the history of a problem, organized from the first sign of trouble to the present.
- **Geography/space.** Example: A presentation about the changing diversity of the workforce, organized by regions in the country (East Coast, West Coast, and so forth).
- **Topic/function/conventional grouping.** Example: A report discussing mishandled airline baggage, organized by names of airlines.
- **Comparison/contrast (pro/con).** Example: A report comparing organic farming methods with those of modern industrial farming.

- **Journalistic pattern.** Example: A report describing how identity thieves can ruin your good name. Organized by *who, what, when, where, why,* and *how.*
- **Value/size.** Example: A report describing fluctuations in housing costs, organized by prices of homes.
- **Importance.** Example: A report describing five reasons a company should move its headquarters to a specific city, organized from the most important reason to the least important.
- **Problem/solution.** Example: A company faces a problem such as declining sales. A solution such as reducing the staff is offered.
- **Simple/complex.** Example: A report explaining genetic modification of plants such as corn, organized from simple seed production to complex gene introduction.
- **Best case/worst case.** Example: A report analyzing whether two companies should merge, organized by the best-case result (improved market share, profitability, employee morale) as opposed to the worst-case result (devalued stock, lost market share, employee malaise).

In the presentation shown in Figure 14.2, Mark arranged the main points by importance, placing the most important point last where it had maximum effect. When organizing any presentation, prepare a little more material than you think you will actually need. Savvy speakers always have something useful in reserve such as an extra handout, transparency, or idea—just in case they finish early. At the same time, most speakers go about 25 percent over the allotted time as opposed to their practice runs at home in front of the mirror. If your speaking time is limited, as it usually is in your classes, aim for less than the limit when rehearsing, so that you don't take time away from the next presenters.

Summarizing in the Conclusion

What do effective conclusions achieve?

Nervous speakers often rush to wrap up their presentations because they can't wait to flee the stage. However, listeners will remember the conclusion more than any other part of a speech. That's why you should spend some time to make it most effective. Strive to achieve three goals:

- Summarize the main themes of the presentation.
- Leave the audience with a specific and memorable take-away.
- Include a statement that allows you to leave the podium gracefully.

Some speakers end limply with comments such as, *I guess that's about all I have to say* or *That's it.* Such lame statements show little enthusiasm and are not the culmination of the talk that listeners expect. Skilled speakers alert the audience that they are finishing. They use phrases such as, *In conclusion, As I end this presentation*, or, *It's time for me to sum up.* Then they proceed immediately to the conclusion. Audiences become justly irritated with a speaker who announces the conclusion but then digresses with one more story or talks on for ten more minutes.

A straightforward summary should review major points and focus on what you want the listeners to do, think, or remember. You might say, *In bringing my presentation to a close, I will restate my major purpose ...*, or, *In summary, my major purpose has been to.... In support of my purpose, I have presented three major points. They are (1) ..., (2) ..., and (3) ....* Notice how Mark Miller, in the conclusion shown in Figure 14.2, summarized his three main points and provided a final focus to listeners.

If you are promoting a recommendation, you might end as follows: *In conclusion, I recommend that we retain Matrixx Marketing to conduct a telemarketing campaign beginning September 1 at a cost of X dollars. To complete this recommendation, I suggest that we (a) finance this campaign from our operations budget, (b) develop a persuasive message describing our new product, and (c) name Lisa Beck to oversee the project.*

A conclusion is akin to a punch line and must be memorable. Think of it as the high point of your presentation, a valuable kernel of information to take away. The valuable kernel of information, or take-away, should tie in with the opening or present a forward-looking idea. Avoid merely rehashing, in the same words, what you said before, but ensure that the audience will take away very specific information or benefits and a positive impression of you and your company. The take-away is the value of the presentation to the audience and the benefit audience members believe they have received. The tension that you built in the early parts of the talk now culminates in the close.

In your conclusion you might want to use an anecdote, an inspiring quotation, or a statement that ties in the opener and offers a new insight. Whatever you choose, be sure to include a closing thought that indicates you are finished. For example, *This concludes my presentation. After investigating many marketing firms, we are convinced that Matrixx is the best for our purposes. Your authorization of my recommendations will mark the beginning of a very successful campaign for our new product. Thank you.*

Building Audience Rapport Like a Pro

LEARNING OBJECTIVE 3
Identify techniques for gaining audience rapport, including (a) using effective imagery, (b) providing verbal signposts, and (c) sending appropriate nonverbal messages.

Good speakers are adept at building audience rapport. They form a bond with the audience; they entertain as well as inform. How do they do it? Based on observations of successful and unsuccessful speakers, we learn that the good ones use a number of verbal and nonverbal techniques to connect with the audience. Their helpful techniques include providing effective imagery, supplying verbal signposts, and using body language strategically.

Effective Imagery

How can you keep the audience's interest?

You will lose your audience quickly if you fill your talk with abstractions, generalities, and dry facts. To enliven your presentation and enhance comprehension, try using some of the following techniques. However, beware of exaggeration or distortion. Keep your imagery realistic and credible.

- **Analogies.** A comparison of similar traits between dissimilar things can be effective in explaining and drawing connections. For example, *Product development is similar to the process of conceiving, carrying, and delivering a baby.* Or, *Downsizing or restructuring is similar to an overweight person undergoing a regimen of dieting, habit changing, and exercising.*
- **Metaphors.** A comparison between otherwise dissimilar things without using the words *like* or *as* results in a metaphor. For example, *Our competitor's CEO is a snake when it comes to negotiating* or *My desk is a garbage dump.*
- **Similes.** A comparison that includes the words *like* or *as* is a simile. For example, *Our critics used our background report like a drunk uses a lamppost—for support rather than for illumination.* Or, *She's as happy as someone who just won the lottery.*
- **Personal anecdotes.** Nothing connects you faster or better with your audience than a good personal story. In a talk about e-mail techniques, you could reveal your own blunders that became painful learning experiences. In a talk to potential investors, the founder of a new ethnic magazine might tell a story about growing up without positive ethnic role models.
- **Personalized statistics.** Although often misused, statistics stay with people—particularly when they relate directly to the audience. A speaker discussing job searching might say, *Look around the room. Only three out of five graduates will find a job immediately after graduation.* If possible, simplify and personalize facts. For example, *The sales of Coca-Cola totaled 2 billion cases last year. That means that every man, woman, and child in the United States consumed six full cases of Coke.*
- **Worst- and best-case scenarios.** Hearing the worst that could happen can be effective in driving home a point. For example, *If we do nothing about our computer backup system now, it's just a matter of time before the entire system crashes and we lose all of our customer contact information. Can you imagine starting from scratch in building all of your customer files again? However, if we fix the system now, we can expand our customer files and actually increase sales at the same time.*

Spotlight on Communicators

© Courtesy of Dianna Booher—Booher Consultants, Inc.

Communication expert Dianna Booher tries to describe the sometimes elusive quality that permits a skillful speaker to establish a rapport with listeners: "Presence may be difficult to define, but it is easy to spot. Most people know it when they see it. It is a manner of moving and interacting that commands attention and creates confidence in the speaker and increases credibility for the content." Although, to some extent, personality may determine presence, the good news is that speaking skills can be learned. You can become an effective speaker by adopting the techniques discussed in this chapter.

How can you ensure that your audience does not get lost?

Verbal Signposts

Speakers must remember that listeners, unlike readers of a report, cannot control the rate of presentation or flip back through pages to review main points. As a result, listeners get lost easily. Knowledgeable speakers help the audience recognize the organization and main points in an oral message with verbal signposts. They keep listeners on track by including helpful previews, summaries, and transitions, such as these:

- **Previewing**

  The next segment of my talk presents three reasons for....

  Let's now consider the causes of....

- **Summarizing**

  Let me review with you the major problems I have just discussed....

  You see, then, that the most significant factors are....

- **Switching directions**

  Thus far we have talked solely about ...; now let's move to....

  I have argued that ... and ..., but an alternate view holds that....

You can further improve any oral presentation by including appropriate transitional expressions such as *first, second, next, then, therefore, moreover, on the other hand, on the contrary,* and *in conclusion*. These transitional expressions, which you learned about in Figure 5.8 on page 156, build coherence, lend emphasis, and tell listeners where you are headed. Notice in Mark Miller's outline, in Figure 14.2, the specific transitional elements designed to help listeners recognize each new principal point.

How can your nonverbal behavior affect the success of your presentation?

Nonverbal Messages

Although what you say is most important, the nonverbal messages you send can also have a potent effect on how well your audience receives your message. How you look, how you move, and how you speak can make or break your presentation. The following suggestions focus on nonverbal tips to ensure that your verbal message is well received.

- **Look terrific!** Like it or not, you will be judged by your appearance. For everything but small in-house presentations, be sure you dress professionally. The rule of thumb is that you should dress at least as well as the best-dressed person in the audience.
- **Animate your body.** Be enthusiastic and let your body show it. Emphasize ideas to enhance points about size, number, and direction. Use a variety of gestures, but don't consciously plan them in advance.
- **Speak extemporaneously.** Do not read from notes or a manuscript, but speak freely. Use your presentation slides to guide your talk. You will come across as more competent and enthusiastic if you are not glued to your notes or manuscript. Use note cards or a paper outline only if presenting without an electronic slideshow.
- **Punctuate your words.** You can keep your audience interested by varying your tone, volume, pitch, and pace. Use pauses before and after important points. Allow the audience to take in your ideas.
- **Get out from behind the podium.** Avoid being glued to the podium. Movement makes you look natural and comfortable. You might pick a few places in the room to walk to. Even if you must stay close to your visual aids, make a point of leaving them occasionally so that the audience can see your whole body.
- **Vary your facial expression.** Begin with a smile, but change your expressions to correspond with the thoughts you are voicing. You can shake your head to show disagreement, roll your eyes to show disdain, look heavenward for guidance, or wrinkle your brow to

Spotlight on Communicators

© Daniel Acker/Bloomberg via Getty Images

Cisco is a worldwide leader in networking that transforms how people connect, communicate, and collaborate. When Chairman and CEO John Chambers introduces new Cisco products to a diverse audience made up of analysts, media, and consumers, he captivates his audience using persuasive communication skills. One of his strategies is to use movement and hand gestures to punctuate every sentence, allowing him to work the crowd. To maintain your listeners' attention, strive to be animated in your voice and body.

show concern or dismay. To see how speakers convey meaning without words, mute the sound on your TV and watch the facial expressions of a talk show personality.

Whenever possible, beginning presenters should have an experienced speaker watch them and give them tips as they rehearse. Your instructor is an important coach who can provide you with invaluable feedback. In the absence of helpers, tape yourself and watch your nonverbal behavior on camera.

Planning Visual Aids and Multimedia Presentations

LEARNING OBJECTIVE 4

Discuss designing visual aids, handouts, and multimedia presentations and using presentation technology competently.

Before you make a business presentation, consider this wise proverb: "Tell me, I forget. Show me, I remember. Involve me, I understand." Your goals as a speaker are to make listeners understand, remember, and act on your ideas. To get them interested and involved, include effective visual aids. Some experts say that we acquire 85 percent of all our knowledge visually: "Professionals everywhere need to know about the incredible inefficiency of text-based information and the incredible effects of images," says developmental molecular biologist John Medina.[5] Therefore, an oral presentation that incorporates visual aids is far more likely to be understood and retained than one lacking visual enhancement.

What purposes do visual aids serve?

Good visual aids have many purposes. They emphasize and clarify main points, thus improving comprehension and retention. They increase audience interest, and they make the presenter appear more professional, better prepared, and more persuasive. Well-designed visual aids illustrate and emphasize your message more effectively than words alone; therefore, they may help shorten a meeting or achieve your goal faster. Visual aids are particularly helpful for inexperienced speakers because the audience concentrates on the aid rather than on the speaker. However, experienced speakers work hard at not being eclipsed or upstaged by their slideshows. Good visuals also serve to jog the memory of a speaker, thus improving self-confidence, poise, and delivery.

Types of Visual Aids

Fortunately for today's speakers, many forms of visual media are available to enhance a presentation. Figure 14.3 describes the pros and cons of a number of visual aids that can guide you in selecting the best one for any speaking occasion. Three of the most popular visuals are multimedia slides, overhead transparencies, and handouts.

Multimedia Slides. With today's excellent software programs—such as Microsoft PowerPoint, Apple Keynote, Lotus Freelance Graphics, Corel Presentations, and Adobe Presenter or Adobe Ovation—you can create dynamic, colorful presentations with your PC. The output from these programs is generally shown on a computer monitor, a TV monitor, an LCD (liquid crystal display) panel, or a screen. With a little expertise and advanced equipment, you can create a multimedia presentation that includes stereo sound, videos, and hyperlinks, as described shortly in the discussion of multimedia presentations.

Overhead Transparencies. Some speakers still rely on the overhead projector for many reasons. Most meeting areas are equipped with projectors and screens. Moreover, acetate transparencies for the overhead are cheap, easily prepared on a computer or copier, and simple to use. Because rooms need not be darkened, a speaker using transparencies can maintain eye contact with the audience. Many experienced speakers create overhead slides in addition to their electronic slides to have a backup plan in the case of malfunctioning presentation technology. More important, though, overhead transparencies are ideal if the speaker needs to draw on the images or data using a marker. A word of caution, though, when using transparencies: stand to the side of the projector so that you don't obstruct the audience's view.

When should you distribute handouts?

Handouts. You can enhance and complement your presentations by distributing pictures, outlines, brochures, articles, charts, summaries, or other supplements. Speakers who use presentation software often prepare a set of their slides along with notes to hand

FIGURE 14.3 **Pros and Cons for Visual Aid Options**

Medium	Pros	Cons
Multimedia slides	Create professional appearance with many color, art, graphic, and font options. Easy to use and transport via removable storage media, Web download, or e-mail attachment. Inexpensive to update.	Present potential incompatibility issues. Require costly projection equipment and practice for smooth delivery. Tempt user to include razzle-dazzle features that may fail to add value.
Transparencies	Give professional appearance with little practice. Easy to (a) prepare, (b) update and maintain, (c) locate reliable equipment, and (d) limit information shown at one time.	Appear to some as an outdated presentation method. Hold speaker captive to the machine. Provide poor reproduction of photos and some graphics.
Handouts	Encourage audience participation. Easy to maintain and update. Enhance recall because audience keeps reference material.	Increase risk of unauthorized duplication of speaker's material. Can be difficult to transport. May cause speaker to lose audience's attention.
Flipcharts or whiteboards	Provide inexpensive option available at most sites. Easy to (a) create, (b) modify or customize on the spot, (c) record comments from the audience, and (d) combine with more high-tech visuals in the same presentation.	Require graphics talent. Difficult for larger audiences to see. Prepared flipcharts are cumbersome to transport and easily worn with use.
Video	Give an accurate representation of the content; strong indication of forethought and preparation.	Create potential for compatibility issues related to computer video formats. Expensive to create and update.
Props	Offer a realistic reinforcement of message content. Increase audience participation with close observation.	Lead to extra work and expense in transporting and replacing worn objects. Limited use with larger audiences.

out to viewers. Timing the distribution of any handout, though, is tricky. If given out during a presentation, your handouts tend to distract the audience, causing you to lose control. Therefore, you should discuss handouts during the presentation but delay distributing them until after you finish.

Speaker's Notes. You have a variety of options for printing hard-copy versions of your presentation. You can, for example, make speaker's notes, which are a wonderful aid for practicing your talk. Beneath the miniature image of each slide is space for you to key in your supporting comments for the abbreviated material in your slides. You can also include up to nine miniature versions of your slides per printed page. These miniatures are handy if you want to preview your talk to a sponsoring organization or if you want to supply the audience with a summary of your presentation. However, resist the temptation to read from your notes during the slide presentation. It might turn off your audience and make you appear insecure and incompetent.

Designing an Impressive Multimedia Presentation

How do businesspeople view PowerPoint and other presentation software?

Few corporate types or entrepreneurs would do without the razzle-dazzle of colorful images to make their points. Electronic slideshows, PowerPoint in particular, have become a staple of business presentations. However, overuse or misuse may be the downside of the ever-present multimedia slideshow. Over the two decades of the software program's existence, millions of poorly created

Zooming In

PART 2

Apple Computer

Do you want to learn presentation secrets from the "world's greatest corporate storyteller," Steve Jobs? The Apple cofounder and CEO is the subject of a book by Carmine Gallo, in which the communication coach reveals the techniques that Jobs uses to deliver "mind-blowing keynote presentations." Jobs' keynotes, or "Stevenotes," inform, educate, and entertain. As Gallo points out, Jobs does not sell computers; he sells an experience: Apple presentations resemble a great theatrical production—a terrific script, heroes and villains, stage props, amazing visuals, and a moment meant to stun the audience.[6]

If you would like to sell your product or ideas the Steve Jobs way, study the following five elements that Gallo culled from hours of Jobs' keynotes:

1. **A headline.** Steve Jobs characterizes every product with a catch phrase that is shorter than a 140-character tweet. Even before it first hit the stores, the iPad was consistently announced as "a magical and revolutionary product at an unbelievable price." All marketing materials use this headline.
2. **A villain.** Rivalry is entertaining and suspenseful. Classic stories feature heroes fighting villains. In the Apple narrative, Microsoft plays the part of the villain, most evident in the "I'm a Mac" TV commercials. Conquering a shared enemy motivates customers and turns them into brand evangelists.
3. **A simple slide.** Jobs' slides are as uncluttered, visual, and simple as Apple products. Powerful images, not bullet points, rule. Just remember the MacBook Air being pulled out of a manila envelope. As opposed to the average 40-word PowerPoint slide, Jobs may use as few as seven words in ten slides.
4. **A demo.** The Apple CEO does not let his audience lose interest. About ten minutes into a presentation, he is demonstrating a new product or feature. His enthusiasm is infectious. Presenting the iPhone in 2007, Jobs showed off Google Maps by looking up Starbucks and just for fun pretended to order 4,000 lattes to go.

©Tony Avelar/Bloomberg via Getty Images

5. **A holy smokes moment.** Jobs creates an emotional experience that becomes truly memorable. He built drama to a crescendo when introducing three new devices, "an iPod, a phone, an Internet communicator," only to stun the audience with the surprising revelation that all three were really one, the new iPhone.

Critical Thinking

- What can you learn from the speaking style of Steve Jobs?
- Why is simplicity important in an oral presentation?
- Communication coach Carmine Gallo says that charismatic speakers such as Steve Jobs are driven by the zeal to make the world a better place and enrich people's lives. If you were an entrepreneur, what would be your sense of mission?

and badly delivered PowerPoint presentations have tarnished PowerPoint's reputation as an effective communication tool. Tools, however, are helpful only when used properly.

Imagine those who sit through the more than 30 million PowerPoint presentations that Microsoft estimates are made each day.[7] No doubt, many of them would say that this "disease" has reached epidemic proportions. As a result, PowerPoint is often ridiculed as an ineffective communication tool. PowerPoint, say its detractors, dictates the way information is structured and presented. They say that the program is turning the nation's businesspeople into a "mindless gaggle of bullet-pointed morons."[8] If you typed *death by PowerPoint* in your favorite search engine, you would score over 1 million hits. However, text-laden, amateurish slides that distract and bore audiences are the fault of their creator and not the software program itself.

In the sections that follow, you will learn to create an impressive multimedia presentation using the most widely used presentation software program, PowerPoint. With any software program, of course, gaining expertise requires an investment of time and effort. You could take a course, or you could teach yourself through an online tutorial such as that at **http://office.microsoft.com/en-us/training/default.aspx**. Another way to master PowerPoint is to read a book such as Doug Lowe's *Microsoft Office PowerPoint 2007 for Dummies*. More advanced guidebooks about effective slideshows abound. If operated by a proficient slide preparer and a skillful presenter, PowerPoint can add a distinct visual impact to any presentation.

Applying the 3-x-3 Writing Process to Slide Presentations

Some presenters prefer to create their slides first and then develop the narrative around their slides. Others prefer to prepare their content first and then create the visual component. The risk associated with the first approach is that you may be tempted to spend too much time making your slides look good and not enough time preparing your content. Remember that great-looking slides never compensate for thin content. In the following discussion, we review the three phases of the writing process and show how they help you develop a visually appealing PowerPoint presentation. In the first phase (prewriting), you analyze, anticipate, and adapt. In the second phase, you research, organize, compose, and design. In the third phase, you revise, edit, and evaluate.

How do you determine presentation content and design?

Analyzing the Situation. Making the best content and design choices for your slides depends greatly on your analysis of the presentation situation. Will your slides be used during a live presentation? Will they be part of a self-running presentation such as in a store kiosk? Will they be saved on a server so that those with Internet access can watch the presentation at their convenience? Will they be sent as a PowerPoint show or a PDF document—also sometimes called a deck—to a client instead of a hard-copy report? Are you converting PowerPoint slideshows for viewing on iPhones, video iPods,[9] or BlackBerry devices?[10]

If you are e-mailing the presentation or posting it online as a self-contained file, the slides will typically feature more text than if they were delivered orally. If, on the other hand, you are creating slides for a live presentation, your analysis will prompt you to choose powerful, telling images over boring text-laden slides.

Anticipating Your Audience. Think about how you can design your presentation to get the most positive response from your audience. Audiences respond, for example, to the colors you use. Primary ideas are generally best conveyed with bold colors such as blue, green, and purple. Because the messages that colors convey can vary from culture to culture, colors must be chosen carefully. In the United States, blue is the color of credibility, tranquility, conservatism, and trust. Therefore, it is the background color of choice for many business presentations. Green relates to interaction, growth, money, and stability. It can work well as a background or an accent color. Purple can also work as a background or accent color. It conveys spirituality, royalty, dreams, and humor.[11]

Just as you anticipate audience members' reactions to color, you can usually anticipate their reactions to special effects. Using animation and sound effects—flying objects, swirling text, clashing cymbals, and the like—only because they are available is not a good idea. Special effects distract your audience, drawing attention away from your main points. You should add animation features only if doing so helps convey your message or adds interest to the content. When your audience members leave, they should be commenting on the ideas you conveyed—not the cool swivels and sound effects.

Which handy rule can help you design effective slides and select proper background and text colors?

Adapting Text and Color Selections. Adapt the amount of text on your slide to how your audience will use the slides. As a general guideline, most graphic designers encourage the 6-x-6 rule: "Six bullets per screen, max; six words per bullet, max."[12] You may find, however, that breaking this rule is sometimes necessary, particularly when your users will be viewing the presentation on their own with no speaker assistance. For most purposes, though, strive to break free from bulleted lists whenever possible and minimize the use of text.

Adapt the colors based on where the presentation will be given. Use light text on a dark background for presentations in darkened rooms. Use dark text on a light background for presentations in lighted rooms. Avoid using a dark font on a dark background, such as red text on a dark blue background. In the same way, avoid using a light font on a light background, such as white text on a pale blue background. Dark on dark or light on light results in low contrast, making the slides difficult to read.

Researching Your PowerPoint Options. You may need to present a complicated idea and will have to learn more about PowerPoint to determine the best way to clarify and simplify its visual presentation. Besides using online tutorials and studying books on the subject, be on the lookout as you view other people's presentations to learn fresh ways to illustrate your content more effectively. Chances are you will learn the most from fellow students and team members who have truly mastered the software.

Organizing Your Slides. When you prepare your slides, translate the major headings in your presentation outline into titles for slides. Then build bullet points using short phrases. In Chapter 5 you learned to improve readability by using graphic highlighting techniques, including bullets, numbers, and headings. In preparing a PowerPoint presentation, you will use those same techniques.

The slides you create to accompany your spoken ideas can be organized with visual elements that will help your audience understand and remember what you want to communicate. Let's say, for example, that you have three points in your presentation. You can create a blueprint slide that captures the three points in a visually appealing way, and then you can use that slide several times throughout your presentation. Near the beginning, the blueprint slide provides an overview of your points. Later, it will provide transitions as you move from point to point. For transitions, you can direct your audience's attention by highlighting the next point you will be talking about. Finally, the blueprint slide can be used near the end to provide a review of your key points.

What are visual clichés, and why should you avoid them?

Working With Templates. All presentation programs require you to (a) create a template that will serve as the background for your presentation and (b) make each individual slide by selecting a layout that best conveys your message. When you craft your template, be cautious about selecting the slide templates that came with the program. They have been seen by millions and amount to what one expert has labeled "visual clichés."[13] Overused templates and even clip art that ship with PowerPoint can weary viewers who have seen them repeatedly in presentations. Instead of using a standard template, search for *PowerPoint template* in Google or your favorite search engine. You will see hundreds of template options available as free downloads. Unless your employer requires that presentations all have the same look, your audience will most likely appreciate fresh templates that complement the purpose of your presentation and provide visual variety.

Office PowerPoint 2007 presentation templates replace the **AutoContent Wizard**. They come with new as well as familiar layouts and themes that you can modify. Templates get you started quickly. They allow you to add your own images or a logo and delete or modify text. Relying only on templates, however, generally leads to text-heavy presentations that lack visual elements. Nevertheless, it's a good start for a PowerPoint newbie. With more experience, you can create backgrounds and layouts from scratch by adding your own elements to each slide.

Composing Your Slideshow. During the composition stage, many users fall into the trap of excessive formatting and programming. They fritter away precious time fine-tuning their slides. They don't spend enough time on what they are going to say and how they will say it. To avoid this trap, set a limit for how much time you will spend making your slides visually appealing. Your time limit will be based on how many "bells and whistles" (a) your audience expects and (b) your content requires to make it understandable. Remember that not every point nor every thought requires a visual. In fact, it's smart to switch off the slides occasionally and direct the focus to yourself. Darkening the screen while you discuss a point, tell a story, give an example, or involve the audience will add variety to your presentation.

Create a slide only if the slide accomplishes at least one of the following purposes:

- Generates interest in what you are saying and helps the audience follow your ideas
- Highlights points you want your audience to remember
- Introduces or reviews your key points
- Provides a transition from one major point to the next
- Illustrates and simplifies complex ideas

In a later section of this chapter, you will find very specific steps to follow as you create your presentation.

Designing for Optimal Effect. Try to avoid long, boring bulleted lists in a presentation. You can alter layouts by repositioning, resizing, or changing the fonts for the placeholders in which your title, bulleted list, organization chart, video clip, photograph, or other elements appear. Figure 14.4 illustrates two of the many layout and design options for creating your slides. The figure shows that you can make your slides visually more appealing and memorable even with relatively small changes.

Notice that the bulleted items on the first slide in Figure 14.4 are not parallel. The slide looks as if the author had been brainstorming or freewriting a first draft. The second and sixth bullet points

FIGURE 14.4 Revising and Enhancing Slides for Greater Impact

Before Revision

Reasons for Selling Online

- Your online business can grow globally.
- Customer convenience.
- Conduct business 24/7.
- No need for renting a retail store or hiring employees.
- Reduce inquiries by providing policies and a privacy statement.
- Customers can buy quickly and easily.

After Revision

Why You Should Sell Online

- Grow business globally.
- Offer convenience to customers.
- Conduct business 24/7.
- Save on rent and staff.
- Create policies to reduce inquiries.

The slide on the left contains bullet points that are not parallel and that overlap in meaning. The second and sixth bullet points say the same thing. Moreover, some bullet points are too long. After revision, the slide on the right has a more convincing title illustrating the "you" view. The bullet points are shorter, and each begins with a verb for parallelism and an emphasis on action. The photo adds interest.

express the same thought, that shopping online is convenient and easy for customers. Some bullet points are too long. The bullets on the improved slide are very short, well within the 6-x-6 rule, although they are complete sentences. The photograph in the revised slide adds interest and illustrates the point. You may use stock photos that you can download from the Web for personal or school use without penalty, or consider taking your own pictures if you own a digital camera.

How can you add pizzazz to your slides?

Figure 14.5 shows how to add variety and pizzazz to your slides. Notice that the information that appeared as bullet points in Figure 14.4 now appears as exciting spokes radiating from the central idea: Why You Should Sell Online. This spoke diagram is just one of numerous **SmartArt graphics** in the **Illustrations** tab in PowerPoint. You can also animate each item in the diagram. Occasionally, try to convert pure text and bullet points to graphics, charts, and other images to add punch to your slideshow. This will keep your audiences interested and help them retain the information you are presenting.

FIGURE 14.5 Converting a Bulleted Slide Into a Diagram

Revised With a SmartArt Graphic

SmartArt Graphics Options

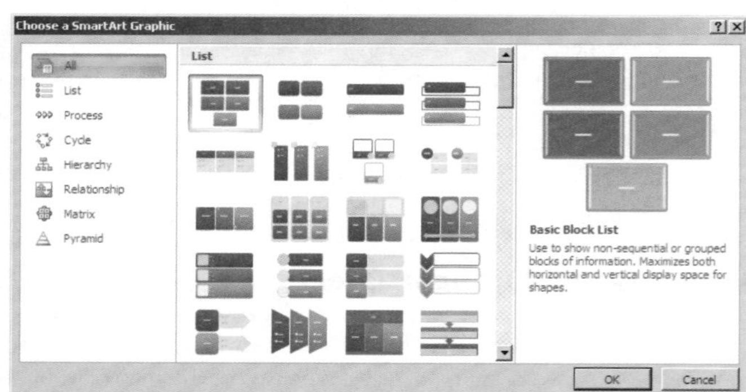

The same content that appears in the Figure 14.4 slides takes on a totally different look when arranged as spokes radiating from a central idea. Add a 3-D effect and a muted background image to the middle shape, for example, and you depart from the usual boring template look. When presenting this slide, you can animate each item and control when it is revealed, further enlivening your presentation. PowerPoint 2007 provides SmartArt graphics with many choices of diagrams and shapes for arranging information.

Revising, Proofreading, and Evaluating Your Slideshow. Use PowerPoint's **Slide Sorter** view to rearrange, insert, and delete slides during the revision process. This is the time to focus on making your presentation as clear and concise as possible. If you are listing items, be sure that all items use parallel grammatical form. Figure 14.6 shows how to revise a slide to improve it for conciseness, parallelism, and other features. Study the design tips described in the first slide and determine which suggestions were not followed. Then compare it with the revised slide.

Notice that both slides in Figure 14.6 feature a blue background, the calming blue serving as the color of choice for most business presentations. However, the background swirls on the first slide are distracting. In addition, the uppercase white font contributes to the busy look, making the slide hard to read. Inserting a transparent overlay and choosing a dark font to mute the distracting waves create a cleaner-looking slide.

As you are revising, check carefully to find spelling, grammar, punctuation, and other errors. Use the PowerPoint spell check, but don't rely on it without careful proofing, preferably from a printed copy of the slideshow. Nothing is as embarrassing as projecting errors on a huge screen in front of an audience. Also, check for consistency in how you capitalize and punctuate points throughout the presentation.

The final stage in applying the 3-x-3 writing process to developing a PowerPoint presentation involves evaluation. Consider whether you have done all you can to use the tools PowerPoint provides to communicate your message in a visually appealing way. In addition, test your slides on the equipment and in the room you will be using during your presentation. Do the colors you selected work in this new setting? Are the font styles and sizes readable from the back of the room? Figure 14.7 shows examples of slides that incorporate what you have learned in this discussion.

The dark purple background and the green and blue hues in the slideshow shown in Figure 14.7 are standard choices for many business presentations. With an unobtrusive dark background, white fonts are a good option for maximum contrast and, hence, readability. The creator of the presentation varied the slide design to break the monotony of bulleted or numbered lists. Images and animated diagrams add interest and zing to the slides.

Using PowerPoint Effectively With Your Audience

What do you have to watch out for with technology?

Many promising presentations have been sabotaged by technology glitches or by the presenter's unfamiliarity with the equipment. Fabulous slides are of value only if you can manage the technology expertly. As we have seen, Apple CEO Steve Jobs is famous for his ability to wow his audiences during his keynote addresses. A *BusinessWeek* cover story described his approach: "Jobs

FIGURE 14.6 Designing More Effective Slides

Before Revision

DESIGN TIPS FOR SLIDE TEXT
1. STRIVE TO HAVE NO MORE THAN SIX BULLETS PER SLIDE AND NO MORE THAN SIX WORDS PER BULLET.
2. IF YOU USE UPPER-AND LOWERCASE TYPE, IT IS EASIER TO READ
3. IT IS BETTER TO USE PHRASES RATHER THAN SENTENCES.
4. USING A SIMPLE, HIGH-CONTRAST TYPE FACE IS EASIER TO READ AND DOES NOT DETRACT FROM YOUR PRESENTATION
5. BE CONSISTENT IN YOUR SPACING, CAPITALIZATION, AND PUNCTUATION.

After Revision

Design Tips for Slide Text
Six bullets per slide or fewer
Six words per bullet or fewer
Upper- and lowercase type
Concise phrases, not sentences
Simple typeface
Consistent spacing, capitalization, and punctuation

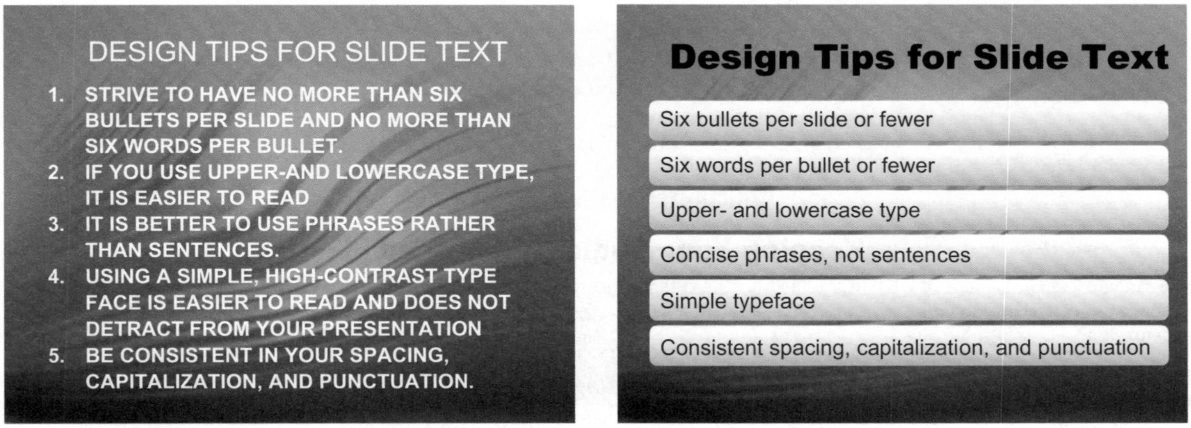

The slide on the left is difficult to read and understand because it violates many slide-making rules. How many violations can you spot? The slide on the right illustrates an improved version of the same information. Which slide do you think viewers would rather read?

FIGURE 14.7 PowerPoint Slides That Summarize and Illustrate Multimedia Presentations

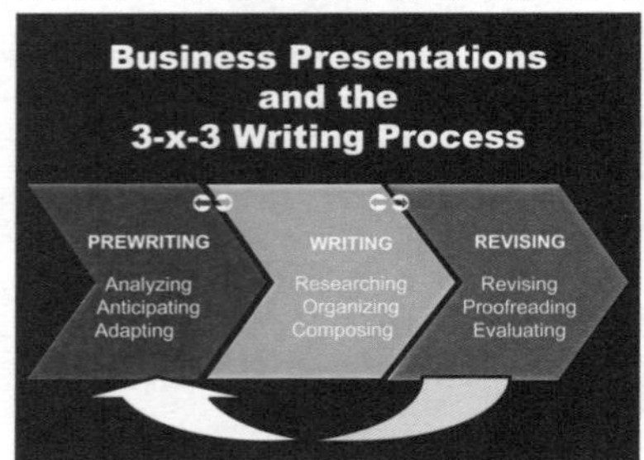

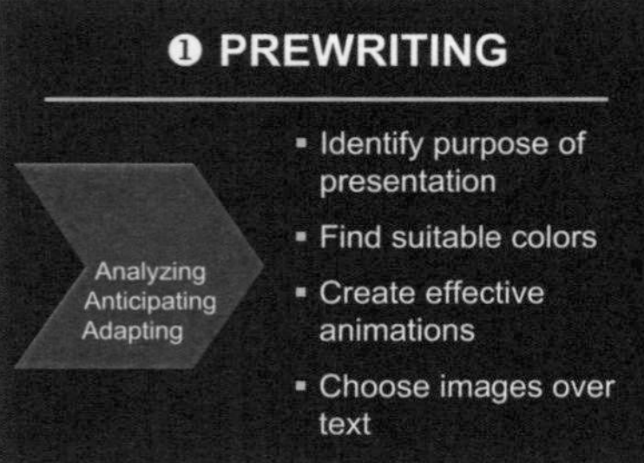

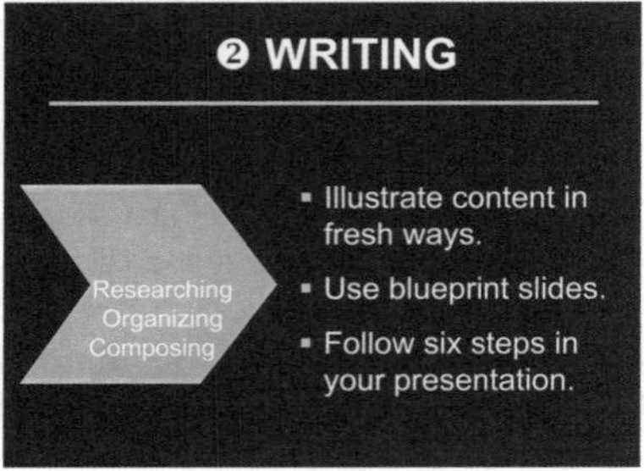

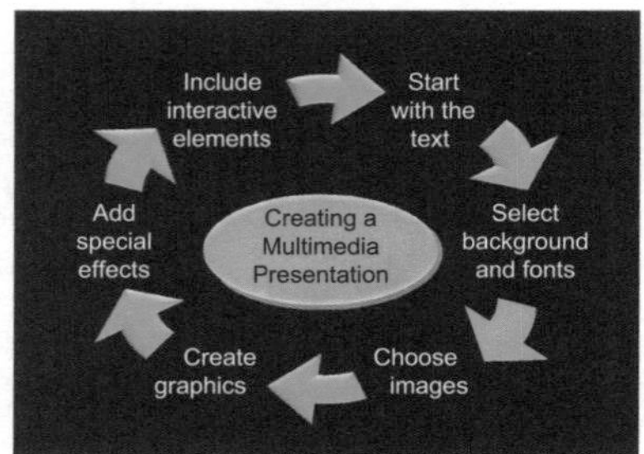

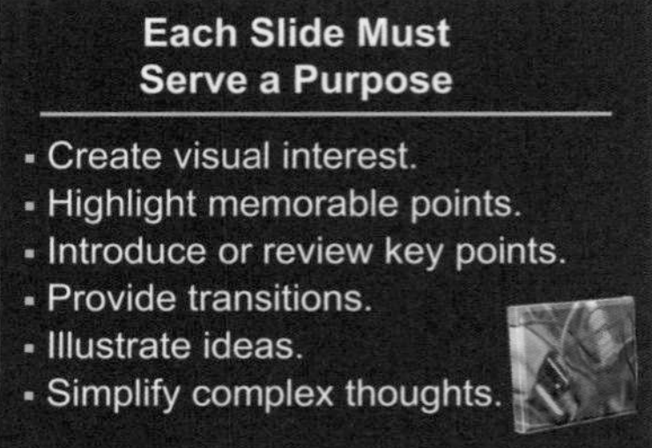

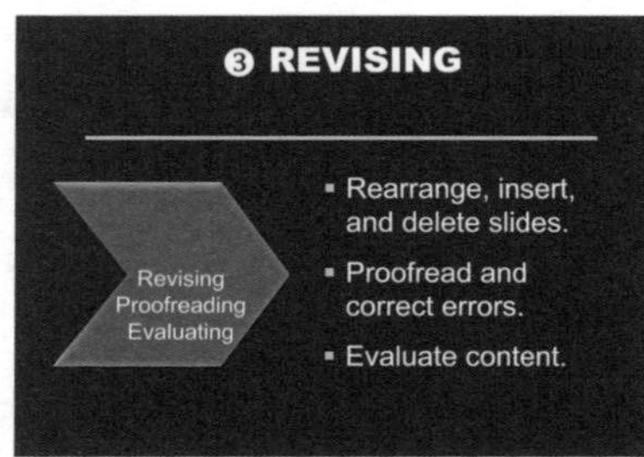

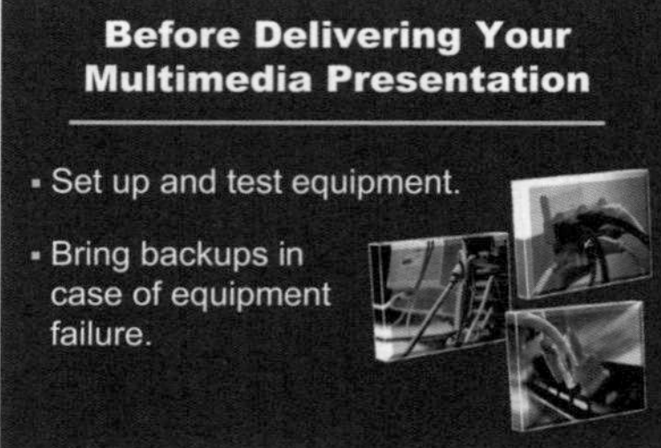

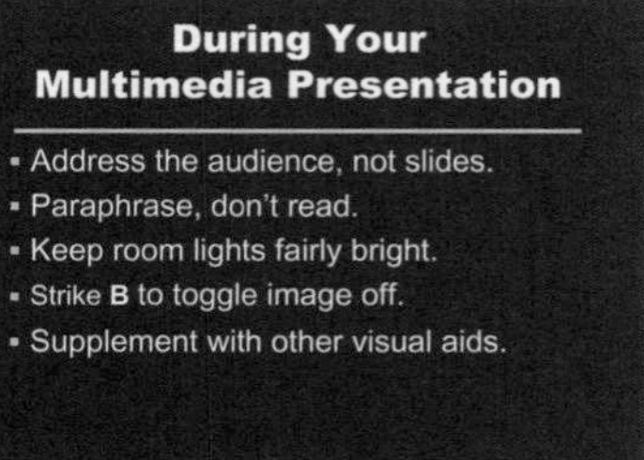

unveils Apple's latest products as if he were a particularly hip and plugged-in friend showing off inventions in your living room. Truth is, the sense of informality comes only after grueling hours of practice."[14] At one of his recent Macworld rehearsals, for example, he spent more than four hours on stage practicing and reviewing every technical and performance aspect of his product launch.

Practicing and Preparing

Allow plenty of time before your presentation to set up and test your equipment.[15] Confirm that the places you plan to stand are not in the line of the projected image. Audience members do not appreciate having part of the slide displayed on your body. Make sure that all links to videos or the Web are working and that you know how to operate all features the first time you try. No matter how much time you put into preshow setup and testing, you still have no guarantee that all will go smoothly. Therefore, you should always bring backups of your presentation. Overhead transparencies or handouts of your presentation provide good substitutes. Transferring your presentation to a CD or a USB flash drive that could run from any available notebook might prove useful as well.

Keeping Your Audience Engaged

How can you keep your audience interested during your presentation?

In addition to using technology to enhance and enrich your message, here are additional tips for performing like a professional and keeping the audience engaged:

- Know your material. This will free you to look at your audience and gaze at the screen, not your practice notes. Maintain genuine eye contact to connect with individuals in the room.
- As you show new elements on a slide, allow the audience time to absorb the information. Then paraphrase and elaborate on what the listeners have seen. Don't insult your audience's intelligence by reading verbatim from a slide.

- Leave the lights as bright as you can. Make sure the audience can see your face and eyes.
- Use a radio remote control (not infrared) so you can move freely rather than remain tethered to your computer. Radio remotes allow you to be up to 50 feet away from your laptop.
- Maintain a connection with the audience by using a laser pointer to highlight slide items to discuss. Be aware, however, that a dancing laser point in a shaky hand may make you appear nervous. Steady your hand.
- Don't leave a slide on the screen when you have finished discussing it. In **Slide Show** view on the **View** tab, strike *B* on the keyboard to turn on or off the screen image by blackening it. Pushing *W* will turn the screen white.

Some presenters allow their PowerPoint slides to steal their thunder. One expert urges speakers to "use their PowerPresence in preference to their PowerPoint."[16] Although multimedia presentations supply terrific sizzle, they cannot replace the steak. In developing a presentation, don't expect your slides to carry the show. You can avoid being upstaged by not relying totally on your slides. Help the audience visualize your points by using other techniques. For example, drawing a diagram on a white board or flipchart can be more engaging than showing slide after slide of static drawings. Demonstrating or displaying real objects or props is a welcome relief from slides. Remember that slides should be used only to help your audience understand the message and to add interest. You are still the main attraction!

Analyzing an Effective Presentation

As you are reviewing the many tips for crafting successful slide presentations, study the sample slides in Figure 14.8. The nine slides in Figure 14.8 shown in PowerPoint's **Slide Sorter** view are taken from a longer slide presentation. Corinne Livesay, a management training consultant, recently used them during a 2½-hour training session for members of the Dayton Chamber of Commerce. They provide several examples of what you have learned about creating slides.

- The photographs used on Slides 1, 5, and 8 were downloaded from Microsoft Office Online. This Web site offers a great variety of royalty-free pictures as opposed to the limited number of images and clip art that ships with the software.
- Slides 2 and 4 were designed using PowerPoint's various **Illustrations** in the **Insert** tab. Slide 2 encourages the audience to interact with the speaker and get involved in the topic of discussion. Even though you can't tell from the image of Slide 4, it is programmed using PowerPoint's **Custom Animation** feature in the **Animations** tab. The presenter brings in elements of the model as they are explained.
- Slides 3 and 6 illustrate how blueprint slides can be used to introduce your main points and later to move from point to point.
- Slide 7 illustrates interactivity with the audience by presenting a polling question. After audience members respond using their handheld devices, the pie chart follows and displays the results.
- Slide 8 illustrates interactivity with the Internet by providing links that can take the audience directly to relevant Web sites.

Eight Steps to Making a Powerful Multimedia Presentation

What is the best process for creating powerful multimedia presentations?

We have now discussed many suggestions for making effective PowerPoint presentations, but you may still be wondering how to put it all together. Here is a step-by-step process for creating a powerful multimedia presentation:

1. **Start with the text.** The text is the foundation of your presentation. Express your ideas using words that are clear, concise, and understandable. Once the entire content of your presentation is in place, you are ready to begin adding color and all the other elements that will make your slides visually appealing.
2. **Select background and fonts.** Select a template that will provide consistent font styles and sizes and a background for your slides. You can create your own template or use one included with PowerPoint. You can also download free templates or pay for templates from

FIGURE 14.8 **Creating Visually Appealing Slides That Engage Your Audience**

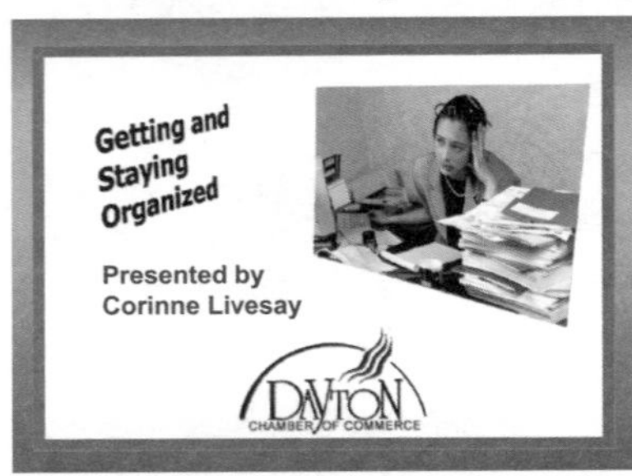

Getting and Staying Organized
Presented by
Corinne Livesay
DAYTON
CHAMBER OF COMMERCE

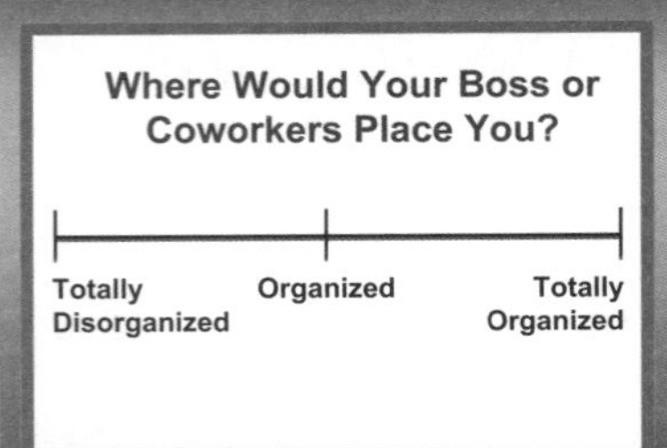

Six Organizing Guidelines

1. Select what should be organized.
2. Unclutter your life.
3. Break tasks into specific steps.
4. Establish a simple system.
5. Stay organized.
6. Prioritize and don't go overboard.

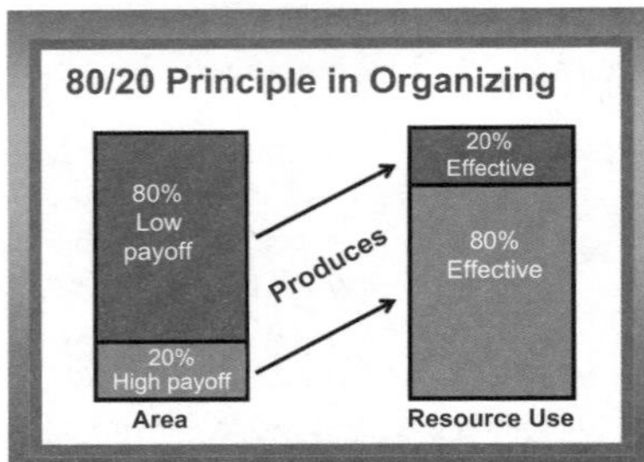

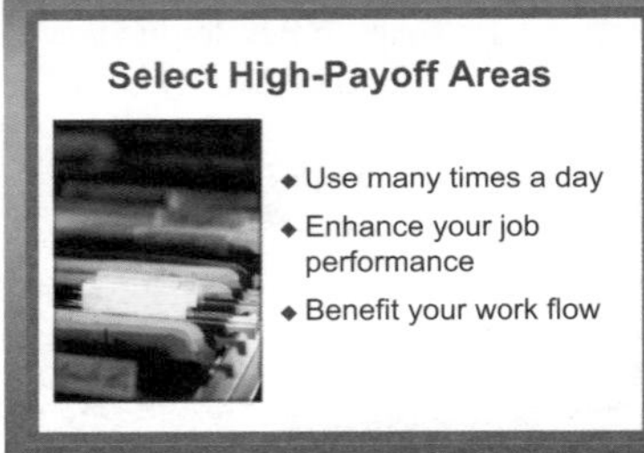

Select High-Payoff Areas
Use many times a day
Enhance your job performance
Benefit your work flow

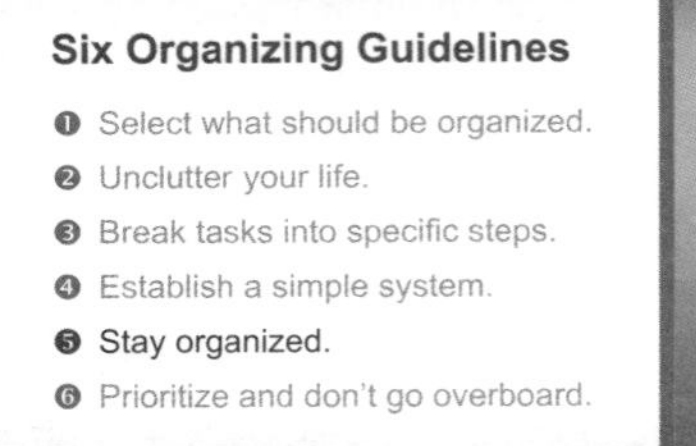

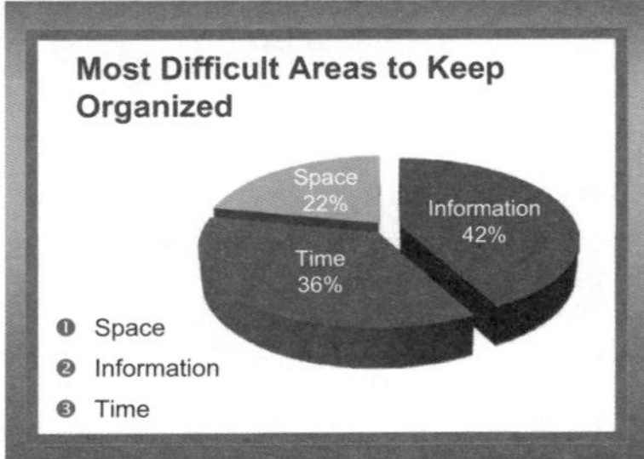

More Information About Organizing:
www.flylady.net
www.organizetips.com
www.getorganizednow.com

Conclusion

- Reclaim your time, space, and information.
- Increase your efficiency.
- Enhance your quality of life.
- Further your career.
- Get organized!

many online sites. You can't go wrong selecting a basic template design with an easy-to-read font, such as Times New Roman or Arial. As a general rule, use no more than two font styles in your presentation. The point size should be between 24 and 36. Title fonts should be larger than text font. The more you use PowerPoint and find out what works and doesn't work, the more you can experiment with bolder, more innovative background and font options that effectively convey your message.

3. **Choose images that help communicate your message.** Images, such as clip art, photographs, and maps, should complement the text. Never use an image that is not immediately relevant. Microsoft Office Online is accessed in PowerPoint and contains thousands of clip art images and photographs, most of which are in the public domain and require no copyright permissions. Before using images from other sources, determine whether permission from the copyright holder is required. Bear in mind that some people consider clip art amateurish, so photographs are usually preferable. In addition, clip art is available to any user, so it tends to become stale fast.

How can you simplify complex information?

4. **Create graphics.** PowerPoint includes a variety of tools to help you simplify complex information or transform a boring bulleted list into a visually appealing graphic. You can use PowerPoint's **Illustrations** tools in the **Insert** tab to create a time line or a flowchart. The **SmartArt** graphic will help you create an organization chart or a cycle, radial, pyramid, Venn, or target diagram. With the **Chart** function, you can select over a dozen chart types including line, pie, and bar charts. All of these tools require practice before you can create effective graphics. Remember that graphics should be easy to understand without overloading your audience with unnecessary details or too much text. In fact, it's a good idea to put such details in handouts rather than cluttering your slides with them.

5. **Add special effects.** To keep your audience focused on what you are discussing, use PowerPoint's **Animations** tab to control when objects or text appear on the screen. Animate points in a bulleted list to appear one at a time, for example, or the boxes in a radial diagram to appear as each is discussed. Keep in mind that the first thing your audience sees on every slide should describe the slide's content. With motion paths and other animation options, you can move objects to various positions on the slide; or to minimize clutter, you can dim or remove them once they have served their purpose.

   In addition, as you move from slide to slide in a presentation, you can select transition effects, such as *wipe down*. The animation and transition options range from subtle to flashy—choose them with care so that the visual delivery of your presentation does not distract from the content of your message. An option at this step is to purchase a PowerPoint add-in product, such as Ovation, that can add professional-looking special effects to your presentation with very little effort.[17]

6. **Create hyperlinks to approximate the Web browsing experience.** Make your presentation more interactive and intriguing by connecting your PowerPoint presentation, via hyperlinks, to other sources that provide content that will enhance your presentation. You can hyperlink to (a) other slides within the presentation or in other PowerPoint files; (b) other programs that will open a second window that displays items such as spreadsheets, documents, or videos; and (c) if you have an Internet connection, Web sites.

   Once you have finished discussing the hyperlinked source or watching the video that opened in a second window, close that window and your hyperlinked PowerPoint slide is in view. In this way, you can break up the monotony of typical linear PowerPoint presentations. Instead, your hyperlinked show approximates the viewing experience of a Web user who enters a site through a main page or portal and then navigates at will to reach second- and third-level pages.

7. **Engage your audience by asking for interaction.** When audience response and feedback are needed, interactive tools are useful. Audience response systems may be familiar to you from game shows, but they are also used for surveys and opinion polls, group decision making, voting, quizzes and tests, and many other applications. To interact with your audience, present polling questions. Audience members submit their individual or team responses using handheld devices read by a PowerPoint add-in program. The audience immediately sees a bar chart that displays the response results.[18]

© John Briggs (www.kiva.org)

When the founders of microlending upstart Kiva make business presentations around the world, audiences respond with enthusiastic applause and even tears. Kiva's online lending platform connects personal lenders with poverty-stricken individuals in developing nations, enabling villagers to start tomato farms, carpet kiosks and other small ventures that improve their lives. Kiva's presentations use heartwarming stories and videos about village entrepreneurs to show that small loans can make a big difference. *What tips can communicators use to deliver powerful, inspirational presentations?*

How can you present slideshows on the Internet?

8. **Move your presentation to the Internet.** You have a range of alternatives, from simple to complex, for moving your multimedia presentation to the Internet or your company's intranet. The simplest option is posting your slides online for others to access. Even if you are giving a face-to-face presentation, attendees appreciate these *electronic handouts* because they don't have to lug them home. The most complex option for moving your multimedia presentation to the Internet involves a Web conference or broadcast.

   Web presentations with slides, narration, and speaker control have emerged as a way for anyone who has access to the Internet to attend your presentation without leaving the office. For example, you could initiate a meeting via a conference call, narrate using a telephone, and have participants see your slides from the browsers on their computers. If you prefer, you could skip the narration and provide a prerecorded presentation. Web-based presentations have many applications, including providing access to updated training or sales data whenever needed.[19]

   Some businesses convert their PowerPoint presentations to PDF documents or send PowerPoint shows (file extension *.PPSX), which open directly in **Slide Show** view, ready to run. Both types of documents are highly suitable for e-mailing. Among their advantages are that they start immediately, can't be easily changed, and typically result in smaller, less memory-hogging files.

Polishing Your Delivery and Following Up

LEARNING OBJECTIVE 5
Specify delivery techniques for use before, during, and after a presentation, and apply reflective thinking skills.

Once you have organized your presentation and prepared visuals, you are ready to practice delivering it. You will feel more confident and appear more professional if you know more about various delivery methods and techniques to use before, during, and after your presentation.

Choosing a Delivery Method

What is extemporaneous delivery, and why is it more convincing than a memorized or read speech?

Inexperienced speakers often feel that they must memorize an entire presentation to be effective. Unless you are an experienced performer, however, you will sound wooden and unnatural. What's more, forgetting your place can be disastrous! That is why we don't recommend memorizing an entire oral presentation. However, memorizing significant parts—the introduction, the conclusion, and perhaps a meaningful quotation—can be dramatic and impressive.

If memorizing your business presentation won't work, is reading from a manuscript the best plan? Definitely not! Reading to an audience is boring and ineffective. Because reading suggests that you don't know your topic very well, the audience loses confidence in your expertise. Reading also prevents you from maintaining eye contact. You can't see audience reactions; consequently, you can't benefit from feedback.

Neither memorizing nor reading creates very convincing business presentations. The best plan, by far, is to present *extemporaneously,* especially when you are displaying an electronic slideshow such as PowerPoint. Extemporaneous delivery means speaking freely, generally without notes, after preparation and rehearsing. It means that in your talk you comment on the electronic slideshow you have prepared and rehearsed several times. Remember, PowerPoint and other presentation software have replaced traditional outlines and notes. Reading notes or a manuscript in addition to PowerPoint slides will damage your credibility.

If you give a talk without PowerPoint, however, you may use note cards or an outline containing key sentences and major ideas, but beware of reading from a script. By preparing and then practicing with your notes, you can talk to your audience in a conversational manner. Your notes should be neither entire paragraphs nor single words. Instead, they should contain a complete sentence or two to introduce each major idea. Below the topic sentence(s), outline subpoints and illustrations. Note cards will keep you on track and prompt your memory, but only if you have rehearsed the presentation thoroughly.

Combating Stage Fright

What is stage fright, and how can you control it?

Nearly everyone experiences some degree of stage fright when speaking before a group. "If you hear someone say he or she isn't nervous before a speech, you're talking either to a liar or a very boring speaker," says corporate speech consultant Dianna Booher.[20] Being afraid is quite natural

CAREER COACH

How to Avoid Stage Fright

Ever get nervous before making a presentation? Everyone does! And it's not all in your head, either. When you face something threatening or challenging, your body reacts in what psychologists call the fight-or-flight response. This physical reflex provides your body with increased energy to deal with threatening situations. It also creates those sensations—dry mouth, sweaty hands, increased heartbeat, and stomach butterflies—that we associate with stage fright. The fight-or-flight response arouses your body for action—in this case, making a presentation.

Because everyone feels some form of apprehension before speaking, it's impossible to eliminate the physiological symptoms altogether. However, you can reduce their effects with the following techniques:

- **Breathe deeply.** Use deep breathing to ease your fight-or-flight symptoms. Inhale to a count of ten, hold this breath to a count of ten, and exhale to a count of ten. Concentrate on your counting and your breathing; both activities reduce your stress.
- **Convert your fear.** Don't view your sweaty palms and dry mouth as evidence of fear. Interpret them as symptoms of exuberance, excitement, and enthusiasm to share your ideas.
- **Know your topic and come prepared.** Feel confident about your topic. Select a topic that you know well and that is relevant to your audience. Test your equipment and arrive with time to spare.
- **Use positive self-talk.** Remind yourself that you know your topic and are prepared. Tell yourself that the audience is on your side—because it is! Moreover, most speakers appear to be more confident than they feel. Make this apparent confidence work for you.
- **Take a sip of water.** Drink some water to alleviate your dry mouth and constricted voice box, especially if you're talking for more than 15 minutes.
- **Shift the spotlight to your visuals.** At least some of the time the audience will be focusing on your slides, transparencies, handouts, or whatever you have prepared—and not totally on you.
- **Ignore any stumbles.** Don't apologize or confess your nervousness. If you keep going, the audience will forget any mistakes quickly.
- **Feel proud when you finish.** You will be surprised at how good you feel when you finish. Take pride in what you have accomplished, and your audience will reward you with applause and congratulations. Your body, of course, will call off the fight-or-flight response and return to normal!

Career Application

Interview someone in your field or in another business setting who must make oral presentations. How did he or she develop speaking skills? What advice can this person suggest to reduce stage fright? When you next make a class presentation, try some or all of the techniques described here and note which are most effective for you.

and results from actual physiological changes occurring in your body. Faced with a frightening situation, your body responds with the fight-or-flight response, discussed more fully in the accompanying Career Coach box. You can learn to control and reduce stage fright, as well as to incorporate techniques for effective speaking, by using the following strategies and techniques before, during, and after your presentation.

Before Your Presentation

Speaking in front of a group will become less daunting if you allow for adequate preparation, sufficient practice, and rehearsals. Interacting with the audience and limiting surprises such as malfunctioning equipment will also add to your peace of mind. Review the following tips for a smooth start:

- **Prepare thoroughly.** One of the most effective strategies for reducing stage fright is knowing your subject thoroughly. Research your topic diligently and prepare a careful sentence outline. Those who try to "wing it" usually suffer the worst butterflies—and make the worst presentations.
- **Rehearse repeatedly.** When you rehearse, practice your entire presentation, not just the first half. In PowerPoint you may print out speaker's notes, an outline, or a handout featuring miniature slides, which are excellent for practice. If you don't use an electronic slideshow, place your outline sentences on separate note cards. You may also wish to include transitional sentences to help you move to the next topic as you practice. Rehearse alone or before friends and family. Also try an audio or video recording of your rehearsals so that you can evaluate your effectiveness.
- **Time yourself.** Most audiences tend to get restless during longer talks. Therefore, try to complete your presentation in no more than 20 minutes. Set a simple kitchen timer during

your rehearsal to keep track of time. Better yet, PowerPoint offers a function called **Rehearse Timings** in the **Slide Show** tab that can measure the length of your talk as you practice.

- **Check the room.** If you are using a computer, a projector, or sound equipment, be certain they are operational. Before you start, check electrical outlets and the position of the viewing screen. Ensure that the seating arrangement is appropriate to your needs.
- **Greet members of the audience.** Try to make contact with a few members of the audience when you enter the room, while you are waiting to be introduced, or when you walk to the podium. Your body language should convey friendliness, confidence, and enjoyment.
- **Practice stress reduction.** If you feel tension and fear while you are waiting your turn to speak, use stress-reduction techniques, such as deep breathing. Additional techniques to help you conquer stage fright are presented in the accompanying Career Coach box.

During Your Presentation

How can you enhance a presentation during delivery?

To stay in control during your talk, to build credibility, and to engage your audience, follow these time-tested guidelines for effective speaking:

- **Begin with a pause.** When you first approach the audience, take a moment to make yourself comfortable. Establish your control of the situation.
- **Present your first sentence from memory.** By memorizing your opening, you can immediately establish rapport with the audience through eye contact. You will also sound confident and knowledgeable.
- **Maintain eye contact.** If the size of the audience overwhelms you, pick out two individuals on the right and two on the left. Talk directly to these people. Don't ignore listeners in the back of the room.
- **Control your voice and vocabulary.** This means speaking in moderated tones but loudly enough to be heard. Eliminate verbal static, such as *ah, er, you know,* and *um*. Silence is preferable to meaningless fillers when you are thinking of your next idea.
- **Put the brakes on.** Many novice speakers talk too rapidly, displaying their nervousness and making it very difficult for audience members to understand their ideas. Slow down and listen to what you are saying.
- **Move naturally.** If you have a lectern, don't remain glued to it. Move about casually and naturally. Avoid fidgeting with your clothing, hair, or items in your pockets. Do not roll up your sleeves or put your hands in your pockets. Learn to use your body to express a point.
- **Use visual aids effectively.** You should discuss and interpret each visual aid for the audience. Move aside as you describe it so that it can be seen fully. Use a pointer if necessary, but steady your hand if it is shaking.
- **Avoid digressions.** Stick to your outline and notes. Don't suddenly include clever little anecdotes or digressions that occur to you on the spot. If it is not part of your rehearsed material, leave it out so that you can finish on time. Remember, too, that your audience may not be as enthralled with your topic as you are.
- **Summarize your main points and arrive at the high point of your talk.** Conclude your presentation by reiterating your main points or by emphasizing what you want the audience to think or do. Once you have announced your conclusion, proceed to it directly.

After Your Presentation

What tasks are best left for after the presentation?

As you are concluding your presentation, handle questions and answers competently and provide handouts if appropriate. Try the following techniques:

- **Distribute handouts.** If you prepared handouts with data the audience will need, pass them out when you finish.
- **Encourage questions.** If the situation permits a question-and-answer period, announce it at the beginning of your presentation. Then, when you finish, ask for questions. Set a time limit for questions and answers.

- **Repeat questions.** Although the speaker may hear the question, audience members often do not. Begin each answer with a repetition of the question. This also gives you thinking time. Then, direct your answer to the entire audience.
- **Reinforce your main points.** You can use your answers to restate your primary ideas (*I'm glad you brought that up because it gives me a chance to elaborate on* ...). In answering questions, avoid becoming defensive or debating the questioner.
- **Keep control.** Don't allow one individual to take over. Keep the entire audience involved.
- **Avoid *Yes, but* answers.** The word *but* immediately cancels any preceding message. Try replacing it with *and*. For example, *Yes, X has been tried. And Y works even better because....*
- **End with a summary and appreciation.** To signal the end of the session before you take the last question, say something like, *We have time for just one more question.* As you answer the last question, try to work it into a summary of your main points. Then, express appreciation to the audience for the opportunity to talk with them.

Organizing Team-Based Written and Oral Presentations

LEARNING OBJECTIVE 6
Organize team-based written and oral presentations, and understand how to communicate in teams.

Companies form teams for many reasons, as discussed in Chapter 2. The goal of some teams is an oral presentation to pitch a new product or to win a high-stakes contract. Before Apple CEO Steve Jobs and his team roll out one of their hotly anticipated new electronic gadgets, you can bet that team members spend months preparing so that his "Stevenote" presentation flows smoothly.[21]

The goal of other teams is to investigate a problem and submit recommendations to decision makers in a report. At BMW, for example, nimble cross-functional teams excel at problem solving across divisions. Such teams speed innovation and the development of new products such as the electronics that now comprise about 20 percent of a new vehicle's value.[22]

The outcome of any team effort is often (a) a written report; (b) a series of self-contained electronic slides, also called a slide deck; or (c) an oral presentation delivered live. The boundaries are becoming increasingly blurred between flat, two-dimensional hard-copy reports and multimedia, hyperlinked slideshows. Both hard-copy reports and multimedia presentations are delivered to clients in business today. This is why team writing and speaking appear side by side in this chapter.

Whether your team's project produces written reports, slide decks, or oral presentations, you generally have considerable control over how the project is organized and completed. If you have been part of any team efforts before, you also know that such projects can be very frustrating—particularly when some team members don't carry their weight or when members cannot resolve conflict. On the other hand, team projects can be harmonious and productive when members establish ground rules and follow guidelines related to preparing, planning, collecting information for, organizing, rehearsing, and evaluating team projects.

Preparing to Work Together

How can teams prepare for a fruitful and smooth collaboration?

Before any group begins to talk about a specific project, members should get together and establish basic ground rules. One of the first tasks is naming a meeting leader to conduct meetings, a recorder to keep a record of group decisions, and an evaluator to determine whether the group is on target and meeting its goals. The group should decide whether it will be governed by consensus (everyone must agree), by majority rule, or by some other method.

The most successful teams make meetings a top priority. They compare schedules to set up the best meeting times, and they meet often. They avoid other responsibilities that might disrupt these meetings.

When teams first organize, they should consider the value of conflict. By bringing conflict into the open and encouraging confrontation, teams can prevent personal resentment and group dysfunction. Confrontation can actually create better final products by promoting new ideas and avoiding groupthink. Conflict is most beneficial when team members can air their views fully. Another important topic to discuss during team formation is how to deal with team members who are not pulling their share of the load. Teams should decide whether they will "fire" members who are not contributing or take some other action in dealing with slackers.

Planning the Document or Presentation

Once teams have established ground rules, members are ready to discuss the target document or presentation. During these discussions, they must be sure to keep a record of all decisions. They should establish the specific purpose for the document or presentation and identify the main issues involved. They must decide on the final format. For a collaborative business report, they should determine what parts it will include, such as an executive summary, figures, and an appendix. They should consider how the report or presentation will be delivered—in person, online, or by e-mail. For a team oral presentation, they should decide on its parts, length, and graphics. For either written or oral projects, they should profile the audience and focus on the questions audience members would want answered. If the report or presentation involves persuasion, they must decide what appeals would achieve the team's purpose.

When work groups plan a team document or presentation, what steps should they follow?

Next the team should develop a work plan (see Chapter 11), assign jobs, and set deadlines. If time is short, members should work backward from the due date. For oral presentations, teams must schedule time for content and creative development as well as for a series of rehearsals. The best-planned presentations can fall apart if they are poorly rehearsed.

For oral presentations, all team members should have written assignments. These assignments should detail each member's specific responsibilities for researching content, producing visuals, developing handout materials, building transitions between segments, and showing up for rehearsals. For written reports, members must decide how the final document will be composed: individuals working separately on assigned portions, one person writing the first draft, the entire group writing the complete document together, or some other method.

Collecting Information

Why must facts in reports and presentations be correct?

One of the most challenging jobs for team projects is generating and collecting information. Unless facts are accurate, the most beautiful report or the most high-powered presentation will fail. As you brainstorm ideas, consider cluster diagramming (see Figure 5.2 on page 140 in Chapter 5). Assign topics and decide who will be responsible for gathering what information. Establishing deadlines for collecting information is important if a team is to remain on schedule. Team members should also discuss ways to ensure the accuracy of the information collected.

Organizing, Writing, and Revising

When a project progresses into the organizing and writing stages, a team may need to modify some of its earlier decisions. Team members may review the proposed organization of the final document or presentation and adjust it if necessary. In composing the first draft of a written report or presentation, team members will probably write separate segments. As they work on these segments, they should use the same version of a word processing or presentation graphics program to facilitate combining files.

Why should teams assign one person to coordinate all the parts of the project?

As individuals work on separate parts of a written report, the team should decide on one person (probably the best writer) to coordinate all the parts. The writer strives for a consistent style, format, and feel in the final product. For oral presentations, team members must try to make logical connections between segments. Each presenter builds a bridge to the next member's topic to create a smooth transition. Team members should also agree to use the same template, and they should allow only one person to make global changes in color, font, and other formatting on the slide and title masters.

Editing, Rehearsing, and Evaluating

The last stage in a collaborative project involves editing, rehearsing, and evaluating. For a written report, one person should assume the task of merging the various files, running a spell checker, and examining the entire document for consistency of design, format, and vocabulary. That person is responsible for finding and correcting grammatical and mechanical errors. Then the entire group meets as a whole to evaluate the final document. Does it fulfill its purpose and meet the needs of the audience?

For oral presentations, one person should also merge all the files and be certain that they are consistent in design, format, and vocabulary. Teams making presentations should practice together several times. If that is not feasible, experts say that teams must schedule at least one full real-time rehearsal with the entire group.[23] Whenever possible, practice in a room that is similar to the location of your talk. Consider video recording one of the rehearsals so that each presenter can critique his or her own performance. Schedule a dress rehearsal with an audience at least two days before the actual presentation. Practice fielding questions.

Successful group documents emerge from thoughtful preparation, clear definitions of contributors' roles, commitment to a group-approved plan, and a willingness to take responsibility for the final product. More information about writing business reports appeared in previous chapters of this book.

Adapting Presentations to Intercultural Audiences

LEARNING OBJECTIVE 7
Explain effective techniques for adapting oral presentations to intercultural audiences, and demonstrate intercultural and diversity understanding.

Every good speaker adapts to the audience, and intercultural presentations call for special adjustments and sensitivity. Most people understand that they must speak slowly, choose simple English, avoid jargon and clichés, use short sentences, and pause frequently when communicating with nonnative speakers of English.

Beyond these basic language adaptations, however, more fundamental sensitivity is often necessary. In organizing a presentation for an intercultural audience, you may need to anticipate and adapt to different speaking conventions, values, and nonverbal behavior. You may also need to contend with limited language skills and a certain reluctance to voice opinions openly.

Understanding Different Values and Nonverbal Behavior

What must you consider when addressing intercultural audiences?

In addressing intercultural audiences, anticipate expectations and perceptions that may differ significantly from what you may consider normal. Remember, for example, that the North American emphasis on getting to the point quickly is not equally prized across the globe. Therefore, think twice about delivering your main idea up front. Many people (notably those in Japanese, Latin American, and Arabic cultures) consider such directness to be brash and inappropriate. Remember that others may not share our cultural emphasis on straightforwardness.[24]

When working with an interpreter or speaking before individuals whose English is limited, you must be very careful about your language. For example, you will need to express ideas in small chunks to give the interpreter time to translate. You may need to slow down as you speak and stop after each thought to allow time for the translation that will follow. Even if your presentation or speech is being translated simultaneously, remember to speak slowly and to pause after each sentence to ensure that your message is rendered correctly in the target language.

The same advice is useful in organizing presentations. Consider breaking your presentation into short, discrete segments. You may want to divide your talk into distinct topics, developing each separately and encouraging discussion periods after each. Such organization enables participants to ask questions and digest what has been presented. This technique is especially effective in cultures where people communicate in "loops." In the Middle East, for example, Arab speakers "mix circuitous, irrelevant (by American standards) conversations with short dashes of information that go directly to the point." Presenters who are patient, tolerant, and "mature" (in the eyes of the audience) will make the sale or win the contract.[25]

ETHICS CHECK
The Robot Presenter
In one of your courses, you are witnessing a PowerPoint presentation, during which it becomes obvious that the speaker has completely memorized her talk. However, she stumbles badly a few times, struggling to remember her lines. Worse yet, you perceive her accent as nearly impenetrable. How should the instructor and the class handle the evaluation of such a presentation?

Match your presentation and your nonverbal messages to the expectations of your audience. In Germany, for instance, successful presentations tend to be dense with facts and precise statistics. Americans might say "around 30 percent" whereas a German presenter might say "30.4271 percent." Similarly, constant smiling is not as valued in Europe as it is in North America. Many Europeans distrust a speaker who is cracking jokes, smiling, or laughing in a business presentation. Their expectation is of a rational—that is, "serious"—fact-based delivery. American-style enthusiasm is often interpreted abroad as hyperbolic exaggeration or, worse, as dishonesty and can lead to misunderstandings. If an American says "Great job!" to offer praise, a Spanish counterpart might believe the American has approved the project. "When Europeans realize there's no commitment implied," warned an intercultural consultant, "they might feel deceived or that the American is being superficial."[26]

Remember, too, that some cultures prefer greater formality than Americans exercise. Instead of first names, use only honorifics (*Mr.* or *Ms.*) and last names, as well as academic or business titles—such as *Doctor* or *Director*. Writing on a flipchart or transparency seems natural and spontaneous in this country. Abroad, though, such informal techniques may suggest that the speaker does not value the audience enough to prepare proper visual aids in advance.[27]

Adjusting Visual Aids to Intercultural Audiences

Although you may have to exercise greater caution with culturally diverse audiences, you still want to use visual aids to help communicate your message. Find out from your international contact whether you can present in English or will need an interpreter. In many countries listeners are too polite to speak up when they don't understand you. One expert advises explaining important concepts in several ways using different words and then requesting

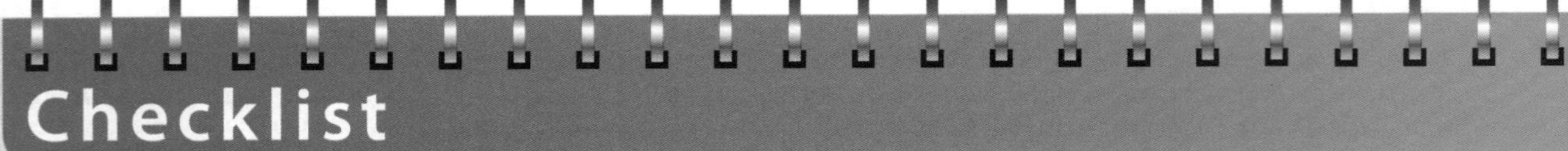

Preparing and Organizing Oral Presentations

Getting Ready to Speak

- **Identify your purpose.** Decide what you want your audience to believe, remember, or do when you finish. Aim all parts of your talk toward this purpose.
- **Analyze the audience.** Consider how to adapt your message (its organization, appeals, and examples) to your audience's knowledge and needs.

Organizing the Introduction

- **Get the audience involved.** Capture the audience's attention by opening with a promise, story, startling fact, question, quote, relevant problem, or self-effacing joke.
- **Establish yourself.** Demonstrate your credibility by identifying your position, expertise, knowledge, or qualifications.
- **Preview your main points.** Introduce your topic and summarize its principal parts.

Organizing the Body

- **Develop two to four main points.** Streamline your topic so that you can concentrate on its major issues.
- **Arrange the points logically.** Sequence your points chronologically, from most important to least important, by comparison and contrast, or by some other strategy.
- **Prepare transitions.** Between major points write "bridge" statements that connect the previous item to the next one. Use transitional expressions as verbal signposts (*first, second, then, however, consequently, on the contrary,* and so forth).
- **Have extra material ready.** Be prepared with more information and visuals in case you have additional time to fill.

Organizing the Conclusion

- **Review your main points.** Emphasize your main ideas in your closing so that your audience will remember them.
- **Provide a strong, final focus.** Tell how your listeners can use this information, why you have spoken, or what you want them to do. As the culmination of your talk, end with a specific audience benefit or thought-provoking final thought (a take-away), not just a lame rehash.

Designing Visual Aids

- **Select your medium carefully.** Consider the pros and cons of each alternative.
- **Highlight main ideas.** Use visual aids to illustrate major concepts only. Keep them brief and simple.
- **Try to replace bullets whenever possible.** Use flowcharts, diagrams, time lines, and so forth, to substitute for bulleted lists when suitable.
- **Use aids skillfully.** Talk to the audience, not to the visuals. Paraphrase their contents.

Developing Multimedia Presentations

- **Learn to use your software program.** Study template and slide layout designs to see how you can adapt them to your purposes.
- **Select colors based on the light level in the room.** Consider how mixing light and dark fonts and backgrounds affects their visibility. Use templates and preset slide layouts if you are new to PowerPoint.
- **Use bulleted points for major ideas.** Make sure your points are all parallel, and observe the 6-x-6 rule.
- **Include multimedia options that will help you convey your message.** Use moderate animation features and hyperlinks to make your talk more interesting and to link to files with related content in the same document, in other documents, or on the Internet.
- **Make speaker's notes.** Jot down the narrative supporting each slide, and use these notes to practice your presentation. Do not read from notes while speaking to an audience, however.
- **Maintain control.** Don't let your slides upstage you. Engage your audience by using additional techniques to help them visualize your points.

members of the audience to relay their understanding of what you have just said back to you. Another expert suggests packing more text on PowerPoint slides and staying closer to its literal meaning. After all, most nonnative speakers of English understand written text much better than they comprehend spoken English. In the United States presenters may spend 90 seconds on a slide, whereas in other countries they may need to slow down to two minutes per slide.[28]

To ensure clarity and show courtesy, provide handouts in English and the target language. Never use numbers without projecting or writing them out for all to see. If possible, say numbers in both languages, but only if you can pronounce or even speak the target language well enough to avoid embarrassment. Distribute translated handouts, summarizing your important information, when you finish.

Spotlight on Communicators

© Nancy Friedman President Telephone Doctor Customer Service Trainer

Instead of commanding telephone callers to "Hold, please," ask politely whether the caller is *able* to hold, advises Telephone Doctor Nancy Friedman. She helps companies improve their employees' telephone skills. One phrase she prohibits is "I don't know." It's better to say, "I will find out." She also recommends that people smile *before* they answer the phone. That prevents "emotional leakage," taking personal frustration out on a caller.

Whether you are speaking to familiar or intercultural audiences, your presentation requires attention to content and strategy. The checklist on the previous page summarizes suggestions for preparing, organizing, and illustrating oral presentations.

Improving Telephone and Voice Mail Skills

LEARNING OBJECTIVE 8

List techniques for improving telephone and voice mail skills to project a positive image.

One form of business presentation involves presenting yourself on the telephone, a skill that is still very important in today's workplace. Despite the heavy reliance on e-mail, the telephone remains an extremely important piece of equipment in offices. With the addition of today's wireless technology, it doesn't matter whether you are in or out of the office. You can always be reached by phone. This section focuses on traditional telephone techniques and voice mail—both opportunities for making a good impression. As a business communicator, you can be more productive, efficient, and professional by following some simple suggestions.

How can telephone and voice mail use promote goodwill and increase productivity?

Making Telephone Calls Efficiently

Before making a telephone call, decide whether the intended call is really necessary. Could you find the information yourself? If you wait a while, will the problem resolve itself? Perhaps your message could be delivered more efficiently by some other means. Some companies have found that telephone calls are often less important than the work they interrupt. Alternatives to telephone calls include instant messaging, texting, e-mail, memos, and calls to automated voice mail systems. If you must make a telephone call, consider using the following suggestions to make it fully productive:

How can you make productive telephone calls?

- **Plan a mini-agenda.** Have you ever been embarrassed when you had to make a second telephone call because you forgot an important point the first time? Before placing a call, jot down notes regarding all the topics you need to discuss. Following an agenda guarantees not only a complete call but also a quick one. You will be less likely to wander from the business at hand while rummaging through your mind trying to remember everything.
- **Use a three-point introduction.** When placing a call, immediately (a) name the person you are calling, (b) identify yourself and your affiliation, and (c) give a brief explanation of your reason for calling. For example: *May I speak to Larry Lopez? This is Hillary Dahl of Sebastian Enterprises, and I'm seeking information about a software program called Power Presentations.* This kind of introduction enables the receiving individual to respond immediately without asking further questions.
- **Be brisk if you are rushed.** For business calls when your time is limited, avoid questions such as *How are you?* Instead, say, *Lisa, I knew you would be the only one who could answer these two questions for me.* Another efficient strategy is to set a contract with the caller: *Look, Lisa, I have only ten minutes, but I really wanted to get back to you.*
- **Be cheerful and accurate.** Let your voice show the same kind of animation that you radiate when you greet people in person. In your mind try to envision the individual

answering the telephone. A smile can certainly affect the tone of your voice, so smile at that person. Keep your voice and throat relaxed by keeping your head straight. Don't squeeze the phone between your shoulder and your ear. Obviously, don't eat food or chew gum while on the phone. Moreover, be accurate about what you say. *Hang on a second; I will be right back* rarely is true. It is better to say, *It may take me two or three minutes to get that information. Would you prefer to hold or have me call you back?*

- **Bring it to a close.** The responsibility for ending a call lies with the caller. This is sometimes difficult to do if the other person rambles on. You may need to use suggestive closing language, such as the following: (a) *I have certainly enjoyed talking with you;* (b) *I have learned what I needed to know, and now I can proceed with my work;* (c) *Thanks for your help;* (d) *I must go now, but may I call you again in the future if I need ...?* or (e) *Should we talk again in a few weeks?*
- **Avoid telephone tag.** If you call someone who's not in, ask when it would be best to call again. State that you will call at a specific time—and do it. If you ask a person to call you, give a time when you can be reached—and then be sure you are in at that time.
- **Leave complete voice mail messages.** Remember that there is no need to rush when you are leaving a voice mail message. Always enunciate clearly and speak slowly when giving your telephone number or spelling your name. Be sure to provide a complete message, including your name, telephone number, and the time and date of your call. Explain your purpose so that the receiver can be ready with the required information when returning your call.

Receiving Telephone Calls Professionally

How do professionals ensure that the telephone calls they receive are productive?

With a little forethought you can project a professional image and make your telephone a productive, efficient work tool. Developing good telephone manners and techniques, such as the following, will also reflect well on you and on your organization.

- **Identify yourself immediately.** In answering your telephone or someone else's, provide your name, title or affiliation, and, possibly, a greeting. For example, *Larry Lopez, Proteus Software. How may I help you?* Force yourself to speak clearly and slowly. Remember that the caller may be unfamiliar with what you are saying and fail to recognize slurred syllables.
- **Be responsive and helpful.** If you are in a support role, be sympathetic to callers' needs. Instead of *I don't know*, try *That's a good question; let me investigate.* Instead of *We can't do that,* try *That's a tough one; let's see what we can do.* Avoid *No* at the beginning of a sentence. It sounds especially abrasive and displeasing because it suggests total rejection.
- **Practice telephone confidentiality.** When answering calls for others, be courteous and helpful, but don't give out confidential information. Better to say, *She's away from her desk* or *He's out of the office* than to report a colleague's exact whereabouts. Also, be tight-lipped about sharing company information with strangers. Security experts insist that employees answering telephones must become guardians of company information.[29]
- **Take messages carefully.** Few things are as frustrating as receiving a potentially important phone message that is illegible. Repeat the spelling of names and verify telephone numbers. Write messages legibly and record their time and date. Promise to give the messages to intended recipients, but don't guarantee return calls.
- **Explain what you are doing when transferring calls.** Give a reason for transferring, and indicate the extension to which you are directing the call in case the caller is disconnected.

Ethics Check

Telling White Lies

Obviously, you wouldn't want to tell callers that your colleague went to the restroom or that your boss is responding to e-mail from a golf course in Hilo, Hawaii. But what about people who, for instance, hide behind voice mail and want you to lie about it? When is it acceptable to tell white lies on the phone to maintain confidentiality and decorum, and when is lying for others wrong?

Making the Best Use of Voice Mail

What are the advantages of voice mail?

Because telephone calls can be disruptive, many businesspeople are making extensive use of voice mail to intercept and screen incoming calls. Voice mail links a telephone system to a computer that digitizes and stores incoming messages. Some systems also provide functions such as automated attendant menus, allowing callers to reach any associated extension by pushing specific buttons.

Voice mail is quite efficient for message storage. Because as many as half of all business calls require no discussion or feedback, the messaging capabilities of voice mail can mean huge savings for businesses. Incoming information is delivered without interrupting potential receivers and without all the niceties that most two-way conversations require. Stripped of superfluous chitchat, voice mail messages allow communicators to focus on essentials. Voice mail also eliminates telephone tag, inaccurate message taking, and time zone barriers.

However, voice mail should not be overused. Individuals who screen all incoming calls cause irritation, resentment, and needless telephone tag. Here are some ways to make voice mail work most effectively for you:

- **Announce your voice mail.** If you rely principally on a voice mail message system, identify it on your business stationery and cards. Then, when people call, they will be ready to leave a message.
- **Prepare a warm and informative greeting.** Make your mechanical greeting sound warm and inviting, both in tone and content. Identify yourself and your organization so that callers know they have reached the right number. Thank the caller and briefly explain that you are unavailable. Invite the caller to leave a message or, if appropriate, call back. Here's a typical voice mail greeting: *Hi! This is Larry Lopez of Proteus Software, and I appreciate your call. You have reached my voice mailbox because I'm either working with customers or talking on another line at the moment. Please leave your name, number, and reason for calling so that I can be prepared when I return your call.* Give callers an idea of when you will be available, such as, *I will be back at 2:30;* or, *I will be out of my office until Wednesday, May 20.* If you screen your calls as a time-management technique, try this message: *I'm not near my phone right now, but I should be able to return calls after 3:30.*
- **Test your message.** Call your number and assess your message. Does it sound inviting? Sincere? Understandable? Are you pleased with your tone? If not, says one consultant, have someone else, perhaps a professional, record a message for you.

This chapter has provided valuable tips for preparing and delivering first-rate oral presentations. You have also learned effective techniques for adapting oral presentations to intercultural audiences. Finally, we illustrated techniques for improving telephone and voice mail skills. All of these techniques and tips can help you be a successful business communicator in an increasingly challenging workplace.

Want to do well on tests and excel in your course? Go to **www.meguffey.com** for helpful interactive resources.

- **Review the Chapter 14 PowerPoint slides to prepare for the first quiz.**

Zooming In — YOUR TURN

Applying Your Skills at Apple Computer

When Steve Jobs unveiled the iPad tablet computer amid much fanfare and hype stoked by months of secrecy, the tech world seemed skeptical at first. Many bloggers were wondering what purpose the "oversized iPhone" would serve or what gap in the Apple product mix and crowded consumer electronics field it would fill. Much derision was leveled at the name of the device for its supposed reference to feminine hygiene products. Marketing experts, however, predicted a huge success for the iPad and argued that the name would have no impact on its wide adoption.

Some of the criticism was aimed at the iPad's technical features. Battery life, compatibility with Adobe's Flash software, and Wi-Fi versus 3G capability ranked high among the hotly debated subjects. The price of the new gadget and Apple's continued exclusive alliance with AT&T in the United States were also discussed.

Your Task

Steve Jobs asks you and other Apple interns to research and monitor the buzz surrounding the company's latest hot gadget. The Apple CEO wants you to monitor traditional news and opinion outlets, but also blogs, tweets, forums, and social media sites. Prepare an outline of your findings. Then use the outline as the basis for creating a simple, image-driven PowerPoint presentation to inform Steve of your findings.

© Tony Avelar/Bloomberg via Getty Images

Summary of Learning Objectives

1 **Discuss two important first steps in preparing effective business presentations.** First, identify what your purpose is and what you want the audience to believe or do so that you can aim the entire presentation toward your goal. Second, know your audience so that you can adjust your message and style to its knowledge and needs.

2 **Explain the major elements in organizing a presentation, including the introduction, body, and conclusion.** The introduction of a good presentation should capture the listener's attention, identify the speaker, establish credibility, and preview the main points. The body should discuss two to four main points, with appropriate explanations, details, and verbal signposts to guide listeners. The conclusion should review the main points, provide a final focus or take-away, and allow the speaker to leave the podium gracefully.

3 **Identify techniques for gaining audience rapport, including (a) using effective imagery, (b) providing verbal signposts, and (c) sending appropriate nonverbal messages.** You can improve audience rapport by using effective imagery including analogies, metaphors, similes, personal anecdotes, statistics, and worst case/best-case scenarios. Rapport is also gained by including verbal signposts that tell the audience when you are previewing, summarizing, and switching directions. Nonverbal messages have a powerful effect on the way your message is received. You should look terrific, animate your body, punctuate your words, get out from behind the podium, and vary your facial expressions.

4 **Discuss designing and using effective visual aids, handouts, and multimedia presentations and using presentation technology competently.** Use simple, easily understood visual aids to emphasize and clarify main points. Choose multimedia slides, transparencies, flipcharts, or other visuals. Generally, it is best to distribute handouts after a presentation. Speakers employing a program such as PowerPoint use templates, layout designs, and bullet points to produce effective slides. A presentation may be enhanced with slide transitions, hyperlinks, sound, animation, video elements, and other multimedia effects. Speaker's notes and handouts may be generated from slides. Web-based presentations allow speakers to narrate and show slides without leaving their home bases. Increasing numbers of speakers are using the Internet to e-mail or post their slides as electronic shows or report deliverables instead of generating paper copies.

5 **Specify delivery techniques for use before, during, and after a presentation, and apply reflective thinking skills.** Before your talk, prepare a sentence outline on note cards or speaker's notes and rehearse repeatedly. Check the room, lectern, and equipment. During the presentation, consider beginning with a pause and presenting your first sentence from memory. Speak freely and extemporaneously, commenting on your PowerPoint slides but using no other notes. Make eye contact, control your voice, speak and move naturally, and avoid digressions. After your talk, distribute handouts and answer questions. End gracefully and express appreciation.

6 **Organize team-based written and oral presentations, and understand how to communicate in teams.** In preparing to work together, teams should name a leader and decide how they will make decisions (by consensus, majority rule, or some other method). They should work out a schedule, discuss the benefits of conflict, and determine how they will deal with members who fail to pull their share. They should decide on the purpose, form, and procedures for preparing the final document or presentation. They must brainstorm ideas, assign topics, and establish deadlines. In composing the first draft of a report or presentation, they should use the same software version and meet to discuss the drafts and rehearsals. For written reports, one person should probably compose the final draft, and the group should evaluate it. For group presentations, team members need to work for consistency of design, format, and wording. Several rehearsals, one of which should be videotaped, will enhance the final presentation.

Are you ready? Get more practice at **www.meguffey.com**

7 Explain effective techniques for adapting oral presentations to intercultural audiences, and demonstrate intercultural and diversity understanding. In presentations before groups whose English is limited, speak slowly, use simple English, avoid jargon and clichés, and opt for short sentences. Pause often to allow an interpreter to keep up with you. Consider building up to your main idea rather than announcing it immediately. Also, consider breaking the presentation into short segments to allow participants to ask questions and digest small parts separately. Beware of appearing too spontaneous and informal. Use visual aids to help communicate your message, but also distribute translated handouts summarizing the most important information.

8 List techniques for improving telephone and voice mail skills to project a positive image. You can improve your telephone calls by planning a mini-agenda and using a three-point introduction (name, affiliation, and purpose). Be cheerful and responsive, and use closing language to end a conversation. Avoid telephone tag by leaving complete messages. In answering calls, identify yourself immediately, avoid giving out confidential information when answering for others, and take careful messages. For your own message, prepare a warm and informative greeting. Tell when you will be available. Evaluate your message by calling it yourself.

Chapter Review

1. Can speaking skills be improved, or do we have to be "born" communicators? (Obj. 1)
2. Why are analyzing an audience and anticipating its reactions particularly important before business presentations, and how would you adapt to the four categories of listeners? (Obj. 1)
3. In preparing an oral presentation, you can reduce your fears and lay a foundation for a professional performance by focusing on what five areas? (Obj. 1)
4. In the introduction of an oral presentation, you can establish your credibility by using what two methods? (Obj. 2)
5. What is Guy Kawasaki's 10/20/30 rule, and what is it good for? (Obj. 2)
6. List six techniques for creating effective imagery in a presentation. Be prepared to discuss each. (Obj. 3)
7. List suggestions that would ensure that your nonverbal messages reinforce your verbal messages effectively. (Obj. 3)
8. What is the picture superiority effect? (Obj. 4)
9. Name specific advantages and disadvantages of multimedia presentation software. (Obj. 4)
10. How is the 6-x-6 rule applied in preparing bulleted points? (Obj. 4)
11. What delivery method is most effective for speakers? (Obj. 5)
12. Why should speakers deliver the first sentence from memory? (Obj. 5)
13. What five issues should be resolved before a team can collaborate productively? (Obj. 6)
14. How might presentations before intercultural audiences be altered to be most effective? (Obj. 7)
15. How can you avoid telephone tag? (Obj. 8)

Critical Thinking

1. Why should even practiced speakers plan their presentations when addressing a business audience instead of just "winging it"? (Obj. 3)
2. "Communicate—don't decorate." This principle is one of 20 rules that graphic designer and educator Timothy Samara discusses in his 2007 book *Design Elements: A Graphic Style Manual*. How could you apply this principle to the design of your PowerPoint presentations? (Obj. 4)
3. How can speakers prevent multimedia presentation software from stealing their thunder? (Obj. 4)
4. Discuss effective techniques for reducing stage fright. (Obj. 5)
5. **Ethical Issue:** Critics of PowerPoint claim that flashy graphics, sound effects, and animation often conceal thin content. Consider, for example, the findings regarding the space shuttle *Challenger* accident that killed seven astronauts. Report authors charged that NASA scientists had used PowerPoint presentations to make it look as though they had done analyses that they hadn't. Overreliance on presentations instead of analysis may have contributed to the shuttle disaster.[30] What lessons about ethical responsibilities when using PowerPoint can be learned from this catastrophe in communication? (Objs. 1, 2, and 4)

Are you ready? Get more practice at **www.meguffey.com**

Activities

14.1 Critiquing a Speech (Objs. 1–4)

Your Task. Search online or your library for a speech that was delivered by a significant businessperson or a well-known political figure. Consider watching Steve Jobs' excellent 15-minute "Stay Hungry, Stay Foolish" commencement speech at Stanford on YouTube. Transcripts of that well-known speech are also available online. Write a memo report to your instructor critiquing the speech in terms of the following:

a. Effectiveness of the introduction, body, and conclusion
b. Evidence of effective overall organization
c. Use of verbal signposts to create coherence
d. Emphasis of two to four main points
e. Effectiveness of supporting facts (use of examples, statistics, quotations, and so forth)

14.2 Knowing Your Audience (Objs. 1, 2)

Your Task. Select a recent issue of *Fortune, Fast Company, BusinessWeek,* or another business periodical approved by your instructor. Based on an analysis of your classmates, select an article that will appeal to them and that you can relate to their needs. Submit to your instructor a one-page summary that includes (a) the author, article title, source, issue date, and page reference; (b) a one-paragraph article summary; (c) a description of why you believe the article will appeal to your classmates; and (d) a summary of how you can relate the article to their needs.

14.3 Overcoming Stage Fright (Obj. 5)

Team

What makes you most nervous when making a presentation before class? Being afraid of becoming tongue-tied? Having all eyes on you? Messing up? Forgetting your ideas and looking silly?
Your Task. Discuss the previous questions as a class. Then, in groups of three or four, talk about ways to overcome these fears. Your instructor may ask you to write a memo, an e-mail, or a discussion board post (individually or collectively) summarizing your suggestions, or you may break out of your small groups and report your best ideas to the entire class.

14.4 Investigating Oral Communication in Your Field (Objs. 1, 5)

Your Task. Interview one or two individuals in your professional field. How is oral communication important in this profession? Does the need for oral skills change as one advances? What suggestions can these people make to newcomers to the field for developing proficient oral communication skills? Discuss your findings with your class.

14.5 Outlining an Oral Presentation (Objs. 1, 2)

One of the hardest parts of preparing an oral presentation is developing the outline.
Your Task. Select an oral presentation topic from the list in **Activity 14.14**, or suggest an original topic. Prepare an outline for your presentation using the format starting at the top of the next column:

Title	
Purpose	
	I. INTRODUCTION
State your name	A.
Gain attention and involve audience	B.
Establish credibility	C.
Preview main points	D.
Transition	
	II. BODY
Main point	A.
Illustrate, clarify, contrast	1.
	2.
	3.
Transition	
Main point	B.
Illustrate, clarify, contrast	1.
	2.
	3.
Transition	
Main point	C.
Illustrate, clarify, contrast	1.
	2.
	3.
Transition	
	III. CONCLUSION
Summarize main points	A.
Provide final focus or take-away	B.
Encourage questions	C.

14.6 Critiquing a Satirical Clip Lampooning PowerPoint (Objs. 1–4)

Watch Don McMillan's now famous YouTube hit "Life After Death by PowerPoint" from 2008 or the expanded version "Life After Death by PowerPoint 2010." Which specific PowerPoint ills is McMillan satirizing? Write a brief summary of the short clips for discussion in class. With your peers discuss whether the bad habits the YouTube videos parody correspond with design principles introduced in this chapter.

14.7 Evaluating and Outlining Podcasts of Apple Keynotes (Objs. 1–4)

To learn from the presentation skills of one of the best corporate speakers today, visit iTunes and watch one or more of the Apple keynotes posted there. They mostly cover Steve Jobs' famous product launches, including that of the iPad, and other important announcements.
Your Task. Download iTunes if you don't yet have a copy of the software and search for *apple keynotes,* or in your browser go to **http://itunes.apple.com/us/podcast/apple-keynotes/id275834665**.

If your instructor directs, watch one of the keynotes and outline it. You may also be asked to critique Steve Jobs' presentation techniques based on the guidelines you have studied in this chapter. Jot down your observations either as notes for a classroom discussion or to serve as a basis for an informative memo or e-mail.

14.8 Creating an Oral Presentation: Outline Your Job Duties (Objs. 1–4)

What if you had to create a presentation for your classmates and instructor, or perhaps a potential recruiter, that describes the multiple tasks you perform at work? Could you do it in a five-minute PowerPoint presentation?

Your instructor, for example, may wear many hats. Most academics (a) teach; (b) conduct research to publish; and (c) provide service to the department, college, university, and the community. Can you see how those aspects of their profession lend themselves to an outline of primary slides (teaching, publishing, service) and second-level slides (instructing undergraduate and graduate classes, presenting workshops, and giving lectures under the *teaching* label)?

Your Task. Now it's your turn to introduce the duties of a current position or a past job, volunteer activity, or internship in a brief, simple, yet well-designed PowerPoint presentation. Your goal is to inform your audience of your job duties in a three- to five-minute talk. Use animation features and graphics where appropriate. Your instructor may show you a completed example of this project.

14.9 Creating an Oral Presentation: Pitch to Guy Kawasaki (Objs. 1–4)

Could you interest an angel investor such as Guy Kawasaki in your business idea? The venture capitalist believes that if you must use more than ten slides to explain your business, you probably don't have one. Furthermore, Kawasaki claims that the ten topics a venture capitalist cares about are the following:

1. Problem
2. Your solution
3. Business model
4. Underlying magic/technology
5. Marketing and sales
6. Competition
7. Team
8. Projections and milestones
9. Status and time line
10. Summary and call to action

Your Task. Dust off that start-up fantasy you may have, and get to work. Prepare a slideshow that would satisfy Kawasaki's 10/20/30 rule: In ten slides and a presentation of no more than 20 minutes, address the ten topics that venture capitalists care about. Make sure that the fonts on your slides are at least 30 points in size. You may want to peek at the coverage of business plans in Chapter 13.

14.10 Delivering an Impromptu Elevator Speech (Objs. 1–4)

"Can you pass the elevator test?" asks presentation whiz Garr Reynolds in a new twist on the familiar scenario.[31] He suggests this technique as an aid in sharpening your core message. In this exercise you need to pitch your idea in a few brief moments instead of the 20 minutes you had been granted with your vice president of product marketing. You arrive at her door for your appointment as she is leaving, coat and briefcase in hand. Something has come up. This meeting is a huge opportunity for you if you want to get the OK from the executive team. Could you sell your idea during the elevator ride and the walk to the parking lot? Reynolds asks. Although this scenario may never happen, you will possibly be asked to shorten a presentation, say, from an hour to 30 minutes or from 20 minutes to 5 minutes. Could you make your message tighter and clearer?

Your Task. Take a business idea you may have, a familiar business topic you care about, or a promotion or raise you wish to request in a time of tight budgets. Create a spontaneous two- to five-minute speech making a good case for your core message. Even though you won't have much time to think about the details of your speech, you should be sufficiently familiar with the topic to boil it down and yet be persuasive.

14.11 Self-Contained Multimedia Activity: Creating a PowerPoint Presentation (No additional research required) (Objs. 2, 3)

You are a consultant who has been hired to improve the effectiveness of corporate trainers. These trainers frequently make presentations to employees on topics such as conflict management, teamwork, time management, problem solving, performance appraisals, and employment interviewing. Your goal is to teach these trainers how to make better presentations.

Your Task. Create six visually appealing slides.* Base the slides on the following content, which will be spoken during the presentation titled Effective Employee Training. The comments shown here are only a portion of a longer presentation.

> Trainers have two options when they make presentations. The first option is to use one-way communication: the trainer basically dumps the information on the employees and leaves. The second option is to use a two-way audience involvement approach. The two-way approach can accomplish many purposes, such as connecting the trainer with the employees, reinforcing key points, increasing employees' retention rates, changing the pace, and adding variety. The two-way approach also encourages employees to get to know each other better. Because today's employees demand more than just a "talking head," trainers must engage their audiences by involving them in a dialogue.
>
> When you include interactivity in your training sessions, choose approaches that suit your delivery style. Also, think about which options your employees would be likely to respond to most positively. Let's consider some interactivity approaches now. Realize, though, that these ideas are presented to help you get your creative juices flowing. After I present the list, we will think about situations in which these options might be effective. We will also brainstorm to come up with creative ideas we can add to this list.

- Ask employees to guess at statistics before revealing them.
- Ask an employee to share examples or experiences.
- Ask a volunteer to help you demonstrate something.
- Ask the audience to complete a questionnaire or worksheet.
- Ask the audience to brainstorm or list something as fast as possible.
- Ask a variety of question types to achieve different purposes.
- Invite the audience to work through a process or examine an object.
- Survey the audience.
- Pause to let the audience members read something to themselves.
- Divide the audience into small groups to discuss an issue.

14.12 Improving the Design and Content of PowerPoint Slides (Objs. 2, 3)

Your Task. Identify ways to improve the design and content of the three slides presented in Figure 14.9. Classify your comments under the following categories: (a) color choices, (b) font choice including style and point size, (c) 6-x-6 rule, (d) listings in parallel grammatical form,

*See the Instructor's Manual and the Instructor's Resource CD.

FIGURE 14.9 PowerPoint Slides Needing Revision

Webcasting Basics

- Hold meetings inexpensively.
- Broadcast via one of many options.
- Include Q&A sessions and live polls.
- Access meetings via Internet.
- View stored presentations when convenient.

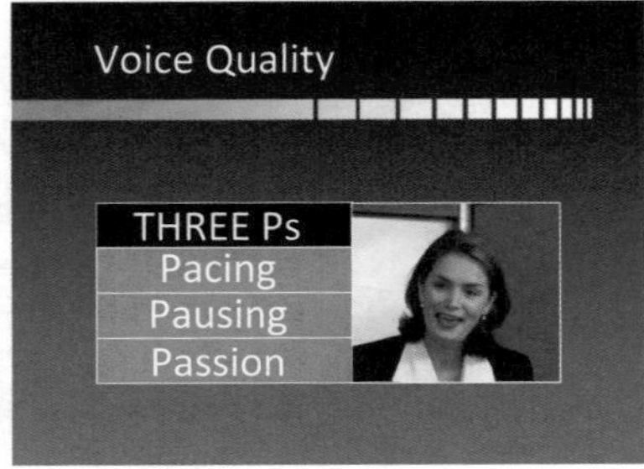

Webcasting Pointers

- Engage audience with personal stories.
- Stand to add energy to your voice.
- Remember that smiles are audible.
- Change slides frequently.
- Conclude with summary after Q&A session.

(e) consistent capitalization and punctuation, and (f) graphics and images. Identify what needs to be improved and exactly how you would improve it. For example, if you identify category (d) as an area needing improvement, your answer would include a revision of the listing. When you finish, your instructor may show you a revised set of slides.*

14.13 Researching *Fortune* List Information (Objs. 1–5)

Web

Your Task. Using an electronic database, perform a search to learn how *Fortune* magazine determines which companies make its annual lists. Research the following lists. Then organize and present a five- to ten-minute informative talk to your class.

a. Fortune 500
b. Global 500
c. 100 Best Companies to Work For
d. America's Most Admired Companies
e. Global Most Admired Companies

14.14 Choosing a Topic for an Oral Presentation (Objs. 1–6)

Team

Your Task. Select a topic from the following list or from the report topics in the activities at the ends of Chapters 11 and 12. For an expanded list of report topics, go to **www.meguffey.com.** Individually or as a team, prepare a five- to ten-minute oral presentation. Consider yourself an expert or a team of experts called in to explain some aspect of the topic before a group of interested people. Because your time is limited, prepare a concise yet forceful presentation with effective visual aids.

If this is a group presentation, form a team of three or four members and conduct thorough research on one of the following topics, as directed by your instructor. Follow the tips on team presentations in this chapter. Divide the tasks fairly, meet for discussions and rehearsals, and crown your achievement with a 15- to 20-minute presentation to your class. Make your PowerPoint presentation interesting and dynamic.

a. Is PowerPoint evil, as Yale professor emeritus Edward Tufte has claimed in his now famous essay? Consider this excerpt: "At a minimum, a presentation format should do no harm. Yet the PowerPoint style routinely disrupts, dominates, and trivializes content. Thus PowerPoint presentations too often resemble a school play—very loud, very slow, and very simple."
b. What information and tools are available at Web job banks to college students searching for full-time employment after graduation? Consider Monster.com and other job banks.
c. How could your peers (in college or in your workplace) be persuaded to make healthful food choices?
d. What simple computer security tips can your company employ to avoid problems?
e. What is telecommuting, and for what kind of workers is it an appropriate work alternative?
f. How could your company use Facebook or Twitter to advantage?
g. How can consumers protect themselves against identity theft?
h. What is the economic outlook for a given product, such as domestic cars, laptop computers, digital cameras, fitness equipment, or a product of your choice?
i. How can your organization or institution improve its image?
j. What are the Webby Awards, and what criteria do the judges use to evaluate Web sites?
k. What brand and model of computer and printer represent the best buy for college students today?
l. What franchise would offer the best investment opportunity for an entrepreneur in your area?
m. What are the differences among casual, business casual, and business formal attire?
n. Which smartphone on the market today offers the best features for businesspeople?
o. Are internships worth the effort?
p. What risks are involved for companies without written policies for e-mail, instant messaging, texting, and social media Web sites?
q. Where should your organization hold its next convention?
r. What is your opinion of the statement "Advertising steals our time, defaces the landscape, and degrades the dignity of public institutions"?[32]
s. What are the advantages and disadvantages of fractional ownership, say, of corporate jets or yachts?
t. What is the outlook for real estate (commercial or residential) investment in your area?
u. What are the pros and cons of videoconferencing for [name an organization]?
v. What do the personal assistants for celebrities do, and how does one become a personal assistant? (Investigate the Association of Celebrity Personal Assistants.)
w. Can a small or midsized company reduce its telephone costs by using Internet phone service?
x. What scams are on the Federal Trade Commission's List of Top 10 Consumer Scams, and how can consumers avoid falling for them?
y. What is fair trade coffee (or cocoa), and why should U.S. businesses such as Starbucks purchase it?
z. Should employees be allowed to use computers in a work environment for anything other than work-related business?

*See the Instructor's Manual and the Instructor's Resource CD.

14.15 Consumer: Will Maxing Out My Credit Cards Improve My Credit Rating? (Objs. 1–5)

Consumer | Web

The program chair for the campus business club has asked you to present a talk to the group about consumer credit. He saw a newspaper article saying that only 10 percent of Americans know their credit scores. Many consumers, including students, have dangerous misconceptions about their scores. Not knowing your score could result in a denial of credit as well as difficulty obtaining needed services and even a job.

Your Task. Using electronic databases and the Web, learn more about credit scores and typical misconceptions. For example, is a higher or lower credit score better? Can you improve your credit score by marrying well? If you earn more money, will you improve your score? If you have a low score, is it impossible to raise it? Can you raise your score by maxing out all your credit cards? (One survey reported that 28 percent of consumers believed the latter statement was true!) Prepare an oral presentation appropriate for a student audience. Conclude with appropriate recommendations.

14.16 Improving Telephone Skills by Role-Playing (Obj. 8)

Your Task. Your instructor will divide the class into pairs. For each scenario take a moment to read and rehearse your role silently. Then play the role with your partner. If time permits, repeat the scenarios, changing roles.

Partner 1	Partner 2
a. You are the personnel manager of Datatronics, Inc. Call Elizabeth Franklin, office manager at Computers Plus. Inquire about a job applicant, Chelsea Chavez, who listed Ms. Franklin as a reference. Respond to Partner 2.	a. You are the receptionist for Computers Plus. The caller asks for Elizabeth Franklin, who is home sick today. You don't know when she will be able to return. Answer the call appropriately.
b. Call Ms. Franklin again the following day to inquire about the same job applicant, Chelsea Chavez. Ms. Franklin answers today, but she talks on and on, describing the applicant in great detail. Tactfully close the conversation.	b. You are now Ms. Franklin, office manager. Describe Chelsea Chavez, an imaginary employee. Think of someone with whom you have worked. Include many details, such as her ability to work with others, her appearance, her skills at computing, her schooling, her ambition, and so forth.
c. You are now the receptionist for Tom Wing, of Wing Imports. Answer a call for Mr. Wing, who is working in another office, at Extension 134, where he will accept calls.	c. You are now an administrative assistant for attorney Michael Murphy. Call Tom Wing to verify a meeting date Mr. Murphy has with Mr. Wing. Use your own name in identifying yourself.
d. You are now Tom Wing, owner of Wing Imports. Call your attorney, Michael Murphy, about a legal problem. Leave a brief, incomplete message.	d. You are now the receptionist for attorney Michael Murphy. Mr. Murphy is skiing in Aspen and will return in two days, but he doesn't want his clients to know where he is. Take a message.
e. Call Mr. Murphy again. Leave a message that will prevent telephone tag.	e. Take a message again as the receptionist for attorney Michael Murphy.

14.17 Presenting Yourself Professionally on the Telephone and in Voice Mail (Obj. 8)

Practice the phone skills you learned in this chapter. Leave your instructor a professional voice mail message. Prepare a mini-agenda before you call. Introduce yourself. If necessary, spell your name and indicate the course and section. Speak slowly and clearly, especially when leaving your phone number. Think of a comment you could make about an intriguing fact, a peer discussion, or your business communication class.

14.18 Presenting Yourself as a Professional When Texting (Obj. 8)

Your phone skills extend not only to voice mail but also to the brief text messages you send to your boss and coworkers. Such *professional* texts are often markedly different in style and tone from the messages you may be exchanging with friends.

Your Task. Send a professional text message to your instructor or to another designated partner in class responding to one of the following scenarios: (a) Explain why you must be late to an important meeting; (b) request permission to purchase a piece of important equipment for the office; or (c) briefly summarize what you have learned in your latest staff development seminar (use a key concept from one of your business classes). Use the recipient's e-mail address to send your text. Do not use abbreviations or smiley faces.

Video Resource

Video Library 1, Effective On-the-Job Oral Presentations

In this video you see Ramon and Sarah in the planning stages of an oral presentation to the board of directors for Integrity Investments. Ramon must persuade the directors that a paid time-off plan makes sense for Integrity employees. Ramon and Sarah brainstorm ideas in the prewriting stage of the writing process. Notice how they apply the 3-x-3 writing process by anticipating the audience and focusing on a purpose. We see Ramon and Sarah go through all three phases of the process, including Ramon's successful presentation.

As you watch the film, be prepared to answer the following questions:

- How is the writing process useful in preparing an oral presentation?
- What techniques can a speaker employ to overcome fear?
- Should every business presentation use PowerPoint? Why or why not?

Are you ready? Get more practice at **www.meguffey.com**

Chat About It

In each chapter you will find five discussion questions related to the chapter material. Your instructor may assign these topics for you to discuss in class, in an online chat room, or on an online discussion board. Some of the discussion topics may require outside research. You may also be asked to read and respond to postings made by your classmates.

Topic 1: How would you classify your classmates as an audience to student presentations: friendly, neutral, uninterested, or hostile? Why?
Topic 2: Why do some presenters avoid making steady eye contact? What might these individuals do to correct this problem?
Topic 3: When might slides with an absolute minimum of text and a maximum of images not be effective?
Topic 4: Do some research to determine what made the "I Have a Dream" speech by Dr. Martin Luther King Jr. so memorable.
Topic 5: When is it acceptable not to return a call when a callback was requested?

Grammar and Mechanics C.L.U.E. Review 14

Total Review

Each of the following sentences has a total of **three** errors in grammar, punctuation, capitalization, usage, or spelling. On a separate sheet, write a correct version. Avoid adding new phrases, starting new sentences, or rewriting in your own words. When finished, compare your responses with the key beginning on page Key-1.

Example: She said that a list of our customers names and addresses were all ready available.
Revision: She said that a list of our **customers'** names and addresses **was already** available.

1. If you are planning a short presentation you should focus on about 3 main points and limit yourself to twenty minutes.
2. Because he was President of the company Mr. Yost made at least 6 major presentations every year.
3. The companys CPA asked me to explain the principle ways we planned to finance the thirty-year mortgage.
4. My accountant and me are greatful to be able to give a short presentation, however, we may not be able to cover the entire budget.
5. The introduction to a presentation should accomplish three goals, (a) Capture attention, (b) establish credibility, and (3) preview main points.
6. Steven wondered whether focusing on what the audience is to remember, and summarizing main points was equally important?
7. A list of suggestions for a speakers ideas are found in the article titled "How To Improve Your Listening Skills."
8. The appearance and mannerisms of a speaker definately effects a listeners evaluation of the message.
9. Melody Hobson, who is an expert speaker said that reading from slides is the Kiss of Death in a presentation.
10. In a poll of three thousand workers only one third felt that there companies valued their opinions.

Are you ready? Get more practice at **www.meguffey.com**

CHAPTER 12

Making the Connection

Understanding the Customer

In the next two chapters, we will continue to look at the functional areas of the company by examining the area of marketing. Marketers make decisions about what products to bring to market in conjunction with the overall strategic direction of the company, and then work with *operations* to design those products and allocate the resources needed to provide them—whether that be production facilities or alliances with other firms if it is a good that is being produced, or layouts and procedures to be followed if it is a service. And, of course, both marketing and operations need to work with *human resources* to make sure people with the needed skills are in place in all areas, as well as with *finance* to make sure the product is financially worthwhile for the company to pursue, and that funds will be available to pursue it. It is an integrated effort. This is evident from the example of Lexus in the chapter. The company "adopted a customer-driven approach with particular emphasis on service" by stressing "product *quality* with a standard of zero defects in manufacturing" and a service goal to "treat each customer as a guest in one's home." Marketing couldn't do this alone. It would have to work with operations to provide this level of product quality as well as human resources to provide this level of customer service. And it would also need an investment of funds to pull it all together.

But just think for a minute what would happen if there were no customer demand for the quality cars sold by Lexus? Just as the decisions that are made in the functional areas to bring a product to market are integrated, the decisions about which products to bring to market obviously have to be integrated with the outside environment—they must come ultimately from the customer. The customer is the central focal point of any successful business. Look at the critical success factors. As we've said many times, you can't *achieve financial success* if you aren't earning revenue, and you can't earn revenue if customers aren't buying your products. And they won't buy your products if they don't at least *meet and at best exceed* their expectations. That is what this chapter is all about—understanding your customers and creating a marketing strategy that satisfies their needs.

This requires that the company keep an eye on all areas of the external environment that may affect marketing decisions, as discussed in the chapter—but particularly on the *social* environment, including demographic changes—to understand the trends that affect customer needs, as well as to better understand the different factors that influence consumer decision making. As the chapter explains, it is important to do market research to understand the customer, and advances in *technology* have made that easier. Technology has also made it possible to create a unique marketing mix for each customer, discussed in the chapter as "one-to-one marketing," based on information kept on customers in the marketing database. The company also has to keep an eye on the *economic* environment to make sure it keeps ahead of the competition and that it takes into consideration the

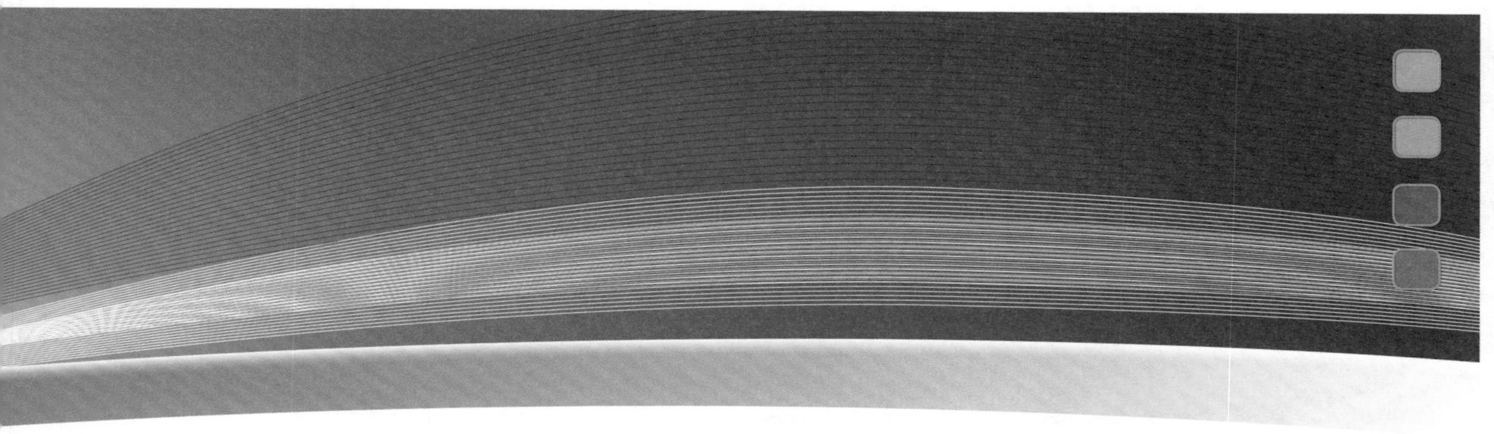

effect of changing incomes and interest rates, etc., as well as the *political* environment to make sure it is meeting all the requirements in its package labelling, etc.

Many concepts in this chapter are important for understanding marketing and its integrative nature. For example, in this chapter you will read about the marketing concept—focusing on customer wants and needs, and integrating the organization's activities in the functional areas to satisfy the customer, but doing so with a responsibility toward the *stakeholders*—profitably for the owners, ethically for the customer, and fairly for the employee. The marketing concept is an important integrative concept as it is the thread that ties all the marketing activities, functional areas, and the business as a whole together to stay focused on the customer and make decisions responsibly so that success is achieved with all the stakeholders in mind and all critical success factors met.

You'll also learn about relationship marketing. This is critical to the long-term success of the company—meeting the critical success factors over time by establishing long-term relationships with customers. This can be done through loyalty programs as one example, but also requires *commitment* from your employees to be customer oriented. As discussed in the chapter, employee attitudes and actions are critical to building relationships. A good example of this is WestJet airlines. Just give them a call and chat with one of their reps, and then call another airline, and you'll see the difference in attitude toward the customer.

Target marketing is another important concept. Identifying a target market helps a company focus marketing efforts on those customers most likely to buy its products. The unique features of the product that appeal to the target group and are seen by the target group as superior to competitive offerings are the company's competitive advantage. If that competitive advantage is cost—operating at a lower cost than competitors and passing this saving on to the customer (as in Wal-Mart)—we see another integration of marketing with the other functional areas. This cost advantage is gained through using less expensive raw materials and/or controlling overhead costs (finance), and making plant operations more efficient and/or designing products that are easier to manufacture (operations), and so on. This is achieved by these areas through people committed to this goal, often with the help of technology.

And finally, the target market of consumers whose needs the company is focusing on is determined after segmenting the market. Though it seems like a purely marketing exercise—dividing up the market of consumers into different groups based on some common characteristics—it has some very definite integrative implications. Take Avon's foray into a new customer segment—teenagers and young women, as discussed in the opening vignette—with a new cosmetics line called "mark." The social environment would have influenced the move, with demographic variables and buying behaviour making the 15- to 24-year-old age group particularly appealing. This in turn caused changes in the functional areas to accommodate the new line, particularly the move to recruit teens as sales representatives, a very innovative move on the part of Avon. Marketing is without a doubt a very central integrative function within a successful business.

CHAPTER 12

Understanding the Customer

LEARNING OUTCOMES

1 Define marketing concept, and relationship marketing.

2 Show how managers create a marketing strategy.

3 Explain marketing mix.

4 Summarize how consumers and organizations make buying decisions.

5 List the five basic forms of market segmentation.

6 Identify how marketing research is used in marketing decision making.

7 List some of the trends in understanding the consumer.

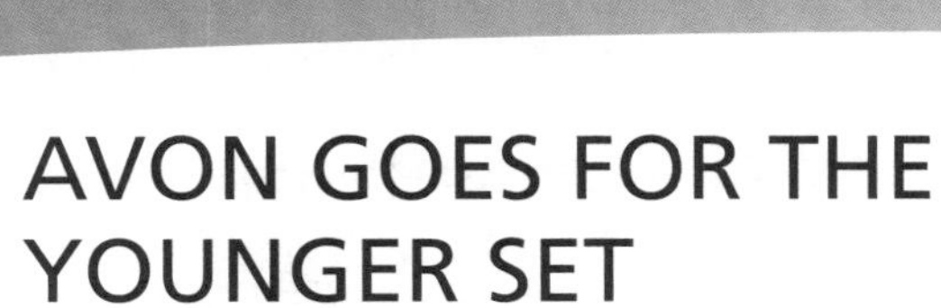

AVON GOES FOR THE YOUNGER SET

Avon Products, Inc. (**www.avon.com**) is attempting to ring the doorbells of a new customer generation: teenagers and young women. The big direct seller of beauty products, eager to reach 16- to 24-year-old shoppers who mostly associate the Avon name with their mothers, launched a cosmetics line called "mark." The hip packaging was distinctly more upscale than other teen-focused brands, including Procter & Gamble's Cover Girl or mass market brands such as Bonne Bell. It was also trendier than Avon's traditional look, which is aimed squarely at 25- to 55-year-old women. However, the $65 million in revenue fell short of the $100 million projected for the first year of mark's introduction. The director of consumer marketing and creative services for the mark brand has focused on new products, new advertising, and new partnerships to attract the younger customers. The brand has become more recognizable through campaigns such as "Girls' empowerment." See the mark branding at (www.meetmark.com) or (www.markcanada.ca).[1]

Avon is recruiting teens as sales representatives, even as it pushes ahead on efforts to boost its main North American sales ranks. Although the company expects some door-to-door selling by its new recruits, it envisions youth sales mostly taking place among groups of friends at slumber parties and other informal gatherings. Avon hopes the opportunity to sell cosmetics to peers will prove more alluring than toiling behind the counter in fast-food restaurants.

About 2.2 million young women in Canada are in the 15- to 24-year-old age group,[2] and many of them spend money on beauty and beauty-related products. "It's not just lip gloss," says Deborah I. Fine, the former publisher of *Glamour* magazine tapped by Avon to lead the youth charge. "It's lip gloss with an earnings opportunity."

Avon executives say research shows that young women have a "neutral to positive" image of the company. But when mark made its debut, its own name was in lights. The name Avon appears, but only in tiny letters.[3]

Critical Thinking Questions

1. **Why do companies identify target customers for their products?**
2. **Why is it important to differentiate a product?**
3. **How does a company like Avon find out what customers and potential customers want in the way of cosmetics?**

SOURCE: Stephanie Thompson, "Avon struggles to make mark on young buyers," in *Advertising Age* (Midwest region edition). Chicago: February 28, 2005; Sally Beatty, "Avon Is Set to Call on Teens," *Wall Street Journal*, October 17. © 2002 by Dow Jones & Co. Inc.

marketing
The process of discovering the needs and wants of potential buyers and customers and then providing goods and services that meet or exceed their expectations.

products
In marketing, any good or service, along with its perceived attributes and benefits, that creates value for the customer.

exchange
The process in which two parties give something of value to each other to satisfy their respective needs.

*Marketing played an important role in Avon's successful launch of mark. Marketing is the process of getting the right goods or services to the right people at the right place, time, and price, using the right promotion techniques. This concept is referred to as the "right" principle. We can say that **marketing** is finding out the needs and wants of potential buyers and customers and then providing goods and services (i.e., **products**—discussed in more detail in Chapter 13) that meet or exceed their expectations. Marketing is about creating exchanges. An **exchange** takes place when two parties give something of value to each other to satisfy their respective needs. In a typical exchange, a consumer trades money for a good or service.*

To encourage exchanges, marketers follow the "right" principle. If your local Avon rep doesn't have the right lipstick for you when you want it, at the right price, you will not exchange money for a new lipstick from Avon. Think about the last exchange (purchase) you made: What if the price had been 30 percent higher? What if the store or other source had been less accessible? Would you have bought anything? The "right" principle tells us that marketers control many factors that determine marketing success. In this chapter, you will learn about the marketing concept and how organizations create a marketing strategy. You will learn how the marketing mix is used to create sales opportunities. Next, we examine how and why consumers and organizations make purchase decisions. Then, we will discuss the important concept of market segmentation, which helps marketing managers focus on the most likely purchasers of their wares. We conclude the chapter by examining how marketing research and decision support systems help guide marketing decision making.

HOT Links

What's new at Avon since it launched its mark line? Browse the company's website, at **(www.avoncompany.com)**, to find out how the teen products are doing.

The Marketing Concept

marketing concept
Identifying consumer needs, and then producing the goods or services that will satisfy them while making a profit for the organization.

If you study today's best organizations, you'll see that they have adopted the **marketing concept**, which involves identifying consumer needs and then producing the goods or services that will satisfy them while making a profit. The marketing concept is oriented toward pleasing consumers by offering value. Specifically, the marketing concept involves

- focusing on customer wants, so the organization can distinguish its product(s) from competitors' offerings;
- integrating all of the organization's activities, including production, to satisfy these wants; and
- achieving long-term goals for the organization by satisfying customer wants and needs legally and responsibly.

Today, companies of every size in all industries are applying the marketing concept. Enterprise Rent-A-Car found that its customers didn't want to have to drive to its offices. Therefore, Enterprise began delivering vehicles to customer homes or places of work. Disney found that some of its patrons really disliked waiting in lines. In response, Disney began offering FastPass at a premium price, which allows patrons to avoid standing in long lines waiting for attractions.

production orientation
An approach in which a firm works to lower production costs without a strong desire to satisfy the needs of customers.

Firms have not always followed the marketing concept. Around the time of the Industrial Revolution in North America (1860–1910), firms had a **production orientation**, which meant that they worked to lower production costs without a strong desire to satisfy the needs of their customers. To do this, organizations concentrated on mass production, focusing internally on maximizing the efficiency of operations, increasing output, and ensuring uniform quality. They also asked such questions as: What can we do best? What can our engineers design? What is economical and easy to produce with our equipment?

There is nothing wrong with assessing a firm's capabilities. In fact, such assessments are necessary in planning. But the production orientation does not consider whether what the firm produces most efficiently also meets the needs of the marketplace. By implementing the marketing concept, an organization looks externally to the consumers in the marketplace and commits to customer value, customer satisfaction, and relationship marketing, as explained in this section.

customer value
The ratio of benefits to the sacrifice necessary to obtain those benefits, as determined by the customer; reflects the willingness of customers to buy a product.

customer satisfaction
The customer's feeling that a product has met or exceeded expectations.

Customer Value

Customer value is the ratio of benefits to the sacrifice necessary to obtain those benefits. The customer determines the value of both the benefits and the sacrifices. Creating customer value is a core business strategy of many successful firms. Customer value is rooted in the belief that price is not the only thing that matters. A business that focuses on the cost of production and price to the customer will be managed as though it were providing a commodity differentiated only by price. In contrast, businesses that provide customer value believe that many customers will pay a premium for superior customer service. Sir Colin Marshall, former chairman of the board of British Airways (BA), is explicit about his commitment to superior customer service, insisting that BA can succeed only by meeting all of its customer value-driven needs, not just price.[4]

The automobile industry also illustrates the importance of creating customer value. To penetrate the fiercely competitive luxury automobile market, Lexus adopted a customer-driven approach, with particular emphasis on service. Lexus stresses product quality with a standard of zero defects in manufacturing. The service quality goal is to treat each customer as one would treat a guest in one's home, to pursue the perfect person-to-person relationship, and to strive to improve continually. This strategy has enabled Lexus to establish a clear quality image and capture a significant share of the luxury car market.

© COURTESY OF GEICO

CONCEPT *in Action* >>>

Geico—the major auto insurer with the scaly mascot—famously boasts a 97 percent customer-satisfaction rating, based on an independent study conducted by Alan Newman Research, 2006. With this claim, communicated through the company's quirky and ubiquitous advertising, consumers get the message that Geico delivers quality insurance coverage at low prices. What factors do you think impact the customer-satisfaction ratings for an auto insurer like Geico?

Customer Satisfaction

Customer satisfaction is a theme that we have stressed throughout the text. **Customer satisfaction** is the customer's feeling that a product or service has met or exceeded expectations. Lexus consistently wins awards for its outstanding customer satisfaction. J. D. Power and Associates surveys car owners two years after they make their purchase. The Customer Satisfaction Survey is made up of four measures that each describes an element of overall ownership satisfaction at two years: vehicle quality/reliability, vehicle appeal, ownership costs, and service satisfaction from a dealer. Lexus continues to lead the industry. Lexus manager Stuart McCullough comments, "In close collaboration with our dealers we aim to provide the best customer service, not only in the car industry, but in any industry. The J. D. Power surveys are a testament to our success in making our customers happy."[5]

At Doubletree Hotels, guests are asked to fill out a CARE card several times during their stay to let staff know how they are doing. Managers check the cards daily to solve guests' problems before they check out. Guests can also use a CARE phone line to call in their complaints at the hotel. A CARE committee continually seeks ways to improve guest services. The goal is to offer a solution to a CARE call in 15 minutes. Embassy Suites goes one step further by offering a full refund to guests who are not satisfied with their stay.

Building Relationships

relationship marketing
A strategy that focuses on forging long-term partnerships with customers by offering value and providing customer satisfaction.

Relationship marketing is a strategy that focuses on forging long-term partnerships with customers. Companies build relationships with customers by offering value and providing customer satisfaction. Companies benefit from repeat sales and referrals that lead to increases in sales, market share, and profits. Costs fall because it is less expensive to serve existing customers than to attract new ones. Keeping an existing customer costs about one-fourth of what it costs to attract a new one, and the probability of retaining a customer is more than 60 percent, whereas the probability of landing a new customer is less than 30 percent.[6]

Customers also benefit from stable relationships with suppliers. Business buyers have found that partnerships with their suppliers are essential to producing high-quality products while cutting costs. Customers remain loyal to firms that provide them greater value and satisfaction than they expect from competing firms.

Customer relationship management (CRM)
The processes used by organizations to track and organize information about current and prospective customers.

Customer relationship management (CRM) are the processes an organization uses to track and organize information regarding current and prospective customers. This includes information about the customers or potential customers, past history with the organization, and future prospects. Usually this involves the implementation of CRM software that can automate the data collection and correlate the data to be used later to increase customer satisfaction and sales.

Loyalty programs, sometimes referred to as frequent-buyer clubs, are an excellent way to build long-term relationships. Most major airlines have frequent-flyer programs. After flying a certain number of miles, you become eligible for a free ticket. Now, cruise lines, hotels, car rental agencies, credit card companies, and even mortgage companies give away "airline miles" with purchases. Consumers patronize the airline and its partners, because they want the free tickets. Thus, the program helps to create a long-term relationship with the customer.

If an organization is to build relationships with customers, its employees' attitudes and actions must be customer oriented. Any person, department, or division that is not customer oriented weakens the positive image of the entire organization. An employee might be the only contact a potential customer has with the firm. In that

CONCEPT *in Action* >>>

As a "guest" on WestJet, you can expect friendly, casual, yet competent service from everyone you encounter, from captain to customer service representative. How does this create customer satisfaction and value to the customer?

PHOTO COURTESY OF WESTJET.

concept check

Explain the marketing concept.

Explain the difference between customer value and customer satisfaction.

What is meant by relationship marketing?

person's eyes, the employee is the firm. If greeted discourteously, the potential customer might well assume that the employee's attitude represents the whole firm.

Building long-term relationships with customers is an excellent way for small businesses to compete against the big chains. Sometimes small firms, with few employees, are in a better position to focus on a tiny segment of the market.

Creating a Marketing Strategy

There is no secret formula for creating goods and services that provide customer value and customer satisfaction. An organization that is committed to providing superior customer satisfaction puts customers at the very centre of its marketing strategy. Creating a customer-focused *marketing strategy* involves four main steps: understanding the external environment, defining the target market, creating a competitive advantage, and developing a marketing mix. In this section, we will examine the first three steps, and in the next section, we will discuss how a company develops a marketing mix.

environmental scanning
The process by which a firm continually collects and evaluates information about its external environment.

Understanding the External Environment

Unless marketing managers understand the external environment, a firm cannot intelligently plan for the future. Thus, many organizations assemble a team of specialists to continually collect and evaluate environmental information, a process called **environmental scanning**. The goal in gathering the environmental data is to identify future market opportunities and threats.

Computer manufacturers understand the importance of environmental scanning to monitor rapidly changing consumer interests. Since the invention of the PC, techies have taken two things for granted: Processor speeds will grow exponentially, and PCs will become indistinguishable from televisions—that there will be, in industry lingo, convergence. The first prediction obviously has come true, and the second is beginning. Consumers may not like to watch movies on their PCs, but they love listening to music on them. They may not like to send e-mail from their couch, but they love having a PC—known as a digital video recorder—attached to the TV to automatically record all their favourite shows. And although they won't buy an old-fashioned TV from Dell or HP, when it comes to flat-screen TVs, they have no problem at all.

For PC makers, it's also good business. Prices and margins for computers keep falling; gross margins in consumer electronics are twice those in the PC world. And now that the music and movies consumers play on those systems are the same zeros and ones that are the foundation of PCs, there is little conversion cost.

In general, six categories of environmental data shape marketing decisions:

- *Social forces*, such as the values of potential customers and the changing roles of families
- *Demographic forces*, such as the ages, birth and death rates, and locations of various groups of people
- *Economic forces*, such as changing incomes, inflation, and recession
- *Technological forces*, such as advances in communications and data retrieval capabilities
- *Political and legal forces*, such as changes in laws and regulatory agency activities
- *Competitive forces* from domestic and foreign-based firms.

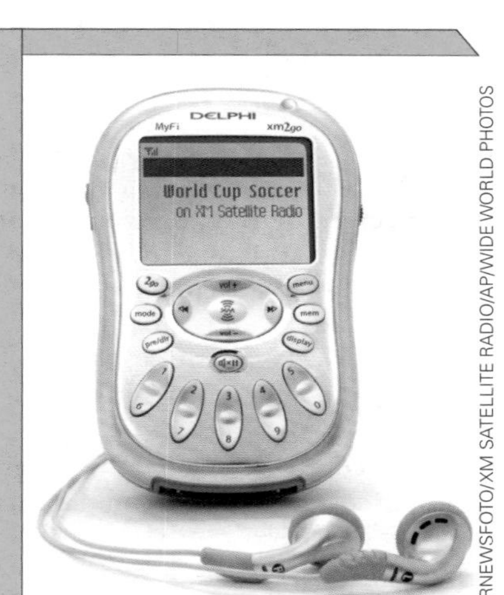

© PRNEWSFOTO/XM SATELLITE RADIO/AP/WIDE WORLD PHOTOS

CONCEPT *in Action* >>>

In the race to be Canada's premier satellite radio provider, two firms lead the pack. XM, the original pioneer of subscriber-based radio, offers listeners the best in entertainment including exclusive digital streams of major league sports and Oprah Winfrey. Rival company Sirius lures subscribers with a programming mix that includes NBA games and edgy adult banter from shock jock Howard Stern. What factors might constitute a competitive advantage for companies in the satellite radio business?

Defining the Target Market

target market
The specific group of consumers toward which a firm directs its marketing efforts.

Managers and employees focus on providing value for a well-defined target market. The **target market** is the specific group of consumers toward which a firm directs its marketing efforts. It is selected from the larger overall market. For instance, Carnival Cruise Lines says its main target market is "blue-collar entrepreneurs," people with an income of $25,000 to $50,000 a year who own auto supply shops, dry cleaners, and the like. Unlike other cruise lines, it does not seek affluent retirees. Laura's Shoppe Canada Limited has several different types of stores, each for a distinct target market: Laura's for average-size women, Laura Petites for petite women, Laura II for plus-size women, and Melanie Lyne for upscale women's apparel featuring designer labels.

Identifying a target market helps a company focus its marketing efforts on those who are most likely to buy its products or services. Concentrating on potential customers lets the firm use its resources efficiently. The target markets for Marriott International's lodging alternatives are shown in Exhibit 12.1. The latest in the Marriott family is SpringHill Suites. The SpringHill idea came from another Marriott chain, Fairfield Suites, an offshoot of Marriott's Fairfield Inns. The suites, opened in the late 1990's, were roomy but devoid of most frills: The closets didn't have doors, and the lobby floors were covered with linoleum. Some franchisees complained to Marriott that the suites were *under*priced: Fairfield Suites guests were saying they would pay a little more for a few more frills, so Marriott began planning an upgrade. To create each of the first 20 or so SpringHill locations, Marriott spent $200,000 renovating an existing Fairfield Suites unit, adding ergonomic chairs, ironing boards, and other amenities. Lobbies at SpringHill hotels are fancier than the rooms themselves: The lobbies have fireplaces, breakfast rooms, crown mouldings at the ceiling, and granite or ceramic tile floors.

Creating a Competitive Advantage

competitive advantage
A set of unique features of a company and its products that are perceived by the target market as significant and superior to those of the competition; also called *differential advantage*.

cost competitive advantage
A firm's ability to produce a product or service at a lower cost than all other competitors in an industry while maintaining satisfactory profit margins.

A competitive advantage, also called a differential advantage, is a set of unique features of a company and its products that are perceived by the target market as significant and superior to those of the competition. As Andrew Grove, CEO of Intel, says, "You have to understand what it is you are better at than anybody else and mercilessly focus your efforts on it." **Competitive advantage** is the factor or factors that cause customers to patronize a firm and not the competition. There are three types of competitive advantage: cost, product/service differential, and niche.

Cost competitive advantage A firm that has a **cost competitive advantage** can produce a product (goods and/or services) at a lower cost than all its competitors

EXHIBIT 12.1 > The Target Markets for Marriott International

	Price Range	Target Market
Fairfield Inn	$45–65	Economizing business and leisure travellers
TownePlace Suites	$55–70	Moderate-tier travellers who stay three to four weeks
SpringHill Suites	$75–95	Business and leisure travellers looking for more space and amenities
Courtyard	$75–105	Travellers seeking quality and affordable accommodations designed for the road warrior
Residence Inn	$85–110	Travellers seeking a residential-style hotel
Marriott Hotels, Resorts, and Suites	$90–235	Grounded achievers who desire consistent quality
Renaissance Hotels and Resorts	$90–235	Discerning business and leisure travellers who seek creative attention to detail
Ritz-Carlton	$175–300	Senior executives and entrepreneurs looking for a unique, luxurious, personalized experience

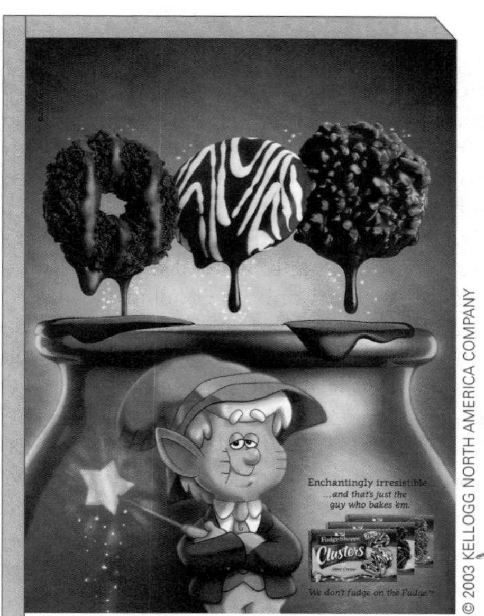

CONCEPT *in Action* >>>

A differential competitive advantage offers a unique value to consumers. The Keebler Company promises chocolate lovers that their Fudge Shoppe Clusters "don't fudge on the fudge." Considering some of the retail stores you are familiar with, what competitive advantages do they have?

while maintaining satisfactory profit margins. Firms become cost leaders by obtaining inexpensive raw materials, making plant operations more efficient, designing products for ease of manufacture, controlling overhead costs, and avoiding marginal customers.

Over time, the cost competitive advantage might fail. Typically, if one firm is using an innovative technology to reduce its costs, then others in the industry will adopt this technology and reduce their costs as well. For example, Bell Labs invented fibre optic cables, which reduced the cost of voice and data transmission by dramatically increasing the number of calls that could be transmitted simultaneously through a 5 cm cable. Within five years, however, fibre optic technology had spread through the industry, and Bell Labs lost its cost competitive advantage. Firms might also lose their cost competitive advantage if competing firms match their low costs by using the same lower cost suppliers. Therefore, a cost competitive advantage might not offer a long-term competitive advantage.

differential competitive advantage
A firm's ability to provide a unique product or service with a set of features that the target market perceives as important and better than the competitor's.

Differential Competitive Advantage A product/service **differential competitive advantage** exists when a firm provides something unique that is valuable to buyers beyond simply offering a low price. Differential competitive advantages tend to be longer lasting than cost competitive advantages, because cost advantages are subject to continual erosion as competitors catch up.

The durability of a differential competitive advantage tends to make this strategy more attractive to many top managers. Common differential advantages are brand names (Lexus), a strong dealer network (Caterpillar Tractor for construction equipment), product reliability (Maytag washers), image (Holt Renfrew in retailing), and service (Federal Express). Brand names such as Coca-Cola, BMW, and Cartier stand for quality the world over. Through continual product and marketing innovations and attention to quality and value, managers at these organizations have created enduring competitive advantages. Arthur Doppelmayr, an Austrian manufacturer of aerial transport systems (Doppelmayr Lifts), believes his main differential advantage, besides innovative equipment design, is his service system which allows the company to come to the assistance of users anywhere in the world within 24 hours. Doppelmayr uses a worldwide system of warehouses and skilled personnel prepared to move immediately in emergency cases.

niche competitive advantage
A firm's ability to target and effectively serve a single segment of the market within a limited geographic area.

Niche Competitive Advantage A company with a **niche competitive advantage** targets and effectively serves a single segment of the market within a limited geographic area. For small companies with limited resources that potentially face giant competitors, "niche-ing" might be the only viable option. A market segment that has good growth potential but is not crucial to the success of major competitors is a good candidate for a niche strategy. Once a potential segment has been identified, the firm needs to make certain it can defend against challengers through its superior ability to serve buyers in the segment. For example, STI Music Private Bank Group follows a niche strategy with its concentration on country music stars and entertainment industry professionals in Nashville. Its office is in the heart of Nashville's music district. STI has decided to expand its niche strategy to Miami, the "epicentre" of Latin music; and Atlanta. The latter is a long-time rhythm-and-blues capital and is now the centre of contemporary "urban" music. Both new markets have the kinds of music professionals—entertainers, record executives, producers, agents, and others—that have made STI so successful in Nashville.

concept check

What is environmental scanning?

What is a target market, and why should a company have one?

Explain the three types of competitive advantages, and provide examples of each.

Developing a Marketing Mix

marketing mix
The blend of product offering, pricing, promotional methods, and distribution system that brings a specific group of consumers superior value.

four Ps (4Ps)
Product, price, promotion, and place (distribution), which together make up the marketing mix.

product strategy
Taking the good or service and selecting a brand name, packaging, colours, a warranty, accessories, and a service program.

pricing strategy
Setting a price based on the demand and cost for a good or service.

distribution strategy
Creating the means by which products flow from the producer to the consumer.

Once a firm has defined its target market and identified its competitive advantage, it can create the **marketing mix**, that is, the blend of product offering, pricing, promotional methods, and distribution system that brings a specific group of consumers superior value. Distribution is sometimes referred to as place, so the marketing mix is based on the **four Ps (4Ps)**: product, price, promotion, and place. Every target market requires a unique marketing mix to satisfy the needs of the target consumers and meet the firm's goals. A strategy must be constructed for each of the 4Ps and blended with the strategies for the other elements. Thus, the marketing mix is only as good as its weakest part. An excellent product with a poor distribution system could be doomed to failure. A successful marketing mix requires careful tailoring. For instance, at first glance you might think that McDonald's and Wendy's have roughly the same marketing mix. After all, they are both in the fast-food business. But McDonald's targets parents with young children through Ronald McDonald, heavily promoted children's Happy Meals, and playgrounds. Wendy's is targeted to a more adult crowd. Wendy's has no playgrounds, but it does have carpeting in some locations (a more adult atmosphere) and has expanded its menu to include items for adult tastes.

Product Strategy

Marketing strategy typically starts with the product. You can't plan a distribution system or set a price if you don't know what you're going to market. Marketers use the term *product* to refer to both *goods*, such as tires, stereos, and clothing, and *services*, such as hotels, hair salons, and restaurants. Thus, the heart of the marketing mix is the good or service. Creating a **product strategy** involves choosing a brand name, packaging, colours, a warranty, accessories, and a service program.

Marketers view products in a much larger context than you might imagine. They include not only the item itself but also the brand name and the company image. The names Ralph Lauren and Gucci, for instance, create extra value for everything from cosmetics to bath towels. That is, products with those names sell at higher prices than identical products without the names. Another example, Holt Renfrew's company image is one of quality and superior service. We buy things not only for what they do but also for what they mean. Product strategies are discussed further in Chapter 13.

© CBS/LANDOV

CONCEPT *in Action* >>>

With their computerized profile-matching capabilities, online dating services are a high-tech way to make a love connection. Today's date-seeking singles want more than automated personals, however. They want advice from experts. At Match.com, popular shrink Dr. Phil guides subscribers towards healthy relationships. At eHarmony.com, Dr. Neil Clark Warren helps the lovelorn find a soul mate. How do Internet dating services use various elements of the marketing mix to bolster the effectiveness of their product strategies?

Pricing Strategy

Pricing strategy is based on demand for the product and the cost of producing it. Some special considerations can also influence the price. Sometimes, for instance, a special introductory price is used to get people to try a new product. Some firms enter the market with low prices and keep them low, such as Carnival Cruise Lines and Suzuki cars. Others enter a market with very high prices and then lower them over time, such as producers of high-definition televisions and personal computers. You can learn more about pricing strategies in Chapter 13.

Distribution Strategy

Distribution strategy is creating the means (the channel) by which a product flows from the producer to the consumer. One aspect of distribution strategy is deciding how many stores and which specific wholesalers and retailers will handle the product in a geographic area. Cosmetics, for instance, are distributed in many different ways. Avon has a sales force of several hundred thousand representatives who call directly on consumers.

Clinique and Estée Lauder are distributed through selected department stores. Cover Girl and Del Laboratories use mostly chain drugstores and other mass merchandisers. Redken sells through beauticians. Revlon uses several of these distribution channels. Distribution is examined in detail in Chapter 13.

Promotion Strategy

promotion strategy
The unique combination of personal selling, advertising, publicity, and sales promotion to stimulate the target market to buy a product or service.

Many people feel that promotion is the most exciting part of the marketing mix. **Promotion strategy** covers personal selling, advertising, public relations, and sales promotion. Each element is coordinated with the others to create a promotional blend. An advertisement, for instance, helps a buyer get to know the company and paves the way for a sales call. A good promotion strategy can dramatically increase a firm's sales. Promotion is examined in Chapter 13.

Public relations plays a special role in promotion. It is used to create a good image of the company and its products. Bad publicity costs nothing to send out, but it can cost a firm a great deal in lost business. Good publicity, such as a television or magazine story about a firm's new product, can be the result of much time, money, and effort spent by a public relations department.

Sales promotion directly stimulates sales. It includes trade shows, catalogues, contests, games, premiums, coupons, and special offers. Tim Hortons discount coupons and "Roll up the rim to win" contests offering money and food prizes are examples of sales promotions.

Not-for-Profit Marketing

HOT Links

Considering a career in marketing? See various options in marketing (or any other field) at **http://www.workopolis.ca**.

Profit-oriented companies are not the only ones that analyze the marketing environment, find a competitive advantage, and create a marketing mix. The application of marketing principles and techniques is also vital to not-for-profit organizations. Marketing helps not-for-profit groups identify target markets and develop effective marketing mixes. In some cases, marketing has kept symphonies, museums, and other cultural groups from having to close their doors. In other organizations, marketing ideas and techniques have helped managers do their jobs better. In the private sector, the profit motive is both an objective for guiding decisions

CONCEPT *in Action* >>>

The Canadian Red Cross, a not-for-profit organization, uses social marketing to remind families to prepare their homes and families for emergencies and disasters. What are differences and similarities in marketing in for-profit and not-for-profit organizations?

HOT Links

Visit the website for the Canadian Museum of Civilization at (www.civilization.ca).

social marketing
The application of marketing techniques to social issues and causes.

and a criterion for evaluating results. Not-for-profit organizations do not seek to make a profit for redistribution to owners or shareholders. Rather, their focus is often on generating enough funds to cover expenses. For example, organized religions do not gauge their success by the amount of money left in offering plates. The Canadian Museum of Civilization does not base its performance evaluations on the dollar value of tokens put into the turnstile.

Not-for-profit marketing is also concerned with social marketing, that is, the application of marketing to social issues and causes. The goals of social marketing are to effect social change (for instance, by creating racial harmony), further social causes (for instance, by helping the homeless), and evaluate the relationship between marketing and society (for instance, by asking whether society should allow advertising on television shows for young children). Individual organizations also engage in social marketing. Mothers Against Drunk Driving (MADD) counsels against drunk driving, and the Canadian Wildlife Federation asks your help in protecting endangered animals and birds and their spaces.

concept check

What is meant by the marketing mix?

What are the components of the marketing mix?

How can marketing techniques help not-for-profit organizations?

Define social marketing.

Buyer Behaviour

LO 4

buyer behaviour
The actions people take in buying and using goods and services.

An organization cannot reach its goals without understanding buyer behaviour. Buyer behaviour is the actions people take in buying and using goods and services. Marketers who understand buyer behaviour, such as how a price increase will affect a product's sales, can create a more effective marketing mix.

To understand buyer behaviour, marketers must understand how consumers make buying decisions. The consumer decision-making process has several steps, which are shown in Exhibit 12.2. The entire process is affected by cultural, social, individual, and psychological factors. The buying process starts with need recognition. This might be as simple as running out of coffee. Yes, I need to purchase more coffee. Or perhaps you recently got married and recognize that you need to start building equity instead of paying rent. Perhaps you are also considering starting a family. Therefore, you decide to buy your first home (Step 1 in Exhibit 12.2).

Next, you begin to gather information about financing, available homes, styles, locations, and so forth (Step 2). After you feel that you have gathered enough information, you begin to evaluate alternatives (Step 3). For example, you might eliminate all homes that cost more than $250,000 or are more than a 30-minute drive to your work. Then an offer is made and, if it is accepted, a purchase is made (Step 4). Finally, you assess the experience and your level of satisfaction with your new home (Step 5).

© THINKSTOCK / GETTY IMAGES

CONCEPT *in Action* >>>

Many companies target consumers reaching retirement age and other baby boomers with advertisements promoting their products. Demographic segmentation is the most common form of market segmentation. What products are specifically targeted to the following groups: age 14–25, 25–50, and over 50?

Influences on Consumer Decision-Making

Cultural, social, individual, and psychological factors have an impact on consumer decision-making from the time a person recognizes a need through post-purchase behaviour. We will examine each of these in more detail.

Culture Purchase roles within the family are influenced by culture. Culture is the set of values, ideas, attitudes, and symbols created to shape human behaviour. Culture is environmentally oriented. The Sami of northern Europe (Kola Peninsula of Russia, Finland, Norway, and Sweden) have developed a culture for Arctic survival. Similarly, the indigenous people of the Brazilian jungle have created a culture suitable for jungle living.

Culture, by definition, is social in nature. It is human interaction that creates values and prescribes acceptable behaviour. Thus, culture gives

EXHIBIT 12.2 > Consumer Decision-Making Process

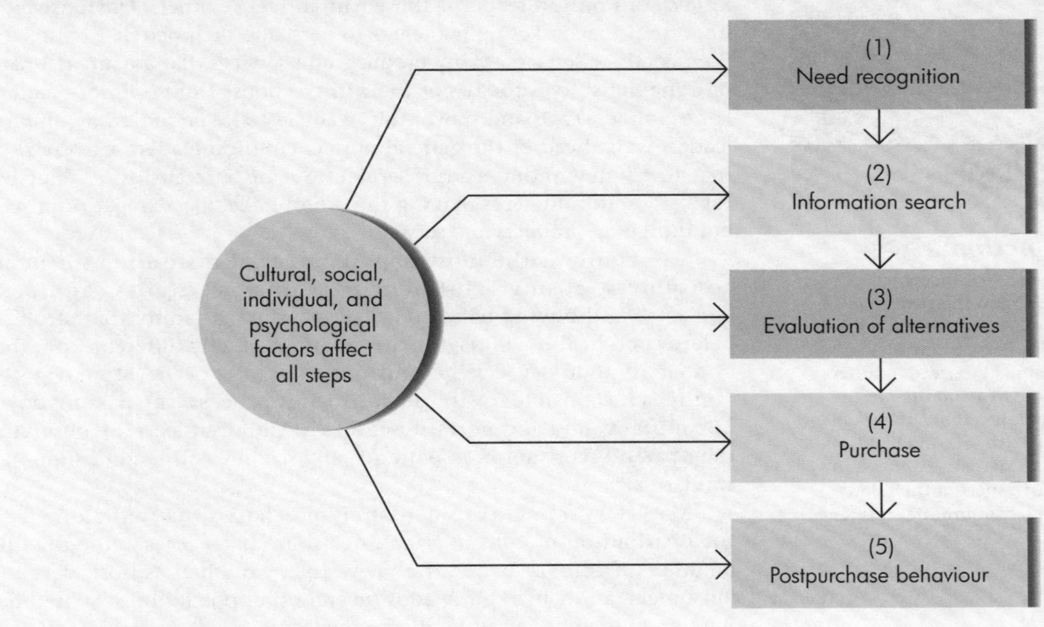

culture
The set of values, ideas, attitudes, and other symbols created to shape human behaviour.

order to society by creating common expectations. Sometimes these expectations are codified into law; for example, if you come to a red light, you stop the car. As long as a value or belief meets the needs of society, it will remain part of the culture; if it is no longer functional, the value or belief recedes. The value that very large families are "good" is no longer held by a majority of Canadians. As Canadians live more in an urban rather than a rural environment, children are no longer needed to perform farm chores.

Culture is not static. It adapts to changing societal needs and evolving environmental factors. The rapid growth of technology has accelerated the rate of cultural change. Inventions such as the elevator made possible modern high-rise cities. Television changed entertainment patterns and family communication flows, and heightened public awareness of political and other news events. The Internet has changed how we communicate and how most of us work.

Social Factors Most consumers are likely to seek out the opinions of others to reduce their search and evaluation effort or uncertainty, especially as the perceived risk of the decision increases. Consumers might also seek out others' opinions for guidance on new products or services, products with image-related attributes, or products where attribute information is lacking or uninformative. Specifically, consumers interact socially with reference groups, opinion leaders, and family members to obtain product information and decision approval. All the formal and informal groups that influence the buying behaviour of an individual are that person's **reference groups**. Consumers might use products or brands to identify with or become a member of a group. They learn from observing how members of their reference groups consume, and they use the same criteria to make their own consumer decisions. A reference

reference groups
Formal and informal groups that influence buyer behaviour.

CONCEPT *in Action* >>>

Since its launching in 2004, Facebook has the become the largest Internet social network with upwards of 50 million users. Originally created for Harvard university students, Facebook quickly spread to other colleges in the Boston area and then to the high schools. In September 2006, it became accessible to anyone with an e-mail address. "Friends" are quick to share their likes and dislikes as well as any aspect of their daily lives. How can online communities influence buyer behaviour?

group might be a fraternity or sorority, a group you work with, or a club to which you belong.

Reference groups frequently include individuals known as group leaders, or opinion leaders—those who influence others. Obviously, it is important for marketing managers to persuade such people to purchase their goods or services. Many products and services that are integral parts of Canadians' lives today got their initial boost from opinion leaders. For example, DVDs and sport utility vehicles were embraced by opinion leaders well ahead of the general public. Opinion leaders are often the first to try new products and services out of pure curiosity. They are typically self-indulgent, making them more likely to explore unproven but intriguing products and services.

The family is the most important social institution for many consumers, strongly influencing values, attitudes, and self-concept—and buying behaviour. For example, a family that strongly values good health will have a grocery list distinctly different from that of a family that views every dinner as a gourmet event. Moreover, the family is responsible for the socialization process, the passing down of cultural values and norms to children. Children learn by observing their parents' consumption patterns, and so they will tend to shop in a similar pattern.

Marketers should consider family purchase situations along with the distribution of consumer and decision maker roles among family members. Ordinary marketing views the individual as both decision maker and consumer. Family marketing adds several other possibilities: Sometimes more than one family member or all family members are involved in the decision; sometimes only children are involved in the decision; sometimes more than one consumer is involved; and sometimes the decision maker and the consumer are different people. For example, a parent will select a dentist for a child to visit.

opinion leaders
Those who influence others.

socialization process
The passing down of cultural norms and values to children.

Individual Influences on Consumer Buying Decisions A person's buying decisions are also influenced by personal characteristics that are unique to each individual, such as gender, personality, and self-concept. Individual characteristics are generally stable over the course of one's life. For instance, most people do not change their gender, and the act of changing personality requires a complete reorientation of one's life.

Physiological differences between men and women result in different needs, such as health and beauty products. Just as important are the distinct cultural, social, and economic roles played by men and women and the effects that these have on their decision-making processes. Men and women also shop differently. Studies show that men and women share similar motivations in terms of where to shop—that is, seeking reasonable prices, merchandise quality, and a friendly, low-pressure environment—but they don't necessarily feel the same about shopping in general. Most women enjoy shopping; their male counterparts claim to dislike the experience and shop only out of necessity. Furthermore, men desire simple shopping experiences, stores with less variety, and convenience.

Each consumer has a unique personality. Personality is a broad concept that can be thought of as a way of organizing and grouping how an individual typically reacts to situations. Thus, personality combines psychological make-up and environmental forces. It includes people's underlying dispositions, especially their most dominant characteristics. Although personality is one of the least useful concepts in the study of consumer behaviour, some marketers believe that personality influences the types and brands of products purchased. For instance, the type of car, clothes, or jewellery a consumer buys can reflect one or more personality traits.

personality
A way of organizing and grouping how an individual reacts to situations.

Self-concept, or self-perception, is how consumers perceive themselves. Self-concept includes attitudes, perceptions, beliefs, and self-evaluations. Although

self-concept
How people perceive themselves.

self-concept can change, the change is often gradual. Through self-concept, people define their identity, which, in turn, provides for consistent and coherent behaviour.

ideal self-image
The way an individual would like to be.

real self-image
How an individual actually perceives him- or herself.

Self-concept combines the **ideal self-image** (the way an individual would like to be) and the **real self-image** (how an individual actually perceives him or herself). Generally, we try to raise our real self-image toward our ideal (or at least narrow the gap). Consumers seldom buy products that jeopardize their self-image. For example, someone who sees herself as a trendsetter wouldn't buy clothing that doesn't project a contemporary image.

Psychological Influences on Consumer Buying Decisions An individual's buying decisions are further influenced by psychological factors such as perception and beliefs and attitudes. These factors are what consumers use to interact with their world. They are the tools consumers use to recognize their feelings, gather and analyze information, formulate thoughts and opinions, and take action. Unlike the other three influences on consumer behaviour, psychological influences can be affected by a person's environment because they are applied on specific occasions. For example, you will perceive different stimuli and process these stimuli in different ways depending on whether you are sitting in class concentrating on the instructor, sitting outside of class talking to friends, or sitting in your dorm room watching television.

perception
The process by which we select, organize, and interpret stimuli into a meaningful and coherent picture.

selective exposure
The process of deciding which stimuli to notice and which to ignore.

belief
An organized pattern of knowledge that an individual holds as true about the world.

attitude
Learned tendency to respond consistently toward a given object, idea, or concept.

The world is full of stimuli. A stimulus is any unit of input affecting one or more of the five senses: sight, smell, taste, touch, and hearing. The process by which we select, organize, and interpret these stimuli into a meaningful and coherent picture is called **perception**. In essence, perception is how we see the world around us and how we recognize that we need some help in making a purchasing decision. People cannot perceive every stimulus in their environment. Therefore, they use **selective exposure** to decide which stimuli to notice and which to ignore. A typical consumer is exposed to more than 250 advertising messages a day but notices only between 11 and 20.

A **belief** is an organized pattern of knowledge that an individual holds as true about his or her world. A consumer might believe that Sony's camcorder makes the best home videos, tolerates hard use, and is reasonably priced. These beliefs might be based on knowledge, faith, or hearsay. Consumers tend to develop a set of beliefs about a product's attributes and then, through these beliefs, a *brand image*—a set of beliefs about a particular brand. In turn, the brand image shapes consumers' attitudes toward the product.

An **attitude** is a learned tendency to respond consistently toward a given object, idea, or concept, such as a brand. Attitudes rest on an individual's value system, which represents personal standards of good and bad, right and wrong, and so forth; therefore, attitudes tend to be more enduring and complex than beliefs. For an example of the nature of attitudes, consider the differing attitudes of consumers around the world toward the practice of purchasing on credit. North Americans have long been enthusiastic about charging goods and services and are willing to pay high interest rates for the privilege of postponing payment. To many European consumers, doing what amounts to taking out a loan—even a small one—to pay for anything seems absurd.

Types of Consumer Buying Decisions

involvement
The amount of time and effort a buyer invests in the searches, evaluations, and decision processes of consumer behaviour.

All consumer buying decisions generally fall along a continuum of three broad categories: routine response behaviour, limited decision-making, and extensive decision-making (see Exhibit 12.3). Goods and services in these three categories can best be described in terms of five factors: level of consumer involvement, length of time to make a decision, cost of the good or service, degree of information search, and the number of alternatives considered. The level of consumer involvement is perhaps the most significant determinant in classifying buying decisions. **Involvement** is the

EXHIBIT 12.3 > Continuum of Consumer Buying Decisions

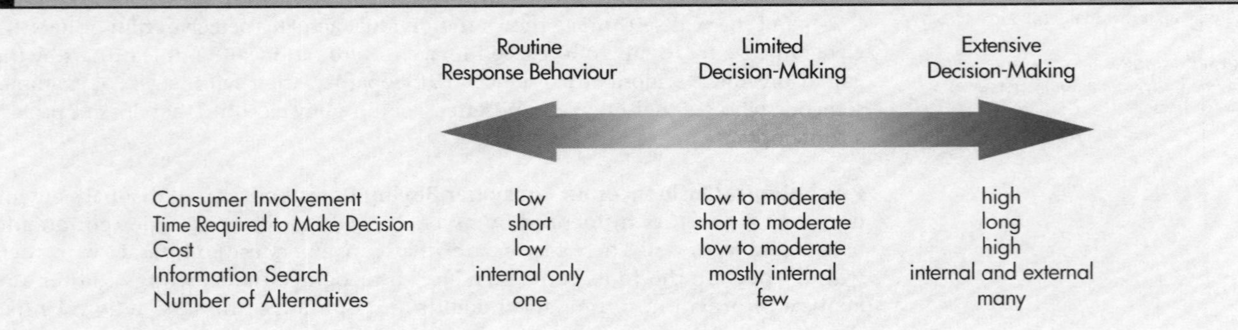

amount of time and effort a buyer invests in the search, evaluation, and decision processes of consumer behaviour.

routine response behaviour
Purchase of low cost, frequently bought items with little search or decision making.

Frequently purchased, low-cost goods and services are generally associated with **routine response behaviour**. These goods and services can also be called low-involvement products, because consumers spend little time on searching and decision-making before making the purchase. Usually, buyers are familiar with several different brands in the product category but stick with one brand. Consumers engaged in routine response behaviour normally don't experience need recognition until they are exposed to advertising or see the product displayed on a store shelf.

limited decision-making
Situation in which a consumer has previous product experience but is unfamiliar with the current brands available.

Limited decision-making typically occurs when a consumer has previous product experience but is unfamiliar with the current brands available. Limited decision-making is also associated with lower levels of involvement (although higher than routine decisions), because consumers do expend moderate effort in searching for information or in considering various alternatives. Suppose the children's usual brand of cereal, Kellogg's Corn Flakes, is unavailable in the grocery store. Completely out of cereal at home, the parent now must select another brand. Before making a final selection, he or she might pull from the shelf several brands similar to Kellogg's Corn Flakes, such as Cheerios, to compare their nutritional value and calories and to decide whether the children will like the new cereal.

extensive decision-making
Purchasing an unfamiliar, expensive, infrequently bought item.

Consumers practice **extensive decision-making** when buying an unfamiliar, expensive product or an infrequently bought item. This process is the most complex type of consumer buying decision and is associated with high involvement on the part of the consumer. This process resembles the model outlined in Exhibit 12.2. These consumers want to make the right decision, so they want to know as much as they can about the product category and available brands. Buyers use several criteria for evaluating their options and spend much time seeking information. Buying a home or a car, for example, requires extensive decision-making.

Business-to-Business Purchase Decision-Making Business buyer behaviour and business markets are different from consumer markets. Business markets include institutions such as hospitals and schools, manufacturers, wholesalers and retailers, and various branches of government. The key difference between a consumer product and a business product is the intended use. If you purchase a certain model of Dell computer for your home so you can surf the Internet, it is a consumer good. If a purchasing agent for MuchMusic buys exactly the same computer for a MuchMusic scriptwriter, it is a business good. Why? The reason is that MuchMusic is a business, so the computer will be used in a business environment.

Characteristics of the Business-to-Business Market The main differences between consumer markets and business markets are as follows:

1. *Purchase volume.* Business customers buy in much larger quantities than consumers. Think how many truckloads of sugar M&M/Mars must purchase to make one day's output of M&Ms. Imagine the number of batteries Sears buys each day for resale to consumers. Think of the number of pens the federal government must use each day.
2. *Number of customers.* Business marketers usually have far fewer customers than consumer marketers. As a result, it is much easier to identify prospective buyers and monitor current needs. Think about how few customers for airplanes or industrial cranes there are compared to the more than 4 million consumer households in the Canada.
3. *Location of buyers.* Business customers tend to be much more geographically concentrated than consumers. For example, the automobile industry is concentrated in Ontario, and the oil industry is concentrated in Alberta. Suppliers to these industries often locate close to the industries to lower distribution costs and facilitate communication.
4. *Direct distribution.* Business sales tend to be made directly to the buyer, because such sales frequently involve large quantities or custom-made items like heavy machinery. Consumer goods are more likely to be sold through intermediaries, such as wholesalers and retailers.

concept check

Explain the consumer decision-making process.

How do business markets differ from consumer markets?

Market Segmentation

market segmentation
The process of separating, identifying, and evaluating the layers of a market to identify a target market.

The study of buyer behaviour helps marketing managers better understand why people make purchases. To identify the target markets that might be most profitable for the firm, managers use **market segmentation**, which is the process of separating, identifying, and evaluating the layers of a market to identify a target market. For instance, a target market might be segmented into two groups: families with children and those without children. Families with young children are likely to buy hot cereals and pre-sweetened cereals. Families with no children are more likely to buy health-oriented cereals. You can be sure that cereal companies plan their marketing mixes with this difference in mind. A business market, on the other hand, might be segmented by large customers and small customers or by geographic area.

The five basic forms of consumer market segmentation are demographic, geographic, psychographic, benefit, and volume. Their characteristics are summarized in Exhibit 12.4 and are discussed in the following sections.

Demographic Segmentation

demographic segmentation
The differentiation of markets through the use of categories such as age, education, gender, income, and household size.

Demographic segmentation uses categories such as age, education, gender, income, and household size to differentiate among markets. This form of market segmentation is the most common. Statistics Canada provides a great deal of demographic data. For example, marketing researchers can use census data to find areas within cities that contain high concentrations of high-income consumers, singles, blue-collar workers, and so forth.

Many products are targeted to various age groups. Most music CDs, Pepsi, Coke, many movies, and thousands of other products are targeted toward teenagers and persons under 25 years old. In contrast, most cruises, medical products, fine jewellery, vacation homes, Buicks, and denture products are targeted toward people 50 years old

EXHIBIT 12.4 > Forms of Consumer Market Segmentation

Form	General Characteristics
Demographic segmentation	Age, education, gender, income, race, social class, household size
Geographic segmentation	Regional location (e.g., Maritimes and Newfoundland and Labrador, Central Canada, Western Canada, Northern Canada); population density (urban, suburban, rural); city or county size; climate
Psychographic segmentation	Lifestyle, personality, interests, values, attitudes
Benefit segmentation	Benefits provided by the good or service
Volume segmentation	Amount of use (light versus heavy)

and up. An example of how Frito Lay targets various age groups for three of its most popular products is shown is Exhibit 12.5.

Certain markets are segmented by gender. These include clothing, cosmetics, personal care items, magazines, jewellery, and footwear. Gillette, for example, is one of the world's best-known marketers of personal care products and has historically targeted men for the most part. Yet women's products have generated most of Gillette's growth since 1992. Gillette's shaving line for women has expanded into a $400 million global business, growing nearly 20 percent annually. Gillette has increased its advertising budget to help it reach a goal of more than $1 billion in revenues from women's shaving products worldwide.

Income is another popular way of segmenting markets. Income level influences consumers' wants and determines their buying power. Housing, clothing, automobiles, and alcoholic beverages are among the many markets segmented by income. Michelina's frozen dinners are targeted to lower income groups, whereas Stouffer's Lean Cuisine line is aimed at higher income consumers.

EXHIBIT 12.5 > Age Segmentation for Fritos, Doritos, and Tostitos

	Name Derivation	Year Introduced	Main Ingredients	Demographic	According to Frito-Lay
Frito	"Little fried bits" (Spanish)	1932	Corn, vegetable oil, salt	33- to 51-year-old males	"Hunger satisfaction"
Doritos	"Little bits of gold"	1964	Corn, vegetable oil, cheddar cheese, salt	Teens, mostly male	"Bold and daring snacking"
Tostitos	"Little toasted bits" (Spanish)	1981	White corn, vegetable oil, salt	Upscale consumers born between 1946 and 1964	"Casual interaction through friends and family . . . a social food that brings people together"

SOURCE: Frito-Lay.

Geographic Segmentation

geographic segmentation
The differentiation of markets by region of the country, city or county size, market density, or climate.

Geographic segmentation means segmenting markets by region of the country, city or county size, market density, or climate. *Market density* is the number of people or businesses within a certain area. Many companies segment their markets geographically to meet regional preferences and buying habits. Both Ford and Chevrolet, for instance, sell more pickup trucks and truck parts in the middle of the country than on either coast.

Psychographic Segmentation

psychographic segmentation
The differentiation of markets by personality or lifestyle.

Ethnic background, income, occupation, and other demographic variables help in developing strategies but often do not paint the entire picture of consumer needs. Demographics provide the skeleton, but psychographics add meat to the bones. **Psychographic segmentation** is market segmentation by personality or lifestyle. People with common activities, interests, and opinions are grouped together and given a "lifestyle name." For example, Harley-Davidson divides its customers into seven lifestyle segments, from "cocky misfits," who are most likely to be arrogant troublemakers, to "laid-back camper types" committed to cycling and nature, to "classy capitalists," who have wealth and privilege.

Benefit Segmentation

benefit segmentation
The differentiation of markets based on what a product will do rather than on customer characteristics.

Benefit segmentation is based on what a product will do rather than on consumer characteristics. For years Crest toothpaste was targeted toward consumers concerned with preventing cavities. Recently, Crest subdivided its market. It now offers regular Crest; Crest Tartar Control, for people who want to prevent cavities and tartar build-up; Crest for kids, with sparkles that taste like bubble gum; another Crest that prevents gum disease, and Crest Vivid White, for people wanting whiter teeth as well as a toothpaste that combines many of these in one tube. Sensodyne toothpaste is aimed at people with highly sensitive teeth.

concept check

Define market segmentation.

List and discuss the five basic forms of market segmentation.

CONCEPT *in Action* >>>

L. L. Bean is a world-renowned outfitter serving people who love the outdoors. Psychographic segmentation is market segmentation by personality or lifestyle. How would you describe the psychographics of L.L. Bean's customers?

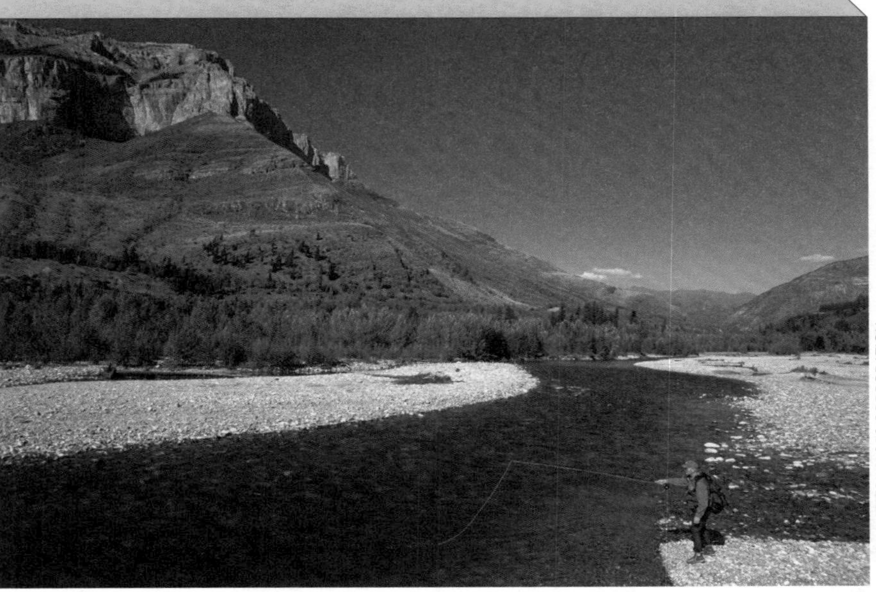

Volume Segmentation

volume segmentation
The differentiation of markets based on the amount of the product purchased.

The fifth main type of segmentation is **volume segmentation**, which is based on the amount of the product purchased. Just about every product has heavy, moderate, and light users, as well as non-users. Heavy users often account for a very large portion of a product's sales. Thus, a firm might want to target its marketing mix to the heavy user segment.

Using Marketing Research to Serve Existing Customers and Find New Customers

marketing research
The process of planning, collecting, and analyzing data relevant to a marketing decision.

HOT Links

A good place to learn more about marketing research is Quirks Marketing research review, **http://www.quirks.com**. In addition to articles, you can link to major marketing research firms.

How do successful companies learn what their customers value? Through marketing research, companies can be sure they are listening to the voice of the customer. **Marketing research** is the process of planning, collecting, and analyzing data relevant to a marketing decision. The results of this analysis are then communicated to management. The information collected through marketing research includes the preferences of customers, the perceived benefits of products, and consumer lifestyles. Research helps companies make better use of their marketing budgets. Marketing research has a range of uses from fine-tuning existing products to discovering whole new marketing concepts.

For example, everything at the Olive Garden restaurant chain, from the décor to the wine list, is based on marketing research. Each new menu item is put through a series of consumer taste tests before being added to the menu. Hallmark Cards uses marketing research to test messages, cover designs, and even the size of the cards. Hallmark's experts know which kinds of cards will sell best in which places. For instance, in geographic regions where engagement parties are popular, engagement cards sell best.

In this section, we examine the marketing research process, which consists of the following steps:

1. Define the marketing problem.
2. Choose a method of research.
3. Collect the data.
4. Analyze the research data.
5. Make recommendations to management.

Define the Marketing Problem

The most critical step in the marketing research process is defining the marketing problem. This involves writing either a problem statement or a list of research objectives. If the problem is not defined properly, the remainder of the research will be a waste of time and money. Two key questions can help in defining the marketing problem correctly:

1. Why is the information being sought? By discussing with managers what the information is going to be used for and what decisions might be made as a result, the researcher can get a clearer grasp of the problem.
2. Does the information already exist? If so, money and time can be saved, and a quick decision can be made.

Choose a Method of Research

After the problem is correctly defined, a research method is chosen. There are three basic research methods: survey, observation, and experiment.

survey research
A marketing research method in which data are gathered from respondents in person, by telephone, by mail, at a mall, or through the Internet to obtain facts, opinions, and attitudes.

observation research
A marketing research method in which the investigator monitors respondents' actions without interacting directly with the respondents; for example, by using cash registers with scanners.

With **survey research**, data are gathered from respondents in person, at a mall, or through the Internet, by telephone, or mail to obtain facts, opinions, and attitudes. A questionnaire is used to provide an orderly and structured approach to data gathering. Face-to-face interviews might take place at the respondent's home, in a shopping mall, or at a place of business.

Observation research is research that monitors respondents' actions without direct interaction. In the fastest-growing form of observation research, researchers use cash registers with scanners that read tags with bar codes to identify the item being purchased. Technological advances are rapidly expanding the future of observation research. For example, ACNielsen has been using black boxes for years on television sets to obtain information on a family's viewing habits silently. But what if the set is on but no one is in the room? To overcome that problem, researchers will soon rely on infrared passive "people meters," which will identify the faces of family members watching the television program. Thus, the meter can duly record when the set is on and no one is watching.

experiment
A marketing research method in which the investigator changes one or more variables—price, packaging, design, shelf space, advertising theme, or advertising expenditures—while observing the effects of these changes on another variable (usually sales).

In the third research method, **experiment**, the investigator changes one or more variables—price, package, design, shelf space, advertising theme, or advertising expenditures—while observing the effects of those changes on another variable (usually sales). The objective of experiments is to measure causality. For example, an experiment might reveal the impact that a change in package design has on sales.

Collect the Data

primary data
Information collected directly from the original source to solve a problem.

secondary data
Information that has already been collected for a project other than the current one but that can be used to solve the current problem.

Two types of data are used in marketing research: **primary data**, which are collected directly from the original source to solve a problem; and **secondary data**, information that has already been collected for a project other than the current one but that can be used to help solve it. Secondary data can come from a number of sources, among them government agencies, trade associations, research bureaus, universities, the Internet, commercial publications, and internal company records. Company records include sales invoices, accounting records, data from previous research studies, and historical sales data.

HOT Links

Find out what information Statistics Canada collects at **http://www.statcan.ca**.

Primary data are usually gathered through some form of survey research. As described earlier, survey research often relies on interviews. See Exhibit 12.6 for the different types of surveys. Today, conducting surveys over the Internet is the fastest-growing form of survey research.

Analyze the Data

After the data have been collected, the next step in the research process is data analysis. The purpose of this analysis is to interpret and draw conclusions from the mass of collected data. Many software statistical programs, such as SAS and SPSS, are available to make this task easier for the researcher.

Make Recommendations to Management

After completing the data analysis, the researcher must prepare the report and communicate the conclusions and recommendations to management. This is a key step in the process, because marketing researchers who want their conclusions acted on must convince the manager that the results are credible and justified by the data collected. Today, presentation software like PowerPoint and Astound provides easy-to-use tools for creating reports and presentations that are more interesting, compelling, and effective than was possible just a few years ago.

concept check

Define marketing research.

Explain the marketing research process.

What are the three basic marketing research methods?

EXHIBIT 12.6 > Common Types of Survey Research

Internet surveys	Conducted on the Internet, often using respondents from huge Internet panels (persons agreeing to participate in a series of surveys).
Executive surveys	Interviews of professionals (e.g., engineers, architects, doctors, executives) or decision makers that are conducted at their place of business.
Mall-intercept surveys	Interviews with consumers that are conducted in a shopping mall or other high-traffic location. Interviews may be done in a public area of the mall, or respondents might be taken to a private test area.
Central location telephone surveys	Interviews are conducted from a telephone facility set up for that purpose. These facilities typically have equipment that permits supervisors to monitor the interviewing unobtrusively while it is taking place. Many of these facilities do national sampling from a single location. An increasing number have computer-assisted interviewing capabilities. At these locations, the interviewer sits in front of a computer terminal attached to a mainframe or personal computer. The questionnaire is programmed into the computer, and the interviewer uses the keyboard to enter responses directly.
Self-administered questionnaires	Self-administered questionnaires are most frequently employed at high-traffic locations, such as shopping malls, or in captive audience situations, such as classrooms and airplanes. Respondents are given general information on how to fill out the questionnaire and are expected to fill it out on their own. Kiosk-based point-of-service touch screens provide a way of capturing information from individuals in stores, health clinics, and other shopping or service environments. Sometimes software-driven questionnaires on diskettes are sent to individuals who have personal computers.
Ad hoc (one-shot) mail surveys	Questionnaires are mailed to a sample of consumers or industrial users, without prior contact by the researcher. Instructions are included, and respondents are asked to fill out the questionnaire and return it via mail. Sometimes a gift or monetary incentive is provided.
Mail panels	Questionnaires are mailed to a sample of individuals who have been pre-contacted. The panel concept has been explained to them, and they have agreed to participate for some period of time in exchange for gratuities. Mail panels typically generate much higher response rates than do ad hoc mail surveys.

Trends in Marketing

To discover exactly what customers value most, organizations are using innovative techniques for collecting customer information. Some of the more sophisticated marketing research techniques that are growing in popularity are the use of the Internet, scanner-based research, capitalizing on loyalty cards, and one-to-one marketing.

Internet Marketing Research

Current methods of conducting some types of research soon may seem as quaint as a steam-engine train. New techniques and strategies for conducting traditional marketing research are appearing online in increasing numbers every day. The growth of Internet marketing research is being fuelled because the Internet:

- Provides more rapid access to business intelligence and thus allows for better and faster decision making.
- Improves a firm's ability to respond quickly to customer needs and market shifts.
- Facilitates conducting follow-up studies and longitudinal research.
- Slashes labour- and time-intensive research activities (and associated costs), including mailing, telephone solicitation, data entry, data tabulation, and reporting.

Expanding Around The Globe

CHALLENGES OF CONDUCTING GLOBAL MARKETING RESEARCH

Global companies, like Research In Motion (RIM), Procter & Gamble, McDonald's, and 3M, want global marketing research to help them make good strategic marketing decisions around the world. Yet, doing marketing research in some countries is not easy.

For example, using the same questionnaire asking "How did you like the taste of the new Pizza Hut crust?" might be followed with a scale that goes (1) excellent through (7) poor. Canadians might rank the new crust at 3.3 and Asians at 1.7. Thus, the conclusion is that the Asians prefer the new crust more than the Canadians. The answer would be wrong! Asians don't like to offend others and therefore rate the new crust higher. In fact, they both liked the new crust the same!

There are many other problems in conducting global research. Cultural habits in some countries virtually prohibit communication with a stranger, particularly for women. For example, a researcher simply may not be able to speak on the phone with a housewife in an Islamic country to find out what she thinks of a particular brand. Second, in many societies, such matters as preferences for hygienic products are too personal to be shared with an outsider. In many Latin American countries, a woman may feel ashamed to talk with a researcher about her choice of a brand of sanitary pad, hair shampoo, or perfume. Third, respondents in many cases may be unwilling to share their true feelings with interviewers because they suspect the interviewers may be agents of the government (for example, seeing information for imposition of additional taxes). Fourth, middle-class people, in developing countries in particular, are reluctant to accept their status and may make false claims to reflect the lifestyle of wealthier people. For example, in a study on the consumption of tea in India, more than 70 percent of the respondents from middle-income families claimed they used one of the several national brands of tea. This finding could not be substantiated because more than 60 percent of the tea sold nationally in India is unbranded, generic tea sold unpackaged. Fifth, many respondents, willing to cooperate, may be illiterate, so that even oral communication may be difficult.[7]

Critical Thinking Questions

- What cultural factors (values, attitudes, ideas, and symbols) may influence the market research conducted in a third-world country?
- How can market researchers improve the accuracy and quality of market research conducted in a foreign country?

Internet surveys have several specific advantages:

- Rapid development, real-time reporting. Internet surveys can be broadcast to thousands of potential respondents simultaneously. The results can be tabulated and posted for corporate clients to view as the returns arrive. Thus, Internet survey results can be in a client's hands in significantly less time than traditional survey results.
- Dramatically reduced costs. The Internet can cut costs by 25 to 40 percent while providing results in half the time it takes to do a traditional telephone survey. Data-collection costs account for a large proportion of any traditional market research budget. Telephone surveys are labour-intensive efforts incurring training, telecommunications, and management costs. Using the Internet eliminates these costs completely.
- Personalization. Internet surveys can be highly personalized for greater relevance to each respondent's own situation, thus speeding the response process. Respondents enjoy answering only pertinent questions, being able to pause and resume the survey as their schedule allows, and having the ability to see previous responses and correct inconsistencies.
- Higher response rates. Busy respondents are growing increasingly intolerant of "snail mail" or telephone-based surveys. Internet surveys take half the time to complete than phone interviews do, can be accomplished at the respondent's convenience (after work hours), and are much more stimulating and engaging. Graphics, interactivity, links to incentive sites, and real-time summary reports make Internet surveys more enjoyable. This results in much higher response rates.
- Ability to contact the hard-to-reach. Busy professionals—doctors, engineers, and top management in Global 2000 firms—are the most difficult to reach through traditional survey methods. Many of these groups are well represented online. Internet surveys provide convenient anytime/anywhere access that makes it easy for busy professionals to participate.[8]

Conducting Internet marketing research is possible only in countries that have a high Internet penetration rate such as in Western Europe. When marketing researchers "go global" they face many challenges, as discussed in the Expanding Around the Globe box.

Scanner-Based Research

scanner-based research
System for gathering information from a single group of respondents by continuously monitoring the advertising, promotion, and pricing they are exposed to and the things that they buy.

Scanner-based research is a system for gathering information from a single group of respondents by continuously monitoring the advertising, promotion, and pricing they are exposed to and the things they buy. The variables measured are advertising campaigns, coupons, displays, and product prices. The result is a huge database of marketing efforts and consumer behaviour. Scanner-based research is bringing ever closer the Holy Grail of marketing research: an accurate, objective picture of the direct causal relationship between different kinds of marketing efforts and actual sales.

The two major scanner-based suppliers are Information Resources, Inc. (IRI), and the ACNielsen Company. Each has about half the market. However, IRI is the founder of scanner-based research.

IRI's first product was called *BehaviorScan*. A household panel (a group of 3,000 long-term participants in the research project) were recruited and maintained in each BehaviorScan town. Panel members shop with an ID card, which is presented at the checkout in scanner-equipped grocery stores and drugstores, allowing IRI to track each household's purchases electronically, item by item, over time. It uses microcomputers to measure TV viewing in each panel household and can send special commercials to panel member television sets. With such a measure of household purchasing, it is possible to manipulate marketing variables, such as TV advertising or consumer promotions, or to introduce a new product and analyze real changes in consumer buying behaviour.

IRI's most successful product is *InfoScan*—a scanner-based sales-tracking service for the consumer packaged-goods industry. Retail sales, detailed consumer purchasing information (including measurement of store loyalty and total grocery basket expenditures), and promotional activity by manufacturers and retailers are monitored and evaluated for all bar-coded products. Data are collected weekly from more than 31,000 supermarkets, drugstores, and mass merchandisers.

Making Ethical Choices

HITTING THE LONG SHOT

As a marketing manager at a beverage company, you are always looking for new products to offer—especially in the under-18 market where you are weak. A hot new drink has been a hit with kids in Japan—sales were up to 75,000 bottles a month—and it is making its way to Europe. Kidsbeer is a cola-like soft drink that is packaged to look like beer. The same colour as lager beer, the drink is formulated to pour with a beer-like foam. It includes guarana, a South American plant extract used in energy drinks. Tomomasu, the Japanese bottler, markets it with the slogan "Even kids cannot stand life unless they have a drink."

The impending arrival of such a drink has raised the ire of consumer groups outside Japan. They are alarmed that any company would glamorize drinking. Already beer drinking is showing up in movies that target kids and teens—for example, DodgeBall and HellBoy. Says Amon Rappaport of the Marin Institute, an alcohol industry watchdog group, "The last thing we need is another product that introduces kids to drinking when the alcohol industry already spends billions doing that."

Nonetheless, you are intrigued and begin to investigate. Besides, several companies still sell candy cigarettes to kids (although some countries have banned them).

Using a Web search tool, locate articles about this topic and then write responses to the following questions. Be sure to support your arguments and cite your sources.

ETHICAL DILEMMA: Kidsbeer would boost your company's revenues, because kids love to mimic their parents' behaviour. Do you recommend it to top management?

SOURCES: "Beer-Flavored Soda Headed for Europe," UPI NewsTrack, September 19, 2005; "Here's Looking at You, Kid," Food Management, October 2005, p. 104; Andrew Adam Newman, "If the Children Can Drink Uncola, What about Unbeer?" New York Times, September 19, 2005, p. C8(L); Andrew Adam Newman, "Youngsters Enjoy Beer Ads, Arousing Industry's Critics," New York Times, February 13, 2006, p. C15(L); "Drink That Looks Like Beer Getting Popular with Kids, Kyodo News International, August 5, 2005.

Loyalty Cards

loyalty cards
Cards issued by a manufacturer, service organization, or retailer that give discounts to loyal and frequent shoppers.

Just swipe the card at the checkout register and get a discount on tomatoes, toothpaste, or other specials. You save money, and the store builds a record that lets it know how to serve its best customers. **Loyalty cards** are cards issued by a service organization, retailer, or manufacturer that give discounts to loyal and frequent shoppers. Most companies require the shopper to fill out a demographic profile questionnaire before the card is issued.

Loyalty cards have been around for a few years now, and supermarket and drugstore chains are beginning to reap the benefits. With a huge amount of data being collected on shoppers, from the types of pop they buy to whether they like to shop late at night, merchants are getting smarter at tracking consumer trends. And they're changing their merchandise, store layout, and advertising accordingly to keep their most loyal customers spending.

Retailers estimate that 20 percent of their shoppers account for 80 percent of store sales, so finding out what their best customers want is essential. By simply scanning purchases, stores track what's selling, but when that information is tied to loyalty cards, merchants obtain richer information on who is buying what. This is the prized asset of supermarkets' future.[9]

One-To-One Marketing

one-to-one marketing
Creating a unique marketing mix for every customer.

marketing database
Computerized file of customers' and potential customers' profiles and purchase patterns.

One-to-one marketing is creating a unique marketing mix for every consumer. The key to creating one-to-one marketing is a good marketing database. The information contained in a marketing database helps managers know and understand customers, and potential customers, on an individual basis. A **marketing database** is a computerized file of customers' and potential customers' profiles and purchase patterns.

In the 1960s, network television enabled advertisers to "get the same message to everyone simultaneously." Database marketing can get a customized, individual message to everyone simultaneously through direct mail. This is why database marketing is sometimes called *micromarketing*. Database marketing can create a computerized form of the old-fashioned relationship that people used to have with the corner grocer, butcher, or baker. "A database is sort of a collective memory," says Richard G. Barlow, president of Frequency Marketing, Inc., a consulting firm. "It deals with you in the same personalized way as a mom-and-pop grocery store, where they knew customers by name and stocked what they wanted."

The size of some databases is impressive: at the Ford Motor Company it contains about 50 million names; Kraft General Foods, 30 million; and Citicorp, 30 million. American Express can pull from its database all cardholders who made purchases at golf pro shops in the past six months, who attended symphony concerts, or who travelled to Europe more than once in the past year, as well as the very few people who did all three.

Companies are using their marketing databases to implement one-to-one marketing. For example, Novartis Seeds, Inc., an agriculture business, produces individually customized, full-colour brochures for 7,000 farmers. Each piece features products selected by Novartis dealers specifically for the farmer based on information collected about the farm operation and the types of crops grown. Instead of the 30-page catalogue Novartis traditionally sent, these customers get a one-page brochure with only the five or six products they need, plus other complementary products dealers feel they should consider.

concept check

Describe how scanner-based research helps measure the effectiveness of marketing.

Explain how loyalty cards are of benefit to manufacturers and retailers.

Describe one-to-one marketing and the role of marketing databases.

Great Ideas to Use Now

As a consumer, you participate in shaping consumer products by the choices you make and the products and services you buy. You can become a better consumer by actively participating in marketing surveys and learning more about the products you buy.

Participate in Marketing Research Surveys

All of us get tired of telephone solicitations where people try to sell us everything from new carpet to chimney cleaning. Recognize that marketing research surveys are different. A true marketing research survey will *never* involve a sales pitch, nor will the research firm sell your name to a database marketer. The purpose of marketing research is to build better goods and services for you and me. Help out the researchers and ultimately help yourself. The Canadian Marketing Association (CMA) is the largest marketing association in Canada. CMA members include major financial institutions, publishers, retailers, charitable organizations, agencies, relationship marketers and those involved in e-business and Internet marketing. A key objective of CMA is to increase consumer confidence in the marketing industry.

Understanding Cognitive Dissonance

cognitive dissonance
The condition of having beliefs or knowledge that are internally inconsistent or that disagree with one's behaviour.

When making a major purchase, particularly when the item is expensive and choices are similar, consumers typically experience cognitive dissonance; that is, they have beliefs or knowledge that are internally inconsistent or that disagree with their behaviour. In other words, instead of feeling happy with their new purchase, they experience doubts, feel uneasy, and wonder if they have done the right thing. Understand that this feeling of uneasiness is perfectly normal and goes away over time. Perhaps the best way to avoid cognitive dissonance is to insist on a strong warranty or money-back guarantee. A second approach is to read everything you can find about your purchase. Go to the Internet, and use the search engines to find articles relevant to your purchase. Find Internet chat rooms about your product, and join in the discussion. And, before you buy, check out the *Consumer Reports* ratings on your product at **http://www.consumerreports.org**. For electronic products, also go to **http://www.CNET.com** and **http://www.ZDNET.com**.

HOT Links

Visit the Canadian Marketing Association at **http://www.the-cma.org** to learn more about how they take a leadership role in responding to consumer concerns and to learn more about their "Code of Ethics and Standards of Practice."

Customer Satisfaction and Quality

We have stressed the importance of product/service quality throughout the text. But how does a company know if it is offering high quality and satisfaction to its customers? The answer is marketing research. Marketing research provides the feedback to managers through customer satisfaction surveys about how well the company is doing.

Conducting a survey is a rather easy task; however, making changes based on the research can be a different story. It all begins with the commitment of top management. If top management makes customer satisfaction a top priority, then the chance of creating satisfied customers increases greatly. For example, Jean Gourdon, General Manager of the Montreal Novotel hotel, consistently earns the highest customer satisfaction ratings in the entire Accor system (more than 3,800 Novotel, Sofitel, Red Roof Inns, Ibis, and Motel 6 hotels). Jean Gourdon is devoted to satisfying customers, and he accomplishes this by making employees number one. Gourdon says,

"I tell my customers that it is staff first, customers second, profit third. I tell them that the management of this hotel does not spend time with customers. I have six department heads who concentrate on the staff. That means being attentive to family life as well, since I believe the organization has a role [to play] in life, not just work."

As a result, it is the employees' responsibility to not only clean rooms or change menus but also to take care of problems and represent the hotel to guests. "These people are the ambassadors of the hotel," Gourdon says. "They are extremely motivated, not just because they don't have supervision, but because they are empowered. It gives their job another dimension and also leverage in the industry." According to Gourdon, customers say it works. "They tell me that when they are here they are treated like kings," he says.[10]

SOURCE: "GM's Winning Vision: Staff First, Profit Follows," *Hotels* (March, 2003), p. 14. Reprinted with permission.

Summary of Learning Outcomes

1 Define the marketing concept, and relationship marketing.

Marketing includes those business activities that are designed to satisfy consumer needs and wants through the exchange process. Marketing managers use the "right" principle—getting the right goods or services to the right people at the right place, time, and price, using the right promotional techniques. Today, many firms have adopted the marketing concept. The marketing concept involves identifying consumer needs and wants and then producing goods or services that will satisfy them while making a profit. Relationship marketing entails forging long-term relationships with customers, which can lead to repeat sales, reduced costs, and stable relationships.

2 Show how managers create a marketing strategy.

A firm creates a marketing strategy by understanding the external environment, defining the target market, determining a competitive advantage, and developing a marketing mix. Environmental scanning enables companies to understand the external environment. The target market is the specific group of consumers toward which a firm directs its marketing efforts. A competitive advantage is a set of unique features of a company and its products that are perceived by the target market as significant and superior to those of the competition.

3 Explain the marketing mix.

To carry out the marketing strategy, firms create a marketing mix—a blend of products, distribution systems, prices, and promotion. Marketing managers use this mix to satisfy target consumers. The mix can be applied to non-business as well as business situations.

4 Summarize how consumers and organizations make buying decisions.

Buyer behaviour is what people and businesses do in buying and using goods and services. The consumer decision-making process consists of the following steps: recognizing a need, seeking information, evaluating alternatives, purchasing the product, judging the purchase outcome, and engaging in post-purchase behaviour. A number of factors influence the process. Cultural, social, individual, and psychological factors have an impact on consumer decision-making. The main differences between consumer and business markets are purchase volume, number of customers, location of buyers, direct distribution, and rational purchase decisions.

5 List the five basic forms of market segmentation.

Success in marketing depends on understanding the target market. One technique used to identify a target market is market segmentation. The five basic forms of segmentation are demographic (population statistics), geographic (location), psychographic (personality or lifestyle), benefit (product features), and volume (amount purchased).

6 Identify how marketing research is used in marketing decision-making.

Much can be learned about consumers through marketing research, which involves collecting, recording, and analyzing data important in marketing goods and services, and communicating the results to management. Marketing researchers can use primary data, which are gathered through door-to-door, mall-intercept, telephone, the Internet, and mail interviews. The Internet is becoming a quick, cheap, and efficient way of gathering primary data. Secondary data are available from a variety of sources including government, trade, and commercial associations. Secondary data save time and money, but they might not meet researchers' needs. A huge amount of secondary data is available on the Internet. Both primary and secondary data give researchers a better idea of how the market will respond to the product. Thus, they reduce the risk of producing something the market doesn't want.

7 List some of the trends in understanding the consumer.

New techniques and strategies for conducting traditional marketing research are appearing online in increasing numbers every day, including Internet marketing research. The growth of Internet marketing research is being fuelled because the

Internet and its acceptance in business today. BehaviorScan uses scanners and television meters to measure the impact of marketing on sales of specific products. BehaviorScan panels can also measure the impact of coupons, free samples, store displays, new packaging, and pricing. A second trend is retailers capitalizing on shopper loyalty cards. These enable managers to track customer shopping patterns. A third trend is the growing use of one-to-one marketing by using databases to target the needs of customers and non-customers more accurately.

Experiential Exercises

1. Can the marketing concept be applied effectively by a sole proprietorship, or is it more appropriate for larger businesses with more managers? Explain.
2. Before starting your own business, you should develop a marketing strategy to guide your efforts. Choose one of the business ideas listed, and develop a marketing strategy for the business. Include the type of market research (both primary and secondary) you will perform and how you will define your target market.
    a. Crafts store to capitalize on the renewed interest in knitting and other crafts
    b. Online corporate-training company
    c. Ethnic restaurant near your campus
    d. Another business opportunity that interests you
3. "Market segmentation is the most important concept in marketing." Why do you think some marketing professionals make this statement? Give an example of each form of segmentation.
4. Pick a specific product that you use frequently, such as a cosmetic or toiletry item, a snack food, article of clothing, book, computer program, or music CD. What is the target market for this product, and does the company's marketing strategy reflect this? Now consider the broader category of your product. How can this product be changed and/or the marketing strategy adjusted to appeal to other market segments?
5. Can marketing research be carried out in the same manner all over the world? Why or why not?
6. Visit the SRI Consulting site, **http://www.sric-bi.com**, and click on the VALS Survey link. First read about the VALS survey and how marketers can use it. Describe its value. Then take the survey to find out which psychographic segment you're in. Do you agree or disagree with the results? Why or why not?
7. How good was the marketing strategy you developed in Question 2? Using advice from the marketing section of *Entrepreneur* (**http://www.entrepreneur.com**) or other resources, revisit your marketing strategy for the business you selected and revise the plan accordingly. (*Entrepreneur*'s article "Write a Simple Marketing Plan" is a good place to start.) What did you overlook? (If you didn't do this exercise, pick one of the businesses and draft a marketing strategy using online resources to guide you.)
8. As the number of people online continues to grow, more of the Web surfers are also buying products online. What do researchers say about the characteristics of the online market? What market segments are appearing? Visit several sites to research this topic, and then prepare a report on the demographics of online markets and other key considerations for marketers. NUA Internet Surveys is a good place to start: **http://www.gdsourcing.ca/**. You'll find summaries of the latest research studies and can search for others by category. From there, you can link to the sites of market research companies. (Many research company sites require registration

or subscriptions; however, you can check press releases for summaries of research findings.) Also search for "Internet marketing" or "online marketing" using search engines and business publication sites such as *Business Week*, *Entrepreneur*, and *Inc.*

Key Terms

attitude 369
belief 369
benefit segmentation 373
buyer behaviour 366
cognitive dissonance 380
competitive advantage 362
cost competitive advantage 362
culture 367
customer satisfaction 359
customer value 359
customer relationship management (CRM) 360
demographic segmentation 371
differential competitive advantage 363
distribution strategy 364
environmental scanning 361
exchange 358
experiment 375
extensive decision-making 370
four Ps (4Ps) 364
geographic segmentation 373
ideal self-image 369
involvement 369
limited decision-making 370
loyalty cards 379
market segmentation 371
marketing 358
marketing concept 358
marketing database 379
marketing mix 364
marketing research 374
niche competitive advantage 363
observation research 375
one-to-one marketing 379
opinion leader 368
perception 369
personality 368
pricing strategy 364
primary data 375
product 358
product strategy 364
production orientation 358
promotion strategy 365
psychographic segmentation 373
real self-image 369
reference groups 367
relationship marketing 360
routine response behaviour 370
scanner-based research 378
secondary data 375
selective exposure 369
self-concept 368
social marketing 366
socialization process 368
survey research 375
target market 362
volume segmentation 374

Review Questions

1. What is marketing? What is an exchange in marketing?
2. What does the marketing concept involve?
3. What is the difference between customer value and customer satisfaction? How are these related to building relationships?
4. Why is it important for marketers to understand the external environment? What are the six general categories of the environment that marketers must evaluate?
5. What is a target market?
6. What are the various competitive advantages that a company can create?
7. What are the four variables in the marketing mix?
8. What influences consumers in their decision-making?
9. What are the characteristics of the business-to-business market?
10. What is market segmentation? What are the five basic forms of consumer market segmentation?
11. What is market research, and what are the steps in the market research process?

CREATIVE THINKING CASE >

Teen Power: A Force to be Reckoned With

Cell phones, surfing gear, X-treme sports, video games—these are just some of the lucrative markets where companies focus major marketing dollars on some very important consumers—teenagers. Understanding youth trends and dynamics in the constantly changing teen market remains an ongoing challenge for companies needing to know how best to spend those dollars.

That's where Teen Research Unlimited (TRU) comes in. Started by youthful entrepreneur Peter Zollo in 1982, TRU was the first company to specialize in teen-focused market research. It keeps companies in touch with teen thinking, making it possible for them to forecast trends and remain a step ahead of the competition. Based in Northbrook, Illinois, TRU has worked closely with many of the world's leading youth brands and advertising agencies, playing a key role in groundbreaking advertising and marketing campaigns, and the development of successful products and services. TRU has worked with over half a million teenagers nationwide to assemble data for use in advertising campaigns, product development, store designs, and other strategic business activities. Last year TRU conducted more than 1,000 focus groups and personal in-depth interviews in addition to several major quantitative studies. TRU also applies its expertise to teen advocacy on important social issues and high-risk youth behaviours such as anti-tobacco and drug use, sexual assault, life safety, education, crisis management, and skin cancer.

So how does TRU gather its data and help its clients create effective marketing strategies? When a burgeoning fashion retailer needed ethnographic research to learn more about their target consumer, they asked TRU to help them. TRU spent months scouring malls, sitting down with shoppers, and carrying out a comprehensive national quantitative analysis to gain a well-rounded view of the client and its competitors. At project completion, TRU was able to provide its client with a strategically sound, actionable plan that built on previous strengths, addressed areas requiring improvement, and set a benchmark for future measurements.

In another study a leading manufacturer of backpacks and luggage hired TRU to explore "personal carrying device" trends. To meet the client's research objective, TRU devised a series of in-home interviews focused on which bags people own, when they use them, and what they use them for. These interviews, as well as "intercepts" on snowy train platforms and the sunny West Coast beaches, were videotaped to reveal an "on-the-street" take on emerging trends.

The only full-service marketing-research firm dedicated solely to understanding teens, TRU's initial vision remains in place today: to develop an unparalleled expertise in the teenage market, and to offer clients virtually unlimited methods for researching teens. And with more businesses than ever focused on marketing to teenage consumers—Abercrombie & Fitch, PepsiCo, Nintendo, and Nokia are just some of TRU's prestigious clients—companies count on TRU's research to remain in touch with what teenagers want.

Critical Thinking Questions

- What makes TRU's research so important?
- In what way is the company unique?
- How does TRU help its customers understand their target market and create effective marketing strategies?

SOURCES: Adapted from the video "Teenage Research Unlimited," http://www.swlearning.com; Parija Bhatnagar, "More Cheese for the 'Mall Rats,'" CNN/Money, February 4, 2005; Ruth Laferla, "Teenagers Shop for Art of the Deal," New York Times, September 22, 2005; Mary Ellen Podmolik, "Teen Stores Leading the Herd," Chicago Tribune, January 14, 2006, p. 1; TRU corporate website (www.teenresearch.com), April 26, 2006.

VIDEO CASE >

Building Customer Relationships—One Kid at a Time

If giving consumers what they want is an excellent way to ensure loyalty and build long-term customer relationships, Fisher-Price has the right idea. Inviting its customers to participate in product design and development studies is an integral part of its marketing research programs. It is also one way Fisher-Price makes sure that products will achieve high levels of customer acceptance and success when they finally do reach the marketplace.

Founded in 1930, Fisher-Price is the most widely recognized brand of infant and preschool toys in the industry, and a trusted name in early childhood development. The company has earned a reputation for designing and producing high-quality toys that provide both developmental benefits and fun for children from birth to age 5.

Shelly Glick Gryfe, Director of Marketing Research at Fisher-Price, is proud of its Play Lab and Mom Talks, which are conducted in-house. Drawing from a list of several thousand volunteers, Gryfe and her team invite mothers with children who meet a specific demographic requirement to spend the day at their facility. In the Play Lab children do arts and crafts, read stories, and are encouraged to interact with a selection of toys. Some of the toys are still in development, whereas others, including those from competing companies, are already on the market.

These sessions are designed to provide the marketing research team with "directional information." Their designers, who observe the children from behind a one-way mirror, are looking for feedback on how they can make Fisher-Price products even better. It was this level of detailed observation that was responsible for the large feet on the company's preschool-age action figures called Rescue Heroes. The designers noted how frustrated the children became when a competitor's action figures kept toppling over.

Mothers are also an important part of the process. After viewing models, videos, and photo boards, and observing children's interactions with the toys, they are consulted on such topics as ranking products in order of desirability and giving opinions on age appropriateness and product pricing. Gryfe says parents participate because they "want to have good toys coming out for their children."

There is no doubt that kids and moms know what they like. Mothers loved the "good guy" theme of the Rescue Heroes line when it was first introduced in 1998 and declared it a winner. CBS television agreed, creating a Rescue Heroes TV series for young viewers, which has helped boost ongoing demand for the products. At Fisher-Price, giving the customer a voice means everyone wins.

Critical Thinking Questions

- How does Fisher-Price's marketing research strategy help build customer loyalty?
- What other "spin-off" benefits does it produce for the company? For the consumer?
- Is there a downside to having customers involved in the product development process? Explain.

SOURCES: Adapted from the video "Fisher-Price: The Pre-School Boy;" and information on Fisher-Price brands from the Mattel corporate Web site, http://www.mattel.com (accessed April 22, 2003).

E-COMMERCE CASE >

Sunworks Organic Farm: For Profit or Health?

In the case of Sunworks Farm, the original idea was to produce organic products to help Sheila, one of the owners, battle fibromyalgia, which had been plaguing her for four years. A naturopath had suggested that Sheila use organic food, and within six weeks, she recovered, marking the beginning of great things for the family. The Hamilton farm has been certified organic since 1997. They started with 80 chickens, and they now raise over 25,000 chickens during the outdoor season. Sunworks Farm provides 600 dozen eggs every week, and they always sell out early in the weekend. The farm also produces whole chickens, roasts, sausages, bison, pork, yogurt, and other products, all organic.

The Hamiltons have a strong family orientation as well, with Sheila's sister raising pigs and lambs, which the Hamiltons then market. Sheila's daughters and their families also work in the business. The Sunworks philosophy is heavily influenced by their ethics. As Ron Hamilton says, "When our customers buy our food, they buy our ethics package." This package includes a concern for the health of the earth as well as people and animals. Only a very small percentage of their products are not sold directly to the consumer primarily through year-round farmers' markets.

By offering a choice to consumers, the Hamiltons are living their values (The animals are raised outdoors when weather permits and graze naturally, supplemented only by organic feed). There are no chemicals, medications, or other toxins applied to their land or fed to their animals. In addition, products such as sausage, wieners, and bacon contain no fillers, nitrates, sulphites, or MSG. The philosophy, as stated on their website (**www.sunworksfarm.com**), is as follows:

We believe that:

1. It is our privilege to be stewards of the land and that we should leave it in a better state than when we got it. We do our best to work with nature and not against it.
2. Our children should be raised in a healthy mental and physical environment.
3. Animals should be treated kindly, humanely, ethically and have access to fresh air, clean water, green grass, and sunshine.
4. A healthy environment and gentle handling grows healthy animals, which reduces disease and the need for medication.
5. We want to grow good healthy food for our customers. We guarantee that you will not taste better meat than our pasture-raised products.

Under this philosophy, based on the ancient Haida saying "We do not inherit the land from our ancestors, we borrow it from our children," Sunworks Farms has continued to prosper, with many customers reaping the benefits of the superior product produced with care and concern for the animals and the earth.

Critical Thinking Questions

1. As a consumer, you might have noticed that organic products are generally more expensive than traditionally mass-produced products. Why are these products more expensive? Are you willing to pay the extra cost? Why or why not?
2. Suggest a marketing strategy for a company such as Sunworks Farm.

SOURCES: Pamela Irving, "Farming for the Love of It: Organic Food," Edmonton Journal, March 22, 2006; and Sunworks Farms Web site, http://www.sunworksfarm.com (accessed September 30th, 2008).

CHAPTER 13

Making the Connection

Creating Marketing Strategies

In this chapter we will continue to look at the functional area of marketing but more specifically at the 4P's of the marketing mix—product, price, place, and promotion. One of the keys to success in marketing is to provide something of unique value to the customer in order to achieve the critical success factor of *meeting their needs*. The second is to market it in such a way that you convince the customer of its benefit. They must believe that it will satisfy their needs or they won't buy it. This is where the 4Ps come in. Not only does marketing have to work with the other functional areas in an integrative fashion, as we discussed last chapter, but the marketing functions themselves must work together in an integrative way to convince the customer of the unique benefit of the product. For example, if a company wants to promote a product that is of better quality than the competition—such as Tivoli Florist in our opening vignette—and therefore designs it to have the features as well as the look of higher quality, promotes it in ways that appeal to high-end customers, distributes it in high-end stores, but prices it below the competition, consumers will be confused as to its quality. All four elements must give a consistent message—they must form an integrative whole—or the customer will be confused rather than convinced.

This is quite evident when you consider, as the chapter explains, that consumers make purchase decisions after considering both the tangible and intangible attributes of the product, including price. They consider the total value package—what they get at the price they have to pay. Another very integrative product concept is that of the product life cycle. It sounds like just a product concept, but the implications of what stage in the life cycle a product is at goes far beyond the product itself and into how it is priced, promoted and distributed.

Integration is also evident in looking at product design alone. The chapter discusses how consumers buy packages of benefits, such as: Burger King sells burgers and fries, but along with that quick food preparation and cleanliness. In other words, the product design must take into consideration *human resource* and *operations* issues as well.

When new products are developed, there are also obvious connections to the other parts of our business model. New product goals are usually financially stated, for example, so that the company only pursues products that help it *achieve financial performance*, and ideas are rejected if they don't meet financial goals. The firm must also determine if it has the operational facilities to produce the product, plus access to the necessary technology, human, and financial resources. New product ideas need to be checked against long-range strategies. Remember that planning takes place at different levels, but all levels are always connected so that they move in the same direction.

Pricing has obvious connections to *finance* of course, just as it affects the total value package for the consumer. The company must set a price that will earn a fair return

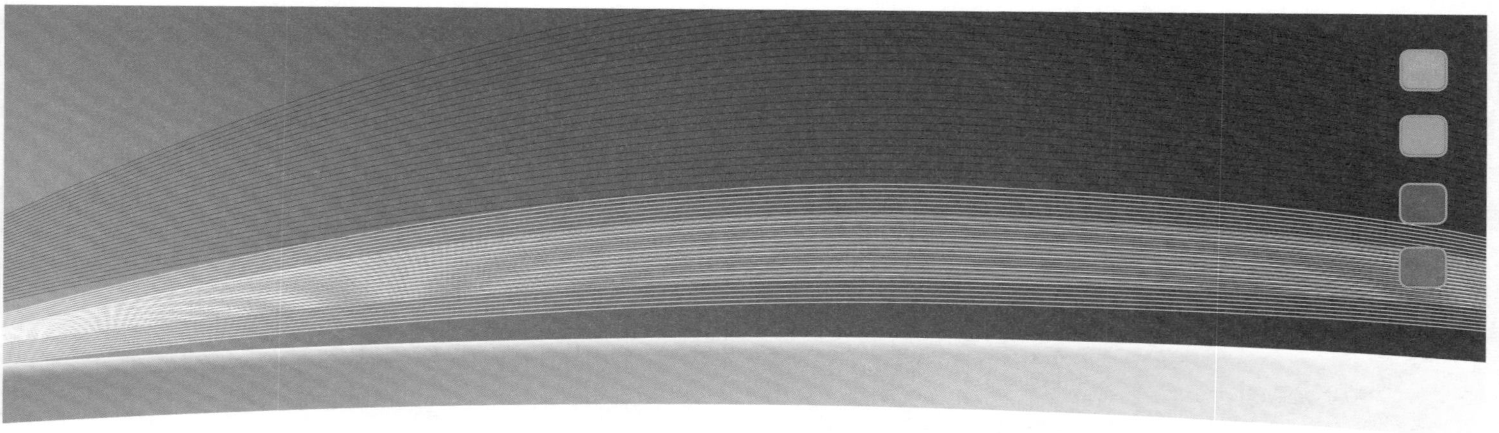

for the company, but provide value to the consumer as well. This connection with finance is no more obvious than in the discussion of breakeven. If the costs from operations, human resources and marketing cannot be covered from the revenue generated by the product, then financially it is not feasible and can't be done within the current cost structure, regardless of its marketing appeal.

Place or distribution is one of the 4Ps that is, by its very nature, the most integrative since any discussion of place must combine two functional areas—operations and marketing. Distribution is typically the responsibility of operations, but is critical to marketing's ability to meet the needs of the customer—getting products to customers when and where they want them. The importance placed on managing the supply chain in today's businesses, that is, the route the product takes from provider to consumer, makes these two areas inseparable.

Promotion appears to most students to be the purest form of marketing, but it is also affected by other areas of the business. For example, one of the elements of a promotional mix is personal selling. This has definite human resource implications. The sales force must be managed to communicate the intended message. And how much is spent on personal selling as opposed to other forms of promotion depends to a great extent on the financial situation of the company. As the chapter suggests, "Money, or the lack of it, is one of the biggest influences on the promotional mix." But the factors in the external environment also affect promotion—the government *(political)* sets guidelines on what can and cannot be done in advertising, the competition has to be monitored carefully to be aware of what message they are projecting vs. your company's message, *social* trends will influence your advertising design and, of course, the *technology* is always changing and expanding the limits of what can be done. For example, the Internet is discussed in the chapter as a potential vehicle for building a brand presence, in fact more quickly than traditional methods, and it is also a powerful tool for tailoring the message to meet the needs of specific consumers. Just go visit (amazon.com).

The clearest example of integration in promotion is the need for integrated marketing communications. Just as all of the 4Ps must project the same message, so must all elements of the promotional mix. If this is not done, the company risks confusing the consumer, and they will simply buy a different product. The area where there is the least control is in personal selling. You are not designing an ad with a consistent message; your salespeople are your message. Therefore, the message may not be the same every time—again you have human resource issues that must be handled very carefully to ensure consistency.

CHAPTER 13

Creating Marketing Strategies

LEARNING OUTCOMES

1. Describe what is meant by a product.
2. Explain the stages of the product life cycle.
3. Discuss the role of pricing and the strategies used for pricing products.
4. Explain distribution and distribution channels.
5. Illustrate how supply chain management can increase efficiency and customer satisfaction.
6. Briefly list the goals of promotional strategy.
7. Discuss the elements of the promotional mix, and integrated marketing communications.
8. Identify the factors that affect the promotional mix.
9. List some of the trends in marketing.

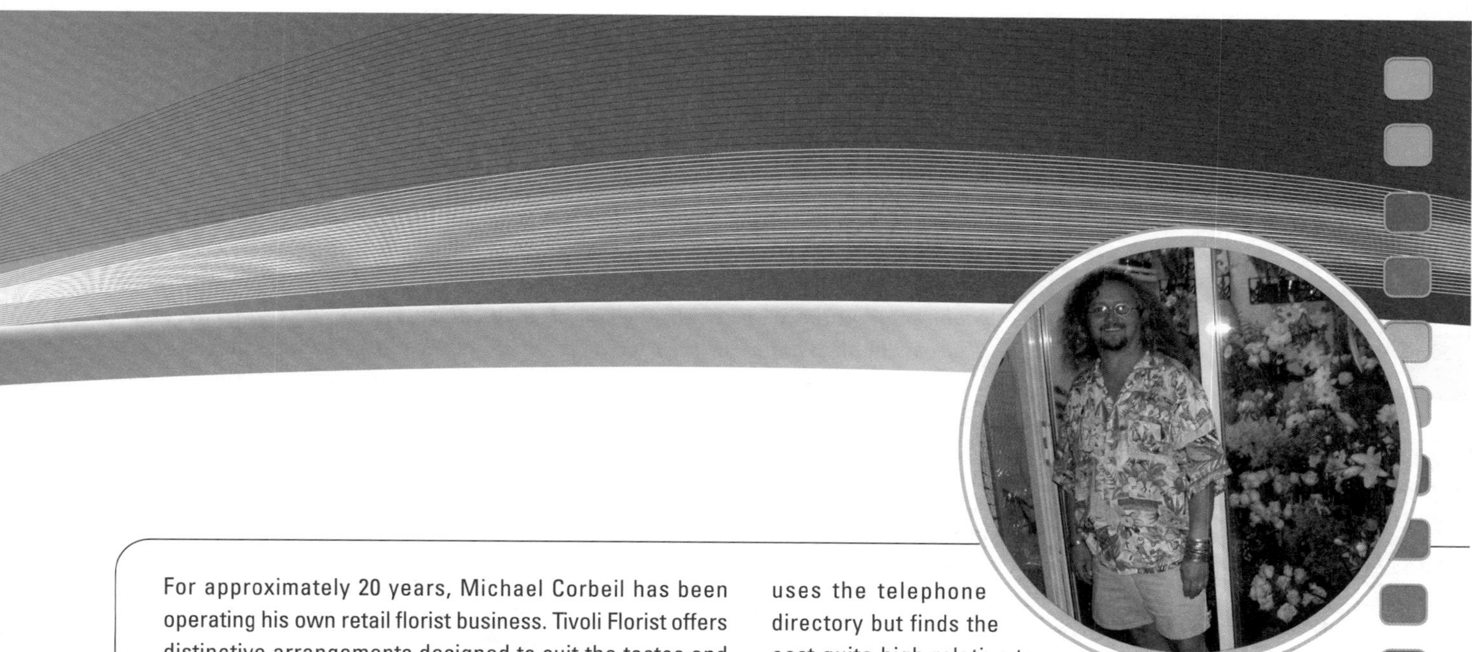

SHIRLEY A. ROSE

For approximately 20 years, Michael Corbeil has been operating his own retail florist business. Tivoli Florist offers distinctive arrangements designed to suit the tastes and requirements of a wide range of clients. Now a successful business owner with two locations, Michael struggled to make the business what it is today. Michael says that he did not realize how long it would take to develop a client base to make the business economically viable. A strong basic knowledge of marketing served him well.

Michael's *product* is several levels up from your run-of-the-mill flower shop. He has 70-80 different types of flowers, none of which are carnations or baby's breath. Fresh flowers arrive daily from such places as Africa, Ecuador, Thailand, Holland, and other European countries. Arrangements are custom designed and range from corporate requirements to weddings, funerals, and other personal occasions. The flowers are fairly-traded and eco-friendly. Other products offered include rare and unusual plants, garden accents, and giftware.

The *price* of Tivoli's flowers reflects the higher quality of the product. In the industry, 3.5 times is the standard markup for an arrangement but some of Tivoli's arrangements are marked up 4 times due to the extra time required to custom design the arrangement. Some of the vases used are very expensive and can be marked up to reflect that, but others are pricey without the same customer appeal, therefore it is sometimes difficult to even get a 1 time markup. At particular times of the year, such as Christmas, Valentine's Day, Easter, and Mother's Day, the markup may be greater, but because of higher shipping costs, the net profit on the arrangement does not increase.

Promotion is done primarily through word-of-mouth. The quality and exclusiveness of the design appeals to the quality-conscious consumer and the reputation of Tivoli Florist spreads throughout the Ottawa area. Michael also uses the telephone directory but finds the cost quite high relative to the results. Tivoli has an attractive website (**www.tivoliflorist.com**) with an interesting array of colourful photographs as well as useful information to inform the inquiring consumer. Another promotional tool used by Michael is the donation of flowers for charitable events that are sponsored by Tivoli's clientele as well as support for and from artistic endeavours.

For now, the *distribution* is from the two existing locations, one a large shop dedicated to Tivoli products, the other a smaller shop as part of another business, Paper Papier, in the Ottawa ByWard Market area. The secondary location is a card and paper store which provides the flowers as a complementary product when customers come in looking for "just the right card" for whatever the occasion. Usually flowers can complete the message the customer wishes to send. Tivoli also offers local and worldwide delivery service.

Obviously in tough economic times, flower sales will suffer since they are covered by one's disposable income. Corporate clients also tend to cut back on non-essentials. But Michael is optimistic, and given his loyal client base and superior product, will probably continue to help brighten the day of his Ottawa customers.

Critical Thinking Questions

1. **In tough economic times, what would you suggest someone like Michael Corbeil might do to maintain the viability of his business?**
2. **What component(s) of the marketing mix should he change? Why? How?**
3. **Check out Michael's website (www.tivoliflorist.com). What suggestions would you make to help encourage more business via the Web?**

The creation of a marketing mix combines the four Ps into a concise plan that will meet or exceed the target market's expectations. Organizations prepare for long-term success by creating and packaging products that add value, and pricing them to meet the organization's financial objectives. The businesses must use the distribution system that enhances the value of the product and determine what methods they will use to move products to locations where consumers wish to buy them. At the same time, the organizations build demand for their products through their promotional strategies. This chapter will discuss the product, price, promotion, and place of goods and services.

What Is a Product?

LO 1

product
In marketing, any good or service, along with its perceived attributes and benefits, that creates value for the customer.

In marketing, a **product** is any good or service, along with its perceived attributes and benefits, that creates value for the customer. Attributes can be tangible or intangible. Among the tangible attributes are packaging and warranties, as illustrated in Exhibit 13.1. Intangible attributes are symbolic, such as brand image. People make decisions about which products to buy after considering both tangible and intangible attributes of a product. For example, when you buy a pair of jeans, you consider price, brand, store image, and style before you buy.

Products are often a blend of goods and services, as shown in Exhibit 13.2. For example, a Honda Civic (a good) would have less value without Honda's maintenance agreement (a service). Although Tim Hortons sells such goods as sandwiches and coffee, customers expect quality service as well, including quick food preparation and cleanliness. When developing a product, an organization must consider how the combination of goods and services will provide value to the customer.

Classifying Consumer Products

Because most things sold are a blend of goods and services, the term *product* can be used to refer to both. After all, consumers are really buying packages of benefits that deliver

EXHIBIT 13.1 > Tangible and Intangible Attributes of a Product Create Value for the Buyer

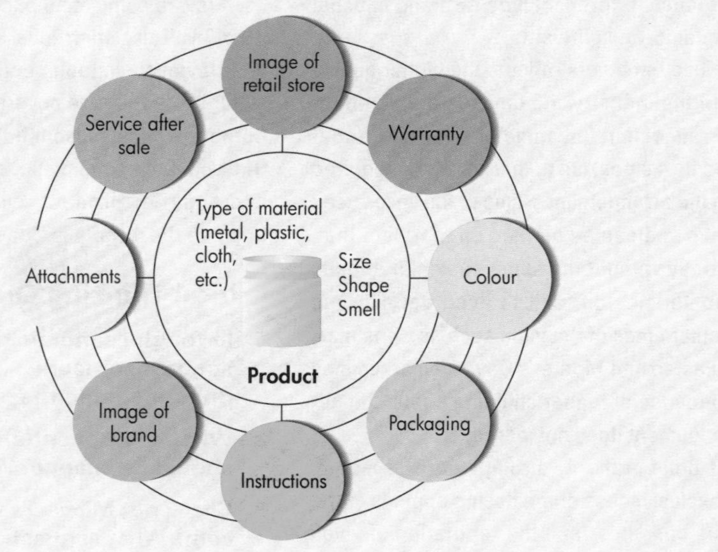

EXHIBIT 13.2 > Products Are Typically a Blend of Goods and Services

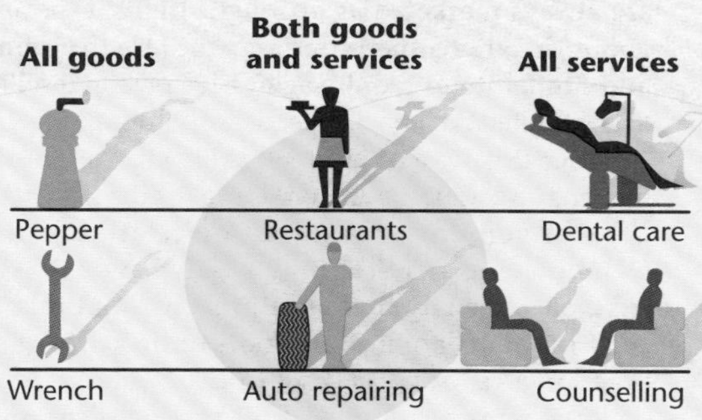

value. The person who buys a plane ride on Air Canada is looking for a quick way to get from one city to another (the benefit). Providing this benefit requires goods (a plane) and services (ticketing, maintenance, piloting).

Marketers must know how consumers view the types of product their companies sell, so that they can design the marketing mix to appeal to the selected target market. To help them define target markets, marketers have devised product categories. Products that are bought by the end user are called *consumer products* (e.g., razors, sandwiches, cars, stereos, magazines, and houses). Consumer products that get used up, such as Lay's potato chips, are called *consumer non-durables*. Those that last for a long time, such as Kenmore washing machines and Apple computers, are *consumer durables*.

Another way to classify consumer products is by the amount of effort consumers are willing to make to acquire them. The four major categories of consumer products are unsought products, convenience products, shopping products, and specialty products, as summarized in Exhibit 13.3.

EXHIBIT 13.3 > Classification of Consumer Products by the Effort Expended to Buy Them

Consumer Product	Examples	Degree of Effort Expended by Consumer
Unsought products	Life insurance Burial plots New products	No effort
Convenience products	Soft drinks Bread Milk Coffee	Very little or minimum effort
Shopping products	Automobiles Homes Vacations	Considerable effort
Specialty products	Expensive jewellery Gourmet dinners Limited-production automobiles	Maximum effort

unsought products
Products that either are unknown to the potential buyer or are known but not actively sought by the buyer.

convenience products
Relatively inexpensive items that require little shopping effort and are purchased routinely without planning.

shopping products
Items that are bought after considerable planning, including brand-to-brand and store-to-store comparisons of price, suitability, and style.

specialty products
Items for which consumers search long and hard, and for which they refuse to accept substitutes.

capital products
Large, expensive items with a long life span that are purchased by businesses for use in making other products or providing a service.

expense items
Items purchased by businesses that are smaller and less expensive than capital products and usually have a life span of less than one year.

Unsought products are products unknown to the potential buyer or known products that the buyer does not actively seek. New products fall into this category until advertising and distribution increase consumer awareness of them. Some goods are always marketed as unsought items, especially products we do not like to think about or care to spend money on. Life insurance, cemetery plots, medical services, and similar items require aggressive personal selling and highly persuasive advertising. Salespeople actively seek leads to potential buyers. Because consumers usually do not seek out this type of product, the company must go directly to them through a salesperson, direct mail, telemarketing, or direct-response advertising.

Convenience products are relatively inexpensive items that require little shopping effort. Soft drinks, candy bars, milk, bread, and small hardware items are examples. We buy them routinely without much planning. This does not mean that such products are unimportant or obscure. Many, in fact, are well known by their brand names—such as Pepsi-Cola, Domino's Pizza, and UPS shipping.

In contrast to convenience products, **shopping products** are bought only after a brand-to-brand and store-to-store comparison of price, suitability, and style. Examples are furniture, automobiles, a vacation in Europe, and some items of clothing. Convenience products are bought with little planning, but shopping products might be chosen months or even years before their actual purchase.

Specialty products are products for which consumers search long and hard, and for which they refuse to accept substitutes. Expensive jewellery, designer clothing, state-of-the-art stereo equipment, limited-production automobiles, and gourmet dinners fall into this category. Because consumers are willing to spend much time and effort to find specialty products, distribution is often limited to one or two sellers in a given region, such as Holt Renfrew, Gucci, or the Porsche dealer.

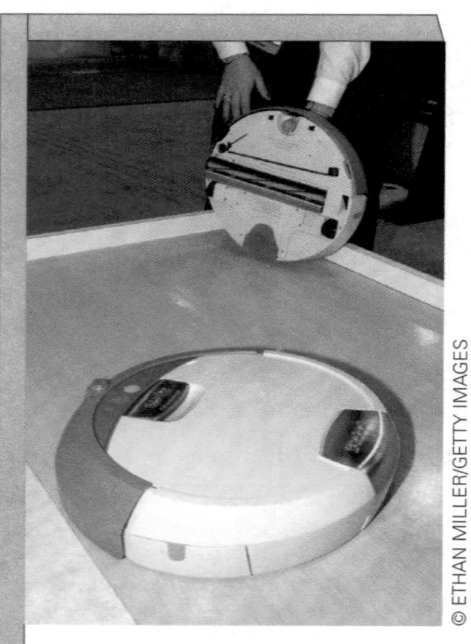

© ETHAN MILLER/GETTY IMAGES

CONCEPT *in Action* >>>

After seeing the Scooba floor-washing robot in action, consumers may never want to touch a mop again. The self-propelled circular bot navigates around hard surfaces, washing and scrubbing floors so they shine like new. A follow-up to the popular Roomba vacuum, Scooba sweeps loose debris, sprays cleaning solution, scrubs surfaces with a brush, and sucks up dirty water—all on its own. How do marketers classify products like the Scooba floor-cleaning robot?

Classifying Business Products

Products bought by businesses or institutions for use in making other products or in providing services are called *business* or *industrial products*. They are classified as either capital products or expense items. **Capital products** are usually large, expensive items with a long life span. Examples are buildings, large machines, and airplanes. **Expense items** are typically smaller, less expensive items that usually have a life span of less than a year. Examples are printer cartridges and paper. Industrial products are sometimes further classified in the following categories:

- *Installations.* These are large, expensive capital items that determine the nature, scope, and efficiency of a company. Capital products like the Ford assembly plant represent a big commitment against future earnings and profitability. Buying an installation requires longer negotiations, more planning, and the judgments of more people than buying any other type of product.
- *Accessories.* Accessories do not have the same long-run impact on the firm as installations, and they are less expensive and more standardized, but they are still capital products. Xerox copy machines, IBM personal computers (PCs), and smaller machines such as Black & Decker table drills and saws are typical accessories. Marketers of accessories often rely on well-known brand names and extensive advertising as well as personal selling.
- *Component parts and materials.* These are expense items that are built into the end product. Some component parts are custom-made, such as a drive shaft for an automobile, a case for a computer, or a special pigment for painting harbour buoys; others are standardized for sale to many industrial users. Intel processors for computers and cement for the construction trade are examples of standardized component parts and materials.
- *Raw materials.* Raw materials are expense items that have undergone little or no processing and are used to create a final product. Examples include lumber, copper, and zinc.

- *Supplies.* Supplies do not become part of the final product. They are bought routinely and in fairly large quantities. Supply items run the gamut from pencils and paper to paint and machine oil. They have little impact on the firm's long-run profits. Bic pens, Unisource copier paper, and Pennzoil machine oil are typical supply items.
- *Services.* These are expense items used to plan or support company operations; for example janitorial cleaning and management consulting.

The Product Life Cycle

LO 2

product life cycle
The pattern of sales and profits over time for a product or product category; consists of an introductory stage, growth stage, maturity, and decline (and death).

Product managers create marketing mixes for their products as they move through the life cycle. The **product life cycle** is a pattern of sales and profits over time for a product (Sunlight dishwashing liquid) or a product category (liquid detergents). As the product moves through the stages of the life cycle, the firm must keep revising the marketing mix to stay competitive and meet the needs of target customers.

Stages of the Life Cycle

As illustrated in Exhibit 13.4, the product life cycle consists of the following stages.

1. *Introduction.* When a product enters the life cycle, it faces many obstacles. Although competition might be light, the *introductory stage* usually features frequent product modifications, limited distribution, and heavy promotion. The failure rate is high. Production and marketing costs are also high, and sales volume is low. Hence, profits are usually small or negative.
2. *Growth stage.* If a product survives the introductory stage, it advances to the *growth stage* of the life cycle. In this stage, sales grow at an increasing rate, profits are healthy, and many competitors enter the market. Large companies might start to acquire small pioneering firms that have reached this stage. Emphasis switches from primary demand promotion to aggressive brand advertising and communicating the differences between brands. For example, the goal changes from convincing people to buy compact DVD players to convincing them to buy Sony versus Panasonic or Sharp.

   Distribution becomes a major key to success during the growth stage, as well as in later stages. Manufacturers scramble to acquire dealers and distributors and to build long-term relationships. Without adequate distribution, it is impossible to establish a strong market position.

   Toward the end of the growth phase, prices normally begin falling and profits peak. Price reductions result from increased competition and from cost reductions from producing larger quantities of items (economies of scale). As well, most firms have recovered their development costs by now, and their priority is in increasing or retaining market share and enhancing profits.
3. *Maturity.* After the growth stage, sales continue to mount—but at a decreasing rate. This is the *maturity stage.* Most products that have been on the market for a long time are in this stage. Thus, most marketing strategies are designed for mature products. One such strategy is to bring out several variations of a basic product (line extension). Kool-Aid, for instance, was originally offered in six flavours. Today there are many flavours, as well as sweetened and unsweetened varieties.
4. *Decline (and death).* When sales and profits fall, the product has reached the decline stage. The rate of decline is governed by two factors: the rate of change in consumer tastes and the rate at which new products enter the market. An example of a product that is at the death stage in Canada is the VCR player. The demand for VCRs is virtually nil (except those that have tapes that have not been converted to DVD).

EXHIBIT 13.4 > Sales and Profits During the Product Life Cycle

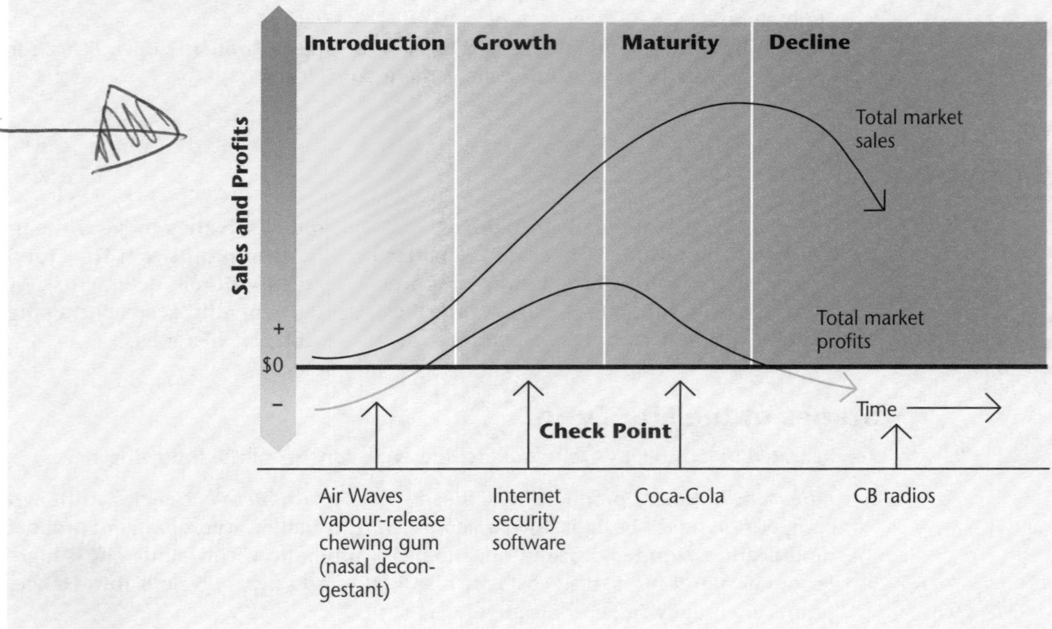

The Product Life Cycle as a Management Tool

The product life cycle can be used in planning. Marketers who understand the cycle concept are better able to forecast future sales and plan new marketing strategies. Exhibit 13.5 is a brief summary of strategic needs at various stages of the product life cycle. Marketers must be sure that a product has moved from one stage to the next before changing the company's marketing strategy. A temporary sales decline should not be interpreted as a sign that the product is dying. Pulling back marketing support can become a self-fulfilling prophecy that brings about the early death of a healthy product.

concept check

What is the product life cycle?

Describe each stage of the product life cycle.

What are the marketing strategies for each stage of the product life cycle?

EXHIBIT 13.5 > Strategies for Success at Each Stage of the Product Life Cycle

Category	Introduction	Growth	Maturity	Decline
Marketing objectives	Encourage trial, establish distribution	Get triers to repurchase, attract new users	Seek new users or uses	Reduce marketing expenses, keep loyal users
Product	Establish competitive advantage	Maintain product quality	Modify product	Maintain product
Distribution	Establish distribution network	Solidify distribution relationships	Provide additional incentives to ensure support	Eliminate trade allowances
Promotional	Build brand awareness	Provide information	Reposition product	Eliminate most advertising and sales promotions
Pricing	Set introductory price (skimming or penetration pricing)	Maintain prices	Reduce prices to meet competition	Maintain prices

Pricing Products Right

LO 3

An important part of the product development process is setting the right price. Price is the perceived value that is exchanged for something else. Value in our society is most commonly expressed in dollars and cents. Thus, price is typically the amount of money exchanged for a good or service. Note that perceived value refers to the time of the transaction. After you've used a product you've bought, you may decide that its actual value was less than its perceived value at the time you bought it. The price you pay for a product is based on the expected satisfaction you will receive and not necessarily the actual satisfaction you will receive.

Although price is usually a dollar amount, it can be anything with perceived value. When goods and services are exchanged for each other, the trade is called barter. If you exchange this book for a math book at the end of the term, you have engaged in barter.

Pricing Objectives

Price is important in determining how much a firm earns. The prices charged customers times the number of units sold equals the gross revenue for the firm. Revenue is what pays for every activity of the company (production, finance, sales, distribution, and so forth). What's left over (if anything) is profit. Managers strive to charge a price that will allow the firm to earn a fair return on its investment.

The chosen price must be neither too high nor too low. And the price must equal the perceived value to target consumers. If consumers think the price is too high, sales opportunities will be lost. Lost sales mean lost revenue. If the price is too low, consumers may view the product as a great value, but the company may not meet its profit goals. Three common pricing objectives are maximizing profits, achieving a target return on the investment, and offering good value at a fair price.

Maximizing Profits

profit maximization
A pricing objective that entails getting the largest possible profit from a product by producing it for as long as the revenue from selling the product exceeds the cost of producing it.

Profit maximization means producing a product for as long as the revenue from selling it exceeds the cost of producing it. In other words, the goal is to get the largest possible profit from the product. For example, suppose Carl Morgan, a builder of houses, sells each house for $300,000. His revenue and cost projections are shown in Exhibit 13.6. Notice in column 3 that the cost of building each house drops for the second through the fifth house. The lower cost per house results from two things: First, by having several houses under construction at the same time, Morgan can afford to hire a full-time crew. The crew is more economical than the independent contractors to whom he would otherwise subcontract each task. Second, Morgan can order materials in greater quantities than usual and thus get quantity discounts on his orders.

Morgan decides that he could sell 15 houses a year at the $300,000 price. But he knows he cannot maximize profits at more than seven houses a year. Inefficiencies begin to creep in at the sixth house. (Notice in column 3 that the sixth house costs more to build than any of the first five houses.) Morgan can't supervise more than seven construction jobs at once, and his full-time crew can't handle even those seven. Thus, Morgan has to subcontract some of the work on the sixth and seventh houses. To build more than seven houses, he would need a second full-time crew.

The exhibit also shows why Morgan should construct seven houses a year. Even though the profit per house is falling for the sixth and seventh houses (column 4), the total profit is still rising (column 5). But at the eighth house, Morgan would go beyond profit maximization. That is, the eighth unit would cost more than its selling price. He would lose $15,000 on the house, and total profit would fall to $154,000 from $169,000 after the seventh house.

EXHIBIT 13.6 > Revenue, Cost, and Profit Projections for Morgan's Houses

(1) Unit of Output (House)	(2) Selling Price (Revenue)	(3) Cost of Building House	(4) Profit on House	(5) Total Profit
1st	$ 300,000	$ 276,000	$ 24,000	$ 24,000
2nd	300,000	275,000	25,000	49,000
3rd	300,000	273,000	27,000	76,000
4th	300,000	270,000	30,000	106,000
5th	300,000	270,000	30,000	136,000
6th	300,000	277,000	23,000	159,000
7th	300,000	290,000	10,000	169,000
8th	300,000	315,000	(15,000)	154,000

Achieving a Target Return on Investment

target return on investment
A pricing objective where the price of a product is set so as to give the company the desired profitability in terms of return on its money.

Another pricing objective used by many companies is **target return on investment,** whereby a price is set to give the company the desired profitability in terms of return on its money. Among the companies that use target return on investment as their main pricing objective are 3M, Procter & Gamble, General Electric, and DuPont.

To get an idea of how target return works, imagine that you are a marketing manager for a cereal company. You estimate that developing, launching, and marketing a new hot cereal will cost $2 million. If the net profit for the first year is $200,000, the return on investment will be $200,000 ÷ $2,000,000, or 10 percent. Let's say that top management sets a 15 percent target return on investment. As a net profit of $200,000 will yield only a 10 percent return, one of two things will happen: Either the cereal won't be produced, or the price and marketing mix will be changed to yield the 15 percent target return.

CONCEPT *in Action* >>>
Some automobile makers have announced Employee-Discount-for-Everyone prices that boosted car sales. But when the bargain blowout ended, so did sales, leaving automakers with an inventory hangover and the need to re-examine their pricing strategies. Some manufacturers switched to value pricing, slashing prices across the board while abandoning incentives like employee discounts and zero-percent financing. Why might some car buyers prefer value pricing to traditional price haggling?

ALAMY

Value Pricing

value pricing
A pricing strategy in which the target market is offered a high-quality product at a fair price and with good service.

Value pricing has become a popular pricing strategy. **Value pricing** means offering the target market a high-quality product at a fair price and with good service. It is the notion of offering the customer a good value. Value pricing doesn't mean high quality that's available only at high prices, nor does it mean bare-bones service or low-quality products. Value pricing can be used to sell a variety of products, from a $30,000 Jeep Wrangler to a $1.99 package of dinner napkins.

A value marketer does the following:

- *Offers products that perform.* This is the price of entry because consumers have lost patience with shoddy merchandise.
- *Gives consumers more than they expect.* Soon after Toyota launched Lexus, the company had to order a recall. The weekend before the recall, dealers phoned every Lexus owner that was affected and arranged to pick up their cars and provide replacement vehicles.
- *Gives meaningful guarantees.* Hyundai offers a five year, 100,000 kilometre power train protection. Michelin recently introduced a tire warranted to last 140,000 kilometres.
- *Gives the buyer facts.* Today's sophisticated consumer wants informative advertising and knowledgeable salespeople.
- *Builds long-term relationships.* The Aeroplan program, Hyatt's Passport Club, and Moen's 800-number hotline all help build good customer relations.

concept check

Explain the concept of price.

What is meant by target return on investment, and how does it differ from profit maximization?

What is value pricing?

How Managers Set Prices

After establishing a pricing objective, managers must set a specific price for the product. Two techniques that are often used to set a price are markup pricing and breakeven analysis.

Markup Pricing

markup pricing
A method of pricing in which a certain percentage (the markup) is added to the product's cost to arrive at the price.

One of the most common forms of pricing is **markup pricing**. In this method, a certain dollar amount is added to a product's cost to arrive at the retail price. (The retail price is thus *cost plus markup*.) The cost is the expense of manufacturing the product or acquiring it for resale. The markup is the amount added to the cost to cover expenses and leave a profit. For the purpose of discussion, there can be two types of markup pricing: one on cost and one on selling price.

For example, if Banana Boat suntan cream costs Shoppers Drug Mart $8 and sells for $11:

based on cost or markup-on-cost,

$$\text{markup amount} = \frac{\text{markup percentage}}{\text{item cost}} \text{ or } \frac{3}{8} = 37.5\%$$

based on selling price or markup-on-selling-price,

$$\text{markup amount} = \frac{\text{markup percentage}}{\text{selling price}} \text{ or } \frac{3}{11} = 27.3\%$$

Several elements influence markups. Among them are tradition, the competition, store image, and stock turnover. Traditionally, department stores used a 40 percent markup. But today, competition and economic conditions have forced retailers to respond to consumer demand and meet competitors' prices. A department store that tried to sell household appliances at a 40 percent markup would lose customers to discounters such as Wal-Mart. However, a retailer trying to develop a prestige image will use markups that are much higher than those used by a retailer trying to develop an image as a discounter.

CONCEPT *in Action* >>>

In recent years, gas prices have soared and fallen. Top producers have defended their pricing methods, citing global demand and political instability as causes of pain at the pump. What are some reasons gas prices rise and fall?

AP/WIDE WORLD PHOTOS

Breakeven Analysis

breakeven point
The price at which a product's costs are covered, so additional sales result in profit.

fixed costs
Costs that do not vary with different levels of output; for example, rent.

variable costs
Costs that change with different levels of output; for example, wages and cost of raw materials.

fixed-cost contribution
The selling price per unit (revenue) minus the variable costs per unit.

total revenue
The selling price per unit times the number of units sold.

total cost
The sum of the fixed costs and the variable costs.

total profit
Total revenue minus total cost.

Manufacturers, wholesalers (companies that buy from manufacturers and sell to retailers and institutions), and retailers (firms that sell to end users) need to know how much of a product must be sold at a certain price to cover all costs. The point at which the costs are covered and additional sales result in profit is the **breakeven point**.

To find the breakeven point, the firm measures the various costs associated with the product:

- **Fixed costs** do not vary with different levels of output. The rent on a manufacturing facility is a fixed cost. It must be paid whether production is one unit or a million.
- **Variable costs** change with different levels of output. Wages and expenses of raw materials are considered variable costs.
- The **fixed-cost contribution** is the selling price per unit (revenue) minus the variable costs per unit.
- **Total revenue** is the selling price per unit times the number of units sold.
- **Total cost** is the total of the fixed costs and the variable costs.
- **Total profit** is total revenue minus total cost.

Knowing these amounts, the firm can calculate the breakeven point:

Breakeven point in units = Total fixed cost ÷ Fixed cost contribution

Let's see how this works: Gray Corporation, a manufacturer of aftershave lotion, has variable costs of $3 per bottle and fixed costs of $50,000. Gray's management believes the company can sell up to 100,000 bottles of aftershave at $5 a bottle without having to lower its price. Gray's fixed-cost contribution is $2 ($5 selling price per bottle minus $3 variable costs per bottle). Therefore, $2 per bottle is the amount that can be used to cover the company's fixed costs of $50,000.

To determine its breakeven point, Gray applies the previous equation:

$$\text{Breakeven point in bottles} = \frac{\$50{,}000 \text{ fixed cost}}{\$2 \text{ fixed-cost contribution}} = 25{,}000 \text{ bottles}$$

HOT Links

Companies are turning to Web-based, smart-pricing software to improve margins on products. Find out how one company's software works at Oracle's website, (**www.oracle.com**).

Gray Corporation will, therefore, break even when it sells 25,000 bottles of aftershave lotion. After that point, at which the fixed costs are met, the $2 per bottle becomes profit. If Gray's forecasts are correct and it can sell 100,000 bottles at $5 a bottle, its total profit will be $150,000 ($2 per bottle × 75,000 bottles).

By using the equation, Gray Corp. can quickly find out how much it needs to sell to break even. It can then calculate how much profit it will earn if it sells more units. A firm that is operating close to the breakeven point might change the profit picture in two ways. Reducing costs will lower the breakeven point and expand profits. Increasing sales will not change the breakeven point, but it will provide more profits.

concept check

Explain how markups are calculated.
Describe breakeven analysis.
What does it mean to "break even"?

Product Pricing Strategies

Managers use various pricing strategies when determining the price of a product, as we explain in this section. Price skimming and penetration pricing are strategies used in pricing new products; other strategies, such as leader pricing and bundling, might be used for established products as well.

Price Skimming

price skimming
The strategy of introducing a product with a high initial price and lowering the price over time as the product moves through its life cycle.

The practice of introducing a new product on the market with a high price and then lowering the price over time is called **price skimming**. As the product moves through its life cycle, the price usually is lowered because competitors are entering the market. As the price falls, more and more consumers can buy the product.

Price skimming has four important advantages. First, a high initial price can be a way to find out what buyers are willing to pay. Second, if consumers find the introductory price too high, it can be lowered. Third, a high introductory price can create an image of quality and prestige. Fourth, when the price is lowered later, consumers might think they are getting a bargain. The disadvantage is that high prices attract competition.

Price skimming can be used to price virtually any new product, such as high-definition televisions, PCs, and colour computer printers. For example, the Republic of Tea has launched new Imperial Republic White Tea, which it says is among the rarest of teas. Because it is minimally processed, white tea is said to retain the highest level of antioxidants and has less caffeine than black and green teas. The company says the tea is picked only a few days each year, right before the leaves open, yielding a small harvest. The product retails for $14 per tin of 50 bags. Products don't have to be expensive to use a skimming strategy.

Penetration Pricing

penetration pricing
The strategy of selling new products at low prices in the hope of achieving a large sales volume.

A company that doesn't use price skimming will probably use **penetration pricing**. With this strategy, the company offers new products at low prices in the hope of achieving a large sales volume. Procter & Gamble did this with SpinBrush. Penetration pricing requires more extensive planning than skimming does, because the company must gear up for mass production and marketing. If the company significantly overestimates demand, its losses are considerable.

Penetration pricing has two advantages. First, the low initial price might induce consumers to switch brands or companies. Using penetration pricing on its jug wines, Gallo has lured customers away from Taylor California Cellars and Inglenook. Second, penetration pricing might discourage competitors from entering the market. Their costs would tend to be higher, so they would need to sell more at the same price to break even.

CONCEPT *in Action* >>>

Dell offers new products at low prices to achieve a high sales volume. In a successful strategy to increase market share, Dell slashed prices of personal computers, requiring competitors Gateway, HP, and Compaq to do the same. What pricing strategy does Dell use?

© AP/WIDE WORLD PHOTOS

Leader Pricing

leader pricing
The strategy of pricing products below the normal markup or even below cost to attract customers to a store where they would not otherwise shop.

loss leader
A product priced below cost as part of a leader pricing strategy.

Pricing products below the normal markup or even below cost to attract customers to a store where they wouldn't otherwise shop is leader pricing. A product priced below cost is referred to as a loss leader. The customers go to the retailer and will often purchase many other products that are competitively priced, not just the loss leader. Retailers hope that this type of pricing will increase their overall sales volume and thus their profit.

Items that are leader priced are usually well known and priced low enough to appeal to many customers. They also are items that consumers will buy at a lower price, even if they have to switch brands. Supermarkets often feature coffee and bacon in their leader pricing. Department stores and specialty stores also rely heavily on leader pricing.

Bundling

bundling
The strategy of grouping two or more related products together and pricing them as a single product.

Bundling means grouping two or more related products together and pricing them as a single product. Weston Hotels' special weekend rates often include the room, breakfast, and one night's dinner. Department stores might offer a washer and dryer together for a price lower than if the units were bought separately. Rogers Communications and Shaw Cable bundle services such as telephone, Internet, and television into one package. This is not only convenient for the customer but, as the next paragraph highlights, allows the companies to sell more products.

The idea behind bundling is to reach a segment of the market that the products sold separately would not reach as effectively. Some buyers are more than willing to buy one product but have much less use for the second. Bundling the second product to the first at a slightly reduced price thus creates some sales that otherwise would not be made. Aussie 3 Minute Miracle Shampoo is typically bundled with its conditioner, because many people use shampoo more than conditioner, so they don't need a new bottle of conditioner.

Odd-Even Pricing

odd-even (psychological) pricing
The strategy of setting a price at an odd number to connote a bargain and at an even number to suggest quality.

Psychology often plays a big role in how consumers view prices and what prices they will pay. Odd-even pricing (or psychological pricing) is the strategy of setting a price at an odd number to connote a bargain and at an even number to imply quality. For years, many retailers have priced their products in odd numbers—for example, $99.95 or $49.95—to make consumers feel that they are paying a lower price for the product.

Some retailers favour odd-numbered prices because they believe that $9.99 sounds much less imposing to customers than $10.00. Other retailers believe that an odd-numbered price signals to consumers that the price is at the lowest level possible, thereby encouraging them to buy more units. Neither theory has ever been proved conclusively, although one study found that consumers perceive odd-priced products as being on sale. Even-numbered pricing is sometimes used to denote quality. Examples include a fine perfume at $100 a bottle, a good watch at $500, or a Holt Renfrew coat at $3,000.

prestige pricing
The strategy of increasing the price of a product so that consumers will perceive it as being of higher quality, status, or value.

Prestige Pricing

The strategy of raising the price of a product so consumers will perceive it as being of higher quality, status, or value is called prestige pricing. This type of pricing is common where high prices indicate high status. In the specialty shops on Rodeo Drive in Beverly Hills, which cater to the super-rich of Hollywood, shirts that would sell for $40 elsewhere sell for at least $150. If the price were lower, customers would perceive them as being of low quality.

concept check

What is the difference between penetration pricing and price skimming?

Explain the concept of price bundling.

Describe odd-even pricing and prestige pricing.

The Nature and Functions of Distribution

LO 4

distribution (logistics)
Efficiently managing the acquisition of raw materials to the factory and the movement of products from the producer to industrial users and consumers.

manufacturer
A producer; an organization that converts raw materials to finished products.

Distribution (or logistics) is efficiently managing the acquisition of raw materials to the factory and the movement of products from the producer or manufacturer to industrial users and consumers. Logistics activities are usually the responsibility of the marketing department and are part of the large series of activities included in the supply chain. As discussed in Chapter 11, a supply chain is the system through which an organization acquires raw material, produces products, and delivers the products and services to its customers. Exhibit 13.7 illustrates a supply chain. Supply chain management helps increase the efficiency of logistics service by minimizing inventory and moving goods efficiently from producers to the ultimate users.

EXHIBIT 13.7 > Supply Chain

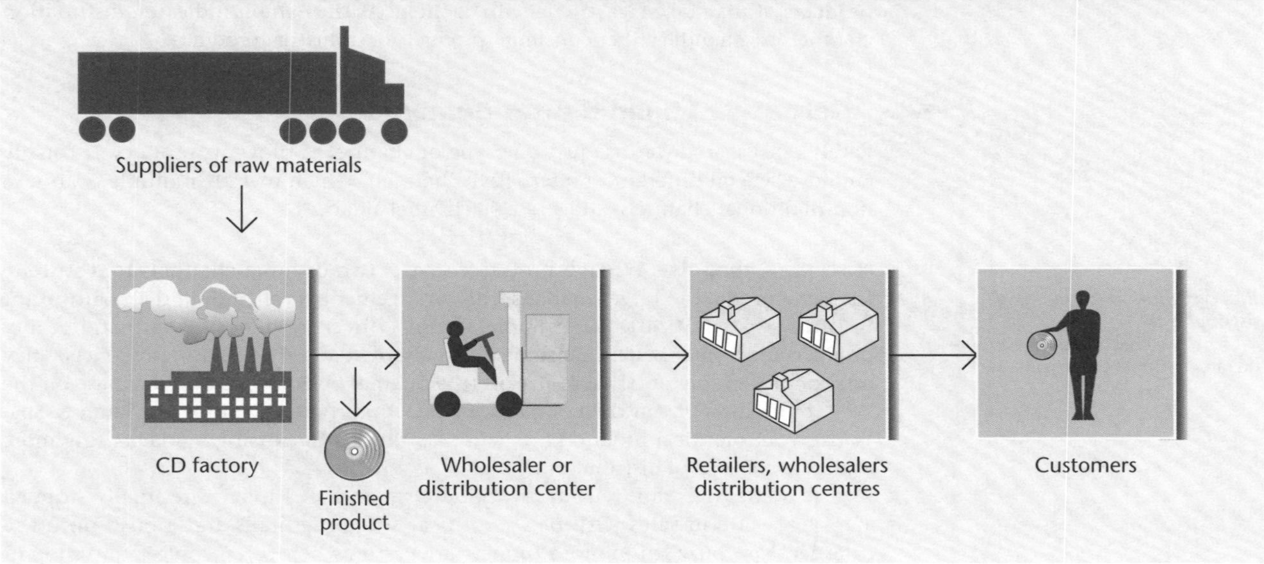

On their way from producers to end users and consumers, goods and services pass through a series of marketing entities known as a distribution channel. We will look first at the entities that make up a distribution channel and then will examine the functions that channels serve.

distribution channel
The series of marketing entities through which goods and services pass on their way from producers to end users.

Marketing Intermediaries in the Distribution Channel

A distribution channel is made up of marketing intermediaries, or organizations that assist in moving goods and services from producers to end users and consumers. Marketing intermediaries are in the middle of the distribution process between the producer and the end user. The following marketing intermediaries most often appear in the distribution channel:

marketing intermediaries
Organizations that assist in moving goods and services from producers to end users.

- *Agents and brokers*. Agents are sales representatives of manufacturers and wholesalers, and brokers are entities that bring buyers and sellers together. Both agents and brokers are usually hired on commission basis by either a buyer or a seller. Agents and brokers are go-betweens whose job is to make deals. They do not own or take possession of goods.
- *Industrial distributors*. Industrial distributors are independent wholesalers that buy related product lines from many manufacturers and sell them to industrial users. They often have a sales force to call on purchasing agents, make deliveries, extend credit, and provide information. Industrial distributors are used in such industries as aircraft manufacturing, mining, and petroleum.
- *Wholesalers*. Wholesalers are firms that sell finished goods to retailers, manufacturers, and institutions (such as schools and hospitals). Historically, their function has been to buy from manufacturers and sell to retailers.
- *Retailers*. Retailers are firms that sell goods to consumers and to industrial users for their own consumption.

agents
Sales representatives of manufacturers and wholesalers.

brokers
Go-betweens that bring buyers and sellers together.

industrial distributors
Independent wholesalers that buy related product lines from many manufacturers and sell them to industrial users.

wholesalers
Firms that sell finished goods to retailers, manufacturers, and institutions.

retailers
Firms that sell goods to consumers and to industrial users for their own consumption.

At the end of the distribution channel are final consumers, like you and me, and industrial users. Industrial users are firms that buy products for internal use or for producing other products or services. They include manufacturers, utilities, airlines, railroads, and service institutions, such as hotels, hospitals, and schools.

Exhibit 13.8 shows various ways marketing intermediaries can be linked. For instance, a manufacturer may sell to a wholesaler that sells to a retailer that in turn sells to a customer. In any of these distribution systems, goods and services are physically transferred from one organization to the next. As each takes possession of the products, it may take legal ownership of them. As the exhibit indicates, distribution channels can handle either consumer products or industrial products.

Alternative Channel Arrangements

Rarely does a producer use just one type of channel to move its product. It usually employs several different or alternative channels, which include multiple channels, non-traditional channels, and strategic channel alliances.[1]

Multiple Channels When a producer selects two or more channels to distribute the same product to target markets, this arrangement is called dual distribution (or multiple distribution). For example, Avon, a direct supplier of health and beauty products for women, offers consumers four alternatives for purchasing products. They can contact a representative in person (the original business model), purchase on the Web, order direct from the company, or pick up products at an Avon Salon & Spa. With Avon, identical products are being distributed to existing markets using more than one channel of distribution.

dual distribution (or multiple distribution)
Two or more channels that distribute the same product to target markets.

Dual channels don't always work out as planned. Tupperware finally stopped a 15-year slide in sales with new booths at shopping malls and a push onto the Internet. New buzz led to more Tupperware parties where salespeople set up shop in

EXHIBIT 13.8 > Channels of Distribution for Industrial and Consumer Products

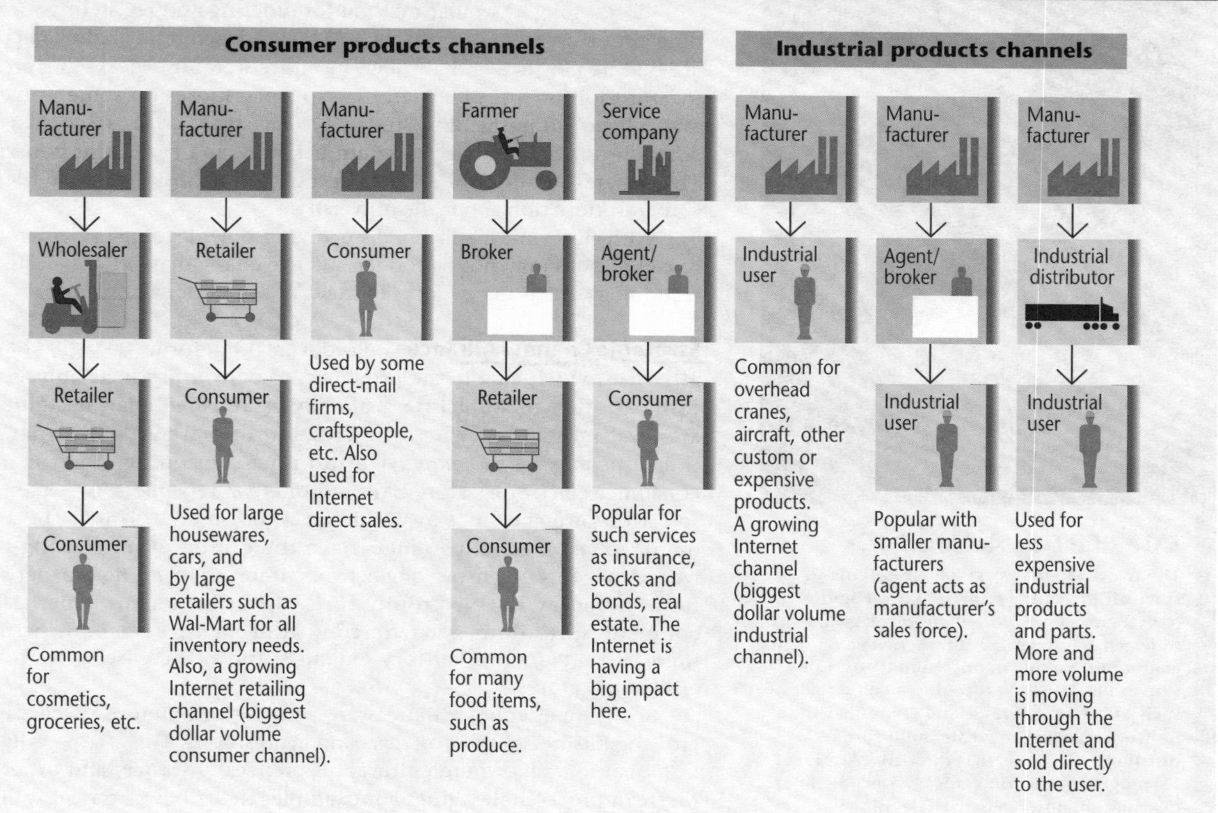

Consumer products channels
Industrial products channels
Manu-facturer
Wholesaler
Retailer
Consumer
Common for cosmetics, groceries, etc.
Manu-facturer
Retailer
Consumer
Used for large housewares, cars, and by large retailers such as Wal-Mart for all inventory needs. Also, a growing Internet retailing channel (biggest dollar volume consumer channel).
Manu-facturer
Consumer
Used by some direct-mail firms, craftspeople, etc. Also used for Internet direct sales.
Farmer
Broker
Retailer
Consumer
Common for many food items, such as produce.
Service company
Agent/ broker
Consumer
Popular for such services as insurance, stocks and bonds, real estate. The Internet is having a big impact here.
Manu-facturer
Industrial user
Common for overhead cranes, aircraft, other custom or expensive products. A growing Internet channel (biggest dollar volume industrial channel).
Manu-facturer
Agent/ broker
Industrial user
Popular with smaller manu-facturers (agent acts as manufacturer's sales force).
Manu-facturer
Industrial distributor
Industrial user
Used for less expensive industrial products and parts. More and more volume is moving through the Internet and sold directly to the user.

people's living rooms to show off plastic food storage containers and such. Then the company decided to place Tupperware in some stores with salespeople in the aisles to demonstrate the merchandise. It looked like the answer to a chronic problem: how to sell face-to-face in an era when shoppers don't have time for a door-to-door sales pitch. Tupperware also figured the move would give it a stream of potential party hosts and sales-force recruits.

But moving into stores turned out to be one of the worst disasters ever at Tupperware. It was so easy to find the company's products that interest in its parties plummeted. Fewer parties meant fewer chances to land other parties and new salespeople—which Tupperware needs to offset turnover that often hits 100 percent a year.[2]

Non-traditional Channels Often non-traditional channel arrangements help differentiate a firm's product from the competition. For example, manufacturers may decide to use non-traditional channels such as the Internet, mail-order channels, or infomercials to sell products instead of going through traditional retailer channels. Although non-traditional channels may limit a brand's coverage, they can give a producer serving a niche market a way to gain market access and customer attention without having to establish channel intermediaries. Non-traditional channels can also provide another avenue of sales for larger firms. For example, a London publisher sells short stories through vending machines in the London

© TERRI MILLER/E-VISUAL COMMUNICATIONS INC.

CONCEPT *in Action* >>>

The television networks are scrambling to stave off the end of television as we know it, as a new generation of viewers has taken to watching streaming Internet video on computers, mobile phones, and iPods. Consumer migration to video download services such as YouTube, In2TV, and iTunes has the networks rushing to create multi-format distribution systems that can deliver Internet TV programming. How might direct digital distribution upset network television's traditional distribution channel?

Underground. Instead of the traditional book format, the stories are printed like folded maps making them an easy-to-read alternative for commuters.

Kiosks, long a popular method for ordering and registering for wedding gifts, dispersing cash through ATMs, and facilitating airline check-in, are finding new uses. Ethan Allen furniture stores use kiosks as a product locator tool for consumers and salespeople. Kiosks on some university and college campuses allow students to register for classes, see their class schedule and grades, check account balances, and even print transcripts. The general public, when it has access to the kiosks, can use them to gather information about the university.

With electronic media rapidly evolving, downloading first-run movies to cell phones may not be too far off! The changing world of electronics technology opens many doors for new, non-traditional channels.

Strategic Channel Alliances Producers often form **strategic channel alliances** which enable the producers to deliver products and services using another manufacturer's already-established channel. Alliances are used most often when the creation of marketing channel relationships may be too expensive and time-consuming. Amazon and a consumer electronics store have a multiyear agreement to expand the selection of electronics available on Amazon.com. Under the agreement, Amazon.com customers have the option of purchasing items from Amazon's inventory of electronic items or from the broader selection offered by the electronic store. The arrangement benefits both companies: it allows Amazon.com to deepen its selection without increasing its own inventory expense, and it increases sales for the electronics store.

Strategic channel alliances are proving to be more successful for growing businesses than mergers and acquisitions. This is especially true in global markets where cultural differences, distance, and other barriers can prove challenging. For example, Heinz has a strategic alliance with Kagome, one of Japan's largest food companies. The companies are

CONCEPT *in Action* >>>

Cabela's started as a two-person, direct-mail operation in the early 1960s. Today, the outdoor outfitter is the world's largest direct marketer and specialty retailer of hunting, fishing, and related merchandise. In addition to operating its famed catalogue business, Cabela's now sells goods to customers through the Internet and at retail superstores. Cabela's showrooms bring the outdoors inside—the stores' museum-quality displays of wildlife, fishing ponds, and mountain replicas are veritable tourist attractions. What logistical challenges arise from using multiple distribution channels?

© AP/WIDE WORLD PHOTOS

CONCEPT *in Action* >>>

An efficient distribution system allows Home Depot to offer customers a vast assortment of building materials, appliances, and tools economically. What do you think the distribution channels for Home Depot are?

strategic channel alliances
One manufacturer using another manufacturer's previously established channel to distribute its goods.

working together to find ways to reduce operating costs while expanding both brands' market presence globally.

The Functions of Distribution Channels

Why do distribution channels exist? Why can't every firm sell its products directly to the end user or consumer? Why are go-betweens needed? Channels serve a number of functions.

Channels Reduce the Number of Transactions Channels make distribution simpler by reducing the number of transactions required to get a product from the manufacturer to the consumer. Assume for the moment that only four students are in your class. Also assume that your professor requires five textbooks, each from a different publisher. If there were no bookstore, 20 transactions would be necessary for all students in the class to buy the books, as shown in Exhibit 13.9. If the bookstore serves as a go-between, the number of transactions is reduced to nine. Each publisher sells to one bookstore rather than to four students. Each student buys from one bookstore instead of from five publishers.

Dealing with channel intermediaries frees producers from many of the details of distribution activity. Producers are traditionally not as efficient or as enthusiastic about selling products directly to end users as channel members are. First, producers may wish to focus on production. They may feel that they cannot both produce and distribute in a competitive way. On the other hand, manufacturers are eager to deal directly with larger retailers, such as Sport Chek. Sport Chek offers huge sales opportunities to producers.

Channels Ease the Flow of Goods Channels make distribution easier in several ways. The first is by sorting, which consists of the following:

- *Sorting out*. Breaking many different items into separate stocks that are similar. Eggs, for instance, are sorted by grade and size.
- *Accumulating*. Bringing similar stocks together into a larger quantity. Twelve large Grade A eggs could be placed in some cartons and 12 medium Grade B eggs in other cartons.
- *Allocating*. Breaking similar products into smaller and smaller lots. (Allocating at the wholesale level is called **breaking bulk**.) For instance, a tank-car load of milk could be broken down into gallon jugs. The process of allocating generally is done when the goods are dispersed by region and as ownership of the goods changes.

breaking bulk
The process of breaking large shipments of similar products into smaller, more usable lots.

EXHIBIT 13.9 > How Distribution Channels Reduce the Number of Transactions

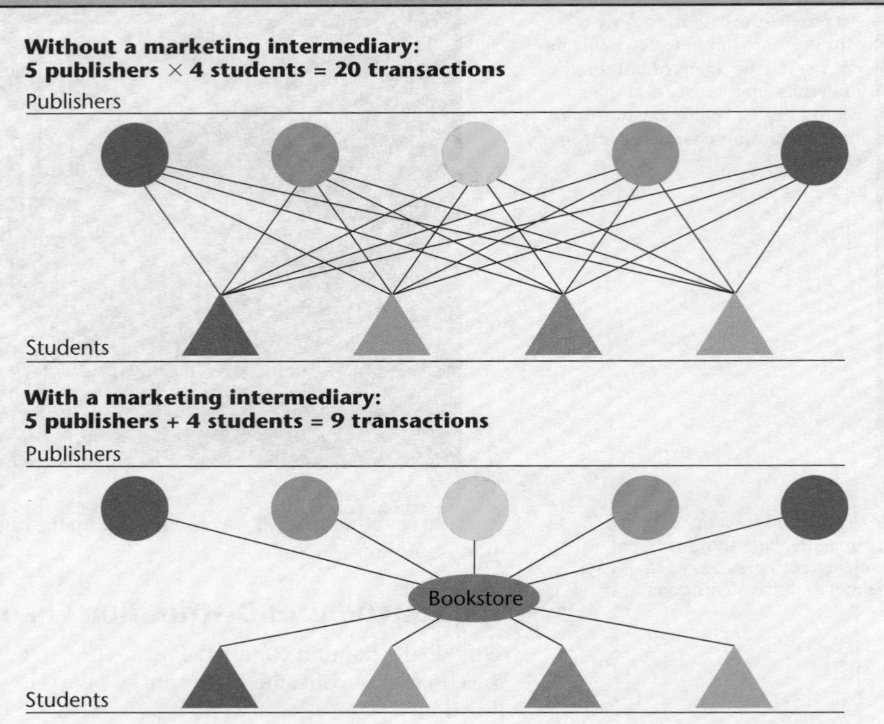

Without the sorting, accumulating, and allocating processes, modern society would not exist. We would have home-based industries providing custom or semicustom products to local markets. In short, we would return to a much lower level of consumption.

A second way channels ease the flow of goods is by locating buyers for merchandise. A wholesaler must find the right retailers to sell a profitable volume of merchandise. A sporting-goods wholesaler, for instance, must find the retailers who are most likely to reach sporting-goods consumers. Retailers have to understand the buying habits of consumers and put stores where consumers want and expect to find the merchandise. Every member of a distribution channel must locate buyers for the products it is trying to sell.

Channel members also store merchandise so that goods are available when consumers want to buy them. The high cost of retail space often means that many goods are stored by the wholesaler or the manufacturer.

Channels Perform Needed Functions The functions performed by channel intermediaries help increase the efficiency of the channel. Yet consumers sometimes feel that the go-betweens create higher prices. They doubt that these intermediaries perform useful functions. Actually, however, if channel intermediaries did not perform important and necessary functions at a reasonable cost, they would cease to exist. If firms could earn a higher profit without using certain channel members, they would not use them.

Channel intermediaries perform three general functions: transactional, logistical, and facilitating. We have already discussed logistics. Transactional functions involve contacting and communicating with prospective buyers to make them aware of goods and services that are available. Sellers attempt to explain why their offerings provide more features, benefits, and value than the competition. The third function is facili-

EXHIBIT 13.10 > Marketing Channel Functions Performed by Intermediaries

Type of Function	Description
Transaction Functions	**Contacting and promoting:** Contacting potential customers, promoting products, and soliciting orders **Negotiating:** Determining how many goods or services to buy and sell, type of transportation to use, when to deliver, and method and timing of payment **Risk taking:** Assuming the risk of owning inventory
Logistical Functions	**Physically distributing:** Transporting and sorting goods **Storing:** Maintaining inventories and protecting goods **Sorting out:** Breaking down a heterogeneous supply into separate homogeneous stocks **Accumulation:** Combining similar stocks into a larger homogeneous supply **Allocation:** Breaking a homogeneous supply into smaller and smaller lots ("breaking bulk") **Assortment:** Combining products into collections or assortments that buyers want available at one place
Facilitating Functions	**Researching:** Gathering information about other channel members and consumers **Financing:** Extending credit and other financial services to facilitate the flow of goods through the channel to the final consumer

tating, which includes financing and market research. Research answers questions such as who is buying the products, where do they like to buy the items, and what are the characteristics of the users. The three basic functions that channel intermediaries perform are summarized in Exhibit 13.10.

A useful rule to remember is that, although channel intermediaries can be eliminated, their functions cannot. The manufacturer must either perform the functions of the intermediaries itself or find new ways of getting them carried out. Publishers can bypass bookstores, for instance, but the function performed by the bookstores then has to be performed by the publishers or by someone else.

concept check

List and define the marketing intermediaries that make up a distribution channel.

Provide an example of a strategic channel alliance.

How do channels reduce the number of transactions?

Expanding Around The Globe

EASY DOES IT ALL

It's just after midnight on the French Riviera, and while the rich and famous sip champagne in Cannes at the annual film festival, something unsightly and orange cruises into the harbour and plops down its anchor among the majestic yachts. An enormous "EasyCruise .com" logo runs down the length of the ship, with all the subtlety of a flashing neon sign. This is the maiden voyage of a new concept in budget cruising, the 14th venture of low-cost superbrand EasyGroup.

The Easy empire was built on experiments in low-cost living like EasyCruise, and life on the inside is a study in value trumping aesthetics. The company is the brainchild of 38-year-old Greek shipping heir Stelios Haji-Ioannou, who popped up on the international radar screen in 1995 when he founded budget airline EasyJet at the tender age of 28. Now, he is merrily slapping the Easy brand on an almost unlimited array of discount products and services, many of which seem to have little in common. There are Easy movie rentals and an Easy shaving cream. There are Easy Internet cafes, Easy pizzas, and an Easy hotel. There's even an Easy wristwatch. "In an industry where consumers are being ripped off, if I can find a way to give them real value, I'm going to do it," he says.

It's an audacious—some would say delusional—notion. But then, nobody thought Stelios had much of a chance with his low-cost debut, the airline. The airline is now fourth only to Lufthansa, Air France, and KLM in the number of passengers carried within Europe. And although it's true that 11 of the other 14 Easy companies have yet to turn an annual profit, they're still young—half have existed for less than a year.

Competitors, however, often feel threatened by Easy's incursions. Stelios starts price wars almost everywhere he goes, and that has earned him plenty of detractors across many industries. "His assumption that he can take any idea and just slap his brand on it is somewhat arrogant," says Paolo Pescatore, a wireless analyst with research firm IDC. Easy's mobile-phone venture, launched in March, illustrates the typical pattern. It sells SIM cards that can be put into existing handsets and then charges for service. Its debut prices were as much as 40 percent below prevailing norms, and rival Carphone Warehouse countered with deep discounts of its own. Orange, a heavyweight in the United Kingdom, sued Easy—for using orange, the same colour that Orange uses in its ads.[3]

Critical Thinking Questions

- With 15 Easy brands on the market, in many different industries, do you think that Stelios has diversified too much? Is he destroying the mystique of the brand?
- Stelios says North America will be "Easy pickings" for the Easy Group. Do you agree? Why or why not?

SOURCE: "Easy Does It All," *Business 2.0*, August 2005, pg. 69–74.

The Intensity of Market Coverage

All types of distribution systems must be concerned with market coverage. How many dealers will be used to distribute the product in a particular area? The three degrees of coverage are exclusive, selective, and intensive. The type of product determines the intensity of the market coverage.

When a manufacturer selects one or two dealers in an area to market its products, it is using **exclusive distribution**. Only items that are in strong demand can be distributed exclusively because consumers must be willing to travel some distance to buy them. If Dentyne chewing gum were sold in only one drugstore per city, Dentyne would soon be out of business. However, Bang and Olufsen stereo components, Jaguar automobiles, and top name designer clothing are distributed exclusively with great success.

exclusive distribution
A distribution system in which a manufacturer selects only one or two dealers in an area to market its products.

selective distribution
A distribution system in which a manufacturer selects a limited number of dealers in an area (but more than one or two) to market its products.

intensive distribution
A distribution system in which a manufacturer tries to sell its products wherever there are potential customers.

A manufacturer that chooses a limited number of dealers in an area (but more than one or two) is using **selective distribution**. Since the number of retailers handling the product is limited, consumers must be willing to seek it out. Timberland boots, a high-quality line of footwear, are distributed selectively. So are Sony televisions, Maytag washers, Waterford crystal, and Tommy Hilfiger clothing. When choosing dealers, manufacturers look for certain qualities. Sony may seek retailers that can offer high-quality customer service. Tommy Hilfiger may look for retailers with high-traffic locations in regional shopping malls. All manufacturers try to exclude retailers that are a poor credit risk or that have a weak or negative image.

A manufacturer that wants to sell its products everywhere there are potential customers is using **intensive distribution**. Such consumer goods as bread, tape, and light bulbs are often distributed intensively. Usually, these products cost little and are bought frequently, which means that complex distribution channels are necessary. Coca-Cola is sold in just about every type of retail business, from gas stations to grocery stores.

concept check

Name the three degrees of market coverage.

Describe the types of products that are distributed using intensive distribution.

Supply Chain Management: Increasing Efficiency and Customer Satisfaction

Distribution is an important part of the marketing mix. Retailers don't sell products they can't deliver, and salespeople don't (or shouldn't) promise deliveries they can't make. Late deliveries and broken promises may mean loss of a customer. Accurate order filling and billing, timely delivery, and arrival in good condition are important to the success of the product.

The goal of supply chain management is to create a satisfied customer by coordinating all of the activities of the supply chain members into a seamless process. Therefore, an important element of supply chain management is that it is completely customer driven. In the mass-production era, manufacturers produced standardized products that were "pushed" down through the supply channel to the consumer. In today's marketplace by contrast, products are being driven by customers who expect to receive product configurations and services matched to their unique needs. For example, Dell only builds computers according to its customers' precise specifications, such as the amount of RAM memory; type of monitor, modem, or CD drive; and amount of hard-disk space. The process begins by Dell purchasing partly built laptops from contract manufacturers. The final assembly is done in Dell factories in Ireland, Malaysia, or China where microprocessors, software, and other key components are added. Those finished products are then shipped to Dell-operated distribution centres in Canada where they are packaged with other items and shipped to the customer.

Through the channel partnership, suppliers, manufacturers, wholesalers, and retailers along the entire supply chain work together toward the common goal of creating customer value. Supply chain management allows companies to respond with the unique product configuration and mix of services demanded by the customer. Today, supply chain management plays a dual role: first, as a communicator of customer demand that extends from the point of sale all the way back to the supplier, and second, as a physical flow process that engineers the timely and cost-effective movement of goods through the entire supply pipeline.

Accordingly, supply chain managers are responsible for making channel strategy decisions, coordinating the sourcing and procurement of raw materials, scheduling production, processing orders, managing inventory, transporting and storing supplies and finished goods, and coordinating customer service activities. Supply chain managers are also responsible for the management of information that flows through the supply chain. Coordinating the relationships between the company and its external partners, such as vendors, carriers and third-party companies, is also a critical function of supply chain management. Because supply chain managers play such a major role in both cost control and customer satisfaction, they are more valuable than ever.

Managing the Logistical Components of the Supply Chain

Logistics, discussed earlier, is a term borrowed from the military that describes the process of strategically managing the efficient flow and storage of raw materials, in-process inventory, and finished goods from the point of origin to the point of consumption. The supply chain team manages the logistical flow. Key decisions in managing the logistical flow are: finding and procuring raw materials and supplies, production scheduling, choosing a warehouse location and type, inventory control, setting up a materials-handling system, and making transportation decisions.

Sourcing and Procurement

One of the most important links in the supply chain is between the manufacturer and the supplier. Purchasing professionals are on the front lines of supply chain management. Purchasing departments plan purchasing strategies, develop specifications, select suppliers, and negotiate price and service levels.

The goal of most sourcing and procurement activities is to reduce the costs of raw materials and supplies and to have the items available when they are needed, for production or for the office, but not before (see just-in-time manufacturing in Chapter 11).

Retailers like 1-800-Flowers.com and FTD use local florists as the backbone of their distribution networks; flowers travel from the farm to a distributor and then to a wholesaler before finally reaching the flower shop. By the time they reach consumers, flowers can be 8 to 12 days old. ProFlowers.com found this procurement system too inefficient and costly. The company developed a network-based system that transforms each domestic flower farm into a self-contained distribution facility. Growers handle everything from receiving real-time flower orders to adding personalized message cards.[4]

Production Scheduling

In traditional mass-market manufacturing, production begins when forecasts call for additional products to be made or inventory control systems signal low inventory levels. The firm then makes a product and transports the finished goods to its own warehouses or those of intermediaries, where the goods wait to be ordered by retailers or customers. Production scheduling based on pushing a product down to the consumer obviously has its disadvantages, the most notable being that companies risk making products that may become obsolete or that consumers don't want in the first place.

In a customer "pull" manufacturing environment, which is growing in popularity, production of goods or services is not scheduled until an order is placed by the customer specifying the desired configuration. This process, known as mass customization, or build-to-order, uniquely tailors mass-market goods and services to the needs of the individuals who buy them. Mass customization was explained in Chapter 11. Companies as diverse as BMW, Dell Computer, Levi Strauss, Mattel, and many Web-based businesses are adopting mass customization to maintain or obtain a competitive edge.

Choosing a Warehouse Location and Type

Deciding where to put a warehouse is mostly a matter of deciding which markets will be served and where production facilities will be located. A storage warehouse is used to hold goods for a long time. For instance, Jantzen makes bathing suits at an even rate throughout the year to provide steady employment and hold down costs. It then stores them in a warehouse until the selling season.

distribution centres
Warehouses that specialize in rapid movement of goods to retail stores by making and breaking bulk.

Distribution centres are a special form of warehouse. They specialize in changing shipment sizes rather than storing goods. Such centres make bulk (put shipments together) or break bulk. They strive for rapid inventory turnover. When shipments arrive, the merchandise is quickly sorted into orders for various retail stores. As soon as the order is complete, it is delivered. Distribution centres are the wave of the future, replacing traditional warehouses. Companies simply can't afford to have a lot of money tied up in idle inventory.

Inventory Control

inventory control system
A system that maintains an adequate assortment of items to meet users' or customers' needs.

Closely interrelated with the procurement, manufacturing, and ordering processes is the inventory control system—a method that develops and maintains an adequate assortment of materials or products to meet manufacturers' or customers' demands.

Inventory decisions, for both raw materials and finished goods, have a big impact on supply chain costs and the level of service provided. If too many products are kept in inventory, costs increase—as do risks of obsolescence, theft, and damage. If too few products are kept on hand, then the company risks product shortages, angry customers, and ultimately lost sales.

Many of the chain retailers have used supply-chain technology to control inventories and dramatically raise profitability. In a matter of seconds, any store manager can tap into the chain's proprietary computer system and pull up real-time data on what products are selling best at that location or across the country.

Setting Up a Materials-Handling System

A materials-handling system moves and handles inventory. The goal of such a system is to move items as quickly as possible while handling them as little as possible. For example, Rival Material Handling Systems Inc. of Ontario specializes in the manufacture and supply of ergonomic industrial and commercial materials-handling products. By using customized materials-handling, companies operate more efficiently at lower costs.

Making Transportation Decisions

Transportation typically accounts for between 5 and 10 percent of the price of goods. Physical-distribution managers must decide which mode of transportation to use to move products from producer to buyer. This decision is, of course, related to all other physical-distribution decisions. The five major modes of transportation are railroads, motor carriers, pipelines, water transportation, and airways. Distribution managers generally choose a mode of transportation on the basis of several criteria:

- *Cost.* The total amount a specific carrier charges to move the product from the point of origin to the destination.
- *Transit time.* The total time a carrier has possession of goods, including the time required for pickup and delivery, handling, and movement between the point of origin and the destination.
- *Reliability.* The consistency with which the carrier delivers goods on time and in acceptable condition.
- *Capability.* The carrier's ability to provide the appropriate equipment and conditions for moving specific kinds of goods, such as those that must be transported in a controlled environment (for example, under refrigeration).

EXHIBIT 13.11 > Criteria for Ranking Modes of Transportation

	Highest				Lowest
Relative cost	Air	Truck	Rail	Pipe	Water
Transit time	Water	Rail	Pipe	Truck	Air
Reliability	Pipe	Truck	Rail	Air	Water
Capability	Water	Rail	Truck	Air	Pipe
Accessibility	Truck	Rail	Air	Water	Pipe
Traceability	Air	Truck	Rail	Water	Pipe

concept check

What is the goal of supply chain management?

Describe the key decisions in managing the logistical flow.

What factors are considered when selecting a mode of transportation?

- *Accessibility*. The carrier's ability to move goods over a specific route or network.
- *Traceability*. The relative ease with which a shipment can be located and transferred.

Using these six criteria, a shipper selects the mode of transportation that will best meet its needs. Exhibit 13.11 shows how the basic modes of transportation rank in terms of these criteria.

Promotional Goals

promotion
The attempt by marketers to inform, persuade, or remind consumers and industrial users to engage in the exchange process.

Very few goods or services can survive in the marketplace without good promotion. Marketers promote their products to build demand. Promotion is an attempt by marketers to inform, persuade, or remind customers and industrial users in order to influence their opinion or elicit a response. Once the product has been created, promotion is often used to convince target customers that it has a differential advantage over the competition. A differential competitive advantage, as explained in Chapter 12, is a set of unique features that the target market perceives as important, and better than the competition's features; the advantage ideally results in purchase of the brand.

Most firms use some form of promotion, a word whose Latin root means "to move forward." Hence, actions that move a company toward its goals are promotional

CONCEPT *in Action* >>>

Reliable and inexpensive water transportation is one of the five major modes of transportation that distribution managers can choose from to move products from the producer to the buyer. What are the other four modes of transportation?

S-OLEG/SHUTTERSTOCK

in nature. Because company goals vary widely, so do promotional strategies. The goal is to stimulate action. In a profit-oriented firm, the desired action is for the consumer to buy the promoted item. McCain's, for instance, wants people to buy more frozen French fries. Not-for-profit organizations seek a variety of actions with their promotions. They tell us not to litter, to buckle up, and to attend the ballet.

Promotional goals include creating awareness, getting people to try products, providing information, retaining loyal customers, increasing the use of products, and identifying potential customers. Any promotional campaign may seek to achieve one or more of these goals:

1. *Creating awareness*. All too often, firms go out of business because people don't know they exist or what they do. Small restaurants often have this problem. Simply putting up a sign and opening the door is rarely enough. Promotion through ads on local radio or television, coupons in local papers, flyers, and so forth can create awareness of a new business or product.
2. *Getting consumers to try products*. Promotion is almost always used to get people to try a new product or to get non-users to try an existing product. Sometimes free samples are given away.
3. *Providing information*. Informative promotion is more common in the early stages of the product life cycle. An informative promotion may explain what ingredients (like fibre) will do for your health, tell you why the product is better (high-definition television versus regular television), inform you of a new low price, or explain where the item may be bought. People typically will not buy a product or support a not-for-profit organization until they know what it will do and how it may benefit them. Thus, an informative ad may stimulate interest in a product. Consumer watchdogs and social critics applaud the informative function of promotion because it helps consumers make more intelligent purchase decisions.
4. *Keeping loyal customers*. Promotion is also used to keep people from switching brands. Slogans such as Campbell's Soups are "M'm! M'm! Good!" and "Intel Inside" remind consumers about the brand. Marketers also remind users that the brand is better than the competition. For years, Pepsi has claimed it has the taste that consumers prefer. Such advertising reminds customers about the quality of the product. Firms can also help keep customers loyal by telling them when a product or service is improved.
5. *Increasing the amount and frequency of use*. Promotion is often used to get people to use more of a product and to use it more often. The most popular promotion to increase the use of a product may be loyalty programs such as, frequent-flyer or -user programs. For example, most larger grocery stores have loyalty cards that reward customers with discounts or redeemable points.
6. *Identifying target customers*. Promotion helps find customers. One way to do this is to list a website. For instance, *Canadian Business* magazine and *Business Week* include web addresses for more information on computer systems, corporate jets, colour copiers and other types of business equipment to help target those who are truly interested.

concept check

What is the objective of a promotional campaign?

How would the promotional campaigns for a new restaurant and an established brand differ?

The Promotional Mix and Integrated Marketing Communications

promotional mix
The combination of advertising, personal selling, sales promotion, and public relations used to promote a product.

The combination of advertising, personal selling, sales promotion, and public relations used to promote a product is called the **promotional mix**. Each firm creates a unique mix for each product. But the goal is always to deliver the firm's message efficiently and effectively to the target audience. These are the elements of the promotional mix:

advertising
Any paid form of non-personal presentation by an identified sponsor.

personal selling
A face-to-face sales presentation to a prospective customer.

sales promotion
Marketing events or sales efforts—not including advertising, personal selling, and public relations—that stimulate buying.

public relations
Any communication or activity designed to win goodwill or prestige for a company or person.

integrated marketing communications (IMC)
The careful coordination of all promotional activities—media advertising, sales promotion, personal selling, and public relations, as well as direct marketing, packaging, and other forms of promotion—to produce a consistent, unified message that is customer focused.

- **Advertising**. Any paid form of non-personal promotion by an identified sponsor.
- **Personal selling**. A face-to-face presentation to a prospective buyer.
- **Sales promotion**. Marketing activities (other than personal selling, advertising, and public relations) that stimulate consumer buying, including coupons and samples, displays, shows and exhibitions, demonstrations, and other types of selling efforts.
- **Public relations**. The linking of organizational goals with key aspects of the public interest and the development of programs designed to earn public understanding and acceptance.

Ideally, marketing communications from each promotional-mix element (personal selling, advertising, sales promotion, and public relations) should be integrated. That is, the message reaching the consumer should be the same regardless of whether it comes from an advertisement, a salesperson in the field, a magazine article, or a coupon in a newspaper insert.

This unintegrated, disjointed approach to promotion has propelled many companies to adopt the concept of **integrated marketing communications (IMC)**. IMC involves carefully coordinating all promotional activities—media advertising, sales promotion, personal selling, and public relations, as well as direct marketing, packaging, and other forms of promotion—to produce a consistent, unified message that is customer focused. Following the concept of IMC, marketing managers carefully work out the roles the various promotional elements will play in the marketing mix. Timing of promotional activities is coordinated, and the results of each campaign are carefully monitored to improve future use of the promotional mix tools. Typically, a marketing communications director is appointed who has overall responsibility for integrating the company's marketing communications.

Pepsi relied on IMC to launch Pepsi One. The $100 million program relied on personal selling in the distribution channels, a public-relations campaign with press releases to announce the product, and heavy doses of advertising and sales promotion. The company toured the country's shopping malls setting up Pepsi One "lounges"—

CONCEPT *in Action* >>>

Whether making a cameo appearance or starring in a major role, brands are top talent in the entertainment world. Coca-Cola sits at the judges' table on American Idol; Under Armour is the performance apparel of choice for the virtual characters in top-selling computer games like Tom Clancy's Ghost Recon 2; and Reese's Pieces are forever immortalized in E.T: The Extra-Terrestrial. Does product placement blur the lines between advertising and content and should viewers be concerned?

F. MICELOTTA/AMERICAN IDOL 2009/GETTY IMAGES FOR FOX

concept check

What is the promotional mix?

What are the features of an integrated marketing communications campaign?

inflatable couches with plastic carpeting—for random taste tests. It also produced 11,000 end-cap displays for supermarket aisles and created stand-up displays for 12-packs to spark impulse purchases. It secured Oscar-winning actor Cuba Gooding Jr. as spokesperson for the ad campaign. The ads made their debut during the World Series. The tagline for the ad campaign was "Only One has it all."

Factors that Affect the Promotional Mix

LO 8

Promotional mixes vary a great deal from product to product and from one industry to the next. Advertising and personal selling are usually a firm's main promotional tools. They are supported by sales promotion. Public relations help develop a positive image for the organization and its products. The specific promotional mix depends on the nature of the product, market characteristics, available funds, and whether a push or a pull strategy is used.

The Nature of the Product

Selling toothpaste differs greatly from selling overhead industrial cranes. Personal selling is most important in marketing industrial products and least important in marketing consumer nondurables (consumer products that get used up). Broadcast advertising is used heavily in promoting consumer products, especially food and other nondurables. Print media and the Internet are used for all types of consumer products. Industrial products may be advertised through special trade magazines. Sales promotion, branding, and packaging are roughly twice as important (in terms of percentage of the promotional budget) for consumer products as for industrial products.

Market Characteristics

When potential customers are widely scattered, buyers are highly informed, and many of the buyers are brand loyal, the promotional mix should include more advertising and sales promotion and less personal selling. But sometimes personal selling is required even when buyers are well informed and geographically dispersed, as is the case with super computers and airplanes. Industrial installations and component parts may be sold to knowledgeable people with much education and work experience. Yet a salesperson must still explain the product and work out the details of the purchase agreement.

detailing
The physical stocking of merchandise at a retailer by the salesperson who delivers the merchandise.

Salespeople are also required when the physical stocking of merchandise—called **detailing**—is the norm. Soft drinks and potato chips, for instance, are generally stocked by the person who makes the delivery, rather than by store personnel. This practice is becoming more common for convenience products as sellers try to get the best display space for their wares.

Available Funds

Money, or the lack of it, is one of the biggest influences on the promotional mix. A small manufacturer with a tight budget and a unique product may rely heavily on free publicity. The media often run stories about new products.

If the product warrants a sales force, a firm with little money may turn to manufacturers' agents. They work on commission, with no salary, advances, or expense accounts. The Duncan Co., which makes parking meters, is just one of the many that rely on manufacturers' agents.

Push and Pull Strategies

Manufacturers may use aggressive personal selling and trade advertising to convince a wholesaler or a retailer to carry and sell their merchandise. This approach is known

push strategy
A promotional strategy in which a manufacturer uses aggressive personal selling and trade advertising to convince a wholesaler or retailer to carry and sell its merchandise.

pull strategy
A promotional strategy in which a manufacturer focuses on stimulating consumer demand for its product, rather than on trying to persuade wholesalers or retailers to carry the product.

as a **push strategy**. The wholesaler, in turn, must often push the merchandise forward by persuading the retailer to handle the goods. A push strategy relies on extensive personal selling to channel members, or trade advertising, and price incentives to wholesalers and retailers. The retailer then uses advertising, displays, and other promotional forms to convince the consumer to buy the "pushed" products. This approach also applies to services. For example, the Jamaican Tourism Board targets promotions to travel agencies, which are members of its distribution channel.

At the other extreme is a **pull strategy**, which stimulates consumer demand in order to obtain product distribution. Rather than trying to sell to wholesalers, a manufacturer using a pull strategy focuses its promotional efforts on end consumers. As they begin demanding the product, the retailer orders the merchandise from the wholesaler. The wholesaler, confronted with rising demand, then places an order from the manufacturer. Thus, stimulating consumer demand pulls the product down through the channel of distribution. Heavy sampling, introductory consumer advertising, cents-off campaigns, buzz marketing, and couponing may all be used as part of a pull strategy. For example, using a pull strategy, the Jamaican Tourism Board may entice travelers to come to its island by offering discounts on hotels or airfare. The push and pull promotional strategies are illustrated in Exhibit 13.12.

Rarely does a company use a pull or a push strategy exclusively. Instead, the mix will emphasize one of these strategies. For example, pharmaceutical company Sanofi Aventis uses a push strategy by using personal selling and sampling of Allegra D, the allergy drug, to physicians and pharmacies. The company also uses print ads in consumer magazines, network TV, newspaper ads, and a Website aimed at final consumers to pull the product through the channel.

concept check

Explain how the nature of the product, market characteristics, and available funds can affect the promotional mix.

Distinguish between push and pull strategies.

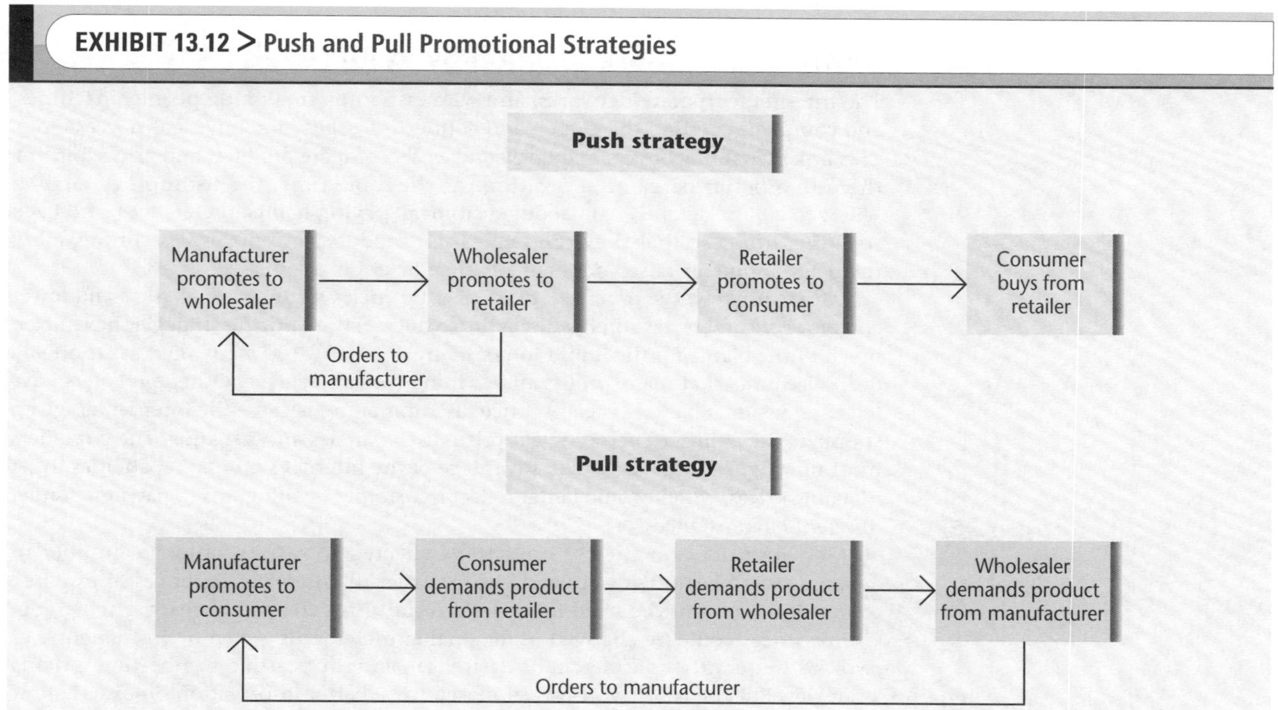

Making Ethical Choices

After working really hard to distinguish yourself, you've finally been promoted to a senior account executive at a major advertising agency and placed in charge of the agency's newest account, a nationally known cereal company. Their product is one you know contains excessive amounts of sugar as well as artificial colorings, and lacks any nutritional value whatsoever. In fact, you have never allowed your own children to eat it.

Your boss has indicated that the cereal company would like to use the slogan, "It's good for you," in their new television and print advertising campaign. You know that a $2 billion lawsuit has been filed against the Kellogg and Viacom corporations for marketing junk food to young children. The suit cited "alluring product packaging, toy giveaways, contests, collectibles, kid-oriented Websites, magazine ads, and branded toys and clothes." In addition, two consumer groups have brought suit against children's television network, Nickelodeon, for "unfair and deceptive junk-food marketing."

Your new role at the agency will be tested with this campaign. Doing a good job on it will cement your position and put you in line for a promotion to vice president. But as a responsible parent you have strong feelings about misleading advertising targeted at susceptible children.

Using a Web search tool, locate articles about this topic and then write responses to the following questions. Be sure to support your arguments and cite your sources.

ETHICAL DILEMMA: Do you follow your principles and ask to be transferred to another account? Or do you help promote a cereal you know may be harmful to children in order to secure your career?

SOURCES: Stephanie Thompson, "Standing Still, Kellogg Gets Hit with a Lawsuit," Advertising Age, January 23, 2006; Stephanie Thompson, "Kellogg Co. Might as Well Have Painted a Bull's-eye on Itself," Advertising Age, January 23, 2006; and Abbey Klaassen, "Viacom Gets Nicked," Advertising Age, January 23, 2006 (all from (http://galenet.thomsonlearning.com).

Trends in Marketing

LO 9

As customer expectations increase and competition becomes fiercer, perceptive marketers will find innovative strategies to satisfy demanding consumers and establish unique products in the market at the right prices. By using new distribution strategies and harnessing new technology to hone their marketing message and reach more customers, companies can boost profits and gain a competitive edge. Some of the significant trends in marketing include: incorporating more technology at all levels, increased use of yield management systems, category management, and outsourcing logistics functions.

Incorporating More Technology at All Levels

The Internet, corporate networks, and wireless setups are linking people, machines, and companies around the globe—and connecting sellers and buyers as never before. This link is enabling buyers to quickly and easily compare products and prices, putting them in a better bargaining position. At the same time, the technology enables sellers to collect detailed data about customers' buying habits, preferences, and even spending limits so that they can tailor their products and prices. For a time, all of these developments raised hopes of a more efficient marketplace.

Unfortunately, the promise of pricing efficiencies for Internet retailers and lower costs for consumers has run headlong into reality. Flawed pricing strategies have taken much of the blame for the implosion of many dot-coms. Too many merchants offered deep discounts that made profits all but impossible to achieve. Other e-retailers have felt the consumer backlash against price discrimination, because the Internet has given shoppers the ability to better detect price discrepancies and bargains. The e-retailers must now figure out how to take advantage of the Internet's unique capabilities to set dynamic prices, which would better reflect a customer's willingness to pay more under different circumstances.

Setting prices on the Internet was expected to offer retailers a number of advantages. To begin with, it would be far easier to raise or lower prices in response to demand, without the need for a clerk to run through a store with a pricing gun. Online prices could be changed in far smaller increments—even by just a penny or two—as frequently as a merchant desired, making it possible to fine-tune pricing strategies. But the real payoff was supposed to be better information on exactly how price-conscious customers are.

The idea was to charge exactly what the market will bear. But putting this into practice online has turned out to be exceptionally difficult, in part because the Internet has also empowered consumers to compare prices to find out if other merchants are offering a better deal or if other consumers are getting a bigger break. And the Internet has also made it easier for consumers to complain.

Online retail sales have been increasing and one reason is the economics of shopping. Think time spent, cost of travel, finding a parking spot, locating your intended store, and then driving home. Now think a mouse click. Countless small businesses have taken the plunge to serve the growing demand of the online shoppers.

The increasing sophistication of search technology and comparison-shopping sites have allowed online businesses cheaply and effectively to market their products to millions of potential customers. Often, these innovations are bringing less-well-known brands and merchants to consumers' attention.

Online merchants can offer a far broader array of merchandise than specialty brick-and-mortar retailers, because they don't have to keep the products on store shelves.

All forms of promotion are applying more and more technology to enhance effectiveness. For example, blogs provide marketers with a real-time dialogue with customers and an avenue to promote their products or services. A blog is an online journal with regularly updated content. This content is pushed to subscribers by RSS (really simple syndication) or e-mail and allows for response and discussion from site visitors. RSS enables users to automatically gather updates from various websites, especially news sites and blogs, and display headlines and a brief summary of those updates in a single location.

As we can see, all areas of marketing are increasing the use of technology to provide better customer service and satisfaction.

Yield Management Systems Help Companies Maximize Their Revenues

yield management systems (YMS)
Mathematical software that helps companies adjust prices to maximize revenue.

When competitive pressures are high, a company must know when it can raise prices to maximize its revenues. More and more companies are turning to yield management systems (YMS) to help adjust prices. First developed in the airline industry, yield management systems use complex mathematical software to profitably fill unused capacity. The software employs techniques such as discounting early purchases, limiting early sales at these discounted prices, and overbooking capacity. YMS now are appearing in other services such as lodging, other transportation forms, rental firms, and even hospitals. A key factor in easy group's success (see the expanding around the globe box) is its use of YMS.

Yield management systems are spreading beyond service industries as their popularity increases. The lessons of airlines and hotels aren't entirely applicable to other industries however, because plane seats and hotel beds are perishable—if they go empty, the revenue opportunity is lost forever. So it makes sense to slash prices to move toward capacity if it's possible to do so without reducing the prices that other customers pay. Cars and steel aren't so perishable. Still, the capacity to make these goods is perishable. An underused factory or mill is a lost revenue opportunity. So it makes sense to cut prices to use up capacity if it's possible to do so while getting other customers to pay full price.

Category Management

Category management
Suppliers manage the inventory of a category of products for a retailer.

Category management is when retailers ask one supplier in a category to determine how the retailer should best stock its shelves. Category management is becoming standard practice at nearly every Canadian grocery store, convenience store, mass merchant, and drugstore chain.

A retailer can increase profits by managing itself not as a collection of products, but product categories. People don't shop for soft drinks the way that they shop for meat.

With soft drinks, it may be more effective to group brands (Pepsi, Coke, store brand) together; in another category, freshness is most important. Sophisticated computer programs and marketing research help decide which products and how much should be carried. Manufacturers that supply most of the category management are called captains. Category captains include: soft drinks—Coca-Cola; shaving—Gillette; pet food—Nestlé Purina; and detergent—Procter & Gamble.

The best retailers are far from passive when it comes to accepting category captains' recommendations. Walmart runs the captain's plan by a "validator," which is a second supplier. So Dole, for example, runs a check on what Del Monte proposes.

Outsourcing Logistics Functions

External partners are becoming increasingly important in the efficient deployment of supply chain management. Outsourcing, or contract logistics, is a rapidly growing segment of the distribution industry in which a manufacturer or supplier turns over the entire function of buying and managing transportation or another function of the supply chain, such as warehousing, to an independent third party. Many manufacturers are turning to outside partners for their logistics expertise in an effort to focus on the core competencies that they do best. Partners create and manage entire solutions for getting products where they need to be, when they need to be there. Logistics partners offer staff, an infrastructure, and services that reach consumers virtually anywhere in the world. Because a logistics provider is focused, clients receive service in a timely, efficient manner, thereby increasing customers' level of satisfaction and boosting their perception of added value to a company's offerings.

Third-party contract logistics enable companies to cut inventories, locate stock at fewer plants and distribution centers, and still provide the same service level or even better. The companies then can refocus investment on their core business.

concept check

What are some ways that technology has been incorporated in marketing?

How are yield management systems and category management used in marketing?

Why are more retailers outsourcing their logistics functions?

Great Ideas to Use Now

Chances are that someday you will be a buyer or seller on eBay. The auction site has more than 100 million registered members from around the world with more than 18,000 categories of items on the auction block. Yet, finding what you want or getting the best deal can be tough. Following are a few helpful tips.

A Buyer's Guide

Browsing/Searching

- Before diving in, get a solid sense of what the items you're interested in are worth. Use the "completed items" advanced search to see the prices that similar items actually sold for, or check eBay's library for the category-specific "inside scoop," which generally features a useful page titled "Factors Influencing Value."
- Search in both related and general categories, as sellers often classify their wares differently. For example, if you're looking for a CD by Elvis Costello, check classic rock, pop, and punk in addition to alternative rock.
- Be descriptive when searching. Specify dates, colours, brands, sizes, and model numbers. Try variations—if a model number has a hyphen, search both with and without it.
- Conduct searches often, as items are constantly added and removed. Save yourself from having to monitor the site on a daily basis by using the "favourite searches" service, which will notify you by e-mail when items matching your search criteria are put up for sale.
- Think eBay for retail too. Many companies, such as Dell and Handspring, off-load surplus inventory at deep discounts, so check here before you try standard retail outlets.

Bidding

- Don't bid if you don't intend to buy, as bids are binding contracts. Bids can be retracted only under exceptional circumstances (e.g., the seller changes the product description after you've placed your bid).
- Don't bid in the first days of an auction. Doing so merely reveals your interest and increases the likelihood of other bidders joining the fray, causing the price to rise quickly. Instead, wait until the auction is near its close (10 to 30 seconds before, depending on the speed of your Internet connection), and then bid the maximum amount you are willing to pay, regardless of any previous bids—a strategy known as sniping. To do this, open a second browser window and fill in all the relevant information, stopping just short of submitting your bid. Watch the auction wind down in the first window, and when the time is right, place your bid in the second. Don't fret—you can always use a professional sniper service to handle this for you automatically.
- Factor in shipping costs, which typically fall on the buyer. If the item is bulky or the seller lives overseas, your "bargain" might end up costing more than you bargained for.
- Try adding a penny or two to your bid. Since many bids are placed in round-number increments, this little extra something can mean the difference between winning by a nose and coming up short.

A Seller's Guide

Listing Online auctions bring out the competitive nature in bidders, especially as the clock runs out. Bidding wars are a seller's dream; to make sure your auction gets significant play, follow these steps:

- Include specifics, such as manufacturer or product name, in both the title and description.
- Be honest in describing imperfections. This gives buyers comfort that you're being honest and could head off conflicts later.
- Set a low initial bid amount to attract more bidders. The mere *possibility* of getting a great deal on that rare Tony Gwynn rookie card encourages competition and increases the likelihood of rival bidders' driving up the price. This can also save you money, as eBay's listing fees are based on the minimum bid you set.
- Include a picture, as most buyers are reluctant to make a big purchase sight unseen. But don't overdo it: Including too many photos, or big ones with large file sizes, slows download times and tends to frustrate buyers with dial-up connections.
- Set a "buy it now" price, which allows buyers to subvert the bidding process and nab an item outright for a predetermined amount.
- Don't set a "reserve" price, which requires bidders to meet or exceed a certain minimum. As bidders can't see this minimum price, many avoid such auctions altogether out of fear that they'll be wasting their time.
- Accept multiple forms of payment, which increases the likelihood that interested buyers will place bids.
- Pay attention to when your auction is scheduled to end. eBay auctions run 3, 5, 7, or 10 days; to get the most traffic, make sure that yours includes a full weekend and ends at a time when people will be around to bid up the price.

Closing the Deal

- Congratulate the winner by e-mail. Include the auction number, a description of the item, the amount of the winning bid, and estimated shipping charges.
- Send the item as soon as the buyer's payment clears, and alert the buyer by e-mail (be sure to include the tracking number).
- Include links to your other auctions in all e-mail correspondence with buyers; if they are satisfied with their experience, they might want to check out what else you have.[5]

Customer Satisfaction and Quality

Distribution is all about getting the right product to the right person, at the right place, at the right time. Even if only one of these things does not occur, then the firm will have a dissatisfied customer. Sophisticated supply chain management programs, using the latest software, have dramatically reduced distribution errors in addition to lowering costs for the firm.

Oracle, the giant software company, has switched from an overly aggressive sales force to making customer service its top priority. "It's more than just the sale," said Paul Ciandrini, former Oracle senior vice president who headed up the company's commercial sales in the western region of North America. "I can make the sale and be a hero, but I can't go back in and expand that sale if it's of no value to the customer."[6]

Even the smallest details have been reconsidered. Oracle used to offer slick presentations on its products and the features that distinguished them from those of SAP AG of Germany. Now, it uses demonstrations that map its customers' specific technology environment, so it can put itself in its customers' shoes by focusing on problems as they see them.

Summary of Learning Outcomes

1 Describe what is meant by a product.

A product is any good or service, along with its perceived attributes and benefits, that creates customer value. Tangible attributes include the good itself, packaging, and warranties. Intangible attributes are symbolic, such as a brand's image. Products are categorized as either consumer products or industrial products. Consumer products are goods and services that are bought and used by the end users. They can be classified as unsought products, convenience products, shopping products, or specialty products, depending on how much effort consumers are willing to exert to get them. Industrial products are those bought by organizations for use in making other products or in rendering services and include capital products and expense items.

2 Explain the stages of the product life cycle.

After a product reaches the marketplace, it enters the product life cycle. This cycle typically has four stages: introduction, growth, maturity, and decline (and possibly death). Profits usually are small in the introductory phase, reach a peak at the end of the growth phase, and then decline. Marketing strategies for each stage are listed in Exhibit 13.5.

3 Discuss the role of pricing and the strategies used for pricing products.

Price indicates value, helps position a product in the marketplace, and is the means for earning a fair return on investment. If a price is too high, the product won't sell well, and the firm will lose money. If the price is too low, the firm might lose money, even if the product sells well. Prices are set according to pricing objectives. Among the most common objectives are profit maximization, target return on investment, and value pricing.

A cost-based method for determining price is markup pricing. A certain percentage is added to the product's cost to arrive at the retail price. The markup is the amount added to the cost to cover expenses and earn a profit. Breakeven analysis determines the level of sales that must be reached before total cost equals total revenue. Breakeven analysis provides a quick look at how many units the firm must sell before it starts earning a profit. The technique also reveals how much profit can be earned with higher sales volumes.

The two main strategies for pricing a new product are price skimming and penetration pricing. Price skimming involves charging a high introductory price and then, usually, lowering the price as the product moves through its life cycle. Penetration pricing involves selling a new product at a low price in the hope of achieving a large sales volume.

Pricing tactics are used to fine-tune the base prices of products. Sellers that use leader pricing set the prices of some of their products below the normal markup or even below cost to attract customers who might otherwise not shop at those stores. Bundling is grouping two or more products together and pricing them as one. Psychology often plays a role in how consumers view products and in determining what they will pay. Setting a price at an odd number tends to create a perception that the item is cheaper than the actual price. Prices in even numbers denote quality or status. Raising the price so an item will be perceived as having high quality and status is called prestige pricing.

4 Explain distribution and distribution channels.

Physical distribution is efficiently managing the acquisition of raw materials to the factory and the movement of products from the producer or manufacturer to industrial users and consumers. Physical distribution activities are usually the responsibility of the marketing department and are part of the large series of activities included in the supply chain. Distribution channels are the series of marketing entities through which goods and services pass on their way from producers to end users. Distribution systems focus on the physical transfer of goods and services and on their legal ownership at each stage of the distribution process. Channels (a) reduce the number of transactions, (b) ease the flow of goods, and (c) increase channel efficiency.

5 Illustrate how supply chain management can increase efficiency and customer satisfaction.

The goal of supply chain management is to coordinate all of the activities of the supply chain members into a seamless process, thereby increasing customer satisfaction. The logistical components of the supply chain include sourcing and procurement, production scheduling, choosing a warehouse location and type, setting up a materials-handling system, and making transportation decisions.

6 Briefly list the goals of promotional strategy.

Promotion aims to stimulate demand for a company's goods or services. Promotional strategy is designed to inform, persuade, or remind target audiences about those products. The goals of promotion are to create awareness, get people to try products, provide information, keep loyal customers, increase use of a product, and identify potential customers.

7 Discuss the elements of the promotional mix, and integrated marketing communications.

The unique combination of advertising, personal selling, sales promotion, and public relations used to promote a product is the promotional mix. Advertising is any paid form of non-personal promotion by an identified sponsor. Personal selling consists of a face-to-face presentation in a conversation with a prospective purchaser. Sales promotion consists of marketing activities—other than personal selling, advertising, and public relations—that stimulate consumers to buy. These activities include coupons and samples, displays, shows and exhibitions, demonstrations, and other selling efforts. Public relations is the marketing function that links the policies of the organization with the public interest and develops programs designed to earn public understanding and acceptance. Integrated marketing communications (IMC) is being used by more and more organizations. It is the careful coordination of all of the elements of the promotional mix to produce a consistent, unified message that is customer focused.

8 Identify the factors that affect the promotional mix.

The factors that affect the promotional mix are the nature of the product, market characteristics, available funds, and whether a push or a pull strategy is emphasized. Personal selling is used more with industrial products, and advertising is used more heavily for consumer products. With widely scattered, well-informed buyers and with brand-loyal customers, a firm will blend more advertising and sales promotion and less personal selling into its promotional mix. A manufacturer with a limited budget might rely heavily on publicity and manufacturers' agents to promote the product.

9 List some of the trends in marketing.

Four trends that we are seeing in marketing include: incorporating more technology at all levels, increased use of yield management systems, category management, and outsourcing logistics functions.

Technology is becoming more prevalent in all aspects of business including marketing. Technology is incorporated from the development of strategies and goals to the final stage – the customer. Companies can use yield management systems (yms) to help them adjust prices to maximize revenue and retailers can use category management to manage the inventory of a category of products for them. Outsourcing, or contract logistics, is a rapidly growing segment of the distribution industry in which a manufacturer or supplier turns over the entire function of buying and managing transportation or another function of the supply chain, such as warehousing, to an independent third party.

Key Terms

advertising 415
agents 404
breakeven point 400
breaking bulk 407
brokers 404
bundling 402
capital products 394
category management 419
convenience products 394
detailing 416
distribution (logistics) 403
distribution centres 412
distribution channel 404
dual distribution (multiple distribution) 404
exclusive distribution 410
expense items 394
fixed costs 400
fixed-cost contribution 400
industrial distributors 404
integrated marketing communications (IMC) 415
intensive distribution 410
inventory control system 412
leader pricing 402
loss leader 402
manufacturer 403
marketing intermediaries 404
markup pricing 399
odd-even (psychological) pricing 402
penetration pricing 401
personal selling 415
prestige pricing 403
price skimming 401
product 392
product life cycle 395
profit maximization 397
promotion 413
promotional mix 414
public relations 415
pull strategy 417
push strategy 417
retailers 404
sales promotions 415
selective distribution 410
shopping products 394
specialty products 394
strategic channel alliances 407
target return on investment 398
total cost 400
total profit 400
total revenue 400
unsought products 394
value pricing 399
variable costs 400
wholesalers 404
yield management systems (YMS) 419

Experiential Exercises

1. Under what circumstances would a jeans maker market the product as a convenience product? A shopping product? A specialty product?
2. Go to the library and look through magazines and newspapers to find examples of price skimming, penetration pricing, and value pricing. Make copies and show them to the class.
3. Write down the names of two brands to which you are loyal. Indicate the reasons for your loyalty.
4. Visit an online retailer such as Amazon.ca (**www.amazon.ca**), PCConnection.com (**www.pcconnection.com**), or Drugstore.com (**www.drugstore.com**). At the site, try to identify examples of leader pricing, bundling, odd-even pricing, and other pricing strategies. Do online retailers have different pricing considerations from "real-world" retailers? Explain.

5. Do a search on Yahoo (**www.yahoo.ca**) for online auctions for a product you are interested in buying. Visit several auctions to get an idea of how the product is priced. How do these prices compare with the price you might find in a local store? What pricing advantages or disadvantages do companies face in selling their products through online auctions? How do online auctions affect the pricing strategies of other companies? Why?
6. Do some comparison shopping. A beauty of the Internet is the ability to comparison shop like never before. Tour and Internet travel companies offer many last-minute specials where travellers can save on their trips. To compare brands, features, and prices of products, go to one of these sites: **(www.airtransat.com)**, **(www.aircanadavacations.com)**, **(www.expedia.com)**, **(www.itravel2000.com)**, and any others that you have researched.
7. Kick the tires before you buy. At some point you are going to buy a car. The Web can simplify the process, help you make an intelligent decision, and save you money. Start at **(www.edmunds.com).** The online version of the respected car buying guide is crammed with information about new and used cars. The site offers thousands of car reviews and current loan rates.
8. Trace the distribution channel for some familiar product. Compose an e-mail explaining why the channel has evolved as it has and how it is likely to change in the future.
9. Go to a successful, independent specialty store in your area that has been in business for quite a while. Interview the manager and try to determine how the store successfully competes with the national chains.
10. Visit a local manufacturer. Interview managers to determine how its supply chain functions. Make a report to the class.
11. One of the biggest challenges for retailers is integrating their various channels to provide a seamless experience for customers, regardless of the channel. Pick two of the following companies, explore their Websites, and compare the channel integration strategies: Staples (**www.staples.com**), Gap (**www.gap.com**), or Borders (**www.borders.com**). In addition to looking at the websites from a channel perspective, you might want to look at the company information and news sites.
12. Protect your privacy online. Here are some pointers to protect yourself against spam.
    - Use free Web-based e-mail services like Microsoft's Hotmail.com to create a second e-mail address to give out when shopping at an e-commerce site. This will prevent your corporate or primary account from being deluged with targeted spam.
    - Use websites like (**www.spychecker.com**) to check if you have unwittingly downloaded spyware—nettlesome programs that are secretly installed when you download many free programs. Visitors to Spychecker are prompted to enter the names of programs, and the site tells them whether the software contains spyware.
    - Activate your Web browser's security functions to block out cookies or alert you when a site is trying to install one on your computer. In Internet Explorer, you would go to Tools, and then click on the Internet Options command. That brings up a series of tabs, including one for Security. Moving the sliding bar to its highest setting will disable all cookies. This, however, might make it difficult to visit many popular Websites, as the sites tend to require the ability to install cookies on your machine.
    - Use e-mail re-mailers like the one at (**www.gilc.org/speech/anonymous/remailer.html**) to bounce your message through a series of computers that forward it on, in theory making it untraceable. Sending anonymous e-mail through these re-mailers also reduces the odds of its being read by hackers, who try to monitor data traffic to and from companies and sites like Hotmail.

- Use privacy software to shield the content and addresses of the Websites you visit from employers and other prying eyes. One of the best such programs is available at (**www.anonymizer.com**).

13. Think of a product that you use regularly. Find several examples of how the manufacturer markets this product, such as ads in different media, sales promotions, and publicity. Assess each example for effectiveness in meeting one or more of the six promotional goals described in the chapter. Then analyze them for effectiveness in reaching you as a target consumer. Consider such factors as the media used, the style of the ad, and ad content. Present your findings to the class.
14. Choose a current advertising campaign for a beverage product. Describe how the campaign uses different media to promote the product. Which medium is used the most, and why? What other promotional strategies does the company use for the product? Evaluate the effectiveness of the campaign. Present your results to the class.
15. The Zenith Media site at (**www.zenithmedia.com**) is a good place to find links to Internet resources on advertising. At the site, click on "Leading Corporate and Brand Sites." Pick three of the company sites listed and review them, using the concepts in this chapter.
16. Does a career in marketing appeal to you? Start your journey at Careers in Marketing, (**www.careers-in-marketing.com**), and explore the five areas listed there: Advertising & Public Relations, Market Research, Non-Profit, Product Management, and Retailing. Which one appeals to you most, and why? Briefly describe the type of work you would be doing, the career path, and how you will prepare to enter this field (courses, part-time jobs, etc.).

Review Questions

1. What is a product? How do products create value for the buyer?
2. What are the four (4) classifications of consumer products?
3. How are business products classified?
4. Discuss the strategies for success at each stage of the product life cycle.
5. What is the role of pricing in marketing?
6. How are product prices determined?
7. What are the various pricing strategies available to managers?
8. What is physical distribution?
9. Define *marketing intermediaries*. What are four common marketing intermediaries?
10. What is the distribution channel? What are the functions of distribution channels?
11. What are some alternative channel arrangements?
12. What are the three (3) degrees of market coverage for consumer products?
13. What is the goal of supply chain management? What are the logistical components of the supply chain?
14. What are some of the key decision in managing the logistical flow of products?
15. Explain some of the criteria that managers must consider when deciding the mode of transportation.
16. What are the goals of promotion?
17. What is the promotional mix, and what options are available in this mix?
18. Explain integrated marketing communications (IMC).
19. List the factors that affect the promotional mix.
20. What are some of the trends in marketing?

CREATIVE THINKING CASE >

Advertisers Score with the World Cup

What sporting event is televised in 213 countries and watched by more passionate fans than any other? If you guessed the Olympics, you'd be wrong. It's the world cup football (soccer) matches, which last a month and are held every four years. An estimated 1.5 billion people watched the 2006 world cup opener, and web surfers registered over 2 billion page views at (www.fifaworldcup.com). Online venues such as chat rooms, blogs, and discussion boards added another media channel for fans to get more of the action.

Soccer's worldwide popularity makes it a prime advertising buy for many global companies, who want to get their message out to these large audiences. More than 240 million players on 1.4 million teams around the world play the game, supporting its claim to be the world's favourite sport. As the FIFA world cup website explains, "the FIFA world cup™ reaches an audience of a size and diversity that is unrivalled by any other single-sports body. Add to this a passion for the game found in all corners of the world, and you have a sporting, social, and marketing phenomenon." As a result, companies vie to become official partners with global marketing rights as well as custom opportunities. The 2006 FIFA world cup™ official partners were Adidas, Avaya, Budweiser, Coca-Cola, Continental, Deutsche Telekom, Emirates, Fujifilm, Gillette, Hyundai, MasterCard, McDonald's, Philips, Toshiba, and Yahoo!.

The world cup's global nature presents major challenges as well as opportunities for its advertisers. Unlike the Grey Cup, which focuses on Canada, the world cup requires even greater levels of creativity to produce ads that make a strong connection with soccer fans from very diverse cultures. Ads may have to appeal to viewers in countries as different as Ireland, Mexico, Malaysia, and Bangladesh.

Companies accomplish this task in various ways. They can select the countries that see their ads. Some have one ad for all countries, whereas others customize ads. MasterCard overcame the language barrier by showing soccer fans from many countries cheering. The only words appear at the end with the company logo: "football fever. Priceless." Anheuser-Busch, which spent more for its 2006 world cup ads than it did for its Olympics or super bowl ads, also opted for a visual rather than verbal ad: people in the stands at a sporting event do the "wave," holding cards that show beer flowing from a Budweiser bottle into a glass, which then empties. "If you get too complicated, you lose people with different cultures and perspectives," says Tony Ponturo, vice president of global sports marketing for the brewer. Gillette starts with the same ad but uses digital techniques so that each ad features the team colors for the country where the spot is showing.

Critical Thinking Questions

- What are some of the challenges global marketers encounter when developing advertising and promotion campaigns? How does the type of product affect the promotional strategies?
- You work for an ad agency that has a world cup sponsor as a client. What approach would you recommend for your agency as it develops a campaign—universal, customized for each geographical region, or something else, and why?
- What types of companies could benefit from placing ads on the fifa website, and how can they use the Internet effectively to promote their products?

SOURCES: Adapted from "Marketing & TV," Fédération Internationale de Football Association, (www.fifa.com), May 3, 2006; Aaron O. Patrick, "World Cup's advertisers hope one size fits all," Wall Street Journal, March 28, 2006, p. B7; "The Wave, " TV commercials, budweiser.com, (www.budweiser.com), May 3, 2006; "World cup advertising analysis," Analyst Wire, March 3, 2006, (http://galenet.thomsonlearning.com); "3 billion eyes to view World Cup opener, (www.worldcupblog.org/world-cup-2006/3-billion-eyes-to-view-world-cup-opener.html), accessed February 26, 2009.

VIDEO CASE >

The Toronto Blue Jays Hit a Home Run with Pricing

Can doubling the number of ticket categories bring more fans out to the ball game? For the Toronto Blue Jays, an improved pricing strategy and additional promotional strategies helped the team raise its profile in its hometown.

Prior to the 1999 baseball season, the Toronto Blue Jays (**www.bluejays.ca**) had just five ticket-pricing categories. After thorough study of their ticket prices, the Blue Jays established a new pricing structure with 10 levels to provide fans different product value. From single-ticket $7 seats to season tickets costing more than $13,000 ($165 per game) for the "In the Action" seats, fans can pick the ticket program that suits them best. In-between seats range from $24 to $49, depending on location. In addition to individual seats and season passes, Blue Jays fans can buy Flex-Packs with 5, 20, or 40 tickets to the games they choose. These packages sell at a discount from the single-ticket price. Group ticket sales, an important component of the Blue Jays product mix, are targeted toward the seats priced at about $40 and under.

As part of the Toronto team's effort to provide a high-quality product at a fair price, the Blue Jays added several regularly occurring special promotions during many home games. For example, every Tuesday home game is a TIM-BR Mart Tuesday. The building supplies chain collaborates with the Blue Jays in a three-part promotion. When a Toronto player hits the official TIM-BR Mart target, a fan chosen at random wins a cottage supplied and built by TIM-BR Mart. Another fan chosen at random gets to watch the game from a custom-built wood deck in the Toronto Rogers Centre. This fan is also provided food and beverage service. A third lucky fan wins a custom-built deck for his or her home by TIM-BR Mart.

Saturday home games have special promotions for children. On Junior Jays Saturdays, sponsored by *The Toronto Star,* children 14 and under are admitted at discounted prices. The gates open early, so fans can watch batting practice, and kids can participate in many activities and contests, win prizes, and get player autographs. Children can enter a drawing to throw out the ceremonial first pitch at the next Junior Jays Saturday game; nine youngsters get to take the field along with the Blue Jays starting lineup, and a child is selected to announce the Blue Jays batters for one inning. Children can also run the bases following the game. Each child 14 and under also receives Blue Jays souvenir giveaways.

The Blue Jays' marketing staff continue to add special promotions to please their fans. For example, they asked fans what they enjoy the most about attending a Blue Jays game and combined many of these elements to create Premium Games. Tickets for these games cost a few dollars more but include a pre-game party, early admission to watch batting practice, autograph signing, giveaway items, and post-game entertainment. Staples Business Depot "Deal of the Game," the FedEx Home Run Club, and Schneider's Juicy Jumbo Toss are among the team's recent promotions.

This well-planned package of special promotions, along with different ticket prices for seats providing different amenities, has increased the Toronto Blue Jays' popularity. As a result, attendance at games is up and the fan base is growing.

Critical Thinking Questions

- How would you describe the Toronto Blue Jays' baseball franchise as a product?
- What decision criteria do you think the Blue Jays used in establishing their new ticket price structure? Do you agree with this pricing strategy?

SOURCE: Toronto Blue Jays web site, (http://toronto.bluejays.mlb.com).

E-COMMERCE CASE >

Success Blooms At 1-800-FLOWERS

Do you need to send flowers for a relative's birthday in Germany, to celebrate your daughter's first big business presentation in the United Kingdom, or to congratulate your neighbours across the street on the birth of their new baby? One call to 1-800- FLOWERS does it all—floral arrangements individually created by the nation's top floral artists, hand-delivered the same day at the peak of freshness and perfection—whether your loved ones are in Australia, the Philippines, Mexico, Italy, Japan, Hawaii, Alaska, or Puerto Rico.

So how do they do it? After opening his first retail store in 1976, Jim McCann, chief executive officer of 1-800-FLOWERS, built a chain of 14 flower shops in the New York metropolitan area before acquiring the 1-800-FLOWERS telephone number in 1986 and continuing to grow his business under that name. His understanding of his customer base and market helped him create a reliable brand his customers could trust.

He knew that when selling such a perishable product, efficient access and distribution is critical to success. The company's sophisticated fulfillment system includes its BloomNet; an international network of florists. BloomNet partners are selected based on their commitment to quality and service and strictly monitored by 1-800-FLOWERS—part of its focus on customer service.

McCann extended his business into other channels, going online in 1992 and opening a website in 1995. He maintains strategic marketing relationships with a number of online services, including America Online, Microsoft Network (MSN), and Yahoo! The company's third-party vendor-direct program allows for easy and efficient delivery of gourmet foods, candies, and gift baskets, among other items. Its collection of brands includes home décor and garden merchandise sold under Plow & Hearth; premium popcorn and other food gifts sold under The Popcorn Factory; chocolates from Fannie May, Godiva, and others; and baked cookies and desserts from Cheryl & Co.

Headquartered on long island, New York, 1-800-FLOWERS, (**www.1800flowers.com**) is today one of the most recognized brands in flower and gift retailing. Available online 24 hours a day, seven days a week, customers can also visit a company-operated or franchised store. The website also allows customers to send free virtual flowers—building their own virtual bouquet complete with flowers, accents, a beautiful vase, and even a personalized message.

1-800-FLOWERS maintains a comprehensive quality assurance program that incorporates ongoing blind test orders, telephone surveys with customers and recipients, in-store and mail surveys, and customer service reports. With customers assured of a 100 percent satisfaction and freshness guarantee on all products and services, the company's fortunes should continue to blossom.

Critical Thinking Questions

1. Describe the unique challenges faced by companies that sell highly perishable products.
2. How does 1-800-FLOWERS meet and address those challenges?
3. What other types of distribution or product access should the company consider?

SOURCES: Adapted from the video "1-800 FLOWERS," (www.swlearning.com); Tim Beyers, "budding growth at 1-800-flowers?" The Motley Fool, (www.fool.com), August 11, 2005; Tony Goins, "1-800-flowers to buy Cheryl & Co.," Business First of Columbus, March 11, 2005; Rich Smith, "1-800-flowers buys Fannie May," The Motley Fool, April 10, 2006, (www.fool.com); 1-800-flowers corporate website, (http://1800flowers.com); April 29, 2006.

CHAPTER 14

Making the Connection

Using Financial Information and Accounting

In the previous four chapters, we examined the functional areas of human resources, operations, and marketing, and saw that they must work together in a very integrative way to achieve the goals of the company. It is obvious that these three areas affect the ability of the company to *gain employee commitment, increase the* level of product *quality* and *innovativeness,* and thus *meet customer needs,* and that they therefore affect the ability of the company to *achieve financial performance.* In this chapter we will begin to look more specifically at the last functional area of *finance,* starting with how a firm develops and uses financial information through the function of accounting.

It's clear from the beginning of this chapter that, regardless of your position in an organization, you need to understand accounting. It is the "financial language of businesses," and all decisions that are made in an organization eventually have financial consequences and therefore show up in the accounting information. For example, on the income statement, you might find advertising expenses and sales revenue from *marketing,* production and operating costs from *operations,* payroll and training costs from *human resources,* and, of course, the interest costs on debt financing to pay for it all. On the statement of financial position, you can also see the impact of each area on the numbers. For example, in the accounts payable section, there might be payments outstanding for employee wages, for marketing expenses, and for operating expenses, as well as for interest on debt financing or dividends payable to shareholders. In the current assets sections, you might find marketable securities (money invested in financial products to earn a return for a short period—a financing decision), accounts receivable from customers for invoices they have not yet paid (a marketing decision), and inventories of goods on hand (an operating decision).

All areas of the company, and employees at all levels, must therefore understand the financial implications of the decisions they make. They must see the integration of their decisions with each area and eventually on the "bottom line." Internal accounting reports help functional areas make these decisions; for example, marketing sales reports can be used to assess how well different marketing strategies are working, and production cost reports help in efforts to control operating costs.

On the other hand, external accounting reports, such as statement of financial position and income statements, which are contained in annual reports to shareholders, are used by many outside *stakeholder* groups. Potential employees use them to assess the stability of a company, and therefore job security and job prospects, before taking job offers, and potential investors use them to assess investment opportunities, just as current shareholders use them to assess the investments they have already made. These stakeholder relationships cannot be dealt with casually, particularly in light of scandals that have called into question

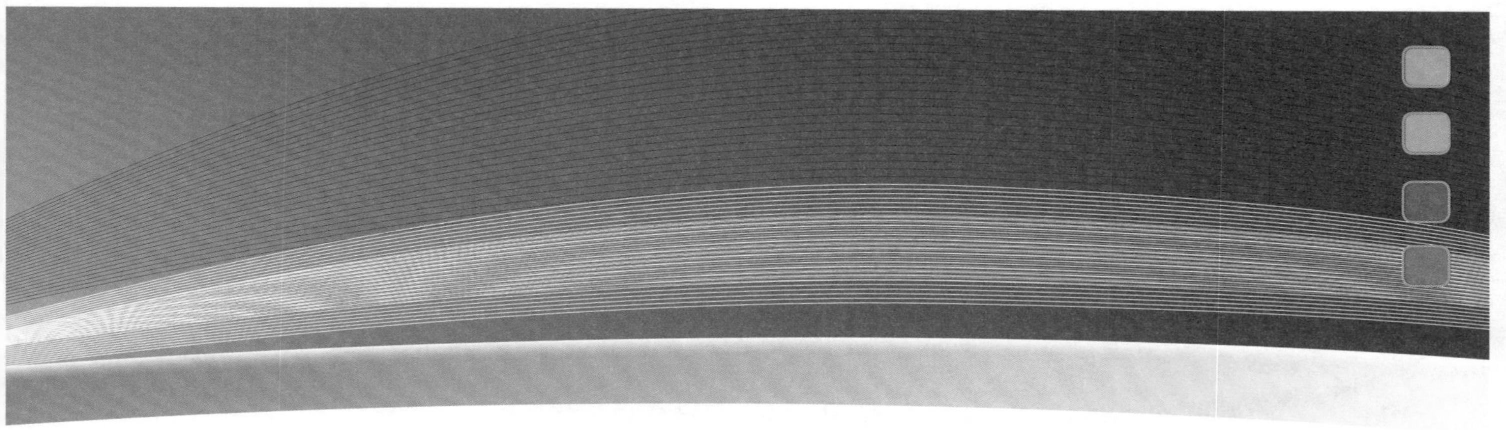

the integrity of the accounting profession. The impact that these scandals, such as those involving WorldCom and Enron, have had on the financial markets (*economic* environment) demonstrate quite clearly the far-reaching integrative impact of financial information and the importance of operating with the highest ethical standards. In fact, this demand for greater ethical conduct (*social* environment) has resulted in many new regulations (*political* environment) governing what firms can and cannot do in reporting accounting information.

The other aspect of the external environment that affects this functional area is *technology*. The advances in technology today have sped up the pace with which accounting information can be gathered and disseminated throughout an organization, thus giving all areas an opportunity to examine the impact of their decisions in an integrative way and focus more on the analysis of the information to make better decisions. In the remaining chapters, we'll continue with the finance area and look at these decisions in more detail.

CHAPTER 14

Using Financial Information and Accounting

LEARNING OUTCOMES

1 Explain the importance of financial reports and accounting information to the targeted users.

2 Show an understanding of the accounting profession.

3 Identify the six steps in the accounting cycle.

4 Understand how a statement of financial position describes the financial condition of an organization.

5 Explain the purpose of the income statement.

6 Describe the importance of the statement of cash flows.

7 Explain how ratio analysis is used to identify a firm's financial strengths and weaknesses.

8 List some of the major trends that are impacting the accounting industry.

ACCOUNTING IN EVERYDAY LIFE

When first introduced to accounting, many students are unsure of what they are getting into. "But," says longtime accounting instructor, Rafik Kurji, "they are already using accounting principles in their everyday lives." Rafik's explains: the individual gets their paycheque (income) and pays the rent (expense), then they make a mortgage payment (reducing a longterm liability), they make a car payment (reducing another liability by paying down the car loan, the car being an asset), a friend pays back the $100.00 he owes (increasing the cash balance and reducing the accounts receivables), etc. At a very basic level, these activities represent accounting. Once on a career path, accounting is important to anyone wishing to move up in the organization.

A marketing manager has to have a sound understanding of accounting principles in order to plan. Many questions need to be answered. What is the revenue stream comprised of? How can it be increased? Can the quantity sold be increased or the cost to produce the goods and services be reduced? Can the other expenses be reduced? Which are fixed expenses and which are variable? What are the assets and what condition are they in? Without this sort of information and knowledge, how can a marketer make recommendations that are in the best interests of the company as a whole? Without careful planning, the company may end up practicing crisis management on a regular basis. The projections on which the plans are based must be constantly compared with the accounting actuals and variances identified and explained. If marketers, HR professionals, purchasers or general managers wish to be active participants in the strategic planning for their companies, they must understand accounting.

SHIRLEY A. ROSE

With the increase in globalization, it has become necessary to standardize accounting around the world. Rafik feels that, without this standardization, we are often comparing apples and oranges. The International Financial Accounting Standards (IFAS) will help accomplish this standardization and enable accountants around the world to more readily understand statements prepared by their counterparts in other countries.

Accountants are always in demand, whether the economy is in a growth or a recessionary period. If the company is not doing well, management still needs to know how just how badly they are doing in order to deal with the situation. As managers sit around the strategic planning table, their knowledge of accounting will serve them well as they contribute valuable information from their own functional areas, enabling the team to make well-informed decisions.

Critical Thinking Questions

As you read this chapter, consider the following questions:

1. **Why is accounting so important to the decision-making activities of managers?**
2. **Can a business be incredibly busy, with high sales volumes, and still not have a good bottom line? If so, explain how this could happen?**
3. **Do you agree that all business students, including marketing, HR and MIS should have a good understanding of accounting? Explain your answer.**

Financial information is central to every organization. To operate effectively, businesses must have a way to track income, expenses, assets, and liabilities in an organized manner. Financial information is also essential for decision making. Managers prepare financial reports using accounting, a set of procedures and guidelines for companies to follow when preparing financial reports. Unless you understand basic accounting concepts, you will not be able to "speak" the standard financial language of business.

All of us—whether we are self-employed, work for a local small business or a multinational Fortune 100 firm, or are not currently in the workforce—benefit from knowing the basics of accounting and financial statements. We can use this information to educate ourselves about companies before interviewing for a job or buying a company's shares or bonds. Employees at all levels of an organization use accounting information to monitor operations. They must also decide which financial information is important for their company or business unit, what those numbers mean, and how to use them to make decisions.

We start this chapter by discussing why accounting is important for businesses and for users of financial information. We then provide a brief overview of the accounting profession and recent problems in the industry, and the new regulatory environment. Following that, we present an overview of accounting procedures, followed by a description of the three main financial statements: the statement of financial position, the income statement, and the statement of cash flows. Using these statements, we then demonstrate how ratio analysis of financial statements can provide valuable information about a company's financial condition. Finally, we will explore current trends affecting the accounting profession.

Accounting: More than Numbers

LO 1

Accounting is the process of collecting, recording, classifying, summarizing, reporting, and analyzing financial activities. It results in reports that describe the financial condition of an organization. All types of organizations—businesses, hospitals, schools,

CONCEPT *in Action* >>>

Financial accounting information, such as asset values, sales, and inventory, helps managers in all types of organizations make business decisions that enhance organizational effectiveness and efficiency. What are some of the consequences of not understanding accounting in business?

© BONNIE KAMIN / PHOTOEDIT

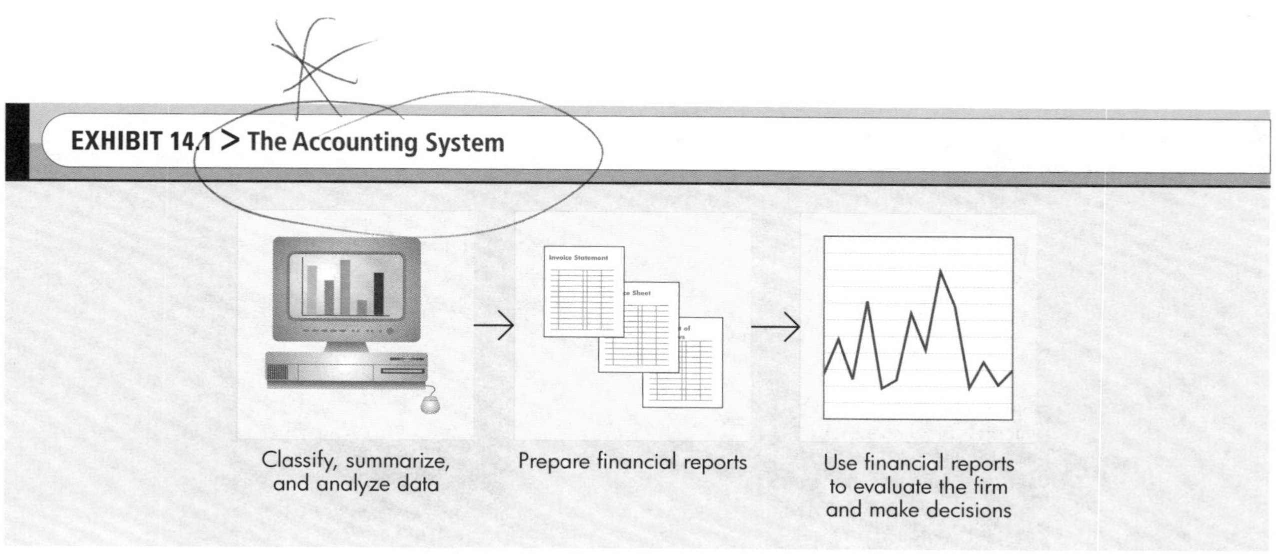
EXHIBIT 14.1 > The Accounting System
Classify, summarize, and analyze data
Prepare financial reports
Use financial reports to evaluate the firm and make decisions

accounting
The process of collecting, recording, classifying, summarizing, reporting, and analyzing financial activities.

government agencies, and civic groups—use accounting procedures. Accounting provides a framework for looking at past performance, current financial health, and possible future performance. It also provides a framework for comparing the financial positions and financial performances of different firms. Understanding how to prepare and interpret financial reports will enable you to evaluate two computer companies and choose the one that is more likely to be a good investment.

As Exhibit 14.1 shows, the accounting system converts the details of financial transactions (sales, payments, purchases, and so on) into a form that people can use to evaluate the firm and make decisions. Data become information, which, in turn, becomes reports. These reports describe a firm's financial position at one point in time and its financial performance during a specified period. Financial reports include *financial statements,* such as the statement of financial position and income statements, and special reports, such as sales and expense breakdowns by product line.

managerial accounting
Accounting that provides financial information that managers inside the organization can use to evaluate and make decisions about current and future operations.

financial accounting
Accounting that focuses on preparing external financial reports that are used by outsiders such as creditors, lenders, suppliers, investors, and government agencies to assess the financial strength of a business.

generally accepted accounting principles (GAAP)
The financial accounting rules, standards, and usual practices followed by accountants in Canada when preparing financial statements, until January 2011.

International Financial Reporting Standards (IFRS)
A set of globally accepted accounting standards adopted in Canada on January 1st, 2011.

HOT Links

Check out what is new at the International Accounting Standards Committee: **(www.iasb.org).**

Who Uses Financial Reports?

The accounting system generates two types of financial reports, as shown in Exhibit 14.2: internal and external. Internal reports are used within the organization. As the term implies, managerial accounting provides financial information that managers inside the organization can use to evaluate and make decisions about current and future operations. For instance, the sales reports prepared by managerial accountants show how well marketing strategies are working. Production cost reports help departments track and control costs. Managers might prepare very detailed financial reports for their own use and provide summary reports to top management.

Financial accounting focuses on preparing external financial reports that are used by outsiders, that is, people who have an interest in the business but are not part of management. Although these reports also provide useful information for managers, they are primarily used by shareholders (the owners of the company), lenders, suppliers, investors, and government agencies to assess the financial strength of a business.

At the time this book was published, accountants in Canada were following the Canadian generally accepted accounting principles (GAAP) to ensure accuracy and consistency in the way financial information is reported. On January 1st, 2011, Canada will adopt the International Financial Reporting Standards (IFRS) for publicly accountable organizations. These organizations must use the IFRS for fiscal periods beginning on or after the January 1st, 2011 date. As well, since financial statements include comparative figures, these companies must present their 2010 financial information using IFRS. The

EXHIBIT 14.2 > Reports Provided by the Accounting System

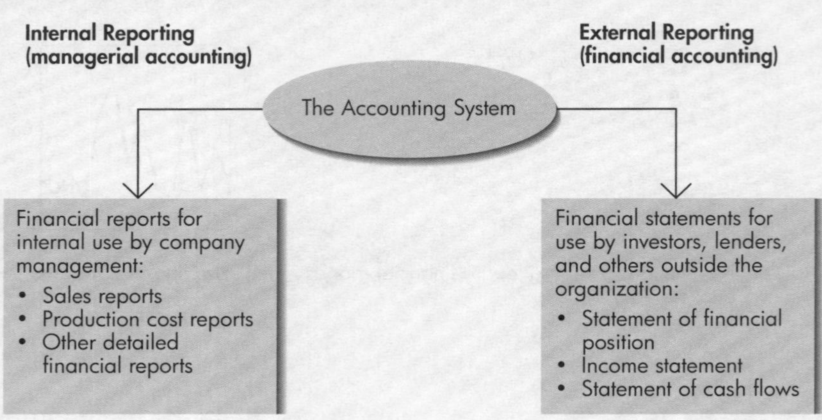

Internal Reporting (managerial accounting)
External Reporting (financial accounting)
The Accounting System
Financial reports for internal use by company management:
• Sales reports
• Production cost reports
• Other detailed financial reports
Financial statements for use by investors, lenders, and others outside the organization:
• Statement of financial position
• Income statement
• Statement of cash flows

annual report
A yearly document that describes a firm's financial status and usually discusses the firm's activities during the past year and its prospects for the future.

adoption of the IFRS was designed to provide consistency in financial reporting internationally and replace the GAAP of over 100 countries.[1] The Expanding Around the Globe box discusses the challenges in changing from GAAP to IFRS.

Financial statements are the chief element of the **annual report**, a yearly document that describes a firm's financial status. Annual reports usually discuss the firm's activities during the past year and its prospects for the future. Three primary financial statements included in the annual report discussed and illustrated later in this chapter are

- the statement of financial position,
- the income statement, and
- the statement of cash flows.

concept check

Explain who uses financial information.

Differentiate between financial accounting and managerial accounting.

Expanding Around The Globe

MOVING TOWARD ONE WORLD OF NUMBERS

Imagine being treasurer of a major multinational company with significant operations in ten other countries. Because the accounting rules in those countries don't conform to IFRS, your staff has to prepare nine sets of financial reports that comply with the host country's rules—and also translate the figures to IFRS for consolidation into the parent company's statements. It's a massive undertaking.

The Canadian Accounting Standards Board (AcSB) and the international accounting standards board (IASB) are working together to develop international accounting standards that will remove disparities between national and international standards, improve the quality of financial information worldwide, and simplify comparisons of financial statements across borders for both corporations and investors.

The AcSB and the IASB desire to create uniform global accounting standards. Presently, there are approximately 100 countries that use IFRS with more signing on each year. As they worked toward convergence, the board members decided to develop a new set of common standards, rather than try to reconcile the two standards. These new standards must be better than existing ones, not simply eliminate differences. Merging GAAP and IFRS into a consistent set of international accounting standards has proven to be very difficult because of different approaches used in the two sets.

However, the convergence project is moving ahead more quickly than the sponsoring groups anticipated. Raising capital outside a corporation's home country overseas will be easier for companies because they will not have to restate their financial reports to conform to either GAAP or IFRS. Because the goal is to develop improved accounting standards, the boards take the big picture view in seeking solutions.[2]

Critical Thinking Questions

- Is it important to have a single set of international accounting standards for at least publicly owned companies? Defend your answer.
- What are some of the major changes from Canadian GAAP to IFRS? (Hint: Use your search engine to find out the answer!)

The Accounting Profession

When you think of accountants, do you picture someone who works alone in a back room, hunched over a desk, scrutinizing pages and pages of numbers? Although today's accountants still must love working with numbers, they now work closely with their clients not only to prepare financial reports but also to help them develop good financial practices. Computers have taken the tedium out of the number-crunching and data-gathering parts of the job and now offer powerful analytical tools as well. Therefore, accountants must keep up with information technology trends. The accounting profession has grown due to the increased complexity, size, and number of businesses and the frequent changes in the tax laws. There are approximately 200,000 accountants in Canada working in the private sector, public sector, or as self-employed accountants.[3]

HOT Links

To find out more about the accounting profession, visit the Canadian Institute of Chartered Accountants site at (**www.cica.ca**), the CMA Canada site at (**www.cma-canada.org**), or the Certified General Accountants site at (**www.cga-canada.org**).

The Accounting Designations

In Canada, there are three accounting associations that grant professional designations. They are the Canadian Institute of Chartered Accountants (CICA), the Society of Management Accountants of Canada (CMA Canada), and the Certified General Accountants Association of Canada (CGA-Canada). Each of the professional accounting associations provides specialized services and has certain educational and work experience requirements for the accountant to be granted the professional designation.

CONCEPT *in Action* >>>

The financial information contained in the CIBC Annual Accountability Report is prepared using generally accepted accounting principles. Lenders, suppliers, investors, and government agencies refer to the annual report to assess the financial strength of a business. What decisions can be made by reviewing a company's annual report?

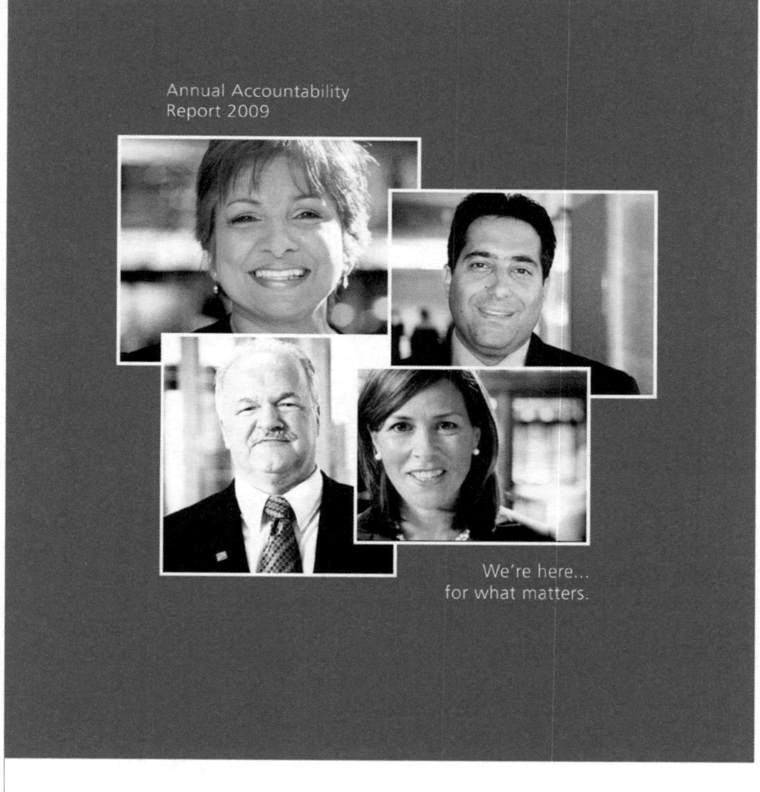

COURTESY CIBC

chartered accountant (CA)
An accountant who has completed an approved bachelor's degree program, completed an educational program, and passed a comprehensive examination.

A **chartered accountant (CA)** typically provides tax, audit, and management services. CAs focus on the external reporting and provide an opinion as to whether the financial statements accurately reflect the company's financial health (this can also be provided by a CGA—discussed below). Most CAs first work for public accounting firms and later become private accountants or financial managers.

CAs generally work in four key areas: public practice, industry, government, or education. In public practice they provide accounting and business advice to clients such as small business taxation, auditing, information technology, personal finance planning, business valuation, receivership, insolvency, and forensic investigation. In industry, CAs develop financial and administrative policies, analyze information, and provide strategic leadership.

certified management accountant (CMA)
An accountant who works primarily in industry and focuses on internal management accounting.

A **certified management accountant (CMA)** works primarily in industry and focuses on internal management accounting. CMAs combine their accounting expertise and business know-how with professional management skills to provide strategic financial management, strategic planning, sales and marketing, information technology, human resources, finance, and operations. According to CMA Canada, *"Working in organizations of all sizes and types, CMAs provide an integrating perspective to business decision making, applying best management practices in strategic planning, finance, operations, sales and marketing, information technology, and human resources to identify new market opportunities, ensure corporate accountability, and help organizations maintain a long-term competitive advantage."*[4]

certified general accountant (CGA)
An accountant who focuses primarily on external financial reporting.

Certified general accountant (CGA) roles have far expanded from the primary focus on external financial reporting. CGAs also provide tax and financial advice to individuals and businesses. Many own their own accounting businesses, whereas others are employed in industry and government. According to CGA Canada, *"CGAs work throughout the world in industry, commerce, finance, government, public practice and other areas where accounting and financial management is required. CGA clients range from major corporations and industries to entrepreneurs. Their expertise is valued in the public sector, government and the corporate world."*[5]

The requirements to become a CA, CMA, or CGA are quite extensive. Each requires a degree plus additional professional studies that cover the full spectrum of financial and business management. Candidates must also complete a period of articling (that results in real-world skills and development of practical problem-solving abilities) and, finally, pass comprehensive exams that demonstrate their knowledge of the profession.

Accountants add value to organizations as CEO/president, treasurer/VP finance, controller, or systems developer. All areas of government require accounting expertise to guide the financial planning and to maintain fiscal control. Additionally, many of Canada's top educators are accountants.

concept check

What are the three accounting designations in Canada?

Basic Accounting Procedures

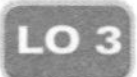

Using generally accepted accounting principles, accountants record and report financial data in similar ways for all firms. They report their findings in financial statements that summarize a company's business transactions over a specified time period. As mentioned earlier, the three major financial statements are the statement of financial position, income statement, and statement of cash flows.

People sometimes confuse accounting with bookkeeping. Accounting is a much broader concept. *Bookkeeping,* the system used to record a firm's financial transactions, is a routine, clerical process. Accountants take bookkeepers' transactions, classify and summarize the financial information, and then prepare and analyze financial reports. Accountants also develop and manage financial systems and help plan the firm's financial strategy.

The Accounting Equation

assets
Things of value owned by a firm.

liabilities
What a firm owes to its creditors; also called *debts*.

owners' equity
The total amount of investment in the firm minus any liabilities; also called *net worth*.

The accounting procedures used today are based on the three main accounting elements of assets, liabilities, and owners' equity. **Assets** are things of value owned by a firm. They might be *tangible,* such as cash, equipment, and buildings, or *intangible,* such as a patent or trademarked name. **Liabilities**—also called *debts*—are what a firm owes to its creditors. **Owners' equity** is the total amount of investment in the firm minus any liabilities. Another term for owners' equity is *net worth.*

The relationship among these three elements is expressed in the accounting equation:

Assets	= Liabilities	+ Owners' equity
(own)	(owe)	(net worth)

The accounting equation must always be in balance (that is, the total of the elements on one side of the equals sign must equal the total on the other side).

Suppose you start a bookstore and put $10,000 in cash into the business. At that point, the business has assets of $10,000 and no liabilities. This would be the accounting equation:

Assets	= Liabilities	+ Owners' equity
$10,000	= $0	+ $10,000

The liabilities are zero, and owner's equity (the amount of your investment in the business) is $10,000. The equation balances.

double-entry bookkeeping
A method of accounting in which each transaction is recorded as at least two entries, so that the accounts or records are changed.

To keep the accounting equation in balance, every transaction must be recorded as at least two entries. As each transaction is recorded, there is an equal and opposite event so that the accounts or records are changed. This method is called **double-entry bookkeeping**.

Suppose that, after starting your bookstore with $10,000 cash, you borrow an additional $10,000 from the bank. The accounting equation will change as follows:

Assets	= Liabilities	+ Owners' equity	
$10,000	= $0	+ $10,000	Initial equation
$10,000	= $10,000	+ $0	Borrowing transaction
$20,000	= $10,000	+ $10,000	Equation after borrowing

Now you have $20,000 in assets—your $10,000 in cash and the $10,000 loan proceeds from the bank. The bank loan is also recorded as a liability of $10,000, because it's a debt that you must repay. Making two entries keeps the equation in balance.

The Accounting Cycle

The *accounting cycle* refers to the process of generating financial statements, beginning with a business transaction and ending with the preparation of the report. Exhibit 14.3 shows the six steps in the accounting cycle. The first step in the cycle is to analyze the data collected from many sources. All transactions that have a financial impact on the firm—sales, payments to employees and suppliers, interest and tax payments, purchases of inventory, and the like—must be documented. The accountant must review the documents to make sure they're complete.

Next, each transaction is recorded in a *journal,* a listing of financial transactions in chronological order. Then the journal entries are recorded in *ledgers,* which show increases and decreases in specific asset, liability, and owners' equity accounts. The ledger totals for each account are summarized in a *trial balance,* which is used to confirm the accuracy of the figures. These values are used to prepare financial statements and management reports. Finally, individuals analyze these reports and make decisions based on the information in them.

EXHIBIT 14.3 > The Accounting Cycle

Step 1:
Analyze business transaction documents
Step 2:
Record business transactions in journal
Accts Rec 12
Cash 11
Step 3:
Post journal entries to ledgers
Step 4:
Prepare trial balance
Balance Sheet
Statement of Cash Flows
Step 5:
Prepare financial statements and management reports from account data
Step 6:
Analyze reports

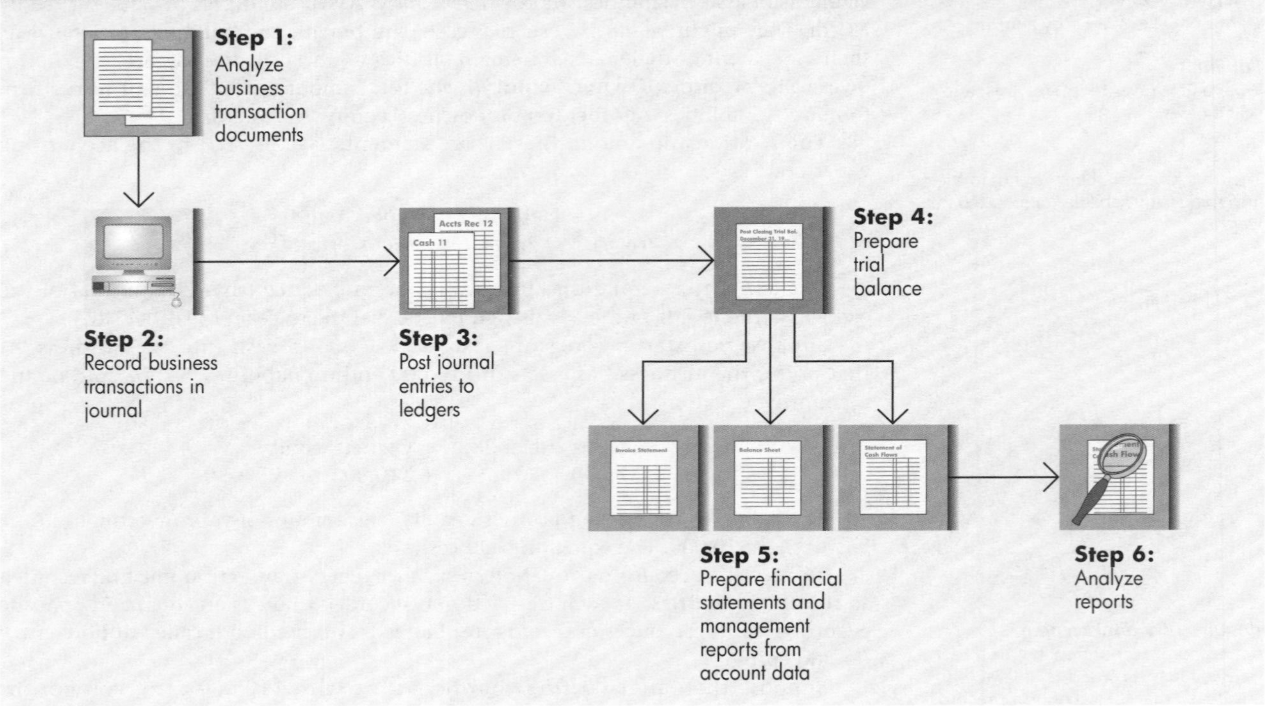

Computers in Accounting

Computerized accounting programs do many different things. Most accounting packages offer six basic modules that handle general ledger, sales order, accounts receivable, purchase order, accounts payable, and inventory control functions. Tax programs use accounting data to prepare tax returns and tax plans. Computerized point-of-sale terminals used by many retail firms automatically record sales and do some of the bookkeeping.

Accounting and financial applications typically represent one of the largest portions of a company's software budget. Accounting software ranges from off-the-shelf programs for small businesses to full-scale customized enterprise resource planning systems for major corporations. Besides the accounting packages mentioned above, many large accounting firms have customized accounting software developed for them and their clients.

concept check

Explain the accounting equation.

Describe the six-step accounting cycle.

What role do computers play in accounting?

The Statement of Financial Position

LO 4

statement of financial position (balance sheet)
A financial statement that summarizes a firm's financial position at a specific point in time.

The **statement of financial position (balance sheet)**, one of three financial statements generated from the accounting system, summarizes a firm's financial position at a specific point in time. It reports the resources of a company (assets), the company's obligations (liabilities), and the difference between what is owned (assets) and what is owed (liabilities), which is known as owners' equity.

liquidity
The speed with which an asset can be converted to cash.

The assets are listed in order of their **liquidity**, the speed with which they can be converted to cash. The most liquid assets come first, and the least liquid are last. Because cash is the most liquid asset, it is listed first. Buildings, on the other hand, have to be sold to be converted to cash, so they are listed after cash. Liabilities are arranged similarly: liabilities due in the short term are listed before those due in the long term.

The statement of financial position at December 31, 2011, for Delicious Desserts, an imaginary manufacturer, is illustrated in Exhibit 14.4. The basic accounting equation is reflected in the three totals highlighted on the statement of financial position: assets of $148,900 equal the sum of liabilities and owners' equity ($70,150 + $78,750). The three main categories of accounts on the statement of financial position are explained below.

EXHIBIT 14.4 > Statement of Financial Position for Delicious Desserts

Delicious Desserts, Inc.
Statement of Financial Position as of December 31, 2011

Assets			
Current assets:			
Cash		$15,000	
Marketable securities		4,500	
Accounts receivable	$45,000		
Less: Allowance for doubtful accounts	1,300	43,700	
Notes receivable		5,000	
Inventory		15,000	
Total current assets			$ 83,200
Fixed assets:			
Bakery equipment	$56,000		
Less: Accumulated depreciation	16,000	$40,000	
Furniture and fixtures	$18,450		
Less: Accumulated depreciation	4,250	14,200	
Total fixed assets			54,200
Intangible assets:			
Trademark		$ 4,500	
Goodwill		7,000	
Total intangible assets			11,500
Total assets			**$148,900**
Liabilities and Owners' Equity			
Current liabilities:			
Accounts payable	$30,650		
Notes payable	15,000		
Accrued expenses	4,500		
Income taxes payable	5,000		
Current portion of long-term debt	5,000		
Total current liabilities		$60,150	
Long-term liabilities:			
Bank loan for bakery equipment	$10,000		
Total long-term liabilities		10,000	
Total liabilities			**$ 70,150**
Owners' equity:			
Common shares (10,000 shares outstanding)		$30,000	
Retained earnings		48,750	
Total owners' equity			**78,750**
Total liabilities and owners' equity			**$148,900**

Assets

current assets
Assets that can or will be converted to cash within the next twelve months.

Assets can be divided into three broad categories: current assets, fixed assets, and intangible assets. Current assets are assets that can or will be converted to cash within the next 12 months. They are important because they provide the funds used to pay the firm's current bills. They also represent the amount of money the firm can raise quickly. Current assets include

- *cash*—funds on hand or in a bank;
- *marketable securities (trading securities)*—temporary investments of excess cash that can readily be converted to cash;
- *accounts receivable*—amounts owed to the firm by customers who bought goods or services on credit;
- *notes receivable*—amounts owed to the firm by customers or others to whom it lent money; and
- *inventory*—stock of goods being held for production or for sale to customers.

fixed assets
Long-term assets used by a firm for more than a year, such as land, buildings, and machinery.

amortization (depreciation)
The allocation of an asset's original cost to the years in which it is expected to produce revenues.

Fixed assets are long-term assets used by the firm for more than a year. They tend to be used in production and include land, buildings, machinery, equipment, furniture, and fixtures. Except for land, fixed assets wear out and become outdated over time. Thus, they decrease in value every year. This declining value is accounted for through amortization. Amortization (also called depreciation) is the allocation of the asset's original cost to the years in which it is expected to produce revenues. A portion of the cost of a depreciable asset—a building or piece of equipment, for instance—is charged to each of the years in which it is expected to provide benefits. This practice helps match the asset's cost against the revenues it provides. As it is impossible to know exactly how long an asset will last, estimates are used. They are based on past experience with similar items or on Canada Revenue Agency's guidelines. Notice that, through 2011, Delicious Desserts has taken a total of $16,000 in amortization on its bakery equipment.

intangible assets
Long-term assets with no physical existence, such as patents, copyrights, trademarks, and goodwill.

Intangible assets are long-term assets with no physical existence. Common examples are patents, copyrights, trademarks, and goodwill. *Patents* and *copyrights* shield the firm from direct competition, so their benefits are more protective than productive. For instance, no one can use more than a small amount of copyrighted material without permission from the copyright holder. *Trademarks* are registered names that can be sold or licensed to others. One of Delicious Desserts' intangible assets is a trademark valued at $4,500. Delicious Desserts' other intangible asset is goodwill of $7,000. *Goodwill* occurs when a company pays more for an acquired firm than the value of its tangible assets.

Liabilities

Liabilities are the amounts a firm owes to creditors. Those liabilities coming due sooner—current liabilities—are listed first on the statement of financial position, followed by long-term liabilities.

current liabilities
Short-term claims that are due within a year of the date of the statement of financial position.

Current liabilities are those due within a year of the date of the statement of financial position. These short-term claims can strain the firm's current assets because they must be paid in the near future. Current liabilities include the following:

- *Accounts payable.* This is the amount that the firm owes for credit purchases due within a year. This account is the liability counterpart of accounts receivable.
- *Notes payable.* These are short-term loans from banks, suppliers, or others that must be repaid within a year. For example, Delicious Desserts has a six-month, $15,000 loan from its bank that is a note payable.
- *Accrued expenses.* These represent expenses, typically for wages and taxes, that have accumulated and must be paid at a specified future date within the year, although no bill has been received by the firm.

CONCEPT *in Action* >>>

On its statement of financial position, a bakery would list its bakery equipment, furniture, and fixtures as fixed assets. The amount it owes its vendors for supplies would appear as a current liability—accounts payable—and its bank loan would be under long-term liabilities. On the income statement, you'll find a summary of revenues and expenses for a particular time period. What information can a potential investor find out from the statement of financial position?

IZAOKAS SAPIRO/SHUTTERSTOCK

- *Income taxes payable.* These are taxes owed for the current operating period but not yet paid. Taxes are often shown separately when they are a large amount.
- *Current portion of long-term debt.* This represents any repayment on long-term debt due within the year. Delicious Desserts is scheduled to repay $5,000 on its equipment loan in the coming year.

long-term liabilities
Claims that come due more than one year after the date of the statement of financial position.

retained earnings
The amounts left over from profitable operations since the firm's beginning; equal to total profits minus all dividends paid to shareholders.

Long-term liabilities come due more than one year after the date of the statement of financial position. They include bank loans (such as Delicious Desserts' $10,000 loan for production equipment), mortgages on buildings, and the company's bonds sold to others.

Owners' Equity

Owners' equity is the owners' total investment in the business after all liabilities have been paid. For sole proprietorships and partnerships, amounts put in by the owners are recorded as capital. In a corporation, the owners provide capital by buying the firm's common shares. For Delicious Desserts, the total common shares investment is $30,000. **Retained earnings** are the amounts left over from profitable operations since the firm's beginning. They are total profits minus all dividends (distributions of profits) paid to shareholders. Delicious Desserts has $48,750 in retained earnings.

concept check

What is a statement of financial position?

What are the three main categories of accounts on the statement of financial position, and how do they relate to the accounting equation?

How do retained earnings relate to owners' equity?

The Income Statement

LO 5

income statement
A financial statement that summarizes a firm's revenues and expenses, and shows its total profit or loss over a period of time.

The statement of financial position shows the firm's financial position at a certain point in time. The **income statement** summarizes the firm's revenues and expenses and shows its total profit or loss over a period of time. Most companies prepare monthly income statements for management and quarterly and annual statements for use by investors, creditors, and other outsiders. The primary elements of the income statement are revenues, expenses, and net income (or net loss). The income statement for Delicious Desserts for the year ended December 31, 2011, is shown in Exhibit 14.5.

EXHIBIT 14.5 > Income Statement for Delicious Desserts

Delicious Desserts, Inc.
Income Statement for the Year Ending December 31, 2011

Revenues			
Gross sales		$275,000	
Less: Sales discounts		2,500	
Less: Returns and allowances		2,000	
Net sales			$270,500
Cost of Goods Sold			
Beginning inventory, January 1		$ 18,000	
Cost of goods manufactured		109,500	
Total cost of goods available for sale		$127,500	
Less: Ending inventory December 31		15,000	
Cost of goods sold			112,500
Gross profit			**$158,000**
Operating Expenses			
Selling expenses			
Sales salaries	$31,000		
Advertising	16,000		
Other selling expenses	18,000		
Total selling expenses		$ 65,000	
General and administrative expenses			
Professional and office salaries	$20,500		
Utilities	5,000		
Office supplies	1,500		
Interest	3,600		
Insurance	2,500		
Rent	17,000		
Total general and administrative expenses		50,100	
Total operating expenses			115,100
Net profit before taxes			**$ 42,900**
Less: Income taxes			10,725
Net profit			**$ 32,175**

Revenues

revenues
The dollar amount of a firm's sales plus any other income it received from sources such as interest, dividends, and rents.

gross sales
The total dollar amount of a company's sales.

net sales
The amount left after deducting sales discounts and returns and allowances from gross sales.

Revenues are the dollar amount of sales plus any other income received from sources such as interest, dividends, and rents. The revenues of Delicious Desserts arise from sales of its products. Revenues are determined starting with gross sales, the total dollar amount of a company's sales. Delicious Desserts had two deductions from gross sales. *Sales discounts* are price reductions given to customers who pay their bills early. For example, Delicious Desserts gives sales discounts to restaurants that buy in bulk and pay at delivery. *Returns and allowances* is the dollar amount of merchandise returned by customers because they didn't like a product or because it was damaged or defective. Net sales is the amount left after deducting sales discounts and returns and allowances from gross sales. Delicious Desserts gross sales were reduced by $4,500, leaving net sales of $270,500.

Expenses

expenses
The costs of generating revenues.

cost of goods sold (COGS)
The total expense of buying or producing a firm's goods or services.

Expenses are the costs of generating revenues. Two types are recorded on the income statement: cost of goods sold and operating expenses.

The cost of goods sold (COGS) is the total expense of buying or producing the firm's goods or services. For manufacturers, cost of goods sold includes all costs directly related to production: purchases of raw materials and parts, labour, and factory overhead (utilities, factory maintenance, and machinery repair). For wholesalers and retailers, it is the cost of goods bought for resale. For all sellers, cost of goods sold includes all the expenses of preparing the goods for sale, such as shipping and packaging.

The value of COGS can be calculated using:

	Beginning Inventories
+	Inventory Purchases
=	Inventories Available for Sale
−	Ending Inventories
=	COGS

Delicious Desserts cost of goods sold is based on the value of inventory on hand at the beginning of the accounting period, $18,000 (from the statement of financial position of the last accounting period). During the year, the company spent $109,500 to produce its manufactured goods. This figure includes the cost of raw materials, labour costs for production workers, and the cost of operating the production area. Adding the cost of goods manufactured to the value of beginning inventory, we get the total cost of goods available for sale, $127,500. To determine the cost of goods sold for the year, we subtract the cost of inventory at the end of the period:

$$\$18,000 + \$109,500 - \$15,000 = \$112,500$$

gross profit
The amount a company earns after paying to produce or buy its products but before deducting operating expenses.

operating expenses
The expenses of running a business that are not directly related to producing or buying its products.

The amount a company earns after paying to produce or buy its products but before deducting operating expenses is the **gross profit**. It is the difference between net sales and cost of goods sold. As service firms do not produce goods, their gross profit equals net sales. Gross profit is a critical number for a company, because it is the source of funds to cover all the firm's other expenses.

The other major expense category is **operating expenses**. These are the expenses of running the business that are not related directly to producing or buying its products. The two main types of operating expenses are selling expenses and general and administrative expenses. *Selling expenses* are those related to marketing and distributing the company's products. They include salaries and commissions paid to salespeople and the costs of advertising, sales supplies, delivery, and other items that can be linked to sales activity, such as insurance, telephone and other utilities, and postage. *General and administrative expenses* are the business expenses that cannot be linked to either cost of goods sold or sales. Examples of general and administrative expenses are salaries of top managers and office support staff; utilities; office supplies; interest expense; fees for accounting, consulting, and legal services; insurance; and rent. Delicious Desserts operating expenses totalled $115,100.

net profit (net income)
The amount obtained by subtracting all of a firm's expenses from its revenues, when the revenues are more than the expenses.

net loss
The amount obtained by subtracting all of a firm's expenses from its revenues, when the expenses are more than the revenues.

Net Profit or Loss

The final figure—or bottom line—on an income statement is the **net profit** (or **net income**) or **net loss**. It is calculated by subtracting all expenses from revenues. If revenues are more than expenses, the result is a net profit. If expenses exceed revenues, a net loss results and is usually shown in brackets.

Several steps are involved in finding net profit or loss. (These are shown in the right-hand column of Exhibit 14.5.) First, the cost of goods sold is deducted from net sales to get the gross profit. Then, total operating expenses are subtracted from gross profit to get the net profit before taxes. Finally, income taxes are deducted to get the net profit. As shown in Exhibit 14.5, Delicious Desserts earned a net profit of $32,175 in 2011.

It is very important to recognize that profit does not represent cash. The income statement is a summary of the firm's operating results during some time period. It does not present the firm's actual cash flows during the period. Those are summarized in the statement of cash flows, which is discussed briefly in the next section.

concept check

What is an income statement? How does it differ from the statement of financial position?

Describe the key parts of the income statement. Distinguish between gross sales and net sales.

How is net profit or loss calculated?

The Statement of Cash Flows

LO 6

statement of cash flows
A financial statement that provides a summary of the money flowing into and out of a firm during a certain period, typically one year.

Net profit or loss is one measure of a company's financial performance. However, creditors and investors are also keenly interested in how much cash a business generates and how it is used. The statement of cash flows, a summary of the money flowing into and out of a firm, is the financial statement used to assess the sources and uses of cash during a certain period, typically one year. All publicly traded firms must include a statement of cash flows in their financial reports to shareholders. The statement of cash flows tracks the firm's cash receipts and cash payments. It gives financial managers and analysts a way of identifying cash flow problems and of assessing the firm's financial viability.

Using income statement and statement of financial position data, the statement of cash flows divides the firm's cash flows into three groups:

- *cash flow from operating activities*—those related to the production of the firm's goods or services;
- *cash flow from investment activities*—those related to the purchase and sale of assets; and
- *cash flow from financing activities*—those related to debt and equity financing.

Delicious Desserts' statement of cash flows for 2011 is presented in Exhibit 14.6. It shows that the company's cash and marketable securities have increased over the last year. Furthermore, during the year, the company generated enough cash flow to increase inventory and fixed assets and to reduce accounts payable, accruals, notes payable, and long-term debt.

HOT Links

Choose any public Canadian company. Search its website for their financial statements, and review the statement of financial position and income statement.

concept check

What is the purpose of the statement of cash flows?

Why has cash flow become such an important measure of a firm's financial condition?

What situations can you cite from the chapter that support your answer?

Analyzing Financial Statements

LO 7

Individually, the statement of financial position, income statement, and statement of cash flows provide insight into the firm's operations, profitability, and overall financial condition. By studying the relationships among the financial statements,

EXHIBIT 14.6 > Statement of Cash Flows for Delicious Desserts

Delicious Desserts, INC.
Statement of Cash Flows for 2011

Cash Flow from Operating Activities		
Net profit after taxes	$ 27,175	
Amortization	1,500	
Decrease in accounts receivable	3,140	
Increase in inventory	(4,500)	
Decrease in accounts payable	(2,065)	
Decrease in accruals	(1,035)	
Cash provided by operating activities		$ 24,215
Cash Flow from Investment Activities		
Increase in gross fixed assets	($ 5,000)	
Cash used in investment activities		($ 5,000)
Cash Flow from Financing Activities		
Decrease in notes payable	($ 3,000)	
Decrease in long-term debt	(1,000)	
Cash used by financing activities		($ 4,000)
Net increase in cash and marketable securities		**$ 15,215**

however, one can gain even more insight into a firm's financial condition and performance.

ratio analysis
The calculation and interpretation of financial ratios using data taken from the firm's financial statements to assess its condition and performance.

Ratio analysis involves calculating and interpreting financial ratios using data taken from the firm's financial statements to assess its condition and performance. A financial ratio states the relationship between financial data on a percentage of three to five years. A firm's ratios can also be compared to industry averages or to basis. For instance, current assets might be viewed relative to current liabilities or sales relative to assets. The ratios can then be compared over time, typically to those of another company in the same industry. Period-to-period and industry ratios provide a meaningful basis for comparison, so that we can answer questions such as, "Is this particular ratio good or bad?"

It's important to remember that ratio analysis is based on historical data and might not indicate future financial performance. Ratio analysis merely highlights potential problems; it does not prove that they exist. However, ratios can help managers monitor the firm's performance from period to period, to understand operations better and identify trouble spots.

Ratios are also important to a firm's present and prospective creditors (lenders), who want to see if the firm can repay what it borrows and assess the firm's financial health. Often loan agreements require firms to maintain minimum levels of specific ratios. Both present and prospective shareholders use ratio analysis to look at the company's historical performance and trends over time.

Ratios can be classified by what they measure: liquidity, profitability, activity, and debt. Using Delicious Desserts' 2011 statement of financial position and income statement (Exhibits 14.4 and 14.5), we can calculate and interpret the key ratios in each group. In Exhibit 14.7, we have summarized the calculations of these ratios for Delicious Desserts. We will now discuss how to calculate the ratios and, more important, how to interpret the ratio value.

Liquidity Ratios

liquidity ratios
Ratios that measure a firm's ability to pay its short-term debts as they come due.

Liquidity ratios measure the firm's ability to pay its short-term debts as they come due. These ratios are of special interest to the firm's creditors. The three main measures of liquidity are the current ratio, the acid-test (quick) ratio, and net working capital.

CONCEPT *in Action* >>>

How is Best Buy doing this quarter compared to historical results? With ratio analysis, managers can track performance. For example, the net profit margin shows how much profit is left after all expenses. Why would a company want to compare their financial ratios with the industry averages?

EXHIBIT 14.7 > Ratio Analysis for Delicious Desserts at Year-End 2011

Ratio	Formula	Calculation	Result
Liquidity Ratios			
Current ratio	Total current assets / Total current liabilities	\$83,200 / \$60,150	1.4
Acid-test (quick) ratio	(Total current assets − inventory) / Total current liabilities	(\$83,200 − \$15,000) / \$60,150	1.1
Net working capital	Total current assets − Total current liabilities	\$83,200 − \$60,150	\$23,050
Profitability Ratios			
Net profit margin	Net profit / Net sales	\$13,175 / \$270,500	11.9%
Return on equity	Net profit / Total owners' equity	\$32,175 / \$78,750	40.9%
Earnings per share	Net profit / Number of shares of common shares outstanding	\$32,175 / 10,000	\$3.22
Activity Ratio			
Inventory turnover	Cost of goods sold / Average inventory		
	Cost of goods sold / (Beginning inventory + Ending inventory)/2	\$112,500 / (\$18,000 + \$15,000)/2	
		\$112,500 / \$16,500	6.8 times
Debt Ratio			
Debt-to-equity ratio	Total liabilities / Owners' equity	\$70,150 / \$78,750	89.1%

current ratio
The ratio of total current assets to total current liabilities; used to measure a firm's liquidity.

acid-test (quick) ratio
The ratio of total current assets excluding inventory to total current liabilities; used to measure a firm's liquidity.

The **current ratio** is the ratio of total current assets to total current liabilities. Traditionally, a current ratio of 2 (\$2 of current assets for every \$1 of current liabilities) has been considered good. Whether it is sufficient depends on the industry in which the firm operates. Public utilities, which have a very steady cash flow, operate quite well with a current ratio well below 2. A current ratio of 2 might not be adequate for manufacturers and merchandisers that carry high inventories and have lots of receivables. The current ratio for Delicious Desserts for 2011, as shown in Exhibit 14.7, is 1.4. This means little without a basis for comparison. If the analyst found that the industry average was 2.4, Delicious Desserts would appear to have low liquidity.

The **acid-test (quick) ratio** is like the current ratio except that it excludes inventory, which is the least liquid current asset. The acid-test ratio is used to measure the firm's ability to pay its current liabilities without selling inventory. The name *acid-test* implies that this ratio is a crucial test of the firm's liquidity. An acid-test ratio of at least 1 is preferred, but again, what is an acceptable value varies by industry. The acid-test ratio is a good measure of liquidity when inventory cannot easily be converted to cash (for instance, if it consists of very specialized goods with a limited market). If inventory is liquid, the current ratio is better. Delicious Desserts' acid-test ratio for 2011 is 1.1. Because Delicious Desserts does not carry large inventories, the values of its acid test and current ratios are fairly close. For manufacturing companies, however, inventory typically makes up a large portion of current assets, so the acid-test ratio will be lower than the current ratio.

net working capital
The amount obtained by subtracting total current liabilities from total current assets; used to measure a firm's liquidity.

Net working capital, though not really a ratio, is often used to measure a firm's overall liquidity. It is calculated by subtracting total current liabilities from total current assets. Delicious Desserts' net working capital for 2011 is $23,050. Comparisons of net working capital over time often help in assessing a firm's liquidity.

Profitability Ratios

profitability ratios
Ratios that measure how well a firm is using its resources to generate profit and how efficiently it is being managed.

net profit margin
The ratio of net profit to net sales; also called *return on sales*. It measures the percentage of each sales dollar remaining after all expenses, including taxes, have been deducted.

To measure profitability, a firm's profits can be related to its sales, equity, or shares value. Profitability ratios measure how well the firm is using its resources to generate profit and how efficiently it is being managed. The main profitability ratios are net profit margin, return on equity, and earnings per share.

The ratio of net profit to net sales is the net profit margin, also called *return on sales*. It measures the percentage of each sales dollar remaining after all expenses, including taxes, have been deducted. Higher net profit margins are better than lower ones. The net profit margin is often used to measure the firm's earning power. "Good" net profit margins differ quite a bit from industry to industry. A grocery store usually has a very low net profit margin, perhaps below 1 percent, whereas a jewellery store's net profit margin would probably exceed 10 percent. Delicious Desserts' net profit margin for 2011 is 11.9 percent. In other words, Delicious Desserts is earning 11.9 cents on each dollar of sales.

return on equity (ROE)
The ratio of net profit to total owners' equity; measures the return that owners receive on their investment in the firm.

The ratio of net profit to total owners' equity is called return on equity (ROE). It measures the return that owners receive on their investment in the firm, a major reason for investing in a company's shares. Delicious Desserts has a 40.9 percent ROE for 2011. On the surface, a 40.9 percent ROE seems quite good, but the level of risk in the business and the ROE of other firms in the same industry must also be considered. The higher the risk, the greater the ROE investors look for. A firm's ROE can also be compared to past values to see how the company is performing over time.

earnings per share (EPS)
The ratio of net profit to the number of common shares outstanding; measures the number of dollars earned by each share.

Earnings per share (EPS) is the ratio of net profit to the number of shares of common shares outstanding. It measures the number of dollars earned by each share. EPS values are closely watched by investors and are considered an important sign of success. EPS also indicates a firm's ability to pay dividends. Note that EPS is the dollar amount earned by each share, not the actual amount given to shareholders in the form of dividends. Some earnings may be put back into the firm. Delicious Desserts' EPS for 2011 is $3.22.

Activity Ratios

activity ratios
Ratios that measure how well a firm uses its assets.

inventory turnover ratio
The ratio of cost of goods sold to average inventory; measures the speed with which inventory moves through a firm and is turned into sales.

Activity ratios measure how well a firm uses its assets. They reflect the speed with which resources are converted to cash or sales. A frequently used activity ratio is inventory turnover.

The inventory turnover ratio measures the speed with which inventory moves through the firm and is turned into sales. It is calculated by dividing cost of goods sold by the average inventory. (Average inventory is estimated by adding the beginning and ending inventories for the year and dividing by 2.) Based on its 2011 financial data, Delicious Desserts' inventory, on average, is turned into sales 6.8 times each year, or about once every 54 days (365 days ÷ 6.8). The acceptable turnover ratio depends on the line of business. A grocery store would have a high turnover ratio, maybe 20 times a year, whereas the turnover for a heavy equipment manufacturer might be only 3 times a year.

Debt Ratios

debt ratios
Ratios that measure the degree and effect of a firm's use of borrowed funds (debt) to finance its operations.

Debt ratios measure the degree and effect of the firm's use of borrowed funds (debt) to finance its operations. These ratios are especially important to

Making Ethical Choices

SUPERMARKETS SHELVE REVENUES AND CAN AUDITORS

As the assistant controller of a major supermarket company, you work closely with the company's independent auditor. Overall, you have been pleased with your auditor's performance and believe that the firm has shown high standards of integrity.

During this year's review of your firm's financial reports and its internal controls, the auditor raised a question about the timing of incentive payments received from vendors and when they would be recognized as revenue. The issue of such incentive payments from vendors is a big one in the grocery industry. Several of your competitors recorded vendor payments received of $2 to $3 billion in 2011—more than those companies' operating profits. You are aware that your chain uses these payment receipts to manipulate earnings, choosing the supplier that offers the largest up-front incentive payments for shelf space to boost quarterly earnings by a sizable amount. Although this is legal, it is a practice that has come under closer scrutiny in the wake of investigations of other accounting irregularities.

You are called into a meeting with the CFO and the controller to discuss what to do about the warning from the audit firm that it might have a "reportable condition" relating to this situation. The CFO wants to fire the audit firm and hire another one. The controller asks for your opinion.

ETHICAL DILEMMA: Should you go along with the CFO and recommend firing the audit firm?

SOURCES: David Henry, "Accounting Games in the Grocer's Aisle," *Business Week*, April 14, 2003, 64; and Stephen Taub, "D&T Warned A&P Dismissed," *CFO.com*, September 19, 2002, (www.cfo.com).

debt-to-equity ratio
The ratio of total liabilities to owners' equity; measures the relationship between the amount of debt financing and the amount of equity financing (owner's funds).

lenders and investors. They want to make sure the firm has a healthy mix of debt and equity. If the firm relies too much on debt, it might have trouble meeting interest payments and repaying loans. The most important debt ratio is the debt-to-equity ratio.

The **debt-to-equity ratio** measures the relationship between the amount of debt financing (borrowing) and the amount of equity financing (owners' funds). It is calculated by dividing total liabilities by owners' equity. In general, the lower the ratio, the better, but it is important to assess the debt-to-equity ratio against both past values and industry averages. Delicious Desserts' ratio for 2011 is 89.1 percent. The ratio indicates that the company has 89 cents of debt for every dollar the owners have provided. A ratio above 100 percent means the firm has more debt than equity. In such a case, the lenders are providing more financing than the owners.

concept check

How can ratio analysis be used to interpret financial statements?

Name the main liquidity and profitability ratios, and explain what they indicate.

What kinds of information do activity ratios give? Why are debt ratios of concern to lenders and investors?

Trends in Accounting

LO 8

The role of accountants has been changing and expanding. Although accountants still perform the important task of assuring that a company's financial reporting conforms to IFRS, they have become a valuable part of the financial team and consult with clients on information technology and other areas as well.

The increasing complexity of today's business environment creates additional challenges for the accounting profession. As we move to a more knowledge-based economy, this creates a problem with being able to value and account for the knowledge assets. By far the most significant accounting change in Canada is the move to IFRS.

HOT Links

Learn more accounting terms at Small Business: Canada, **(http://sbinfocanada.about.com/od/accounting)** or **(http://sbinfocanada.about.com/cs/businessinfo/a/biztermsall.htm).**

Accountants Expand Their Role

Moving beyond their traditional task of validating a company's financial information, accountants now take an active role in advising their clients on systems and procedures, accounting software, and changes in accounting regulations. They also delve into operating information to discover what's behind the numbers. By examining the risks and weaknesses in a company, they can help managers develop financial controls and procedures to prevent future trouble spots. For example, auditors in a manufacturing company might spend a significant amount of time on inventory, a likely problem area.

Accounting firms have greatly expanded the consulting services they provide clients. As a result, accountants have become more involved in the operations of their clients. This raises the question of potential conflicts of interest. Can auditors serve both the public and the client? Auditors' main purpose is to certify financial statements. Will they maintain sufficient objectivity to raise questions while auditing a client that provides them with significant consulting revenues? Can auditors review systems and methods that they recommended? According to one expert, "If the financial markets don't believe in a firm's audit, the firm has nothing."

Valuing Knowledge Assets

As the world's economy becomes knowledge-based rather than industrial-based, more of a company's value might come from internally generated, intangible intellectual assets. Intellectual capital is an important resource to any organization, but are we serious about actually attaching a dollar value to it? Dr. Nick Bontis, a researcher and practitioner in knowledge management, intellectual capital, and organizational learning at McMaster University in Hamilton, Ontario, discovered that the main reason cited by his research subjects for leaving their employment was that they felt they were underutilized. With voluntary turnover in Canadian organizations reaching 15 percent, we are watching these knowledge assets walk out the door.[6]

Whether and how to value intangibles are controversial issues. Some people believe that because intangibles are uncertain and risky, they do not belong on the statement of financial position. Costs related to intangibles might bear no relationship to their actual value. On the other hand, placing a value on intangibles allows companies to know whether they are earning adequate returns on R&D, whether patents are worth renewing, and whether they should invest more to build brands. Clearly, there are no quick and easy solutions to this issue, which will continue to be studied in the coming years.

Canada Moves to International Financial Reporting Standards (IFRS)

The most significant trend in accounting presently is the move to IFRS. As we have seen, international trade and investment is important to the Canadian economy and our standard of living. As more and more Canadian companies are operating globally, the various accounting methods used internationally has created duplicate work and more expenses. By moving to IFRS, international companies can use one accounting method. This creates many advantages.

Some of the advantages include: lower costs associated with preparation of financial information, consistency in reports internationally, ease of financial comparisons with other companies, etc. Some notable changes to IFRS include: revenue is called income, the balance sheet is called the Statement of Financial Position and the cash flow statement is called the Statement of Cash Flows.

concept check

What new roles are accountants playing? Do you see any potential problems from these new roles?

What are knowledge assets, and why have they become so important?

How will Canada's moving to IFRS benefit our companies?

Great Ideas to Use Now

By now it should be very clear that basic accounting knowledge is a valuable skill to have, whether you start your own company or work for someone else. Analyzing a company's financial statements before you take a job there can tell you quite a bit

Customer Satisfaction and Quality

The recent upheaval in corporate financial reporting makes customer satisfaction and quality very relevant to financial statement preparation and the accounting profession. As noted earlier, auditing firms often gave good reports to companies later charged with accounting irregularities.

The customers for financial reports are not just the corporate clients who hire the auditors. The investing public—both institutions who buy large blocks of shares and individuals—rely heavily on the quality and reliability of reported financial information to make investment decisions. They are demanding that auditors and corporations demonstrate their compliance with higher standards.

Companies are now giving new respect to the external auditing process. "If you want an audit that will detect management fraud, you must be willing to pay more for it and pay far greater attention to the process and what will be included and analyzed," says Robert G. Eccles, PricewaterhouseCoopers senior fellow and coauthor of *Building Public Trust: The Future of Corporate Reporting.* "The audit committee must be the customer for the audit, and this will require more time on the part of the audit committee."

Better quality control will result from new corporate governance standards and financial disclosure practices. Management at Airgas Inc., an industrial gases distributor, now spends more time on these issues. It was already in compliance with the latest legislative and regulatory reforms. Recently, the company implemented a more formal approach to financial quality control. The audit committee will hold a special meeting every year to review current business issues. "This focus is closely tied to our growth strategy," says Roger Millay, Airgas senior vice-president and CFO. "Good governance, and the perception and understanding of good governance, are important to our growth strategy. The market's confidence in our governance is essential to attracting capital."

SOURCE: Outlook 2003: More Changes, Greater Challenges, (www.businessfinancemag.com), December 2002. Reprinted with permission from Penton Media.

about its financial health. Once you are on the job, you need to understand how to read financial statements and how to develop financial information for business operations. It's almost impossible to operate effectively in a business environment otherwise. In a small company, you will wear many hats, and having accounting skills may help you get the job. In addition, accounting will help you manage your personal finances.

If you own your own firm, you can't rely on someone else to take charge of your accounting system. You must decide what financial information you need to manage your company better and to track its progress. If you can't understand the reports your accountant prepares, you will have no idea whether they are accurate.

Summary of Learning Outcomes

1 Explain the importance of financial reports and accounting information to the targeted users?

Accounting involves collecting, recording, classifying, summarizing, reporting, and analyzing a firm's financial activities according to a standard set of procedures. The financial reports resulting from the accounting process give managers, employees, investors, customers, suppliers, creditors, and government agencies a way of analyzing a company's past, current, and future performance. Financial accounting is concerned with the preparation of financial reports using generally accepted accounting principles. Managerial accounting provides financial information that management can use to make decisions about the firm's operations.

2 Show an understanding of the accounting profession.

Although today's accountants still must love working with numbers, they now work closely with their clients not only to prepare financial reports but also to help them develop good financial practices. Computers have taken the tedium out of the number-crunching and data-gathering parts of the job and now offer powerful analytical tools as well. Therefore, accountants must keep up with information technology trends.

In Canada there are three accounting associations that grant professional designations. They are the Canadian Institute of Chartered Accountants (CICA), the Society of Management Accountants of Canada (CMA Canada), and the Certified

General Accountants Association of Canada (CGA-Canada). Each of the professional accounting associations provides specialized services and has certain educational and work experience requirements for the accountant to be granted the professional designation.

3 Identify the six steps in the accounting cycle.

The accounting cycle refers to the process of generating financial statements. It begins with analyzing business transactions, recording them in journals, and posting them to ledgers. Ledger totals are then summarized in a trial balance that confirms the accuracy of the figures. Next, the accountant prepares the financial statements and reports. The final step involves analyzing these reports and making decisions.

4 Understand how a statement of financial position describes the financial condition of an organization.

The statement of financial position represents the financial condition of a firm at one moment in time, in terms of assets, liabilities, and owners' equity. The key categories of assets are current assets, fixed assets, and intangible assets. Liabilities are divided into current and long-term liabilities. Owners' equity, the amount of the owners' investment in the firm after all liabilities have been paid, is the third major category.

5 Explain the purpose of the income statement.

The income statement is a summary of the firm's operations over a stated period of time. The main parts of the statement are revenues (gross and net sales), cost of goods sold, operating expenses (selling and general and administrative expenses), taxes, and net profit or loss.

6 Describe the importance of the statement of cash flows.

The statement of cash flows summarizes the firm's sources and uses of cash during a financial-reporting period. It breaks the firm's cash flows into those from operating, investment, and financing activities. It shows the net change during the period in the firm's cash and marketable securities.

7 Explain how ratio analysis is used to identify a firm's financial strengths and weaknesses.

Ratio analysis is a way to use financial statements to gain insight into a firm's operations, profitability, and overall financial condition. The four main types of ratios are liquidity ratios, profitability ratios, activity ratios, and debt ratios. Comparing a firm's ratios over several years and comparing them to ratios of other firms in the same industry or to industry averages can indicate trends and highlight financial strengths and weaknesses.

8 List some of the major trends that are impacting the accounting industry.

The accounting industry is responding to the rise in information technology in several ways. The role of accountants has expanded beyond the traditional audit and tax functions and now includes management consulting in areas such as computer systems, human resources, and electronic commerce. A major issue facing the industry is how to treat key intangible assets—knowledge assets such as patents, brands, and research and development—and whether they should be valued and included on a company's statement of financial position. The most significant trend is Canada's move to the IFRS. This allows Canadian companies operating internationally to potentially benefit from decreased costs of financial reporting, consistency in financial reporting, ease of financial comparisons, etc.

Key Terms

accounting 434
acid-test (quick) ratio 448
activity ratios 449
amortization (depreciation) 442
annual report 436
assets 439
certified general accountant (CGA) 438
certified management accountant (CMA) 438
chartered accountant (CA) 438

Experiential Exercises

1. Learn to read financial statements. To become more familiar with annual reports and key financial statements, head for IBM's "Guide to Understanding Financials" at (**www.ibm.com/investor/financialguide**). The material offers a good overview of financial reporting and shows you what to look for when you read these documents.
2. **Prepare personal financial statements.** One of the best ways to learn about financial statements is to prepare them. Put together your personal statement of financial position and income statement, using Exhibits 14.4 and 14.5 as samples. You will have to adjust the account categories to fit your needs. Here are some suggestions:
   - Current assets–cash on hand, balances in savings and chequing accounts.
   - Investments–shares and bonds, retirement funds.
   - Fixed assets–real estate, personal property (cars, furniture, jewellery, etc.).
   - Current liabilities–credit card balances, loan payments due in one year.
   - Long-term liabilities–auto loan balance, mortgage on real estate, other loan balances that will not come due until after one year.
   - Income–employment income, investment income (interest, dividends).
   - Expenses–housing, utilities, food, transportation, medical, clothing, insurance, loan payments, taxes, personal care, recreation and entertainment, and miscellaneous expenses.

   After you complete your personal financial statements, use them to see how well you are managing your finances. Consider the following questions:

   - Should you be concerned about your debt ratio?
   - Would a potential creditor conclude that it is safe or risky to lend you money?
   - If you were a company, would people want to invest in you? Why or why not? What could you do to improve your financial condition?
3. Your firm has been hired to help several small businesses with their year-end financial statements.

a. Based on the following account balances, prepare the Marbella Design Enterprises statement of financial position as of December 31, 2011:

Cash	$30,250
Accounts payable	28,500
Fixtures and furnishings	85,000
Notes payable	15,000
Retained earnings	64,450
Accounts receivable	24,050
Inventory	15,600
Equipment	42,750
Accumulated amortization on fixtures and furnishings	12,500
Common shares (50,000 shares outstanding)	50,000
Long-term debt	25,000
Accumulated amortization on equipment	7,800
Marketable securities	13,000
Income taxes payable	7,500

b. The following are the account balances for the revenues and expenses of the Windsor Gift Shop for the year ending December 31, 2011. Prepare the income statement for the shop.

Rent	$15,000
Salaries	23,500
Cost of goods sold	98,000
Utilities	8,000
Supplies	3,500
Sales	195,000
Advertising	3,600
Interest	3,000
Taxes	12,120

4. During the year ended December 31, 2011, Lawrence Industries sold $2 million worth of merchandise on credit. A total of $1.4 million was collected during the year. The cost of this merchandise was $1.3 million. Of this amount, $1 million has been paid, and $300,000 is not yet due. Operating expenses and income taxes totalling $500,000 were paid in cash during the year. Assume that all accounts had a zero balance at the beginning of the year (January 1, 2011). Write a brief report for the company controller that includes calculation of the firm's (a) net profit and (b) cash flow during the year. Explain why there is a difference between net profit and cash flow.

5. A friend has been offered a sales representative position at Draper Publications, Inc., a small publisher of computer-related books, but wants to know more about the company. Because of your expertise in financial analysis, you offer to help analyze Draper's financial health. Draper has provided the following selected financial information:

Account balances on December 31, 2011:	
Inventory	$ 72,000
Net sales	450,000
Current assets	150,000
Cost of goods sold	290,000
Total liabilities	180,000
Net profit	35,400
Total assets	385,000
Current liabilities	75,000
Other information	
Number of common shares outstanding	25,000
Inventory at January 1, 2011	48,000

Calculate the following ratios for 2011: acid-test (quick) ratio, inventory turnover ratio, net profit margin, return on equity (ROE), debt-to-equity ratio, and earnings per share (EPS). Summarize your assessment of the company's financial performance, based on these ratios, in a report for your friend. What other information would you like to have to complete your evaluation?

6. Two years ago, Rebecca Mardon started a computer consulting business, Mardon Consulting Associates. Until now, she has been the only employee, but business has grown enough to support an administrative assistant and another consultant this year. Before she adds staff, however, she wants to hire an accountant and computerize her financial record keeping. Divide the class into small groups, assigning one person to be Rebecca and the others to represent members of a medium-sized accounting firm. Rebecca should think about the type of financial information systems her firm requires and develop a list of questions for the firm. The accountants will prepare a presentation, making recommendations to her as well as explaining why their firm should win the account.
7. Do annual reports confuse you? Many websites can take the mystery out of this important document. See IBM's "Guide to Understanding Financials" at (**www.prars.com/ibm/ibmframe.html**). Moneychimp's "How to Read an Annual Report" features an interactive diagram that provides a big picture view of what the report's financial information tells you: (**www.moneychimp.com/articles/financials/fundamentals.htm**). Which site was more helpful to you, and why?
8. Can you judge an annual report by its cover? What are the most important elements of a top annual report? Go to Sid Cato's Official Annual Reportwebsite, (**www.sidcato.com**), to find his 15 standards for annual reports and read about the reports that receive his honours. Then, get a copy of an annual report and evaluate it using Cato's 135-point scale. How well does it compare to his top picks?

Review Questions

1. What is accounting? What is the difference between managerial and financial accounting?
2. What is IFRS? What is its function?
3. Discuss the accounting profession in terms of public versus private accountants, CAs, CMAs, and CGAs.
4. What is the accounting equation?
5. Explain the various categories of a statement of financial position.
6. What is the purpose of the income statement? What does it include?
7. What is the purpose of a statement of cash flows?
8. What is ratio analysis?
9. Name and provide the formulas of the liquidity ratios mentioned in the chapter.
10. What do profitability ratios tell us? Which ratios are mentioned in the chapter?
11. What are activity ratios and which ones are mentioned in the chapter?
12. What do debt ratios measure? What does the debt-to-equity ratio measure?
13. What trends are happening in the accounting field?

CREATIVE THINKING CASE >

Accounting: Who Are We Responsible To?

Arthur Andersen started the accounting firm that bore his name in 1913. From the start, he embraced the highest business ethics, refusing to manipulate unsatisfactory financial results at a client's request. Andersen's motto, "Think straight, talk straight," was the foundation of the company's culture of honesty and integrity. The company was known for its disciplined and strict attention to accounting standards.

By the 1990s, the Andersen culture had strayed far from its founder's philosophy. Andersen was "a place where the mad scramble for fees had trumped good judgment," says Barbara Ley Toffler, author of *Final Accounting: Ambition, Greed and the Fall of Arthur Andersen*. These fees came not only from auditing but increasingly from the rapidly growing consulting practices of Andersen and its industry colleagues. Business units competed with each other and were rewarded for bringing in revenues, not for evaluating a deal's risks.

The growth of consulting revenues was in itself a problem. Andersen often provided business services to the same companies it audited, earning as much from consulting as auditing. This conflict of interest placed pressure on the auditors to go along with aggressive accounting practices in order to preserve the consulting relationships and earnings.

Andersen's culture also placed a loyalty to the firm before loyalty to clients or shareholders. Partners who raised questions were penalized. This attitude went straight down the line, as Toffler discovered when leading a meeting of young Andersen employees. She asked how they would respond if a supervisor told them to do something they considered wrong. Only one person spoke up: "If he insisted I do it, yes, I would." Toffler then asked if he would tell anyone about it: "No. It could hurt my career."

Turning a blind eye to accounting irregularities at clients was a common practice. Says Toffler, who—ironically—ran Andersen's business ethics consulting practice from 1995 to 1999, "High-level members of that organization knew much of what was going on." As Enron's wrongdoings became public, the firm's top management became Enron's partner in duplicity instead of demonstrating the industry leadership its founder would have expected.

In June 2002, Andersen was convicted of obstruction of justice in the Enron case for shredding documents. Later that summer, the doors shut at the accounting firm that once set the standards to which other firms aspired.

Critical Thinking Questions

- Toffler says that Andersen executives expected that aggressive accounting would have an impact when the economy tanked but issued few warning memos and did nothing to change the culture of greed. With the benefit of hindsight, what steps could Andersen's leadership have taken to preserve the firm as the accounting scandals unfolded?
- Andersen's Enron audit team was aware of monkey business as early as 1987, when management covered up the oil-trading scandal mentioned in the chapter opener. It also caved in to pressure to sign off on questionable deals and participated in document destruction that led to its obstruction-of-justice conviction. Suggest procedures that auditors and corporations should adopt and enforce to prevent these abuses.
- Discuss why providing consulting services to audit clients in such areas as business strategy, financial strategy, human resources, and information technology systems planning, design, and implementation can create a conflict of interest.

SOURCES: Greg Farrell, "Former Andersen Exec Tells of Stressful Internal Culture," *USA Today*, March 3, 2003; William J. Holstein, "Lessons of a Fallen Rival for Accounting's Big 4," *The New York Times*, February 23, 2003; and Rob Walker, "Inside a Culture of Greed," *Newsday*, March 6, 2003.

VIDEO CASE >

Doug Hall Fixes Tofino

Tofino is a remote community on the west coast of Vancouver Island. Many of the small businesses there depend on the tourism industry, which is, to a large degree, seasonal. Doug Hall is a successful business consultant who has been hired to advise three of Tofino's entrepreneurs on how to be more profitable. The operations include a fish/ice-cream market, Mike's Market; a whale-watching/museum company, and a cleaning business, Dust Bunnies. Each enterprise is able to cover its expenses and make a bit of money, but the profits are small, and there is virtually no growth. The owners report working long hours at their respective endeavours and are interested in what a high-profile American consultant might suggest.

The fish market owner has several other businesses and lacks focus. The whale-watching entrepreneur has tried to differentiate by offering whale bones for the tourists to admire as part of his museum. The owner of the cleaning service, although successful, is simply tired of cleaning toilets.

An analysis of each statement of financial position might show a reasonable current ratio and acid-test ratio but nothing particularly strong. The ROE ratios might not look very good for the fish market and the whale-watching, as each of these probably has significant owner's equity. To help these businesses increase their cash flow, Doug Hall suggests strategies such as diversification for the whale-watching business, greater focus and branding for the fish/ice-cream market, and the addition of a totally new operation for the owner of the cleaning business.

In an area that depends heavily on tourism, it is more difficult to have money coming in regularly, and the stress of having to make enough money in the summer to last the entire year is enormous. The whale-watching does occur year-round, but summer is the busiest time. Dust Bunnies primarily cleans vacation rentals, and Mike's Market, although serving the locals, depends on the tourists as well.

Doug Hall makes excellent recommendations to the owners, and the results are interesting.

Critical Thinking Questions

- If these three entrepreneurs were to implement Doug's suggestions, how would they finance the changes?
- Why would having significant owner's equity negatively affect the ROE for the market and the whale-watching businesses?
- Which of the three companies profiled in the video found a strategy to allow year-round income? Check (**www.tofinotime.com/main**) and look at Bodi Bikes. Also look at (**www.tofinowhalecentre.com**).

SOURCE: CBC, *Venture*, "Doug Hall Fixes Tofino Part 1, 2, and 3," February 20, 2005.

E-COMMERCE CASE >

Accounting for the Dollars Spent on the Gun Registry

Whether you disagree philosophically with the Canadian gun registry or not, most Canadian taxpayers would certainly disagree with the amount of tax dollars spent on it.

Criticisms of the gun registry have been voiced for years, and with a cost of approximately $2 billion, have we spent our tax dollars wisely? The annual cost of the registry is $2.9 million a year with daily usage of 9400 inquiries per day by police officials, a cost of $308.51 per inquiry. How can we assign a dollar value to a human life? Does the use of the Registry reduce the incidence of murder by firearms?

The rate of spousal murder by firearms has dropped considerably and the RCMP report these are the most common weapons used in domestic disputes. A Swiss study suggests that the gun registry may, in fact, be saving Canada money by lowering the costs associated with firearms injuries. Their estimated savings, based on costing studies, is a savings of $1.4 billion a year. Others argue that it is impossible to establish a direct causal link to the gun control and do not agree that the decreases in deaths and injuries can be attributed to the gun registry.

The Conservatives are still attempting to abolish the gun registry and have put forward a third bid to do so. They are aware of the importance of the rural vote and recognize that most rural constituents do not support the gun registry. Since 2006, the government has granted amnesties, fee rebates, and has overall not collected a possible $56.5 million while spending $35.9 million to run the registry.

Critical Thinking Questions

1. From an accounting perspective, can you justify the money spent on the gun registry to date? In this chapter, we discussed valuing knowledge assets and other intangibles. How would you attach a dollar value to a human life? If this could be done, could you then make an argument for the money spent on the gun registry?
2. Check online to determine if the Conservatives have, in fact, abolished the registry. What research can you find on valuing intangible assets? What further research has been done on the effectiveness of the Registry or gun control in general?

SOURCES: Tonda MacCharles, "Conservatives make Third Attempt to Kill Gun Registry," TheStar.com, April 1, 2009; Nathanial Gronewold, "Swiss study says Canada's gun registry may help cut costs from violence," Canadian Press, June 27, 2006; and Frances Russell, " Canadian Police want to keep gun registry going, Winnipeg Free Press, Apr. 1, 2009.

CHAPTER 16

Making the Connection

Managing the Firm's Finances

In this chapter, we will continue to look at the finance area of business. The primary role of the financial manager is to maximize the value of the firm for the owners, achieving the main critical success factor of *financial performance*. This, we know, cannot be done without the other four success factors, reiterating the need for managers in all departments to work closely with one another, and the finance area in particular.

As we saw in Chapter 15, the relationship between finance and the major *stakeholders*, particularly the owners, is a difficult but important one. Financial managers make many important decisions regarding the acquisition, disposition, and management of financial resources to maximize the value of the firm for its owners. They must decide what projects to invest the firm's money into, and how to finance those projects, whether through issuing debt—borrowing the money—or selling more shares—equity financing. Each has its own advantages and disadvantages, or rewards and risks in 'finance speak.' If the firm chooses to use equity financing, one of the major decisions that will affect this stakeholder group is how much of the company's profit will be distributed to the shareholders in the form of a dividend. The shareholders expect a return, so if a regular dividend is not paid, then they expect the return in the form of an increased share price. This can happen only if the investing community sees potential in the value of the shares. If neither of these happens, the price of the shares will fall as shareholders sell their shares. The company must therefore consider the stakeholder response to the decisions it makes, as they will affect its ability to maximize the value of the firm for the owners.

As we also saw in Chapter 15, all decisions have financial consequences, but financial decisions have consequences in other areas as well. For example, policies for granting credit affect *marketing's* ability to generate sales. Just imagine if BMW did not offer financing packages on its vehicles. Furthermore, money spent on research and development or new production facilities has an impact on what *operations* is capable of doing, just as the company's policies on payroll costs have an impact on attracting and keeping key employees (*human resources*). To make money, the firm must first spend money, but it must also control that money to continue to be profitable and stay viable. A fine balance must be achieved between taking the risks and reaping the rewards—one that the finance manager must consider and that affects all areas of the company.

Cash flow provides an example of this need for integration and balance. To aid marketing in selling the firm's products, the supply chain must be set up to make sure that inventory is available for customers and that credit is generally extended. However, that means that finance must balance the time that it takes to sell the inventory and then collect the accounts receivable from customers with the payments on that inventory and other expenses. If it does not

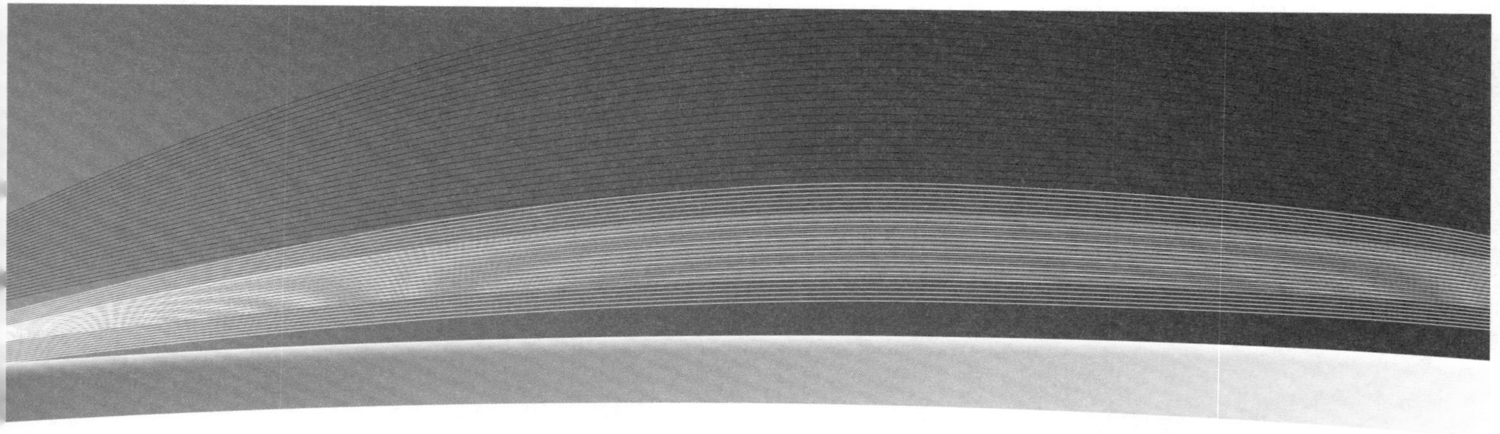

do this, the company will not have enough cash coming in to pay its bills and will go bankrupt! Another example is with inventory. The operations area needs raw materials on hand to avoid delays in production, and marketing needs enough finished goods on hand to *satisfy customers*, but finance must balance these needs with the cost of carrying inventory, and therefore tries to keep inventory levels at a minimum. In Chapter 11, we discussed techniques for dealing with inventory and saw that technology provides many new options.

Technology is just one of the many environmental factors that must be taken into account in making financial decisions. For example, as market demand changes (*social* environment), funds need to be shifted between projects. As discussed in this chapter, the social environment has also had a significant impact on changing the role of the typical CFO in an organization—from being "just numbers people" to helping to develop and implement the firm's overall *strategy* and "re-establish public trust" in the wake of recent financial scandals. As interest and exchange rates fluctuate (*economic* environment), some projects and methods of financing projects either will need to be abandoned or will become more possible. General economic conditions in domestic and world markets, like the recent global meltdown created by the sub-prime mortgage crisis, might cause firms to speed up or slow down the rate of investment in different projects, and government policies in the home and foreign countries (*political* environment) might make investment in certain projects more attractive than others. Finally, as *technology* advances and costs drop, some projects become more accessible.

In the internal business environment, when budgets are set, the finance area must work with the other functional areas to develop *plans* for financing the company that help it meet its strategic goals. Each area has a role to play in helping the organization achieve its strategic goals, and the resources they will need must be considered by the finance area. Finance uses various forecasts, as discussed in the chapter, to develop financial plans for the business to ensure that its goals are met in a way that balances risks and rewards, maximizing the value of the firm for its owners.

CHAPTER 16

Managing the Firm's Finances

LEARNING OUTCOMES

1 Explain the roles finance and the financial manager play in the firm's overall strategy.

2 Describe how a firm develops its financial plans, including forecasts and budgets.

3 List the types of short- and long-term expenditures a firm makes.

4 Summarize the main sources and costs of unsecured and secured short-term financing.

5 Identify and compare the two primary sources of long-term financing.

6 Understand the major types, features, and costs of long-term debt.

7 Discuss how firms issue equity, and the costs to the company.

8 Understand risk, how it can be managed and what makes a risk insurable.

9 Describe the types of insurance coverage that businesses should consider.

10 List some of the trends that are affecting the practice of financial management.

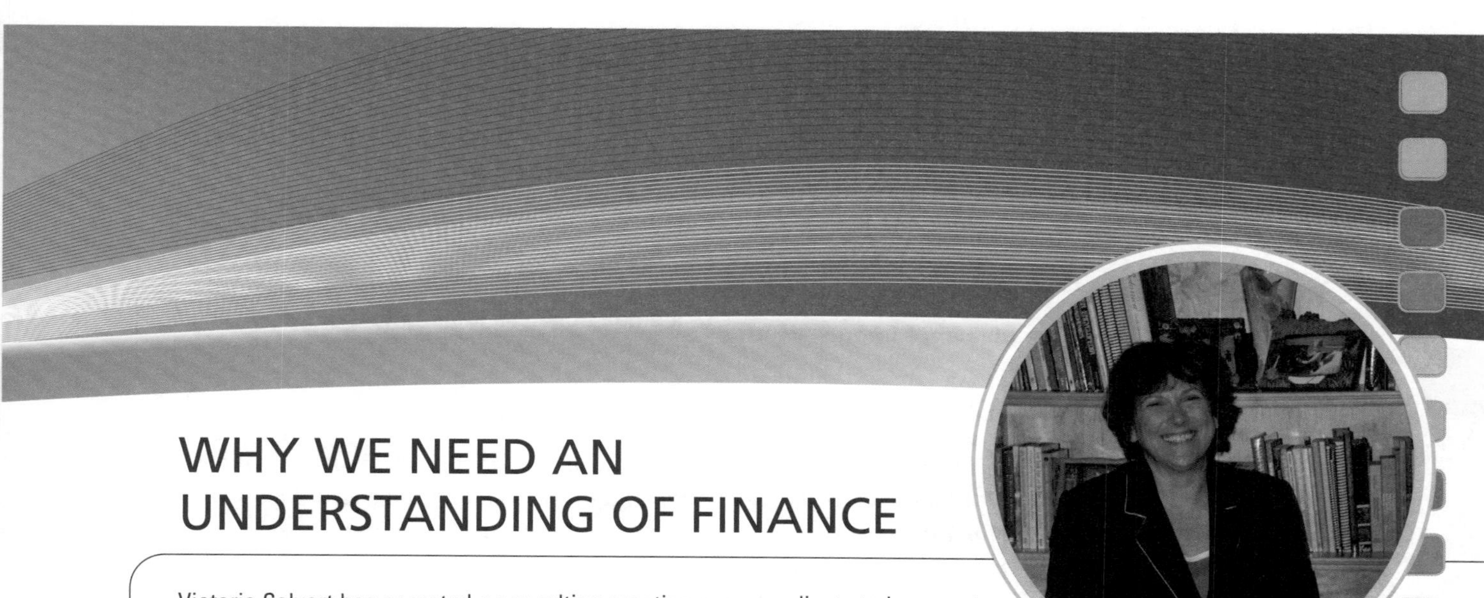

WHY WE NEED AN UNDERSTANDING OF FINANCE

SHIRLEY A. ROSE

Victoria Calvert has operated a consulting practice specializing in venture launch and expansion since 1984. Having guided clients through both recessions and periods of rapid expansion has required her to develop financing strategies to both downsize and expand client operations.

Calvert indicated that there would be significant opportunities for acquisition and expansion despite slower economic conditions in the 2010 to 2012 period. She said "A report published by the Canadian Federation of Business implied that almost 500,000 ventures would be for sale in the 2010 to 2015 period as owners retire. That ownership transfer will require a great deal of financial creativity. As banks may still be reluctant to lend to new owners, a patchwork financial strategy could be employed. Buyers could ask for a long term loan from the current owner, as well as issuing shares to friends and family (love money). In a crunch, the new owner can use their credit card, as many entrepreneurs do, to finance short-term assets such as inventory."

Calvert reflected that many clients have had to deal with short-term cash shortages. She suggested that managers of small- and medium-sized organizations tend to focus on marketing issues rather than managing their cash flow. They have costs (such as rent) that may increase dramatically; ensuring that their sales or profit margins have increased in a similar manner is essential. While she does not recommend cutting advertising and promotion during tight economic times, she does have her clients critically evaluate each of their products or service lines to ensure they are contributing to profits. Cut the dogs; get rid of products that are not turning over or that have thin margins. She does, however, caution clients to keep up to date on some important expenses, indicating, "Don't forget to pay for your insurance; a lawsuit or fire damage will put you out of business if you are not covered."

Clients are advised to match the type of financing to the operation needed by their business. She suggests that short-term financing, such as operating lines or short-term loans, be used to fund inventory or accounts receivable. Alternatively, long-term assets such as equipment or buildings, should be funded with long-term financing—long-term loans, the issuing of shares, or a mortgage. She laughs as she remembers one client who used six different credit cards for short term cash requirements, and got a call from the bank to cancel his account. He had been busy, and focused only on staff and customers, forgetting to manage the money. "We took some time, assessed the profitability of his activities, sold some materials and equipment, and restructured his funding to give him some cash to pay bills. He introduced a better software package and manages the finances now. He even has enough equity to consider a second location."

Calvert recommends clients track their expenses and prepare trend analyses; if margins start slipping they can address the problem quickly. She also provides them with standard costs for their industry by referring them to (www.sme.ic.gc.ca). She suggests, "If they know what is common for their industry, they can aim to contain their expenses to the industry norm—it provides a goalpost for them."

When asked if she had any parting words of advice for new managers she quipped, "Sure. It is not what you earn, it is what you keep that is important."

Critical Thinking Questions

1. **Why is a basic knowledge of finance important to *any* manager?**
2. **What can happen if you tend to ignore the implications of financial issues in your day-to-day operations? In your strategic planning?**
3. **What financial strategies might you suggest to a small business looking to expand, given the current economic climate?**

In today's fast-paced global economy, managing a firm's finances is more complex than ever. A thorough command of traditional finance activities—financial planning, investing money, and raising funds—is only part of the job. Financial managers are more than number crunchers. As part of the top-management team, chief financial officers (CFOs) need a broad understanding of their firm's business and industry, as well as leadership ability and creativity. They must never lose sight of the primary goal of the financial manager: to maximize the value of the firm to its owners.

All firms, whether start-up companies with three employees or major multinational corporations with billions of dollars in annual revenue, need to manage their finances efficiently and effectively. Otherwise, the firm will not have the resources it needs to pay its bills and run its daily operations or to make investments in future growth.

Financial management—spending and raising a firm's money—is both a science and an art. The science part is analyzing numbers and flows of cash through the firm. The art is answering questions like these: Is the firm using its financial resources in the best way? Aside from costs, why choose a particular form of financing? How risky is each option?

Whether you are a marketing manager, purchasing agent, or systems analyst, knowledge of finance will help you to do your job better. You'll be able to understand your company's financial statements, its financial condition, and management's investment and financing decisions. Financial information also provides feedback on how well you are doing and identifies problems. On a more practical note, you may be asked to prepare a budget for your department or unit. Employees who understand the financial decision-making process will be able to prepare proposals that address financial concerns. As a result, they will be more likely to get the resources they require to accomplish the firm's goals.

If you own a business, you must pay close attention to financial management. Without financial plans you may find yourself running out of cash. It's easy to get so caught up in growing sales that you neglect your billing and collection methods. In fact, managing accounts receivable is often one of the more challenging aspects of running a young company.

This chapter focuses on the financial management of a firm. We'll start with an overview of the role of finance and of the financial manager in the firm's overall business strategy. Next we consider the basics of financial planning: forecasts and budgets. Discussions of short- and long-term uses of funds and sources of short- and long-term financing follow. The importance of understanding and managing risk and insurance is examined, and finally, we'll look at key trends affecting financial management.

The Role of Finance and the Financial Manager

Any company—whether it's a two-lawyer law partnership or an integrated oil company, such as Suncor Energy—needs money to operate. To make money, it must first spend money—on inventory and supplies, equipment and facilities, and employee wages and salaries. Therefore, finance is critical to the success of all companies. It might not be as visible as marketing or production, but management of a firm's finances is just as much a key to the firm's success.

financial management
The art and science of managing a firm's money so that it can meet its goals.

Financial management—the art and science of managing a firm's money so that it can meet its goals—is not just the responsibility of the finance department. All business decisions have financial consequences. Managers in all departments must work closely with financial personnel. If you are a sales representative, for example, the company's credit and collection policies will affect your ability to make sales.

HOT Links

What challenges do today's financial managers face? To find out, browse through recent issues of *CFO* magazine at **(www.cfo.com)**.

Revenues from sales of the firm's products should be the chief source of funding, but money from sales doesn't always come in when it's needed to pay the bills. Financial managers must track how money is flowing into and out of the firm (see Exhibit 16.1). They work with the firm's other department managers to determine how available funds will be used and how much money is needed. Then they choose the best sources to obtain the required funding.

For example, a financial manager will track day-to-day operational data such as cash collections and disbursements to ensure that the company has enough cash to meet its obligations. Over a longer time horizon, the manager will thoroughly study whether and when the company should open a new manufacturing facility. The manager will also suggest the most appropriate way to finance the project, raise the funds, and then monitor the project's implementation and operation.

Financial management is closely related to accounting. In most firms, both areas are the responsibility of the vice-president of finance or the CFO (many of whom have an accounting designation). But the accountant's main function is to collect and present financial data. Financial managers use financial statements and other information prepared by accountants to make financial decisions. Financial managers focus on **cash flows**, the inflows and outflows of cash. They plan and monitor the firm's cash flows to ensure that cash is available when needed.

cash flows
The inflows and outflows of cash for a firm.

CONCEPT *in Action* >>>

Because all business decisions have financial consequences, managers in all departments must work closely with financial personnel. A company's credit and collection policies, for example, might impact a sales representative's ability to close a sale. Who is responsible for making key financial decisions for businesses?

EXHIBIT 16.1 > How Cash Flows Through a Business

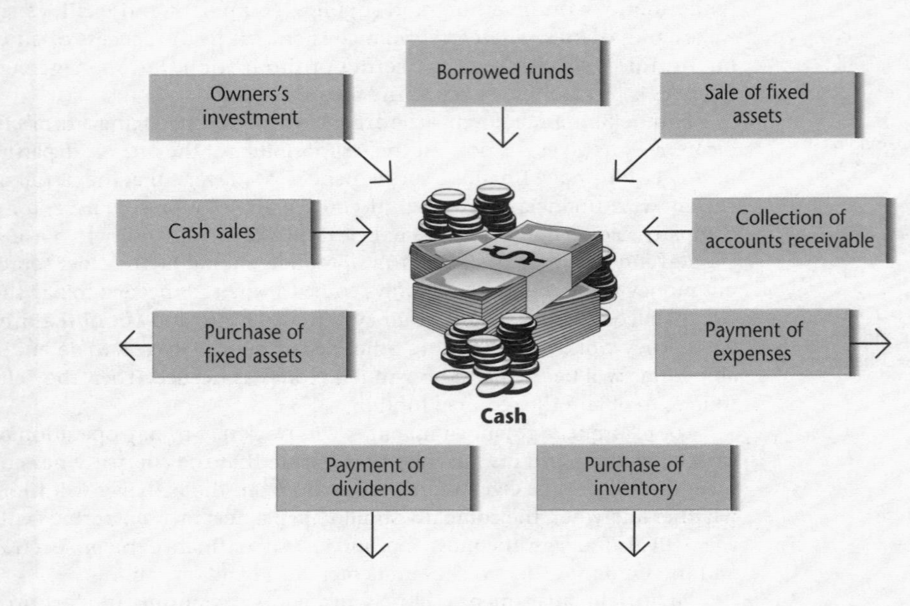

The Financial Manager's Responsibilities and Activities

Financial managers have a complex and challenging job. They analyze financial data prepared by accountants, monitor the firm's financial status, and prepare and implement financial plans. One day they might be developing a better way to automate cash collections; the next they might be analyzing a proposed acquisition. The key activities of the financial manager are

- *financial planning*—preparing the financial plan, which projects revenues, expenditures, and financing needs over a given period;
- *investment (spending money)*—investing the firm's funds in projects and securities that provide high returns in relation to their risks; and
- *financing (raising money)*—obtaining funding for the firm's operations and investments and seeking the best balance between debt (borrowed funds) and equity (funds raised through the sale of ownership in the business).

HOT Links

When you come across a finance term you don't understand, visit **(www.fiscalagents.com/newsletter/gloss/Glossary/a.shtml).**

The Goal of the Financial Manager

How can financial managers make wise planning, investment, and financing decisions? The main goal of the financial manager is *to maximize the value of the firm to its owners.* The value of a publicly owned corporation is measured by the share price of its shares. A private company's value is the price at which it could be sold.

To maximize the firm's value, the financial manager has to consider both short- and long-term consequences of the firm's actions. Maximizing profits is one approach, but it should not be the only one. Such an approach favours making short-term gains over achieving long-term goals. What if a firm in a highly technical and competitive industry did no research and development? In the short run, profits would be high because research and development are very expensive, but in the long run, the firm might lose its ability to compete because of its lack of new products.

This is true regardless of a company's size or point in its life cycle. David Deeds was cofounder of a company that developed an innovative computer-aided design hardware and software package for architects and engineers. He and his partners made some decisions early in the company's life to pursue opportunities such as consulting projects that generated revenue quickly. The company saw its profits grow, adding staff and offices to handle the increased business, but this sidetracked the founders from their initial vision: designing revolutionary new products to address client needs. "We managed ourselves into a niche where we could survive and make a little money but never offer anything unique or grow significantly," says Deeds. Although they built a reasonably successful small business, the desire for the quick buck overrode the long-term goal of building a $100 million company.[1]

return
The opportunity for profit.

risk
The potential for loss or the chance that an investment will not achieve the expected level of return.

risk–return trade-off
A basic principle in finance that holds that the higher the risk, the greater the return that is required.

Financial managers constantly strive for a balance between the opportunity for profit and the potential for loss. In finance, the opportunity for profit is termed **return**; the potential for loss, or the chance that an investment will not achieve the expected level of return, is **risk**. A basic principle in finance is that the higher the risk, the greater the return that is required. This widely accepted concept is called the **risk–return trade-off**. Financial managers consider many risk and return factors when making investment and financing decisions. Among them are changing patterns of market demand, interest rates, general economic conditions, market conditions, and social issues (such as environmental effects and equal employment opportunity policies).

concept check

What is the role of financial management in a firm?

How do the three key activities of the financial manager relate?

What is the main goal of the financial manager? How does the risk–return trade-off relate to the financial manager's main goal?

Financial Planning: Looking Ahead

As we learned in Chapter 7, companies use several types of plans to determine how to achieve organizational objectives. A company's *financial plan* is part of the overall company plan and guides the firm toward its business goals and the maximization of its value. The financial plan enables the firm to estimate the amount and timing of its investment and financing needs.

To prepare a financial plan, the financial manager must first consider existing and proposed products, the resources available to produce them, and the financing needed to support production and sales. Forecasts and budgets are essential to the firm's financial planning. They should be part of an integrated planning process that links them to strategic plans and performance measurement.

Forecasting the Future

The financial-planning process starts with financial forecasts, or projections of future developments within the firm. The estimated demand for the firm's products (the sales forecast) and other financial and operating data are key inputs. At Ford Motor Company, economic analysts estimate expected production and sales for each line of cars and trucks. Then, financial analysts prepare detailed short- and long-term financial forecasts based on these assumptions.

short-term forecasts
Projections of revenues, costs of goods, and operating expenses over a one-year period.

Short-term forecasts, or *operating plans,* project revenues, costs of goods, and operating expenses over a one-year period. Using short-term forecasts, financial managers at Ford estimate the next year's expenses for inventory, labour, advertising, and other operating activities. These estimates form the basis for cash budgets (described next), which forecast cash inflows and outflows over the same period.

long-term forecasts
Projections of a firm's activities and the funding for those activities over a period that is longer than a year, typically 2 to 10 years.

Long-term forecasts, or strategic plans, cover a period that is longer than a year, typically 2 to 10 years, and take a broader view of the firm's financial activities. With these forecasts, management can assess the financial effects of various business strategies: What would be the financial results of investing in new facilities and equipment? Of developing new products? Of eliminating a line of business? Of acquiring other firms? Long-term forecasts also show where the funding for these activities is expected to come from.

Lenders typically ask potential borrowers for forecasts that cover the period during which the loan will be outstanding. The forecasts are used to evaluate the risk of the loan and to see that adequate cash flow will be available to pay off the debt. Then they structure loan terms and covenants (requirements that the company comply with certain operating and financial measures during the loan period) based on those statements.

Budgets

budgets
Formal written forecasts of revenues and expenses that set spending limits based on operational forecasts; include cash budgets, capital budgets, and operating budgets.

Businesses prepare budgets to plan and control their future financial activities. Budgets are formal written forecasts of revenues and expenses that set spending limits based on operational forecasts. All budgets begin with forecasts. Budgets provide a way to control expenses and compare the actual performance to the forecast. By monitoring actual revenues and expenses and comparing them to budgets on a regular basis, companies gain critical information about operations. When variances to the budget occur, managers can analyze them to determine if they need to take steps to correct them. Suppose the owner of a small printing company sees that May sales are down and expenses are over budget because a major press broke down and the company was unable to fulfill many orders on time. This situation would require asking such questions as: How old is the press, has it broken down before, should the company continue to repair it or is it time to replace it, can the company afford a new press, and how would it finance the new press? A back-up plan to prevent lost orders would be another possible outcome of this budget review.

cash budgets
Budgets that forecast a firm's cash inflows and outflows and help the firm plan for cash surpluses and shortages.

capital budgets
Budgets that forecast a firm's outlays for fixed assets (plant and equipment), typically covering a period of several years.

operating budgets
Budgets that combine sales forecasts with estimates of production costs and operating expenses to forecast profits.

Firms use several types of budgets, most of which cover a one-year period:

- Cash budgets forecast the firm's cash inflows and outflows, and help the firm plan for cash surpluses and shortages. Because having enough cash is so critical to their financial health, many firms prepare annual cash budgets subdivided into months or weeks. Then they project the amount of cash needed in each shorter time period.
- Capital budgets forecast outlays for fixed assets (plant and equipment). They usually cover a period of several years and ensure that the firm will have enough funds to buy the equipment and buildings it needs.
- Operating budgets combine sales forecasts with estimates of production costs and operating expenses to forecast profits. They are based on individual budgets for sales, production, purchases of materials, factory overhead, and operating expenses. Operating budgets then are used to plan operations: dollars of sales, units of production, amounts of raw materials, dollars of wages, and so forth.

concept check

What is a financial plan? Name two types of financial-planning documents.

Distinguish between short- and long-term forecasts. How are both used by financial managers?

Briefly describe three types of budgets.

Budgets are routinely used to monitor and control the performance of a division, a department, or an individual manager. When actual outcomes differ from budget expectations, management must take action.

CONCEPT *in Action* >>>

Budgets of all types help companies plan and control their future financial activities. What types of fixed assets would a fast-growing, outdoor video-billboard company include in its capital budget?

© KRISTIINA PAUL

How Organizations Use Funds

LO 3

To grow and prosper, a firm must keep investing money in its operations. The financial manager decides how best to use the firm's money. Short-term expenses support the firm's day-to-day activities. For instance, an athletic-apparel maker regularly spends money to buy raw materials such as leather and fabric, and to pay employee salaries. Long-term expenses are typically for fixed assets. For the athletic-apparel maker, these would include outlays to build a new factory, buy automated manufacturing equipment, or acquire a small manufacturer of sports apparel.

Short-Term Expenses

Short-term expenses, often called *operating expenses,* are outlays used to support current selling and production activities. They typically result in current assets, which include cash and any other assets (accounts receivable and inventory) that can be converted to cash within a year. The financial manager's goal is to manage current assets so the firm has enough cash to pay its bills and to support its accounts receivable and inventory.

cash management
The process of making sure that a firm has enough cash on hand to pay bills as they are due, and to meet unexpected expenses.

Cash Management: Assuring Liquidity Cash is the lifeblood of business. Without it, a firm could not operate. An important duty of the financial manager is cash management, or making sure that enough cash is on hand to pay bills as they are due and to meet unexpected expenses.

Businesses use budgets to estimate the cash requirements for a specific period. Many companies keep a minimum cash balance to cover unexpected expenses or changes in projected cash flows. The financial manager arranges loans to cover any shortfalls. If the size and timing of cash inflows closely match the size and timing of cash outflows, the company needs to keep only a small amount of cash on hand. A company whose sales and receipts are fairly predictable and regular throughout the year needs less cash than a company with a seasonal pattern of sales and receipts. A toy company, for instance, whose sales are concentrated in the fall, spends a great deal of cash during the spring and summer to build inventory. It has excess cash during the winter and early spring, when it collects on sales from its peak selling season.

Because cash held in current accounts earns little, if any, interest, the financial manager tries to keep cash balances low and to invest the surplus cash. Surpluses are invested temporarily in marketable securities, short-term investments that are easily converted into cash. The financial manager looks for low-risk investments that offer high returns. Three of the most popular marketable securities are Treasury bills, certificates of deposit, and **commercial papers**. (Commercial paper is unsecured short-term debt—an IOU—issued by a financially strong corporation.)

commercial paper
Unsecured short-term debt—an IOU—issued by a financially strong corporation.

Companies with overseas operations face even greater cash management challenges, as the Expanding Around the Globe box explains. Developing the systems for international cash management may sound simple in theory, but in practice it's extremely complex. In addition to dealing with multiple foreign currencies, treasurers must understand and follow banking practices and regulatory and tax requirements in each country. Regulations may impede their ability to move funds freely across borders. Also, issuing a standard set of procedures for every office may not work because local business practices differ from country to country. Moreover, local managers may resist the shift to a centralized structure because they don't want to give up control of cash generated by their units. Corporate financial managers must be sensitive to and aware of local customs and adapt the centralization strategy accordingly.

In addition to seeking the right balance between cash and **marketable securities**, the financial manager tries to shorten the time between the purchase of inventory or services (cash outflows) and the collection of cash from sales (cash inflows). The three key strategies are to collect money owed to the firm (accounts receivable) as quickly as possible, to pay money owed to others (accounts payable) as late as possible without damaging the firm's credit reputation, and to turn inventory quickly to minimize the funds tied up in it.

marketable securities
Short-term investments that are easily converted into cash.

Expanding Around the Globe

FOLLOW THE MONEY

If you think it's hard to balance your chequing account, imagine trying to deal with $4 billion or more in 1,400 accounts in 46 different currencies for 233 legal entities, at 145 banks worldwide! That's the job facing Jim Colby, assistant treasurer of Honeywell International Inc., and his counterparts at other multinational companies who grapple with complex treasury operations like this on a daily basis. With so much at stake, international cash management becomes a priority for financial managers.

Many companies are joining Honeywell in the quest for more efficient global cash management systems. Corporate treasurers want to identify and pool cash from overseas operations so that these cash balances can be put to work. In addition, recent regulatory changes have brought huge amounts of cash back to North America from overseas operations—and too much cash can be as much of a problem as too little. "Cash is a wonderful thing to have, but when it's yielding 3.5 percent pre-tax, then it's also a burden. That is not a viable return on a large asset," says David O'Brien, assistant treasurer of EDS Corp.

At Honeywell, Colby and his team turned to a Web-based technology solution to improve its global cash pooling system. Prior to 2002, Honeywell couldn't track its cash, most of which was outside North America and earning little or no interest. The company launched a centralized Web portal in 2002, and Honeywell's business units began reporting their cash holdings. By 2005, Honeywell upgraded to an automated treasury platform.

Once Honeywell knew where its cash holdings were, it could manage this cash more efficiently and profitably. Treasury managers developed budgets and goals for interest income that were tied to cash balance forecasts, exchange rates in each country, and other factors. Next, they pooled cash from individual bank accounts and invested it in marketable securities. The interest income goals established performance benchmarks and were factored into incentive compensation. The results were significant. Today, most of Honeywell's cash is now actively managed and the interest income is about twice what it was in 2002. The company can also quickly identify which cash reserves are available to make an acquisition or fund a large capital project.[2]

Critical Thinking Questions

- Why is managing cash such an important part of a financial manager's job? Why is having too much cash a problem?
- What were the benefits from Honeywell's new cash management procedures worldwide? For a multinational company? Are there any disadvantages?

Adapted from Richard Gamble,"Got Cash? Who Doesn't?" Treasury & Risk Management, December 2005/January 2006, http://www.treasuryandrisk.com; Richard Gamble, Susan Kelly, and John Labate, "The 2005 Alexander Hamilton Award Winners: Cash Management; Bronze Award Winner: Honeywell International," Treasury & Risk Management, November 2005, all from http://www.treasuryandrisk.com; and Karen M. Kroll, "Treasury Today: To Centralize or Not?" Business Finance, April 2006, http://businessfinancemag.com.

accounts receivable
Sales for which a firm has not yet been paid.

Managing Accounts Receivable Accounts receivable represent sales for which the firm has not yet been paid. Because the product has been sold but cash has not yet been received, an account receivable amounts to a use of funds. For the average manufacturing firm, accounts receivable represent about 15 to 20 percent of total assets.

The financial manager's goal is to collect money owed to the firm as quickly as possible while offering customers credit terms attractive enough to increase sales. Accounts receivable management involves setting *credit policies,* guidelines on offering credit, and *credit terms,* specific repayment conditions, including how long customers have to pay their bills and whether a cash discount is given for quicker payment. Another aspect of accounts receivable management is deciding on *collection policies,* the procedures for collecting overdue accounts.

Setting up credit and collection policies is a balancing act for financial managers. On the one hand, easier credit policies or generous credit terms (a longer repayment period or larger cash discount) result in increased sales. On the other hand, the firm has to finance more accounts receivable, and the risk of uncollectible accounts receivable rises. Businesses consider the impact on sales, timing of cash flow, experience with bad debt, customer profiles, and industry standards when developing their credit and collection policies.

Companies that want to speed up collections actively manage their accounts receivable rather than passively letting customers pay when they want to. Companies that take this approach can usually collect from anyone.

Technology plays a big role in helping companies improve their credit and collections performance. When the tech sector fell on hard times, Cisco saw its global Days Sales Outstanding (DSO) climb to a high of 47 days. The company then developed Web-based reporting tools that improved overall cash management. Managers received frequently updated accounts receivable and cash collection reports, along with real-time collection and credit reports. The new system also flagged potential problems with customers. Within nine months of implementation, Cisco exceeded its goal of reducing DSO to 30 days, slashing that number to 24 days.[3]

Inventory One use of funds is to buy inventory needed by the firm. In a typical manufacturing firm, inventory is nearly 20 percent of total assets. The cost of inventory includes not only its purchase price but also ordering, handling, storage, interest, and insurance costs.

Production, marketing, and finance managers usually have differing views about inventory. Production managers want lots of raw materials on hand to avoid production delays. Marketing managers want lots of finished goods on hand so that customer orders can be filled quickly, but financial managers want the least inventory possible without harming production efficiency or sales. Financial managers must work closely with production and marketing to balance these conflicting goals. Techniques for reducing the investment in inventory—inventory management, the just-in-time system, and materials requirement planning—were described in Chapter 11.

Long-Term Expenditures

capital expenditures
Investments in long-lived assets such as land, buildings, machinery, and equipment, that are expected to provide benefits extending beyond one year.

A firm also uses funds for its investments in long-lived assets—such items as land, buildings, machinery, equipment, and information systems. These are called capital expenditures. Unlike operating expenses, which produce benefits within a year, the benefits from capital expenditures extend beyond one year. For instance, a printer's purchase of a new printing press with a usable life of seven years is a capital expenditure. It appears as a fixed asset on the firm's balance sheet. Paper, ink, and other supplies, however, are expenses. Mergers and acquisitions, discussed in Chapter 5, are also considered capital expenditures.

Firms make capital expenditures for many reasons. The most common are to expand and to replace or renew fixed assets. Another reason is to develop new products. Most manufacturing firms have a big investment in long-term assets. Boeing Company, for instance, puts millions of dollars a year into airplane-manufacturing facilities.

Because capital expenditures tend to be costly and have a major effect on the firm's future, the financial manager must analyze long-term projects and select those that offer the best returns, while maximizing the firm's value. This process is called capital budgeting. Decisions involving new products or the acquisition of another business are especially important. Managers look at project costs and forecast the future benefits the project will bring—for example, from increased productivity, staff reductions, and other cost savings—to calculate the firm's estimated return on the investment.

capital budgeting
The process of analyzing long-term projects and selecting those that offer the best returns while maximizing the firm's value.

For instance, consider the period during which Air Canada or WestJet Airlines is planning for new aircraft. Before going ahead, the company must consider not only its present aircraft and load factors (i.e., how many seats are typically full during any of its routes) but also the actual acquisition costs, maintenance costs, how to finance the aircraft (i.e., debt capital or equity capital), the amount that the aircraft will actually be flying (and therefore making revenue), and the anticipated payback period (i.e., how long will it take for the revenue that the aircraft generates to pay off its costs).

concept check

Distinguish between short- and long-term expenses.

What is the financial manager's goal in cash management? List the three key cash management strategies.

Describe the firm's main motives in making capital expenditures.

Obtaining Short-Term Financing

How do firms raise the funding they need? They borrow money (debt), sell ownership shares (equity), and retain earnings (profits). The financial manager must assess all of these sources and choose the one most likely to help maximize the firm's value.

Like expenses, borrowed funds can be divided into short- and long-term loans. A short-term loan comes due within a year; a long-term loan has a maturity greater than one year. Short-term financing is shown as a current liability on the balance sheet and is used to finance current assets and support operations. Short-term loans can be unsecured or secured.

Unsecured Short-Term Loans

unsecured loans
Loans for which the borrower does not have to pledge specific assets as security.

Unsecured loans are made on the basis of the firm's creditworthiness and the lender's previous experience with the firm. An unsecured borrower does not have to pledge specific assets as security. The three main types of *unsecured short-term loans* are trade credit, bank loans, and commercial paper.

trade credit
The extension of credit by the seller to the buyer between the time the buyer receives the goods or services and when it pays for them.

accounts payable
Purchase for which a buyer has not yet paid the seller.

Trade Credit: Accounts Payable When Magna International Inc. (Magna) sells auto parts to its customers; the customers do not have to pay cash on delivery. Instead, Magna regularly bills its customers for the purchases, and they pay at a later date. This is an example of trade credit: The seller extends credit to the buyer between the time the buyer receives the goods or services and when it pays for them. Trade credit is a major source of short-term business financing. The buyer enters the credit on its books as an account payable. In effect, the credit is a short-term loan from the seller to the buyer of the goods and services. Until the customers pay Magna, Magna has an account receivable from its customers and the customers have an account payable to Magna.

Bank Loans Unsecured bank loans are another source of short-term business financing. Companies often use these loans to finance seasonal (cyclical) businesses. For instance, a swimwear manufacturer has strong sales in the spring and summer and lower sales during the fall and winter. It needs short-term bank financing to increase inventories before its strongest selling season and to finance accounts receivable during late winter and early spring, as shown in Exhibit 16.2. The company repays these bank loans when it sells the inventory and collects the receivables.

EXHIBIT 16.2 > Swimwear Manufacturer's Seasonal Cash Flows

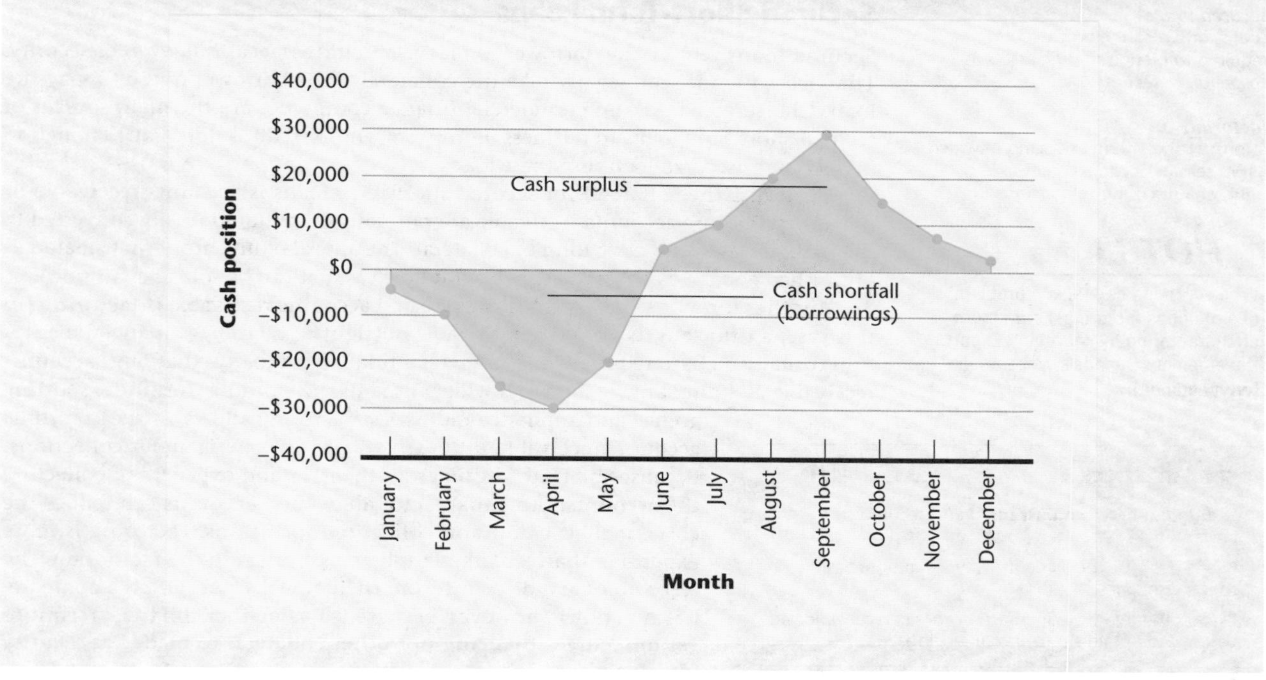

line of credit
An agreement between a bank and a business that specifies the maximum amount of short-term borrowing the bank will make available to the business or an individual.

revolving credit agreement (or revolving line of credit)
A line of credit that allows the borrower to have access to funds again once it has been repaid.

Unsecured bank loans include lines of credit and revolving credit agreements (although in Canada most are secured). A **line of credit** is an agreement between a bank and a business or an individual. It specifies the maximum amount of short-term borrowing the bank will make available to the firm or the individual. This allows the borrower to obtain a number of loans without reapplying each time, as long as they do not exceed the prearranged amount.

Most lines of credit are a **revolving credit agreement (or revolving line of credit)**. A revolving credit agreement allows the borrower to continue to have access to funds as long as the maximum has not been exceeded. Therefore, the business or individual can pay off the line of credit and have access to the available funds again. Most credit cards offer revolving lines of credit.

Firms often obtain annual lines of credit based on their expected seasonal needs. Then they can quickly borrow without having to reapply to the bank each time funds are needed. Suppose the swimwear manufacturer projected a cash shortfall of $80,000 for the period from February to June. The financial manager might get a $100,000 line of credit from the bank. (The extra $20,000 would be there to cover any unexpected outlays.) The firm could borrow funds as needed—$10,000 in February, $25,000 in March, $30,000 in April. Then it could gradually repay the loan as it collects cash during the summer months.

Commercial Paper As noted earlier, *commercial paper* is an unsecured short-term debt—an IOU—issued by a financially strong corporation. Thus, it is a short-term investment for firms with temporary cash surpluses, and it is a financing option for major corporations. Corporations issue commercial paper in multiples of $100,000 for periods ranging from 3 to 270 days. Many big companies use commercial paper instead of short-term bank loans because the interest rate on commercial paper is usually 1 to 3 percent below bank rates.

secured loans
Loans for which the borrower is required to pledge specific assets as *collateral*, or security.

factoring
A form of short-term financing in which a firm sells its accounts receivable outright, at a discount, to a *factor*.

Secured Short-Term Loans

Secured loans require the borrower to pledge specific assets as *collateral*, or security. The secured lender can legally take the collateral if the borrower doesn't repay the loan. Chartered banks and commercial finance companies are the main sources of secured short-term loans to business. Borrowers whose credit is not strong enough to qualify for unsecured loans use these loans.

Typically, the collateral for secured short-term loans is accounts receivable or inventory. Because accounts receivable are normally quite liquid (easily converted to cash), they are an attractive form of collateral. The appeal of inventory—raw materials or finished goods—as collateral depends on how easily it can be sold at a fair price.

Another form of short-term financing using accounts receivable is factoring. In this case, a firm sells its accounts receivable outright to a *factor*, a financial institution (usually a chartered bank or commercial finance company) that buys accounts receivable at a discount. Factoring is widely used in the clothing, furniture, sporting goods, and appliance industries. Factoring allows a firm to turn its accounts receivable into cash without worrying about collections. Because the factor assumes all the risks and expenses of collecting the accounts, firms that factor all of their accounts can reduce the costs of their credit and collection operations. Factoring is more expensive than a bank loan, however, because the factor buys the receivables at a discount from their actual value. Often a company has no choice, however, because it has neither the track record to get unsecured financing nor other collateral to pledge as security for a loan.

HOT Links

When working capital is a problem, one option is factoring. Learn more about factoring by searching Export Development Canada's website at **(www.edc.ca)**.

concept check

Distinguish between unsecured and secured short-term loans.

Briefly describe the three main types of unsecured short-term loans.

Discuss the two ways in which accounts receivable can be used to obtain short-term financing.

CONCEPT *in Action* >>>

For businesses with steady orders but a lack of cash to make payroll or other immediate payments, factoring is a popular way to obtain financing. In factoring, a firm sells its invoices to a third-party funding source for cash. The factor purchasing the invoices then collects on the due payments over time. Trucking companies with voluminous accounts are good candidates for factoring. Why might firms choose factoring instead of loans?

© ROBERT MCGOUEY/ALAMY

Raising Long-Term Financing

A basic principle of finance is to match the term of the financing to the period over which benefits are expected to be received from the associated outlay. Short-term items should be financed with short-term funds, and long-term items should be financed with long-term funds. Long-term financing sources include both debt (borrowing) and equity (ownership). Equity financing comes either from selling new ownership interests or from retaining earnings.

Debt Versus Equity Financing

Say that Bombardier plans to spend $2 billion over the next four years to build and equip new factories to make regional jets. The company's top management will assess the pros and cons of both debt and equity and then consider several possible sources of the desired form of long-term financing.

The major advantage of debt financing is the deductibility of interest expense for income tax purposes, which lowers its overall cost. In addition, there is no loss of ownership. The major drawback is **financial risk**: the chance that the firm will be unable to make scheduled interest and principal payments. The lender can force a borrower that fails to make scheduled debt payments into bankruptcy. Most loan agreements have restrictions to ensure that the borrower operates efficiently.

financial risk
The chance that a firm will be unable to make scheduled interest and principal payments on its debt.

Equity, on the other hand, is a form of permanent financing that places few restrictions on the firm. The firm is not required to pay dividends or repay the investment. However, equity financing gives common shareholders voting rights that provide them with a voice in management. Equity is more costly than debt. Unlike the interest on debt, dividends to owners are not tax-deductible expenses. Exhibit 16.3 summarizes the major differences between debt and equity financing.

concept check

Discuss the major differences between debt and equity financing.

What is financial risk?

Financial managers try to select the mix of long-term debt and equity that results in the best balance between cost and risk. If a company's debt load gets too high, in the view of investors and securities analysts, the costs of borrowing will rise. Company policies about the mix of debt and equity vary. Some companies have high debt

EXHIBIT 16.3 > Major Differences Between Debt and Equity Financing

	Debt Financing	Equity Financing
Voice in management	Creditors typically have none, unless borrower defaults on payments. Creditors may be able to place restraints on management in event of default.	Common shareholders have voting rights.
Claim on income and assets	Debt holders rank ahead of equity holders. Payment of interest and principal is a contractual obligation of the firm.	Equity owners have a residual claim on income (dividends are paid only after interest and any scheduled principal payments are paid) and assets. The firm has no obligation to pay dividends.
Maturity	Debt has a stated maturity and requires repayment of principal by a specified maturity date.	The company is not required to repay equity, which has no maturity date.
Tax treatment	Interest is a tax-deductible expense.	Dividends are not tax-deductible and are paid from after-tax income.

compared to equity. Debt as a percentage of equity is 163 percent at International Paper, a capital-intensive manufacturer. Others keep debt to a minimum. The long-term debt-to-equity ratio for Nike is about 12 percent; Starbucks, 4 percent; Microsoft, 3 percent; and Apple Computer, 0 percent.

Long-Term Debt Financing

Long-term debt is used to finance long-term (capital) expenditures. The initial maturities of long-term debt typically range between 5 and 20 years. Three important forms of long-term debt are term loans, bonds, and mortgage loans.

term loan
A business loan with an initial maturity of more than one year; can be unsecured or secured.

A **term loan** is a business loan with an initial maturity of more than one year. Term loans generally have 5- to 12-year maturities and can be unsecured or secured. They are available from chartered banks, insurance companies, pension funds, commercial finance companies, and manufacturers' financing subsidiaries. A contract between the borrower and the lender spells out the amount and maturity of the loan, the interest rate, payment dates, the purpose of the loan, and other provisions, such as operating and financial restrictions on the borrower to control the risk of default. Term loans may be repaid on a quarterly, semiannual, or annual schedule. The payments include both interest and principal, so the loan balance declines over time. Borrowers try to arrange a repayment schedule that matches the forecast cash flow from the project being financed.

bonds
Long-term debt obligations (liabilities) issued by corporations and governments.

Bonds are long-term debt obligations (liabilities) issued by corporations and governments. Like term loans, corporate bonds are issued with formal contracts that set forth the obligations of the issuing corporation and the rights of the bondholders. Most bonds are issued in multiples of $1,000 (par value) with initial maturities of 10 to 30 years. The stated interest rate, or *coupon rate*, is the percentage of the bond's par value that the issuer will pay each year as interest.

mortgage loan
A long-term loan made against real estate as collateral.

A **mortgage loan** is a long-term loan made against real estate as collateral. The lender takes a mortgage on the property, which lets the lender seize the property, sell it, and use the proceeds to pay off the loan if the borrower fails to make the scheduled payments. Long-term mortgage loans are often used to finance office buildings, factories, and warehouses. Life insurance companies are an important source of these loans. They make billions of dollars' worth of mortgage loans to businesses each year.

concept check

What is a long-term loan used for?

What is a term loan? A bond? A mortgage loan?

Equity Financing

Equity is the owners' investment in the business. In corporations, the preferred and common shareholders are the owners. A firm obtains equity financing by selling new ownership shares (external financing), by retaining earnings (internal financing), or, for small and growing, typically high-tech companies, through venture capital (external financing).

common shares
A security that represents an ownership interest in a corporation.

Selling New Issues of Common Shares **Common shares** are securities that represent an ownership interest in a corporation. In March 2006, Tim Hortons offered 29 million shares of common shares at the initial price of $27 and began trading on the Toronto Stock Exchange and the New York Stock Exchange.

HOT Links

What are some of the IPOs available today? Check out the premium investor resource centre at **(http://ipo.investcom.com)**.

The Tim Hortons offering is an example of a company *going public*—its first sale of shares to the public. Usually, a high-growth company has an *initial public offering* (IPO), because it needs to raise funds to finance continuing growth. An IPO often enables existing shareholders, usually employees, family, and friends who bought the shares privately, to earn big profits on their investment. (Companies that are already public can also issue and sell additional common shares to raise equity funds.)

But going public has some drawbacks. For one thing, there is no guarantee an IPO will sell. It is also expensive. Big fees must be paid to investment bankers, brokers, lawyers, accountants, and printers. And once the company is public, it is watched closely by regulators, shareholders, and securities analysts. The firm must reveal information such as operating and financial data, product details, financing plans, and operating strategies. Providing this information is often costly.

Going public can be successful when a company is well established and market conditions are right. Strong equity markets in the late 1990s and into 2000 prompted many companies, especially very young Internet-related companies, to go public. Frequently companies that were only a year or two old rushed to go public to take advantage of market conditions. Their prices popped up to what many believed were unrealistic levels. When the recession started in 2008 and capital markets dried up, far fewer companies were willing to brave the IPO waters. Instead, they turned to other financing sources to tide them over until the market for new issues picked up.

dividends
Payments to shareholders from a corporation's profits.

share or stock dividends
Payments to shareholders in the form of more shares; can replace or supplement cash dividends.

Dividends and Retained Earnings Dividends are payments to shareholders from a corporation's profits. A company does not have to pay dividends to shareholders, but if investors buy the shares expecting to get dividends and the firm does not pay them, the investors might sell their shares. If too many sell, the value of the shares decreases. Dividends can be paid in cash or in shares. Share dividends are payments in the form of more shares. Share dividends may replace or supplement cash dividends. After a share dividend has been paid, more shares have a claim on the same company, so the value of each share often declines.

At their quarterly meetings, the company's board of directors (with the advice of its financial managers) decides how much of the profits to distribute as dividends and how much to reinvest. A business's basic approach to paying dividends can greatly affect its share price. A stable history of dividend payments indicates good financial health. If a firm that has been making regular dividend payments cuts or skips a dividend, investors start thinking it has serious financial problems. The increased uncertainty often results in lower share prices. Thus, most firms set dividends at a level they can keep paying. They start with a relatively low dividend payout ratio, so that they can maintain a steady or slightly increasing dividend over time.

retained earnings
Profits that have been reinvested in a firm.

Retained earnings, profits that have been reinvested in the firm, have a big advantage over other sources of equity capital: They do not incur underwriting costs. Financial managers strive to balance dividends and retained earnings to maximize the value of the firm. Often the balance reflects the nature of the firm and its industry. Well-established and stable firms and those that expect only modest growth, such as public utilities, financial services companies, and large industrial corporations, typically pay out much of their earnings in dividends.

Most high-growth companies, like those in technology-related fields, finance much of their growth through retained earnings and pay little or no dividends to shareholders.

preferred shares
Equity securities for which the dividend amount is set at the time the shares are issued.

Preferred Shares Another form of equity is preferred shares. Unlike common shares, preferred shares usually have a dividend amount that is set at the time the shares are issued. These dividends must be paid before the company can pay any dividends to common shareholders. Furthermore, if the firm goes bankrupt and sells its assets, preferred shareholders get their money back before common shareholders do. Preferred shares are described in greater detail in Chapter 15.

Like debt, preferred shares increase the firm's financial risk because it obligates the firm to make a fixed payment, but preferred shares are more flexible. The firm can miss a dividend payment without suffering the serious results of failing to pay back a debt.

Making Ethical Choices

THE FRIENDS AND FAMILY IPO PLAN

As a financial analyst at an up-and-coming high-technology firm, you are involved in your most exciting project to date: helping to prepare pro forma financial statements (pro forma is a projection or estimate of what will happen in the future based on what is happening now) for the prospectus for the firm's initial public offering.

During your visits to various departments, you hear rumours about promises of IPO shares for favoured customers and suppliers. Researching if this is legal, you learn your company can give up to 5 percent of its offering to anyone it chooses. Because this price is not offered to the general public, inviting these "friends and family" to buy shares at the IPO price presents an attractive opportunity. At the height of the bull market, IPO share prices were jumping an average of 65 percent on the first day. Even though times are more normal now, the growth prospects make these shares a good buy. "Companies are continuing to be approached for shares by analysts and others who wield influence," says David Helfrich, a venture capitalist.

However, some legal experts believe that allocating IPO share to customers and vendors borders on bribery and creates conflicts of interest. Those receiving shares could feel pressured to send business to your firm. Yet such practices are common; other businesses in your industry use shares to gain a competitive advantage (perhaps as a way of saying "thank you" or of obtaining obligations from people who they want to help them in the future).

If your company is giving out only small allocations of shares, such as 100 to 200 shares, and the offering price is $18 to $20, the profit from flipping the shares on the first days is negligible and the potential for conflicts of interest reduced. If the invitation is for larger amounts, at what point does it become a problem?

ETHICAL DILEMMA: Should you bring this situation to your superiors' attention and urge them to develop a corporate policy that covers offers to sell shares at special prices?

SOURCES: Linda Himelstein, "CEOs to Eliot Spitzer: 'Give It Back? No Way!' " *Business Week*, June 9, 2003, 113; and Linda Himelstein and Ben Elgin, "High Tech's Kickback Culture," *Business Week*, February 10, 2003, 74–77.

HOT Links

Which companies are getting funding from venture capital firms? For this and other information, visit vFinance.com at (**www.vfinance.com**).

HOT Links

Find out about the Canada's Venture Capital & Private Equity Association at (**www.cvca.ca**).

Preferred shares are more expensive than debt financing, however, because preferred dividends are not tax-deductible. Furthermore, because the claims of preferred shareholders on income and assets are second to those of debt holders, preferred shareholders require higher returns to compensate for the greater risk.

Venture Capital As we learned in Chapter 6, *venture capital* is another source of equity capital. It is most often used by small and growing firms that aren't big enough to sell securities to the public. This type of financing is especially popular among high-tech companies that need large sums of money.

Venture capitalists invest in new businesses in return for part of the ownership, sometimes as much as 60 percent. They look for new businesses with high growth potential, and they expect a high investment return within 5 to 10 years. By getting in on the ground floor, venture capitalists buy shares at a very low price. They earn profits by selling the shares at a much higher price when the company goes public. Venture capitalists generally get a voice in management through a seat on the board of directors.

Getting venture capital is difficult, even though there are many private venture capital firms in this country. Most venture capitalists finance only about 1 to 5 percent of the companies that apply. Venture capital investors, many of whom experienced losses from their investments in failed dot-coms, are less willing nowadays to take risks on very early-stage companies with unproven technology. They are looking for companies with high growth potential that are already on a demonstrated track to profitability.

As a result, other sources of venture capital, including private foundations, governments, and wealthy individuals (called *angel investors*), are helping start-up firms find equity capital. These private investors are motivated by the potential for earning a high return on their investment. Accountants, lawyers, business associates, financial consultants, bankers, and others can help the small firm find an angel.

concept check

Define each of the following:

- Common shares
- Dividends
- Share or stock dividends
- Retained earnings
- Preferred shares
- Venture capital

Managing Risk And Insurance

Every day, businesses and individuals are exposed to many different kinds of risk. Investors who buy shares or speculate in commodities can earn a profit, but they also take the risk of losing all or part of their money. Illness is another type of risk, involving financial loss from not only the cost of medical care but also the loss of income.

Businesses, too, are exposed to many types of risk. Market risks, such as lower demand for a product or worsening economic conditions, can hurt a firm. Other risks involve customers—they could be injured on a company's premises or by a company's product. Like homes and cars owned by individuals, business property can be damaged or lost through fire, floods, and theft. Businesses must also protect themselves against losses from theft by dishonest employees. The loss of a key employee is another risk, especially for small firms.

It is impossible to avoid all risks, but individuals and businesses can minimize risks or buy protection—called insurance—against them. Although some risks are uninsurable, many others are insurable. Let's now look at basic risk concepts and the types of insurance available to cover them.

Risk Management

risk management
The process of identifying and evaluating risks and selecting and managing techniques to adapt to risk exposures.

Every business faces risks like the ones previously listed. **Risk management** involves analyzing the firm's operations, evaluating the potential risks, and figuring out how to minimize losses in a cost-efficient manner. In today's complex business environment, the concern for public and employee welfare and the potential for lawsuits have both increased. Risk management thus plays a vital role in the overall management of a business.

peril
A hazard or a source of danger.

speculative risk
The chance of either loss or gain, without insurance against the possible loss.

Types of Risk Individuals and firms need to protect themselves against the economic effects of certain types of risk. In an insurance sense, risk (sometimes called *pure risk*) is the chance of financial loss due to a **peril** (a hazard or a source of danger). Insurable risks include fire, theft, auto accident, injury or illness, a lawsuit, or death. **Speculative risk** is the chance of either loss or gain. Someone who buys shares in the hope of later selling it at a profit is taking a speculative risk and cannot be insured against it.

HOT Links

Learn about how Reuters Risk Management Services, at **(http://risk.reuters.com)**, helps companies with global operations identify, measure, and manage financial risk.

Strategies to Manage Risk Risk is part of life. Nevertheless, people have four major ways of dealing with it.

- *Risk avoidance.* This means staying away from situations that can lead to loss. A person can avoid the risk of a serious injury by choosing not to go skydiving. A daycare centre could avoid risk by not transporting children to and from the facility or taking them on field trips. Manufacturers who wish to avoid risks could produce only goods that have a proven track record, but these risk-avoidance strategies could stifle growth in the long run. Thus, risk avoidance is not good for all risks.
- *Risk Retention (Self-insurance).* This is the willingness to bear a risk without insurance, also called *risk assumption.* This offers a more practical way of handling many types of risks. Many large firms with warehouses or stores spread out over Canada might choose not to insure them. They assume that even if disaster strikes one location, the others won't be harmed. The losses will probably be less than the insurance premiums for all of the locations. Many companies retain losses, because it is cheaper to assume some risks than to insure against them. Some choose to pay small claims and insure only for catastrophic losses. Others "go naked," paying for all claims from current company funds. This is clearly the most risky strategy. A big claim could cripple the firm or lead to bankruptcy.

THE CANADIAN PRESS/HAMILTON-SPECTATOR-JOHN RENNISON

CONCEPT *in Action* >>>
Companies must constantly manage risk which is often not foreseen. What ways can businesses manage unforeseen risks?

insurance
The promise of compensation for certain financial losses.

- *Risk Control (Risk reduction).* This is done by adopting techniques to prevent financial losses. For example, companies adopt safety measures to reduce accidents. Construction workers are required to wear hard hats and safety glasses. Airlines keep their aircraft in good condition and require thorough training programs for pilots and flight attendants. Hotels install smoke alarms, sprinkler systems, and firewalls to protect guests and minimize fire damage.
- *Risk transfer.* This means paying someone else to bear some or all of the risk of financial loss for certain risks that can't be avoided, assumed, or controlled to acceptable levels. One way to transfer risk is through insurance. Individuals and organizations can pay a fee (a *premium*) and get the promise of compensation for certain financial losses. The companies that take on the risks are called *insurance companies*.

concept check

What is risk management?

What are the types of risk?

What are some strategies for managing risk?

Insurance Concepts

LO 9

insurance policy
A written agreement that defines what the insurance covers and the risks that the insurance company will bear for the insured party.

underwriting
A review process of all insurance applications and the selection of those who meet the standards.

Companies purchase insurance to cover insurable risks. An insurance policy is the written agreement that defines what the insurance covers and the risks that the insurance company will bear for the insured party. It also outlines the policy's benefits (the maximum amount that it will pay in the event of a loss) and the premium (the cost to the insured for coverage). Any demand for payment of losses covered by the policy is a *claim*.

Before issuing a policy, an insurance company reviews the applications of those who want a policy and selects those that meet its standards. This underwriting process also determines the level of coverage and the premiums. Each company sets its own underwriting standards based on its experience. For instance, a life insurance company might decide not to accept an applicant who has had a heart attack within the previous five years (or to charge a 50 to 75 percent higher premium). A property insurer might refuse to issue a policy on homes near brush-filled canyons, which present above-average fire hazards.

insurable interest
An insurance applicant's chance of loss if a particular peril occurs.

To get insurance, the applicant must have an **insurable interest**: the chance of suffering a loss if a particular peril occurs. In most cases, a person cannot insure the life of a friend, because the friend's death would not be considered a financial loss. But business partners can get life insurance on each other's lives, because the death of one of them would have a financial impact on their firm.

insurable risk
A risk that an insurance company will cover. It must meet certain criteria.

Insurable Risks Insurance companies are professional risk takers, but they won't provide coverage against all types of risk. Some risks are insurable; some are not. For instance, changes in political or economic conditions are not insurable. An **insurable risk** is one that an insurance company will cover. For a risk to be insurable, it must meet these criteria:

- *The loss must not be under the control of the insured.* The loss must be accidental—that is, unexpected and occurring by chance. Insurance companies do not cover losses purposely caused by the insured party. No insurance company will pay for the loss of a clothing store that the insured set on fire, nor will most companies pay life insurance benefits for a suicide.
- *There must be many similar exposures to that peril.* Insurance companies study the rates of deaths, auto accidents, fires, floods, and many other perils. They know about how many of these perils will occur each year. The **law of large numbers** lets them predict the likelihood that the peril will occur and then calculate premiums.

law of large numbers
Insurance companies' predictions of the likelihood that a peril will occur; used to calculate premiums.

Suppose that an insurance company has 150 policies in a city. The company knows from past experience that these policyholders are likely to have a total of 12 car accidents a year and that the average payment for a claim in this city has been $1,000. The total claims for one year's car accidents in the city would be $12,000 (12 accidents × $1,000). Thus, the company would charge each policyholder a premium of at least $80 ($12,000 ÷ 150). Profits and administrative expenses would serve to increase the premium from this base rate.

- *Losses must be financially measurable.* The dollar amount of potential losses must be known, so that the insurance company can figure the premiums. Life insurance is for a fixed amount specified at the time the policy is bought. Otherwise, the company and the beneficiary (the one who gets the funds) would have to agree on the value of the deceased's life at the time of death. Premiums have to be calculated before then, however.
- *The peril must not be likely to affect all the insured parties at the same time.* Insurance companies must spread out their risks by insuring many people and businesses in many locations. This strategy helps minimize the chance that a single calamity will wipe out the insurance company.
- *The potential loss must be significant.* Insurance companies cannot afford to insure trivial things for small amounts. Many policies have **deductibles**, amounts that the insured must pay before insurance benefits begin.
- *The company must have the right to set standards for insurance coverage.* Insurance companies can refuse to cover people with health problems such as AIDS, cancer, or heart trouble, a poor driving record, or a dangerous job or hobby. They can also charge higher premiums because of the higher risks they are covering.

deductibles
The amounts that the insured must pay before insurance benefits begin.

Premium Costs Insurance policies must be economical—relatively low in cost compared to the benefits—so that people will want to buy them. Yet the premiums must also cover the risks that the insurance company faces. Insurance companies collect statistics on many perils. Then specially trained mathematicians called *actuaries* use the law of large numbers to develop actuarial tables, which show how likely each peril is. Actuarial tables are the basis for calculating premiums. For example, actuaries use a mortality table showing average life expectancy and the expected number of deaths per 1,000 people at given ages to set life insurance premiums.

Almost every homeowner buys insurance to cover the perils of fire, theft, vandalism, and other home-related risks. With such a large pool of policyholders, homeowners' policies are usually inexpensive. Annual premiums are about 0.5 percent (or less) of the value of the home. This low cost encourages people to buy policies and thereby helps spread the insurance companies' risk over many homes throughout the country.

When setting premiums, insurers also look at the risk characteristics of certain groups to assess the probability of loss for those groups. For instance, smokers tend to die younger than non-smokers do and thus pay higher life insurance premiums. Female drivers under the age of 25 have a lower rate of accidents than male drivers, so their car insurance premiums are lower.

Insurance Providers Insurers can be either public or private. Public insurance coverage is offered by specialized government agencies (e.g., provincial health care plans and employment insurance). Private insurance coverage is provided by privately organized (non-government) companies.

Public Insurance Government-sponsored insurance can be regulated by either the provinces or the federal government. These are some of the main programs:

employment insurance
Payment of benefits to laid-off workers while they seek new jobs.

workers' compensation
Payments to cover the expenses of job-related injuries and diseases, including medical costs, rehabilitation, and job retraining if necessary.

Canada Pension Plan
Insurance that provides retirement, disability, death, and health benefits.

provincial health care
Health insurance programs provided by the provinces.

- *Employment Insurance (EI).* The employment insurance program pays laid-off workers weekly benefits while they seek new jobs. Persons who terminate their employment voluntarily or are fired for cause are generally not eligible for **employment insurance**. These programs also provide job counselling, education opportunities, and placement services. The size of the weekly benefit depends on the workers' previous income. Employment insurance is funded by the employees and through contributions by the employers.
- *Workers' compensation.* The provinces and territories have laws requiring employers in many industries to fund **workers' compensation** insurance to cover the expenses of job-related injuries and diseases, including medical costs, rehabilitation, and job retraining if necessary. It also provides disability income benefits (salary and wage payments) for workers who can't perform their jobs. Employers can buy workers' compensation policies or self-insure. A company's premium is based on the amount of its payroll and the types of risks present in the workplace. For instance, a construction company would pay a higher premium for workers' compensation insurance than would a jewellery store.
- *Canada Pension Plan (CPP).* The **Canada Pension Plan** provides retirement, disability, survivor benefits, and death benefits. CPP is funded by equal contributions from workers and employers. Canadians that have paid into the plan can collect as early as age 60. The province of Quebec administers its own pension plan.
- *Provincial health care.* Health care is provided to all Canadians through their respective **provincial health care** programs. In some provinces the premiums are not collected separately but are included in other taxes, and in others there are direct payments to the provincial health care insurance program.

Private Insurance Companies Private insurance companies sell property and liability insurance, health insurance, and life insurance. Generally they can be either not-for-profit (e.g., Blue Cross) or shareholder insurance companies (e.g., Manulife Financial).

For example, all eligible residents in every province and territory can obtain Blue Cross coverage through their provincial/territorial independent member plan. Blue Cross provides products such as health care, dental care, life insurance, and disability income.

Just like other publicly owned corporations, *shareholder insurance companies* are profit-oriented companies owned by shareholders. The shareholders do not have to be policyholders, and the policyholders do not have to be shareholders. Their profits come from insurance premiums in excess of claim payments and operating expenses and from investments in securities and real estate.

Types of Insurance

Most companies offer group health and life insurance plans for their employees as a fringe benefit. Employers typically pay some of the health insurance premiums, and employees pay the rest. The cost is usually considerably less than for individual policies, although it pays to check before signing up. For example, companies might pay for the entire cost of life insurance equal to one or two times the employee's annual salary, with an option to purchase more under the group plan, but the premiums might be more expensive than buying an individual policy.

Businesses often insure the lives of key employees, such as top executives, salespeople, inventors, and researchers, whose death could seriously limit the income or value of a firm. To protect themselves, businesses buy **key person life insurance**, a life insurance policy that names the company as beneficiary. In the case of a partnership, which is dissolved when a partner dies, key person insurance is often bought for each partner, with the other partner named as the beneficiary, so that the surviving partner can buy the partnership interest from the estate of the deceased and continue operating.

key person life insurance
A term insurance policy that names the company as beneficiary.

Property and Liability Insurance Property and liability insurance is important for businesses that wish to protect against losses of property and lawsuits arising from harm to other people. *Property insurance* covers financial losses from damage to or destruction of the insured's assets as a result of specified perils, whereas *liability insurance* covers financial losses from injuries to others and damage to or destruction of others' property when the insured is considered to be the cause. It also covers the insured's legal defence fees up to the maximum amount stated in the policy. Automobile liability insurance is an example. It would pay for a fence damaged when the insured person lost control of his or her car. Commercial and product liability insurance also fall into this category.

Commercial liability insurance covers a variety of damage claims, including harm to the environment from pollution. In the case of *product liability,* if a defective furnace exploded and damaged a home, the manufacturer would be liable for the damages. If the manufacturer were insured, the insurance company would cover the losses or pay to dispute the claim in court.

Property and liability insurance is a broad category. Businesses buy many types of property and liability insurance. These protect against loss of property due to fire, theft, accidents, or employee dishonesty, and financial losses arising from liability cases. Landlords and owners of business property buy *building insurance,* a type of property coverage, for protection against both property damage and liability losses. For instance, if a person broke an arm slipping on a wet floor in a hardware store, the business's insurance policy would cover any claim.

Special Types of Business Liability Insurance Businesses also purchase several other types of insurance policies, depending on their particular needs.

- *Business interruption insurance.* This optional coverage is often offered with fire insurance. It protects business owners from losses occurring when the business must be closed temporarily after property damage. **Business interruption insurance** might cover costs such as rental of temporary facilities, wage and salary payments to employees, payments for leased equipment, fixed payments (for instance, rent and loans), and profits that would have been earned during the period. *Contingent business interruption insurance* covers losses to the insured in the event of property damage to a major supplier or customer.
- *Theft insurance.* Businesses also want to protect their property against financial losses due to crime. **Theft insurance** is the broadest coverage and protects businesses against losses from an act of stealing. Businesses can also buy more limited types of theft insurance.

business interruption insurance
Covers costs such as rental of temporary facilities, wage and salary payments to employees, payments for leased equipment, fixed payments, and profits that would have been earned during that period.

theft insurance
A broad insurance coverage that protects businesses against losses from an act of stealing.

- *Fidelity and surety bonds.* What if a firm has a dishonest employee? This situation is covered by a *fidelity bond*, an agreement that insures a company against theft committed by an employee who handles company money. If a restaurant manager is bonded for $50,000 and steals $60,000, the restaurant will recover all but $10,000 of the loss. Banks, loan companies, and retail businesses that employ cashiers typically buy fidelity bonds.

  A *surety bond,* also called a *performance bond,* is an agreement to reimburse a firm for non-performance of acts specified in a contract. This form of insurance is most common in the construction industry. Contractors buy surety bonds to cover themselves in case the project they are working on is not completed by the specified date or does not meet specified standards. In practice, the insurance company often pays another contractor to finish the job or to redo shoddy work when the bonded contractor fails to perform.
- *Title insurance.* A title policy protects the buyer of real estate against losses caused by a defect in the title—that is, a claim against the property that prevents the transfer of ownership from seller to purchaser. It eliminates the need to search legal records to be sure that the seller was actually the owner of (had clear title to) the property.
- *Professional liability insurance.* This form of insurance covers financial losses (legal fees and court-awarded damages up to specific limits) resulting from alleged malpractice by professionals in fields like medicine, law, architecture, and dentistry. *Directors and officers insurance* is a type of professional liability insurance designed to protect top corporate management, who have also been the target of malpractice lawsuits. It pays for legal fees and court-awarded damages up to specific limits.

professional liability insurance
Insurance designed to protect top corporate management, who have been the target of malpractice lawsuits.

concept check

What is an insurance policy? Underwriting? Insurable interest?

What are premiums and deductibles?

What types of insurance policies are available? What is the purpose of each?

Trends in Financial Management

Finance has moved from a relatively isolated, inward-looking function to a unit that is heavily involved in shaping and implementing a company's overall strategic objectives. Many of the key trends shaping the practice of financial management echo those in other disciplines. For example, technology is improving the efficiency with which financial managers run their operations. The "Customer Satisfaction and Quality" box, on page 515, describes how Dell Computer uses technology to improve its cash forecasts. The continued expansion of the financial manager's role in risk management is a natural outgrowth of the new regulations in the United States, as Canadian companies that trade on the United States exchanges must adhere not only to Canadian law but also American standards (e.g., the Sarbanes-Oxley Act).

The CFO's Role Continues to Expand

During the 1990s, CFOs expanded their jobs beyond the ordinary finance responsibilities. No longer just numbers people, they joined top management in developing and implementing the firm's strategic direction. Negotiating billion-dollar mergers and finding creative financing vehicles were all part of the day's work. They were the company's face to the Bay Street analysts, who watched to see if the company would meet each quarter's earnings estimates.

CFOs are more highly visible and active in company management than ever before. They serve as both business partner to the chief executive and a fiduciary to the board. "Today, in what I'll call the post-Enron, post-WorldCom era, there's been a restored emphasis on the fiduciary and control aspects," says Robert Lumpkins, vice chairman and CFO of Cargill Inc., a privately owned international agricultural and industrial products company. "Finance today is well-balanced between what

I'll call the value-adding and the value-preservation aspects." In global organizations such as Cargill, with 142,000 employees in 61 countries, finance managers must also be sensitive to cultural differences and different approaches to solving problems.[4]

Finance professionals need to have a broad view of company operations to communicate effectively with business unit managers, board members, creditors, and investors. Douglas Oberheim, a group president at Caterpillar, credits his years as CFO with providing him the broad perspective to see the company from the shareholder's viewpoint and the understanding of the importance of cross-functional activities. In addition to such traditional duties as arranging mergers and acquisitions, raising and allocating capital, and managing treasury operations, CFOs are also key players in matters pertaining to information technology, human resources, and the supply chain. Interpersonal skills are essential because they must motivate employees and encourage a positive environment that promotes accountability and ethical behaviour down through the organization. Finance managers must learn to be team players who can work with employees in other functional areas. At times finance and business unit executives have differing positions, and it takes careful negotiation to resolve issues. For example, business units may want to maintain larger cash balances than finance recommends. Educating unit managers about the cost of idle cash and establishing appropriate incentives can change corporate culture.[5]

Weighing the Risks

The job of managing a company's risk, which became even more difficult after the September 11, 2001 terrorist attacks, continues to be challenging for financial executives. Adding to the complexity are the volatile economy and financial markets at home and abroad. No longer does risk management focus narrowly on buying insurance to protect against loss of physical assets and interruption of business. Instead, more companies now consider **enterprise risk management (ERM)** a priority. ERM goes beyond just identifying, monitoring, and lowering risk to include a strategic approach to defining and managing all elements of a company's risk.

enterprise risk management (ERM)
A company-wide, strategic approach to identifying, monitoring, and managing all elements of a company's risk.

CONCEPT *in Action* >>>

The CFO-as-busy-bean counter image has undergone an extreme makeover, as today's financial chiefs increasingly perform highly visible decision-making roles alongside CEOs. Intense pressure for financial reporting compliance along with expectations of beating the numbers each quarter are major factors behind both the rising prominence and turnover of financial officers. And as responsibility increases, so does pay. Have CFOs become chief executive material?

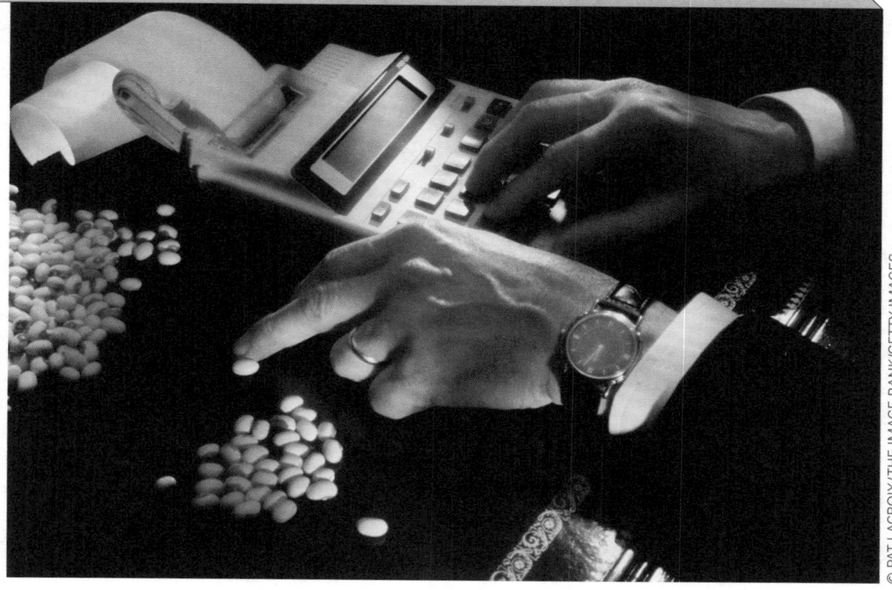

© PAT LACROIX/THE IMAGE BANK/GETTY IMAGES

© AP/WIDE WORLD PHOTOS

CONCEPT *in Action* >>>

Many companies have created a new position, chief risk officer, to study risk potential and coordinate risk management procedures throughout the company. How can a company anticipate catastrophic events and minimize the devastating impact on business?

As the risk management function expands beyond its traditional role, companies recognize that ERM can make significant contributions to financial performance and shareholder returns. Because a failure in a company's risk control procedures can lead to substantial financial losses, corporate CFOs and treasurers are taking a proactive, leadership role in ERM. This requires them to get more involved with operations and form partnerships with business unit executives. "Effective risk management requires the ability to walk in the shoes of operations," says David Kelsey, senior vice president and CFO of Sealed Air Corp., a packaging products manufacturer. "Risk management can't be perceived as getting in the way of what business wants to do. Risk management needs to manage exposures, but not by creating more work or increasing costs."[6]

Companies face a wide range of risks, including:

- credit risk—exposure to loss as a result of default on a financial transaction, or a reduction in a security's market value due to decline in the credit quality of the debt issuer;
- market risk—risk resulting from adverse movements in the level or volatility of market prices of securities, commodities, and currencies; and
- operational risk—the risk of unexpected losses arising from deficiencies in a firm's management information, support, and control systems and procedures.

Jennifer Ceran, treasurer of eBay Inc., was an early adopter of ERM. Ceran recognized the need for the finance area to go beyond the traditional risk tasks assigned to the treasury operation, such as insurance, and take a broader view of all the risks affecting the company. Evaluating all types of risk and their impact on each other is critical to reducing overall risk for any company. As Rossini Zumwalt, assistant treasurer and director of finance at software firm Symantec explains,

> "We identified the risks we already knew about, but what were we leaving out? It's not just the risk you know. It's the risks you don't know. We forgot the 'E' in ERM. I think that's why companies are challenged. It's important to attach the 'E,' to go beyond traditional risks."[7]

Companies are also using risk management in response to new corporate governance guidelines. Better risk management procedures are important to shareholders in the post-Enron era. They want to know that companies have taken steps to minimize risks that would affect the company's values.

concept check

How has the role of CFO changed since the passage of the Sarbanes-Oxley Act?

Why are improved risk management procedures important to shareholders?

Great Ideas to Use Now

Whether you are a marketing manager, purchasing agent, or systems analyst, knowledge of finance will help you to do your job better. You'll be able to understand your company's financial statements, its financial condition, and management's investment and financing decisions. Financial information also provides feedback on how well you are doing and identifies problems. On a more practical note, you might be asked to prepare a budget for your department or unit. Employees who understand the financial decision-making process will be able to prepare proposals that address financial concerns. As a result, they will be more likely to be given the resources they require to accomplish the firm's goals.

If you own a business, you must pay close attention to financial management. Without financial plans, you might find yourself running out of cash. It's easy to get so caught up in growing sales that you neglect your billing and collection methods. In fact, managing accounts receivable is often one of the more challenging aspects of running a young company. But you can't rely on revenue increases to solve your cash flow problems. Good receivables practices start with credit policies. Be choosy when it comes to offering trade credit, and check customers' credit references and payment history thoroughly. Set the initial credit limit fairly low until the customer establishes a prompt payment history. Here are some other ways to improve collections.

- Bill frequently, not just at the end of the month, so that money flows in throughout the month. Send bills when milestones are reached, such as making a presentation or completing a phase of a project.
- Clearly state payment terms, and make sure that the language on the invoice matches the contract.
- Establish regular and frequent follow-up procedures. Some companies call to notify the customer that the bill has been sent and to make sure the customer is satisfied. Weekly calls are in order for late payments.
- Try to get a firm date by which you will be paid, and be prepared to say what you will do if you aren't paid on time—for example, stopping work on a project or not shipping the next part of the order.
- Keep detailed notes of all conversations relating to a collection: your contact, date of the call, what was promised, and what you replied. You can then e-mail this as confirmation of your understanding and as another reminder.
- Monitor results of outstanding receivables collection.
- Don't fill new orders from customers who are continually delinquent.[8]

Customer Satisfaction and Quality

Because an organization's finance department affects every other area of the firm, it must adhere to the highest quality standards. "Our decision-making needs to be near-perfect, if not perfect," says Ruth Ann M. Gillis, former CFO of Exelon, an electric utility company.

Reliable and consistent financial reports and analyses are critical for managers throughout the firm and also to investors, creditors, suppliers, and customers. Because CEOs and CFOs must now certify the company's financial reports under the Sarbanes-Oxley Act (although this is American legislation, Canadian companies listed on U.S. exchanges must also adhere to the act), they are demanding that their managers adhere to strict quality control procedures and guidelines. To minimize risks of errors, companies are establishing formal rules and procedures for corporate finance. Some CFOs, including Home Depot's Carol Tomé and Consolidated Edison's Joan Freilich, ask key finance managers to sign personal statements that the financial statements they submit are correct.

Financial managers are continually looking for ways to improve the quality of their forecasts and budgets. Unhappy with the level of accuracy in its cash forecasts, Dell Computer developed the Enzo Liquidity Forecasting Tool. It chose the name in honour of race car designer Enzo Ferrari, to underscore the speed of Dell's cash forecasts. Complex cash flow forecasts now take one person an afternoon to prepare instead of three people working for two days. Accuracy is extremely high: The variance is less than $30 million on an accounts payable balance of $5 billion, a 99.4 percent accuracy level. Better cash forecasts were one reason Dell was able to raise its investment income above $1.5 million annually. In addition, Enzo's sophisticated analytical powers give financial managers a broader view of the cash picture. "Any question you can have about a scenario, you can answer," says Nathan Brunner, senior finance consultant at Dell.

SOURCES: Joseph Weber, "CFOs on the Hot Seat," *Business Week*, March 17, 2003, 67–70; and "Stand Back! Enzo Has Arrived," in Jay Sherman and Susan Kelly, "Uphill Racer—The 2002 Alexander Hamilton Award Winners," *Treasury & Risk Management*, October 2002, (www.treasuryandrisk.com).

Summary of Learning Outcomes

1 Explain the roles finance and the financial manager play in the firm's overall strategy.

Finance is the art and science involved in managing the firm's money. The financial manager must decide how much money is needed and when, how best to use the available funds, and how to get the required financing. The financial manager's responsibilities include financial planning, investing (spending money), and financing (raising money). Maximizing the value of the firm is the main goal of the financial manager, whose decisions often have long-term effects.

2 Describe how a firm develops its financial plans, including forecasts and budgets.

Financial planning enables the firm to estimate the amount and timing of the financial resources it needs to meet its business goals. The planning process begins with forecasts based on the demand for the firm's products. Short-term forecasts project expected revenues and expenses for one year. They are the basis for cash budgets, which show the flow of cash into and out of the firm and are used to plan day-to-day operations. Long-term forecasts project revenues and expenses over more than a year, typically 2 to 10 years. These strategic plans allow top management to analyze the impact of different options on the firm's profits.

3 List the types of short- and long-term expenditures a firm makes.

A firm invests in short-term expenses—supplies, inventory, and wages—to support current production, marketing, and sales activities. The financial manager manages the firm's investment in current assets, so that the company has enough cash to pay its bills and support accounts receivable and inventory. Long-term expenditures (capital expenditures) are made for fixed assets such as land, buildings, machinery, and equipment. Because of the large outlays required for capital expenditures, financial managers carefully analyze proposed projects to determine which offer the best returns.

4 Summarize the main sources and costs of unsecured and secured short-term financing.

Short-term financing comes due within one year. The main sources of unsecured short-term financing are trade credit, bank loans, and commercial paper. Secured loans require a pledge of certain assets, such as accounts receivable or inventory, as security for the loan. Factoring, or selling accounts receivable outright at a discount, is another form of short-term financing.

5 Identify and compare the two primary sources of long-term financing.

Financial managers must choose the best mix of debt and equity for their firm. The main advantage of debt financing is the tax-deductibility of interest, but debt involves financial risk, because it requires the payment of interest and principal on specified dates. Equity—common and preferred shares—is considered a permanent form of financing on which the firm might or might not pay dividends. Dividends are not tax-deductible.

6 Understand the major types, features, and costs of long-term debt.

The main types of long-term debt are term loans, bonds, and mortgage loans. Term loans can be secured or unsecured and generally have 5- to 12-year maturities. Bonds usually have initial maturities of 10 to 30 years. Mortgage loans are secured by real estate. Long-term debt usually costs more than short-term financing because of the greater uncertainty that the borrower will be able to make the scheduled loan payments.

7 Discuss how firms issue equity and the costs to the company.

The chief sources of equity financing are common shares, retained earnings, and preferred shares. The cost of selling shares includes issuing costs and potential dividend payments. Retained earnings are profits reinvested in the firm. For the issuing firm, preferred shares are more expensive than debt, because its dividends are not tax-deductible and its claims are secondary to those of debt holders, but less expensive than common shares. Venture capital is often a source of equity financing for small and growing, typically high-tech companies.

8 Understand risk, how it can be managed, and what makes a risk insurable.

Risk is the potential for loss or the chance that an investment will not achieve the expected level of return. Risk can be managed by identifying and evaluating the potential risks and selecting and managing techniques to adapt to risk exposures.

To get insurance, the applicant must have an insurable interest: the chance of suffering a loss if a particular peril occurs. An insurable risk is one that an insurance company will cover. To qualify, the following conditions must be met: The loss must not be under the control of the insured; there must be many similar exposures to that peril; losses must be financially measurable; the peril must not be likely to affect all the insured parties at the same time; the potential loss must be significant; and the company must have the right to set standards for insurance coverage.

9 Describe the types of insurance coverage that businesses should consider.

The main types of insurance that businesses should consider include property and liability, commercial liability, business interruption, theft, fidelity and surety bonds, title insurance, and professional liability insurance.

10 List some of the trends that are affecting the practice of financial management.

The role of the CFO has changed, with CFOs taking the central role in overseeing corporate compliance with the various regulations and re-establishing public trust. They must balance the roles of corporate cop and strategic planner. The continued expansion of the financial manager's role in risk management is a natural outgrowth as companies face a wide range of risks, including credit, market, and operational risk. More companies are adopting risk management to identify and evaluate risks and select techniques to control and reduce risk.

Key Terms

accounts payable 500
accounts receivable 499
bonds 504
budgets 496
business interruption insurance 511
Canada Pension Plan 510
capital budgeting 500
capital budgets 496
capital expenditures 499
cash budgets 496
cash flows 493
cash management 497
commercial paper 498
common shares 504
deductibles 509
dividends 505
employment insurance 510
enterprise risk management (ERM) 513
factoring 502
financial management 493
financial risk 503
insurable interest 509
insurable risk 509
insurance 508
insurance policy 508
key person life insurance 511
law of large numbers 509
line of credit 501
long-term forecasts 496
marketable securities 498
mortgage loan 504
operating budgets 496
peril 507
preferred shares 505
professional liability insurance 512
provincial health care 510
retained earnings 505
return 495
revolving credit agreement† (revolving line of credit) 501
risk 495
risk management 507
risk-return trade-off 495
secured loans 502
share or stock dividends 505
short-term forecasts 495
speculative risk 507
term loan 504
theft insurance 511
trade credit 500
underwriting 508
unsecured loans 500
workers' compensation 510

Experiential Exercises

1. Prepare a personal budget. A personal budget is one of the most valuable tools for personal financial planning. It will help you evaluate your current financial situation, spending patterns, and goals. Use the following steps to create your budget.

   Using credit card receipts, cheque records, and other documents, record your income and expenses for the past 30 days. Based on this information, develop a personal budget for the next month. Record your budget in the "Planned" column of the worksheet in Exhibit 16.4. Include scholarships or grants as other income sources.

   Track your actual income and expenses for one month. Write down everything you spend on a daily basis, or you will forget little things (like snacks) that add up over the course of a month. Record your actual totals in the "Actual" column of the worksheet.

   At the end of the budget period, compare your budget to your actual results. Record any differences between the "Planned" and "Actual" values in the "Variance" column of the worksheet. How close were you to your budget estimates? In what categories did you overspend? Where did you underspend? Did creating the budget have any impact on how you allocated your money to different categories and how you spent your money?

   Optional: Use the results of your first month's budget to project next month's income and expenses. Repeat the monitoring process.
2. The head of your school's finance department has asked you to address a group of incoming business students about the importance of finance to their overall business education. Develop an outline with the key points you would cover in your speech.
3. As a financial manager at Nature's Food Company, you are preparing forecasts and budgets for a new line of high-nutrition desserts. Why should the finance department prepare these plans for the product development group? What factors would you consider in developing your projections and assessing their impact on the firm's profits?
4. You are the cash manager for a chain of sporting goods stores facing a cash crunch. To date, the chain has always paid accounts payable within the credit period. The CFO wants to consider extending payments beyond the due date. Write a memo that discusses the pros, cons, and ethics of stretching accounts payable as well as other cash-saving options to investigate.
5. You are the chief financial officer of Discovery Labs, a privately held, five-year-old biotechnology company that needs to raise $3 million to fund the development of a new drug. Prepare a report for the board of directors that discusses the types of long-term financing available to the firm, their pros and cons, and the key factors to consider in choosing a financing strategy.
6. GetSmart **(www.getsmart.com)** is an information service that offers advice on personal loans. Try the questionnaires in each area, using different answers, to see what is necessary to qualify for that financing option.
7. If factoring accounts receivable is still a mystery to you, visit the 21st Financial Solutions site, **(www.21stfinancialsolutions.com).** Follow the links on the home page to answer these questions: What are factoring's advantages? What are the additional benefits, and what types of companies can use factoring to their advantage? Then summarize the factoring process.
8. Visit your bank's website to learn about the bank's products and services for corporate customers. Describe briefly each type of loan it offers. Then do the same for another financial institution.
9. Visit the Treasury Board of Canada Secretariat website at **(www.tbs-sct.gc.ca/tbs-sct/index-eng.asp)** to learn more about risk management.

EXHIBIT 16.4 > Monthly Budget Worksheet

Name: ____________________

Month of ____________________

	Planned	Actual	Variance
Income			
Wages (take-home pay)	____	____	____
Support from relatives	____	____	____
Loans	____	____	____
Withdrawals from savings	____	____	____
Other ________	____	____	____
Other ________	____	____	____
(1) Total Available Income	____	____	____
Expenses			
Fixed Expenses			
Housing	____	____	____
Automobile payment	____	____	____
Insurance	____	____	____
Loan repayment	____	____	____
Savings for goals	____	____	____
Tuition and fees	____	____	____
Other ________	____	____	____
Subtotal, Fixed Expenses	____	____	____
Flexible Expenses			
Food	____	____	____
Clothing	____	____	____
Personal care	____	____	____
Entertainment and recreation	____	____	____
Transportation	____	____	____
Telephone	____	____	____
Utilities (electricity, gas, water)	____	____	____
Cable TV	____	____	____
Medical and dental	____	____	____
Books, magazines, educational supplies	____	____	____
Gifts	____	____	____
Other ________	____	____	____
Other ________	____	____	____
Subtotal, Flexible Expenses	____	____	____
(2) Total Expenses	____	____	____
Cash Surplus (Deficit) [(1)–(2)]	____	____	____

Review Questions

1. What is financial management?
2. List the responsibilities of the financial manager.
3. What is the goal of the financial manager? What are risk, return, and the risk-return trade-off?
4. What is the purpose of the three types of budgets mentioned in this chapter?

5. What is cash management, and why is it important in business?
6. How can technology be used to help companies improve their credit and collection performance?
7. What are the sources of short-term financing?
8. How do companies obtain long-term financing?
9. Describe the major differences between debt and equity financing.
10. What are dividends and retained earnings?
11. What is the difference between common shares and preferred shares?
12. What is risk management? What are some strategies to manage risk?
13. What are the various types of insurance available to businesses?

CREATIVE THINKING CASE >

Investors Hang Up on Vonage

Founded in 2002, Vonage quickly became a major player in Voice over Internet Protocol (VoIP) phone service. Using Internet connections instead of traditional phone lines, it offered customers an attractive flat rate of about $25 a month for calls to the United States, Canada, and many European countries. By its May IPO, Vonage had 1.7 million customers and more than half the U.S. market for Internet phone service. Vonage claimed to be the fastest growing phone company in the United States. Revenues in 2005 were almost triple 2004 levels.

Management thought the time was right to go public and raise funds for expansion. Investors were again interested in IPOs after several years of low demand. So on May 24, 2006, it sold 31.25 million shares and raised $531 million. It also offered its individual customers—usually closed out of high-profile IPOs—the chance to buy 100 shares at the IPO price, an unusual move. So why was the Vonage IPO the worst in two years?

Timing is everything, and Vonage's timing was off. The market fell sharply on inflation concerns. The shares opened on the New York Stock Exchange at $17, fell to $14.85 by the end of the first day, and were trading below $7 by September 2006.

The offer to individual investors worked against Vonage, sending a message to some analysts that institutions were not interested in buying the stock and that Vonage needed help from its customers. Chad Brand of Peridot Capital Management considered this a "huge red flag. . . . If that's not a sign that nobody else wanted their stock, I don't know what is," he posted on his website.

Several factors negatively affected the Vonage offering. Increased competition creates pricing pressure. Rivals range from small VoIP players similar to Vonage to Internet powerhouses including Google, Yahoo, and MSN. Cable companies such as Time Warner, that offer phone service bundled with television and broadband services, and Verizon and other traditional providers are lowering prices as well. Vonage's sales are already falling, while costs-per-subscriber are rising. The company's marketing costs are very high, and the per-line cost of providing service is also rising at the same time as customer complaints about service quality are mounting.

Regulatory uncertainty adds another layer of complexity. Telecommunications providers are campaigning to charge for carrying other company's calls. This would add to Vonage's costs. As Vonage grows, it will be required to collect sales tax and other fees, pushing customer bills well above the $25 flat rate they were expecting to pay and removing pricing advantages.

These are just a few of the issues that stand in the way of Vonage's profitability. In fact, Vonage's IPO prospectus says that it will focus on growth rather than profitability and went so far as to say that it might never become profitable. As a public company, Vonage will be under greater pressure to execute its business plan and also face close scrutiny from its investors. Only time will tell if investors hang up when Vonage calls.

Critical Thinking Questions

- What issues should executives of a company such as Vonage consider before deciding to go public? In your opinion, was the company ready for an IPO, and why?
- How else could Vonage have raised funds to continue to grow? Compare the risks of raising private equity to going public.
- Use a search engine and a site such as Yahoo Finance to learn about Vonage's current situation. Prepare a brief summary, including its current financial situation. Is it still a public company, and how has its stock fared?

SOURCES: David A. Gaffen, "Tale of Two IPOs," Wall Street Journal Online, May 24, 2006, (www.wsj.com); Olga Kharif, "Vonage's Iffy IPO," Business Week Online, February 9, 2006, (www.businessweek.com); Timothy J. Mullaney, "Vonage's Lackluster IPO," Business Week Online, May 24, 2006, (www.businessweek.com); Shawn Young and Li Yuan, "Vonage Faces User Complaints as IPO Looms," Wall Street Journal, May 18, 2006, p. B1; Shawn Young and Lynn Cowan, "Vonage Lacks Voltage in Its IPO, with Weakest Debut in 2 Years," Wall Street Journal, May 25, 2006, p. C4; Shawn Young and Randall Smith, "How Vonage's High-Profile IPO Stumbled on the Stock Market," Wall Street Journal, June 3, 2006, p. A1.

VIDEO CASE >

Debt Nation

Many Canadians are finding themselves in deep financial trouble, even though they make a reasonable income. The primary contributing factor seems to be credit card debt. Many items purchased with major credit cards are intangible, which means that you have nothing to show for it when the bill comes in. For example, trips, restaurant meals, shows, and gas are often purchased with credit cards. And the credit card companies are pushing hard.

In 2003, there were approximately 23.9 million *retailer-issued* credit cards in circulation in Canada. These are the ones at 28.8 percent interest (e.g., HBC/Zellers). Students often start out in debt simply from educational expenses, with the average amount being $22,700 for four-year programs. Add that to a credit card (or two, or three,) and financial trouble can follow.

Family 1, Wayne and Theresa, are not that unusual, and many Canadians behave in a similar manner—the ostrich approach: If I can't see it, it's not a problem. Family 2, Joanne and Travis, admit that Joanne is a shopaholic. Some people get a genuine high from shopping, similar to that of drugs and alcohol. For Family 3, Hanna Laura might have to forgo her trip to England to curb her debt. How did this happen to ordinary Canadians? In 2001, Canadians received 208.3 million credit card solicitations. If you pay your monthly amount regularly, what happens? The credit card company probably raises your limit! This is a very slippery slope. With an increase in credit card debt of 90 percent between 1997 and 2001, as well as an estimated household debt owed by Canadians in 2003 of $731 billion compared to saving of $9.39 billion, it is obvious we need to step back and look at what we are doing.

Critical Thinking Questions

- If a large number of Canadians suddenly stopped using their credit cards (and did not have the cash to make intended purchases) what effect would this have on the Canadian economy?
- Are the credit card companies acting responsibly by encouraging Canadians to accept more cards? How might they build their business in a more ethical matter?

SOURCES: CBC, *Marketplace*, "Debt Nation Part 1," January 15, 2006.
CBC, *Marketplace*, "Debt Nation Part 2," January 22, 2006.

E-COMMERCE CASE >

Investing Your Money: Is the Target of Your Investment Managing Risk Adequately?

An important aspect of managing a firm's finances (the chapter title) involves understanding and managing risk. Do we have enough assets to cover our liabilities? Currently some Canadian corporate pension plans do *not* have enough assets to cover the value of the current pension plan obligations. In fact, these plans are underfunded. For example, Air Canada had a pension plan deficit of $3.2 billion on January 1st, 2009.

Investors in pension plans are sometimes unaware of this problem, as it is not readily apparent from the financial statements. An item such as pension plan underfunding would have to be discovered by examining the off-balance sheet obligations of the company.

What are the implications of an underfunded plan for the investor? A cash infusion might be required in a few cases; however, there is an impact on the share value. Keeping in mind that the asset value of the fund is an estimate, as is the value of future obligations, is this really a serious problem? It depends. Interest rates are relatively low right now—as this book is being printed—and when they rise, the current value of future obligations will decrease. Furthermore, the assets supporting the plan should appreciate in value, causing the underfunding gap to disappear. Again, given that the numbers reflect management estimates, of greater concern might be the trust in the firm's management.

Al Rosen, a commentator for *Canadian Business Online,* feels that attention needs to be given to the lack of accounting principles that might prevent the pension plan underfunding issue. In his opinion, the inadequacy of a system that does not look out for the interests of investors is the problem, with the pension issues being only a symptom.

SOURCE: (www.theglobeandmail.com/servlet/story/LAC.20090326.Race26/TPStory/Business), accessed March 29, 2009.

Critical Thinking Questions

1. Do you agree or disagree with Al Rosen's point of view? Why?
2. Choose a Canadian company at random, and see if you can tell from the financial statements whether the pension plan is adequately funded. Does the result of the exercise change your answer to question 1?

SOURCES: Al Rosen, "Time Bombs," *Canadian Business,* 79 no. 10 (Summer 2006), 23; Al Rosen, "The Pension Fun Never Stops," *Canadian Business,* 76 no. 13 (July 7–21, 2003), 23; April 29, 2003; and Boston Beer Company corporate website, www.bostonbeer.com, accessed May 1, 2003.

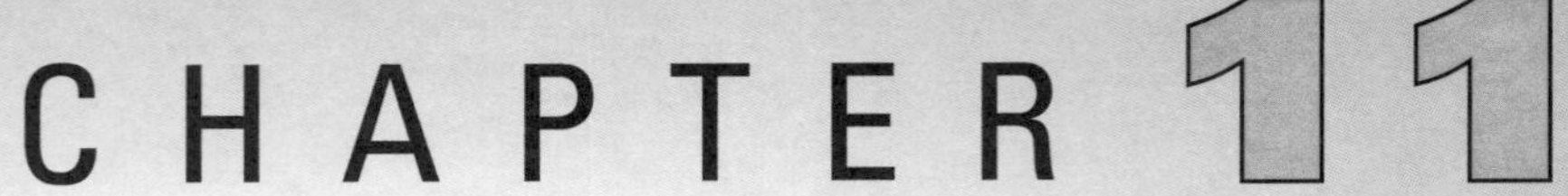

CHAPTER 11

Making the Connection

Achieving World-Class Operations Management

This chapter, on the management of the operations area of a business, starts with a discussion of Harley-Davidson's operations. This example is very appropriate to the title of the chapter, as Harley definitely epitomizes world-class operations and offers many lessons for companies struggling to get there. For years Harley tried to sell freedom and adventure but with a poor-quality product sold at a high price because of outdated and inefficient facilities. Its *financial performance* was extremely poor, because it simply did not *meet customer needs*—poor *quality* at a high price did not provide the customer with anything of value. Once it stopped trying to produce quantity and focused instead on quality, Harley turned it all around. Today the company is a leader in quality management. But it required a view of the business as a whole—meeting the needs of the customer (*marketing*) through *committed employees* (*human resources*) and providing quality (*operations*) at the lowest cost to improve the bottom line (*finance*) while uniting all the *stakeholders* in the "Harley-Davidson family."

As explained in the chapter, sound operations management is vital to the financial success of the company because this area accounts for as much as three-quarters of the company's costs. It is a wonderful example of the integrative nature of business, as it must work very closely with the other functional areas to achieve maximum financial performance. Most obviously, operations must develop processes to provide for the demand created and forecasted by marketing, but it must also work with marketing to develop and design products so that the operations processes used to provide them are the most efficient and effective and the distribution of those products—both an operations and a marketing issue—is done efficiently, cost-effectively, and in a manner that meets the customers' needs. Similarly, operations must work with human resources to have the right numbers of the best-qualified people available to produce products and service customers, as well as deciding whether to replace this human effort with robots or other computerized techniques. In fact, most of the decisions made in the operations area have wider functional implications. For example, the choice of location can affect transportation costs and thus the final cost of the product as well as the availability and cost of labour, whereas implementing a flexible manufacturing system is expensive but needs little labour to operate, and provides consistent quality products that meet individual customer specifications.

An excellent example in the chapter of the need for a successful business to integrate operations with the other functional areas is that of Designlore with its "Right the First Time" approach to designing products. Designlore recognizes the need to integrate innovative design that meets customer needs with traditional engineering and operations principles, in order to provide products that are designed in a way that keeps all members of the supply chain satisfied from engineering right through to the final

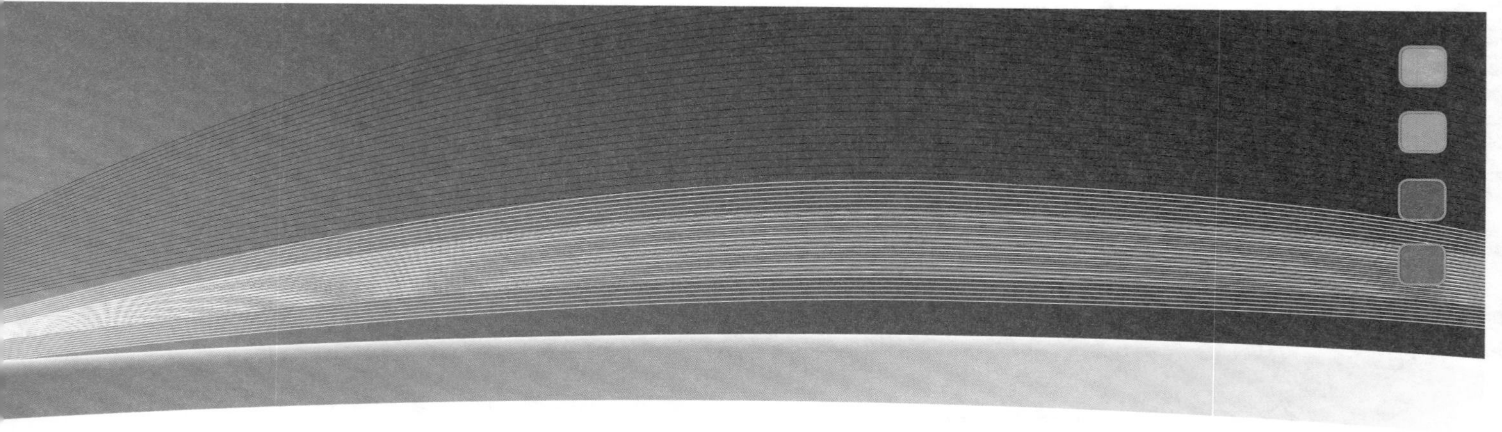

consumer. Another area where we can see the integration of operations with the other facets of our business model is in the external environment. Many businesses today are faced with environmental challenges in an effort to meet their operational goals. For example, in the *social* environment, consumers are expecting customized products of greater quality delivered in a timely manner at a reasonable price. This requires using whatever *technology* is available to allow the company to stay ahead of the competition and improving relationships with suppliers and vendors (both important stakeholder groups), so that there is a smooth flow from provider to consumer. If consumers don't get what they want, they will simply go to the increasing number of competitors in the global *economic* environment who can often produce at a lower cost, and they will frequently do this at breakneck speed, using technology to shop over the Internet, switching their loyalties at the click of a mouse!

The technology that is available to the operations area of a business has improved tremendously. In this chapter, we outline many of these *innovations*. One of the most integrative examples of technology is manufacturing resource planning (MRPII). It uses a complex computerized system to integrate data from the different departments of the company, so that they are all working as one to meet customer needs. Enterprise resource planning (ERP) takes this a step further by going outside the business and integrating information about suppliers and customers into the system. These technologies and others help to manage the supply chain so that the entire sequence, from securing inputs into the process to delivering goods to the consumer, is done in a manner that meets the needs of the customer at the highest possible level.

Operations management is also an excellent example of the management process at work. You will read in the chapter about production *planning* and *control*, and the specific tools and techniques that are used to plan and control the production process. Quality control is a particularly important issue for management in meeting the customers' needs for a quality product. Part of the process is also deciding on the layout for the production or service facility, which involves *organizing* the company's resources in the most appropriate way to produce goods or provide services to the customer efficiently. The final management function is pivotal—*motivating*—as we know that workers must be committed to the task for it all to come together. Operations managers working directly with the workers that produce the goods or services for the customers have the ultimate responsibility to gain that commitment.

In this chapter, you'll learn about many trends in operations that allow companies to both enhance innovation to meet changing customer needs in a timely manner, and adapt to changes in technology. At the same time, they are improving quality, keeping costs down, and gaining employee commitment by involving teams of employees throughout the process. And isn't that what it's all about—meeting critical success factors by integrating the functional areas within the dynamic business environment?

CHAPTER 11

Achieving World-Class Operations Management

LEARNING OUTCOMES

1. Discuss why production and operations management is important in both manufacturing and service firms.
2. List the types of production processes used by manufacturers and service firms.
3. Describe how organizations decide where to put their production facilities and what choices must be made in designing the facility.
4. Explain why resource-planning tasks like inventory management and supplier relations are critical to production.
5. Discuss how operations managers schedule and control production.
6. Evaluate how quality management and lean-manufacturing techniques help firms improve production and operations management.
7. Identify the roles that technology and automation play in manufacturing and service industry operations management.
8. List some of the key trends affecting the way companies manage production and operations.

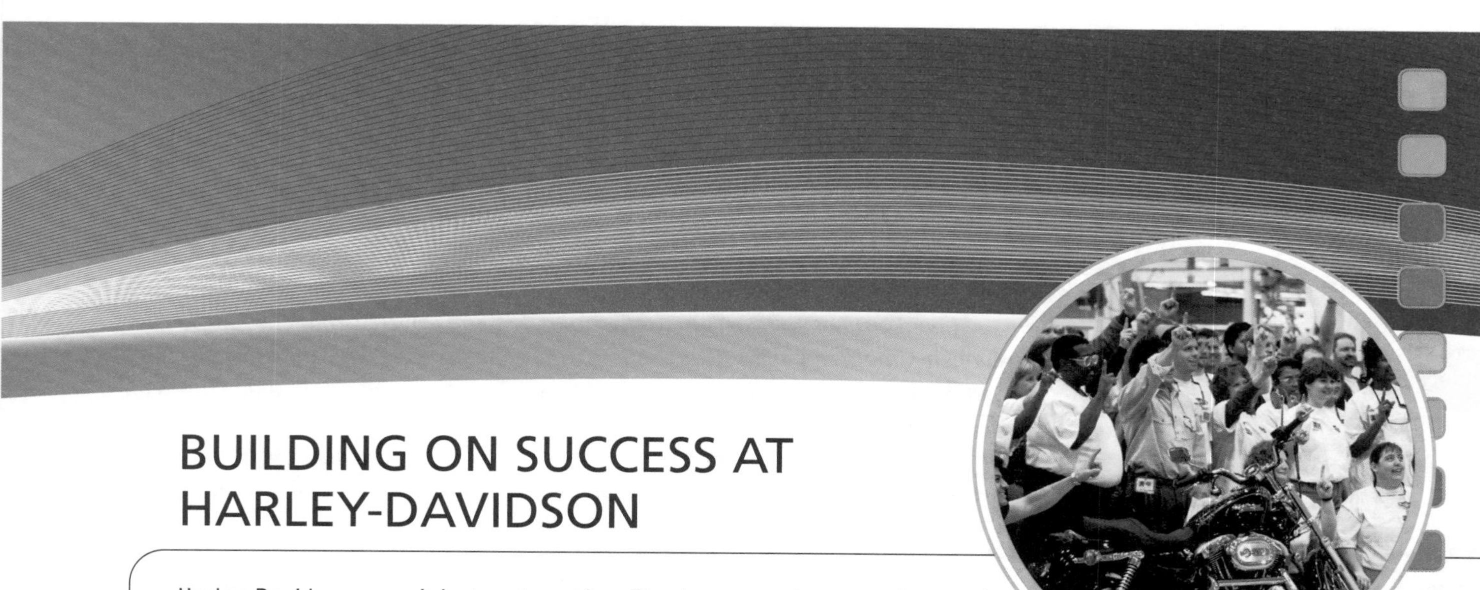

BUILDING ON SUCCESS AT HARLEY-DAVIDSON

Harley-Davidsons aren't just motorcycles. They're an American legend, known for their unique style, sound, and power ever since the first one was assembled in a backyard workshop in 1903. "People want more than two wheels and a motor," explains former Harley-Davidson CEO Jeffrey Bleustein. "Harleys represent something very basic—a desire for freedom, adventure, and individualism."

Twenty years ago, Harley also represented everything that was wrong with American manufacturing. The company's production facilities were outdated and inefficient, keeping prices high. Quality was so poor that owners sometimes joked they needed two Harleys—one to ride and one for parts. As fed-up consumers turned to motorcycles made by Japanese and German manufacturers, Harley-Davidson's sales plummeted, and the company teetered on bankruptcy.

Today, however, Harley-Davidson (**www.harley-davidson.com**) is a company reborn. While 2007 was not as strong as 2006, with a decrease in revenue of 2.3%, Harley-Davidson Motorcycles still posted a revenue figure of $4.4 billion. The company's manufacturing facility in York, Pa. suffered a three week strike which impacted production at the Milwaukee plant as well.

The quest for excellence begins with product design. Every component in a Harley bike is put through a rigorous design process that examines its manufacturability according to quality standards. Special software estimates the cost of each design proposal, so that expenses can be carefully controlled. Vendors hoping to supply various components to Harley-Davidson automatically receive this same information electronically, integrating it into the product development cycle.

Lasers and robots automate many production tasks. Components ready for assembly are loaded onto specially designed carts that swivel 360 degrees and can be lowered or raised to suit different workers or tasks. The carts then move into workstations where groups of employees assemble them into motorcycle frames. No motorcycle leaves a Harley-Davidson plant without a final quality inspection. A team of test drivers revs up and rides each motorcycle, checking operating quality and listening for the classic Harley sound.

© AP / WIDE WORLD PHOTOS

Employees play a critical role in Harley's production facilities. Working in teams, many employees are cross-trained to perform a variety of production tasks. Each work team is asked to look constantly for ways to build better motorcycles. The company has implemented many employee-generated ideas for improving equipment, factory layout, and production processes. They depend on their dealers and distributors as well, to create demand for their products and services.

Industry analysts say Harley-Davidson's rebirth and continued growth is intimately tied to its dedication to quality and efficiency in its operations and production processes. "Harley-Davidson succeeded because they aligned all stakeholders—from customers to shareholders to employees and suppliers," says consultant Stephen Shapiro. "They created the Harley-Davidson family, where everyone, including unions, are united in a common purpose."[1]

Critical Thinking Questions

As you read this chapter, consider the following questions as they relate to Harley-Davidson:

1. **How has focusing on quality in its operations and production supported Harley-Davidson's growth?**
2. **What external factors have led to this focus?**
3. **What future production decisions will Harley need to make if it is to continue to grow?**

Finding the most efficient and effective methods of producing the goods or services it sells to customers is an ongoing focus of nearly every type of business organization. Today more than ever, changing consumer expectations, technological advances, and increased competition are all forcing business organizations to rethink where, when, and how they will produce products or services.

Like Harley-Davidson, manufacturers have discovered that it is no longer enough simply to push products through the factory and onto the market. Consumers demand high quality at reasonable prices. They also expect manufacturers to deliver products in a timely manner. Firms that can't meet these expectations often face strong competition from businesses that can. To compete, many manufacturers are reinventing how they make their products by automating their factories, developing new production processes, using quality control techniques, and tightening their relationships with suppliers.

Service organizations are also facing challenges. Their customers are demanding better service, shorter waits, and more individualized attention. Just like manufacturers, service organizations are using new methods to deliver what customers need and want. Banks, for example, are using technology such as ATMs and the Internet to make their services more easily accessible to customers. Many universities and colleges now offer weekend and even online courses for students who find it more convenient. Tax services are filing tax returns via computer.

In this chapter, we examine how manufacturers and service firms manage and control the creation of products and services. We'll discuss production planning, including the choices firms must make concerning the type of production process they will use, the location where production will occur, the design of the facility, and the management of resources needed in production. Next, we'll explain routing and scheduling, two critical tasks for controlling production and operations efficiency. Many businesses are improving productivity by employing quality control methods and automation. We'll discuss these methods before summarizing some of the trends affecting production and operations management.

Production and Operations Management—An Overview

production
The creation of products and services by turning inputs, such as natural resources, raw materials, human resources, and capital, into outputs, which are products and services.

operations management
Management of the production process.

Production, the creation of products and services, is an essential function in every firm. Production turns inputs, such as natural resources, raw materials, human resources, and capital, into outputs, which are products and services. This process is shown in Exhibit 11.1. Managing this conversion process is the role of operations management.

In the 1980s, many Canadian industries, such as automotive and steel, lost customers to foreign competitors because their production systems could not provide the quality customers demanded. As a result, most Canadian companies, both large and small, now consider a focus on quality to be a central component of effective operations management.

The goal of customer satisfaction, closely linked to quality, is also an important part of effective production and operations. In the past, the manufacturing function in most companies was focused inward. Manufacturing had little contact with customers and didn't always understand their needs and desires. Today, however, stronger links between marketing and manufacturing have encouraged production managers to be more outwardly focused and to consider decisions in light

CONCEPT *in Action* >>>

With oil reserves second only to Saudi Arabia, Canada's Alberta province is set to become a vast supplier of crude oil worldwide. Unlike the smooth petroleum that gushes from Arabian wells, however, most of Alberta's black gold has to be mined from oil-rich sands. The process is rigorous: 400-ton trucks transport excavated bitumen to crushers and mixers that separate the sands from the oil and the resulting slurry travels miles of pipeline to North American refineries. What are key inputs in the mining of oil sands?

BLOOMBERG VIA GETTY IMAGES

of their effect on customer satisfaction. Service companies have also found that making operating decisions with customer satisfaction in mind can be a competitive advantage.

Operations managers, the personnel charged with managing and supervising the conversion process, play a vital role in today's firm. They often control about three-fourths of a firm's assets, including inventories, wages, and benefits. They work closely with other major functions of the firm, such as marketing, finance, accounting, and human resources, to help ensure that the firm produces its goods

EXHIBIT 11.1 > Production Process for Products and Services

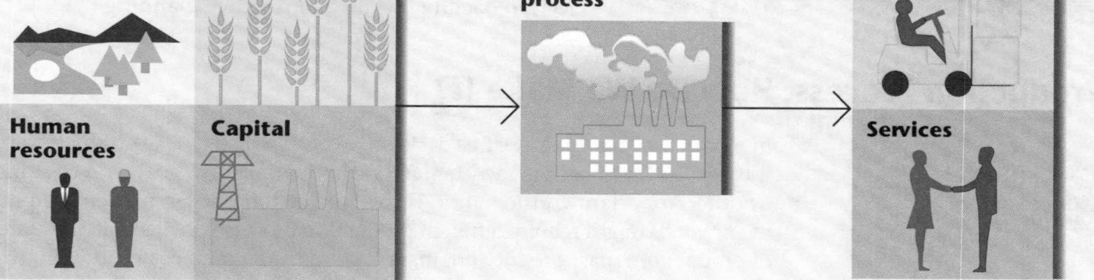

© SUNSET BOULEVARD/CORBIS SYGMA

CONCEPT *in Action* >>>

From its storied creation in post-war Italy to its big-screen immortalization in movies like Roman Holiday and Quadrophenia, the Vespa scooter has a reputation for romance, rebellion, and style. Manufactured by Italy's Piaggio, the Vespa's svelte, stainless-steel chassis and aeronautic-inspired designs are seen everywhere in Europe and more and more in the United States. The Piaggio Group presently operates factories in Italy, Spain, India, and China. What important production-planning decisions does Piaggio need to make as it considers expanding into overseas markets?

production planning
The aspect of operations management in which the firm considers the competitive environment and its own strategic goals in an effort to find the best production methods.

concept check

Define production.

What is production planning? Production control?

profitably and continually satisfies customers. They face the challenge of combining people and other resources to produce high quality goods on time and at a reasonable cost. Working with marketing, they help to decide which products to make or which services to offer. They become involved with the development and design of goods and determine what production processes will be most effective.

Production and operations management involves three main types of decisions that are made at three different stages:

1. Production planning. The first decisions facing operations managers come at the planning stage. At this stage, managers decide where, when, and how production will occur. They obtain resources and determine site locations.
2. Production control. At this stage, the decision-making process focuses on scheduling, controlling quality and costs, and the day-to-day operations of running a factory or service facility.
3. Improving production and operations. The final stage of operations management focuses on developing more efficient methods of producing the firm's goods or services.

These three types of decisions are ongoing and often occur simultaneously. In the following sections, we will take a closer look at the decisions and considerations firms face in each of these stages of production and operations management.

Gearing Up: Production Planning

An important part of operations management is production planning. During production planning, the firm considers the competitive environment and its own strategic goals in an effort to find the best production methods. Good production planning balances goals that might conflict, such as providing high quality service while keeping operating costs down, or keeping profits high while maintaining adequate inventories of finished products. Sometimes accomplishing all of these goals is quite difficult.

Production planning involves three phases. Long-term planning has a time frame of three to five years. It focuses on which goods to produce, how many to produce, and where they should be produced. Medium-term planning decisions cover about two years. They concern the layout of the factory or service facilities, where and how to obtain the resources needed for production, and labour issues. Short-term planning, with a one year time frame, converts these broader goals into specific production plans and materials management strategies.

Four important decisions must be made in production planning. They involve the type of production process that will be used, site selection, facility layout, and resource planning.

The Production Process: How Do We Make It?

LO 2

production process
The way in which a good is made.

In production planning, the first decision involves which type of production process—the way in which a good is made—best fits with the company's goals and customer demands. Another important consideration is the type of good or service being produced, as different goods might require different production processes. In general, there are three types of production: mass production, mass customization, and customization. In addition to production type, operations managers also classify production processes in two ways: by how inputs are converted into outputs and by the timing of the process.

mass production
The ability to manufacture many identical goods at once.

One for All: Mass Production Mass production, manufacturing many identical goods at once, was a product of the Industrial Revolution. Henry Ford's Model T automobile is a good example of mass production. Each car turned out by Ford's factory was identical, right down to its colour. If you wanted a car in any colour except black, you were out of luck. Canned goods, over-the-counter drugs, and household appliances are examples of goods that are still mass produced. The emphasis in mass production is on keeping manufacturing costs low by producing highly uniform products using repetitive and standardized processes. Mass production, therefore, relies heavily on standardization, mechanization, and specialization. As many products become more complicated to produce, however, mass production is becoming more complex. Automobile manufacturers, for example, must now incorporate more sophisticated electronics into their car designs. As a result, the number of assembly stations in most automobile manufacturing plants has increased.

mass customization
A manufacturing process in which goods are mass produced up to a point and then custom tailored to the needs or desires of individual customers.

Just for You: Customizing Goods In mass customization, goods are produced using mass production techniques but only up to a point. At that point, the product or service is custom tailored to the needs or desires of individual customers. Many Canadian furniture manufacturers use mass customization to produce couches and chairs to customer specifications, usually within 30 days. The basic frames used to make the furniture are the same, but automated machinery pre-cuts the colour and type of leather or fabric ordered by each customer. These coverings are then added to the frame through mass production techniques. Dynasty Furniture Mfg. Ltd of Mississauga, Ontario uses mass customization for its sofas and other products.

customization
The production of goods or services one at a time according to the specific needs or wants of individual customers.

job shop
A manufacturing firm that produces goods in response to customer orders.

Customization is the opposite of mass production. In customization, the firm produces goods or services one at a time according to the specific needs or wants of individual customers. Unlike mass customization, each product or service produced is unique. For example, a print shop might handle a variety of projects, including newsletters, brochures, stationery, and reports. Each print job varies in quantity, type of printing process, binding, colour of ink, and type of paper. A manufacturing firm that produces goods in response to customer orders is called a job shop.

Some types of service businesses also deliver customized services. Doctors, for instance, usually must consider the individual illnesses and circumstances of each patient before developing a customized treatment plan. Real estate agents also develop a customized service plan for each customer based on the type of house the person is selling or wants to buy. The differences between mass production, mass customization, and customization are summarized in Exhibit 11.2.

concept check

What is mass production?

Differentiate mass customization from customization.

Converting Inputs to Outputs Production involves converting *inputs* (raw materials, parts, human resources) into *outputs* (products or services). In a manufacturing company, the inputs, the production process, and the final outputs are usually obvious. Harley-Davidson, for instance, converts steel, rubber, paint, and other inputs into motorcycles. The production process in a service company involves a less obvious conversion. For example, a hospital converts the knowledge and skills of its medical personnel, along with equipment and supplies from a variety of sources, into health care services for patients. Exhibit 11.3 provides examples of the inputs and outputs used by several other types of businesses.

process manufacturing
A production process in which the basic input is *broken down* into one or more outputs (products).

assembly process
A production process in which the basic inputs are either *combined* to create the output or *transformed* into the output.

There are two basic processes for converting inputs into outputs. In process manufacturing, the basic input (raw materials, parts) is *broken down* into one or more outputs (products). For instance, bauxite (the input) is processed to extract aluminum (the output). The assembly process is just the opposite. The basic inputs, like parts, raw materials, or human resources, are either *combined* to create the output or *transformed* into the output. An airplane, for example, is created by assembling thousands of parts. Steel manufacturers use heat to transform iron and other materials into steel.

EXHIBIT 11.2 > Classification of Production Types

Mass Production	Mass Customization	Customization
Highly uniform products or services. Many products made sequentially.	Uniform standardized production to a point, then unique features added to each product.	Each product or service produced according to individual customer requirements.
Examples: Breakfast cereals, soft drinks, and computer keyboards.	**Examples:** Dell Computers, tract homes, and TaylorMade golf clubs.	**Examples:** Custom homes, legal services, and haircuts.

In services, customers may play a role in the transformation process. For example, a tax preparation service combines the knowledge of the tax preparer with the client's information about personal finances to complete tax returns.

continuous process
A production process that uses long production runs lasting days, weeks, or months without equipment shutdowns; generally used for high-volume, low-variety products with standardized parts.

Production Timing A second consideration in choosing a production process is timing. A continuous process uses long production runs that can last days, weeks, or months without equipment shutdowns. It is best for high-volume, low-variety products with standardized parts, such as nails, glass, and paper. Some services also use a continuous process. Your local electric company is one example. Per-unit costs are low, and production is easy to schedule.

CONCEPT *in Action* >>>

Mass customization has produced a thriving build-to-order society. This revolution in manufacturing is fueled, in part, by pop culture, where the compulsion to parade individuality is a hot commodity. Expressing oneself has never been easier. Consumers can design a new pair of sneakers with Vans Customs, build their own bags at Timbuk2, and customize a snowboard using the Burton Series 13 customization program—all while munching a pack of personalized M&M's candies. What developments have made mass customization a viable method of production?

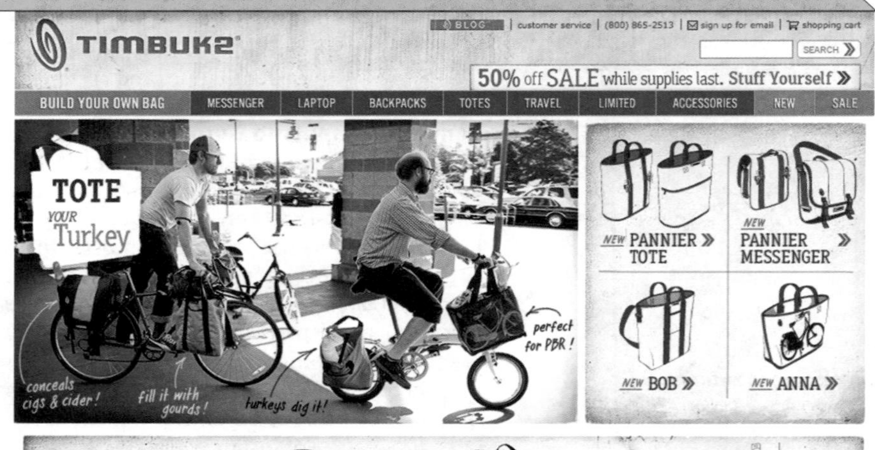

COURTESY OF TIMBUK2

EXHIBIT 11.3 > Converting Inputs to Outputs

Type of Organization	Input	Output
Airline	Pilots, crew, flight attendants, reservations system, ticketing agents, customers, airplanes, fuel, maintenance crews, ground facilities	Movement of customers and freight
Grocery store	Merchandise, building, clerks, supervisors, store fixtures, shopping carts, customers	Groceries for customers
High school	Faculty, curriculum, buildings, classrooms, library, auditorium, gymnasium, students, staff, supplies	Graduates, public service
Manufacturer	Machinery, raw materials, plant, workers, managers	Finished products for consumers and other firms
Restaurant	Food, cooking equipment, serving personnel, chefs, dishwashers, host, patrons, furniture, fixtures	Meals for patrons

intermittent process
A production process that uses short production runs to make batches of different products; generally used for low-volume, high-variety products.

In an **intermittent process**, short production runs are used to make batches of different products. Machines are shut down to change them to make different products at different times. This process is best for low-volume, high-variety products, such as those produced by mass customization or customization. Job shops are examples of firms using an intermittent process.

Although some service companies use continuous processes, most rely on intermittent processes. For instance, a restaurant preparing gourmet meals, a physician performing physical examinations or surgical operations, and an advertising agency developing ad campaigns for business clients all customize their services to suit each customer. They use the intermittent process. Note that their "production runs" might be very short—one grilled salmon or one eye exam at a time.

concept check

Define process manufacturing and the assembly process.

What is the difference between continuous and intermittent processes?

Location, Location, Location: Where Do We Make It?

A big decision that managers must make early in production and operations planning is where to put the facility, be it a factory or a service office. The facility's location affects operating and shipping costs and, ultimately, the price of the product or service and the company's ability to compete. Mistakes made at this stage can be expensive, because moving a factory or service facility once production begins is difficult and costly. Firms must weigh a number of factors to make the right decision.

Availability of Production Inputs As we discussed earlier, organizations need certain resources to produce products and services for sale. Access to these resources, or inputs, is a huge consideration in site selection. Executives must assess the availability of raw materials, parts, and equipment for each production site under consideration. The costs of shipping raw materials and finished goods can be as much as 25 percent of a manufacturer's total cost, so locating a factory where these and other costs are as low as possible can make a major contribution to a firm's success. Companies that use heavy or bulky raw materials, for example, might choose to be located near suppliers. Metal refiners want to be near ore deposits, oil refiners near oil fields, paper mills near forests, and food processors near farms.

The availability and cost of labour are also critical to both manufacturing and service businesses, and the unionization of local labour is another point to consider

Making Ethical Choices

SWEATING IT OUT AT NEW ERA CAP

As production manager for New Era Cap, the largest North American manufacturer of ball caps, you supervise operations at three factories. The oldest plant, in Derby, New York, has 600 workers and produces 120,000 caps a week, the lowest production rate of the three plants. The Derby factory also has the highest worker absentee rate of any plant, with as many as 13 percent of workers calling in sick on any given day.

In an attempt to bring the Derby plant up to the same level of efficiency as the other two, you've implemented several changes in the past few years. You've introduced new production schedules, made staff cuts, and tried to reduce absentee rates.

Unhappy with the changes you've made, Derby workers went on strike 10 months ago. After New Era executives refused to settle with the striking workers' demands for reduced hours and pay raises, their union, the Communications Workers of America (CWA), issued public statements accusing the Derby plant of "sweatshop" working conditions. At the CWA's urging, the United Students Against Sweatshops (USAS) started a campaign to get colleges and universities to boycott New Era caps. Several universities have already joined the boycott.

You are convinced that the Derby plant is not a sweatshop. You've shifted most of Derby's production to New Era's other two factories with minimal problems. The union now says it will end the strike and call off the boycott if the company grants immediate pay raises and health benefit increases to all Derby workers. You feel this is blackmail.

ETHICAL DILEMMA: Should you recommend that New Era's president agree to the union's demands?

SOURCES: "New Era Union Plans Boycott," *Buffalo Business First*, July 20, 2001; "Cap Maker Shifts Production after Walkout," *Buffalo Business First*, July 16, 2001; "New Era Says 'Sweatshop' Label Is False," *Buffalo Business First*, June 4, 2002; "New Era Cap Makes New Offer to CWA Strikers," *Buffalo Business First*, February 26, 2002; all sources downloaded from (http://buffalo.bizjournals.com).

in many industries. Payroll costs can vary widely from one location to another due to differences in the cost of living, the number of jobs available, and the size, skills, and productivity of the local workforce.

HOT Links

Learn more about the products Globe Motors manufactures at **(www.globe-motors.com).**

Low labour costs were one reason why Globe Motors, a manufacturer of motors and power steering systems for automotive, aerospace, and defence applications, chose Portugal as the site for its production facility. In addition to low labour costs, Portugal offers manufacturers the lowest operating costs in the European Union.[2]

Marketing Factors Businesses must also evaluate how their facility location will affect their ability to serve their customers. For some firms, it might not be necessary to be located near customers. Instead, the firm will need to assess the difficulty and costs of distributing its goods to customers from the chosen location.

Other firms might find that locating near customers can provide marketing advantages. When a factory or service centre is close to customers, the firm can often offer better service at a lower cost. Other firms might gain a competitive advantage by locating their facilities so that customers can easily buy their products or services. The location of competitors might also be a factor. Businesses with more than one facility might also need to consider how far to spread their locations to maximize market coverage. Globe Motors decided to build its new production facility in Europe because the continent is a major market for Globe's products. By building its motors closer to this large customer base, rather than exporting them to Europe after producing them elsewhere, Globe believes it will be able to improve customer service and response time.[3]

Manufacturing Environment Another factor to consider is the manufacturing environment in a potential location. Some localities have a strong existing manufacturing base. When a large number of manufacturers, perhaps in a certain industry, are already located in an area, that area is likely to offer greater availability of resources, such as manufacturing workers, better accessibility to suppliers and transportation, and other factors that can increase a plant's operating efficiency.

HOT Links

What characteristics contribute to a city's manufacturing climate? Find out by reading more at Industry Week's website: **(www.industryweek.com).**

Industry Week magazine conducts a regular survey of the manufacturing climate offered by areas around the world. Each area is rated on the productivity of its manufacturing sector, the percentage of the local workforce employed in manufacturing, the contribution of manufacturing to the area's overall economy, and several other factors. One such area that has been identified as a global "hot spot" is Turkey.[4]

Local Incentives Incentives offered by countries, states, or cities might also influence site selection. Tax breaks are a common incentive. A locality might reduce the amount of taxes the firm will pay on income, real estate, utilities, or payroll. Local governments also sometimes offer exemption from certain regulations or financial assistance to attract or keep production facilities in their area. For example, Portugal helped entice Globe Motors by offering $7.6 million USD in financial incentives, as well as tax breaks and assistance with employee-training programs.[5]

concept check

Discuss how each of the following impacts the location of production:

- Availability of production inputs
- Marketing factors
- Manufacturing environment
- Local incentives
- International location considerations

International Location Considerations Like Globe Motors, many manufacturers have chosen to move much of their production to international locations in recent years. There are often sound financial reasons for considering this step. Labour costs are considerably lower in countries like Singapore, China, and Mexico. Foreign countries might also have fewer regulations governing how factories operate. A foreign location might place production closer to new markets. As we've seen, all of these considerations motivated Globe Motors to build a new production facility in Portugal.

Designing the Facility

After the site location decision has been made, the next focus in production planning is the facility's layout. Here, the goal is to determine the most efficient and effective design for the particular production process. A manufacturer might opt for a U-shaped production line, for example, rather than a long, straight one to allow products and workers to move more quickly from one area to another.

Service organizations must also consider layout, but they are more concerned with how it affects customer behaviour. It might be more convenient for a hospital to place its freight elevators in the centre of the building, for example, but doing so might block the flow of patients, visitors, and medical personnel between floors and departments.

There are three *main* types of facility layouts: process, product, and fixed-position layouts. All three are illustrated in Exhibit 11.4. Cellular manufacturing is another type of facility layout.

process layout
A facility arrangement in which work flows according to the production process. All workers performing similar tasks are grouped together, and products pass from one workstation to another.

Process Layout: All Welders Stand Here The process layout arranges workflow around the production process. All workers performing similar tasks are grouped together. Products pass from one workstation to another (but not necessarily to every workstation). For example, all grinding would be done in one area, all assembling in another, and all inspection in yet another. The process layout is best for firms that produce small numbers of a wide variety of products, typically using general-purpose machines that can be changed rapidly to new operations for different product designs. For example, a manufacturer of custom machinery would use a process layout.

product (assembly line) layout
A facility arrangement in which workstations or departments are arranged in a line with products moving along the line.

Product Layout: Moving Down the Line Products that require a continuous or repetitive production process use the product (or assembly line) layout. When large quantities of a product must be processed on an ongoing basis, the workstations or departments are arranged in a line with products moving along the line. Automobile and appliance manufacturers, as well as food-processing plants, usually use a product layout. Service companies may also use a product layout for routine processing operations. For example, overnight film processors use assembly line techniques.

fixed-position layout
A facility arrangement in which the product stays in one place and workers and machinery move to it as needed.

Fixed-Position Layout: Staying Put Some products cannot be put on an assembly line or moved about in a plant. A fixed-position layout lets the product stay in one place while workers and machinery move to it as needed. Products that are impossible to move—ships, airplanes, and construction projects—are typically produced using a fixed-position layout. Limited space at a project site often means that parts of the product must be assembled at other sites, transported to the fixed site, and then assembled. Other examples of the fixed-position layout are on-site services like housecleaning services, pest control, and landscaping.

EXHIBIT 11.4 > Facility Layouts

Process layout arranges workflow around the production process. All workers performing similar tasks are grouped together.

© RIA NOVOSTI / ALAMY

Products that require a continuous or repetitive production process use the **product layout**.

© LOU LINWEI / ALAMY

A **fixed-position layout** lets the product stay in one place while workers and machinery move to it as needed.

© JUSTIN KASE Z07Z / ALAMY

cellular manufacturing
Production technique that uses small, self-contained production units, each performing all or most of the tasks necessary to complete a manufacturing order.

Cellular Manufacturing: A Start-to-Finish Focus Cellular manufacturing combines some aspects of both product and fixed-position layout. Work cells are small, self-contained production units that include several machines and workers arranged in a compact, sequential order. Each work cell performs all or most of the tasks necessary to complete a manufacturing order. There are usually between 5 and 10 workers in a cell, and they are trained to perform all of the steps in the production process. The goal is to create a team environment where team members are involved in production from beginning to end. Clothing manufacturing can use cellular manufacturing by having small work cells completing all the work of each order.

Pulling It Together: Resource Planning

As part of the production-planning process, firms must ensure that the resources needed for production, such as raw materials, parts, and equipment, will be available at strategic moments in the production process. This can be a huge challenge. The components used to build just one Boeing airplane, for instance, number in the millions. Cost is also an important factor. In many industries, the cost of materials and supplies used in the production process amounts to as much as half of sales revenues. Resource planning is therefore a big part of any firm's production strategy.

bill of material
A list of the items and the number of each required to make a given product.

purchasing
The process of buying production inputs from various sources; also called *procurement*.

Resource planners begin by specifying which raw materials, parts, and components will be required, and when, in order to produce finished goods. To determine the amount of each item needed, the expected quantity of finished goods to be produced must be forecast. A bill of material is then drawn up that lists the items and the number of each required to make the product. Purchasing, or *procurement*, is the process of buying production inputs from various sources.

make-or-buy decision
The determination by a firm of whether to make its production materials or buy them from outside sources.

outsourcing
The purchase of items from an outside source rather than making them internally.

Make or Buy? The firm must decide whether to make its production materials or buy them from outside sources. This is the make-or-buy decision. The quantity of items needed is one consideration. If a part is used in only one of many products, buying the part might be more cost-effective than making it. Buying standard items, such as screws, bolts, rivets, and nails, is usually cheaper and easier than producing them internally. Sometimes purchasing larger components from another manufacturing firm is cost-effective as well. Purchasing items from an outside source instead of making them internally is called outsourcing. Harley-Davidson, for example, purchases its tires, brake systems, and other motorcycle components from other businesses that make them to Harley's specifications. If a product has special design features that need to be kept secret to protect a competitive advantage, however, a firm might decide to produce all parts internally.

HOT Links

How do companies decide whether to make or buy? Find out more at the Outsourcing Institute, a professional association where buyers and sellers network and connect: **(www.outsourcing.com)**.

In deciding whether to make or buy, a firm must also consider whether outside sources can provide high-quality supplies in a reliable manner. Having to shut down production because vital parts weren't delivered on time can be a costly disaster. Just as bad are inferior parts or materials, which can damage a firm's reputation for producing high-quality goods. Therefore, firms that buy some or all of their production materials from outside sources should pay close attention to building strong relationships with quality suppliers.

inventory
The supply of goods that a firm holds for use in production or for sale to customers.

inventory management
The determination of how much of each type of inventory a firm will keep on hand and the ordering, receiving, storing, and tracking of inventory.

Inventory Management: Not Just Parts A firm's inventory is the supply of goods it holds for use in production or for sale to customers. Deciding how much inventory to keep on hand is one of the biggest challenges facing operations managers. With large inventories, the firm can meet most production and customer demands. Buying in large quantities can also allow a company to take advantage of quantity discounts. On the other hand, large inventories can tie up the firm's money, are expensive to store, and can become obsolete.

Inventory management involves deciding how much of each type of inventory to keep on hand and the ordering, receiving, storing, and tracking of it. The goal of inventory management is to keep down the costs of ordering and holding inventories while maintaining enough on hand for production and sales. Good inventory management enhances product quality, makes operations more efficient, and increases profits. Poor inventory management can result in dissatisfied customers, financial difficulties, and even bankruptcy.

One way to determine the best inventory levels is to look at three costs: the cost of holding inventory, the cost of reordering frequently, and the cost of not keeping enough inventories on hand. Managers must measure all three costs and try to minimize them.

perpetual inventory
A continuously updated list of inventory levels, orders, sales, and receipts.

To control inventory levels, managers often track the use of certain inventory items. Most companies keep a perpetual inventory, a continuously updated list of inventory levels, orders, sales, and receipts, for all major items. Today, companies often use computers to track inventory levels, calculate order quantities, and issue purchase orders at the right times.

materials requirement planning (MRP)
A computerized system of controlling the flow of resources and inventory. A master schedule is used to ensure that the materials, labour, and equipment needed for production are at the right places in the right amounts at the right times.

Computerized Resource Planning Many manufacturing companies have adopted computerized systems to control the flow of resources and inventory. Materials requirement planning (MRP) is one such system. MRP uses a master schedule to ensure that the materials, labour, and equipment needed for production are at the right places in the right amounts at the right times. The schedule is based on forecasts of demand for the company's products. It says exactly what will be manufactured during the next few weeks or months and when the work will take place. Sophisticated computer programs coordinate all the elements of MRP. The computer comes up with materials requirements by comparing production needs to the materials the company already has on hand. Orders are placed so that items will be on hand when they are needed for production. MRP helps ensure a smooth flow of finished products.

manufacturing resource planning II (MRPII)
A complex computerized system that integrates data from many departments to allow managers to forecast and assess the impact of production plans on profitability more accurately.

enterprise resource planning (ERP)
A computerized resource-planning system that incorporates information about the firm's suppliers and customers with its internally generated data.

Manufacturing resource planning II (MRPII) was developed in the late 1980s to expand on MRP. It uses a complex computerized system to integrate data from many departments, including finance, marketing, accounting, engineering, and manufacturing. MRPII can generate a production plan for the firm as well as management reports, forecasts, and financial statements. The system lets managers make more accurate forecasts and assess the impact of production plans on profitability. If one department's plans change, the effects of these changes on other departments are transmitted throughout the company.

Whereas MRP and MRPII systems are focused internally, enterprise resource planning (ERP) systems go a step further and incorporate information about the

CONCEPT *in Action* >>>

Wal-Mart's retail dominance is built upon advanced logistics and inventory management. The company's vendor-managed inventory system puts the burden on suppliers to maintain stock until needed in stores and radio frequency identification tags (RFID) help automate the flow of goods. Wal-Mart's remarkable 2:1 sales-to-inventory ratio is expected to shrink further to a theoretical "zero inventory" state in which it won't pay for products until they're purchased by consumers. What costs are associated with keeping too much or too little inventory?

©TERRI MILLER/E-VISUAL COMMUNICATIONS INC.

CONCEPT *in Action* >>>

Manufacturing product labels for over 9,000 Estée Lauder cosmetics products would be impossible without enterprise resource planning (ERP). A daily data feed between ERP systems at Estée Lauder and label-supplier Topflight ensures that machines produce only the labels necessary for the next production run. The data-transfer link is flexible enough to accommodate dynamic design changes to colours and label copy while eliminating purchase orders, invoices, and price negotiations. What quality and cost benefits does ERP deliver to manufacturers and

firm's suppliers and customers into the flow of data. ERP unites all of a firm's major departments into a single software program. For instance, production can call up sales information and know immediately how many units must be produced to meet customer orders. By providing information about the availability of resources, including both human resources and materials needed for production, the system allows for better cost control and eliminates production delays. The system automatically notes any changes, such as the closure of a plant for maintenance and repairs on a certain date or a supplier's inability to meet a delivery date, so that all functions can adjust accordingly. Both large and small organizations use ERP to improve operations.

Keeping the Goods Flowing: Supply Chain Management

In the past, the relationship between purchasers and suppliers was often competitive and antagonistic. Businesses used many suppliers and switched among them frequently. During contract negotiations, each side would try to get better terms at the expense of the other. Communication between purchasers and suppliers was often limited to purchase orders and billing statements.

Today, however, many firms are moving toward a new concept in supplier relationships. The emphasis is increasingly on developing a strong supply chain. The supply chain can be thought of as the entire sequence of securing inputs, producing goods, and delivering goods to customers. If any links in this process are weak, chances are that customers—the end point of the supply chain—will end up dissatisfied.

supply chain
The entire sequence of securing inputs, producing goods, and delivering goods to customers.

Effective supply chain strategies reduce costs. For example, integration of the shipper and customer's supply chains allows companies to automate more processes and save time. Technology also improves supply chain efficiency by tracking goods through the various supply chain stages and also helping with logistics. With better information about production and inventory, companies can order and receive goods at the optimal point to keep inventory holding costs low.

Companies also need contingency plans for supply chain disruptions. Is there an alternative source of supply if a blizzard closes the airport so that cargo planes can't land or a drought causes crop failures? By thinking ahead, companies can avert major losses. The length and distance involved in a supply line is also a consideration. Importing parts from or outsourcing manufacturing to Asia creates a long supply chain for a manufacturer in Europe or Canada. Perhaps there are closer suppliers or manufacturers who can meet a company's needs at a lower overall cost. Companies should also re-evaluate outsourcing decisions periodically.

Strategies for Supply Chain Management

Ensuring a strong supply chain requires that firms implement supply chain management strategies. Supply chain management focuses on smoothing transitions along the supply chain, with the ultimate goal of satisfying customers with quality products and services. A critical element of effective supply chain management is to develop tighter bonds with suppliers. In many cases, this means reducing the number of suppliers used and asking those suppliers to offer more services or better prices in return for an ongoing relationship. Instead of being viewed as "outsiders" in the production process, many suppliers are now playing an important role in supporting the operations of their customers. They are expected to meet higher quality standards, offer suggestions that can help reduce production costs, and even contribute to the design of new products. The Expanding Around the Globe box shows the critical role of supply-chain management for global companies.

supply chain management
The process of smoothing transitions along the supply chain, so that the firm can satisfy its customers with quality products and services; focuses on developing tighter bonds with suppliers.

Talk to Us: Improving Supplier Communications Effective supply chain management requires the development of strong communications with suppliers. Technology,

CONCEPT *in Action* >>>

Managing an efficient supply chain is critical for businesses, especially when the product being delivered is a bouquet of fresh-cut flowers. To ensure that only the freshest, most colourful floral arrangement arrives for that special someone, Internet florist ProFlowers ships directly from the flower fields, bypassing the middleman. This direct-from-the-grower strategy, combined with coordinated carrier scheduling and a 100 percent product-inspection policy, enables ProFlowers to deliver flowers twice as fresh as the competition. What strategies help businesses create and maintain an effective supply chain?

AP/WIDE WORLD PHOTOS

e-procurement
The process of purchasing supplies and materials using the Internet.

particularly the Internet, is providing new ways to do this. E-procurement, the process of purchasing supplies and materials online, is booming. Some manufacturing firms use the Internet to keep key suppliers informed about their requirements. Intel, for example, has set up a special website for its suppliers and potential suppliers. Would-be

Expanding Around The Globe

SOPHISTICATED SUPPLY-CHAIN STRATEGIES KEEP PRODUCTS ON THE MOVE

Headquartered in Tokyo but with offices around the world, shipping company MOL is taking integrating with its customers to new levels. It is joining its customers in a series of joint ventures to build and operate dedicated vessels for as long as 25 years. One such joint venture teamed MOL with a Chinese steel mill, to build and sail ships bringing Brazilian iron ore and coal across the Pacific Ocean for processing.

Sophisticated supply-chain systems that control every aspect of production and transportation are the key to making offshore manufacturing work. Supply-chain software that monitors operations and continually makes adjustments ensures that all processes are running at peak efficiency. By tightly mapping an entire sequence—from order to final delivery—and by automating it as much as possible, supply-chain management can deliver products from across the world while at the same time cutting costs. Companies that can carry a small inventory and get paid faster improve their cash flow and profitability.

Acer, a $7 billion Taiwanese computer and electronics maker, brings components from around the world and assembles them at factories in Taiwan and mainland China—into everything from PC notebooks to TVs. It then reverses the flow by shipping these products to international buyers. "In 2004, Acer sold 4 million portable systems. Without a solid supply-chain infrastructure behind us, we couldn't hope to do it," says Sumit Agnihotry, Acer's American director of notebook product marketing.

The synchronizing of trade is essential. If goods don't get into the stores in time, sales might be lost or the company might have to carry larger inventories to avoid sell-outs, which would cut into its profits. Companies need to continually monitor demand and react quickly by adjusting production. "This gets increasingly difficult when the supply chain stretches across thousands of miles and a dozen time zones," says David Bovet, managing director of Mercer Management Consulting, a Boston-based firm that advises on business tactics. "There are strategies that smart companies are using to bring costs down to earth. Getting the most of lower labour costs overseas requires an emphasis on transportation, and supply-chain skills are a required core competency," he says. His advice to global manufacturers: Cooperate with shippers and integrate supply chains into one cohesive system.

The acknowledged master of supply-chain dynamics is Dell, with its global logistics control room lined with big screens that monitor its shipping lanes at all times. Alongside Dell executives are representatives of its logistics suppliers for guidance and quick action if anything goes wrong.

Risk is the name of the game when it comes to international trade, and companies need to decide whether to play it safe with extra inventory or scramble if a disaster like a port strike occurs. Either way, they need to have contingency plans and be ready to react, and solid supply-chain strategies will ensure they are prepared for any eventuality.[6]

Critical Thinking Questions

- Why are solid supply-chain strategies so important?
- What problems is a company likely to experience without such strategies in place?

suppliers can visit the site to get information about doing business with Intel; once they are approved, they can access a secure area to make bids on Intel's current and future resource needs.

The Internet also streamlines purchasing by providing firms with quick access to a huge database of information about the products and services of hundreds of potential suppliers. Many large manufacturers now participate in *reverse auctions* online, whereby the manufacturer posts its specifications for the materials it requires. Potential suppliers then bid against each other to get the job. Reverse auctions can slash procurement costs.

However, there are risks with reverse auctions. For example, it can be difficult to establish and build ongoing relationships with specific suppliers using reverse auctions, because the job ultimately goes to the lowest bidder. Therefore, reverse auctions might not be an effective procurement process for critical production materials.[7]

electronic data interchange (EDI)
The electronic exchange of information between two trading partners.

Another communications tool is **electronic data interchange (EDI)**, in which two trading partners exchange information electronically. EDI can be conducted via a linked computer system or over the Internet. The advantages of exchanging information with suppliers electronically include speed, accuracy, and lowered communication costs.

Dana Corporation, a manufacturer of auto and truck frames, has only one customer, New United Motor Manufacturing Inc. (NUMMI), a joint venture between Toyota and General Motors. In the past, NUMMI could give Dana only a six-week production forecast. A fax was sent to Dana each day updating NUMMI's needs. Dana and NUMMI then installed an EDI system that continually alerts Dana about NUMMI's purchasing requirements on an hourly basis. As a result, Dana has been able to cut its inventory, smooth its production scheduling, and meet NUMMI's needs more efficiently and rapidly.[8]

concept check

What four important decisions must be made in production planning?

What factors does a firm consider when making a site selection decision?

How is technology being used in resource planning?

Production and Operations Control

Every company needs to have systems in place to see that production and operations are carried out as planned and to correct errors when they are not. The coordination of materials, equipment, and human resources to achieve production and operating efficiencies is called *production control*. Two of its key aspects are routing and scheduling.

Routing: Where to Next?

routing
The aspect of production control that involves setting out the workflow, the sequence of machines and operations through which the product or service progresses from start to finish.

value-stream mapping
Routing technique that uses simple icons to visually represent the flow of materials and information from suppliers through the factory and to customers.

Routing is the first step in production control. It sets out a workflow, that is, the sequence of machines and operations through which a product or service progresses from start to finish. Routing depends on the type of goods being produced and the facility layout. Good routing procedures increase productivity and cut unnecessary costs.

One useful tool for routing is **value-stream mapping**, where production managers "map" the flow from suppliers through the factory to customers. Simple icons represent the materials and information needed at various points in the flow. Value-stream mapping can help identify where bottlenecks might occur in the production process and is a valuable tool for visualizing how to improve production routing.

Electronics manufacturer Rockwell Collins used value-stream mapping to automate more of its purchasing operations. The company evaluated 23 areas to identify where process changes would improve efficiency. Based on the study, managers decided to automate three steps: request for quote, quote receipt and total purchase cost, and automated purchase order. The company implemented a new system that automatically sends requests for quotes to appropriate suppliers and evaluates the responses to determine which best meets Rockwell Collins' requirements. Once in place, the new systems allowed purchasing professionals to focus on strategic rather than routine activities.[9]

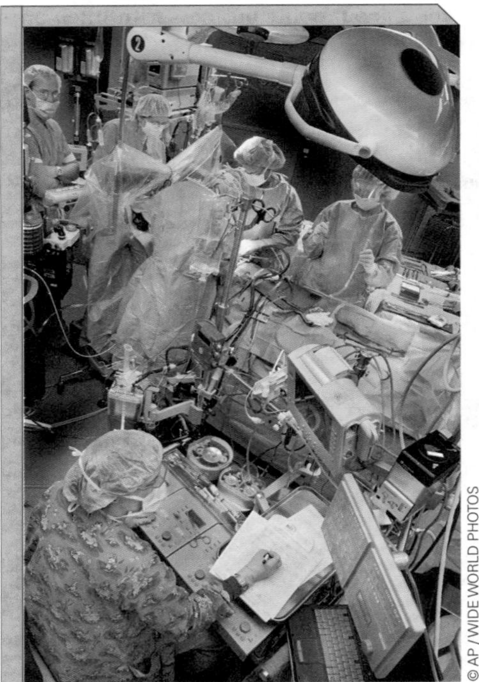
© AP/WIDE WORLD PHOTOS

CONCEPT *in Action* >>>

Routing and scheduling are just as important to service organizations as they are to manufacturing firms. Hospitals, for instance, must carefully schedule the equipment, personnel, and facilities needed to conduct patient surgeries and other treatments. What are some of the consequences if we do not properly plan the route and scheduling of services?

Scheduling: When Do We Do It?

Closely related to routing is scheduling. Scheduling involves specifying and controlling the time required for each step in the production process. The operations manager prepares timetables showing the most efficient sequence of production and then tries to ensure that the necessary materials and labour are in the right place at the right time.

Scheduling is important to both manufacturing and service firms. The production manager in a factory schedules material deliveries, work shifts, and production processes. Trucking companies schedule drivers, clerks, truck maintenance, and repair with customer transportation needs. Scheduling at a polytechnic, college, or university entails deciding when to offer which courses, in which classrooms, with which instructors. A museum must schedule its special exhibits, ship the works to be displayed, market its services, and conduct educational programs and tours.

Scheduling can range from simple to complex. Giving numbers to customers waiting to be served in a bakery and making interview appointments with job applicants are examples of simple scheduling. Organizations that must produce large quantities of products or services, or service a diverse customer base, face more complex scheduling problems.

Three common scheduling tools used for complex situations are Gantt charts, the critical path method, and PERT.

Tracking Progress with Gantt Charts Named after their originator, Henry Gantt, Gantt charts are bar graphs plotted on a timeline that show the relationship between scheduled and actual production. Exhibit 11.5 is an example. On the left, the chart lists the activities required to complete the job or project. Both the scheduled time and the actual time required for each activity are shown, so the manager can easily judge progress.

Gantt charts are most helpful when only a few tasks are involved, when task times are relatively long (days or weeks rather than hours), and when job routes are short and simple. One of the biggest shortcomings of Gantt charts is that they are static. They also fail to show how tasks are related. These problems can be solved, however, by using two other scheduling techniques, the critical path method and PERT.

scheduling
The aspect of production control that involves specifying and controlling the time required for each step in the production process.

Gantt charts
Bar graphs plotted on a timeline that show the relationship between scheduled and actual production.

The Big Picture: Critical Path Method and PERT To control large projects, operations managers need to closely monitor resources, costs, quality, and budgets. They also must be able to see the "big picture"—the interrelationships of the many tasks necessary to complete the project. Finally, they must be able to revise scheduling and divert resources quickly if any tasks fall behind schedule. The critical path method (CPM) and the program evaluation and review technique (PERT) are related project management tools that were developed in the 1950s to help managers accomplish this.

In the critical path method (CPM), the manager identifies all of the activities required to complete the project, the relationships between these activities, and the order in which they need to be completed. Then, he or she develops a diagram that uses arrows to show how the tasks are dependent on each other. The longest path through these linked activities is called the critical path. If the tasks on the critical path are not completed on time, the entire project will fall behind schedule.

To understand better how CPM works, look at Exhibit 11.6, which shows a CPM diagram for constructing a house. All of the tasks required to finish the house and an

critical path method (CPM)
A scheduling tool that enables a manager to determine the critical path of activities for a project—the activities that will cause the entire project to fall behind schedule if they are not completed on time.

critical path
The longest path through the linked activities in a critical path method network.

EXHIBIT 11.5 > A Typical Gantt Chart

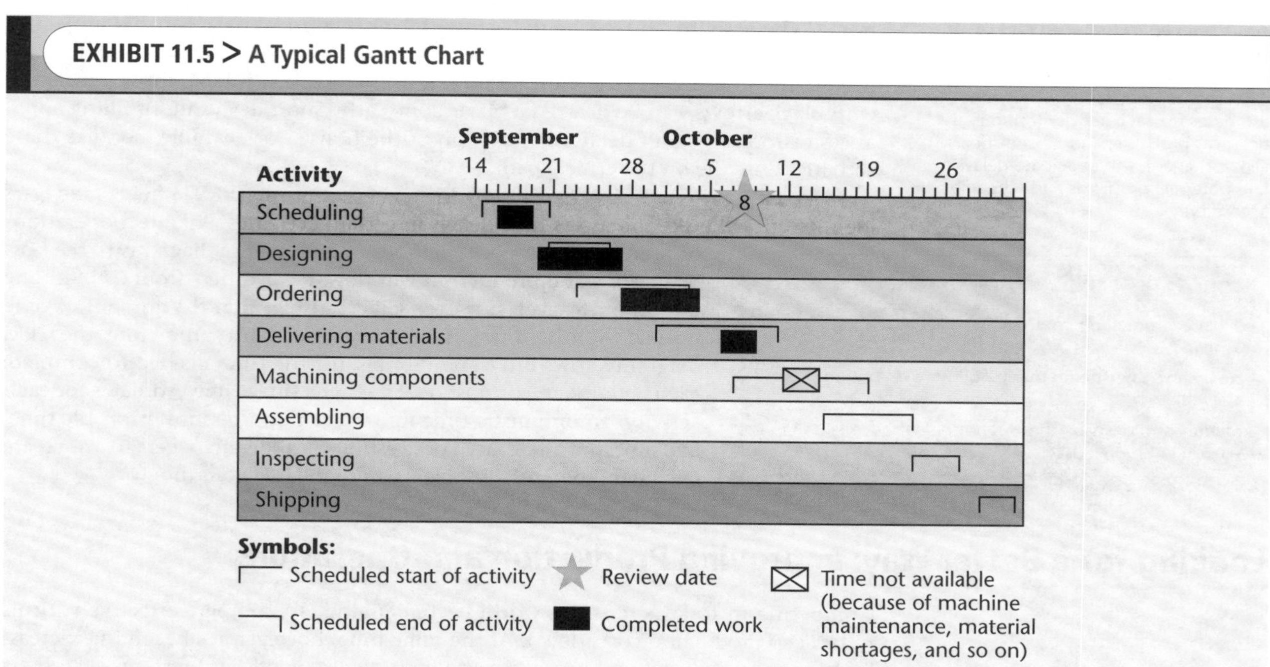

estimated time for each have been identified. The arrows indicate the links between the various steps and their required sequence. As you can see, most of the jobs to be done can't be started until the house's foundation and frame are completed. It will take five days to finish the foundation and an additional seven days to erect the house

EXHIBIT 11.6 > A CPM Network for Building a House

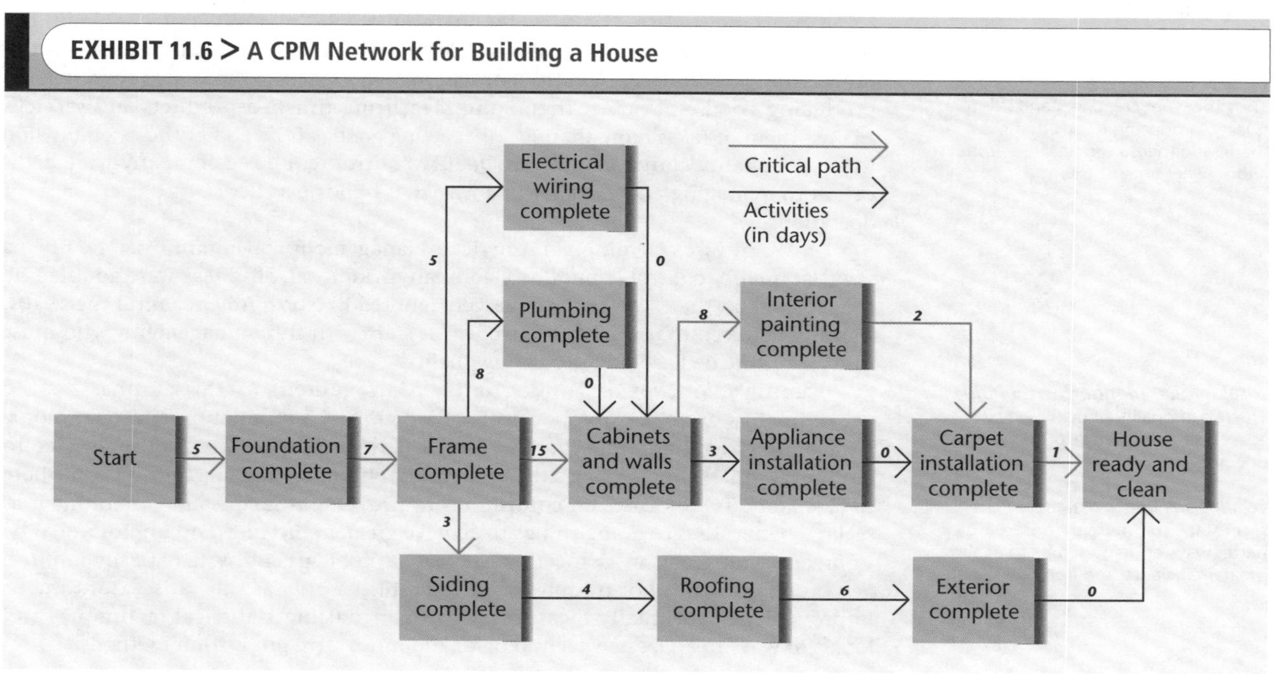

program evaluation and review technique (PERT)
A scheduling tool that is similar to the CPM method but assigns three time estimates for each activity (optimistic, most probable, and pessimistic); allows managers to anticipate delays and potential problems and schedule accordingly.

frame. The activities linked by red arrows form the critical path for this project. It tells us that the fastest possible time the house can be built is 38 days, the total time needed for all of the critical path tasks. The non-critical path jobs, those connected with black arrows, can be delayed a bit or done early. Short delays in installing appliances or roofing won't delay construction of the house, for example, because these activities don't lie on the critical path.

Like CPM, **program evaluation and review technique (PERT)** helps managers identify critical tasks and assess how delays in certain activities will affect operations or production. In both methods, managers use diagrams to see how operations and production will flow. PERT differs from CPM in one important respect, however. CPM assumes that the amount of time needed to finish a task is known with certainty; therefore, the CPM diagram shows only one number for the time needed to complete each activity. In contrast, PERT assigns three time estimates for each activity: an optimistic time for completion, the most probable time, and a pessimistic time. These estimates allow managers to anticipate delays and potential problems and schedule accordingly.

concept check

What is production control, and what are its key aspects?

How can value-stream mapping improve routing efficiency?

Identify and describe three commonly used scheduling tools.

Looking for a Better Way: Improving Production and Operations

Competing in today's business world is challenging. To compete effectively, firms must keep production costs down. At the same time, however, it's becoming increasingly complex to produce and deliver the high-quality goods and services customers demand. Methods to help meet these challenges include quality management techniques, lean manufacturing, and automation.

Putting Quality First

quality
Goods and services that meet customer expectations by providing reliable performance.

Successful businesses recognize that quality and productivity must go hand in hand. **Quality** goods and services meet customer expectations by providing reliable performance. Defective products waste materials and time, increasing costs. Worse, poor quality causes customer dissatisfaction, which usually means lost sales.

quality control
The process of creating standards for quality, producing goods that meet them, and measuring finished products and services against them.

A consumer measures quality by how well a good serves its purpose. From the company's point of view, quality is the degree to which a good conforms to a set of predetermined standards. **Quality control** involves creating those quality standards, producing goods that meet them, and measuring finished products and services against them. It takes more than just inspecting goods at the end of the assembly line to ensure quality control, however. Quality control requires a company-wide dedication to managing and working in a way that builds excellence into every facet of operations.

Dr. W. Edwards Deming, an American management consultant, was the first to say that quality control should be a company-wide goal. His ideas were adopted by the Japanese in the 1950s but were largely ignored in North America until the 1970s. Deming believed that quality control must start with top management, who must foster a culture dedicated to producing quality.

total quality management (TQM)
The use of quality principles in all aspects of a company's production and operations.

continuous improvement
A constant commitment to seeking better ways of doing things to achieve greater efficiency and improved quality.

Deming's concept of **Total Quality Management (TQM)** emphasizes the use of quality principles in all aspects of a company's production and operations. It recognizes that all employees involved with bringing a product or service to customers—marketing, purchasing, accounting, shipping, manufacturing—contribute to its quality. TQM focuses on **continuous improvement**, a constant commitment to seeking better ways of doing things to achieve greater efficiency and improve quality. Company-wide teams work together to prevent problems and systematically improve key processes instead of troubleshooting problems only as they arise. Continuous improvement continually measures performance using statistical techniques and looks for ways to apply new technologies and innovative production methods.

Sustainable Business, Sustainable World

One of the ways that a sustainable business can make the most impact is in its operations. One company that is making a real effort to be truly sustainable is the Hudson's Bay Company (Hbc). The Hudson's Bay Company, Canada's largest diversified general merchandise retailer, operates the Bay, Zellers, Home Outfitters, and Fields. It's commitment to sustainability can be seen very clearly in the statement on the front of its Corporate Social Responsibility Report: *"At Hbc, we understand that every one of us has a role to play in creating the kind of world we want to live in and pass on to our children. The possibilities are boundless when we act with a Global Mind."*

This global mindset is evident in Hbc's three core principles designed to reduce its environmental footprint: "#1. Continuous evaluation of our environmental policies and procedures; #2. Environmental improvement in our operations; and #3. Educating associates, customers and partners."

Hbc's Environmental Sustainability Team meets monthly and reports directly to Hbc senior management. It conducts annual audits of the company's operations to determine the amount of waste diverted from landfill, the amount of packaging and harmful PVCs in its private label products, energy consumption by store, and greenhouse gas (GHG) emissions. And most importantly, it continually looks for ways to improve its policies and practices.

Some of the new environmental improvements that Hbc introduced in its operations in 2007 include committing to zero waste, recycling in its stores, preserving water, opening green stores, increasing its number of biodiesel fuel trucks, and performing lighting retrofits. In fact Hbc's head office became the first office tower in Canada to be certified zero waste by Zero Waste International Alliance. This distinction for achieving a more than 95% diversion rate of waste away from landfills was also awarded to two other Hbc office buildings and seven of its retail locations. Now that's commitment. In 2007 Hbc also opened its greenest Zellers ever in Waterdown, Ontario. Some of the energy conservations measures include the use of two wind generators and solar panels to provide energy, a white roof to reflect heat, energy recovery ventilators, and heating/ventilating and air conditioning units that use non-ozone depleting refrigerant.

Hbc's efforts have won it several awards, including a 2007 Ontario Waste Minimization Award. This Facilities Platinum Award was presented to the Simpson Tower on Bay Street in Toronto in recognition of excellence and commitment to a sustainable environment. As well, the BOMA Go Green Plus Certificate of Achievement was awarded to the same building for environmental excellence in the management of the building.

How does your new knowledge of Hbc's commitment to environmental sustainability affect you and your decisions regarding where to shop? Should companies become more sustainable in their operations because it's the right thing to do for our planet or because it's better for the bottom line—leading to greater revenue generation by more conscious consumers, or both? Do you think that society is becoming sufficiently more conscious that environmental sustainability will pay off in terms of more customers, or does it simply pay off in more efficient operations? Is there an integrative effect?

SOURCE: www.hbc.com

Six Sigma
A quality control process that relies on defining what needs to be done to ensure quality, measuring and analyzing production results statistically, and finding ways of improving and controlling quality.

Another quality control method is the Six Sigma quality program. Six Sigma is a company-wide process that focuses on measuring the number of defects that occur and systematically eliminating them to get as close to "zero defects" as possible. In fact, Six Sigma quality aims to have every process produce no more than 3.4 defects per million. Six Sigma focuses on designing products that not only have fewer defects but also satisfy customer needs. A key process of Six Sigma is called *DMAIC*. This stands for Define, Measure, Analyze, Improve, and Control. Employees at all levels define what needs to be done to ensure quality, then measure and analyze production results using statistics to see if the standards are met. They are also charged with finding ways of improving and controlling quality.

HOT Links

Learn more about Six Sigma at the Knowledge Management Group's website, **(www.tkmg.org/services.html)**.

General Electric was one of the first companies to institute Six Sigma throughout the organization. All GE employees are trained in Six Sigma concepts, and many analysts believe this has given GE a competitive manufacturing advantage. Service firms have applied Six Sigma to their quality initiatives as well.

ISO 9000
A set of five technical standards of quality management created by the International Organization for Standardization to provide a uniform way of determining whether manufacturing plants and service organizations conform to sound quality procedures.

ISO 14000
A set of technical standards designed by the International Organization for Standardization to promote clean production processes to protect the environment.

Worldwide Excellence: International Quality Standards The International Organization for Standardization (ISO), located in Belgium, is an industry organization that has developed standards of quality that are used by businesses around the world. ISO 9000, introduced in the 1980s, is a set of five technical standards designed to offer a uniform way of determining whether manufacturing plants and service organizations conform to sound quality procedures. To register, a company must go through an audit of its manufacturing and customer service processes, covering everything from how it designs, produces, and installs its goods to how it inspects, packages, and markets them. More than 500,000 organizations worldwide have met ISO 9000 standards.

ISO 14000, launched after ISO 9000, is designed to promote clean production processes in response to environmental issues such as global warming and water pollution. To meet ISO 14000 standards, a company must commit to improving environmental management continually and reducing pollution resulting from its

CONCEPT *in Action* >>>

The Six Sigma quality program directly involves production employees in setting quality standards and in measuring and analyzing finished goods to ensure that quality has been achieved. Here, a worker in an electronics factory inspects a finished circuit board, looking for any defects. How can a service company (e.g., accountancy firm or dry cleaners) ensure quality?

© AP/WIDE WORLD PHOTOS

production processes. Some accredited ISO 14000 organizations include ASQR Canada, Intertek Testing Services NA Limited, and KPMG Performance Registrar Inc.

Lean Manufacturing Trims the Fat

lean manufacturing
Streamlining production by eliminating steps in the production process that do not add benefits customers are willing to pay for.

just-in-time (JIT)
A system in which materials arrive exactly when they are needed for production rather than being stored on-site.

Manufacturers are discovering that they can respond better to rapidly changing customer demands, while keeping inventory and production costs down, by adopting lean manufacturing techniques. **Lean manufacturing** streamlines production by eliminating steps in the production process that do not add benefits customers are willing to pay for. In other words, *non–value-added production processes* are cut, so that the company can concentrate its production and operations resources on items essential to satisfying customers. Toyota was a pioneer in developing these techniques, but today manufacturers in many industries subscribe to the lean-manufacturing philosophy.

Another Japanese concept, **just-in-time (JIT)**, goes hand in hand with lean manufacturing. JIT is based on the belief that materials should arrive exactly when they are needed for production rather than being stored on-site. Relying closely on computerized systems such as MRP, MRPII, and ERP, manufacturers determine what parts will be needed and when, and then order them from suppliers, so they arrive "just in time." Under the JIT system, inventory and products are "pulled" through the production process in response to customer demand. JIT requires close teamwork between vendors and purchasing and production personnel, because any delay in deliveries of supplies could bring JIT production to a halt.

HOT Links

Quality Management Products of Oakville, Ontario, helps its customers to improve their organization with a comprehensive line of quality software products and services. Visit their website at **(www.qmproducts.com)**.

Transforming the Factory Floor with Technology

LO 7

Technology is helping many firms improve their operating efficiency and ability to compete. Computer systems, in particular, are enabling manufacturers to automate factories in ways never before possible.

Among the technologies helping to automate manufacturing are computer-aided design and manufacturing systems, robotics, flexible manufacturing systems, and computer-integrated manufacturing.

computer-aided design (CAD)
The use of computers to design and test new products and modify existing ones.

computer-aided manufacturing (CAM)
The use of computers to develop and control the production process.

CAD/CAM systems
Linked computer systems that combine the advantages of *computer-aided design* and *computer-aided manufacturing*. The system helps design the product, control the flow of resources, and operate the production process.

Computer-Aided Design and Manufacturing Systems Computers have transformed the design and manufacturing processes in many industries. In computer-aided design (CAD), computers are used to design and test new products and modify existing ones. Engineers use these systems to draw products and look at them from different angles. They can analyze the products, make changes, and test prototypes before making even one item. Computer-aided manufacturing (CAM) uses computers to develop and control the production process. The systems analyze the steps required to make the product. They then automatically send instructions to the machines that do the work. CAD/CAM systems combine the advantages of CAD and CAM by integrating design, testing, and manufacturing control into one linked computer system. The system helps design the product, control the flow of resources needed to produce the product, and operate the production process.

Cardianove Inc., a Montreal-based manufacturer of medical and surgical equipment, used CAD software to develop the world's smallest heart pump. The company says using computer-aided design shaved two years off the normal design time for cardiac devices. The company's CAD program ran complex three-dimensional simulations to confirm that the design would function properly inside the human body. Cardionove Inc. tested more than 100 virtual prototypes using the software before the top three designs were actually produced for real-life testing.[10]

robotics
The technology involved in designing, constructing, and operating computer-controlled machines that can perform tasks independently.

Robotics *Robots* are computer-controlled machines that can perform tasks independently. Robotics is the technology involved in designing, constructing, and operating robots. The first robot, or "steel-collar worker," was used by General Motors in 1961. Today robots are used by many companies in many different industries.

Robots can be mobile or fixed in one place. Fixed robots have an arm that moves and does what the computer instructs. Some robots are quite simple, with limited movement for a few tasks such as cutting sheet metal and spot welding. Others are complex, with hands or grippers that can be programmed to perform a series of movements. Some robots are even equipped with sensing devices for sight and touch.

Robots usually operate with little or no human intervention. Replacing human effort with robots is most effective for tasks requiring accuracy, speed, or strength. Although manufacturers such as Harley-Davidson, as described at the beginning of this chapter, are most likely to use robots, some service firms are also finding them useful. Some hospitals, for example, use robots to sort and process blood samples, freeing medical personnel from a tedious, sometimes hazardous, repetitive task.

HOT Links

Want to know more about how robots work? Find out at **(http://electronics.howstuffworks.com/robot.htm)**.

flexible manufacturing system (FMS)
A system that combines automated workstations with computer-controlled transportation devices—automatic guided vehicles (AGVs)—that move materials between workstations and into and out of the system.

Adaptable Factories: Flexible Manufacturing Systems A flexible manufacturing system (FMS) automates a factory by blending computers, robots, machine tools, and materials-and-parts-handling machinery into an integrated system. These systems combine automated workstations with computer-controlled transportation devices. Automatic guided vehicles (AGVs) move materials between workstations and into and out of the system.

Flexible manufacturing systems are expensive. Once in place, however, a system requires little labour to operate and provides consistent product quality. The system can be changed easily and inexpensively. FMS equipment can be programmed to perform one job and then quickly be reprogrammed to perform another. These systems work well when small batches of a variety of products are required or when each product is made to individual customer specifications.

computer-integrated manufacturing (CIM)
The combination of computerized manufacturing processes (such as robots and flexible manufacturing systems) with other computerized systems that control design, inventory, production, and purchasing.

Quick Change with Computer-Integrated Manufacturing Computer-integrated manufacturing (CIM) combines computerized manufacturing processes (like robots and FMS) with other computerized systems that control design, inventory, production, and purchasing. With CIM, when a part is redesigned in the CAD system, the changes are quickly transmitted both to the machines producing the part and to all other departments that need to know about and plan for the change.

Technology and Automation at Your Service

> **concept check**
>
> Define total quality management, lean manufacturing, and just-in-time, and explain how each can help a firm improve its production and operations.
>
> How are both manufacturing and non-manufacturing firms using technology and automation to improve operations?

Manufacturers are not the only businesses benefiting from technology. Non-manufacturing firms are also using automation to improve customer service and productivity. Banks now offer services to customers through automated teller machines (ATMs), via automated telephone systems, and over the Internet. Retail stores of all kinds use point-of-sale (POS) terminals that track inventories, identify items that need to be reordered, and tell which products are selling well. Wal-Mart, the leader in retailing automation, has its own satellite system connecting POS terminals directly to its distribution centres and headquarters.

Trends in Production and Operations Management

Some manufacturing employment has been eliminated as manufacturers attempt to cut operating costs. Many of these jobs have been moved overseas, where manufacturers have opened new production facilities or contracted out production to foreign firms with lower operating and labour costs. Continued growth in global competition, increasingly complex products, and more demanding consumers continue to force manufacturers to plan carefully how, when, and where they produce the goods they sell. New production techniques and manufacturing technologies are vital to keeping production costs as low as possible and productivity levels high. At the same time, many firms are re-evaluating the productivity of their production facilities and, in some cases, are deciding to close underperforming factories.

Non-manufacturing firms must carefully manage how they use and deploy their resources, while keeping up with the constant pace of technological change. Non-manufacturing firms must be ever vigilant in their search for new ways of streamlining service production and operation to keep their overall costs down.

Asset Management

In a tight economy, businesses must be careful about how their operating assets are used. From raw materials to inventories and manufacturing equipment, wasted, malfunctioning, or misused assets are costly. For example, one telephone company reported it had lost track of $5 billion worth of communications equipment. "I would say that every big company I have worked with has lost track of many major assets and a plethora of minor ones," said one executive. In fact, when chief financial officers of large companies were surveyed by *CFO Magazine*, 70 percent reported that asset management in their firms was "inefficient" or "erratic."[11]

Asset management software systems, many of which are Internet based, are beginning to help fix this problem. These programs automatically track materials, equipment, and inventory. They also automate inventory management, and maintenance and repairs scheduling.

ChevronTexaco has successfully implemented this type of system in its enormous production facility in Bakersfield, California. The facility is one of the largest outdoor factories in the world, stretching 160 kilometres from north to south, and containing a maze of storage tanks, filtering installations, and pipelines. In all, there are 230,000 separate pieces of equipment and machinery in hundreds of categories in the facility. To manage all of these assets, ChevronTexaco has installed an automated asset management system that schedules preventive maintenance for all equipment and tracks where surplus equipment and supplies are stored. ChevronTexaco estimates it is saving millions of dollars a year in the facility because of more effective asset management.[12]

Modular Production

Increasingly, manufacturers are relying on *modular production* to speed up and simplify production. Modular production involves breaking a complex product, service, or process into smaller pieces that can be created independently and then combined quickly to make a whole. Modular production not only cuts the cost of developing innovative products but also gives businesses a tool for meeting rapidly changing conditions. It also makes implementation of mass or pure customization strategies easier.

Johnson Controls Inc. (JCI), a manufacturer, works closely with its suppliers to build automotive interiors modularly. JCI uses 11 major components from 35 suppliers to build Jeep Liberty cockpits. The parts, designed to fit and function together, are then assembled in JCI's factory. "Our product development strategy is to build from the best capabilities and technologies in the world, but that doesn't mean they have to be owned and operated by us," says JCI vice-president Jeff Edwards.[13]

Designing Products for Production Efficiency

Today's operations managers recognize that production efficiency must begin *before* the first part reaches the factory floor. As a result, many manufacturers are investing in new methods of integrating product design and engineering with the manufacturing supply chain.

Designlore of Toronto, Ontario offers solutions and customized product design services to entrepreneurs and corporations. They specialize in taking product ideas to the finished product phase including: engineering, industrial and mechanical design, research and development, etc. The company prides itself on "Right the First Time" approach using innovative design with traditional engineering principles.

CONCEPT *in Action* >>>

Toyota focuses design and engineering on "crossover vehicles"—car model designs that appeal to different consumer segments yet are built using many of the same components and parts. This has allowed Toyota's factories to become flexible and modular. What other industries incorporate modular production?

concept check

Explain modular production.

Why does production efficiency have to begin before the first part reaches the factory floor?

Another developing trend is the use of factory simulation tools for product design. These tools allow product designers to see the effects their designs will have on production equipment. For example, if a design calls for a specific size of drilled hole on a product, factory simulation tools will specify which particular drill bit and machine will be necessary for the task.

Great Ideas to Use Now

As we've seen throughout this chapter, every organization produces something. Cereal manufacturers turn grains into breakfast foods. Law firms turn the skills and knowledge of lawyers into legal services. Retailers provide a convenient way for consumers to purchase a variety of goods. Colleges and universities convert students into educated individuals. Therefore, no matter what type of organization you end up working for in the future, you will be involved, to one degree or another, with your employer's production and operations processes.

Some employees, such as plant managers and quality control managers, will have a direct role in the production process. However, employees of manufacturing firms are not the only ones involved with production. Software developers, bank tellers, medical personnel, magazine writers, and a host of other employees are also actively involved in turning inputs into outputs. If you manage people in these types of jobs, you'll need insight into the tools used to plan, schedule, and control production processes. Understanding production processes, resource management, and techniques for increasing productivity is vital to becoming a more valuable employee, one who sees how his or her job fits into "the big picture" of the firm's operating goals.

If you plan to start your own business, you'll also face many production and operations decisions. You can use the information from this chapter to help you find suppliers, design an operating facility (no matter how small), and put customer-satisfying processes in place. This information can also help you make decisions about whether to manufacture goods or rely on outside contractors to handle production.

Customer Satisfaction and Quality

Although we have talked a great deal in this chapter about methods for producing products faster and less expensively, it is important to remember that the most efficient factory in the world would be deemed a failure if the products it made broke soon after customers purchased them. Underlying every production and operations management decision is a very simple question: How will this affect our customers' satisfaction? To compete in today's marketplace, businesses must make sure they have the right answer.

The Honeywell Control Products plant realized it didn't have the right answer. The plant makes electromechanical snap-action switches that are used in machines such as icemakers and washing machines. In the face of foreign competition in the early 1990s, the plant had developed a successful strategy to improve productivity and reduce manufacturing costs. By 1998, however, it was clear that customers weren't happy. Complaints and returns were constantly rising.

The problem? "We were driving the wrong behaviours," says Cynthia Knautz, manufacturing engineer at the plant. "All of our employee goals were set on output. Our production employees could build 36,000 bad switches in a day and still get rewarded." The plant set up new processes to help track and control quality and tied employee incentives to quality and customer satisfaction. As a result, customer reject rates have dropped dramatically, while production rates have actually increased.

SOURCE: Best Plant Winners 2002: Honeywell Control Products, *Industry Week Online*, 2002. Reprinted with permission of Penton Media. (http://www.industryweek.com/articles/iw_best_plants_profile_-_2002_9937.aspx).

Summary of Learning Outcomes

1 Discuss why production and operations management is important in both manufacturing and service firms.

In the 1980s, many manufacturers lost customers to foreign competitors because their production and operations management systems did not support the high-quality, reasonably priced products consumers demanded. Service organizations also rely on effective operations management to satisfy consumers. Operations managers, the personnel charged with managing and supervising the conversion of inputs into outputs, work closely with other functions in organizations to help ensure quality, customer satisfaction, and financial success.

2 List the types of production processes used by manufacturers and service firms.

Products are made using one of three types of production processes. In mass production, many identical goods are produced at once, keeping production costs low. Mass production, therefore, relies heavily on standardization, mechanization, and specialization. When mass customization is used, goods are produced using mass production techniques up to a point, after which the product or service is custom tailored to individual customers by adding special features. When a firm's production process is built around customization, the firm makes many products one at a time according to the very specific needs or wants of individual customers.

3 Describe how organizations decide where to put their production facilities and what choices must be made in designing the facility.

Site selection affects operating costs, the price of the product or service, and the company's ability to compete. In choosing a production site, firms must weigh the availability of resources—raw materials, human resources, and even capital—needed for production, as well as the ability to serve customers and take advantage of marketing opportunities. Other factors include the availability of local incentives and the manufacturing environment. Once a site is selected, the firm must choose an appropriate design for the facility. The three main production facility designs are process, product, and fixed-position layouts. Cellular manufacturing is another type of facility layout.

4 Explain why resource-planning tasks like inventory management and supplier relations are critical to production.

Production converts input resources, such as raw materials and labour, into outputs, finished products, and services. Firms must ensure that the resources needed for production will be available at strategic moments in the production process. If they are not, productivity, customer satisfaction, and quality might suffer. Carefully managing inventory can help cut production costs while maintaining enough supply for production and sales. Through good relationships with suppliers, firms can get better prices, reliable resources, and support services that can improve production efficiency.

5 Discuss how operations managers schedule and control production.

Routing is the first step in scheduling and controlling production. Routing involves analyzing the steps needed in production and setting out a workflow, the sequence of machines and operations through which a product or service progresses from start to finish. Good routing increases productivity and can eliminate unnecessary costs. Scheduling involves specifying and controlling the time and resources required for each step in the production process. Operations managers use three methods to schedule production: Gantt charts, the critical path method, and program evaluation and review techniques.

6 Evaluate how quality management and lean-manufacturing techniques help firms improve production and operations management.

Quality and productivity go hand in hand. Defective products waste materials and time, increasing costs. Poor quality also leads to dissatisfied customers. By implementing quality control methods, firms often reduce these problems and streamline production. Lean manufacturing also helps streamline production by eliminating unnecessary steps in the production process. When activities that don't add value for customers are eliminated, manufacturers can respond to changing market conditions with greater flexibility and ease.

7 **Identify the roles that technology and automation play in manufacturing and service industry operations management.**

Many firms are improving their operational efficiency by using technology to automate parts of production. Computer-aided design and manufacturing systems, for example, help design new products, control the flow of resources needed for production, and even operate much of the production process. By using robotics, human time and effort can be minimized. Factories are being automated by blending computers, robots, and machinery into flexible manufacturing systems that require less labour to operate. Service firms are automating operations too, using technology to cut labour costs and control quality.

8 **List some of the key trends affecting the way companies manage production and operations.**

The manufacturing sector has been faced with growing global competition, increased product complexity, and more demanding customers, so manufacturers must carefully plan how, when, and where they produce the goods they sell. New production techniques and manufacturing technologies can help keep costs as low as possible. Managing assets like inventory, raw materials, and production equipment is increasingly important. Asset management software systems automatically track materials and inventory to help reduce waste, misuse, and malfunctions. Modular production allows manufacturers to produce products using high-quality parts without investments in expensive technology. Production efficiency must begin before the factory floor. Many firms are using tools that integrate product design and engineering with the manufacturing supply chain to understand the cost and quality implications of producing new products.

Experiential Exercises

1. Track a project with a Gantt chart. Your instructor has just announced a huge assignment, due in three weeks. Where do you start? How can you best organize your time? A Gantt chart can help you plan and schedule more effectively. You'll be able to see exactly what you should be doing on a particular day.
   - First, break the assignment down into smaller tasks: pick a topic, conduct research at the library or on the Internet, organize your notes, develop an outline, and write, type, and proofread the paper.
   - Next, estimate how much time each task will take. Be realistic. If you've spent a week or more writing similar papers in the past, don't expect to finish this paper in a day.
   - At the top of a piece of paper, list all of the days until the assignment is due. Along the side of the paper, list all of the tasks you've identified in the order in which they need to be done.
   - Starting with the first task, block out the number of days you estimate each task will take. If you run out of days, you'll know you need to adjust how you've scheduled your time. If you know that you will not be able to work on some days, note them on the chart as well.
   - Hang the chart where you can see it.
2. Look for ways in which technology and automation are used at your school, in the local supermarket, and at your doctor's office. As a class, discuss how automation affects the service you receive from each of these organizations. Does one organization use any types of automation that might be effectively used by one of the others? Explain.
3. Pick a small business in your community. Make a list of the resources critical to the firm's production and operations. What would happen if the business suddenly couldn't acquire any of these resources? Discuss strategies that small businesses can use to manage their supply chain.
4. Today's Fashions is a manufacturer of women's dresses. The company's factory has 50 employees. Production begins when the fabric is cut according to specified patterns. After being cut, the pieces for each dress style are placed into bundles,

which then move through the factory from worker to worker. Each worker opens each bundle and does one assembly task, such as sewing on collars, hemming dresses, or adding decorative items such as appliqués. Then, the worker puts the bundle back together and passes it on to the next person in the production process. Finished dresses are pressed and packaged for shipment. Draw a diagram showing the production process layout in the Today's Fashions factory. What type of factory layout and process is Today's Fashions using? Discuss the pros and cons of this choice. Could Today's Fashions improve the production efficiency by using a different production process or factory layout? How? Draw a diagram to explain how this might look.

5. As discussed in this chapter, many firms have moved their manufacturing operations to overseas locations in the past decade. Although there can be sound financial benefits to this choice, moving production overseas can also raise new challenges for operations managers. Identify several of these challenges, and offer suggestions for how operations managers can use the concepts in this chapter to minimize or solve them.

6. Reliance Systems is a manufacturer of computer keyboards. The company plans to build a new factory and hopes to find a location with access to low-cost but skilled workers, national and international transportation, and favourable government incentives. As a team, use the Internet and your school library to research possible site locations, both domestic and international. Choose a location you feel would best meet the company's needs. Make a group presentation to the class explaining why you have chosen this location. Include information about the location's labour force, similar manufacturing facilities already located there, availability of resources and materials, possible local incentives, the political and economic environments, and any other factors you feel make this an attractive location. After all teams have presented their proposed locations, as a class rank all of the locations and decide the top two that Reliance should investigate further.

7. Find the supplier information websites of several firms by using the Google search engine, **(www.google.ca)**, to conduct a search for "supplier information." Visit two or three of these sites. Compare the requirements the companies set for their suppliers. How do the requirements differ? How are they similar?

8. Find out about the manufacturing environment in Canada by using **(www.google.ca)** and searching for manufacturing in Canada. You will have many options for learning more about the manufacturing opportunities.

9. Using a search engine such as Excite (**www.excite.com**) or Info Seek (**www.infoseek.com**), search for information about technologies like robotics, CAD/CAM systems, or ERP. Find at least three suppliers for one of these technologies. Visit their websites and discuss how their clients are using their products to automate production.

Key Terms

assembly process 327
bill of material 333
CAD/CAM systems 343
cellular manufacturing 333
computer-aided design (CAD) 343
computer-aided manufacturing (CAM) 343
computer-integrated manufacturing (CIM) 343
continuous improvement 340
continuous process 328
critical path 338
critical path method (CPM) 338
customization 327
electronic data interchange (EDI) 337
enterprise resource planning (ERP) 334
e-procurement 336
fixed-position layout 331
flexible manufacturing system (FMS) 343
Gantt charts 338
intermittent process 329

inventory 333
inventory management 333
ISO 9000 341
ISO 14000 341
job shop 327
just-in-time (JIT) 342
lean manufacturing 342
make-or-buy decision 333
manufacturing resource planning II (MRPII) 334
mass customization 327
mass production 327
materials requirement planning (MRP) 334
operations management 324
outsourcing 333
perpetual inventory 334
process layout 331
process manufacturing 327
product (or assembly line) layout 331
production 324
production planning 326
production process 326
program evaluation and review technique (PERT) 340
purchasing 333
quality 340
quality control 340
robotics 343
routing 337
scheduling 338
Six Sigma 341
supply chain 335
supply chain management 335
total quality management (TQM) 340
value-stream mapping 337

Review Questions

1. Define production and operations management.
2. What is production planning? What is the production process, and what options are available to manufacturers?
3. What are some of the considerations when determining the location of production facilities?
4. After management has decided on a location for the facilities, they need to design the facilities' layout. What are some options in the design?
5. What are the considerations when we are formulating our resource planning?
6. What are supply chain and supply chain management?
7. What is scheduling? What are the three (3) common scheduling tools available to management?
8. Discuss some ways of improving production and operations.
9. How can technology be used to improve operating efficiencies and the ability for companies to compete?
10. Discuss the importance of asset management.
11. What is modular production?

CREATIVE THINKING CASE >

Innovation Labs Spark Creativity

With sales of 12.5 million units in less than a year, no one is questioning why designers of the sleek Razr, Motorola's ultra-light, half-inch-thick cell phone, broke some internal rules in bringing the phone to market. Leaving their cubicles at the company's traditional research facility, engineers joined with designers and marketers at the company's innovation lab known as Moto City. Open space and waist-high cubicles—even for senior executives—fostered team spirit and a breaking down of barriers, which contributed to the project's success. Customary practices like running new product ideas past regional managers were bypassed. "We did not want to be distracted by the normal inputs we get," says Gary R. Weis, senior director of mechanical engineering. "It would not have allowed us to be as innovative."

Innovation labs are fast becoming a key element in the effort to revamp old-style research and development (R&D). In the past, scientists and engineers toiled away for years in pursuit of patents, and then handed their work over to product developers and marketers for eventual shipment to consumers. But today's sophisticated production and operations technology, as well as ferocious competition, can mean new innovations grow old quickly, so companies must work fast to get products to market. To keep pace with consumer demand, Motorola introduced new colours for the Razr, as well as follow-up phones like the Razr2, the candy-bar shaped Slvr and the rounded Pebl.

But the need for speed in innovation stretches beyond high-tech companies. Businesses as varied as Mattel, Boeing, Wrigley, Procter & Gamble, and even the Mayo Clinic also use such labs to shatter the bureaucratic barriers that existed among inventors, engineers, researchers, designers, marketers, and others. Now, teams of people from different disciplines gather to focus on a problem—brainstorming, tinkering, and toying with different approaches—and generate answers to test on customers. Successful products are then sped to the market.

Although innovation labs are typically created to generate new product ideas, they are also used to improve manufacturing processes. Large organizations have discovered that innovation labs can be a powerful tool for cutting through bureaucratic bloat. At Boeing Company, for instance, nearly 3,000 engineers and finance and program management staffers from scattered locations were moved last year to the factory that assembles 737 jetliners. To urge people to mingle, Boeing created common break areas where mechanics and engineers could talk shop over coffee or a snack, building informal relationships that improved both daily working processes and innovations.

But innovation labs are not panaceas. If ideas that emerge from these facilities are flawed, the products will undoubtedly be failures. And some older workers, especially baby boomers, may have a hard time giving up cherished perks such as private offices. Yet for companies in a creative rut, innovation labs can be places where something magical gets started.

Critical Thinking Questions

- How do innovation labs contribute to successful production and operations management?
- In what significant ways do they differ from a more traditional research and development approach?
- What market conditions lead companies to use innovation labs?

SOURCES: Joseph Weber, Stanley Holmes, and Christopher Palmieri, "'Mosh Pits of Creativity," Business Week, November 7, 2005, (www.businessweek.com); Rebecca Fannin, "Unlocking Innovation: CEOs Are Learning How to Better Tap University R & D," The Chief Executive, June 2005, (www.findarticles.com); Innovation Labs website, (www.innovationlabs.com) (May 22, 2006).

VIDEO CASE >

Big Blue Turns Small Businesses into Large Competitors

"It is like music, once it is in place and working," says Susan Jain, a marketing executive with IBM Global Services. She is talking about Enterprise Resource Planning, or ERP, complex software modules that do just about everything to help companies run more efficiently and competitively.

"The old systems couldn't relate one piece of information to another," she says. Separate databases meant information systems weren't integrated, so day-to-day operations were cumbersome and management reporting often inaccurate. With ERP, information is accessible immediately, greatly improving overall operating efficiency and speeding up and shortening internal reporting procedures, and even reducing the time it takes to bring new products to market.

ERP is a "relational database" that ties all aspects of information gathering and dissemination together in a tidy package. For example, ERP software modules can receive an order, check raw material stocks to make sure the order can be produced, order any additional materials that might be needed, place the order in the production schedule, and send it to shipping and invoicing. Its human resources module will even help hire and train the staff needed to produce and fulfill the order.

Companies no longer need to predict what products customers might want, or keep tons of product on warehouse shelves gathering dust. ERP literally allows companies to "build to order"—in fact, IBM has an automobile customer that does just that. It builds to order, one car at a time, eliminating the customary guessing games of what colours or styles might be popular at a given time.

Even small companies are investing in ERP systems to enable them to grow and compete, despite the substantial investment in time and dollars that is required. Jain is candid about the costs involved. The software costs about $1 million dollars, with an equal expenditure required for new hardware. Implementation, training, and education can cost two to three times that amount and take years in the case of very large companies.

IBM Global Financing supports all elements of an ERP acquisition with a broad array of financing offerings with flexible payment options. But after all that expense, return on investment is difficult to measure. With so many variables driving business success, good results could be due to other factors, such as changes in working styles or a general upswing in the current business environment. IBM's promotional material asks "Are You Ready for IBM?" It's a big decision for small companies to make.

Critical Thinking Questions

- As the production manager for a large manufacturing company, you recommend the acquisition of ERP software to your bosses. Be specific in describing how such a system would help your company be more competitive.
- What kind of information would you want such a system to integrate for your company?
- Explain how you would propose to track performance to justify the cost of installing such a system.

SOURCE: Adapted from material in the video "Are You Ready for IBM?" Information Management Systems at IBM, (www.ibm.com) (accessed April 8, 2003).

E-COMMERCE CASE >

Magna Moves Forward

In moving his company from a tool and die shop in Ontario to an automobile parts manufacturer and an auto-maker, Frank Stronach has practiced world-class operations management. Stronach began his rise to fame and fortune in 1957 with a business called Multimatic, employing only 10 people. In 1960, Multimatic produced sun visor brackets for General Motors Canada. Today, Magna international, Inc. (named in 1973) operates in 25 countries with over 70,000 employees and more than 300 facilities that focus on manufacturing, research and development, engineering and sales.

How has Stronach managed to remain successful in such a volatile industry as automobile manufacturing? Magna is on the cutting edge of the technological advances related to the industry. By engaging in the design, development and manufacture of systems, components and modules, as well as assembling vehicles, they have been able to control not only the research and development of many aspects of the final products, but also the design of the production process, if not the facility itself. Magna is able to control the inventory management, schedule production, monitor quality and effect lean manufacturing techniques. However, the industry profile is changing rapidly with GM declaring bankruptcy. Where does that leave auto parts manufacturers such as Magna? Apparently well positioned to move forward.

Magna is leading a consortium of partners in a bid to take over Opel, Germany's second largest automaker. The partnership is expected to include GM at 35%, Sherbank (Russian state-owned creditor of OAO GAZ, Russia's second largest automaker) at 35%, Magna at 20% and Opel employees at 10%. There are many advantages to this venture including access to the Russian market which is expected to become the largest in Europe, access to OAO GAZ excess factory capabilities, access to Opel's 10 vehicle assembly plants in Germany, Britain, Spain, Portugal, and Poland, and access to Opel's vast engineering expertise.

Magna is the only parts manufacturer to ever move into the realm of auto manufacturing. If the joint venture goes ahead as planned, the opportunities will be exciting, but, of course, the challenges of such a combination of players, all with their own agendas, will be just that ... a challenge.

Critical Thinking Questions

1. What operations management challenges can you see in moving from one plant located in Austria to ten plants located in various countries?
2. With a 20% share in the joint venture, how much control over the production process would Magna actually have?
3. Check out (www.Magna.com) to see the status of the joint venture today.

SOURCES: Mike Ramsey, "Magna may build cars here for Europeans; Strong euro gives edge to N. A. assembly," The Windsor Star, June 7, 2007, accessed June 17, 2009; David Olive, "Car czar Stronach opening new opportunities; the road ahead for reviving Opel may be tough to navigate but Canadian auto-parts mogul is in the driver's seat," Toronto Star, June 14, 2009, accessed June 17, 2009 and (http://cobrands.hoovers.com) accessed June 17, 2009.

CHAPTER 10

Making the Connection

Managing Human Resources and Labour Relations

In this section of the text we will take a look at the internal environment of a business or, more simply, the functional areas of a business. These areas are what most people think of when they think of a business or a career in business—human resources, operations, marketing, accounting, and finance.

Before we take a look inside each of the functional areas in detail, in separate chapters, one very important message must be communicated clearly at the outset. Even though each of these areas is discussed separately in different chapters of introductory textbooks, and later in separate courses in business schools, they cannot act separately if the business is to be successful. They are all part of the integrated business model that has been the central theme of this text. Each of these areas must work together to make the business successful overall. For example, a company cannot design and market a product for which it does not have the human, operational, and financial resources. Just imagine The Bay attempting to produce a new all-terrain vehicle and introduce it to the market. It could perhaps alter its store setup to sell the vehicle, but does it have the facilities and people skills to produce it? Would it even have the financial resources to put toward this type of endeavour, considering the tight budgets most businesses are working with today to keep their core business alive?

It was clear from Chapter 7, which deals with management and planning, that all decisions made at the tactical level in the functional areas come from decisions made at a higher *strategic* level that affect the whole company. Top management first scans the external environment (PEST model) to look for opportunities and threats and matches those with the strengths and weaknesses of the company in the different functional areas to decide the direction for the company. It is therefore unlikely that a decision like this one would ever be made by The Bay. Even if there were opportunities in the market for ATVs, it would not match with the strengths of the company. Financial resources would therefore not be released for this type of project to begin with.

In this chapter we'll take a look at our first functional area. The old adage "last but not least" certainly applies here. As we discussed earlier, *gaining the commitment of employees* is the most critical factor, because all of the other four critical success factors are achieved through the people in the company. Without a strong human resource area and the strong commitment of the employees toward organizational goals, the company simply cannot be successful in any functional area or overall.

The business environment today provides many challenges for the human resource manager. In the *political* environment, regulations govern many aspects of the human resource function, such as how workers can be selected (e.g., drug testing, human rights legislations governing the application and interview process). The mix of people hired is also regulated for some companies through employment equity legislation. Issues relating to diversity are critically important, because without a diverse workforce, companies will have a difficult time both understanding the global marketplace and, subsequently, designing products and marketing plans to appeal to this multifaceted society. Therefore, companies must consider this trend toward greater diversity in the make-up of society very seriously, taking proactive steps rather than just reacting to government legislation. The importance of diversity to a company's success can be seen in the example of PepsiCo in the opening vignette to this chapter. PepsiCo has

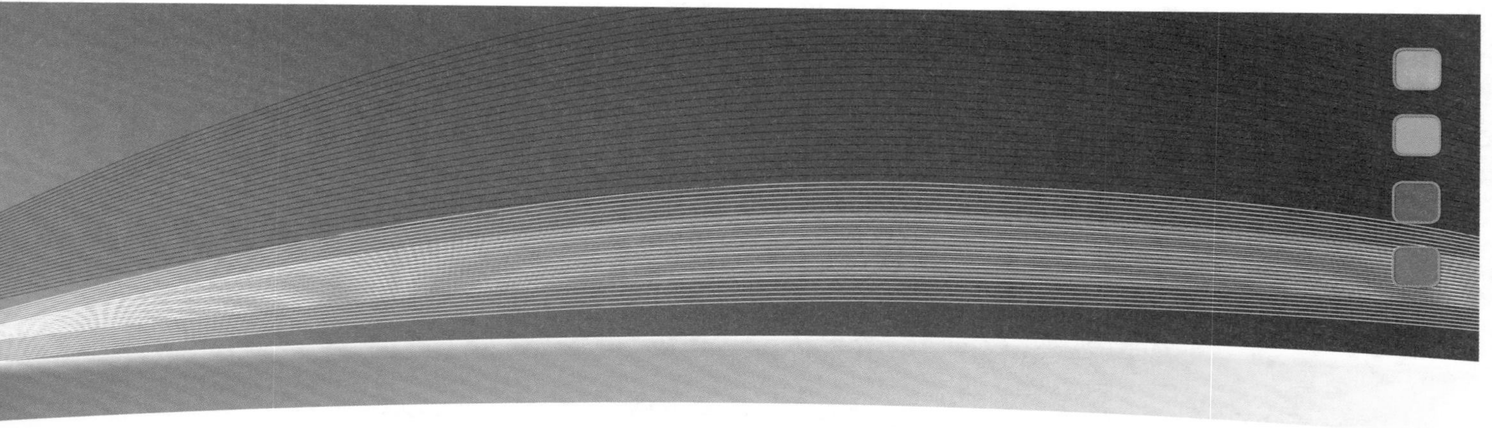

a long-standing commitment to diversity within its marketing and human resources that has made it both more responsive to the marketplace and a better place to work, giving it a competitive advantage. In the *economic* environment, organizations are competing not only for customers but also for a shrinking pool of qualified job applicants, and they must also pay attention to the salaries of the competition to remain competitive. In the *social* environment, workers are seeking to better balance their home and work lives, making it more critical and more difficult to gain commitment in the traditional ways;the aging workforce is also creating difficulties. The *technological* environment is reshaping how work is done, offering options to human labour and changing the nature of many jobs and the skills required to do them. Technology also affects how the human resource department does its job. You'll find many examples both in the chapter and in trying to find a job yourself, such as using the Internet to recruit workers and using specially designed software to pick out key phrases from résumés to sort through them more quickly.

An environmental factor that has a dramatic impact on how a company operates is the presence of unions. This is a very integrative factor as it has implications for all the environmental factors and all the areas of the business. It is *political,* because legislation governs how unions become involved with a group of workers and how the union-management relationship works; it is social, because the culture and attitude of the workers affect how they view unions and whether they would want to work in a unionized environment; it is technological, because the union contract could impact the rights of management to use technology if it replaces workers; and it is economic, because a unionized workplace often has less flexibility and higher compensation costs than a non-unionized environment, and that can impact a company's competitiveness. Unions can therefore affect the financial success of the company, and they can definitely signal an issue with respect to worker commitment when the workers feel compelled to have a third party represent them with management. This point stresses the importance of management operating with the commitment of the workers foremost in its mind if it wishes to operate without a union. It is management's job to create a work environment that gains commitment and loyalty, where the human resource policies are so worker focused that unions are the last thought on the workers' minds.

As with the other functional areas, the main basis for all decisions in the human resource area is the company's goals and *strategy.* The role of the human resource area is to provide the right numbers of the right kinds of people in the right places at the right times to assist the other functional areas to help the organization achieve its objectives. To do this, the human resource area must work very closely with *marketing, operations,* and *finance* to understand their objectives and thus their human resource requirements. It must also understand the jobs that need to be done to determine the skills that it must recruit and train for.

One area in which human resources must work especially closely with finance is in the area of employee compensation and benefits. Because of the relative size of this expense, it has a tremendous impact on the bottom line on the one hand, but on the other it also affects the level of commitment from employees. Therefore, an integrative approach must be taken in determining compensation. This matter is becoming more important as workers are changing jobs more often.

Compensation is just one decision area in which the human resource manager must develop and implement policies in an integrative way to create a more committed workforce. For example, one common approach in recruitment and selection is to promote first from within. This practice shows employees that the organization is committed to them, which is an essential ingredient in gaining commitment from employees. Another particularly integrative way to increase commitment is by offering telecommuting. The technological environment has made telecommuting possible, thus improving the productivity of workers and saving companies money. This, in turn, has helped firms retain key people who would otherwise have to leave. In training and development as well, the organization can show its commitment to the employees by helping them to achieve their potential. Again, employees will be more committed to an organization that shows commitment to them in its human resource policies. This effort to train and develop employees makes them both better at their jobs and more loyal, which translates into being more *innovative,* providing greater *quality,* and working harder to meet and exceed *customer needs,* thereby allowing the organization to *achieve financial performance* both through lower turnover and through greater customer satisfaction.

CHAPTER 10

Managing Human Resources and Labour Relations

LEARNING OUTCOMES

1 Discuss the human resource management process, and how human resource needs are determined.

2 Explain how firms recruit applicants.

3 Summarize how firms select qualified applicants.

4 List some of the types of training and development programs organizations offer their employees.

5 Show how performance appraisals are used to evaluate employee performance.

6 Analyze the various methods for compensating employees.

7 Explain how labour–management relations are different in a unionized environment.

8 Describe some of the key laws and federal agencies affecting human resource management and labour relations.

9 List some of the trends and issues affecting human resource management and labour relations.

PEPSICO IS COMMITTED TO DIVERSITY

PepsiCo (**www.pepsico.com**) is the parent company of some of Canada's best-known brands, including Pepsi, Frito-Lay, Tropicana, and Quaker Oats. With more than 185,000 employees around the world, PepsiCo employees share a common set of values and goals. Top executives and human resource managers know that success takes the work of talented and dedicated people who are committed to making an impact every day. Their ability to grow year after year is driven by their ability to attract, develop, and retain world-class people who will thrive in a dynamic environment. To achieve this, PepsiCo recognizes that they need employees who are anxious to be part of a dynamic, results-oriented company, with powerful brands and top-notch people.

Early in the firm's history—as far back as the 1940s—Pepsi-Cola acknowledged the importance of diversity within its workplaces and in the marketplace. Recognizing the importance of tailoring its marketing to minority groups, Pepsi pioneered advertising specifically to minority groups. These ads featured minority actors and actresses and focused on minority lifestyles. The company also developed education and sports programs spotlighting minorities, and sponsored major musical tours by entertainers such as Michael Jackson and Tina Turner. The firm also spends millions of dollars advertising in minority media such as *Ebony* and *Black Enterprise.*

PepsiCo has been nationally recognized as one of the top places for women and minorities to work. The firm has been hiring minorities in professional positions for more than 65 years. Pepsi was the first Fortune 500 Company to have an African American vice-president. PepsiCo has developed a number of diversity initiatives to ensure that the firm's core value of diversity is a competitive advantage. These initiatives include the following:

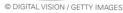

© DIGITAL VISION / GETTY IMAGES

- Within Pepsi-Cola, Frito-Lay, and Tropicana operating divisions, executives are completely dedicated to managing diversity in the workplace.
- Multiyear strategic plans for diversity are developed with the same vigour and goal-setting process as other business issues. Goals include turnover reduction, increased diversity hiring, and creation of an "inclusion" culture.
- An External Diversity Advisory Board consisting of educators, politicians, practitioners, and customers advises PepsiCo senior management on how to leverage diversity in the marketplace.
- Annual employee reviews incorporate the need to "Act with Integrity," "Create a Positive Work Environment," and "Align and Motivate Teams."
- A mandatory annual Affirmative Action Planning process is in place.
- An annual organizational health survey incorporates diversity questions and requires analysis of the minority and female employees. Senior management is held accountable for results.
- A corporate program is dedicated to training employees on how to work and manage in an inclusive environment.
- Employee networks mentor and support minority and female employees.

Critical Thinking Questions

As you read this chapter, consider these questions as they relate to PepsiCo:

1. **How can diversity in the workplace be an advantage to PepsiCo?**
2. **What role does the federal government play in ensuring that diversity exists at PepsiCo and all other companies?**

Human resource management and labour relations involve acquisition, development, use, and maintenance of a human resource mix (people and positions) to achieve strategic organizational goals and objectives. Successful human resource management is based on a company's ability to attract and hire the best employees, equip them with the knowledge and skills they need to excel, compensate them fairly, and motivate them to reach their full potential and perform at high levels. Today's business environment presents numerous challenges to effectively managing employees:

- *Technology continues to advance, which places great importance on knowledge workers, especially when demand outstrips the supply of high talent individuals.*
- *Global business operations involve rapid data transfer and necessitate accelerated decision making by executive and technical employees.*
- *The workforce is increasingly more diversified and multicultural, which places increased emphasis on communication and cultural understanding.*
- *Work life and family priorities are more difficult to balance as dual worker families populate the labour force.*
- *Employment and labour laws continue to greatly influence employee recruitment and hiring, compensation decisions, and employee retention and turnover in both union and non-union organizations.*

Each day, human resource experts and front-line supervisors deal with these challenges while sharing responsibility for attracting and retaining skilled, motivated employees. Whether faced with a large or small human resource problem, supervisors need some understanding of difficult employee relations issues, especially if there are legal implications.

In this chapter, you will learn about the elements of the human resource management process, including human resource planning and job analysis and design, employee recruitment and selection, training and development of employees, performance planning and evaluation, and compensation of the workforce. The chapter also describes labour unions and their representation of millions of Canadian workers in construction, manufacturing, transportation, and service-based industries.

© PHOTODISC RED/GETTY IMAGES

CONCEPT *in Action* >>>

As business expands around the globe, human resource managers need to develop communication systems and training strategies that build teamwork among diverse employees who may be located around the world. What human resource challenges are caused by increasing globalization of Canadian companies?

Achieving High Performance Through Human Resource Management

LO 1

human resource management
The process of hiring, developing, motivating, and evaluating employees to achieve organizational goals.

Human resource (HR) management is the process of hiring, developing, motivating, and evaluating employees to achieve organizational goals. The goals and strategies of the firm's business model form the basis for making human resource management decisions. HR practices and systems comprise the firm's human resource decision support system that is intended to make employees a key element for gaining competitive advantage. To this end, the HR management process contains the following sequenced activities:

EXHIBIT 10.1 > Human Resource Management Process

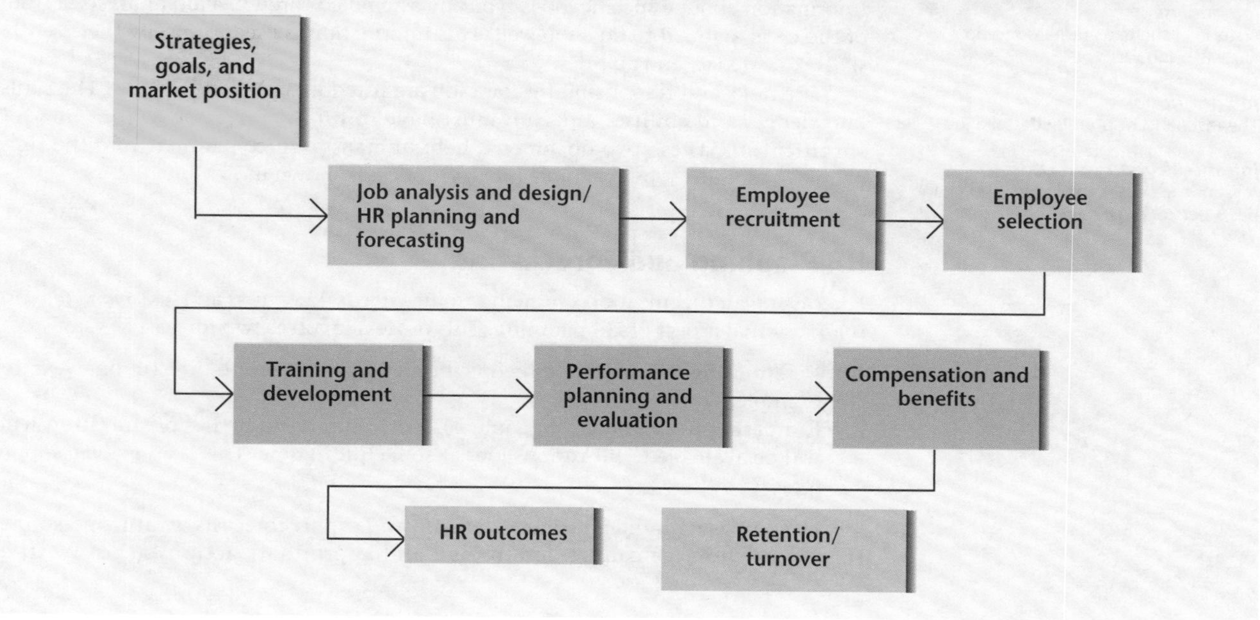

- job analysis and design,
- human resource planning and forecasting,
- employee recruitment,
- employee selection,
- training and development,
- performance planning and evaluation, and
- compensation and benefits.

The human resource management process shown in Exhibit 10.1 encourages the development of high performance employees. The process is sequential because employees can't be trained and paid until selected and placed in jobs, which follows recruitment, which is preceded by human resource planning and job analysis and design. Good HR practices used along this sequence foster performance improvement, knowledge and skill development, and loyal employees who desire to remain with the organization.

concept check

Define human resource management.

Describe the human resource management process.

HR Planning and Job Analysis and Design

Two important, and somewhat parallel, aspects of the human resource management process are determining the employee needs of the firm and the jobs to be filled. Firms need to have the right number of people, with the right training, in the right jobs, to do the organization's work when it needs to be done. Human resource specialists are the ones who must determine future human resource needs and assess the skills of the firm's existing employees to see if new people must be hired or existing ones retrained.

human resource (HR) planning
Creating a strategy for meeting future human resource needs.

Creating a strategy for meeting future human resource needs is called **human resource (HR) planning**. Two important aspects of HR planning are job analysis and forecasting the firm's people needs. The HR planning process begins with a review

job analysis
A study of the tasks required to do a particular job well.

job description
The tasks and responsibilities of a job.

job specification
A list of the skills, knowledge, and abilities a person must have to fill a job.

of corporate strategy and policy. By understanding the mission of the organization, planners can understand its human resource needs.

Human resource planners must know what skills different jobs require. Information about a specific job is typically assembled through a job analysis, a study of the tasks required to do a job well. This information is used to specify the essential skills, knowledge, and abilities.

The tasks and responsibilities of a job are listed in a job description. The skills, knowledge, and abilities a person must have to fill a job are spelled out in a job specification. These two documents help human resource planners find the right people for specific jobs. A sample job description is shown in Exhibit 10.2.

HR Planning and Forecasting

Forecasting an organization's human resource needs, known as an HR *demand forecast,* is an essential aspect of HR planning. This process involves two forecasts:

1. Determining the number of people needed by some future time (in one year, for example).
2. Estimating the number of people currently employed by the organization who will be available to fill various jobs at some future time. This is an *internal* supply forecast.

By comparing human resource demand and supply forecasts, a future personnel surplus or shortage can be determined and appropriate action taken. WestJet,

EXHIBIT 10.2 > Job Description

Position: College Recruiter
Reports to: Vice President of Human Resources
Location: Corporate Offices
Classification: Salaried/Exempt

Job Summary: Member of HR corporate team. Interacts with managers and department heads to determine hiring needs for college graduates. Visits 20 to 30 college and university campuses each year to conduct preliminary interviews of graduating students in all academic disciplines. Following initial interviews, works with corporate staffing specialists to determine persons who will be interviewed a second time. Makes recommendations to hiring managers concerning best-qualified applicants.

Job Duties and Responsibilities:

Estimated time spent and importance

15 percent	Working with managers and department heads, determines college recruiting needs.
10 percent	Determines colleges and universities with degree programs appropriate to hiring needs to be visited.
15 percent	Performs college relations activities with numerous colleges and universities.
25 percent	Visits campuses to conduct interviews of graduating seniors.
15 percent	Develops applicant files and performs initial applicant evaluations.
10 percent	Assists staffing specialists and line managers in determining who to schedule for second interviews.
5 percent	Prepares annual college recruiting report containing information and data about campuses, number interviewed, number hired, and related information.
5 percent	Participates in tracking college graduates who are hired to aid in determining campuses that provide the most outstanding employees.

Job Specification (Qualifications):

Bachelor's degree in human resource management or a related field. Minimum of two years of work experience with the firm in HR or department that annually hires college graduates. Ability to perform in a team environment, especially with line managers and department heads. Very effective oral and written communication skills. Reasonably proficient in Excel, Word, and Windows computer environment and familiar with PeopleSoft.

a low-cost airline, has continuously added planes and routes that require adding personnel. In contrast, some other airlines have reduced flights and decreased employee head count. In both cases, the firms had to forecast the number of employees needed, given their respective competitive positions with the industry. Exhibit 10.3 summarizes the process of planning and forecasting an organization's people needs.

contingent workers
Persons who prefer temporary employment, either part- or full-time.

Many firms with employee shortages are hiring **contingent workers**, or persons who prefer temporary employment, either part- or full-time. Postsecondary students and retired persons make up a large portion of Canada's contingent workforce. Other people who want to work but don't want to be permanent employees can join a temporary employment agency. A temporary employment agency performs staffing, training, and compensation functions by contracting with a business to provide employees for a specified period. A firm with a shortage of accountants can rent or lease an accountant from the temporary employment agency for the expected duration of the shortage.

concept check

Distinguish between job analysis, job description, and job specification.

Describe the job analysis and design process.

What is the process for human resource forecasting?

EXHIBIT 10.3 > Human Resource Planning Process

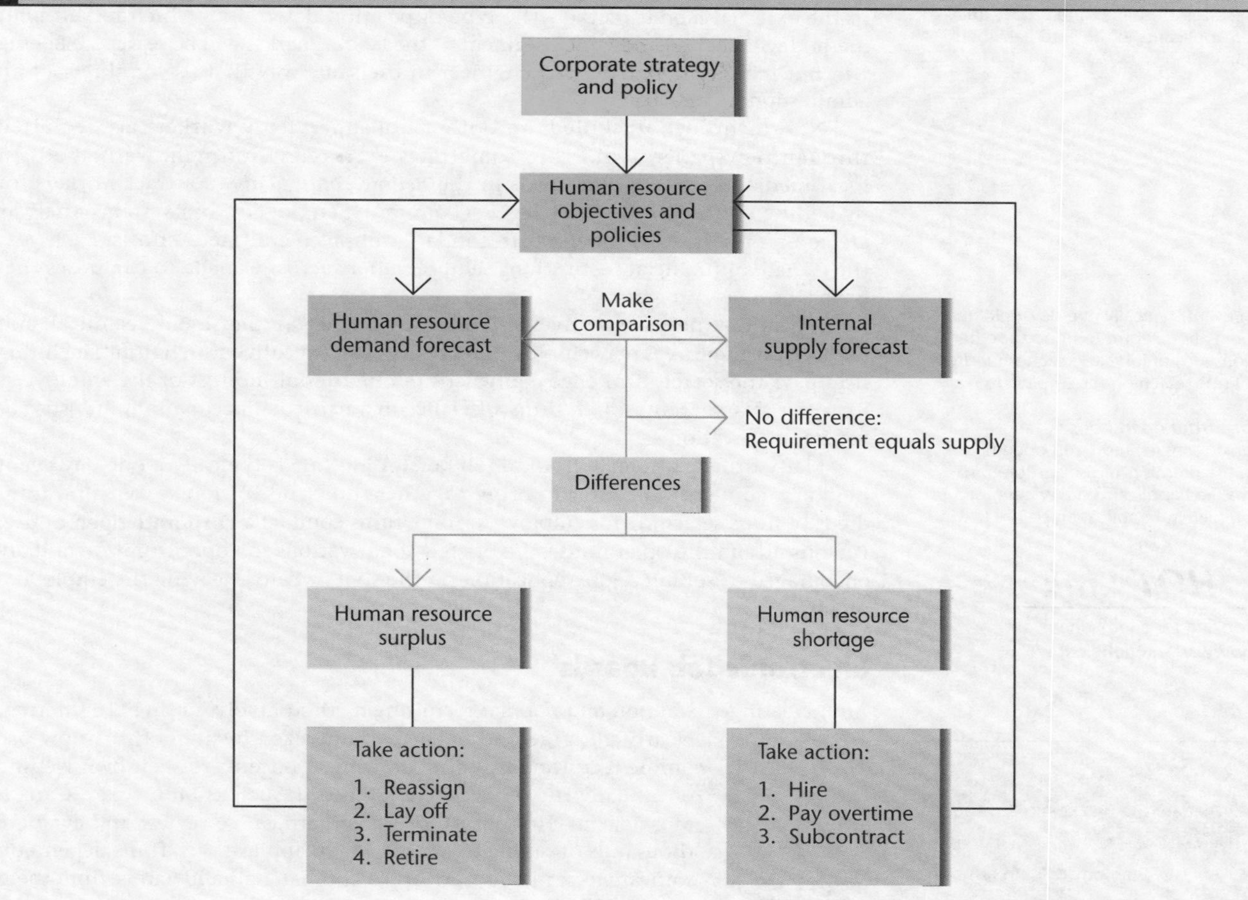

Employee Recruitment

When a firm creates a new position or an existing one becomes vacant, it starts looking for people with qualifications that meet the requirements of the job. Two sources of job applicants are the internal and external labour markets. The internal labour market consists of employees currently employed by the firm; the external labour market is the pool of potential applicants outside the firm.

Internal Labour Market

Internal recruitment can be greatly facilitated by using a human resource information system containing a skills inventory, or computerized employee database of information about an employee's previous work experience, education and certifications, job and career preferences, performance, and attendance. Promotions and job transfers are the most common results of internal recruiting. Most companies, including UPS, WestJet Airlines, and Wal-Mart, follow a policy of promotion from within and try to fill positions with their existing employees. The internal search for job applicants usually means that a person must change his or her job. People are typically either promoted or transferred.

External Labour Market

recruitment
The attempt to find and attract qualified applicants in the external labour market.

If qualified job candidates cannot be found inside the firm, the external labour market must be tapped. **Recruitment** is the attempt to find and attract qualified applicants in the external labour market. The type of position determines which recruitment method will be used and which segment of the labour market will be searched. Boeing will not recruit an experienced engineer in the same way that it would recruit an admin support person.

Non-technical, unskilled, and other nonsupervisory workers are recruited through newspaper, radio, and sometimes even television help-wanted ads in local media. Starbucks placed ads in the *Beijing Youth Daily* to attract workers for its Beijing coffee shops. Entry-level accountants, engineers, and systems analysts are commonly hired through postsecondary campus recruitment efforts. Each year the Canadian financial institutions send recruiters across Canada to campuses that have a business program.

job fair
An event, typically one day, held at a convention centre to bring together thousands of job seekers and hundreds of firms searching for employees.

corporate open house
Persons are invited to an open house on the premises of the corporation. Qualified applicants are encouraged to complete an application before leaving.

A firm that needs executives and other experienced professional, technical, and managerial employees may employ the services of an executive search firm. The hiring firm pays the search firm a fee equivalent to one to four months of the employee's first-year salary. Many search firms specialize in a particular occupation, industry, or geographic location.

Many firms participate in local job fairs. A **job fair** is typically a one-day event held at a convention center to bring together thousands of job seekers and hundreds of firms searching for employees. Some firms conduct a **corporate open house**. Persons attend the open house, are briefed about various job opportunities, and are encouraged to submit a job application on the spot or before leaving the employer's premises.

HOT Links

Looking for a job? Check out **(www.workopolis.ca).**

Electronic Job Boards

An increasingly common and popular recruiting method involves using the Internet. Nearly all large and most medium-sized business firms now use online recruiting by either drawing applicants to their own website or utilizing the services of a job board, such as Monster.ca, CareerMosaic.com, Hotjobs.ca, or CareerPath.ca. To review and evaluate thousands of online résumés and job applications, firms depend on software to scan and track applicant materials and gather from them critical information for applicant selection.

concept check

What are the two labour markets?

Describe different ways that employees are recruited.

How is technology helping firms find the right recruits?

CONCEPT *in Action* >>>

Job fairs bring together hundreds of employers and thousands of job seekers. Job fairs are one of the ways human resource managers identify employees from the external job market. What are some of the benefits of job fairs to employers and potential employees?

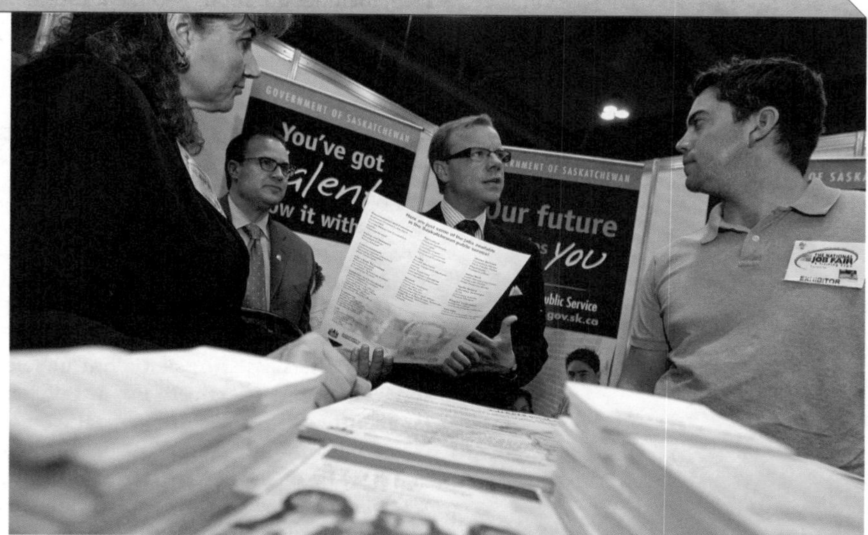

AP/WIDE WORLD PHOTOS

Employee Selection

selection
The process of determining which persons in the applicant pool possess the qualifications necessary to be successful on the job.

After a firm has attracted enough job applicants, employment specialists begin the selection process. **Selection** is the process of determining which persons in the applicant pool possess the qualifications necessary to be successful on the job. The steps in the employee selection process are shown in Exhibit 10.4. An applicant who can jump over each step, or hurdle, will very likely receive a job offer; thus, this is known as the successive hurdles approach to applicant screening. Alternatively, an applicant can be rejected at any step or hurdle. Selection steps or hurdles are described below:

1. *Initial screening.* During the initial screening, an applicant usually completes an application form and has a brief interview of 30 minutes or less. The application

EXHIBIT 10.4 > Steps of the Employee Selection Process

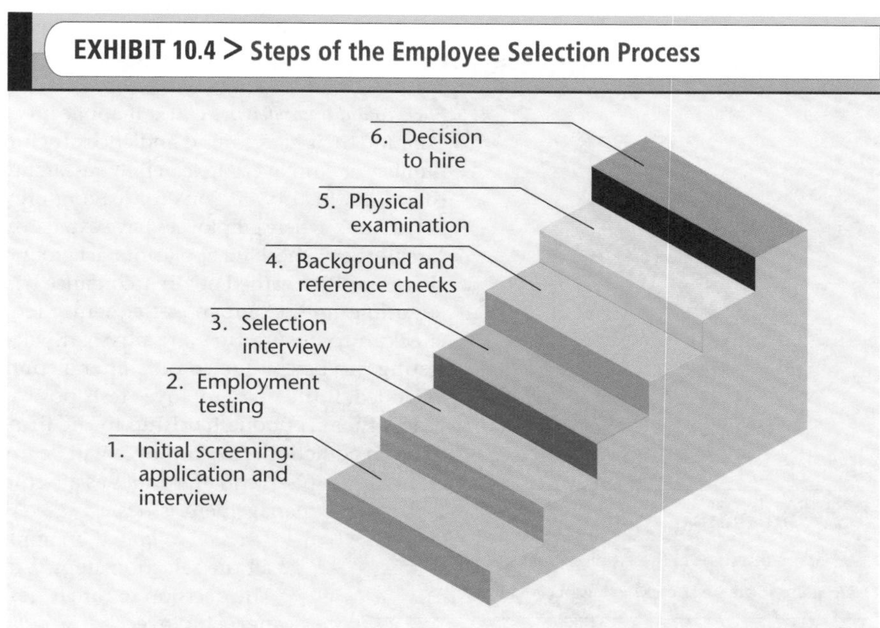

form includes questions about education, work experience, and previous job duties. A personal résumé may be substituted for the application form. If the potential employer believes that the potential employee is suitable, then the next step is the interview. The interview is normally structured, consisting of a short list of specific questions. For example: Are you familiar with any accounting software packages? Did you supervise anyone in your last job? Did you use a company car when making sales calls?

2. *Employment testing.* Following the initial screening, an applicant may be asked to take one or more employment tests, such as the Wonderlic Personnel Test, a mental-ability test. Some tests are designed to measure special job skills, others measure aptitudes, and some are intended to capture characteristics of one's personality. The Myers-Briggs Type Indicator is a personality and motivational instrument widely used on college campuses as an aid in providing job and career counselling as well as assisting a student in selecting his or her major. In recent years some firms have begun to use a test that assesses one's emotional intelligence. Frequently called the e-quotient, the emotional intelligence quotient reveals how well a person understands his or her own emotions and the emotions of others, and how he or she behaves based on this understanding.
3. *Selection interview.* The tool most widely used in making hiring decisions by Intel, Merck, and other firms is the **selection interview**, an in-depth discussion of an applicant's work experience, skills and abilities, education, and career interests. For managerial and professional positions, an applicant may be interviewed by several persons, including the line manager for the position to be filled. This interview is designed to determine an applicant's communication ability and motivation. It is also a means for gathering additional factual information from the applicant such as college major, years of part-time work experience, computer equipment used, and reason for leaving the last job. The applicant may be asked to explain how to solve a particular management problem or how she or he provided leadership to a group in a previous work situation when an important problem had to be solved quickly. United Airlines asks prospective flight attendants how they handled a conflict with a customer or coworker in a previous job.

   Carolyn Murray, a recruiter for W. C. Gore and Associates, makers of Gore-Tex, says she pays little attention to a candidate's carefully scripted responses to her admittedly easy questions. Instead, she listens for a casual remark that reveals the reality behind an otherwise thought-out reply. Using a baseball analogy, Carolyn's examples of how three job candidates struck out are presented in Exhibit 10.5.[1]

selection interview
An in-depth discussion of an applicant's work experience, skills and abilities, education, and career interests.

4. *Background and reference check.* If applicants pass the selection interview, most firms examine their background and check their references. In recent years an increasing number of employers are carefully researching applicants' backgrounds, particularly their legal history, reasons for leaving previous jobs, and even creditworthiness. Retail firms, where employees have extensive contact with customers, tend to be very careful about checking applicant backgrounds. It is important to note that reference checks must be carried out in accordance with current regulations and legislations.
5. *Physical exams.* Companies frequently require job candidates to have a medical checkup to ensure they are physically able to perform a job. In Canada, drug testing can be conducted only after a conditional offer of employment has been extended. If the new employee tests positive, he or she will probably still be hired unless there is undue hardship to the firm as a result. If the condition turns out to be an addiction, the employee will be treated under the new employer's benefit plan, and any issues as a result of the addiction become performance management issues.[2]
6. *Decision to hire.* If an applicant progresses satisfactorily through all the selection steps, a decision to hire the individual is made. The decision to hire is nearly always made by the manager of the new employee.

concept check

What are the steps in the employee selection process?

Describe some ways in which applicants are tested.

EXHIBIT 10.5 > Striking Out with Gore-Tex

The Pitch (Question to Applicant)	The Swing (Applicant's Response)	The Miss (Interviewer's Reaction to Response)
"Give me an example of a time when you had a conflict with a team member."	"Our leader asked me to handle all of the FedExing for our team. I did it, but I thought that FedExing was a waste of my time."	"At Gore, we work from a team concept. Her answer shows that she won't exactly jump when one of her teammates needs help."
"Tell me how you solved a problem that was impeding your project."	"One of the engineers on my team wasn't pulling his weight, and we were closing in on a deadline. So I took on some of his work."	"The candidate may have resolved the issue for this particular deadline, but he did nothing to prevent the problem from happening again."
"What's the one thing that you would change about your current position?"	"My job as a salesman has become boring. Now I want the responsibility of managing people."	"He's probably not maximizing his current territory, and he is complaining. Will he find his next role 'boring' and complain about that role, too?"

Employee Training and Development

training and development
Activities that provide learning situations in which an employee acquires additional knowledge or skills to increase job performance.

orientation
Training that prepares a new employee to perform on the job; includes information about job assignments, work rules, equipment, and performance expectations, as well as about company policies, salary and benefits, and parking.

To ensure that both new and experienced employees have the knowledge and skills to perform their jobs successfully, organizations invest in **training and development** activities. Training and development involves learning situations in which the employee acquires additional knowledge or skills to increase job performance. Training objectives specify performance improvements, reductions in errors, job knowledge to be gained, and/or other positive organizational results. Training is done either on or off the job. The process of creating and implementing training and development activities is shown in Exhibit 10.6.

New employee training is essential and usually begins with **orientation**, which entails getting the new employee ready to perform on the job. Formal orientation (often a half-day classroom program) provides information about company policies, salary and benefits, and parking. Although this information is very helpful, the more important orientation is about job assignments, work rules, equipment, and performance expectations provided by the new employee's supervisor and coworkers. This second briefing tends to be more informal and can last for several days or even weeks.

EXHIBIT 10.6 > Employee Training and Development Process

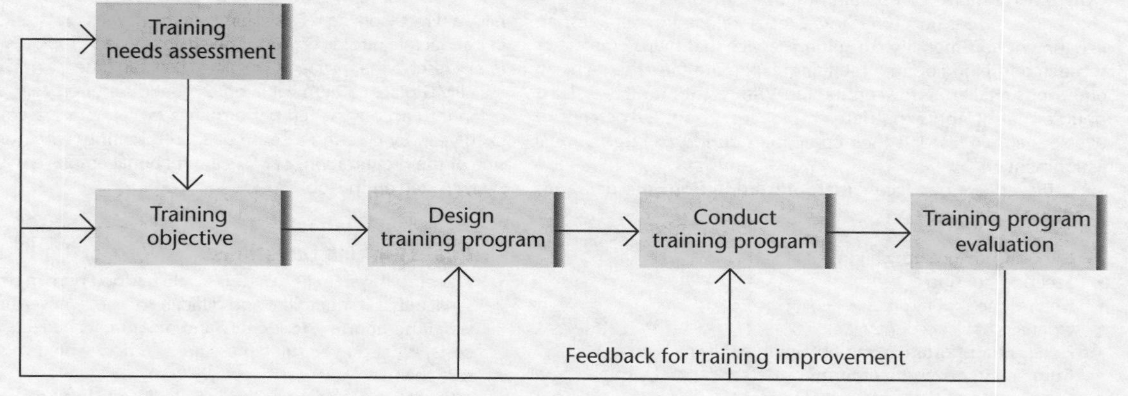

HOT Links

For the latest news in the human resources field, visit the website of the Society for Human Resource Management at **(www.shrm.org)**.

on-the-job training
Training in which the employee learns the job by doing it with guidance from a supervisor or experienced coworker.

job rotation
Reassignment of workers to several different jobs over time so that they can learn the basics of each job.

apprenticeship
A form of on-the-job training that combines specific job instruction with classroom instruction.

mentoring
A form of on-the-job training in which a senior manager or other experienced employee provides job- and career-related information to a protégé.

On-the-Job Training

Continuous training for both new and experienced employees is important to keep job skills fresh. Job-specific training, designed to enhance a new employee's ability to perform a job, includes on-the-job training, during which the employee learns the job by doing it with guidance from a supervisor or experienced coworker.

On-the-job training takes place at the job site or workstation and tends to be directly related to the job. This training involves specific job instructions, coaching (guidance given to new employees by experienced ones), special project assignments, or job rotation. Job rotation is the reassignment of workers to several different jobs over time. It is not uncommon for management trainees to work sequentially in two or three departments, such as customer service, credit, and human resources, during their first year on the job.

An apprenticeship usually combines specific on-the-job instruction with classroom training. It might last as long as four years and can be found in the skilled trades of carpentry, plumbing, and electrical work.

With mentoring, another form of on-the-job training, a senior manager or other experienced employee provides job- and career-related information to a protégé. Inexpensive and providing instantaneous feedback, mentoring is becoming increasingly popular with many firms. For an example of mentoring for cultural orientation, explore Expanding Around the Globe.

Expanding Around The Globe

EMPLOYEES ON THE (INTERNATIONAL) MOVE

Is an international job assignment a step up the ladder to a more rewarding career path or a potential mine-field of professional and family risk? The answer depends as much on an employee's family situation as their ambition, according to a new survey that explores worldwide employee-relocation trends. And it also depends on how well their company supports and handles a transfer to an international location.

Working abroad at one of the Canadian or foreign multinational firms can be exciting and look good on your résumé. Increasing numbers of recent college graduates and experienced professionals are offered opportunities for overseas work assignments ranging from a few days to 24 months, or longer. But acclimating to a new country and culture, as well as a new work environment, can be daunting and involves some unique challenges. According to GMAC Global Relocation Services, an assignment and mobility consulting service that helps employees settle in a foreign country, retaining expatriate talent remains an enormous challenge for companies. With attrition rates at least double that of non-expatriate employees, about 21 percent of overseas employees left their companies during an international assignment.

Other challenges face expatriates aside from the demands of work:

- Choosing schools for children
- Securing housing
- Finding medical facilities
- Opening bank accounts
- Finding transportation and obtaining a driver's license
- Completing government forms
- Locating stores that sell familiar foods
- Learning about community and entertainment offerings

With 1,200 to 1,500 employees working outside of their home countries at any given time, KPMG International, one of the world's largest accounting firms with a presence in 144 countries, attempts to deal with employee relocation adjustment issues by utilizing a "buddy" system. At work, the KPMG Global Code of Conduct, entitled "Performance with Integrity," sets out guidelines of ethical conduct that KPMG requires of all its employees worldwide. The code applies equally to partners and employees of all KPMG member firms regardless of their title or position.

To ease the social and cultural burden for new expatriates, the firm links the employee to a buddy for one-on-one support during the length of their assignment, which is typically 24 months. Timothy Dwyer, national director for international human resource advisory services at KPMG, points out that buddies—who usually do not have a direct working relationship with the new expatriate—function in a social role outside of work. They help the new employee and the family resolve the myriad of problems that can arise.

KPMG places a high value on the buddy support role, which is taken into account when performance evaluations are conducted each year. By creating a sense of shared identity within and outside of the organization, KPMG's international employees are more likely to stay on the job.[3]

Critical Thinking Questions

- The buddy system at KPMG is a value-added human resource service that is intangible and difficult to assess; nevertheless, it is important to identify and measure its benefits and costs. What do you think these are and how would you measure them?
- What are the top four or five job qualifications an employee should have to be considered for an overseas assignment?

Off-the-Job Training

Even with the advantages of on-the-job training, many firms recognize that it is often necessary to train employees away from the workplace. With off-the-job training, employees learn their duties away from the job. There are numerous popular methods of off-the-job training. Frequently, it takes place in a classroom, where cases, role-play exercises, films, videos, lectures, and computer demonstrations are utilized to develop workplace skills.

programmed instruction
A form of computer-assisted off-the-job training.

simulation
A scaled down version or mock-up of equipment, process, or work environment.

Web-based technology is being increasingly used along with more traditional off-the-job training methods. E-learning and e-training involve online computer presentation of information for learning new job tasks. Many companies with widely dispersed employees can deliver training materials electronically to save time and travel costs. For example, transportation companies can deliver technical and safety training through **programmed instruction**, a computer-assisted, self-paced, and highly structured training method that presents trainees with concepts and problems using a modular format. Software can make sure that employees receive, undergo, and complete, as well as sign off on, various training modules.

Computer-assisted training can also be done using a **simulation**, a scaled-down version of a manufacturing process or even a mock cockpit of a jet airplane. Air Canada uses a training simulator for pilots to practice hazardous flight manoeuvres or learn the controls of a new aircraft in a safe, controlled environment with no passengers. The simulator allows for more direct transfer of learning to the job.

concept check

Describe several types of on-the-job training.

What are the advantages of programmed instruction and simulation?

How is technology impacting off-the-job training?

Performance Planning and Evaluation

Along with employee orientation and training, new employees learn about performance expectations through performance planning and evaluation. Managers provide employees with expectations about the job. These are communicated as job objectives, schedules, deadlines, and product and/or service quality requirements. As an employee performs job tasks, the supervisor periodically evaluates the employee's efforts. A **performance appraisal** is a comparison of actual performance with expected performance to assess an employee's contributions to the organization and to make decisions about training, compensation, promotion, and other job changes. The performance planning and appraisal process is shown in Exhibit 10.7 and is described below:

performance appraisal
A comparison of actual performance with expected performance to assess an employee's contributions to the organization.

1. Performance standards are established.
2. The employee works to meet the standards and expectations.

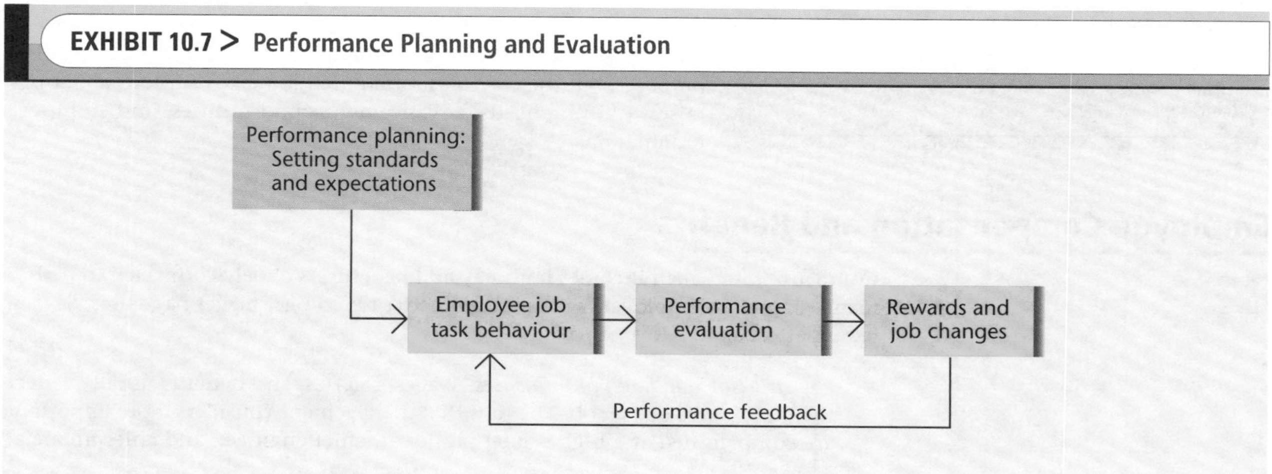

CONCEPT *in Action* >>>

During a performance appraisal, a manager evaluates an employee's performance, comparing actual performance to expected performance goals. At General Electric, employees receive feedback from work teams, peers, and customers to develop perspective on their management style and skills. How does the performance appraisal help the employee and the organization?

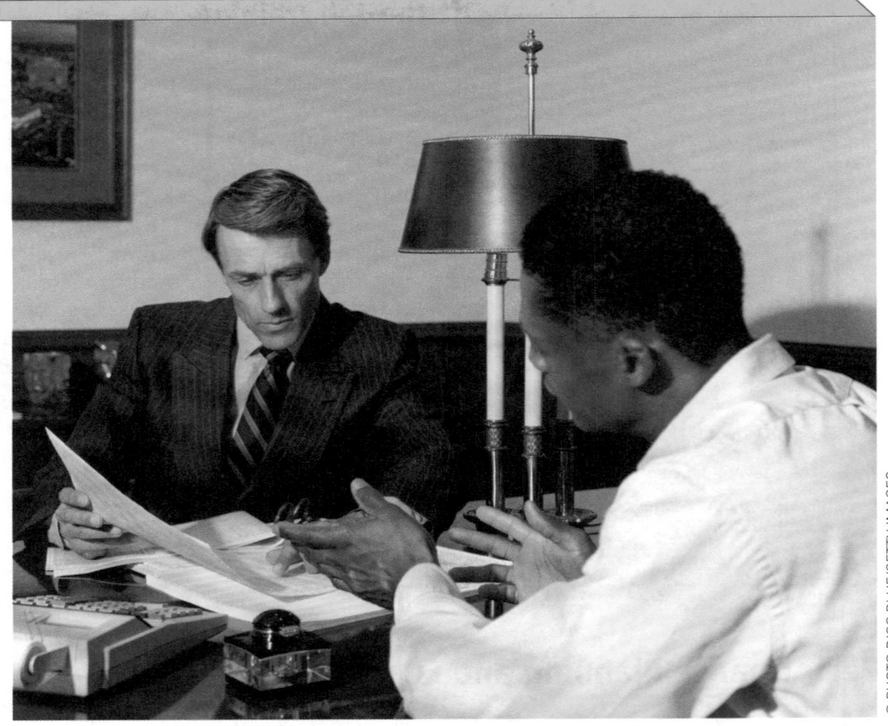

© PHOTO DISC BLUE/GETTY IMAGES

3. The employee's supervisor evaluates the employee's work in terms of quality and quantity of output and various characteristics such as job knowledge, initiative, relationships with others, and attendance and punctuality.
4. Following the performance evaluation, reward (pay raise) and job change (promotion) decisions can be made.
5. Rewards are positive feedback and provide reinforcement, or encouragement, for the employee to work harder in the future.

concept check

What are the steps in the performance planning and appraisal process?

What purposes do performance appraisals serve?

Describe some sources of information for the performance appraisal..

Information for performance appraisals can be assembled using rating scales, supervisor logs of employee job incidents, and reports of sales and production statistics. Regardless of the source, performance information should be accurate and a record of the employee's job behaviour and efforts. Performance appraisals serve a number of purposes, but they are most often used to make decisions about pay raises, training needs, advancement opportunities, and employee terminations.

Employee Compensation and Benefits

LO 6

Compensation, which includes both pay and benefits, is closely connected to performance appraisal. Employees who perform better tend to get bigger pay raises. Several factors affect an employee's pay:

1. *Pay structure and internal influences.* Wages, salaries, and benefits usually reflect the importance of the job. The jobs that management considers more important are compensated at a higher rate; president, chief engineer, and chief financial

officer are high-paying jobs. Likewise, different jobs of equal importance to the firm are compensated at the same rate. For instance, if a drill-press operator and a lathe operator are considered of equal importance, they might both be paid $21 per hour.

2. *Pay level and external influences.* In deciding how much to pay workers, the firm must also be concerned with the salaries paid by competitors. If competitors are paying much higher wages, a firm might lose its best employees. Larger firms conduct salary surveys to see what other firms are paying. Wage and salary surveys conducted by Statistics Canada, for example, can also be useful.

An employer can decide to pay at, above, or below the going rate. Most firms try to offer competitive wages and salaries within a geographic area or an industry. If a company pays below-market wages, it might not be able to hire skilled people. The level, or competitiveness, of a firm's compensation is determined by the firm's financial condition (or profitability), efficiency, and employee productivity, as well as the going rates paid by competitors.

Types of Compensation or Pay

There are two basic types of compensation: direct and indirect. Direct pay is the wage or salary received by the employee; indirect pay consists of various employee benefits and services. Employees are usually paid directly on the basis of the amount of time they work, the amount they produce, or some combination of time and output. Hourly rates of pay or a monthly salary are considered base pay, or an amount of pay received by the employee regardless of output level.

The following are the most common types of compensation:

- *Hourly wages.* These will vary depending on the positions and job market. Each province and territory in Canada is responsible to set a "minimum hourly wage."
- *Salaries.* Managerial and professional employees are usually paid an annual salary on either a biweekly or a monthly basis.
- *Piecework and commission.* Some employees are paid according to how much they produce or sell. A car salesperson might be paid $500 for each car sold or a 3 percent commission on the car's sale price. Thus, a salesperson who sold four cars in one week at $500 per car would earn $2,000 in pay for that week. Alternatively, a 3 percent commission on four cars sold with total sales revenue of $70,000 would yield $2,100 in pay.

  Increasingly, business firms are paying employees using a base wage or salary and an incentive. The incentive feature is designed to increase individual employee, work group, and/or organizational performance. Incentive pay plans are commonly referred to as variable or contingent pay arrangements.
- *Accelerated commission schedule.* A salesperson could be paid a commission rate of 3 percent on the first $50,000 of sales per month, 4 percent on the next $30,000, and 5 percent on any sales beyond $80,000. For a salesperson that made $90,000 of sales in one month, the monthly pay would be as follows:

  3 percent × $50,000 = $1,500
  4 percent × $30,000 = $1,200
  5 percent × $10,000 = $ 500
  $90,000 → $3,200
- *Bonus.* A bonus is a payment for reaching a specific goal; it may be paid on a monthly, quarterly, or annual basis. A bank with several offices or branches might set monthly goals for opening new accounts, making loans, and customer service. Each employee of a branch that meets all goals would be paid a monthly bonus of $100. Although the bonuses are paid to the employees

concept check

How does a firm establish a pay scale for its employees?

What is the difference between direct and indirect pay?

Making Ethical Choices

KEEPING SECRETS

Working on national security issues for a consulting firm with the Canadian Security Intelligence Service contracts has been both exciting and increasingly stressful. The excitement comes from the actual work of investigating and evaluating potential terrorist threats to Canada. The stress is a result of a greatly increased workload and much closer scrutiny of your work. When you started your job in June, 40- to 45-hour weeks were common. Since the increased terrorist attacks around the world, your workload has increased dramatically, and you now must work 55 to 65 hours per week. Managers appear to be monitoring employees' activities and paying closer attention to their mental state for evidence of instability. Along with your fellow workers, you are concerned that the heightened security measures might change the policies with regard to confidentiality of medical records.

Because the consulting firm's culture doesn't support open discussion, you don't feel comfortable talking with your colleagues or your supervisor about the stress you are experiencing. Instead, you seek counsel from HR and are given names of several psychotherapists who participate in the company's employee assistance plan. You assume that your visit to HR and the subject of that visit are as secret as the nature of your work. Your psychotherapist has advised you that your visits and the content of all sessions are confidential.

You begin to sense that your supervisor is aware of your 90-minute absences, even though you made sure to schedule visits to the therapist on a different day and different time each week. The idea that your supervisor might know you are seeking psychological counselling only increases your stress level.

ETHICAL DILEMMA Does your employer have the right to know about your visits to a psychotherapist?

SOURCES: Tybe Diamond, "American Psychoanalytic Association Files a Lawsuit to Challenge the Bush Administration HIPPA Abuses," e-mail, April 14, 2003; "Protecting Privacy and Personal Security—Our World's Need for a Careful Balance and the 10 Commandments of Ethical Surveillance," *PRNewsire*, September 13, 2001, (www.findarticles.com); and Jonathan A. Segal, "Security vs. Privacy: To Ensure a Secure Environment for All Workers Avoid Violating the Privacy of Any One Individual," *HR Magazine*, February 2002, (www.findarticles.com).

NORM BETTS / LANDOV

CONCEPT *in Action* >>>

Determining a CEO's fair salary isn't easy. CEOs are responsible for making decisions that can impact tens of thousands of employees and dramatically increase or decrease the value of a company. Indigo CEO Heather Reisman's compensation package would have to reflect her 25 years of extensive business experience. How do you think executive salaries should be determined?

individually, the employees must function as an effective, high-performing group to reach the monthly goals.

- *Profit sharing.* A firm that offers profit sharing pays employees a portion of the profits over a preset level. For example, profits beyond 10 percent of gross sales might be shared at a 50 percent rate with employees. The company retains the remaining profits. All employees might receive the same profit shares, or the shares might vary according to base pay.
- *Fringe benefits.* **Fringe benefits** are indirect compensation and include pensions, health insurance, vacations, and many others. Some fringe benefits are required by law (e.g., paid vacations and holidays, employment insurance [EI] and Canada or Quebec Pension Plan [CPP or QPP], the EI and CPP/QPP are paid at least in part by the employer).

Many employers also offer fringe benefits not required by law. Among these are paid time off (e.g., extra vacations, sick days), insurance (health care, disability, life, dental, vision, and accidental death and dismemberment), pensions and retirement savings accounts, and stock purchase options.

Some firms with numerous fringe benefits allow employees to mix and match benefit items or select items based on individual needs. This is a flexible, or cafeteria-style, benefit plan. A younger employee with a family might desire to purchase medical, disability, and life insurance, whereas an older employee might want to put more benefit dollars into a retirement savings plan. All employees are allocated the same number of benefit dollars but can spend these dollars on different items and in different amounts.

fringe benefits
Indirect compensation, such as pensions, health insurance, and vacations.

Understanding Labour Relations in a Unionized Environment

LO 7

labour union
An organization that represents workers in dealing with management over issues involving wages, hours, and working conditions.

A **labour union** is an organization that represents workers in dealing with management over issues involving wages, hours, and working conditions. The labour relations process that produces a union–management relationship consists of three phases: union organizing, negotiating a labour agreement, and the day-to-day administering of the agreement. In Phase 1, a group of employees within a firm might form a union on their own, or an established union may target an employer and organize many of

collective bargaining
The process of negotiating labour agreements that provide for compensation and working arrangements mutually acceptable to the union and to management.

the firm's workers into a local labour union. The second phase constitutes **collective bargaining**, which is the process of negotiating labour agreements that provide for compensation and working arrangements mutually acceptable to the union and to management.

Finally, the third phase of the labour relations process involves the daily administering of the labour agreement primarily through the handling of worker grievances and other workforce management problems that require interaction between managers and labour union officials.

Modern Labour Movement

local union
A branch or unit of a national union that represents workers at a specific plant or in a specific geographic area.

national union
A union that consists of many local unions in a particular industry, skilled trade, or geographic area and thus represents workers throughout an entire country.

A **local union** is a branch or unit of a **national union** that represents workers at a specific plant or over a specific geographic area. In conformance to national union rules, local unions determine the number of local union officers, procedures for electing officers, the schedule of local meetings, financial arrangements with the national organization, and the local's role in negotiating labour agreements.

The largest national union is the Canadian Union of Public Employees (CUPE) with more than half a million members across Canada. CUPE represents workers in airlines, education, emergency services, health care, libraries, municipalities, public utilities, social services, transportation, and universities. Under the CUPE national union are the various local unions (e.g., CUPE local 774 in Abbotsford, British Columbia).

The three main functions of the local union are collective bargaining, worker relations and membership services, and community and political activities. Collective bargaining generally takes place every two or three years. Local union officers and shop stewards oversee worker-management relations on a day-to-day basis. A **shop steward** is an elected union official who represents union members to management when workers have issues. For most union members, his or her primary contact with the union is through union officials at the local level.

shop steward
An elected union official who represents union members to management when workers have issues.

Negotiating Union Contracts

A union contract is created through collective bargaining. Typically, both management and union negotiating teams are made up of a few persons. One person on each side is the chief spokesperson.

Bargaining begins with union and management negotiators setting a bargaining agenda, a list of contract issues that will be discussed. Much of the bargaining over the specific details takes place through face-to-face meetings and the exchange of written proposals. Demands, proposals, and counterproposals are exchanged during several rounds of bargaining. The resulting contract must then be approved by top management and by union members. The collective bargaining process is shown in Exhibit 10.8.

The union contract is a legally binding agreement that typically covers such issues as union security, management rights, wages and benefits, job security, and grievance procedures. Each of these is discussed in this section.

closed shop
A company where only union members can be hired.

union shop
A company where non-union workers can be hired but must then join the union.

agency shop
A company where employees are not required to join the union but must pay it a fee to cover its expenses in representing them.

Union Security One of the key issues in a contract is union security. From the union's perspective, the most secure arrangement is the **closed shop**, a company where only union members can be hired. The union serves, in effect, as an employment agency for the firm. Today, the most common form of union security is the **union shop**. Non-union workers can be hired, but then they must join the union, normally within 30 or 60 days.

An **agency shop** does not require employees to join the union, but to keep working at the company, employees must pay the union a fee to cover its expenses in representing them. The union must fairly represent all workers, including those who do not become members.

EXHIBIT 10.8 > The Process of Negotiating Labour Agreements

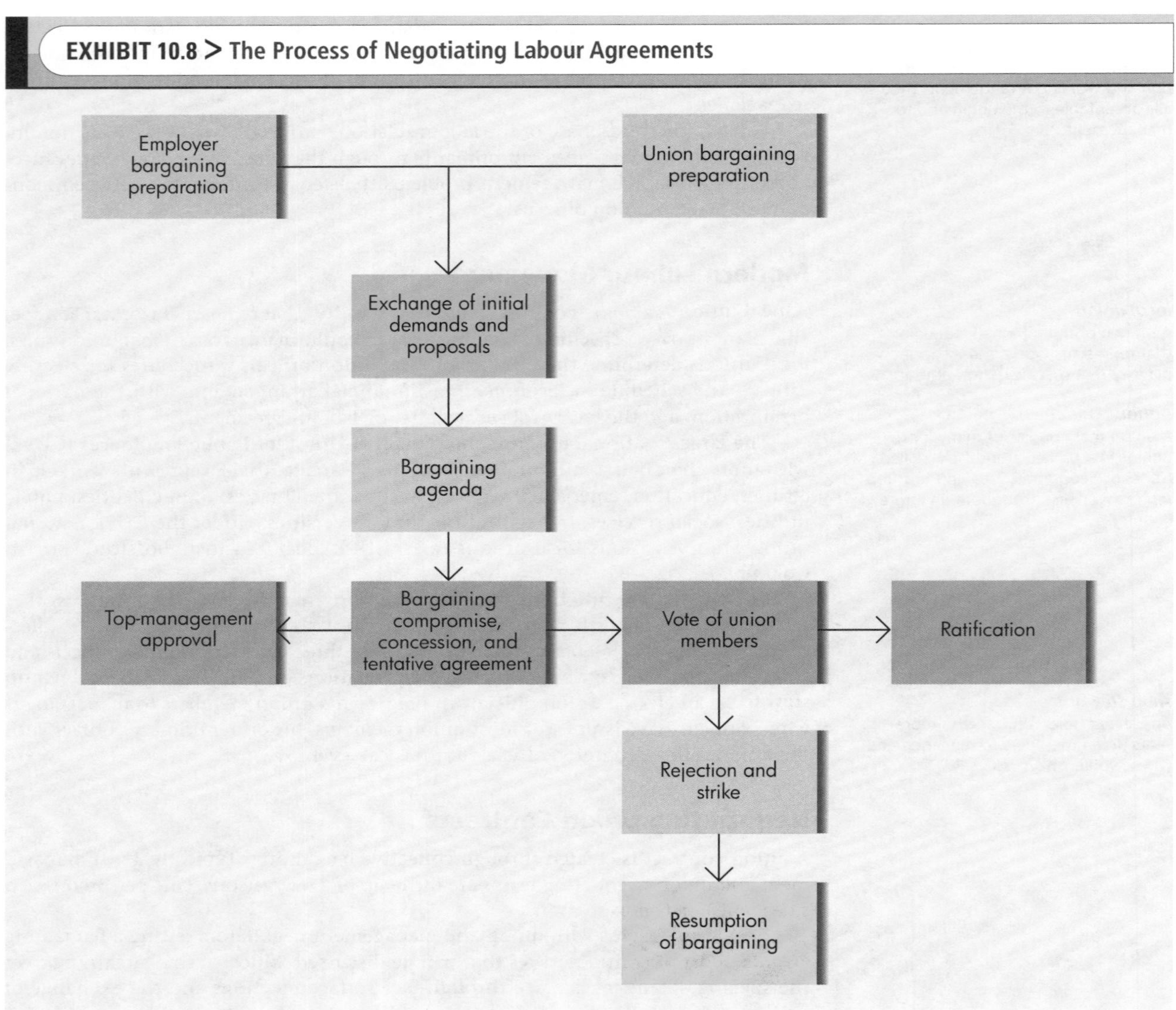

open shop
A company where employees do not have to join the union or pay dues or fees to the union; established under right-to-work laws.

When employees can work at a unionized company without having to join the union, this arrangement is commonly known as an open shop. Workers don't have to join the union or pay dues or fees to the union.

Management Rights When a company becomes unionized, management loses some of its decision-making abilities. But management still has certain rights that can be negotiated in collective bargaining.

One way to lessen a union's influence in the management of an organization is by having a *management rights clause* in the labour agreement. Most union contracts have one. A typical clause gives the employer all rights to manage the business except as specified in the contract. For instance, if the contract does not specify the criteria for promotions, with a management rights clause managers will have the right to use any criteria they wish. Another way to preserve management rights is to list areas that are not subject to collective bargaining. This list might secure management's right to schedule work hours, hire and fire workers, set production standards, determine the number of supervisors in each department, and promote, demote, and transfer workers.

Wages and Benefits Much bargaining effort goes into wage increases and improvements in fringe benefits. Once agreed to, they remain in effect for the life of the contract. Some contracts provide for a cost-of-living adjustment (COLA), under which wages increase automatically as the cost of living goes up.

cost-of-living adjustment (COLA)
A provision in a labour contract that calls for wages to increase automatically as the cost of living rises (usually measured by the consumer price index).

Other contracts provide for *lump-sum wage adjustments*. The workers' base pay remains unchanged for the contract period (usually two or three years), but each worker receives a bonus (or lump sum) once or twice during the contract.

The union and the employer are usually both concerned about the firm's ability to pay higher wages. The firm's ability to pay depends greatly on its profitability. But even if profits have declined, average to above-average wage increases are still possible if labour productivity increases.

In addition to requests for wage increases, unions usually want better fringe benefits. In some industries, such as steel and auto manufacturing, fringe benefits are 40 percent of the total cost of compensation. Benefits might include higher wages for overtime work, holiday work, and less desirable shifts; insurance programs (life, health and hospitalization, dental care); payment for certain non-work time (rest periods, vacations, holidays, sick time); pensions; and income maintenance plans. A fairly common income maintenance plan is a *supplementary unemployment benefits fund* set up by the employer to help laid-off workers.

Job Security and Seniority Cost-of-living adjustments, supplementary unemployment benefits, and certain other benefits give employees some financial security. But most financial security is directly related to job security—the assurance, to some degree, that workers will keep their jobs. Of course, job security depends primarily on the continued success and financial well-being of the company.

Seniority, the length of an employee's continuous service with a firm, is discussed in about 90 percent of all labour contracts. Seniority is a factor in job security; usually, unions want the workers with the most seniority to have the most job security.

concept check

Discuss the difference between a local and national union.

Explain the collective bargaining process.

Explain each of the following: closed shop, union shop, agency shop, and open shop.

Grievance and Arbitration The union's main way of policing the contract is the grievance procedure. A grievance is a formal complaint, by an employee or by the union, that management has violated some part of the contract. Under a typical contract, the employee starts by presenting the grievance to the supervisor, either in person or in writing. The typical grievance procedure is illustrated in Exhibit 10.9.

grievance
A formal complaint, filed by an employee or by the union, charging that management has violated the contract.

If the problem isn't solved, the grievance is put in writing. The employee, one or more union officials, the supervisor, and perhaps the plant manager then discuss the grievance. If the matter still can't be resolved, another meeting takes place with higher level representatives of both parties present. If top management and the local union president can't resolve the grievance, it goes to arbitration.

Arbitration is the process of settling a labour-management dispute by having a third party—a single arbitrator or a panel—make a decision. The arbitrator is mutually chosen by labour and management and is expected to be impartial. The decision is final and binding on the union and the employer. The arbitrator reviews the grievance at a hearing and then makes the decision, which is presented in a document called the award.

arbitration
The process of settling a labour-management dispute by having a third party—a single arbitrator or a panel—make a decision, which is binding on both the union and the employer..

Similar to arbitration is mediation, the process of settling issues in which the parties present their case to a neutral mediator. The mediator (the specialist) holds talks with union and management negotiators at separate meetings and at joint sessions. The mediator also suggests compromises. Mediators cannot issue binding decisions or impose a settlement on the disputing parties. Their only tools are communication and persuasion. Mediation almost always produces a settlement between the union and a firm, but sometimes the process takes months or even a year, and either or both sides can reject the mediator's assistance.

mediation
A method of attempting to settle labour issues in which a specialist (the mediator) tries to persuade management and the union to adjust or settle their dispute.

EXHIBIT 10.9 > Typical Grievance Procedure

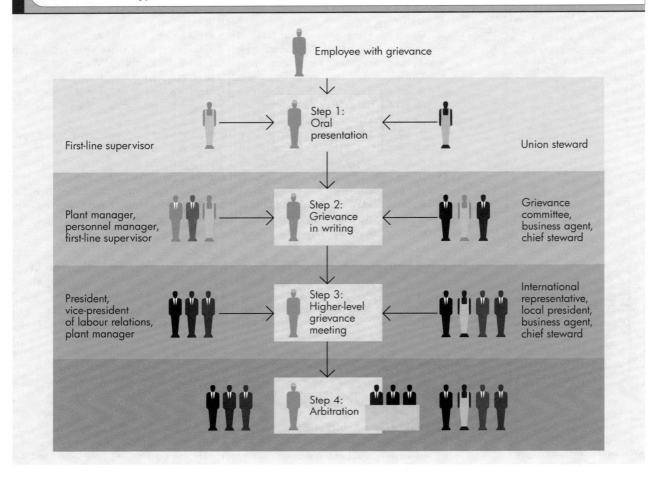

Tactics for Pressuring a Contract Settlement

Virtually all labour agreements specify peaceful resolution of conflicts, usually through arbitration. However, when a contract expires and a new agreement has not been reached, the union is free to strike or engage in other efforts to exert economic pressure on the employer. A strike occurs when employees refuse to work. Likewise, the employer can put pressure on the union through a lockout or hiring strike replacements if the union has called a strike. Some services which are seen to be critical do not have the option of a strike or lockout. Other strategies to force a contract settlement are listed in Exhibit 10.10.

concept check

Describe the grievance procedure.

What is the distinction between arbitration and mediation?

In what ways do arbitrators act like judges?

Laws Affecting Human Resource Management

Federal laws help ensure that job applicants and employees are treated fairly and not discriminated against. Hiring, training, and job placement must be unbiased. Promotion and compensation decisions must be based on performance. These laws help all Canadians who have talent, training, and the desire to get ahead.

EXHIBIT 10.10 > Strategies of Unions and Employers

Union Strategies		Employer Strategies	
Strike:	Employees refuse to work.	**Lockout:**	Employer refuses to let Employees enter plant to work.
Boycott:	Employees try to keep customers and others from doing business with employer.	**Strike replacements:**	Employer uses non-union employees to do jobs of striking union employees.
Picketing:	Employees march near entrance of firm to publicize their view of dispute and discourage customers.	**Mutual-aid pact:**	Employer receives money from other companies in industry to cover some of income lost because of strikes.
Corporate campaign:	Union disrupts shareholder meetings or buys company stock to have more influence over management.	**Shift production:**	Employer moves production to non-union plant or out of country.

CONCEPT *in Action* >>>

Strikes are powerful union tools, usually used as a last resort when labour and management cannot reach agreement on issues such as wages, pensions, vacation time, and other benefits. What other strategies are available to both unions and managements to force a contract?

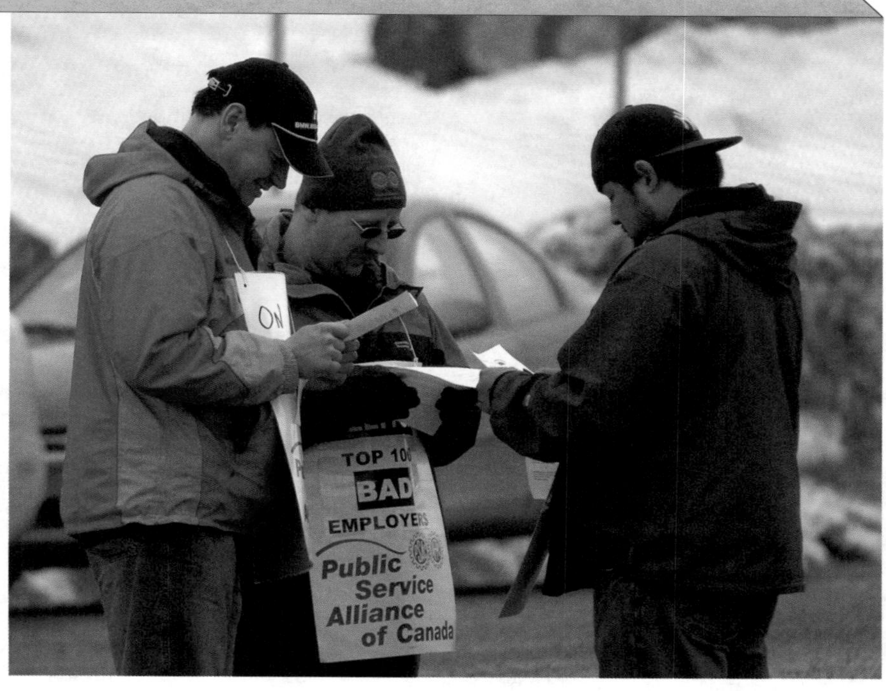

CP PHOTO (BRENT REANEY)

HOT Links

Learn more about the Employment Equity Act by searching The Department of Justice Canada at (**www.justice.gc.ca**).

New legislation and the continual interpretation and reinterpretation of existing laws will continue to make the jobs of human resource managers challenging and complicated. The key laws that currently affect human resource management are shown in Exhibit 10.11.

Employers may not discriminate against persons with disability. They must make "reasonable accommodations," so that qualified employees can perform the job, unless doing so would cause "undue hardship" for the business. Altering

EXHIBIT 10.11 > Laws Impacting Human Resource Management

Law	Purpose	Applicability
Charter of Rights and Freedoms (contained in the Constitution Act of 1982)	Provides the right to live and seek employment anywhere in Canada	Takes precedence over all other laws
Human rights legislation	Provides equal opportunity for members of protected groups in areas such as accommodation, contracts, provision of goods and services, and employment	Comprised of federal, provincial, and territorial laws with a common objective
Canadian Human Rights Act (1977)	Prohibits discrimination on a number of grounds	Applies to federal government agencies, Crown corporations, and businesses under federal jurisdiction
Employment Equity Act (amended in 1996)	Attempts to remove employment barriers and promote equality for the members of four designated groups: women, visible minorities, Aboriginal people, and persons with disabilities	Every employer must implement the Act and make every reasonable accommodation to ensure that people in the designated groups are represented in their organization. The degree of representation in each occupational group should reflect the Canadian workforce and be consistent with their ability to meet reasonable occupational requirements
Occupational Health and Safety Act	Designed to protect the health and safety of workers by minimizing work-related accidents and illness	All provinces, territories, and the federal jurisdiction have occupational health and safety legislation
WHMIS (Workplace Hazardous Materials Information System)	Designed to protect workers by providing information about hazardous materials in the workplace	Canada-wide legally mandated system

work schedules, modifying equipment so a wheelchair-bound person can use it, and making buildings accessible by ramps and elevators are considered reasonable. Two companies often praised for their efforts to hire people with disabilities are McDonald's and IBM Canada.

Canada's overall employment equity record of the past decade has been mixed. The employment of women in professional occupations continues to grow, but minority representation among professionals has not significantly increased, even though professional jobs have been among the fastest-growing areas. Technical jobs have the most equitable utilization rates of minorities. Almost 400 federal and federally regulated organizations submit annual reports to Human Resources Development Canada (HRDC) under the Employment Equity Act. The organizations are then graded on an alphabetical scale.

concept check

What are the key laws affecting employment?

What is employment equity?.

Trends in Human Resource Management

Some of today's most important trends in human resource management are using employee diversity as a competitive advantage, improving efficiency through outsourcing and technology, and hiring employees who fit the organizational culture.

CONCEPT *in Action* >>>

For some occupations, danger is part of the job description. Tallies of work-related casualties routinely identify loggers, pilots, commercial fishermen, and steel workers as holding the most deadly jobs in industry. Job fatalities are often linked to the use of heavy or outdated equipment. However, many work-related deaths also happen in common highway accidents or as homicides. What laws and agencies are designated to improve occupational safety?

© NATALIE FOBES/CORBIS

Employee Diversity and Competitive Advantage

competitive advantage
A set of unique features of an organization that are perceived by customers and potential customers as significant and superior to the competition.

Canadian society and its workforce are becoming increasingly more diverse in terms of racial and ethnic status, age, educational background, work experience, and gender. A company with a demographic employee profile that looks like its customers may be in a position to gain a competitive advantage, which is a set of unique features of a company and its product or service that are perceived by the target market as superior to those of the competition. Competitive advantage is the factor that causes customers to patronize a firm and not the competition. Many things can be a source of competitive advantage: for WestJet Airlines it is route structure and high asset utilization; for the Four Seasons Hotels it is very high quality guest services; for Toyota it is manufacturing efficiency and product durability; and for Tim Hortons it is location, service, and outstanding coffee products. For these firms, a competitive advantage is also created by their HR practices.

Many firms are successful because of employee diversity which can produce more effective problem solving, a stronger reputation for hiring women and minorities, even greater employee diversity, quicker adaptation to change, and more robust product solutions because a diverse team can generate more options for improvement.[4]

In order for an organization to use employee diversity for competitive advantage, top management must be fully committed to hiring and developing women and minority individuals.

Outsourcing HR and Technology

outsource
The assignment of various functions, such as human resources, accounting, or legal work, to outside organizations.

The role of the HR professional has changed noticeably over the past 20 years. One significant change has been the use of technology in handling relatively routine HR tasks, such as payroll processing, initial screening of applicants, and benefits enrolments. Many businesses have purchased specialized software (SAP and Oracle/PeopleSoft) to perform the information processing aspects of many HR tasks. Other firms outsource, or contract out these tasks to HR service providers.

HR outsourcing is done when another firm can perform a task better and more efficiently, thus saving costs. Sometimes HR activities are outsourced because HR requirements are extraordinary and too overwhelming to execute in-house in a timely fashion. Frequently, HR activities are simply outsourced because a provider has greater expertise.

Organizational Culture and Hiring for Fit

Regardless of general business and economic conditions, many firms are expanding operations and hiring additional employees. For many growing firms, corporate culture can be a key aspect of developing employees into a competitive advantage for the firm. Corporate culture refers to the core values and beliefs that support the mission and business model of the firm and guide employee behaviour. Companies frequently hire for fit with their corporate cultures. This necessitates recruitment and selection of employees who exhibit the values of the firm. The companies might use carefully crafted applicant questionnaires to screen for values and behaviours that support corporate culture. In addition to cultural fit, firms are increasingly hiring for technical knowledge and skills fit to the job.

concept check

How can employee diversity give a company a competitive advantage?

What are some of the advantages and disadvantages to outsourcing services?

Explain the concept of hiring for fit.

Great Ideas to Use Now

Planning Your Career

It's never too early to start thinking about your career in business. No, you don't have to decide today, but it's important to decide fairly soon to plan your life's work. A very practical reason for doing so is that it will save you a lot of time and money. We have seen too many students who aren't really sure what they want to do after graduation. The longer you wait to choose a profession, the more credit hours you might have to take in your new field, and the longer it will be before you start earning real money.

A second reason to choose a career field early is that you can get a part-time or summer job and "test-drive" the profession. If it's not for you, you will find out very quickly.

Your school career centre can give you plenty of information about various careers in business. We also describe many career opportunities at the end of each part of this text. Another source of career information is the Internet. Go to any search engine, such as Excite or Lycos, and enter "careers in business," or narrow your search to a specific area such as management or marketing.

Career planning will not end when you find your first professional job. It is a lifelong process that ends only with retirement. Your career planning will include conducting a periodic self-assessment of your strengths and weaknesses, gathering information about other jobs both within the firm and externally, learning about other industries, and setting career goals for yourself. You must always think about your future in business.

Human Resources Decision Making

During your professional career in business, you will likely have the opportunity to become a manager. As a manager, you will have to make many human resource decisions, including hiring, firing, promoting, giving a pay raise, sending an employee to a training program, disciplining a worker, approving a college tuition reimbursement request, and reassigning an employee to a different job. In short, you will be involved in virtually every human resource decision or activity affecting the employees you manage. Always treat people as you wish to be treated when making human resource decisions. Be fair, be honest, offer your experience and advice, and communicate frequently with your employees. If you follow this simple advice, you will be richly rewarded in your career.

Customer Satisfaction and Quality

Interviewing for a job can be a nerve-wracking experience. You show up on time in your interview suit expecting to meet someone equally prepared. But that is not always the case. One hears plenty of horror stories of personnel recruiters keeping interviewees waiting while they nonchalantly carry out some unimportant task, like watering their plants. Your meeting with a human resource representative is often your first exposure to the company you are applying to work for, and nothing is more demeaning than to be shown a lack of respect. Firms need to provide good customer service to applicants if they expect to hire the most qualified employees.

The following are further examples of poor customer service when dealing with job applicants:

- A firm reschedules your interview but doesn't let you know about the change
- A firm fails to acknowledge receiving your job application or résumé
- The interviewer eats his or her lunch during your job interview
- The interviewer interrupts the interview to answer cell phone calls that are clearly personal
- The firm fails to contact you for several weeks after your interview
- The interviewer is obviously not prepared to conduct the interview

Firms have several opportunities to create a positive impression of their organization during these key points in the employee selection process. These include a variety of communication channels, such as:

- in-person greetings at a job fair or at the interview itself,
- phone calls to a prospective employee from a human resource professional to set up the interview and any follow-up conversations between human resources and the applicant,
- e-mail correspondence to acknowledge receipt of an application and to thank applicants for submitting their job application,
- information packets given to the applicant, and
- a thank-you note from the employer following the second interview.

A firm that is recognized for treating prospective employees especially well is the Ritz-Carlton Hotel, a subsidiary of Marriott International. Ritz managers want to make a good impression, because an applicant could be a future Ritz-Carlton hotel guest. A department head or hotel executive greets each attendee personally at Ritz-Carlton job fairs. Every applicant receives a personal, formal thank-you note for coming to the job fair, and those who are considered for positions but later rejected receive another note. All job fair applicants complete a behavioural questionnaire and are briefly interviewed.

"The Ritz-Carlton knows how to take care of its employees and customers and the upshot is that it has amazing customer service," says David Saxby, president of Measure-X, a company that specializes in helping utilities improve their customer service and sales. "Ritz-Carlton officials know their efforts create a win-win-win situation. Employees feel good about themselves, guests are happy and the company stays in business."[5]

Critical Thinking Questions

- What are the benefits of an employer treating a job applicant like a customer? Are there costs associated with treating applicants poorly?
- Assume you are a hiring manager. What things can you do to ensure that applicants develop a favourable impression of your firm?

Summary of Learning Outcomes

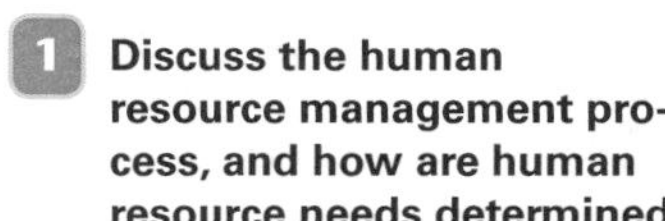

1 Discuss the human resource management process, and how are human resource needs determined

The human resource management process consists of a sequence of activities that begins with job analysis and HR planning; progresses to employee recruitment and selection; then focuses on employee training, performance appraisal, and compensation; and ends when the employee leaves the organization.

Creating a strategy for meeting human resource needs is called human resource planning, which begins with job analysis. Job analysis is the process of studying a job to determine its tasks and duties for setting pay, determining employee job performance, specifying hiring requirements, and designing training programs. Information from the job analysis is used to prepare a job description, which lists the tasks and responsibilities of the job. A job specification describes the skills, knowledge, and abilities a person needs to fill the job described in the job description. By examining the human resource demand forecast and the internal supply forecast, human resource professionals can determine if the company faces a personnel surplus or shortage.

2 Explain how firms recruit applicants.

When a job vacancy occurs, most firms begin by trying to fill the job from within. If a suitable internal candidate is not available, the firm begins an external search. Firms use local media to recruit non-technical, unskilled, and non-supervisory workers. To locate highly trained recruits, employers use college recruiters, executive search firms, job fairs, and company websites to promote job openings.

3 Summarize how firms select qualified applicants.

Typically, an applicant submits an application or résumé and then receives a short, structured interview. If an applicant makes it past the initial screening, he or she might be asked to take an aptitude, personality, or skills test. The next step is the selection interview, which is an in-depth discussion of the applicant's work experience, skills and abilities, education, and career interests.

4 List some of the types of training and development programs organizations offer their employees.

Training and development programs are designed to increase employees' knowledge, skills, and abilities to foster job performance improvements. Formal training (usually classroom in nature and off-the-job) takes place shortly after being hired. Development programs prepare employees to assume positions of increasing authority and responsibility. Job rotation, executive education programs, mentoring, and special-project assignments are examples of employee development programs.

5 Show how performance appraisals are used to evaluate employee performance.

A performance appraisal compares an employee's actual performance with the expected performance. Performance appraisals serve several purposes but are typically used to determine an employee's compensation, training needs, and advancement opportunities.

6 Analyze the various methods for compensating employees.

Direct pay is the hourly wage or monthly salary paid to an employee. In addition to the base wage or salary, direct pay may include bonuses and profit shares. Indirect pay consists of various benefits and services. Some benefits are required by law: unemployment compensation, worker's compensation, Canada or Quebec Pension Plan, and paid vacations and holidays. Others are voluntarily made available by employers to employees. These include pensions, health and other insurance products, employee wellness programs, and college tuition reimbursement.

7 Explain how labour-management relations are different in a unionized environment

Many organizations have unionized employees. A labour union is organized to represent workers in dealing with management over issues involving wages, hours, and working conditions. Contracts are negotiated that set out the responsibilities of management and the workers through collective bargaining.

8 Describe some of the key laws and federal agencies affecting human resource management and labour relations.

A number of federal, provincial, and territorial laws affect human resource management. These include the Charter of Rights and Freedoms (contained in the Constitution Act of 1982), the Canadian Human Rights Act (1977), the Employment Equity Act (amended in 1995), the Occupational Health and Safety Act, and the Workplace Hazardous Materials Information System.

9 List some of the trends and issues affecting human resource management and labour relations.

Today, more and more companies are actively recruiting minorities. A diverse workforce often leads to increased market share and profits. Organizations are becoming proactive in their management of diversity. Companies are creating initiatives to build effective multicultural organizations.

Outsourcing is becoming more popular as a means to increased cost savings and ease of obtaining expertise. Technology continues to improve the efficiency of human resource management. It also enables firms to outsource many functions done internally in the past. In addition to normal job requirements, selected workers must have the ability to adapt to a local culture and perhaps to learn a foreign language.

KEY TERMS

agency shop 305
apprenticeship 300
arbitration 307
closed shop 305
collective bargaining 305
competitive advantage 311
contigent workers 295
corporate open house 296
cost-of-living adjustment (COLA) 307
fringe benefits 304
grievance 307
human resource (HR) planning 293
human resource management 292
job analysis 294
job description 294
job fair 296
job rotation 300
job specification 294
labour union 304
layoff
local union 305
mediation 307
mentoring 300
mutual-aid pact
national union 305
on-the-job training 300
open shop 306
orientation 299
outsource 311
performance appraisal 301
programmed instruction 301
recruitment 296
selection 297
selection interview 298
shop steward 305
simulation 301
training and development 299
union shop 305

Experiential Exercises

1. Make telecommuting work for you. Maybe a part-time job requires too much driving time. Perhaps there are simply no jobs in the immediate area that suit you. Try telecommuting right now. Is telecommuting for you? Many people are more satisfied with their personal and family lives than before they started working at home. But telecommuting is not for every person or every job, and you'll need plenty of self-discipline to make it work for you. Ask yourself if you can perform your duties without close supervision. Think also about whether you would miss your coworkers. If you decide to give telecommuting a try, consider these suggestions to maintain your productivity:

   - *Set ground rules with your family.* Spouses and small children have to understand that even though you're in the house, you are busy earning a living. It's fine to throw in a few loads of laundry or answer the door when the plumber comes. It's another thing to take the kids to the mall or let them play games on your office PC.
   - *Clearly demarcate your work space by using a separate room with a door you can shut.* Let your family know that, emergencies excepted, the space is off-limits during working hours.
   - *If you have small children, you might want to arrange for childcare during your working hours.*
   - *Stay in touch with your coworkers and professional colleagues.* Go into the office from time to time for meetings to stay connected.

   Above all, you can make telecommuting work for you by being productive. Doing your job well, whether on-site or telecommuting, will help assure you of a bright future.

2. The fringe benefit package of many employers includes numerous voluntarily provided items such as health care insurance, life insurance, a pension plan, tuition reimbursement, employee price discounts on products of the firm, and paid sick leave. At your age, what are the three or four most important benefits? Why? Twenty years from now, what do you think will be your three or four most important benefits? Why?

3. As a corporate recruiter, you must know how to screen prospective employees. The Integrity Center website, at (**www.integctr.com**), offers a brief tutorial on pre-employment screening, a glossary of key words and phrases, and related information. Prepare a short report that tells your assistant how to go about this process.
4. Go to the Monster Board at (**http://resume.monster.ca**) to learn how to prepare an electronic résumé that will get results. Develop a list of rules for creating effective electronic résumés, and revise your own résumé into electronic format.
5. Working as a contingent employee can help you explore your career options. Visit the Manpower website at (**www.manpower.com**), and search for several types of jobs that interest you. What are the advantages of being a temporary worker? What other services does Manpower offer job seekers?
6. Web-based training is becoming popular at many companies as a way of bringing a wider variety of courses to more people at lower costs. The Web-Based Training Information Center site, at (**www.webbasedtraining.com**), provides a good introduction. Learn about the basics of online training at its Primer page. Then link to the Resources section, try a demo, and explore other areas that interest you. Prepare a brief report on your findings, including the pros and cons of using the Web for training, to present to your class.
7. Your 250-employee company is considering outsourcing some of its HR functions because it wants to offer a wider range of services. You've been asked to prepare a report on whether it should proceed and if so, how. Visit BuyerZone.com, (**www.buyerzone.com**), click on HR Outsourcing and then HR Outsourcing Buyer's Guide, to learn more about why companies are going outside for this important function and the advantages and disadvantages of doing so. Summarize your finding and make a recommendation. Then use a search engine to locate two to three firms that offer HR outsourcing services. Compare them and recommend one, explaining the reasons for your choice.

Review Questions

1. Why is human resource management in today's organization instrumental in driving an organization toward its goals?
2. What is the human resource management process?
3. Why is human resource planning and forecasting so important?
4. What is recruitment? What are some recruitment methods?
5. What are the steps in employee selection?
6. Differentiate between training and development.
7. What are the steps in performance evaluation?
8. What is compensation? How is it determined?
9. Discuss the types of compensation.
10. What is a labour union?
11. How are labour agreements negotiated?
12. What are the management and union strategies for dealing with conflict?
13. What are the primary laws that affect human resource management?
14. Discuss the trends in HRM.

CREATIVE THINKING CASE >

"People First" at FedEx

FedEx founder and CEO Frederick Smith wants employees to be an integral part of the decision-making process at FedEx. He believes that putting the people first leads to better service for the customer and this leads, ultimately, to higher profits for the company. The People-Service-Profit (P-S-P) focus ensures that employee satisfaction, empowerment, risk taking, and innovation are encouraged, leading to 100 percent customer satisfaction, 100 percent of the time, and resulting in corporate profits.

FedEx Canada employs more than 5,000 people in 56 locations, with more 1,300 drop-off locations, and three call centres dealing with more than 35,000 calls per day. To emphasize the "people first" approach, the president traded jobs with one of his couriers for a week, and had the experience televised. An unusual exercise such as this sent a clear message to customers and employees alike. "We are serious about putting people first."

To help employees with the P-S-P focus, the following processes are in place at FedEx:

- An annual employee satisfaction survey
- A promotion-from-within policy
- Employee recognition and reward programs
- Leadership evaluation
- Open communication including e-mail, print, broadcast and face-to-face
- Pay-for-performance remuneration
- An employee appeal procedure and guaranteed fair treatment policies.

The P-S-P philosophy, supported by the appropriate policies, leads to motivated employees who go beyond what might be delineated in the usual job description. Corporate legend reports a story of an employee who looked after a customer's cat after the cat was inadvertently wrapped into a package by the customer. Another story describes how a FedEx manager personally flew to Ottawa to hand-deliver lifesaving medication to a customer. These examples illustrate the service commitment FedEx has encouraged and obtained from their employees. Many companies profess that "people are our greatest asset," but FedEx has managed actually to live this philosophy through their "people first" focus.

Critical Thinking Questions

- To maintain the culture FedEx has developed, it is important to hire employees who "fit." How might FedEx do this?
- Look at the compensation and evaluation aspects of HR. Suggest strategies for FedEx in keeping with their P-S-P focus.

SOURCES: Brenda McWillams and Gary Burkett, "Empowered Employees," *Marketing*, 3 no. 22 (June 19, 2006), 40; FedEx Canada History, (www.fedex.com/ca) (accessed July 10, 2006); FedEx Philosophy, (www .fedex.com/ca) (accessed December 7, 2008).

VIDEO CASE >

PepsiCo: More than Just Personnel

How does a company with a massive international presence, doing business in multiple time zones and languages, manage its employees? PepsiCo does it with a Values Statement and Code of Conduct that spells out what the company stands for, the rules it lives by—and Strategic Human Resources Management. The Values Statement—which reflects the company's aspirations—and the Code of Conduct—which provides the operating principles to achieve those goals—apply to every PepsiCo (**www.pepsico.com**)

employee and to every business transaction the company makes worldwide. Chairman and chief executive officer Steven S. Reinemund believes the company's continued success comes from its employees' dedication to these principles.

At PepsiCo, Strategic Human Resources Management (SHRM) develops strategies that contribute to company expansion and innovation. It is fully integrated into the organization, "partnering" with every division of PepsiCo's business, and must produce hard line results.

One mode of SHRM divides the work into four "quadrants":

Administrative Experts manage basic human resource functions like paying employees, dealing with their benefits, ensuring they are treated fairly, and more.

Employee Champions represent the employees' perspective to management with a view to maximizing their contribution to the company.

Change Agents develop systems and processes to facilitate change within the organization.

Strategic Business Partners devise strategies for growth in the organization.

Let's look at SHRM in action. Darryl Claiborne, a human resources director for Frito-Lay, a PepsiCo snack division, sometimes heads out on field trips. "There's times that I actually jump on a route truck and spend a day with an employee. As we ride we talk about understanding the business and how to drive the numbers," he says.

In a conventional company, human resource personnel rarely leave their offices. But PepsiCo believes that it is important for HR managers to achieve a more complete integration into the organization's various departments, to everyone's benefit. For example, employee retention has improved as a result of this type of direct communication between managers and employees in the trenches.

When a sales rep asks Darryl about career advancement, Darryl suggests he first meet the obligations of his current job—improving sales figures and establishing a rapport with his customers—before taking advantage of the company's self-nomination procedure which allows employees to inform management they are interested in promotion. In some cases it could mean following an established progression of advancement before moving into management.

PepsiCo recognizes the value of a human resource function that goes beyond the basics to deliver strategies and measurable hard line results that contribute to the company's success.

It judges employee performance according to the person's contribution to company results and is committed to equal opportunity for all employees and job applicants. PepsiCo's focus on SHRM helps the company grow and innovate—keys to flourishing in today's competitive corporate environment.

Critical Thinking Questions

- What challenges do human resource organizations face in today's competitive business environment? How is PepsiCo meeting those challenges?
- Strategic Human Resources Management refers to an integrated personnel/human resource function. Describe the components of the SHRM planning process and how each one contributes to PepsiCo's corporate development and growth.
- PepsiCo believes in an integrated human resource function, even sending senior human resource personnel out into the field. What important benefits have resulted from this unusual activity?

SOURCES: Adapted from the video case, "Human Resources Management—PepsiCo"; Society for Human Resource Management (SHRMOnline) (www.shrm.org); (October 15, 2005); Lin Grensing-Pophal, "First Day Impressions Set Stage for Retention," White Paper for The Society for Human Resources Management, CareerJournal.com, (www.careerjournal.com) (October 15, 2005); PepsiCo corporate Website, (www.pepsico.com) (October 15, 2005).

E-COMMERCE CASE >

Is Trust in the Workplace *Really* Important?

According to the Great Place to Work Institute in San Francisco, which spent two and a half decades researching workplace culture, the answer is a resounding "YES." But does this finding hold true in Canada? "YES" again. The Great Place to Work Institute Canada conducted an analysis of almost 10,000 employee surveys in the fall of 2005. The Great Place to Work Model focuses on workplace trust as opposed to the usual attention-getters, such as compensation, benefits, and other perks. The Trust Index comprises 57 questions in the areas of credibility, respect, fairness, pride, and camaraderie. Accepted applicants for the Best Workplaces list are able to access the Trust Index as part of the employee survey section of the application process.

TD Bank Financial Group ranked high in the survey. With 74,000 employees, the merger of TD Bank and Canada Trust was the largest bank merger in Canadian history. Merging two different cultures could have been a huge problem, but obviously, management handled it well, with Ed Clark, of the acquired company, Canada Trust, becoming the new CEO. TD tends to focus on instilling pride in its employees as one aspect of its trust-based culture. Volunteerism is important in the company, and employees can access paid time off for volunteer activities.

Graham Lowe, one of the founding partners of the Great Place to Work Institute Canada, provides a number of principles to help managers move toward a "great" workplace. These include talking about employee trust openly, being aware of trust-building and breaking actions, focusing on a few trust-building changes and pursuing them, focusing on the *process* rather than the end result of these changes, and celebrating what already works well. By creating a high-trust culture, management can increase the company's competitive advantage, which benefits employees, management, shareholders, and customers.

Critical Thinking Questions

1. What sort of corporate culture would you, as an employee, prefer?
2. Focus on a potential employer, and investigate the culture through secondary research.
3. Look at (**www.greatplacetowork.ca**) and determine how this company would rank using the criteria discussed on the website.

SOURCES: Andrew Wahl "Best Workplaces," *Canadian Business*, April 10–23, 2006, 64–66; Andrew Wahl, "On the Money," *Canadian Business*, April 10–23, 2006, 68–69; and Peter Evans, "TD Bank Financial Group," *Canadian Business*, April 10–23, 2006, 77–79; (www/greatplacetowork.ca/best/list-ca.htm), accessed December 7, 2008.

GLOSSARY

A

absolute advantage The situation when a country can produce and sell a product at a lower cost than any other country or when it is the only country that can provide the product.

accounting The process of collecting, recording, classifying, summarizing, reporting, and analyzing financial activities.

accounts payable Purchase for which a buyer has not yet paid the seller.

accounts receivable Sales for which a firm has not yet been paid.

acid-test (quick) ratio The ratio of total current assets excluding inventory to total current liabilities; used to measure a firm's liquidity.

acquisition The purchase of a corporation by another corporation or by an investor group; the identity of the acquired company can be lost.

activity ratios Ratios that measure how well a firm uses its assets.

administrative law The rules, regulations, and orders passed by boards, commissions, and agencies of government (municipal, provincial, and federal).

advertising Any paid form of non-personal presentation by an identified sponsor.

agency shop A company where employees are not required to join the union but must pay it a fee to cover its expenses in representing them.

agents Sales representatives of manufacturers and wholesalers.

amortization (depreciation) The allocation of an asset's original cost to the years in which it is expected to produce revenues.

angel investors Individual investors or groups of experienced investors who provide funding for start-up businesses.

annual report A yearly document that describes a firm's financial status and usually discusses the firm's activities during the past year and its prospects for the future.

application service providers (ASPs) A service company that buys and maintains software on its servers and distributes it through high-speed networks to subscribers for a set period and price.

apprenticeship A form of on-the-job training that combines specific job instruction with classroom instruction.

arbitration A method of settling disputes in which the parties agree to present their case to an impartial third party and are required to accept the arbitrator's decision.

assembly process A transformation process in which the basic inputs are either combined to create the output or transformed into the output.

assets Possessions of value owned by a firm.

Association of Southeast Asian Nations (ASEAN) Organization initially established in 1967 to promote economic growth, social progress, and cultural development in the region; currently has 10 members.

attitude Learned tendency to respond consistently toward a given object, idea, or concept.

authority Legitimate power, granted by the organization and acknowledged by employees, that allows an individual to request action and expect compliance.

autocratic leaders Directive leaders who prefer to make decisions and solve problems on their own with little input from subordinates.

B

baby boomers People born between the late 1940s (after World War II) and the mid-1960s.

balance of payments A summary of a country's international financial transactions showing the difference between the country's total payments to and its total receipts from other countries.

balance of trade The differences between the value of a country's exports and the value of its imports during a certain time.

balance sheet See statement of financial position.

Bank of Canada Canada's central bank whose objective is to "promote the economic and financial well-being of Canada."

bank rate The interest rate that the Bank of Canada charges on one-day loans to financial institutions.

bankruptcy The legal procedure by which individuals or businesses that cannot meet their financial obligations are relieved of some, if not all, of their debt.

barriers to entry Factors, such as technological or legal conditions, that prevent new firms from competing equally with a monopoly.

batch processing A method of updating a database in which data are collected over some time period and then processed together.

bear markets Markets in which securities prices are falling.

belief An organized pattern of knowledge that an individual holds as true about the world.

benefit segmentation The differentiation of markets based on what a product will do rather than on customer characteristics.

bill of material A list of the items and the number of each required to make a given product.

board of directors A group of people elected by the shareholders to handle the overall management of a corporation, such as setting corporate goals and policies, hiring corporate officers, and overseeing the firm's operations and finances.

bond ratings Letter grades assigned to bond issues to indicate their quality, or level of risk; assigned by rating agencies such as Moody's and Standard & Poor's (S&P).

bonds Securities that represent long-term debt obligations (liabilities) issued by corporations and governments.

breach of contract The failure by one party to a contract to fulfill the terms of the agreement without a legal excuse.

breakeven point The price at which a product's costs are covered, so additional sales result in profit.

breaking bulk The process of breaking large shipments of similar products into smaller, more usable lots.

broker markets (organized stock exchanges) Organizations on whose premises securities are resold using an auction-style trading system.

brokers Go-betweens that bring buyers and sellers together.

budgets Formal written forecasts of revenues and expenses that set spending limits based on operational forecasts; include cash budgets, capital budgets, and operating budgets.

bull markets Markets in which securities prices are rising.

bundling The strategy of grouping two or more related products together and pricing them as a single product.

business An organization that strives for a profit by providing goods and services desired by its customers.

business cycles Upward and downward changes in the level of economic activity.

Business Development Bank of Canada (BDC) Bank that provides small and medium-sized businesses with flexible financing, affordable consulting services, and venture capital.

business interruption insurance Covers such costs as rental of temporary facilities, wage and salary payments to employees, payments for leased equipment, fixed payments, and profits that would have been earned during that period.

business law The body of law that governs commercial dealings.

business plan A formal written statement that describes in detail the idea for a new business and how it will be carried out; includes a general description of the company, the qualifications of the owner(s), a description of the product or service, an analysis of the market, and a financial plan.

business-to-business (B2B) e-commerce Electronic commerce that involves transactions between companies.

business-to-consumer (B2C) e-commerce Electronic commerce that involves transactions between businesses and the end user of the goods or services; also called *e-tailing*.

business-to-enterprise (B2E) Electronic collecting, storing, updating, and using of information within the business.

buyer behaviour The actions people take in buying and using goods and services.

C

CAD/CAM systems Linked computer systems that combine the advantages of *computer-aided design* and *computer-aided manufacturing*. The system helps design the product, control the flow of resources, and operate the production process.

caisses populaires Credit unions operating in Quebec and other areas of Canada with francophone populations.

Canada Deposit Insurance Corporation (CDIC) A federal Crown Corporation created in 1967 to provide deposit insurance and contribute to the stability of Canada's financial system.

Canadian Charter of Rights and Freedoms Legislation that guarantees the rights and freedoms of Canadians.

Canada Pension Plan Insurance that provides retirement, disability, death, and health benefits.

capital Tools, machinery, equipment, and buildings used to produce goods and services and get them to the consumer. Sometimes refers to the money that buys machinery, factories, and other production and distribution facilities.

capital budgeting The process of analyzing long-term projects and selecting those that offer the best returns while maximizing the firm's value.

capital budgets Budgets that forecast a firm's outlays for fixed assets (plant and equipment), typically for a period of several years.

capital expenditures Investments in long-lived assets, such as land, buildings, machinery, and equipment, that are expected to provide benefits over a period longer than one year.

capital products Large, expensive items with a long life span that are purchased by businesses for use in making other products or providing a service.

cartel An agreement between enterprises to lessen competition.

cash budgets Budgets that forecast a firm's cash inflows and outflows and help the firm plan for cash surpluses and shortages.

cash flows The inflow and outflow of cash for a firm.

cash management The process of making sure that a firm has enough cash on hand to pay bills as they come due and to meet unexpected expenses.

category management Suppliers manage the inventory of a category of products for a retailer.

cellular manufacturing Production technique that uses small, self-contained production units, each performing all or most of the tasks necessary to complete a manufacturing order.

centralization The degree to which formal authority is concentrated in one area or level of an organization.

certified general accountant (CGA) An accountant who focuses primarily on external financial reporting.

certified management accountant (CMA) An accountant who works primarily in industry and focuses on internal management accounting.

chain of command The line of authority that extends from one level of an organization's hierarchy to the next, from top to bottom, and makes clear who reports to whom.

chartered accountant (CA) An accountant who has completed an approved bachelor's degree program, completed an educational program, and passed a comprehensive examination. Only a CA can issue an auditor's opinion on a firm's financial statements.

chartered banks Profit-oriented financial institutions that accept deposits, make business and consumer loans, invest in government and corporate securities, and provide other financial services.

chief information officer (CIO) An executive with responsibility for managing all information resources in an organization.

circular flow The movement of inputs and outputs among households, businesses, and governments; a way of showing how the sectors of the economy interact.

civil code A body of written law that sets out the private rights of the citizens.

code of ethics A set of guidelines prepared by a firm to provide its employees with the knowledge of what the firm expects in terms of their responsibilities and behaviour toward fellow employees, customers, and suppliers.

coercive power Power that is derived from an individual's ability to threaten negative outcomes.

cognitive dissonance The condition of having beliefs or knowledge that are internally inconsistent or that disagree with one's behaviour.

collective bargaining The process of negotiating labour agreements that provide for compensation and working arrangements mutually acceptable to the union and to management.

command economy An economic system characterized by government ownership of virtually all resources and economic decision-making by central government planning; also known as a *planned economy*.

commercial paper Unsecured short-term debt (an IOU) issued by a financially strong corporation.

committee structure An organizational structure in which authority and responsibility are held by a group rather than an individual.

common law The body of unwritten law that has evolved out of judicial (court) decisions rather than being enacted by a legislature; also called *case law*.

common shares Securities that represent one form of ownership interest in a corporation.

competitive advantage A set of unique features of a company and its products that are perceived by the target market as significant and superior to those of the competition; also called *differential advantage*.

component lifestyle A lifestyle made up of a complex set of interests and choices.

computer network A group of two or more computer systems linked together by communications channels to share data and information.

computer virus A computer program that copies itself into other software and can spread to other computer systems.

computer-aided design (CAD) The use of computers to design and test new products and modify existing ones.

computer-aided manufacturing (CAM) The use of computers to develop and control the production process.

computer-integrated manufacturing (CIM) The combination of computerized manufacturing processes (such as robots and flexible manufacturing systems) with other computerized systems that control design, inventory, production, and purchasing.

conceptual skills A manager's ability to view the organization as a whole, understand how the various parts are interdependent, and assess how the organization relates to its external environment.

conglomerate merger A merger of companies in unrelated businesses; done to reduce risk.

consensual leaders Leaders who encourage discussion about issues and then require that all parties involved agree to the final decision.

consultative leaders Leaders who confer with subordinates before making a decision but who retain the final decision-making authority.

consumer price index (CPI) A measure of retail price movements that compares a representative "shopping basket" of goods and services.

consumerism A movement that seeks to increase the rights and powers of buyers vis-à-vis sellers.

consumer-to-business (C2B) e-commerce Electronic commerce that involves transactions between consumers and businesses initiated by the consumer.

consumer-to-consumer (C2C) e-commerce Electronic commerce that involves transactions between consumers.

contingency plans Plans that identify alternative courses of action for very unusual or crisis situations; typically stipulate the chain of command, standard operating procedures, and communication channels the organization will use during an emergency.

contingent workers Persons who prefer temporary employment, either part- or full-time.

continuous improvement A constant commitment to seeking better ways of doing things to achieve greater efficiency and improve quality.

continuous process A production process that uses long production runs lasting days, weeks, or months without equipment shutdowns; generally used for high-volume, low-variety products with standardized parts.

contract An agreement that sets for the relationship between parties regarding the performance of a specified action; creates a legal obligation and is enforceable in a court of law.

contract manufacturing The practice in which a foreign firm manufacturers private-label goods under a domestic firm's brand name.

contractionary policy The use of monetary policy by the Bank of Canada to tighten the money supply by selling government securities or raising interest rates.

controlling The process of assessing the organization's progress toward accomplishing its goals; includes monitoring the implementation of a plan and correcting deviations from the plan.

convenience products Relatively inexpensive items that require little shopping effort and are purchased routinely without planning.

conventional ethics The second stage in the ethical development of individuals in which people move from an egocentric viewpoint to consider the expectations of an organization or society; also known as social ethics.

convertible bonds Corporate bonds that are issued with an option that allows the bondholder to convert them into common shares.

cooperatives Legal entities typically formed by people with similar interests, such as customers or suppliers, to reduce costs and gain economic power. A cooperative has limited liability, an unlimited life span, an elected board of directors, and an administrative staff; all profits are distributed to the member-owners in proportion to their contributions.

copyright A form of protection established by the government for creators of works of art, music, literature, or other intellectual property; gives the creator the exclusive right to use, produce, and sell the creation during the lifetime of the creator and the creator's estate for 50 years thereafter.

corporate culture The set of attitudes, values, and standards of behaviour that distinguishes one organization from another.

corporate governance The way in which an organization is being governed, directed, and administered.

corporate open house Persons are invited to an open house on the premises of the corporation. Qualified applicants are encouraged to complete an application before leaving.

corporate philanthropy The practice of charitable giving by corporations; includes contributing cash, donating equipment and products, and supporting the volunteer efforts of company employees.

corporation A legal entity with an existence and life separate from its owners who, therefore, are not personally liable for the entity's debts. A corporation has many of the same legal rights and responsibilities as that of a person: it can own property, enter into contracts, sue and be sued, and engage in business operations.

cost competitive advantage A firm's ability to produce a product or service at a lower cost than all other competitors in an industry while maintaining satisfactory profit margins.

cost of goods sold (COGS) The total expense of buying or producing a firm's goods or services.

cost-of-living adjustment (COLA) A provision in a labour contract that calls for wages to increase automatically as the cost of living rises (usually measured by the consumer price index).

cost-push inflation Inflation that occurs when increases in production costs push up the prices of final goods and services.

costs Expenses incurred in creating and selling goods and services.

countertrade A form of international trade in which part or all of the payment for goods or services is in the form of other goods and services.

credit unions Not-for-profit, member-owned financial cooperatives.

critical path In a critical path method network, the longest path through the linked activities.

critical path method (CPM) A scheduling tool that enables a manager to determine the critical path of activities for a project—the activities that will cause the entire project to fall behind schedule if they are not completed on time.

cross-functional teams Teams of employees who are from about the same level in the organizational hierarchy but from different functional areas; for example, task forces, organizational committees, and project teams.

crowding out The situation that occurs when government spending replaces spending by the private sector.

Crown corporations Companies that only the provincial and federal government can set up.

culture The set of values, ideas, attitudes, and other symbols created to shape human behaviour.

currency Bank notes and coins used as a medium of exchange.

current assets Assets that can or will be converted to cash within the next 12 months (within the next fiscal year).

current liabilities Short-term claims that are due within a year of the date of the balance sheet.

current ratio The ratio of total current assets to total current liabilities; used to measure a firm's liquidity.

custom regulations Regulations on products that are different from generally accepted international standards.

customer departmentalization Departmentalization that is based on the primary type of customer served by the organizational unit.

customer relationship management (CRM) The processes used by organizations to track and organize information about current and prospective customers.

customer satisfaction The customer's feeling that a product has met or exceeded expectations.

customer value (in economics) The customer's perception of the ratio of benefits (functionality, performance, durability, design, ease of use, and serviceability) to the sacrifice (of money, time, and effort) necessary to obtain those benefits.

customer value (in marketing) The ratio of benefits to the sacrifice necessary to obtain those benefits, as determined by the customer; reflects the willingness of customers to buy a product.

customization The production of goods or services one at a time according to the specific needs or wants of individual customers.

cyclical unemployment Unemployment that occurs when a downturn in the business cycle reduces the demand for labour throughout the economy.

D

database An electronic filing system that collects and organizes data and information.

data mart Special subset of a data warehouse that deals with a single area of data and is organized for quick analysis.

data warehouse An information technology that combines many databases across a whole company into one central database that supports management decision making.

dealer markets Securities markets where buy and sell orders are executed through dealers, or "market makers" linked by telecommunications networks.

debentures Unsecured bonds that are backed only by the reputation of the issuer and its promise to pay the principal and interest when due.

debt A form of business financing consisting of borrowed funds that must be repaid with interest over a stated time period.

debt ratios Ratios that measure the degree and effect of a firm's use of borrowed funds (debt) to finance its operations.

debt-to-equity ratio The ratio of total liabilities to owners' equity; measures the relationship between the amount of debt financing and the amount of equity financing.

decentralization The process of pushing decision-making authority down the organizational hierarchy.

decision support system (DSS) An interactive, flexible, computerized information system that allows managers to make decisions quickly and accurately; used to conduct sales analyses, forecast sales, evaluate advertising, analyze product lines, and keep tabs on market trends and competitors' actions.

decisional roles A manager's activities as an entrepreneur, resource allocator, conflict resolver, or negotiator.

deductibles The amounts that the insured must pay before insurance benefits begin.

delegation of authority The assignment of some degree of authority and responsibility to persons lower in the chain of command.

demand The quantity of a good or service that people are willing to buy at various prices.

demand curve A graph showing the quantity of a good or service that people are willing to buy at various prices.

demand deposits Money kept in chequing accounts that can be withdrawn by depositors on demand.

demand-pull inflation Inflation that occurs when the demand for goods and services is greater than the supply.

democratic leaders Leaders who solicit input from all members of the group and then allow the members to make the final decision through a vote.

demographic segmentation The differentiation of markets through the use of categories such as age, education, gender, income, and household size.

demography The study of people's vital statistics, such as their age, race and ethnicity, and location.

departmentalization The process of grouping jobs together so that similar or associated tasks and activities can be coordinated.

depreciation (amortization) The allocation of an asset's original cost to the years in which it is expected to produce revenues; also referred to as *amortization*.

deregulation The removal of rules and regulations governing business competition.

detailing The physical stocking of merchandise at a retailer by the salesperson who delivers the merchandise.

devaluation A lowering of the value of a nation's currency relative to other currencies.

differential competitive advantage A firm's ability to provide a unique product or service that offers something of value to buyers besides simply a lower price.

distribution (logistics) Efficiently managing the acquisition of raw materials to the factory and the movement of products from the producer to industrial users and consumers.

distribution centres Warehouses that specialize in changing shipment sizes rather than in storing goods.

distribution channel The series of marketing entities through which goods and services pass on their way from producers to end users.

distribution strategy The part of the marketing mix that involves deciding how many stores and which specific wholesalers and retailers will handle the product in a geographic area.

diversity Employee differences in age, race and ethnicity, gender, educational background, and work experience.

dividends Payments to shareholders from a corporation's profits.

division of labour The process of dividing work into separate jobs and assigning tasks to workers.

double-entry bookkeeping A method of accounting in which each transaction is recorded as two entries so that two accounts or records are changed.

dual distribution (or multiple distribution) Two or more channels that distribute the same product to target markets.

dumping The practice of charging a lower price for a product in foreign markets than in the firm's home market.

E

earnings per share (EPS) The ratio of net profit to the number of common shares outstanding; measures the number of dollars earned by each share.

economic growth An increase in a nation's output of goods and services.

economic system The combination of policies, laws, and choices made by a nation's government to establish the systems that determine what goods and services are produced and how they are allocated.

economics The study of how a society uses scarce resources to produce and distribute goods and services.

effectiveness The ability to produce the desired result or good (doing the right thing).

efficiency Using the least amount of resources to accomplish the organization's goals (doing things right).

electronic business (e-business) The entire process that involves the full value chain (the entire value-adding process, from the raw materials to the eventual end user, including the disposing of the packaging after use) and how all units of a business operate.

electronic commerce (e-commerce) The actual transaction of selling a product or service via the Internet.

electronic data interchange (EDI) The electronic exchange of information between two trading partners.

embargo A total ban on imports or exports of a product.

employment insurance Payment of benefits to laid-off workers while they seek new jobs.

empowerment The process of giving employees increased autonomy and discretion to make decisions, as well as control over the resources needed to implement those decisions.

enterprise portal A customizable internal website that provides proprietary corporate information to a defined user group, such as employees, supply chain partners, or customers.

enterprise resource planning (ERP) A computerized resource planning system that includes information about the firm's suppliers and customers as well as data generated internally.

enterprise risk management (ERM) A company-wide, strategic approach to identifying, monitoring, and managing all elements of a company's risk.

entrepreneurs People with vision, drive, and creativity who are willing to take the risk of starting and managing a new business to make a profit or greatly changing the scope and direction of an existing firm.

environmental scanning The process in which a firm continually collects and evaluates information about its external environment.

e-procurement The process of purchasing supplies and materials online using the Internet.

equilibrium The point on the supply and demand curve at which quantity demanded equals quantity supplied.

equity A form of business financing consisting of funds raised through the sale of stock in a business.

equity theory A theory of motivation that holds that worker satisfaction is influenced by employees' perceptions about how fairly they are treated compared with their coworkers.

ethics A set of moral standards for judging whether something is right or wrong.

European Union (EU) An organization of 15 European nations (as of early 2004) that works to foster political and economic integration in Europe; formerly called the European Community.

exchange The process in which two parties give something of value to each other to satisfy their respective needs.

exchange controls Laws that require a company earning foreign exchange (foreign currency) from its exports to sell the foreign exchange to a control agency, such as a central bank.

exchange-traded fund (ETF) A basket of marketable securities in a category, such as industry sector, investment objective, or geographical area, or that track an index. ETFs are similar to mutual funds but trade like shares.

excise taxes Taxes that are imposed on specific items such as gasoline, alcoholic beverages, and tobacco.

exclusive distribution A distribution system in which a manufacturer selects only one or two dealers in an area to market its products.

executive information system (EIS) A management support system that is customized for an individual executive; provides specific information for strategic decisions.

expansionary policy The use of monetary policy by the Bank of Canada to increase the growth of the money supply.

expectancy theory A theory of motivation that holds that the probability of an individual acting in a particular way depends on the strength of that individual's belief that the act will have a particular outcome and on whether the individual values that outcome.

expense items Items, purchased by businesses, that are smaller and less expensive than capital products and usually have a life span of less than one year.

expenses The costs of generating revenues.

experiment A marketing research method in which the investigator changes one or more variables—price, packaging, design, shelf space, advertising theme, or advertising expenditures—while observing the effects of these changes on another variable (usually sales).

expert power Power that is derived from an individual's extensive knowledge in one or more areas.

expert system A management support system that gives managers advice similar to what they would get from a consultant; it uses artificial intelligence to enable computers to reason and learn to solve problems in much the same way humans do.

exporting The practice of selling domestically produced goods to buyers in another country.

exports Goods and services produced in one country and sold in other countries.

express contract A contract in which the terms are specified in either written or spoken words.

extensive decision making Purchasing an unfamiliar, expensive, infrequently bought item.

F

factoring A form of short-term financing in which a firm sells its accounts receivable outright at a discount to a *factor*.

factors of production The resources that are necessary to produce goods and services: labour, capital, entrepreneurs, physical resources, and information.

federal budget deficit The condition that occurs when the federal government spends more for programs than it collects in taxes.

financial accounting Accounting that focuses on preparing external financial reports that are used by outsider stakeholders such as creditors, suppliers, investors, and government agents to assess the financial strength of a business.

financial intermediation The process in which financial institutions act as intermediaries between the suppliers and demanders of funds.

financial management The art and science of managing a firm's money so that it can meet its goals.

financial risk The chance that a firm will be unable to make scheduled interest and principal payments on its debt.

fiscal policy The government's use of taxation and spending to affect the economy.

fixed assets Long-term assets used by a firm for more than a year, such as land, buildings, and machinery; also referred to as *capital assets* or *property, plant, and equipment (PPE).*

fixed costs Costs that do not vary with different levels of output; for example, rent.

fixed-cost contribution The selling price per unit (revenue) minus the variable costs per unit.

fixed-position layout A facility arrangement in which the product stays in one place and workers and machinery move to it as needed.

flexible manufacturing system (FMS) A system that combines automated workstations with computer-controlled transportation devices—automatic guided vehicles (AGVs)—that move materials between workstations and into and out of the system.

floating exchange rates A system in which prices of currencies move up and down based upon the demand for and supply of the various currencies.

foreign direct investment Active ownership of a foreign company or of manufacturing or marketing facilities in a foreign country.

formal organization The order and design of relationships within a firm; consists of two or more people working together with a common objective and clarity of purpose.

four Ps (4Ps) Product, price, promotion, and place (distribution), which together make up the marketing mix.

franchise agreement A contract setting out the terms of a franchising arrangement, including the rules for running the franchise, the services provided by the franchisor, and the financial terms. Under the contract, the franchisee is allowed to use the franchisor's business name, trademark, and logo.

franchisee In a franchising arrangement, the individual or company that sells the goods or services of the franchisor in a certain geographic area.

franchising A form of business organization based on a business arrangement between a franchisor, which supplies the product concept, and the franchisee, who sells the goods or services of the franchisor in a certain geographic area.

franchisor In a franchising arrangement, the company that supplies the product concept to the franchisee.

free-rein (laissez-faire) leadership A leadership style in which the leader turns over all authority and control to subordinates.

free trade The policy of permitting the people of a country to buy and sell where they please without restrictions.

free trade zone An area where the nations allow free, or almost free, trade among each other while imposing tariffs on goods of nations outside the zone.

frictional unemployment Short-term unemployment that is not related to the business cycle.

friendly takeover A takeover that is supported by the management and board of directors of the targeted company.

fringe benefits Indirect compensation such as pensions, health insurance, and vacations.

full employment Situation when the economy is producing to its maximum sustainable capacity, using labour, technology, land, capital, and other factors of production to their fullest potential.

functional departmentalization Departmentalization that is based on the primary functions performed within an organizational unit.

futures contracts Legally binding obligations to buy or sell specified quantities of commodities or financial instruments at an agreed-on price at a future date.

G

Gantt charts Bar graphs plotted on a time line that show the relationship between scheduled and actual production.

general partners Partners who have unlimited liability for all of the firm's business obligations and who control its operations.

general partnership A partnership in which all partners share in the management and profits. Each partner can act on behalf of the firm and has unlimited liability for all its business obligations.

generally accepted accounting principles (GAAP) The financial accounting standards followed by accountants in Canada in preparing financial statements.

Generation X Those born between the mid-1960s and the late 1970s.

Generation Y Those born from the early 1980s to the mid 1990s.

geographic departmentalization Departmentalization based on the geographic segmentation of the organizational units.

geographic segmentation The differentiation of markets by region of the country, city or county size, market density, or climate.

global management skills A manager's ability to operate in diverse cultural environments.

global vision The ability to recognize and react to international business opportunities, be aware of threats from foreign competition, and use international distribution networks effectively to obtain materials and move finished products to customers.

goal-setting theory A theory of motivation based on the premise that an individual's intention to work toward a goal is a primary source of motivation.

goods Tangible items manufactured by businesses.

grievance A formal complaint, filed by an employee or by the union, charging that management has violated the contract.

gross domestic product (GDP) The total market value of all final goods and services produced within a nation's borders each year.

gross national product (GNP) The total market value of all final goods and services produced by a country regardless of where the factors of production are located.

gross profit The amount a company earns after paying to produce or buy its products but before deducting operating expenses.

gross sales The total dollar amount of a company's sales.

group cohesiveness The degree to which group members want to stay in the group and tend to resist outside influences.

H

Hawthorne effect The phenomenon that employees perform better when they feel singled out for attention or feel that management is concerned about their welfare.

high-yield (junk) bonds High-risk, high-return bonds.

horizontal merger A merger of companies at the same stage in the same industry; done to reduce costs, expand product offerings, or reduce competition.

hostile takeover A takeover that goes against the wishes of the target company's management and board of directors.

human relations skills A manager's interpersonal skills that are used to accomplish goals through the use of human resources.

human resource (HR) planning Creating a strategy for meeting future human resource needs.

human resource management (HRM) The process of hiring, developing, motivating, and evaluating employees to achieve organizational goals.

hygiene factors Extrinsic elements of the work environment that do not serve as a source of employee satisfaction or motivation.

I

ideal self-image The way an individual would like to be.

implied contract A contract that depends on the acts and conduct of the parties to show agreement; the terms are not specified in writing or orally.

import quota A limit on the quantity of a certain good that can be imported; also known as a *quantitative restraint.*

imports Goods and services that are bought from other countries.

income statement A financial statement that summarizes a firm's revenues and expenses and shows its total profit or loss over a period of time; also referred to as a *profit and loss statement* or *statement of earnings.*

income taxes Taxes that are based on the income received by businesses and individuals.

industrial distributors Independent wholesalers that buy related product lines from many manufacturers and sell them to industrial users.

inflation The situation in which the average of all prices of goods and services is rising.

informal organization The network of connections and channels of communication based on the informal relationships of individuals inside an organization.

information system (IS) The hardware, software, people, data, and so on, that provide information about all aspects of a firm's operations.

information technology (IT) The equipment and techniques used to manage and process information.

informational roles A manager's activities as an information gatherer, an information disseminator, or a spokesperson for the company.

infrastructure The basic institutions and public facilities upon which an economy's development depends.

initial public offer (IPO) A company's first issuance of shares to the public.

institutional investors Investment professionals who are paid to manage other people's money.

insurable interest An insurance applicant's chance of loss if a particular peril occurs.

insurable risk A risk that an insurance company will cover. It must meet certain criteria.

insurance The promise of compensation for certain financial losses.

insurance policy A written agreement that defines what the insurance covers and the risks that the insurance company will bear for the insured party.

intangible assets Long-term assets with no physical existence, such as patents, copyrights, trademarks, and goodwill.

integrated marketing communications (IMC) The careful coordination of all promotional activities—media advertising, sales promotion, personal selling, and public relations, as well as direct marketing, packaging, and other forms of promotion—to produce a consistent, unified message that is customer focused.

intensive distribution A distribution system in which a manufacturer tries to sell its products wherever there are potential customers.

interest A fixed amount of money paid by the issuer of a bond to the bondholder on a regular schedule, typically every six months; stated as the *coupon rate.*

intermittent process A production process that uses short production runs to make batches of different products; generally used for low-volume, high-variety products.

International Financial Reporting Standards (IFRS) A set of globally accepted accounting standards to be adopted in Canada on January 1st, 2011.

International Monetary Fund (IMF) An international organization, founded in 1945, that promotes trade, makes short-term loans to member nations, and acts as a lender of last resort for troubled nations.

interpersonal roles A manager's activities as a figurehead, company leader, or liaison.

intranet An internal corporate-wide area network that uses Internet technology to link employees in many locations and with different types of computers.

intrapreneurs Entrepreneurs who apply their creativity, vision, and risk taking within a large corporation, rather than starting a company of their own.

inventory The supply of goods that a firm holds for use in production or for sale to customers.

inventory control system A system that maintains an adequate assortment of items to meet a user or customer's needs.

inventory management The determination of how much of each type of inventory a firm will keep on hand and the ordering, receiving, storing, and tracking of inventory.

inventory turnover ratio The ratio of cost of goods sold to average inventory; measures the speed with which inventory moves through a firm and is turned into sales.

investment bankers Firms that act as underwriters, buying securities from corporations and governments and reselling them to the public.

involvement The amount of time and effort a buyer invests in the searches, evaluations, and decision processes of consumer behaviour.

ISO 14000 A set of five technical standards of quality management created by the International Organization for Standardization to provide a uniform way of determining whether manufacturing plants and service organizations conform to sound quality procedures.

ISO 9000 A set of technical standards designed by the International Organization for Standardization to promote clean production processes to protect the environment.

J

job analysis A study of the tasks required to do a particular job well.

job description The tasks and responsibilities of a job.

job enlargement The horizontal expansion of a job by increasing the number and variety of tasks that a person performs.

job enrichment The vertical expansion of a job by increasing the employee's autonomy, responsibility, and decision-making authority.

job fair An event, typically one day, held at a convention centre to bring together thousands of job seekers and hundreds of firms searching for employees.

job rotation Reassignment of workers to several different jobs over time so that they can learn the basics of each job; also called *cross-training*.

job sharing A scheduling option that allows two individuals to split the tasks, responsibilities, and work hours of one 40-hour-per-week job.

job shop A manufacturing firm that produces goods in response to customer orders.

job specification A list of the skills, knowledge, and abilities a person must have to fill a job.

joint venture An agreement in which a domestic firm buys part of a foreign firm to create a new entity.

justice What is considered fair according to the prevailing standards of society; in the 21st century, an equitable distribution of the burdens and rewards that society has to offer.

just-in-time (JIT) A system in which materials arrive exactly when they are needed for production, rather than being stored on site.

K

key person life insurance A term insurance policy that names the company as beneficiary.

knowledge The understanding or awareness of information about a subject.

knowledge management (KM) A worker who develops or uses knowledge, contributing to and benefiting from information used in performing various tasks, including planning, acquiring, searching, analyzing, organizing, storing, programming, producing, distributing, marketing, or selling functions.

knowledge worker A worker who develops or uses knowledge, contributing to and benefiting from information used in performing various tasks, including planning, acquiring, searching, analyzing, organizing, storing, programming, producing, distributing, marketing, or selling functions.

L

labour Economic contributions of people.

labour union An organization that represents workers in dealing with management over issues involving wages, hours, and working conditions.

law of large numbers Insurance companies' predictions of the likelihood that a peril will occur, used to calculate premiums.

laws The rules of conduct in a society, created and enforced by a controlling authority, usually the government.

leader pricing The strategy of pricing products below the normal markup or even below cost to attract customers to a store where they would not otherwise shop.

leadership The process of guiding and motivating others toward the achievement of organizational goals.

leadership style The relatively consistent way that individuals in leadership positions attempt to influence the behaviour of others.

lean manufacturing Streamlining production by eliminating steps in the production process that do not add benefits that customers are willing to pay for.

legitimate power Power that is derived from an individual's position in an organization.

leveraged buyout (LBO) A corporate takeover financed by large amounts of borrowed money; can be done by outside investors or by a company's own management.

liabilities What a firm owes to its creditors; also called *debts*.

licensing The legal process whereby a firm agrees to allow another firm to use a manufacturing process, trademark, patent, trade secret, or other proprietary knowledge in exchange for the payment of a royalty.

limited decision-making Situation in which a consumer has previous product experience but is unfamiliar with the current brands available.

limited liability partnership (LLP) In a limited liability partnership, each individual partner is protected from responsibility for the acts of other partners, and each party's liability is limited to harm resulting from that party's own actions.

limited partners Partners whose liability for the firm's business obligations is limited to the amount of their investment. They help to finance the business and/or promote the business, but do not participate in the firm's day-to-day operations.

limited partnership A partnership with one or more general partners who have unlimited liability, and one or more limited partners whose liability is limited to the amount of their investments.

line of credit An agreement between a bank and a business that specifies the maximum amount of unsecured short-term borrowing the bank will allow the firm over a given period, typically one year.

line organization An organizational structure with direct, clear lines of authority and communication flowing from the top managers downward.

line positions All positions in the organization directly concerned with producing goods and services and which are directly connected from top to bottom.

line-and-staff organization An organizational structure that includes both line and staff positions.

liquidity The speed with which an asset can be converted to cash.

liquidity ratios Ratios that measure a firm's ability to pay its short-term debts as they come due.

local area network (LAN) A network that connects computers at one site, enabling the computer users to exchange data and share the use of hardware and software from a variety of computer manufacturers.

local union A branch or unit of a national union that represents workers at a specific plant or in a specific geographic area.

logistics management The management of the physical distribution process.

long-term forecasts Projections of a firm's activities and the funding for those activities over a period that is longer than a year; from a financial point typically covers 2 to 10 years.

long-term liabilities Claims that come due more than one year after the date of the balance sheet.

loss leader A product priced below cost as part of a leader pricing strategy.

loyalty cards Cards issued by a manufacturer, service organization, or retailer that give discounts to loyal and frequent shoppers.

M

Maastricht Treaty A 1993 treaty concluded by the members of the European Community (now the European Union) that outlines plans for tightening bonds among the members and creating a single market; officially called the Treaty on European Union.

macroeconomics The sub-area of economics that focuses on the economy as a whole by looking at aggregate data for large groups of people, companies, or products.

make-or-buy decision The determination by a firm of whether to make its own production materials or buy them from outside sources.

management The process of guiding the development, maintenance, and allocation of resources to attain organizational goals.

management information system (MIS) The methods and equipment that provide information about all aspects of a firm's operations

management support system (MSS) A dynamic information system that helps managers make decisions by allowing them to analyze data, identify business trends, make forecasts, and model business strategies.

managerial accounting Accounting that provides financial information that managers inside the organization can use to evaluate and make decisions about current and future operations.

managerial hierarchy The levels of management within an organization; typically includes top, middle, and supervisory management.

manufacturer A producer; an organization that converts raw materials to finished products.

manufacturing resource planning II (MRPII) A complex computerized system that integrates data from many departments to control the flow of resources and inventory.

market economy An economic system based on competition in the marketplace and private ownership of the factors of production (resources); also known as the *private enterprise system* or *capitalism*.

market segmentation The process of separating, identifying, and evaluating the layers of a market to design a marketing mix.

market structure The number of suppliers in a market.

marketable securities Short-term investments that are easily converted into cash.

marketing The process of discovering the needs and wants of potential buyers and customers and then providing goods and services that meet or exceed their expectations.

marketing concept Identifying consumer needs and then producing the goods or services that will satisfy them while making a profit for the organization.

marketing database Computerized file of customers' and potential customers' profiles and purchase patterns.

marketing intermediaries Organizations that assist in moving goods and services from producers to end users.

marketing mix The blend of product offering, pricing, promotional methods, and distribution system that brings a specific group of consumers superior value.

marketing research The process of planning, collecting, and analyzing data relevant to a marketing decision.

markup pricing A method of pricing in which a certain percentage (the markup) is added to the product's cost to arrive at the price.

Maslow's hierarchy of needs A theory of motivation developed by Abraham Maslow; holds that humans have five levels of needs and act to satisfy their unmet needs. At the base of the hierarchy are fundamental physiological needs, followed in order by safety, social, esteem, and self-actualization needs.

mass customization A manufacturing process in which modules are mass-produced and then assembled to meet the needs or desires of individual customers.

mass production The ability to manufacture many identical goods or provide many identical services at once.

materials requirement planning (MRP) A computerized system of controlling the flow or resources and inventory. A master schedule is used to ensure that the materials, labour, and equipment needed for production are at the right places in the right amounts at the right times.

matrix structure (project management) An organizational structure that combines functional and product departmentalization by bringing together people from different functional areas of the organization to work on a special project.

mechanistic organization An organizational structure that is characterized by a relatively high degree of job specialization, rigid departmentalization, many layers of management, narrow spans of control, centralized decision-making, and a long chain of command.

mediation The intervention of a third party with a view to persuading the parties to adjust or settle their dispute.

mentoring A form of on-the-job training in which a senior manager or other experienced employee provides job- and career-related information to a protégé.

Mercosur A trade agreement among Argentina, Brazil, Paraguay, and Uruguay that eliminates most tariffs among the member nations.

merger The combination of two or more firms to form a new company, which often takes on a new corporate identity.

microeconomics The sub area of economics that focuses on individual parts of the economy such as households or firms.

middle management Managers who design and carry out tactical plans in specific areas of the company.

mission An organization's purpose and reason for existing; its long-term goals.

mission statement The formalized statement of an organization's purpose and reason for existing.

mixed economies Economies that combine several economic systems; for example, an economy where the government owns certain industries but others are owned by the private sector.

monetary policy The measures taken by the Bank of Canada to regulate the amount of money in circulation to influence the economy.

money Anything that is acceptable as payment for goods and services.

monopolistic competition A market structure in which many firms offer products that are close substitutes and in which entry is relatively easy.

monopoly A situation in which there is no competition and the benefits of a free market are lost.

mortgage bonds Corporate bonds that are secured by property, such as land, equipment, or buildings.

mortgage loan A long-term loan made against real estate as collateral.

motivating factors Intrinsic job elements that lead to worker satisfaction.

multiculturalism The condition when all major ethnic groups in an area, such as a city, county, or province, are about equally represented.

multinational corporations Corporations that move resources, goods, services, and skills across national boundaries without regard to the country in which their headquarters are located.

mutual fund A financial service company that pools its investors' funds to buy a selection of securities that meet its stated investment goals.

mutual-aid pact An agreement by companies in an industry to create a fund that can be used to help cover fixed costs of any member company whose workers go on strike.

N

National Association of Securities Dealers Automated Quotation (NASDAQ) system The first electronic-based stock market and the fastest-growing part of the stock market.

national debt The accumulated total of all of the federal government's annual budget deficits.

national union A union that consists of many local unions in a particular industry, skilled trade, or geographic area and thus represents workers throughout an entire country.

nationalism A sense of national consciousness that boosts the culture and interests of one country over those of all other countries.

natural resources Commodities that are useful inputs in their natural state.

net loss The amount obtained by subtracting all of a firm's expenses from its revenues, when the expenses are more than the revenues.

net profit (net income or net earnings) The amount obtained by subtracting all of a firm's expenses from its revenues, when the revenues are more than the expenses.

net profit margin The ratio of net profit to net sales; also called *return on sales*. It measures the percentage of each sales dollar remaining after all expenses, including taxes, have been deducted.

net sales The amount left after deducting sales discounts and returns and allowances from gross sales.

net working capital The amount obtained by subtracting total current liabilities from total current assets; used to measure a firm's liquidity.

niche competitive advantage A firm's ability to target and effectively serve a single segment of the market within a limited geographic area.

non-programmed decisions Responses to infrequent, unforeseen, or very unusual problems and opportunities where the manager does not have a precedent to follow in decision-making.

North American Free Trade Agreement (NAFTA) An agreement, launched in 1994, creating a free-trade zone including Canada, the United States, and Mexico.

not-for-profit organization An organization that exists to achieve some goal other than the usual business goal of profit.

O

observation research A marketing research method in which the investigator monitors respondents' actions without interacting directly with the respondents; for example, by using cash registers with scanners.

odd-even (psychological) pricing The strategy of setting a price at an odd number to connote a bargain and at an even number to suggest quality.

office automation system An information system that uses information technology tools such as word processing systems, e-mail systems, cellular phones, pagers, and fax machines to improve communications throughout an organization.

oligopoly A market structure in which a few firms produce most or all of the output and in which large capital requirements or other factors limit the number of firms.

one-person corporation A corporation with only one person as the shareholder; common in professional practices (e.g., medical doctors, accountants, or lawyers).

one-to-one marketing Creating a unique marketing mix for every customer.

on-line (real-time) processing A method of updating a database in which data are processed as they become available.

on-the-job training Training in which the employee learns the job by doing it with guidance from a supervisor or experienced coworker.

open market operations The purchase or sale of Canadian government securities by the Bank of Canada to stimulate or slow down the economy.

open shop A company where employees do not have to join the union or pay dues or fees to the union; established under right-to-work laws.

operating budgets Budgets that combine sales forecasts with estimates of production costs and operating expenses to forecast profits.

operating expenses The expenses of running a business that are not directly related to producing or buying its products.

operational planning The process of creating specific standards, methods, policies, and procedures that are used in specific functional areas of the organization; helps guide and control the implementation of tactical plans.

operations management The design and management of the transformation process.

opinion leaders Leaders who influence others.

options Contracts that entitle holders to buy or sell specified quantities of common shares or other financial instruments at a set price during a specified time.

orientation Training that prepares a new employee to perform on the job; includes information about job assignments, work rules, equipment, and performance expectations, as well as about company policies, salary and benefits, and parking.

organic organization An organizational structure that is characterized by a relatively low degree of job specialization, loose departmentalization, few levels of management, wide spans of control, decentralized decision-making, and a short chain of command.

organization chart A visual representation of the structured relationships among tasks and the people given the authority to do those tasks.

organized stock exchanges Organizations on whose premises securities are resold using an auction-style trading system.

organizing The process of coordinating and allocating a firm's resources to carry out its plans.

outsource The assignment of various functions, such as human resources, accounting, or legal work, to outside organizations. Also refers to the purchase of items from an outside source rather than making them internally.

over-the-counter (OTC) market A sophisticated telecomunications network that links dealers and enables them to trade securities.

owners' equity The total amount of investment in the firm minus any liabilities; also called *net worth*.

P

participative leaders Leaders that share decision making with group members and encourages discussion of issues and alternatives; includes democratic, consensual, and consultative styles.

partnership An association of two or more persons who agree to operate a business together for profit.

patent A form of protection (limited monopoly) established by the government to inventors; gives an inventor the exclusive right to manufacture, use, and sell an invention for 20 years.

payroll taxes Income taxes that are collected by the employer and remitted to the federal government, usually in the form of a deduction from the employee's pay.

penetration pricing The strategy of selling new products at low prices in the hope of achieving a large sales volume.

pension funds Large pools of money set aside by corporations, unions, and governments for later use in paying retirement benefits to their employees or members.

perception The process by which we select, organize, and interpret stimuli into a meaningful and coherent picture.

perfect (pure) competition A market structure in which a large number of small firms sell similar products, buyers and sellers have good information, and businesses can be easily opened or closed.

performance appraisal A comparison of actual performance with expected performance to assess an employee's contributions to the organization.

peril A hazard or a source of danger.

perpetual inventory A continuously updated list of inventory levels, orders, sales, and receipts.

personal selling A face-to-face sales presentation to a prospective customer.

personality A way of organizing and grouping how an individual reacts to situations.

physical distribution (logistics) The movement of products from the producer to industrial users and consumers.

planning The process of deciding what needs to be done to achieve organizational objectives, identifying when and how it will be done, and determining by whom it should be done.

postconventional ethics The third stage in the ethical development of individuals in which people adhere to the ethical standards of a mature adult and are less concerned about how others view their behaviour than about how they will judge themselves in the long run; also known as *principled ethics*.

power The ability to influence others to behave in a particular way.

preconventional ethics A stage in the ethical development of individuals in which people behave in a childlike manner and make ethical decisions in a calculating, self-centred way, based on the possibility of immediate punishment or reward; also known as *self-centred ethics*.

preferential tariff A tariff that is lower for some nations than for others.

preferred shares Equities for which the dividend amount is set at the time the stock is issued.

prestige pricing The strategy of increasing the price of a product so that consumers will perceive it as being of higher quality, status, or value.

price skimming The strategy of introducing a product with a high initial price and lowering the price over time as the product moves through its life cycle.

pricing strategy The part of the marketing mix that involves establishing a price for the product based on the demand for the product and the cost of producing it.

primary data Information collected directly from the original source to solve a problem.

primary market The securities market where *new* securities are sold to the public.

principal The amount borrowed by the issuer of a bond; also called *par value*.

principle of comparative advantage The concept that each country should specialize in the products that it can produce most readily and cheaply and trade those products for those that other countries can produce more readily and cheaply.

private corporation A corporation that does not trade publicly and, therefore, is not listed on a stock exchange.

private law The law relating to the relationship between individuals, businesses, or individuals and businesses.

problem-solving teams Teams of employees from the same department or area of expertise and from the same level of the organizational hierarchy who meet regularly to share information and discuss ways to improve processes and procedures in specific functional areas.

process The way a good is made or a service provided.

process departmentalization Departmentalization that is based on the production process used by the organizational unit.

process layout A facility arrangement in which work flows according to the production process. All workers performing similar tasks are grouped together, and products pass from one workstation to another.

process manufacturing A transformation process in which the basic input is broken down into one or more outputs (products).

producer price index (PPI) An index of the prices paid by producers and wholesalers for various commodities such as raw materials, partially finished goods, and finished products.

product In marketing, any good or service, along with its perceived attributes and benefits, that creates value for the customer.

product (assembly line) layout A facility arrangement in which workstations or departments are arranged in a line with products moving along the line.

product departmentalization Departmentalization that is based on the goods or services produced or sold by the organizational unit.

product liability The responsibility of manufacturers and sellers for defects in the products they make and sell.

product life cycle The pattern of sales and profits over time for a product or product category; consists of an introductory state, growth stage, maturity, and decline (and death).

product strategy The part of the marketing mix that involves choosing a brand name, packaging, colours, a warranty, accessories, and a service program for the product.

production The creation of products and services by turning inputs, such as natural resources, raw materials, human resources, and capital, into outputs, which are products and services.

production orientation An approach in which a firm works to lower production costs without a strong desire to satisfy the needs of customers.

production planning The aspect of operations management in which the firm considers the competitive environment and its own strategic goals in an effort to find the best production methods.

production process The way in which a good is made.

professional liability insurance Insurance designed to protect top corporate management, who have been the target of malpractice lawsuits.

profit The money left over after all expenses are paid.

profit maximization A pricing objective that entails getting the largest possible profit from a product by producing the product as long as the revenue from selling it exceeds the cost of producing it.

profitability ratios Ratios that measure how well a firm is using its resources to generate profit and how efficiently it is being managed.

program evaluation and review technique (PERT) A scheduling tool that is similar to the CPM method but assigns three time estimates for each activity (optimistic, most probable, and pessimistic); allows managers to anticipate delays and potential problems and schedule accordingly.

programmed decisions Decisions made in response to frequently occurring routine situations.

programmed instruction A form of computer-assisted off-the-job training.

promotion (in marketing) The attempt by marketers to inform, persuade, or remind consumers and industrial users to engage in the exchange process.

promotion strategy The part of the marketing mix that involves personal selling, advertising, public relations, and sales promotion of the product.

promotional mix The combination of advertising, personal selling, sales promotion, and public relations used to promote a product.

property taxes Taxes that are imposed on real and personal property based on the assessed value of the property.

protectionism The policy of protecting home industries from outside competition by establishing artificial barriers such as tariffs and quotas.

protective tariffs Tariffs that are imposed to make imports less attractive to buyers than domestic products are.

provincial health care Health insurance programs provided by the provinces.

psychographic segmentation The differentiation of markets by personality or lifestyle.

public corporation Corporation that has the right to issue shares to the public.

public law The law relating to the relationship between the individual or business and the government (or its agencies).

public relations Any communication or activity designed to win goodwill or prestige for a company or person.

pull strategy A promotional strategy in which a manufacturer focuses on stimulating consumer demand for its product rather than on trying to persuade wholesalers or retailers to carry the product.

purchasing The process of buying production inputs from various sources; also called *procurement*.

purchasing power The value of what money can buy.

pure monopoly A market structure in which a single firm accounts for all industry sales and in which there are barriers to entry.

push strategy A promotional strategy in which a manufacturer uses aggressive personal selling and trade advertising to convince a wholesaler or retailer to carry and sell its merchandise.

Q

quality Goods and services that meet customer expectations by providing reliable performance.

quality control The process of creating standards for quality and then measuring finished products and services against them.

quality of life The general level of human happiness based on such things as life expectancy, educational standards, health, sanitation, and leisure time.

R

ratio analysis The calculation and interpretation of financial ratios taken from the firm's financial statements to assess its condition and performance.

real self-image How an individual actually perceives him- or herself.

recession A decline in GDP that lasts for at least two consecutive quarters.

recruitment The attempt to find and attract qualified applicants in the external labour market.

re-engineering The complete redesign of business structures and processes to improve operations.

reference groups Formal and informal groups that influence buyer behaviour.

referent power Power that is derived from an individual's personal charisma and the respect and/or admiration the individual inspires.

relationship management The practice of building, maintaining, and enhancing interactions with customers and other parties to develop long-term satisfaction through mutually beneficial partnerships.

relationship marketing A strategy that focuses on forging long-term partnerships with customers by offering value and providing customer satisfaction.

retailers Firms that sell goods to consumers and to industrial users for their own consumption.

retained earnings (in accounting) Profits that have been reinvested in a firm.

retained earnings (in financial management) The amounts left over from profitable operations since the firm's beginning; equal to total profits minus all dividends paid to shareholders.

return The opportunity for profit.

return on equity (ROE) The ratio of net profit to total owners' equity; measures the return that owners receive on their investment in the firm.

revenues The money a company earns from providing services or selling goods to customers.

revolving credit agreement (revolving line of credit) A guaranteed line of credit whereby a bank agrees that a certain amount of funds will be available for a business to borrow over a given period.

reward power Power that is derived from an individual's control over rewards.

risk (financial) The potential for loss or the chance that an investment will not achieve the expected level of return.

risk (general) The potential for losing time and money or otherwise not being able to accomplish an organization's goals.

risk management The process of identifying and evaluating risks and selecting and managing techniques to adapt to risk exposures.

risk-return trade-off A basic principle in finance that holds that the higher the risk, the greater the return that is required.

robotics The technology involved in designing, constructing, and operating computer-controlled machines that can perform tasks independently.

routine response behaviour Purchase of low-cost, frequently bought items with little search or decision making.

routing The aspect of production control that involves setting out the workflow—the sequence of machines and operations through which the product or service progresses from start to finish.

S

sales promotions Marketing events or sales efforts—not including advertising, personal selling, and public relations—that stimulate buying.

sales taxes Taxes that are levied on goods and services when they are sold; calculated as a percentage of the price.

scanner-based research System for gathering information from a single group of respondents by continuously monitoring the advertising, promotion, and pricing they are exposed to and the things that they buy.

scheduling The aspect of production control that involves specifying and controlling the time required for each step in the production process.

scientific management A system of management developed by Frederick W. Taylor and based on four principles: developing a scientific approach for each element of a job, scientifically selecting and training workers, encouraging cooperation between workers and managers, and dividing work and responsibility between management and workers according to who can better perform a particular task.

seasonal unemployment Unemployment that occurs during specific seasons in certain industries.

secondary data Information that has already been collected for a project other than the current one but that can be used to solve the current problem.

secondary market The securities market where (already issued) old securities are traded among investors; includes the organized stock exchanges, the over-the-counter market, and the commodities exchanges.

secured bonds Corporate bonds for which specific assets have been pledged as collateral.

secured loans Loans for which the borrower is required to pledge specific assets as collateral, or security.

securities Investment certificates issued by corporations or governments that represent either equity or debt.

selection The process of determining which persons in the applicant pool possess the qualifications necessary to be successful on the job.

selection interview An in-depth discussion of an applicant's work experiences, skills and abilities, education, and career interests.

selective distribution A distribution system in which a manufacturer selects a limited number of dealers in an area (but more than one or two) to market its products.

selective exposure The process of deciding which stimuli to notice and which to ignore.

self-concept How people perceive themselves.

self-managed work teams Highly autonomous teams of employees who manage themselves without any formal supervision and take responsibility for setting goals, planning and scheduling work activities, selecting team members, and evaluating team performance.

servers Computers that store data and "serve" information to other computers, called clients, on request.

services Intangible offerings of businesses that can't be held, touched, or stored.

share or stock dividends Payments to shareholders in the form of more shares; can replace or supplement cash dividends.

shareholders The owners of a corporation, who hold shares of stock that provide certain rights; also known as *stockholders*.

shop steward An elected union official who represents union members to management when workers have issues.

shopping products Items that are bought after considerable planning, including brand-to-brand and store-to-store comparisons of price, suitability, and style.

short-term forecasts Projections of revenues, costs of goods, and operating expenses over a one-year period.

simulation A scaled down version or mock-up of equipment, process, or work environment.

Six Sigma A quality control process that relies on defining what needs to be done to ensure quality, measuring and analyzing production results statistically, and finding ways of improving and controlling quality.

small business A business that is independently owned, is owned by an individual or a small group of investors, is based locally, and is not a dominant company in its industry.

social investing The practice of limiting investments to securities of companies that behave in accordance with the investor's beliefs about ethical and social responsibility.

social marketing The application of marketing techniques to social issues and causes.

social responsibility The concern of businesses for the welfare of society as a whole; consists of obligations beyond those required by law or contracts.

socialism An economic system in which the basic industries are owned either by the government itself or by the private sector under strong government control.

socialization process The passing down of cultural norms and values to children.

software The general term for various programs used to operate computers; a set of instructions that directs a computer's activities.

sole proprietorship A business that is established, owned, operated, and often financed by one person.

span of control The number of employees a manager directly supervises; also called span of management.

specialization The degree to which tasks are subdivided into smaller jobs.

specialty products Items for which consumers search long and hard and for which they refuse to accept substitutes.

speculative risk The chance of either loss or gain, without insurance against the possible loss.

staff positions Positions in an organization held by individuals who provide the administrative and support services that line employees need to achieve the firm's goals.

stakeholders Individuals or groups (including organizations) to whom the business has a responsibility; including the investors or shareholders (those with a financial interest), employees, customers, suppliers (business partners), governments, local communities, the environment, and society as a whole.

standard of living A country's output of goods and services that people can buy with the money they have.

statement of cash flows A financial statement that provides a summary of the money flowing into and out of a firm.

statement of financial position A financial statement that summarizes a firm's financial position at a specific point in time.

statute law (or statutory law) Written law enacted by a legislature (municipal, provincial, or federal).

stock dividends See share dividends.

stockbroker A person who is licensed to buy and sell securities on behalf of clients.

strategic alliance A cooperative agreement between business firms; sometimes called a *strategic partnership*.

strategic channel alliances One manufacturer using another manufacturer's previously established channel to distribute its goods.

strategic giving The practice of tying philanthropy closely to the corporate mission or goals and targeting donations to regions where a company operates.

strategic planning The process of creating long-range (one to five years), broad goals for the organization and determining what resources will be needed to accomplish those goals.

strict liability A concept in products-liability laws under which a manufacturer or seller is liable for any personal injury or property damage caused by defective products or packaging that do not meet industry standards.

structural unemployment Unemployment that is caused by a mismatch between available jobs and the skills of available workers in an industry or region; not related to the business cycle.

supervisory management Managers who design and carry out operational plans for the ongoing daily activities of the firm.

supply The quantity of a good or service that businesses will make available at various prices.

survey research A marketing research method in which data are gathered from respondents in person, by telephone, by mail, at a mall, or through the Internet to obtain facts, opinions, and attitudes.

supply chain The entire sequence of securing inputs, producing goods, and delivering goods to customers.

supply chain management The process of using information along the supply chain so that the firm can satisfy its customers with quality products and services; includes working closely with suppliers.

supply curve A graph showing the quantity of a good or service that a business will make available at various prices.

T

tactical planning The process of beginning to implement a strategic plan by addressing issues of coordination and allocating resources to different parts of the organization; has a shorter time frame (less than one year) and more specific objectives than strategic planning.

target for the overnight rate The signal to the major participants in the money market as to what the Bank of Canada is aiming for when participants borrow and lend one-day funds to each other.

target market The specific group of consumers toward which a firm directs its marketing efforts.

target return on investment A pricing objective where the price of a product is set so as to give the company the desired probability in terms of return on its money.

tariff A tax imposed on imported goods.

technical skills A manager's specialized areas of knowledge and expertise, as well as the ability to apply that knowledge.

telecommuting An arrangement in which employees work at home and are linked to the office by phone, fax, and computer or other communication devices.

term deposits Deposits at a bank or other financial institution that pay interest but cannot be withdrawn on demand.

term loan A business loan with a maturity of more than one year; can be unsecured or secured.

theft insurance A broad insurance coverage that protects business against losses for an act of stealing.

Theory X A management style, formulated by Douglas McGregor, which is based on a pessimistic view of human nature and assumes that the average person dislikes work, will avoid it if possible, prefers to be directed, avoids responsibility, and wants security above all.

Theory Y A management style, formulated by Douglas McGregor, that is based on a relatively optimistic view of human nature; assumes that the average person wants to work, accepts responsibility, is willing to help solve problems, and can be self-directed and self-controlled.

Theory Z A theory developed by William Ouchi that combines U.S. and Japanese business practices by emphasizing long-term employment, slow career development, moderate specialization, group decision-making, individual responsibility, relatively informal control over the employee, and concern for workers.

time deposits Interest-bearing deposits that cannot be withdrawn on demand.

top management The highest level of managers; includes CEOs, presidents, and vice-presidents, who develop strategic plans and address long-range issues.

tort A civil, or private, act that harms other people or their property.

total cost The sum of the fixed costs and the variable costs.

total profit Total revenue minus total cost.

total quality management (TQM) The use of quality principles in all aspects of a company's production and operations.

total revenue The selling price per unit times the number of units sold.

trade credit The extension of credit by the seller to the buyer between the time the buyer receives the goods or services and when it pays for them.

trade deficit An unfavourable balance of trade that occurs when a country imports more than it exports.

trade surplus A favourable balance of trade that occurs when a country exports more than it imports.

trademark The legally exclusive design, name, or other distinctive mark that a manufacturer uses to identify its goods in the marketplace.

training and development Activities that provide learning situations in which an employee acquires additional knowledge or skills to increase job performance.

transaction processing system (TPS) An information system that handles the daily business operations of a firm. The system receives and organizes raw data from internal and external sources for storage in a database.

trust company A financial institution that conduct the same activities as a bank but can also administer estates, trusts, pension plans, and agency contracts.

U

underwriting The process of buying securities from corporations and governments and reselling them to the public; the main activity of investment bankers.

unemployment rate The percentage of the total labour force that is not working but is actively looking for work.

union shop A company where non-union workers can be hired but must then join the union.

unsecured loans Short-term loans for which the borrower does not have to pledge specific assets as security.

unsought products Products that either are unknown to the potential buyer or are known but the buyer does not actively seek them.

Uruguay Round A 1994 agreement by 117 nations to lower trade barriers worldwide.

utilitarianism A philosophy that focuses on the consequences of an action to determine whether it is right or wrong; holds that an action that affects the majority adversely is morally wrong.

V

value pricing A pricing strategy in which the target market is offered a high-quality product at a fair price and with good service.

value-stream mapping Routing technique that uses simple icons to visually represent the flow of materials and information from suppliers through the factory and to customers.

variable costs Costs that change with different levels of output; for example, wages and cost of raw materials.

venture capital Financing obtained from investment firms that specialize in financing small, high-growth companies and receive an ownership interest and a voice in management in return for their money.

vertical merger A merger of companies at different states in the same industry; done to gain control over supplies of resources or to gain access to different markets.

virtual corporation A network of independent companies linked by information technology to share skills, costs, and access to one another's markets; allows the companies to come together quickly to exploit rapidly changing opportunities.

virtual private networks (VPNs) Private corporate networks connected over a public network, such as the Internet. VPNs include strong security measures to allow only authorized users to access the network.

volume segmentation The differentiation of markets based on the amount of the product purchased.

W

warranty A guarantee of the quality of a good or service.

whistle blower An employee, former employee, or any other member of an organization that reports misconduct by others in the organization that have the power to take corrective action.

wholesalers Firms that sell finished goods to retailers, manufacturers, and institutions.

wide area network (WAN) A network that connects computers at different sites via telecommunications media such as phone lines, satellites, and microwaves.

work groups Groups of employees who share resources and coordinate efforts so as to help members perform their individual duties and responsibilities better. The performance of the group can be evaluated by adding up the contributions of the individual group members.

work teams Groups of employees who not only coordinate their efforts, but also collaborate by pooling their knowledge, skills, abilities, and resources in a collective effort to attain a common goal, causing the performance of the team to be greater than the sum of the members' individual efforts.

workers' compensation Payments to cover the expenses of job-related injuries and diseases, including medical costs, rehabilitation, and job retraining if necessary.

World Bank An international bank that offers low-interest loans, as well as advice and information, to developing nations.

World Trade Organization (WTO) An organization established by the Uruguay Round in 1994 to oversee international trade, reduce trade barriers, and resolve disputes among member nations.

yield management system (YMS) Mathematical software that helps companies adjust prices to maximize revenue

COMPANY INDEX

A

B

C

D

E

F

Q

R

S

T

U

V

W

X

Y

Z

SUBJECT INDEX

A

B

C

D

E

F

G

H

I

J

K

L

M

N

O

P

Q

R

S

T

U

V

W

Y